GREAT
PSYCHOLOGISTS
and THEIR TIMES

GREAT
PSYCHOLOGISTS
and THEIR TIMES

SCIENTIFIC INSIGHTS INTO

PSYCHOLOGY'S HISTORY

DEAN KEITH SIMONTON

American Psychological Association • Washington D.C.

Published by
American Psychological Association
750 First Street, NE
Washington, DC 20002
www.apa.org

To order
APA Order Department
P.O. Box 92984
Washington, DC 20090-2984
Tel: (800) 374-2721, Direct: (202) 336-5510
Fax: (202) 336-5502, TDD/TTY: (202) 336-6123
On-line: www.apa.org/books/
E-mail: order@apa.org

In the U.K., Europe, Africa, and the Middle East, copies may be ordered from
American Psychological Association
3 Henrietta Street
Covent Garden, London
WC2E 8LU England

Typeset in Goudy by AlphaWebTech, Mechanicsville, MD

Printer: Data Reproductions Corporation, Auburn Hills, MI
Cover Designer: Naylor Design, Washington, DC
Technical/Production Editor: Jennifer L. Macomber

The opinions and statements published are the responsibility of the authors, and such opinions and statements do not necessarily represent the policies of the American Psychological Association.

Library of Congress Cataloging-in-Publication Data

Simonton, Dean Keith.
    Great psychologists and their times : scientific insights into psychology's history / Dean Keith Simonton.—1st ed.
        p. cm.
    Includes bibliographical references and index.
    ISBN 1-55798-896-X (alk. Paper)
    1. Psychologists—Psychology. I. Title.

BF109.A1 S56 2002
150'.92'2—dc21   2001055302

British Library Cataloguing-in-Publication Data
A CIP record is available from the British Library.

Printed in the United States of America
First Edition

To David A. Kenny,
who earned his PhD under Donald T. Campbell,
who earned his PhD under Robert C. Tryon,
who earned his PhD under Edward C. Tolman,
who earned his PhD under Edwin B. Holt,
who earned his PhD under William James,
whose name was given to the Harvard psychology building
where I earned my PhD under David A. Kenny.

CONTENTS

PREFACE

Who becomes a great psychologist? What must psychologists do to earn themselves a lasting place in psychology's history? Why did their contributions have such a high impact on the field? Do highly influential psychologists possess a telltale cognitive style or a distinctive set of personality traits? What are their most typical theoretical and methodological commitments? What kind of family backgrounds do they have? Where do they get their training, and under whom do they study? How do their lives and careers unfold, and how do they terminate? Are notable psychologists born or made? To attain greatness, must they be the right person at the right place and the right time? If so, what aspects of the sociocultural context are most conducive to the emergence of illustrious psychologists? To what extent is the appropriate milieu defined by what is happening within psychological science, and to what extent is the milieu defined by external circumstances? Do these sociocultural conditions affect not just the magnitude of achievement but also the very nature of that achievement? Are the ideas of great psychologists contingent on political events, economic circumstances, or cultural values? Can all of these questions be given scientific answers? If so, how? And how may the scientific study of great psychologists increase the chances that great psychologists will continue to populate the discipline far into the future? How can this scientific knowledge be used to enhance psychology as a science?

These are just a sample of the many issues that are addressed throughout this book. My goal is to look at the individuals who have contributed most to the advancement of psychological science. Moreover, I examine these distinguished psychologists and thinkers from a scientific perspective—especially from the standpoint of psychological science; that is, I answer the questions raised in the previous paragraph using the best available empirical findings and theoretical models. Is such an aim too ambitious, perhaps even a little audacious? I obviously don't think so. To help readers appreciate why, I need to put this book in the context of my overall research program.

To a large degree, this project was the inevitable fulfillment of the scientific inquiries in which I have been engaged for more than 25 years. Starting with my 1974 doctoral dissertation, I have been systematically studying individuals who have some claim to greatness. These luminaries have included eminent scientists and inventors, great philosophers, literary giants, illustrious artists, classical composers, presidents of the United States, absolute monarchs of Europe, and other distinguished achievers in almost every domain of accomplishment. Moreover, this research program has so far generated more than 240 publications, including more than 100 articles in professional journals in the sciences and humanities. Among these publications are seven books, such as *Genius, Creativity, and Leadership: Historiometric Inquiries* (Simonton, 1984d); *Why Presidents Succeed: A Political Psychology of Leadership* (Simonton, 1987d); *Scientific Genius: A Psychology of Science* (Simonton, 1988d); and *Origins of Genius: Darwinian Perspectives on Creativity* (Simonton, 1999b). In these I examined such factors as intelligence, precocity, personality, values, motivation, family environment, genetics, education, political circumstances, and the broad sociocultural milieu.

Yet despite all of the fascinating findings, I began to realize that my research had completely overlooked one particular form of outstanding achievement—a form of special relevance to me as a psychologist. Hence, beginning in 1985, I turned my research interests toward the psychologists who have done the most to make psychology what it is today. This growing curiosity received some external encouragement when I was invited to contribute an empirical study in commemoration of the 100th anniversary of the founding of the American Psychological Association. The resulting article, "Leaders of American Psychology, 1879–1967: Career Development, Creative Output, and Professional Achievement" (Simonton, 1992b) was published as the lead article and American Psychological Association Centennial Feature in the first 1992 issue of the *Journal of Personality and Social Psychology*. This experience got me really hooked on an idea: to carve out a specialty of the psychology of science, one even more specialized than the psychology of psychology. In particular, this field would be devoted to expanding a scientific understanding of individuals who attained distinction in the discipline.

This notion of a psychology of great psychologists received an added push when I began teaching my department's course on the history of psychology in the winter quarter of 1989. In the process of reading many of the top-selling textbooks on that subject, I began to notice the many examples of "historical generalizations" that dealt with this very substantive question. That is, the authors would frequently evoke some general principle or behavioral law to explain the impact of some particular notable in the field. Very often, these remarks represented implicit hypotheses quite worthy of empirical scrutiny. This realization led me to have my research assistants gather a diverse collection of examples from many textbooks. On the basis of this inventory I wrote the article "Behavioral Laws in Histories of Psychology: Psychological Science, Metascience, and the Psychology of Science" (Simonton, 1995a), which served as a target article for peer commentary in a 1995 issue of *Psychological Inquiries*. The reactions revealed a striking bifurcation in the discipline: Psychologists committed to the psychology of science tended to welcome the essay, whereas those dedicated to the history of psychology tended to be highly critical.

This differential response provoked me to consider putting together a summary of everything known so far about the psychologists who have earned a place in the annals of psychology. This extensive review would look at the phenomenon from the standpoint of cognitive processes, individual differences, life span development, and sociocultural influences—basically all of the core approaches of the psychology of science. The upshot is this volume on the psychology of great psychologists.

So, who should read this book? One obvious audience would be individuals who are fascinated with psychology's history and who believe that psychology itself might have something interesting to say about the figures who occupy a conspicuous place in that history. This group of readers would not be confined to psychology's own historians but rather could encompass general historians of science as well as psychohistorians who do case studies of notable scientists. This group could also include many psychologists whose commitment to the discipline extends beyond their own particular subdiscipline. Another audience would be people who wonder about the scientific status of psychology and who realize that this status might be clarified if psychology's history and the people who made it were better understood. These readers might want to know how great psychologists compare with other great scientists, or they might be curious as to whether scientific change operates in psychology in the same manner as it does in other scientific disciplines. Yet another audience would be individuals dedicated to the psychology of science and who are willing to count psychology among the sciences. These readers would necessarily believe that the scientific enterprise is very much a psychological creation—a product of the scientist's cognitive processes, personal dispositions, and life experiences. For this readership the book would constitute a case study of how psychology permeates one particular scientific discipline. I guess the book's potential audience consists ultimately of all psychologists, scientists, and historians who are willing to ponder the provocative overlap among psychology, science, and history.

Because of the breadth of this potential audience, I have tried to keep technical details to the barest essentials. As a rough estimate, only about 5% of the text really requires anything more than a liberal arts education. Most of that 5% can be easily understood by anyone with the knowledge and expertise provided by introductory psychology courses, including basic methods and statistics. Nonetheless, it is fair to say that the greater is a reader's knowledge about psychology and its history, the more he or she will appreciate the scientific insights presented throughout the text. After all, the bulk of this book is devoted to applying the discoveries and techniques of psychological science to the history of psychology as a science.

Many individuals made this book possible. I first thank all of the numerous research assistants who helped me gather a rich inventory of historical generalizations from history of psychology textbooks. These were Jeff Ancker, Ken Andersson, Marc Bartolome, Stony Beck, Rayna Broome, Lois Campbell, James Chan, Suzanne Dahnert, Elisabeth Dean, Carolyn Dodge, Nadia Gemmellaro, John M. Gotelli, Aaron Grey, Alysia Hall, Jennifer Idlor, Kathryn Kaney, Andrea Lim, Kristin Lipman, Christopher Lucich, Brenna McKinley, Rick Moen, Scott Morris, Manoj Perera, Linda Plachy, Stephen Price, Daniel J. Seitz, Darren T. Seitz, Julie Silva, Rachel Silverman, Wendy Etsuko Siu, David Smiler, Heidi Soltis, Heather Weibel, Diane Wenzler, Becky Wong, and Kai Yang. Next I must express gratitude to those who collected biographical data about specific historical figures: Jennifer Bovolick, Robin Chand, Elaine Chinn, Tracé Conway, Joy Donny, Kelley Elkins, Vida Fereydouni, Sean Follette, Calvin Fong, Othon Franco, Kuldip Gill, Rick Gonzales, Jacob Grosz, Beverly Kwong, Phong La, Hanh Le, May Chao Lee, Susan Lovercheck, Crystal Martin, Renae McCann, Christian McClellan, Heather McCormick, Pamela Nyon, Kim Pham, Lillian Sanchez, Mundeep Sidhu, Marco Tam, Harjot Walia, Russell Wong, and Timmie Yamada. Special thanks go to Ann Ulibarri, who tabulated the data used for Figure 12.1, and to W. Scott Terry, who provided me with many of the birth order data used in Table 9.1. Of course, I also must thank my family for their support, especially my wife Melody and daughter Sabrina. Last listed, but foremost in gratitude, I must mention David A. Kenny, the chair of my doctoral thesis committee. His encouragement and openness enabled me to make my doctoral dissertation the first exemplar of how I wanted to spend the rest of my career. It is for this reason that he receives the book's dedication.

I

THE SCIENTIFIC HISTORY OF PSYCHOLOGY

INTRODUCTION: THE SCIENTIFIC HISTORY OF PSYCHOLOGY

William James's 1890 *The Principles of Psychology* is widely regarded as one of the field's classic textbooks. Appropriately enough, the first line of the first chapter opens with a definition of the discipline: "Psychology is the science of mental life, both of its phenomena and of their conditions," where "the phenomena are such things as we call feelings, desires, cognitions, reasonings, decisions, and the like" (W. James, 1890/1952, p. 1). Although some psychologists might tinker with James's definition in various ways—most notably by inserting "behaviors" into the list of its phenomena—the definition remains very close to the word's Greek etymology. Psychology is the study of the mind in the same way that biology is the study of life and sociology is the study of society. Also like those two scientific enterprises, certain individuals have had an exceptional impact on the field's evolution as a science. Just as there are great biologists and great sociologists, so too, are there great psychologists. Although James can certainly be counted among the discipline's greats, he must rub elbows with hundreds of other worthy contributors (R. I. Watson, 1974; Zusne, 1984). At the same time, these great psychologists represent only a small percentage of all the psychologists who have ever lived. Not all colleagues manage to make some signal contribution that ensures their continued place in the annals of the discipline. Moreover, even among those who have made their mark, not all can boast the same exalted level of impact. Whereas some psychologists are well known to all members of the discipline, others have reputations that are confined to particular specialties or to circumscribed periods in psychology's history. For every psychologist with the status of a William James there are dozens of more obscure colleagues whose contributions have mostly esoteric or historic interest.

What makes a psychologist great in the first place? Why are some psychologists so highly acclaimed while others attain, at best, the status of also-rans? As will soon become evident, this issue cannot be properly addressed without first completing two preliminary tasks. First, I must specify what it exactly means to attain an illustrious place in the discipline's history. Second, I must discuss the dimensions by which a discipline's history can be understood, including those dimensions that can be most properly considered scientific rather than humanistic. The first task is accomplished in chapter 1; the second, in chapter 2.

1

EMINENCE IN PSYCHOLOGY

How does one determine who can be included among psychology's notables? How does one gauge the magnitude of their greatness? As I discuss more fully in chapter 3, several measurement strategies are actually available to any investigator. Therefore, at this point I would like to mention just one: expert nominations. James McKeen Cattell (1903b), himself a distinguished American psychologist, was the first to introduce this practice, and the technique has been used sporadically ever since (e.g., K. E. Clark, 1957; S. F. Davis, Thomas, & Weaver, 1982; Korn, Davis, & Davis, 1991). In this method, recognized leaders in the field identify and rate the major figures who have contributed the most to the discipline. An excellent example is the study Annin, Boring, and Watson conducted in 1968. They began with an initial list of 1,040 candidates who (a) had attained some degree of prominence, (b) lived between 1600 and 1967, and (c) were presumed deceased at the time of the study. These candidates were then rated by a panel of nine distinguished jurors from four countries: Edwin G. Boring (Harvard), Richard J. Herrnstein (Harvard), Ernest R. Hilgard (Stanford), Robert I. Watson (New Hampshire), Michael Wertheimer (Colorado), Robert B. MacLeod (Cornell), Megumi Imada (Kyoto), Paul Fraisse (Sorbonne), and Joseph R. Nuttin (Louvain).

In essence, the ratings were made along a 4-point scale on which the highest score was given to candidates who would most properly belong among the top 500 most "important psychologists" in the discipline's history. The final list of the supposed greats actually contained 538 notables, but that was close enough. The 53 who received the highest possible ratings from all nine raters are shown in Exhibit 1.1. It is not surprising that this list included such big names as Wilhelm Wundt, John B. Watson, Wolfgang Köhler, Gordon W. Allport, and Charles E. Spearman, as well as the already-mentioned William James. It is interesting that Edward B. Titchener and Max Wertheimer also appear in this elite subset. Boring earned his PhD under the first, and Michael Wertheimer was the son of the second. Even so, because their placement among the top 10% was unanimous, this honor was probably well deserved by both psychologists.

A different problem appears, nonetheless. Close inspection reveals that many of those who made the final cut are, technically, not psychologists. In fact, according to a follow-up study by R. I. Watson and Merrifield (1973), only 42% of the 538 luminaries can be considered psychologists in the strictest sense, albeit another 6% can be considered psychiatrists and yet another 3% psychoanalysts, both closely related achievement domains. On the other hand, this still leaves nearly half of psychology's history in the hands of notables who might not be considered psychologists, psychiatrists, or psychoanalysts. This substantial remainder falls almost entirely into two categories: scientists and philosophers. Some might argue that some individuals in these last two groups might not properly belong in a list of great psychologists. The "psychological eminence" credited to the scientists and philosophers can be distinguished from the status credited to genuine "eminent psychologists" (Henley & Thorne, 1992).

This issue essentially revolves around whether scholars wish to use an inclusive or exclusive definition of psychology and its history. The divergence is reflected in many histories of the field. Some texts begin with the philosophers of antiquity (D. E. Robinson, 1986), whereas others start the historical narrative proper when psychology became a discipline divorced from philosophy and separate from the other sciences (E. G. Boring, 1950). The former, inclusive position is the one adopted in this book—that is, although I place the most emphasis on what we know about great psychologists in the narrowest sense, I also give some space to others who have left their indelible mark on the discipline. Thus, this volume is about three general groups of contributors—the philosophers, the scientists, and the psychologists—with proper concentration on members of the last group. I now turn to what these three categories are taken to represent. This helps justify adopting an inclusive perspective on psychology's history.

PHILOSOPHERS

Hermann Ebbinghaus certainly belongs in the elite group of eminent psychologists (see Exhibit 1.1). Although he is best known for his pioneering

EXHIBIT 1.1
The 53 Most Highly Rated Important Psychologists, 1600–1967

Philosophers

Franz Brentano (1838–1917)
René Descartes (1596–1650)
John Dewey (1859–1952)
Gustav Theodor Fechner (1801–1887)
Johann Friedrich Herbart (1776–1841)
David Hume (1711–1776)
William James (1840–1910)
John Locke (1632–1704)
James Mill (1773–1836)
John Stuart Mill (1806–1873)
Herbert Spencer (1820–1903)

Scientists

Vladimir Mikhailovich Bekhterev
   (1857–1927)
Walter Bradford Cannon (1871–1945)
Jean-Martin Charcot (1825–1893)
Charles Darwin (1809–1882)
Hermann von Helmholtz (1821–1894)
Ewald Hering (1834–1918)
Ivan Pavlov (1849–1936)
Karl Pearson (1857–1936)
Charles Scott Sherrington (1857–1952)
Ernst Heinrich Weber (1795–1878)

Psychologists

Alfred Adler (1870–1937)
Gordon W. Allport (1897–1967)
James R. Angell (1869–1949)
Alfred Binet (1857–1911)

Hermann Ebbinghaus (1850–1909)
Sigmund Freud (1856–1939)
Francis Galton (1822–1911)
G. Stanley Hall (1844–1924)
Clark L. Hull (1884–1952)
Pierre Janet (1859–1947)
Carl Jung (1875–1961)
Kurt Koffka (1886–1941)
Wolfgang Köhler (1887–1967)
Emil Kraepelin (1856–1926)
Oswald Külpe (1862–1915)
Karl S. Lashley (1890–1958)
William McDougall (1871–1938)
Clifford Thomas Morgan (1915–1976)
Henri Piéron (1881–1964)
Edgar John Rubin (1886–1951)
Charles E. Spearman (1863–1945)
Carl Stumpf (1848–1936)
Lewis M. Terman (1877–1956)
Edward L. Thorndike (1874–1949)
L. L. Thurstone (1887–1955)
Edward B. Titchener (1867–1927)
Edward C. Tolman (1886–1959)
John B. Watson (1878–1958)
Max Wertheimer (1880–1943)
Robert S. Woodworth (1869–1962)
Wilhelm Wundt (1832–1920)
Robert M. Yerkes (1876–1956)

Note. Names are those listed in Annin, Boring, and Watson (1968; see also Zusne & Dailey, 1982). Individuals are assigned to their general domains of achievement according to the designations given by R. I. Watson and Merrifield (1973). The scientists entail psychologists, neurologists, biologists, and statisticians, and the psychologists include psychiatrists and psychoanalysts.

research on memory, he also made the famous observation that "psychology has a long past, yet its real history is short" (Ebbinghaus, 1908, p. 3). This assertion has been frequently quoted in history texts for most of this century (albeit often in a different translation; see, e.g., E. G. Boring, 1950, p. ix). Less often quoted is the following sentence, which asserts that "for thousands of years it has existed and has been growing older" (Ebbinghaus, 1908, p. 3). That is a very long past. Yet at the same time, psychology has a short history as a bona fide scientific discipline. When Ebbinghaus was writing, the discipline was younger than 50 years old. The philosophers mostly filled the vast temporal gap between psychology's past and its history. Thus, in the list of the 538 eminent psychologists, thinkers make up the second-largest single group: Ninety-two are so identified, along with 1 logician and 1 theologian, yielding a percentage of 17% (R. I. Watson & Merrifield, 1973).

Actually, this proportion understates the representation of this category in the annals of the discipline, for it includes only historical figures living between 1600 and 1967 (Annin et al., 1968). Needless to say, the number of distinguished philosophers who failed to satisfy this criterion is very large, and many of them have made outstanding contributions to psychology. Ebbinghaus (1908) gave the specific case of Aristotle, "that giant thinker" who around 340 BC had "built it up into an edifice comparing very favorably with any other science of that time" (p. 3). Aristotle's treatises *On the Soul* and *On Memory and Reminiscence*, for instance, still contain observations and speculations that remain worthy of discussion today.

To be sure, Ebbinghaus (1908) also added that Aristotle's psychology did not go anywhere. Even so, that does not mean that he or any other great thinker from psychology's long past can be ignored. The ancient philosophers, after all, raised some very critical questions. What are the origins of human knowledge? How does one know that what one believes is true? What is the relation between the soul and body, or between the mind and the brain? Is there something that can be called "human nature" and, if so, what is it like? What are the foundations of human happiness? How can one best lead the "good life," and what is the basis of one's knowledge of good and evil, the foundation of one's moral sense? These issues, which have dominated philosophical thought for centuries, all date back to the great Greek thinkers of the distant past. The philosopher Alfred North Whitehead (1929) once observed that the "the safest general characterization of the European philosophical tradition is that it consists of a series of footnotes to Plato" (p. 63), the author of the famous dialogues and Aristotle's own teacher at the Academy. By this assertion Whitehead did "not mean the systematic scheme of thought which scholars have doubtfully extracted from his writings"; rather, he was alluding "to the wealth of general ideas scattered through them" that "have made [Plato's] writing an inexhaustible mine of suggestion" (p. 63).

To a very large extent, the same may be said of psychology, which grew out of that same intellectual tradition. For example, psychologist Howard Gardner (1983) claimed

> that a key ingredient in contemporary cognitive science is the agenda of issues, and the set of concerns, which have long exercised epistemologists in the Western philosophical tradition. To my mind, it is virtually unthinkable that cognitive science would exist, let alone assume its current form, had there not been a philosophical tradition dating back to the time of the Greeks. (p. 7)

The philosophers may admittedly not have provided modern answers, but at least they should receive credit for raising the questions. As Albert Einstein and Leopold Infeld (1938) once noted, in a different context,

> The formulation of a problem is often more essential than its solution, which may be merely a matter of mathematical or experimental skill. To

raise new questions, new problems, to regard old problems from a new angle, requires creative imagination and marks real advances in science. (p. 95)

Before turning to the next category of contributions, a caveat is in order. The European philosophical tradition is not the only great one, by any means. Alfred Kroeber (1944), the eminent cultural anthropologist, identified many other major intellectual configurations, including the Indian, Arab–Muslim, and Chinese. The last tradition alone features more than 300 notable philosophers (Simonton, 1988b). Moreover, many of these non-Western thinkers have speculated about matters of patent psychological relevance. From the Indian subcontinent, for instance, came the Upanishads of the ancient Hindus and the revelations of the Buddha, the first discussing the nature of the human mind and the second treating the psychological origins of human happiness. Nevertheless, these non-Western philosophies have only a minor place in psychology's history. Scientific psychology emerged directly out of European intellectual history, and only relatively recently has it opened itself up to influences outside that core tradition (e.g., humanistic and transpersonal psychologies). Hence, the focus here reflects that differential influence of the world's great philosophers.

SCIENTISTS

Many eminent contributors to psychology's history were neither psychologists nor philosophers. Ivan Pavlov, for example, was a distinguished physiologist—and one who even looked somewhat disdainfully on psychology's claims to scientific status. In fact, in the list of 538 illustrious figures the physiologists constitute the third-largest group, after the psychologists and philosophers (cf. Exhibit 1.1). Fully 10% can be so identified (R. I. Watson & Merrifield, 1973). Yet along with them can be added biologists, sociologists, physicists, anatomists, anthropologists, and neurologists (2% each) and astronomer–mathematicians, mathematicians, statisticians, ophthalmologists, chemists, and geneticists (1% each), yielding a total proportion of 29%—which exceeds by a substantial margin the percentage due the philosophers. Nonetheless, because this list goes as far back as 1600, most of the major scientists since the Scientific Revolution are included, such as Galileo and Kepler (but not Copernicus or Vesalius). So it is a moot point whether the proportion would continue to far surpass that for the philosophers if it were extended back to antiquity. Yet it is also a point not worth much debate. It suffices to conclude that psychology's history owes a great deal to the scientists who have distinguished its past.

When one examines the record more carefully, however, it becomes apparent that scientists enter psychology's annals for a diversity of reasons.

Many are there because they actually made direct contributions to psychology as a scientific enterprise. Charles Darwin's work on *The Expressions of Emotions in Man and Animals* as well as his developmental study of his first-born son can be considered such. All of the scientists listed in Exhibit 1.1 fall into this group. On the other hand, often scientists have attained prominence in the history of psychology for reasons other than their direct contributions to the discipline.

Take Isaac Newton, for example. This illustrious mathematician and physicist made it into the select group of 538 "important psychologists" (Annin et al., 1968). Yet what are his direct contributions to psychology? Newton's theory of colors has the most obvious relevance. With the exception of Goethe's offbeat views, all psychological theories of color vision begin with Newton's spectral theory as the physical foundation. Newton also devised the calculus, a mathematical tool of great utility in quantitative psychology, but it is hard to see this as sufficient justification. Most likely the main reason for Newton's inclusion is his *Mathematical Principles of Natural Philosophy*, which is frequently claimed to be the greatest single scientific monograph ever written. Yet despite its profound influence on the physical sciences and even general philosophy, this work's impact on psychology is far more indirect. Newton's magnum opus served as an exemplar of how the best science is done in the best sciences. Neobehaviorist Clark L. Hull so admired the book that a copy was displayed on his desk, almost like a copy of the Bible. Hull's learning theory also clearly aspired to the same mathematical and hypothetico–deductive method that makes Newton's book such a remarkable treatise. Hence, Newton's influence on psychology in this case seems to have been largely that of a methodological standard or paradigm to which the most ambitious psychologists could aspire.

Nicolaus Copernicus provides an even more striking case. Although he died before 1600, and therefore could not be honored with inclusion among the 538, he enjoys a very conspicuous presence in biographical dictionaries and histories of the discipline (Zusne, 1984; Zusne & Dailey, 1982). Unlike Newton, moreover, his contribution is confined to a single major work—*On the Revolutions of the Heavenly Spheres*—in which he presented his heliocentric theory of the solar system. Yet a close reading of Copernicus's masterpiece will fail to yield anything of significance for psychological science. It provides neither the substantive basis for psychological theory nor a novel methodology for the psychologist's emulation. So what is the rationale for his prominence in the discipline's history? The main reason was clearly the revolutionary nature of his theory, which completely overturned the Ptolemaic system inherited from antiquity. Moreover, humanity's own earth was removed from its privileged position at the center of the universe to just one of several planets orbiting the sun. So revolutionary was this system that it was eventually condemned by the Roman Catholic authorities, thus launching the antagonism between religion and science that has punctuated intellectual history ever since. Hence, what inspired philosophers and scientists after Copernicus was not his specific ideas but rather the fact that he had overthrown tradition, dethroned the earth, and provoked powerful opposition from the more conservative forces in society. The history of psychology accordingly contains several instances where its innovators have compared their ideas directly to the Copernican revolution. Immanuel Kant (1787/ 1952) did just this in the preface to the second edition of his epochal *Critique of Pure Reason,* and Sigmund Freud (1917/1953) did the same in his speculative essay on "A Difficulty in the Path of Psycho-Analysis." Copernicus is thus most important in psychology for providing the first modern prototype of the scientific revolutionary who turns the intellectual world topsy-turvy.

It is probably erroneous to conclude that neither Newton nor Copernicus belongs in psychology's history. Their contributions may have been indirect, but their impact was probably far greater than many psychologists, whose contributions were direct but relatively minor. Moreover, their indirect influence can be negative as well as positive. To what extent can Newton be held accountable for the "physics envy" that has led many psychologists to attempt prematurely to convert their discipline into an exact science? To what degree can the example of Copernicus be held responsible for giving psychologists unjustified confidence in eccentric novelties that are more wacky than revolutionary?

PSYCHOLOGISTS

What remains is the category of "important psychologists," which consists of individuals who can be called psychologists. The justification for including notable psychologists in the history of psychology seems too obvious to deserve detailed discussion, yet what is obvious is not always so simple. The term *psychologist* can at once be too narrow and too broad, depending on what it means for someone to "do psychology."

On the one hand, it would certainly be a mistake to confine the term to individuals who acquired PhDs in psychology. That would exclude many earlier figures who earned their degrees in periods when it was impossible to obtain doctoral training in the field. Indeed, Wundt and James would be excluded by this criterion; both the "father of psychology" and the "father of American psychology" were MDs rather than PhDs. Of course, this same status holds for almost all great psychiatrists and psychoanalysts, such as Emil Kraepelin and Carl Jung (Otto Rank and Eric Fromm being among the rare exceptions among such notables). Even worse, many of psychology's luminaries who received their doctorates did so in fields other than psychology. Karl S. Lashley's PhD was in genetics, Edwin Guthrie's was in philosophy, and Jean Piaget's was in biology—all three earned these degrees in periods when doctoral programs in psychology were already well established. Several others, such as Francis Galton, did not even earn a degree beyond the baccalaureate. These cases show that psychologists can hold almost any degree and still rise among the greats in the field—*qua* psychologists.

On the other hand, the discipline of psychology has broadened considerably since its founding, so that psychologists form a far more heterogeneous group than in days of old. This heterogeneity holds even for those who obtained doctoral degrees in the discipline. This Spencerian evolution is seen throughout the world, but it is perhaps most conspicuous in the history of the American Psychological Association (APA; see, e.g., Howard et al., 1986). Founded in 1892 by G. Stanley Hall, its first members were almost entirely academic researchers. Their view was that psychology was a scientific discipline dedicated to the advancement of research and theory. APA's first conferences and publications continued this emphasis. Over time, however, the number of applied psychologists and psychotherapists increased, a growth that accelerated immensely after World War II, especially in the area of clinical psychology. By the 1980s, these practitioners represented the overwhelming majority of the APA membership. As a result, APA began to function ever more as a professional organization, such as the American Medical Association, than a scientific organization, such as the American Sociological Association. At the beginning, APA presidents were usually distinguished scientists, but after awhile this ceased to be a prerequisite, the top spot largely being replaced by highly accomplished practitioners instead. In 1966, the APA president, Dorothy Cantor, was distinguished by having received a PsyD (a practice degree) rather than a PhD (a research degree). This event was symptomatic of a larger trend: Increasingly more practitioners were obtaining their graduate training from "free-standing" professional schools rather than from graduate schools associated with research institutions. In 1988 these radical transformations in APA motivated the more scientifically oriented psychologists to form a new organization, the American Psychological Society. There thus exist more than one psychology in the United States.

So how should these newfangled psychologists be treated? If psychiatrists and psychoanalysts, and even geneticists and philosophers, can all be counted among the great psychologists, how can these practitioners be excluded? To me the only fair answer is to continue to adopt an inclusive view of the field. However, this inclusiveness must operate according to the same rigorous criteria by which other notables have entered the annals of the discipline. Sigmund Freud, for example, was technically a practitioner rather than a scientist. He held no full-time appointment at a research institution; instead, his whole career was rooted in his own private practice. He also may have been a very great therapist—many psychoanalysts might say the greatest ever. Yet Freud's name did not get emblazoned in psychology's history because he was a great practitioner. Freud was a highly prolific author of scholarly books and articles. He was also a great professional, founding and promoting organizations and journals to promulgate psychoanalysis as a recognized school of psychology. Furthermore, Freud's impact was eventually even felt among academic psychologists, who began to test his theories or incorporate his ideas into different psychological terms. Freud earned his distinctive status as one of psychology's greats for the magnitude and duration of the influence he had on psychological research and practice—not even considering his pervasive reverberations in intellectual and popular culture. In short, Freud made history. All other psychologists, whatever their training and occupation, must be held to the same standard to attain greatness.

2

HISTORY AND SCIENCE

In the preceding chapter, I argued that there are three major routes to attaining greatness in psychology. First, one can contribute to the history of those philosophical issues that have direct relevance to the debates that dominate psychology today. Second, one can make a contribution to the history of those scientific disciplines that have the most intimate linkages with psychological science. Third and last, the luminary can contribute to the history of psychology as a bona fide psychologist. What these three pathways share is the assumption that a psychologist's greatness is to be defined by his or her contribution to history.

This common requirement of greatness, then, suggests that to understand the nature of greatness demands that one first comprehend the nature of history. Hence, I open this chapter with a discussion of how historical understanding can be obtained. It will become evident that among the various approaches to the attainment of such understanding is the use of scientific analysis. Therefore, I close the chapter with a discussion of the prospects for a scientific study of psychology's history. It will then become apparent that among the various scientific options is the constructive use of the psychology of science, including the psychology of psychological science.

UNDERSTANDING HISTORY

How is history understood? The best approach to addressing this difficult question is to discuss the central issues that plague the understanding of history. Six issues are the most critical: genius versus zeitgeist as causal agents, internal versus external influences, presentist versus historicist narratives, idiographic versus nomothetic interpretations, quality versus quantity in phenomena, and deterministic versus stochastic descriptions.

Genius Versus Zeitgeist as Causal Agents

When claiming that a great psychologist "makes history," people implicitly assume that individuals can in fact do such a thing. Many historians believe that this is indeed possible. For instance, English historian and essayist Thomas Carlyle (1841) maintained, in his essay *On Heroes*, that "Universal History, the history of what man has accomplished in this world, is at bottom the History of the Great Men who have worked here" (p. 1). This Great Person theory of history had a direct impact on psychology's conception of genius. This is apparent in Francis Galton's (1869) classic work *Hereditary Genius*, in which he defined genius in terms of enduring reputation, as gauged by "the opinion of contemporaries, revised by posterity the reputation of a leader of opinion, of an originator, of a man to whom the world deliberately acknowledges itself largely indebted" (Galton 1892/1972, p. 77). One obvious approach to acknowledging this indebtedness is the allotment of eponymic status; that is, the Great Person's name provides a label for an important school, syndrome, illusion, technique, measurement unit, or the like and is thereby assigned credit for the contribution, discovery, movement, or event. Widespread eponyms in psychology run into the hundreds; Table 2.1 provides a partial listing (for many more examples, see Zusne, 1987b).

This individualistic perspective appears quite compatible with psychology's own disciplinary disposition. Psychological research is largely dedicated to the study of individual cognition, emotion, and behavior. In line with this affinity, the Great Person or genius theory also motivates the organization and emphasis of many textbooks on psychology's history, such as R. I. Watson's (1963) *The Great Psychologists: From Aristotle to Freud* and Raymond Fancher's (1979) *Pioneers of Psychology*. In histories like these, the titles of headings and sometimes of whole chapters are often merely the names of illustrious psychologists. Nevertheless, not all historians of psychology favor this perspective. The most prominent opponent was E. G. Boring, who has long been recognized as one of the major figures in the emergence of the history of psychology as a scholarly discipline. Through his various articles and chapters (E. G. Boring, 1963), and especially through his 1950 classic *A History of Experimental Psychology*, Boring has had a considerable impact on

TABLE 2.1
Representative Eponyms in the History of Psychology

Domain	Eponyms
Schools	Aristotelian, Cartesian, Comptian, Hegelian, Kantian, Machian, Marxist, Platonist, Thomist, Watsonian
Therapeutics	Adlerian, Bernheim's, Freudian, Jungian, Pinel's system, Rankian, Reichian, Rogerian
Theories	Cannon–Bard, Darwinian, Hebb's, Heider's, Hering's, James–Lange, Ladd–Franklin, Lamarckian, Malthusian, Thurstone's, Young–Helmholtz
Laws	Bell–Magendie, Donders's, Emmert's, Fechner's, Galton's, Heinis, Mendel's, Müller–Schumann, Ribot's, Steven's, Weber, Yerkes–Dodson, Zipf's
Syndromes	Brown–Séquard, Down's, Klinefelter's, Korsakoff's, Selye's, Tourette
Diseases	Alzheimer's, Charcot's, Daltonism, Janet's, Parkinson's
Symptoms	Broca's aphasia, Charcot's triad, Wernicke's agnosia
Neuroanatomy	Bekhterev nucleus, Bell's circle of nerves, Golgi apparatus, Purkinje cell
Phenomena	Aubert, Féré, Köhler–Restorff
Effects	Brewster, Broadbent, Brücke, Garcia, Gibson, Greenspoon, Rosenthal, Stroop, Zeigarnik
Illusions	Aristotle's, Ebbinghaus, Hering, Jastrow, Müller–Lyer, Ponzo, Wundt
Figures	Ebbinghaus, Lissajou's, Purkinje, Rubin's
Reflexes	Babinski, Darwinian, Moro
Triangles	Hellwag's, Helmholtz, Koenig, Maxwell's, Pascal's
Scales	Bayley, Guttman, Likert, Oseretsky, Thorndike's, Thurstone, Wechsler–Bellevue
Experiments	Cannon–Washburn, Fechner's, Franklin, Stratton's
Test	Bárány, Bender, Goodenough, Fourier's, Henmon–Nelson, Jung, McNemar, Otis, Rorschach, Stanford–Binet, Torrance, Turing, Vygotsky
Measurement units	Angstrom, Celsius, decibel, Fahrenheit, hertz, Kelvin, ohm, volt
Curves	Ebbinghaus, Gaussian, Gomopertz, Laplacean, Vincent
Techniques	Aubert diaphragm, Dunlap chronoscope, Erdmann–Dodge tachistoscope, Galton's whistle, galvanometer, Gesell observation dome, Jastrow cylinders, Koenig cylinders, Lashley's jumping stand, Luria technique, Seashore's audiometer, Skinner box, Thorndike's puzzle box, Wundt gravity phonometer, Yerkes–Watson discrimination apparatus
Statistics	Bayes theorem, Bernoulli trials, Cronbach's alpha, Fisher distribution, Pearsonian correlation, Poisson distribution, Spearman's g
Mathematics	Boolean algebra, Fourier's law, Markov process Shannon–Weiner information measure
Paradoxes	Fechner's, Leonardo's, Lord's, Zeno's
Miscellaneous	Ames demonstration, Asch situation, Bekhterev's nystagmus, Berger rhythm, Brunswik ratio, Buridan's ass, Freudian slip, Galenic temperaments, Hering's afterimage, Ishihara plates, Jungian typology, Kraepelin's classification, Lloyd Morgan's canon, mesmerism, Montessori method, Newton's color circle, Occam's razor, Pavlovian conditioning, Purkinje afterimage, statue of Condillac, Titchener's circles

both research and teaching in the field. Boring explicitly rejected the genius theory, arguing that it is excessively "personalistic." In contrast, he argued for a "naturalistic" perspective that explicates the major events of psychology's history in terms of the *zeitgeist*, the German word for "spirit of the times." The psychologists who are called "great" are merely the eponymic agents of larger, impersonal forces operating in the intellectual climate of the discipline. Indeed, Boring believed that in the future history could be written without the supposed big names because their causal status would be reduced to mere epiphenomena. "When that day comes," concluded Boring (1963), "we shall look back—surely we shall or rather our posterity will—on the personalized history of science of the twentieth century with an indulgent smile and think: How egocentric and immature they all were in those days!" (p. 25).

This zeitgeist theory of history has exerted its own distinctive influence on how historians have chosen to narrate the origins and development of psychology (e.g., Furumoto, 1989). Boring's influence is conspicuous in quotations such as the following:

> A Copernicus or a Marie Curie does not single-handedly change the course of history through sheer force of genius. He or she does so only because the way has already been cleared. We shall see that this has been true for every major figure in the history of psychology. (Schultz & Schultz, 1992, p. 18)

Boring's impact is also apparent in many excellent textbooks that adopt a "history of ideas" approach. A fine example is Thomas Hardy Leahey's (1997) *A History of Psychology: Main Currents in Psychological Thought*. None of its 15 chapter titles features the proper name of a single psychologist, scientist, or philosopher, neither do such names appear in any of the headings for the principal sections of each chapter. Even when a figure's name shows up in secondary section titles, it is often in an understated manner, such as "The Reassertion of Metaphysics: Immanuel Kant (1724–1804)" (p. 138), with the intellectual movement or trend preceding the name. In addition, many historical figures, such as William James, find themselves spread across different sections and even chapters, according to how they fit the flow of ideas rather than the progression of their lives.

Boring and many of his followers saw genius and zeitgeist as rival conceptions of history. Yet the two theories do not have to be perceived as so antagonistic. The events that make up the history of psychology or any other human activity may be the joint product of both individual and situational factors. Certainly this is true in the case of historic leaders, such as monarchs and presidents (Simonton, 1984f, 1987c), and there is ample evidence that the same holds for creative domains as well (Simonton, 1994a). One of my central goals is to show how the concept of genius can be inserted into psychology's history in a naturalistic fashion while concomitantly acknowledging the impact of the zeitgeist.

Internal Versus External Influences

Although E. G. Boring (1950, 1963) gave the zeitgeist a powerful causal role in psychology's history, he never really provided a precise and rigorous definition of the term (Ross, 1969; cf. B. Hyman & Shephard, 1980). Instead, he left it as a kind of amorphous force that he would juxtapose against the proverbial genius. Still, it is clear from his writings that he tended to view zeitgeist in a relatively restricted manner. It was defined according to intellectual movements within the discipline, such as the prevailing set of theories, problems, techniques, and findings. On the other hand, zeitgeist can also be granted a more encompassing definition. Rather than having one zeitgeist for psychologists, another for sociologists, and yet another for biologists, it might be conceived as a more inclusive milieu that entails every sociocultural phenomenon that helps shape individual beliefs. That milieu might even include political, economic, and technological circumstances that operate well beyond the confines of the intellectual domain. For example, whereas part of Charles Darwin's theory of evolution might reflect the accumulation of knowledge in biology, geology, and paleontology, another part might reflect the concurrent stage in the development of British capitalism and imperialism.

This definitional spread captures two rival accounts of scientific history, including the history of psychology. On the one hand, internalist interpretations assume that the key forces underlying evolution and revolution in the sciences are internal to the discipline itself. A well-known example is the theory of scientific change advanced by philosopher and scientist Thomas Kuhn (1970). Put in simple terms, the scientists making up a particular discipline all subscribe to a received paradigm, which constitutes a field-specific zeitgeist. This paradigm defines the theoretical constructs and methodological techniques that characterize the problem-solving research of normal science. With time, however, the paradigm begins to generate anomalies—findings that are inconsistent with paradigmatic expectations. If enough of these anomalies accumulate, the discipline enters a state of crisis. In scientific revolutions, this crisis is resolved by the discovery and promulgation of a new paradigm. Hence, Albert Einstein's relativity theory purported to resolve certain anomalies that plagued Newtonian mechanics. The main point is that a complete account of scientific change in Kuhn's model requires only reference to transformations occurring within the particular science.

Externalist accounts have a contrary outlook. Ideas are mostly a reflection of more powerful forces pervading all of society. When those forces change, intellectual history must follow suit. This is the position taken by

Marxists, who argue that the history of ideas is a manifestation of more fundamental transformations in material conditions, as defined by the economic system. Classical, medieval, capitalist, and socialist systems must have correspondingly contrasting ideologies. Karl Marx made explicit the contrast between internalist and externalist perspectives when he compared his own dialectical materialism with the dialectic idealism advocated by the German philosopher Georg Hegel, who had proposed an extremely internalist philosophy of history:

> My dialectic method is not only different from the Hegelian, but is its direct opposite. To Hegel, the life-process of the human brain, i.e., the process of thinking, which, under the name of "the Idea," he even transforms into an independent subject, is the demiurge of the real world, and the real world is only the external, phenomenal form of "the Idea." With me, on the contrary, the ideal is nothing else than the material world reflected by the human mind, and translated into forms of thought. (Marx, 1873/1952, p. 11)

It is crucial that historians of psychology not fall into the error of the either–or. The ideas that populate the history of psychology are very likely the joint product of both internal and external factors. A comprehensive account of the rise and fall of its various theories and schools will largely incorporate both disciplinary and sociocultural forces. This is a point that I amply document in Part V of this book.

Presentist Versus Historicist Narratives

When historians narrate significant events and people they often slip into the "fallacy of presentism," a kind of anachronism whereby the past is viewed only through glasses deeply colored by the obsessions of the present (D. H. Fisher, 1970, p. 135). A classic illustration is presented in English historian Herbert Butterfield's (1951) *Whig Interpretation of History*. *Whig history* is defined as the

> tendency in many historians to write on the side of Protestants and Whigs, to praise revolutions provided they have been successful, to emphasize certain principles of progress in the past and to produce a story which is the ratification if not the glorification of the present. (p. v)

Presentism is a commonplace problem in intellectual histories that appraises the ideas of premodern thinkers according to the standards of modern times (e.g., Randall, 1940). It is no accident, therefore, that thinkers who espouse opinions more consistent with contemporary views tend to attain more acclaim than do those whose opinions now appear obsolete (Simonton, 1976f). Needless to say, because histories of psychology are likewise histories of ideas, they frequently have presentist biases as well. It definitely appears whenever psychologists are called great for being "ahead of their times" or for "anticipating" modern beliefs.

The alternative to presentism is *historicism*, which can be defined as "the commitment to understanding the past for its own sake" (Stocking, 1965, p. 212). The historian examines events, ideas, and persons of previous eras as they are embedded in the appropriate historical context. The past is understood in its own terms, without respect to long-term consequences or contemporary meanings. This contextual understanding must supersede any misplaced desire to pass judgment according to the hindsight of the present. This approach can accordingly serve as an antidote to the presentist practice of judging great psychologists according to standards inappropriate for their times. To illustrate, most modern psychologists must feel not a little embarrassment when reading Galton's (1869) *Hereditary Genius*, so replete as it is with sexist and racist opinions. Yet, placed in the context of his Victorian times, Galton's outdated ideas would look much more mainstream than they do today.

There exists a third perspective on history that is neither presentist nor historicist. Rather than place all the emphasis on either the present or the past, equal weight can be placed on *all* the persons, ideas, and events that constitute the relevant historical record from its beginnings to the contemporary times. In this approach the researcher transcends history by adopting a scientific perspective that is fundamentally ahistorical. Major contributors to the discipline become "subjects" or "participants" who provide data points in an egalitarian fashion. Just as significant is that this alternative permits the simultaneous incorporation of both individual and situational factors. The rationale for this scientific "transhistorical" strategy will make more sense in the discussion that follows.

Idiographic Versus Nomothetic Analyses

What student has not lamented that history is so full of "names, dates, and places"? Proper nouns and chronological delimiters abound. Even scholars who have written psychology's story from a history-of-ideas perspective have not avoided this necessity (e.g., Leahey, 1997). Page after page presents the names and vital statistics of great psychologists, the titles and publication dates of their key works, and an inventory of predecessors and successors that is equally riddled with proper nouns. This appearance departs dramatically from what appears in the typical scientific journal article. Generalizations and abstractions are ubiquitous; proper nouns and dates are almost entirely relegated to citations of other publications. Almost never is the name of a subject or participant given, neither would any reader have any interest if it were.

Gordon Allport (1937) made much of the distinction between the idiographic and the nomothetic (cf. Allport, 1962). History is an idiographic enterprise, full of particulars, intimately tied to specifics. Science is a nomothetic enterprise, dedicated to abstractions and generalizations that transcend the particular and specific. Psychology, as a science, has strongly allied itself with the nomothetic, with the search for general laws of cognition, emotion, and behavior. The history of psychology, in contrast, has dedicated itself to the idiographic, with the narration and interpretation of the unique and often unlawful.

What happens, though, when psychological science combines with historical phenomena? There are two main outcomes (Simonton, 1999c). On the one hand, the idiographic nature of history may predominate over the nomothetic nature of science. The outcome is psychohistory and psychobiography, an enterprise represented by such seminal works as Sigmund Freud's (1910/1964) *Leonardo da Vinci and a Memory of His Childhood* and Erik Erikson's (1958) *Young Man Luther: A Study in Psychoanalysis and History* (Elms, 1994; Runyan, 1982). Although the reliance on psychoanalytic principles is obvious, the expressed goal is to explicate the distinctive features of an individual life, not to make major contributions to nomothetic knowledge. On the other hand, history and science may combine so that the quest for universal and abstract laws or regularities predominates (Simonton, 1990d). Classic examples include Galton's (1869) *Hereditary Genius* and Catharine Cox's (1926) *The Early Mental Traits of Three Hundred Geniuses*, which constitutes the second volume of Lewis Terman's monumental *Genetic Studies of Genius*. In both works a multiple-case rather than single-case strategy was used to test hypotheses that transcend the idiosyncracies of any one individual. It is telling that Leonardo da Vinci shows up as a "subject" in both Galton's and Cox's studies, and that Martin Luther appears as a "subject" in Cox's investigation, but in all of these appearances these historical figures become submerged in the mass of other cases that are collectively used to discover behavioral regularities.

One special asset of the latter approach is the ability to incorporate into a single data analysis all of the variables that are deemed critical in making a psychologist "great" (Simonton, 1990d). The variables can include both individual and situational factors, and the latter can entail both internal (disciplinary) and external (sociocultural) influences. Once all the pertinent variables are measured, they can be subjected to statistical analyses and mathematical modeling techniques. This methodological approach necessarily presumes that historical phenomena can be quantified.

Quality Versus Quantity in Phenomena

Historical narratives have historically been qualitative rather than quantitative. The numbers are almost exclusively confined to dates, and even these dates are only handles for conveying the sequence and location of people and events in the flow of history. In contrast, scientific investigations are far more inclined to stress the quantitative aspects of phenomena. This inclination is especially conspicuous in the exact, or "hard" sciences, such as astronomy, physics, and chemistry, disciplines in which measurements, numbers, parameters, and formulae abound. Indeed, a strong tendency exists to judge a discipline's scientific advancement according to the degree that its theories and findings can be expressed in quantitative and mathematical terms. The opposite of *exact* is *inexact*; the opposite of *hard* is *soft*.

Admittedly, not all history is qualitative, neither is all science quantitative. In the former case, several historians have introduced quantitative methods into their discipline, often under the name *cliometrics* (e.g., Aydelotte, 1971). This approach has been especially fruitful in economic history, where it has earned its most distinguished practitioners the Nobel Prize for Economics (Whaples, 1991). In the case of the sciences, many notable contributions have been qualitative rather than quantitative in orientation. Darwin's *Origin of Species* (1860/1952) is a prime example, for his argument and documentation depended on neither numbers nor mathematics. Even so, it is often only in the early stages of a science that work can be of such high quality and remain purely qualitative. The history of evolutionary theory since Darwin has displayed an increased use of quantitative methods, including both measurement and mathematical analysis. For example, Gregor Mendel used quantitative techniques to discover genetic laws, after which Mendelian genetics was mathematically integrated with evolutionary theory in such works as R. A. Fisher's (1930) *The Genetical Theory of Natural Selection*. Ensuing work in population genetics converted Darwinism from a qualitative to a quantitative theory.

Of course, not everyone is enthusiastic about quantification, the opposition being particularly strong in humanistic disciplines, such as history, that purport to deal with intrinsically qualitative phenomena (e.g., Barzun, 1974). Even so, as Edward L. Thorndike (1921) once said, "Whatever exists, exists in some amount. To measure it is simply to know its varying amounts" (p. 379). The "greats" who populate the history books should be no exception to this general observation. In fact, Thorndike practiced what he preached by becoming one of the pioneers in the application of quantitative methods to historical figures. In 1936 Thorndike published the paper "The Relation Between Intellect and Morality in Rulers," and his very last scientific investigation—published posthumously by his son Robert in 1950—was on "Traits of Personality and Their Intercorrelations as Shown in Biographies." The latter was a singlehanded attempt to assess 91 great creators and leaders on 48 characteristics, such as intelligence, emotionality, agreeableness, depression, dominance, and sexual proclivity. Among the 91 were several whose names often show up in histories of psychology, including Isaac Newton, Benjamin Franklin, Johann Goethe, and Charles Darwin. Thus, Thorndike's swan song provides a concrete illustration of how some of the greats of psychology's history might be subjected to quantitative analysis.

Why should history be quantified in the first place? What possible advantage is there to reducing the incredible richness of the historical record to Arabic numerals and algebraic equations? One asset is that the mere act of quantification can reduce the overwhelming details of history to a more concise representation. Human information processing has many limitations that make it very difficult to make correct inferences from complex data (Faust, 1984). Quantitative reduction can therefore render the implicit patterns more accessible to the human mind. A straightforward illustration of this potential is found in Scottish biographer James Boswell's (1791/1952) *The Life of Samuel Johnson*:

> BOSWELL. Sir Alexander Dick tells me, that he remembers having a thousand people in a year to dine at his house: that is, reckoning each person as one, each time that he dined there. JOHNSON. That, Sir, is about three a day. BOSWELL. How your statement lessens the idea. JOHNSON. That, Sir, is the good of counting. It brings everything to a certainty, which before floated in the mind indefinitely. (pp. 507–508)

It took only a simple arithmetic manipulation of two numbers to convert the amazing to the mundane. A truly sophisticated mathematical analysis of even more impressive numerical arrays can boast ever greater reductive power. For example, E. L. Thorndike's (1950) last publication contains a table showing how the 91 subjects were scored on the 48 characteristics. Each row represents the scores received for each eminent individual. Although that amounts to 48 items of information about each individual, each number summarizes a much larger amount of information extracted from the biographies that Thorndike read about each one. That alone amounts to a valuable encapsulation of a vast quantity of data, yet that still yields a 91 × 48 data matrix with 4,368 numbers 1 or 2 digits long. To consolidate matters still further, Thorndike calculated the correlations among the 48 traits, thereby discovering what characteristics go together. The correlation matrix then replaces the data matrix, the number of separate numbers being reduced by almost one quarter, or 1,128 (= 0.5 × 48 × 47).

Unfortunately, Thorndike died before he could complete his study, but subsequent investigators have analyzed his data still further. A factor analysis of his published correlation matrix indicates that the associations among the 48 variables can be reduced to just four factors: Intelligence, Industriousness, Extraversion, and Aggressiveness (Simonton, 1991d; also see Knapp, 1962). That reduction results in only 192 data points, just 4 per eminent participant (viz., 48 × 4 factor loadings). As a final coup de grâce, it was also demonstrated that only two of these factors—Intelligence and Aggressiveness—predict the long-term eminence of each of the 91 historical figures (Simonton, 1991d). Even with a new variable (eminence) added, the rich complexity found in the hundreds of biographies that Thorndike read can be reduced to two simple nomothetic relationships (i.e., two regression coefficients).

Deterministic Versus Stochastic Descriptions

Perhaps the impressive aspect about the physical sciences is the seeming precision of the equations that describe natural phenomena: $V = gt^2$, $PV = wRT$, $F = kq_1q_2/r^2$, $E = mc^2$, and so on (just to give some of the simpler formulae). These equations not only look exact, but also most often are. Any minor empirical discrepancies can normally be dismissed as failures in instrumentation rather than failures of theory. Moreover, that precision is often accompanied by tremendous explanatory and predictive breadth. James Clerk Maxwell's equations, for instance, provide a complete description of electric and magnetic fields in just four compact formulae. Just as impressive is the fact that this precision and comprehensiveness usually obtain with a relatively small number of crucial variables. To be sure, in several areas of the physical sciences, these special assets are compromised—most notably in quantum physics, where the predictions are inherently probabilistic. Even so, a complete inventory of all nomothetic principles in the physical sciences will show that precision, comprehensiveness, and parsimony characterize the overwhelming majority.

This situation contrasts greatly with what holds in psychology. Equations that are precise, comprehensive, and parsimonious are extremely rare. For instance, although we have the Fechner law $R = k \log S$, this case is somewhat deceiving. For one thing, the equation originates in a branch of psychology closest to physics, namely, psychophysics. Gustav Fechner was in fact a physicist before becoming a psychologist. In addition, the law is only apparently precise, for it holds for only a somewhat narrow range of the independent variable (and its accuracy varies according to the sensory modality besides). It is best considered an approximation. As one ventures into areas of psychology that deal with phenomena farther removed from the physical sciences, one will notice two things. First, the number of independent variables in the equations usually increases. Human behaviors, cognitions, and emotions are multiply determined, and the more causes are included, so the more predictors must be included. Second, the predictive precision normally declines, as recorded by the typical amount of residual errors. Most commonly the amount of variance left unexplained exceeds the amount of variance explained, and often by a very ample margin. That is, psychologists usually must rely on a general linear model (e.g., multiple regression, analysis of variance, multivariate analysis of variance) in which the error term represents more variance than all of the independent variables combined.

In short, whereas the physical sciences most often describe phenomena using deterministic equations, the psychological sciences most frequently rely on stochastic equations that allow for the heavy intrusion of chance. Matters naturally get even worse when the phenomena under investigation reach historical proportions. For example, this book addresses the topic of what makes a psychologist great. Very likely hundreds of individual and situational factors contribute to whether a psychologist becomes one of the discipline's true luminaries (Eysenck, 1995; Simonton, 1999b), yet usually a researcher studies only a dozen or so, leaving most of the variance in greatness unexplained (see, e.g., Helmreich, Spence, Beane, Lucker, & Matthews, 1980; Simonton, 1992b). This means that the behavioral laws by which history can be explained most often operate in a very general way. Psychology's nomothetic principles function only as rough "covering laws" (Hempel, 1965) that outline the main patterns but not the nitty-gritty specifics. The situation is like what Charles Darwin claimed about his own attempts to explain a complex phenomenon: "I am inclined to look at everything as resulting from designed laws, with the details, whether good or bad, left to the working out of what we can call chance" (F. Darwin, 1892/1958, p. 24). Even after Darwin's theory was given more mathematical treatment in the 20th century, it still handles the general pattern of evolution rather better than the minuscule details.

I hasten to point out that the distinction between deterministic and stochastic descriptions is one of degree rather than kind. The chance component is merely an index of researchers' scientific ignorance. Theoretically, at least, researchers can keep adding more and more independent variables to the prediction equations, sacrificing parsimony for the sake of precision. The error term would then become ever smaller. Assuming that all variables are measured with perfect reliability—a big assumption!—residual errors would uniformly reduce to zero after all predictors are incorporated (and their functional relations correctly specified). An equation lacking the stochastic term would thereby convert into a deterministic equation. Practically speaking, the likelihood of such an outcome is probably very small, but it remains possible in principle.

SCIENTIFIC ANALYSES

It should have become apparent in the foregoing section that history can be understood from multiple perspectives. Yet among those viewpoints is the scientific one. The researcher or scholar can adopt the quantitative methods and nomothetic goals that predominate in the sciences—that is, history can be the subject of scientific inquiry. Yet science, too, can be the subject of scholarly scrutiny. In fact, the scientific enterprise has so impressed the world with its discoveries and inventions that it has itself become the subject of intellectual scrutiny, yielding various disciplines known collectively as *metasciences*. Some metascientific disciplines, such as the philosophy and history of science, are humanistic in emphasis. In the former discipline science is studied from the standpoint of supposed philosophical universals, whereas in the latter science is examined from the perspective of historical particulars.

Yet other metasciences, such as the sociology of science, are themselves sciences (Gaston, 1978; Mulkay, 1980). This might seem a strange concept.

Having scientists studying science might seem like having foxes guard the chicken coop. Yet the practice is consistent with the definition of science as "observation, identification, description, experimental investigation, and theoretical explanation of phenomena" (*American Heritage Electronic Dictionary*, 1992). Science itself consists of a set of phenomena worthy of scientific treatment, such as the training of scientists or the process of scientific discovery. From the standpoint of this book, one particular science of science has exceptional utility: the psychology of science.

The Psychology of Science

Although not always explicitly identified as such, the psychology of science has a long and distinguished history (Feist & Gorman, 1998; Fisch, 1977; Gholson, Shadish, Neimeyer, & Houts, 1989). Past contributors have included such great psychologists as Francis Galton (1874), William James (1880), Hermann von Helmholtz (1891/1898), Ernst Mach (1896), James McKeen Cattell (1903a), S. S. Stevens (1939), Walter Cannon (1940), Max Wertheimer (1945/1982), Louis M. Terman (1954), Paul Meehl (1954), B. F. Skinner (1959), David McClelland (1962), R. B. Cattell (1963), Abraham Maslow (1966), Jean Piaget (1970), and Herbert Simon (1977). The psychology of science essentially is simply the psychological study of the scientific enterprise, including the scientists who make up that enterprise (Grover, 1981; Mahoney, 1976; Mansfield & Busse, 1981; Simonton, 1988d).

Just as psychology is broken into subdisciplines, the psychology of science assumes several forms. Four subtopics are perhaps the most prominent, namely, those that correspond to psychology's cognitive, differential and personality, developmental, and social subdisciplines (Feist & Gorman, 1998).

1. *Cognitive psychologists* concentrate on the mental processes and strategies that underlie the origination and acceptance of scientific discoveries (Tweney, 1999; Tweney, Doherty, & Mynatt, 1981).
2. *Differential and personality psychologists* examine how individual differences in scientific performance or achievement correlate with cross-sectional variation in intellect, motivation, disposition, interests, or values (e.g., R. B. Cattell & Drevdahl, 1955; Chambers, 1964).
3. *Developmental psychologists* focus on the experiences and conditions that affect scientific development and performance across the life span (e.g., Dennis, 1954b; Simonton, 1991a).
4. *Social psychologists* study how interpersonal influences and group processes influence scientific performance or achievement (Shadish & Fuller, 1994).

This impressive range of subdisciplinary perspectives is augmented all the more by the tremendous variety of methodological approaches adopted by researchers (Feist & Gorman, 1998; Fisch, 1977; Tweney et al., 1981). The methods can include computer simulations, laboratory experiments, longitudinal studies, psychometric assessments, content analyses, meta-analyses, citation assessments, and biographical data. The units of analysis can be as small as single discoveries and as large as whole generations, and the sample sizes can vary from single-case studies to inquiries with thousands of cases. The research participants can range from adolescents who have exhibited scientific talent to mature scientists who have entered the final years of their careers. Moreover, the scientists who serve as participants in these investigations can vary from regular academic and industrial researchers to scientists of the first rank, including Nobel laureates and members of the National Academy of Sciences.

Of special interest, however, is the occasion when the research participants studied by psychologists are themselves psychologists. The result is a species of the psychology of science that can be called the *psychology of psychological science*.

The Psychology of Psychological Science

Psychologists have engaged in scholarly self-examination in several ways. Sometimes researchers will study future psychologists, such as undergraduates pursuing psychology majors or graduate students enrolled in doctoral programs (e.g., Hirschberg & Itkin, 1978). Other times investigators will examine fellow professionals, whether practitioners or researchers or both (e.g., Coan, 1973; Krasner & Houts, 1984; Zachar & Leong, 1992). To the extent that these investigations look at cognitive, personality, developmental, and social variables they may be taken as legitimate examples of the psychology of psychological science.

One special variety of the psychology of science is the scientific study of exceptional scientists, including scientific geniuses (Simonton, 1988d). Such research dates from the pioneering studies of Galton (1874) and J. M. Cattell (1910). This particular substantive focus has its counterpart in the psychology of psychological science as well; that is, researchers will scrutinize psychologists who have secured a conspicuous place in the annals of the discipline. As befits the methodological and theoretical diversity of psychology, there exist more than one approach to the psychological study of eminent psychologists. Sometimes illustrious psychologists become the subjects of single-case studies, such as Fancher's (1998) psychobiographical examination of Galton. Other times two or more luminaries are compared and contrasted, as in George Welsh's (1975) use of the Adjective Check List to differentiate the personalities of Freud and Carl Jung.

However, from the current perspective the most critical inquiries are those that apply quantitative techniques to multiple cases to draw generalizations that transcend the idiosyncratic features of any one psychologist. These quantitative and nomothetic studies fall into two main categories: psychometric and historiometric.

1. *Psychometric* studies apply regular assessment techniques, such as surveys and personality inventories, to contemporary psychologists who have some claim to enduring fame. An example is a study (Roe, 1953b) in which 14 eminent psychologists were administered the Thematic Apperception Test and Rorschach test along with measures of verbal, mathematical, and spatial intelligence. The members of this elite sample were nominated by such experts as E. G. Boring, E. R. Hilgard, D. B. Lindsley, and L. M. Terman.

2. *Historiometric* studies, on the other hand, exploit archival data to examine psychologists who have convincingly attained the status of historical figures in the discipline (for the original definition, see Woods, 1909, 1911). One example is my inquiry (Simonton, 1992b), in which I used content analysis, citation measures, and biographical data to examine 69 psychologists who were prominent in American psychology from 1879 to 1967 (according to Annin, Boring, & Watson, 1968).

Whether psychometric or historiometric, the psychology of psychological science specialty has already displayed nearly as much breadth as seen in the psychology of science as a whole. Indeed, when this literature is coupled with other research in the science of science, it becomes possible to present a scientific analysis of what it most likely takes to make history as a psychologist. Hence, the main purpose of this book is to provide an integrated review of the principal empirical findings. I begin the review in Part II by scrutinizing both individual differences and longitudinal changes in the productivity and influence of psychologists. In many respects, this part contains the core chapters, because it depicts what is most directly required to leave a lasting imprint on the discipline. In Part III I examine the personal characteristics that differentiate the more productive and influential psychologists from those much less so. In Part IV I turn to the developmental correlates of a psychologist's greatness, adopting a truly life span perspective. Then in Part V I survey the sociocultural context, including the internal and external zeitgeist. In the last section, Part VI, I discuss some of the major implications of this literature for teaching and research in the discipline.

II

LIFETIME OUTPUT OF PSYCHOLOGISTS AND THEIR IMPACT ON THE FIELD

INTRODUCTION: LIFETIME OUTPUT OF PSYCHOLOGISTS AND THEIR IMPACT ON THE FIELD

Near the beginning of the play *Julius Caesar*, William Shakespeare has Cassius complain to Brutus about the title character's intimidating greatness:

Why, man, he doth bestride the narrow world
Like a Colossus, and we petty men
Walk under his huge legs and peep about
To find ourselves dishonourable graves.
(quoted in Craig & Bevington, 1973, p. 774)

To some extent, some psychologists might voice a comparable complaint about one or another great psychologist. A psychoanalyst might feel that way about Sigmund Freud, a developmental psychologist about Jean Piaget, or a behaviorist about B. F. Skinner. Conflated admiration and envy are certainly not unique to the political world. It was too easy for Alexander Pope to praise Isaac Newton with the famous couplet "Nature and Nature's laws lay hid in night: / God said *Let Newton be!* and all was light" (quoted in *Who Said What When*, 1991, p. 129). As a poet, Pope's genius was not preempted by Newton's awesome achievements. Newton's fellow scientists, in both his day and after, would sometimes display a more ambivalent reaction. The great mathematician Joseph-Louis Lagrange once remarked that Newton was "not only the greatest genius that had ever existed, but was also the most fortunate, for, as there is only one universe, it can fall to only one man in the world's history to interpret its laws" (quoted in Jeans, 1942, p. 710). After Newton, everyone else was left with the scraps.

In the next three chapters I examine the truth of such opinions, as applied to the psychologists who most conspicuously figure in the discipline's history. I begin chapter 3 by examining individual differences in output and influence, whereas in chapter 4 I investigate how these indicators of greatness vary across the life span. In chapter 5 I look at the research programs and publications that are most likely to leave a lasting impact on the field.

3

INDIVIDUAL DIFFERENCES
IN GREATNESS

Contrary to what I just suggested in the introduction to Part II, not everyone agrees that a few great geniuses tend to dominate the scientific enterprise. According to the Spanish philosopher Ortega y Gasset (1932/1957),

> it is necessary to insist upon this extraordinary but undeniable fact: experimental science has progressed thanks in great part to the work of men astoundingly mediocre, and even less than mediocre. That is to say, modern science, the root and symbol of our actual civilization, finds a place for the intellectually commonplace man and allows him to work therein with success. (pp. 110–111)

Nobel laureate Sir Howard Florey concurred:

> Science is rarely advanced by what is known in current jargon as a "breakthrough," rather does our increasing knowledge depend on the activity of thousands of our colleagues throughout the world who add small points to what will eventually become a splendid picture much in the same way that the Pointillistes built up their extremely beautiful canvasses. (quoted in Crowther, 1968, p. 363)

These greatness-debunking views show up in psychology as well. "Advancement of science proceeds through the patient work of the many as well as through that of the eminent few," said one noted historian of the discipline (R. I. Watson, 1963, p. 479). More striking is that James McKeen Cattell (1910), who devoted much of his career to studying eminent scientists, still conceded that "we do not know whether progress is in the main due to a large number of faithful workers or to the genius of a few" (p. 634).

Nevertheless, a considerable amount of empirical research has been dedicated to this question since the foregoing scholars expressed their antielitist views. Sociologists of science, for instance, have addressed whether the evidence truly supports the "Ortega hypothesis" (J. R. Cole & Cole, 1972). I cite these studies later in the chapter, when I review individual differences in output. These dramatic results will be reinforced by a second set of investigations that focus on individual differences in a psychologist's eminence.

PRODUCTIVITY

If the greatest psychologists are the most prolific in lifetime output, then there is little doubt that the discipline's founder, Wilhelm Wundt, stands at or near the pinnacle of greatness. According to E. G. Boring (1950),

> his daughter's bibliography cites 491 items, where an "item" is taken as any writing, from one of less than a single page up to the entire 2,353 pages of the last edition of the *Physiologishe Psychologie*. If we exclude mere reprinted editions, but include all the pages of every revised edition, an adding-machine shows that Wundt in these 491 items wrote about 53,735 pages in the sixty-eight years between 1853 and 1920. In spite of all the many one-page items, Wundt's average adventure into print was about 110 pages long, with over seven such adventures in the average year. If there are 24,836 days in sixty-eight years, then Wundt wrote or revised at the average rate of 2.2 pages a day from 1853 to 1920, which comes to about one word every two minutes, day and night, for the entire sixty-eight years. (p. 345)

This is a truly prodigious amount of writing. Although it possible that Jean Piaget exceeded this magnitude of output (Zusne & Blakely, 1985), it can also be argued that Boring may have underestimated Wundt's total output (Bringmann & Balk, 1983). So perhaps the safest conclusion to draw is that Wundt and Piaget may jointly anchor the upper end of the productivity distribution in psychology, at least among deceased psychologists.

The top point of the scale thus defined, how should the bottom end be demarcated? Again, there are two alternative operational definitions, albeit for a rather different reason. Lifetime output constitutes an unambiguous example of a ratio scale; that is, there exists a bona fide zero point consisting of all those psychologists who have published absolutely nothing at all. Therefore, one option is to take all unproductive individuals as anchoring the bottom portion of the distribution. To make this group more meaningful, these individuals might be defined as all those who are technically capable of publishing but have failed to do so. In most research, this restriction entails the stipulation that the person received a PhD in psychology and therefore had the potential of publishing his or her thesis research (e.g., Rodgers & Maranto, 1989). Yet even within this restricted group the nonpublishers usually represent a fairly large proportion of all degree-earning psychologists. Because no variation in output exists within this subset of unproductive colleagues, many researchers opt for a truncated distribution instead (e.g., Dennis, 1954a, 1954c): Only those psychologists are included who have made at least one contribution to the field. Whether an investigation starts at 0 or 1 on the scale largely depends on the nature of the available data and the hypotheses under scrutiny.

The extreme points now defined, the only thing that remains is a rule for gauging how any given psychologist is placed along the ratio scale. Here the number of measurement options increases dramatically. One solution is to adopt the method used by E. G. Boring (1950): counting the number of printed pages. Productivity scores would then range from 0 or 1 page of published text to as many as 53,735 (Wundt) or 62,935 (Piaget). One special asset of this operational definition is that it provides an extremely fine-grained measure—tens of thousands of tick marks divide the greats from the also-rans. It also nicely weights works according to size. Monographs automatically count more than articles, articles more than research notes, research notes more than brief commentaries or letters to the editor. On the other hand, this method is not generally very practical. In some cases the pertinent information about page numbers is not available, not even counting the formatting differences across various publications that might introduce disparities. The more severe objection, however, is that the method is simply too cumbersome for use in multiple-case investigations, whether psychometric or historiometric. It is one task to count pages for Wundt and Piaget, quite another to count them for dozens if not hundreds of psychologists (e.g., Helmreich, Spence, Beane, Lucker, & Matthews, 1980; Rodgers & Maranto, 1989; Simonton, 1992b). Hence, it should come as no surprise that page counts are rather rare in the published literature in the metasciences.

A second approach is far more commonplace: publication counts. The bottom of the scale would then still be anchored by either 0 or 1 publication. The top score may not necessarily be set by Wundt anymore, because much of his output was in very large works, such as the multivolume *Folk Psychology* (*Völkerpsychologie*, 1900–1920). According to one estimate (Bringmann & Balk, 1983) none other than E. G. Boring, with a score of 505 publications, holds down the upper end of this productivity distribution! Wundt comes in with a very close second-place finish, at 503 publications. Other great psychologists for whom figures are available include Sigmund Freud (330), William James (307), Johannes Müller (285), Gustav Fechner (267), Hermann von Helmholtz (229), Alfred Binet (227), Francis Galton (227), Abraham Maslow (165), and Charles Darwin (119; Bringmann & Balk, 1983). To put these figures into perspective, physicist Albert Einstein could claim 607 publications, mathematician Henri Poincaré 530. Consequently, the greatest of the psychologists—including one illustrious historian of the discipline—do not fall too far short of those who attained high distinction in other sciences.

Although counting publications is much more efficient than counting pages, the former suffers from a methodological disadvantage that the other does not. In a straight count, a massive book will weigh no more than a one-page comment. Psychologists could easily accumulate a huge productivity score simply by publishing their ideas in the smallest possible units. Metascientific researchers have consequently made many recommendations about how to remove this clear injustice. The most common is to assign some weighting scheme to the publications (e.g., Manis, 1951; McDowell, 1982). For example, one investigation used the following scheme: texts and other scholarly books = 20, edited books = 10, book chapters = 6, journal articles = 4, magazine articles = 2, reprint articles = 2, book reviews = 2, and unpublished reports = 1, with a complicated formula for apportioning differential credit in cases of multiple authorship (Furnham & Bonnett, 1992). As these weights indicate, any single scheme is likely to appear a bit arbitrary and controversial. Most do not count unpublished reports, for instance, and some will weight articles according to the journal quality (e.g., Clemente, 1973; Stephan & Levin, 1991). There also is no consensus on how to handle best the problem of multiple authorship; some researchers have used a simple fraction based on the number of authors (e.g., Kyvik, 1990) and others have not made any accommodation at all (e.g., Segal, Busse, & Mansfield, 1980). Some investigators even avoid the problem of weights altogether by counting only journal articles, a procedure that implicitly assigns the weightings of article = 1 and everything else = 0 (e.g., Blackburn, Behymer, & Hall, 1978).

Before one despairs of finding any universally acceptable method, one must first consider the aims of a particular inquiry. On the one hand, if the goal is to make fine distinctions at the upper end of the productivity distribution, then the choice of operational definition will determine the outcome. For example, Piaget surpasses Wundt in page counts, but not in publication counts. In the first case, Piaget has the advantage of more than 9,000 pages, whereas in the second case Wundt enjoys an edge of almost 200 publications. Yet such disparities across alternative instruments are commonplace in psychometrics. Two standard IQ tests, for instance, cannot be expected to make equivalent discriminations among extremely bright individuals. On the other hand, if the purpose of the study is to assess individual differences in output across the full available range, then it matters very little which operational definition is adopted. The cross-sectional variance then overwhelms the method variance. Accordingly, not only will alternative measures correlate very highly with each other, but they also will exhibit extremely similar correlations with other variables, such as personality traits and biographical experiences (e.g., Simonton, 1992b). One sees operating here the well-known psychometric principle of "it don't make no nevermind" (e.g., Wainer, 1976).

Because the findings are so robust across alternative indicators, it is usually unnecessary to make fine distinctions when discussing individual differences in output. Next I look at the some of the implications following aspects of this variation: the cross-sectional distribution, the relation between quantity and quality, the longitudinal stability of individual differences in output, the impact of the type of contribution, and the long-term fate of a psychologist's life work.

Variation and Distribution

Psychologists are prone to assume that most psychological attributes are distributed according to the normal, Gaussian, or bell-shaped (normal) curve. According to this symmetrical distribution, most individuals have average levels of a given trait. The odds of finding a person who departs from the average decline as a negative (but nonlinear) function of the degree of the departure, whether positive or negative. In particular, 67% of the population should have scores within 1 standard deviation of the mean, 95% within 2 standard deviations, and 99% within 3. From Galton's (1869) day on, this distribution has been said to describe human abilities, and empirical evidence suggests that the normal curve provides a very close approximation to the actual cross-sectional distribution of intelligence (Burt, 1963). However, because scientific output can be considered a form of exceptional performance, it is much less likely to be described by a normal distribution (Simonton, 1999d; Walberg, Strykowski, Rovai, & Hung, 1984); that is, scientific creativity constitutes a behavior that most human beings cannot even do, and only a tiny percentage of those who can do it are able do it exceedingly well. The expected distribution in such cases is highly skewed toward the right rather than symmetric about the mean. In particular, a very small percentage of the scientists should account for a huge proportion of the total output in any given scientific discipline.

This expectation has been verified in a large number of empirical studies (Simonton, 1997b). Of these, the most relevant and interesting may be that conducted by psychologist Wayne Dennis (1954c). The question he explicitly addressed was "whether the aggregate publications of any generation of scientists are made up primarily of the work of the highly productive minority or are composed chiefly of the contributions of the less productive majority" (p. 191). Dennis gathered four groups of data from various sources, all indicating the differential output of American psychologists. Group I included 160 individuals covered in Carl Murchison's (1932) *Psychological Reg-*

ister, II involved 587 individuals treated in a study published by Samuel Fernberger (1938), III contained an unspecified number from a study later published by Kenneth E. Clark (1957), and IV included 229 individuals who had published original articles in the *American Journal of Psychology* (between 1887 and 1900) and the *Psychological Review* (between 1894 and 1900). For Groups II and III *Psychological Abstracts* was used as the indicator of output. For each group Dennis divided the psychologists into deciles according to their level of output and then calculated the percentage of total contributions attributed to the individuals in each decile. The results are shown in Table 3.1, along with my own calculation of the average percentages across all four groups. The overall pattern is quite consistent. Psychologists in the top 10% in terms of output account for between 37% and 47% of all publications, with a mean of 41%. The bottom 10%, in contrast, ranges from 0% to 3%, with an average of less than 1%. In fact, the top half of the most productive psychologists are responsible for 90% of the total output, leaving the bottom half with the remaining 10%. Hence, the bulk of the psychological research can be credited to a highly prolific elite.

Dennis (1954c) provided more details for Group I. The range of publications listed in the *Psychological Register* ranged from 0 to 130. The latter figure cannot be directly compared with numbers given earlier for various great psychologists, because these counts came from a specific cohort of psychologists born prior to 1879 and still living in 1932. Hence, the tabulations underestimate the total lifetime output of these individuals. In addition, not all works were included in the bibliographies. Nonetheless, it is clear that the dispersion is impressive. According to Dennis (1954c), "the most productive man published more titles than the 80 persons who make up the lower five deciles" (p. 191). Furthermore, the 16 psychologists who make up the top decile represent almost uniformly a distinguished group. Dennis listed them in alphabetical order as follows: Mary W. Calkins, June Downey, Knight Dunlap, C. E. Ferree, Shepard I. Franz, M. E. Haggerty, C. H. Judd, J. H. Leuba, Max F. Meyer, L. M. Terman, E. L. Thorndike, J. E. W. Wallin, H. C. Warren, M. F. Washburn, J. B. Watson, and R. M. Yerkes. Of these 16, only 2—Haggerty and Wallin—were not among the 538 "important psychologists" identified by Annin, Boring, and Watson in 1968. Moreover, several of these individuals have served as president of the American Psychological Association, including the first two women to occupy that position, Calkins and Washburn. The latter was also the second woman elected to the National Academy of Sciences, indicating Washburn's greatness as a scientist as well as a psychologist.

The elitist distribution that Dennis (1954c) demonstrated for psychologists is not unique to psychology. On the contrary, the same skewed distribution holds for other sciences as well as for the arts and humanities (Huber, 1999; Simonton, 1999b). Dennis (1955) himself showed that the same conclusions held for domains as diverse as American secular music; books in the

TABLE 3.1
Productivity Distribution for Psychologists: Percentage Contributed by Decile for Four Groups

Decile	Group I	II	III	IV	M
1	47	37	42	37	40.75
2	21	21	21	21	21.00
3	12	14	14	11	12.75
4	8	10	9	9	9.00
5	5	8	6	5	6.00
6	3	6	4	3	4.00
7	2	3	2	3	2.50
8	1	1	1	3	1.50
9	1	0	1	3	1.25
10	0	0	0	3	0.75

Note. The four groups represented distinct samples using different archival sources and definitions of output. Table compiled from various statistics reported in (Dennis, 1954c).

Library of Congress; and publications in gerontology and geriatrics, geology, infantile paralysis, chemistry, and linguistics. Moreover, the distribution holds for both lifetime output and for output for any fixed period of a career (Fulton & Trow, 1974; Helmreich et al., 1980; Huber, 1998a, 1998b; Lehman, 1946; Shockley, 1957). So robust is this finding that it has actually been described according to two laws:

1. The *Price law*, proposed by Derek Price (1963), a historian of science who became a notable advocate for quantitative methods (perhaps reflecting his prior training as a physicist), proposes that if k is the number of scientists who have made at least one contribution to a given field, then half of all those contributions can be credited to $\sqrt{k}$. When this law is applied to the Dennis data it appears that psychology is slightly less elitist than predicted. In Group IV, for instance, there were 229 psychologists, implying that 15 would account for half of all the publications. Yet the top decile, which consists of 23 psychologists, can claim only 37% of the total.

2. The *Lotka law*, formulated by Alfred Lotka (1926), an eminent population geneticist, claims that the number of scientists who claim n publications is inversely proportional to the square of n. Expressed more formally, $f(n) = c\,n^{-2}$, where c is a constant that varies according the discipline and other factors. By taking logarithms of both sides of the equation, the Lotka law becomes $\log f(n) = \log c - 2 \log n$, yielding a straight line (e.g., if $f[n]$ and n were plotted on double-log

graph paper). When this line is fit to the appropriately transformed frequencies that Dennis (1954c) provided for Group I, 91% of the variance is explained. This is a reasonably close approximation (Price, 1963).

The fact that the Price and Lotka laws are approximate rather than exact should not blind one to the fundamental nature of the observed cross-sectional distributions, which remain extremely skewed in shape. Although Dennis (1954c) suggested that the observed curve might represent the upper portion of the normal curve, with the lower half or so cut off, Herbert Simon (1954, 1955)—himself a prolific psychologist and Nobel laureate—showed that this interpretation is definitely incorrect. The upper tail of the distribution is far more elongated, and thus far more elitist, than the upper tail of the bell-shaped curve. Simon (1955) even provided a mathematical model that purported to provide a theoretical rationale for the distinctive cross-sectional distribution (also see Simonton, 1997b, 1999d).

Given these considerations, one generalization is secure: The empirical distribution clearly contradicts the Ortega hypothesis that sciences largely advance by means of those scientists who are "astoundingly mediocre, and even less than mediocre." On the contrary, the statistics lend stronger endorsement to what the eminent psychiatrist Cesare Lombroso (1891) once affirmed in his classic book *The Man of Genius*, namely that "the appearance of a single great genius is more than equivalent to the birth of a hundred mediocrities" (p. 120). The wording might appear crude and insensitive, yet it remains true that the majority of the psychologists can be credited with only about 10% of the total contributions to the field. This immense disparity between the great and the small would seem to provide a strong justification for any history of psychology that adopts a Great Person perspective. A historical narrative that refers to only 10% of psychologists will cover 41% of the discipline, a rather efficient strategy.

Quantity and Quality

It now should be evident that psychology's history is dominated by a productive elite in a manner that flatly contradicts the Ortega hypothesis. Hence, a psychologist's greatness might be objectively defined according to his or her lifetime output. Yet within this operational definition hides another difficulty: Where exactly should a historian draw the line? As noted earlier, productivity is inherently a ratio scale that runs by consecutive integers from 0 to whatever the maximum happens to be in terms of total pages or publications. Dennis (1954c) might have divided the productivity levels into deciles, but that division is purely arbitrary. Hence, as one descends from the most prolific to the least, the attribution of greatness weakens gradually, and by virtually continuous amounts. The attribution is fairly secure at the extreme ends of the distribution, such as the top and bottom decile, but much less so in the middle. Take Wayne Dennis himself as an example. Having produced several classic studies on early child development, he certainly has some claim to being an important developmental psychologist. He also served as editor of the *Psychological Bulletin*, one of the more prestigious journals in the discipline (Rushton & Roediger, 1978). Dennis even earned an entry in a biographical dictionary devoted to eminent psychologists (Zusne, 1984). Yet, at best, his name has a very marginal status within the discipline's history. Because his lifetime output of 130 publications falls below what is witnessed in the truly great, perhaps Dennis falls close to the lower bound between the great and the also-rans. The English–Canadian psychologist George Sidney Brett and Belgian psychologist Ovide Jean Decroly are two others with the same level of productivity as Dennis, and with about the same degree of historical obscurity. Perhaps the minimal criterion for psychological greatness is to have published more than Dennis, Brett, and Decroly.

Yet this solution faces two objections. First, there exist ample numbers of great psychologists—such as Anna Freud, Leta Hollingworth, Pierre Janet, and Karl L. Lashley—who might not satisfy this productivity criterion. These would constitute false negatives. Second, there are a respectable number of obscure psychologists who might still satisfy this same cutoff. Remember that Dennis identified M. E. Haggerty and J. E. W. Wallin among the 16 who defined the top decile in a particular cohort—yielding a false-positive rate of 1 out of 8. The problem seems to be that so far output has been defined in terms of quantity rather than quality; that is, a psychologist's influence has been evaluated according to a single dimension of raw output that ranges from 0 to the maximal values seen in the discipline. S. Cole and Cole (1973), two sociologists of science, called those anchoring the bottom end the *Silent* and those at the top the *Prolific*. Yet the Coles observed that the Silents and the Prolifics might define only placement along the quantity dimension. Another dimension might gauge the quality of a scientist's work. Accordingly, it is conceivable that two other types of scientists might appear, namely, what the Coles called the *Perfectionists* and the *Mass Producers*. The Perfectionists publish very little, but almost everything they do produce is high impact. They are like jewelers who dote on each well-polished gem. The Mass Producers just publish and publish and publish, and much of it is rubbish. They are often the masters of the "least publishable unit," churning out hundreds of little notes and comments on topics of only transient interest. Perhaps the single magnum opus of a Perfectionist is worth more than all the publications of a Mass Producer put together.

In theory, the quantity and quality dimensions could be orthogonal, at least for all psychologists who have published at least one item. To the extent that they are correlated, the more rare become the Perfectionists and the Mass Producers, and the more common are the psychologists who occupy the dimension anchored by the Silents and the Prolifics. On the other hand, if the dimensions are truly uncorrelated, then great psychologists will consist of two distinct groups: the Prolifics and the Perfectionists, with the Mass Producers occupying some nebulous position between them and the Silents. So are there two kinds of great psychologists, or only one?

Answering this question obviously requires an operational definition of *quality*, which is defined as the impact a psychologist has on the field. In recent years, the most accepted practice in the sociology and psychology of science has been to use citation counts (e.g., J. Cole & Cole, 1971; Rushton, 1984). These essentially take two forms: (a) the number of publications that are cited in the literature and (b) the number of citations those publications received. The citations are usually calculated using either the *Science Citation Index* or the *Social Science Citation Index*, with the latter serving as the most commonly used source for evaluating psychological research (cf. Myers, 1970; Ruja, 1956). The citations are most often for periods of either 1 or 5 years, but longer accumulations are sometimes used as well.

As with any other measurement technique, citation measures have come under considerable criticism as assessments of scientific quality (e.g., Bonzi, 1992; Lindsey, 1989; A. L. Porter, 1977). The various complaints include the following: (a) the lack of a universally accepted way to handle multiple authorship (e.g., Ashton & Oppenheim, 1978; Lindsey, 1980); (b) the biasing effects of the prestige of the institutions from which the publications originate (S. Cole, 1970; cf. J. A. Stewart, 1983); (c) the fact that many citations actually contain criticisms rather than endorsements (Moravcsik & Murugesan, 1975); and (d) the possibility that some scientists might "chalk up high citation counts by simply writing barely publishable papers on fashionable subjects which will then be cited as perfunctory, 'also ran' references" (Moravcsik & Murugesan, 1975, p. 91). However, these and other problems have been shown to be insufficient to undermine the validity of citation counts, whether in the sciences in general or in psychology in particular (e.g., J. Cole & Cole, 1971; Rushton, 1984). Either these potential artifacts account for too little method variance or they prove to be too transient to affect the measures in the long term.

Because later in this chapter I provide more explicit evidence for the validity of citation counts, for the moment I simply take this measure as the best available indicator of the quality of a scientist's research. Given that assumption, then the empirical literature has demonstrated most emphatically that quality and quantity are by no means orthogonal dimensions. On the contrary, both the number of citations and the number of cited publications are positive functions of the total number of publications, cited or not cited (Crandall, 1978). These relationships hold not just for psychology (e.g., Rodgers & Maranto, 1989; Simonton, 1992b) but also for all other sciences (e.g., Busse & Mansfield, 1984; Feist, 1993; J. A. Stewart, 1983). In psychology, the typical intercorrelations range between .50 and .70, meaning that between one quarter and one half of the variance is shared between any two variables (Rodgers & Maranto, 1989; Simonton, 1992b). Moreover, these correlations are not contingent on the particular operational definitions used. For example, essentially the same results obtain regardless of whether self-citations are included among the total citations (e.g., Helmreich et al., 1980), and alternative methods of handling multiple authorship yield pretty much the same results (J. Cole & Cole, 1971; Rushton, 1984). Hence, the best conclusion is that quality of output is a positive function of quantity of output: The more publications one produces, the higher the odds that one will get cited, and the higher the number of citations one's best work will receive (J. Cole & Cole, 1971; Rushton, 1984). Frank Barron (1963), the distinguished creativity researcher, put it this way:

> The biography of the inventive genius commonly records a lifetime of original thinking, though only a few ideas survive and are remembered to fame. Voluminous productivity is the rule and not the exception among the individuals who have made some noteworthy contribution. (p. 139)

As a corollary of this conclusion, the more items one can list in one's bibliography, the more items one must have that receive few or no citations. The more successes there are, the more failures there are as well.

This last point must be amplified with a closely related finding: The quantity–quality relation is governed by the *equal-odds rule* (Simonton, 1997b): The ratio of citations to total publications (or the ratio of total cited publications to all publications) does not systematically vary according to a researcher's output (Platz, 1965; Simonton, 1985b; K. G. White & White, 1978). For example, the number of citations per publication is not larger for those who are the most prolific (R. A. Davis, 1987; K. G. White & White, 1978). Hence, the most productive psychologists have not figured out a way to increase their success rate. These findings are mathematically most consistent with a straightforward model that specifies the number of citations to be a positive linear function of the number of publications plus a random error term that has roughly the same variance as total publications. It is interesting that a secondary analysis of Group I of Dennis's (1954c) study actually found a slightly negative association between citations per publication and the total number of publications (Platz & Blakelock, 1960). The psychologists in the upper half of the productivity distribution had an average citation rate of 12%, whereas those in the lower half had a citation rate of 28%, a difference that came close to statistical significance ($p = .051$). Although this particular finding has not been replicated in other studies (e.g., K. G. White & White, 1978), it does demonstrate that the greatest psychologists are not necessarily Perfectionists and might even have a leaning toward being Mass Producers (also see Feist, 1997). This seems to contradict the common view that a scientist's reputation is undermined by the production of low-quality publications (cf. S. C. Hayes, 1983).

Although quality and quantity are functionally related, the two factors have rather contrasting cross-sectional distributions. Specifically, the distributions are much more elitist for citations than for publications (Redner, 1998). This means that if the Ortega hypothesis has been proven inconsistent with the publication data, then it is even more flatly contradicted by the citation data (J. Cole & Cole, 1972). For instance, of 299 Australian academic psychologists studied in the 1970–1975 period, the top 10% in output accounted for 36% of the total publications but could be credited with 60% of the total citations (K. G. White & White, 1978). In a study of 196 American academic psychologists, 11% had no citations during a 3-year period, another 25% averaged 2 or fewer citations per year, and only 10% averaged more than 50 citations per year (Helmreich et al., 1980). Also, according to a rather comprehensive study of 48,903 psychologists who published in major English-language psychology journals from 1962 to 1967, more than half were cited only once, and a mere 6% were cited at least a half dozen times (Myers, 1970). Solely 18 out of the 48,903 received more than 200 citations, including such notable psychologists as Kenneth Spence (378), Neal Miller (362), Leon Festinger (298), Clark Hull (267), Edward Thorndike (241), and J. P. Guilford (201). Highly skewed statistics such as these emerge even when the samples of psychologists are confined to those who are associated with major research institutions. For instance, of the faculty at the 100 top-rated university departments of the United States, Canada, and Great Britain, 22% received no citations in a single year, and only 3% had more than 100 citations in a 5-year period (Endler, Rushton, & Roediger, 1978).

What makes figures like these so remarkable is that the citations are aggregated across the cumulative work of any given psychologist. Therefore, when psychologists receive no citations in a given period, that means that they have not published a single item during their entire careers up to the year of citation that at least one other scientist found worth mentioning. As academic psychologists, these uncited individuals must be publishing, but for the purposes of assessing impact they must be grouped with the Silents. Indeed, sociological research on the Ortega hypothesis has underlined the minimal impact of scientists who publish only minor articles (J. Cole & Cole, 1972; Oromaner, 1985). Not only do influential articles disproportionately cite other influential publications, but also the unimportant publications even cite disproportionately the influential publications. One study of the criminology literature, for instance, found that "less important works (those with few citations) are rarely utilized by much more important papers (those with the highest citation counts)" (Green, 1981, p. 45). More than half of the research, in fact, was not cited at all! That represents a huge quantity of silent research.

One final aspect of the quantity–quality association must be noted. Although the correlation is very high, it is far from perfect. Even a correlation of .70 leaves room for considerable scatter around the bivariate regression line. As a consequence, nothing prevents an investigator from creating artificial groups of Silents, Prolifics, Perfectionists, and Mass Producers from any given data set. All the researcher has to do is to split the productivity and citation counts at their respective medians. The result would be four groups defined by low productivity and low citations (the Silents), high productivity and high citations (the Prolifics), low productivity and high citations (the Perfectionists), and high productivity and low citations (the Mass Producers). Even so, whenever a researcher performs this methodological legerdemain on real data, the Prolifics and Silents outnumber the Perfectionists and Mass Producers by well over 2 to 1 (see, e.g., J. Cole & Cole, 1972; Feist, 1997; Helmreich, Spence, & Thorbecke, 1981). Moreover, it is evident that the errors around the regression line are such that the Perfectionists and Mass Producers do not form taxonomically distinct groups (e.g., both lack identifiable clusters of outliers). Accordingly, the safest scientific conclusion remains that quality is a positive linear function of quantity but that the association is not so strong as to rule out an occasional Perfectionist or Mass Producer.

It is curious that the preceding methodological tactic suggests a potential operational definition of the great psychologist. Perhaps the minimum requirement for being called "great" is that the psychologist be in the upper half of the distribution with respect to both publications and citations. In other words, all Prolific psychologists make the first cut. I express this as a necessary but not sufficient criterion, because individuals who are above the median in both quantity and quality will constitute as much as one third of the total (J. Cole & Cole, 1972; Feist, 1997). For most tastes, that percentage might appear a bit on the liberal side. So it is very likely some additional criteria would have to be imposed.

Longitudinal Stability

An important methodological issue may be lurking in the preceding section. Very often publication and citation counts are based on a relatively thin slice of a scientist's career. Most commonly, the figures will come from between somewhere between 1 and 6 years. For example, studies that rely on the *Social Science Citation Index* typically use either a single year's compilation or the 5-year cumulative compilations that are periodically published. Therefore, it is essential to ask whether a small temporal sampling of a psychologist's career can provide a reliable gauge of his or her relative standing in the discipline. For instance, can a Silent psychologist in one year become a Prolific psychologist in the next? According to a considerable body of research, the answer is simply: It is quite unlikely. The likelihood is low for two reasons.

First, citation rates are extremely stable over time. This stability holds for all scientific disciplines, including psychology (e.g., Bonzi, 1992; Rushton,

1984). For instance, a sample of 82 personality and social psychologists who had received their PhDs in 1960 or earlier were scrutinized in 1965, 1970, and 1975 (Helmreich et al., 1981). The 1965 citation rate correlated .46 and .42 with the rates in 1970 and 1975, respectively, and the citations received in the latter two years correlated .88. The latter figure is more indicative of the temporal stability of citations, because the psychologists by then were at least 10 years into their careers. In appraising the magnitude of these "test–retest reliabilities" it is essential to realize that citations counted within single years will be less reliable than those counted within 5-year periods (Allison, 1977). For example, a study of 69 eminent American psychologists (who were deceased as of 1969) counted the citations they received in the 5-year cumulative indexes for 1971–1975 and 1981–1985 (Simonton, 1992b). The correlation between the two counts was .94.

Second, publication rates also display considerable temporal stability, albeit not usually so much as citations (Blackburn et al., 1978; Bonzi, 1992; S. Cole, 1979). This stability has been demonstrated in several samples of psychologists (e.g., Over, 1982a, 1982b; Rushton, 1990). However, apparently the first demonstration was conducted by Dennis (1954b) in a study that involved only two groups. Group I included 43 psychologists born between 1850 and 1860 who had their publications listed in Murchison's (1932) *Psychological Register*. The sample included such notables as Havelock Ellis, with 240 publications; Sigmund Freud, with 201; and Hendrick Zwaardmaker, with 162. Of course, there were many more psychologists who were much less productive (up to age 70, for this cohort). Dennis tabulated the output for each psychologist in five age periods (i.e., the 20s, 30s, 40s, 50s, and 60s) and then calculated the productivity correlations between consecutive and nonconsecutive decades. The correlations tended to be quite high. From the 30s to the 60s, adjacent correlation coefficients ranged from .71 to .82. Although the decade of the 20s had somewhat lower correlations with the other decades, the productivity during this period still correlated .58 with output in the 30s and .53 with output in the 60s (also see Horner, Rushton, & Vernon, 1986; Rodgers & Maranto, 1989). Group II of Dennis's (1954b) study included a sample of 41 members of the National Academy of Sciences (NAS; excluding all psychologists) and obtained the same results. Again excluding the decade of the 20s, when most careers were still getting off the ground, adjacent decades were correlated between .79 and .86. Even productivity in those first 10 years was a reasonably good predictor of later output (also see Christensen & Jacomb, 1992; Chubin, Porter, & Broeckmann, 1981).

To assert that citation and publication counts exhibit temporal stability is not equivalent to asserting that these measures of output and impact inexorably increase from year to year. The facts prove otherwise. For instance, the cumulative output of some academic psychologists is affected after receiving tenure, with productivity leveling off after having increased since the onset of the career (Bridgwater, Walsh, & Walkenbach, 1982). Yet this effect does not change the relative ranking of various psychologists. On the contrary, because the plateau does not appear for psychologists who hold positions at high-prestige institutions, the distance separating them from the less productive members of their cohort will actually increase (also see Blackburn et al., 1978). Hence, it is the relative standing of a psychologist within a given cohort that stays fairly stable, not the rate of output for each psychologist.

It follows that most psychologists will not jump back and forth among the categories of the Silents, Prolifics, Perfectionists, and Mass Producers. The category to which a psychologist belongs can usually be determined relatively early in his or her career. Furthermore, the identification becomes all the more secure with each passing year. The assignment becomes almost certain once the psychologist's career is completed and the cumulative output and impact more reliably assessed.

Contribution Type

In chapter 13 I examine whether a scientific analysis of psychology's history can contribute to the evaluation of psychology's status as a science. Yet one potential criterion might be inferred from the supposed relation between productivity and scientific greatness. If the great psychologists are those who publish many influential works, how do their output and impact compare with the acknowledged greats of the most successful scientific disciplines? Are psychology's luminaries in the same league as those of the exact, hard, or natural sciences? Earlier I noted that Wundt's lifetime output compared favorably with that of Henri Poincaré and fell only about 100 publications short of Einstein's. Unhappily, however, those are not the only comparisons that might be made. The illustrious mathematicians Augustin Cauchy, Leonhard Euler, and Arthur Cayley claimed totals of 789, 856, and 995, respectively, and the eminent chemist Wilhelm Ostwald accumulated an awesome bibliography of 5,545 publications (Bringmann & Balk, 1983). Is one to conclude that psychology pales in comparison to mathematics? Must one surmise that the best chemistry has to offer has more than 10 times the genius as the best that psychology can claim?

These inferences seem dubious. Many studies have shown that disciplines differ tremendously in the level of output expected of their researchers. For example, one survey of 27,000 faculty in American higher education found substantial variation in the current publication activities across different disciplines (Fulton & Trow, 1974). In the biological sciences, 84% were active researchers, a figure that declined to 75% for the social sciences and to 60% for education. Even within the social sciences substantial differences can appear, as is evident in the low scholarly productivity of those who serve on the editorial boards of social work journals (Lindsey, 1976; Pardek, Chung, & Murphy, 1996). Within psychology, too, clinical and counseling psychologists are noticeably less productive than research psychologists (Brems, Johnson, & Gallucci, 1996). These contrasts may ensue in part from distinct norms operating in various scientific disciplines, some of which place more emphasis on other activities, such as teaching, administration, and public service. However, another part likely arises from the different types of publications that are likely to be produced in various disciplines and subdisciplines. Thus, scholarship in the humanities is more likely to take the form of books, unlike research in the sciences, which is more likely to take the form of journal articles. It should not surprise one, then, that scientists tend to be more productive (in item counts) than humanists (Fulton & Trow, 1974).

Hence, comparisons of output across disciplines must assume that a unit of publication in one field is truly comparable to a publication unit in another; otherwise, the counts are not on the same scale. It would be like measuring the height of one mountain in feet and another in meters and then asking which is taller. As noted before, it is for this reason that many researchers weight publication counts according to the nature of the contribution (e.g., Furnham & Bonnett, 1992; Manis, 1951). Moreover, different types of contributions should differ not only according to the magnitude of effort that researchers must invest in their production but also according to the impact the contributions are likely to have on the field. For example, although it is true that E. G. Boring's total output slightly exceeded that of Wilhelm Wundt, a different picture emerges if books and articles are excluded from both counts. Boring's output includes 45 book reviews and 202 editorials (Zusne, 1984), whereas Wundt's includes 197 book reviews and 28 miscellaneous publications (Bringmann & Balk, 1983). Because it is likely that editorials have less impact on the field than do book reviews, and all of these publications have less impact than articles and books, the edge would seem to reside with Wundt.

At the other extreme, what about the influence of books? Despite the emphasis on publishing journal articles, it is conceivable that books offer integrative advantages that mere journal articles cannot. A study of 69 eminent American psychologists found some evidence for such superiority (Simonton, 1992b). For each psychologist the proportion of his or her output that was represented by books rather than journal articles was calculated. This measure was then correlated with the number of cited publications, the total number of citations, and the number of citations to his or her single most cited work (using a 5-year accumulation for 1971–1975). In all three cases the correlations were statistically and substantively significant (i.e., about 10% of the variance was explained). The superior impact of the more ambitious publications was also shown by looking at the psychologist's most frequently cited work. Although books only accounted for 17% of all the publications credited to these 69 psychologists, books represented 45% of the works that received the most citations. Examples of such high-impact book-length contributions include Gordon Allport's *The Nature of Prejudice*

(198 citations) and Carl I. Hovland's *Communication and Persuasion* (135 citations).

Corroborative results were found in an earlier study in which a dramatically different methodology was used (Heyduk & Fenigstein, 1984). The investigators sent letters to eminent psychologists asking them to identify those "texts or articles which have significantly influenced your work and though, both past and present, in your major area of psychology" (p. 556). As many as 10 works could be identified by each survey respondent. Sigmund Freud's contributions came out on top, with such works as *The Psychopathology of Everyday Life*, *A General Introduction to Psychoanalysis*, *The Interpretation of Dreams*, and *Introductory Lectures on Psychoanalysis* leaving a mark on many great psychologists after him. Yet, it is astonishing that extremely few articles were mentioned and, in every case but one, when a scientific article was deemed influential, a book or monograph by the same author proved even more so. For instance, Clark L. Hull's articles on "A Functional Interpretation of the Conditioned Reflex" and "The Goal Gradient Hypothesis and Maze Learning" were each mentioned twice, but his book on the *Principles of Behavior* was mentioned 7 times. Only 1 author out of the 39 most influential psychologists had more impact through an article rather than a book: Lee Cronbach, in his classic 1957 article "The Two Disciplines of Scientific Psychology." That means that fewer than 3% of these eminent contributors staked their fame on an article rather than a book. Furthermore, 92% of the works that influenced eminent psychologists were books or monographs, leaving only 8% to be credited to articles.

These results suggest that, to become great, psychologists should choose their projects wisely. Publishing exclusively articles, even if in the best journals, is not the optimal strategy. Every so often psychologists should consolidate their ideas into more comprehensive syntheses. This implies that the Prolific contributors tend to strike a delicate compromise between the Mass Producers, who churn out article after article, and the Perfectionists, who concentrate on a magnum opus or two. Greatness consists in the right mixture of the small but many and the few but big.

Long-Term Influence

Critics of citation measures have noted a quirk that seems to invalidate the measurement's justification: Methodological works tend to be cited more than theoretical or empirical contributions (e.g., Folly, Hajtman, Nagy, & Ruff, 1981; Peritz, 1983). That by itself might not be a bad thing. After all, science depends very much on the use of the right methods and techniques. Individuals who devise a way to enhance the rigor and precision of investigation might indeed deserve a special increment in credit. It is their work that enables the theorists and experimentalists to do better science. However, this fairness often disappears when one looks at the specific nature of the citations. I concluded the previous section by observing the greater impact of book-length contributions. The explanation for this superiority assumed that these books contained original ideas that can be attributed to their authors. Yet that does not have to be the case. There are also textbooks, including methodological and statistics textbooks, and these do not have to contain a single original idea of the author. On the contrary, such texts need only present a difficult subject in a manner accessible to students and researchers trying to master the techniques.

Contemplate the outcome of one pioneering citation study (Myers, 1970). The most frequently cited authors were identified according to the references to their work over a 6-year period in more than a dozen prestigious journals, including *Psychological Review*, *Journal of Experimental Psychology*, *British Journal of Psychology*, *Canadian Journal of Psychology*, *Journal of Personality and Social Psychology*, and *Journal of Abnormal Psychology*. The 99th percentile in citation counts included some obvious big names in the field, such as W. K. Estes, L. Festinger, H. F. Harlow, C. I. Hovland, C. L. Hull, J. Piaget, B. F. Skinner, and E. L. Thorndike. Yet this group also included some surprises, such as A. L. Edwards, S. Siegel, E. F. Linquist, and B. J. Winer. Neither was the latter group near the bottom of the pile in this elite. Whereas the obvious luminaries claimed between 166 and 298 citations each, the nonobvious citation celebrities could boast between 224 and 377 citations each! And what do these four authors in the second group have in common? Every single one published a bestselling statistics or methods textbook. Indeed, it is likely that a whole generation of psychologists was raised on their texts. For instance, I'm sure I am not the only psychologist who earned a PhD in the mid-1970s who learned the analysis of variance from Winer's (1962) *Statistical Principles in Experimental Design*. Neither are the results of this analysis unusual. A similar outcome appeared when researchers identified the 100 most-cited psychologists in the 1975 *Social Science Citation Index* (Endler et al., 1978). The top 10 included S. Freud, J. Piaget, A. Bandura, H. J. Eysenck, D. T. Campbell, E. Goffman, B. F. Skinner, and E. H. Erikson, as well as B. J. Winer and S. Siegel, the former in 3rd place on the list (after Freud and Piaget) and the latter in 10th!

What is one to make of these citation anomalies? On the one hand, there can be no doubt that the measures do indeed assess relative influence. The psychologists who cited Winer were not doing so to be nice but to give credit where credit was due. On the other hand, there is really no basis for believing that Winer was being cited for the same reasons as Skinner and Piaget. The Winer book was normally receiving citations by authors who needed to specify the particular techniques adopted in the statistical analyses, whereas Skinner and Piaget were receiving citations for their original contributions to theory and research. Moreover, as soon as a better textbook comes along, Winer will immediately fall by the wayside in a manner that would seem unthinkable in the case of the two great psychologists. Hence, probably the optimal decision is simply to label these cases transient aberrations in an otherwise-valid criterion. With time, these irregularities would slowly vanish.

Yet this raises the issue of what happens to citations in the long term. It is one thing to show that citations tend to be relatively stable during the course of a psychologist's career, but it is another to prove that the same stability holds after his or her career has ceased. Although the final count of cumulative output seldom changes after a scientist dies—except for occasional posthumous publications—the influence that output has on the discipline might change in either direction. In some cases the scientist's work might have proven merely fashionable and sink rapidly into oblivion. In other cases the life work might have a sleeper effect and gradually increase in impact. The more typical pattern, however, is probably somewhere in between. Citation of a deceased author's work gradually decays over time, but it never disappears altogether (Simonton, 1984g, 1992b). The first big drop likely occurs some time after the scientist dies, as the social obligation to cite an old mentor or colleague becomes less potent (Trimble, 1986). After that, however, citation rates will continue to decline either because the work becomes manifestly obsolete or because the research becomes fully incorporated into the common knowledge of the discipline (e.g., Abt, 1983; Barnett, Fink, & Debus, 1989; MacRae, 1969; Price, 1965). Nevertheless, if the contribution is truly one that survives the tests of time, the citations will not reduce to zero.

An excellent illustration of this process occurring among the great psychologists is what happened to F. C. Donders (see Goodman, 1971). This Dutch ophthalmologist first introduced mental reaction times as a technique in mental chronometry back in 1865 (in Dutch) and 1868 (in German). Even after his method became assimilated as an integral part of experimental psychology, he continued to receive some degree of recognition. To be sure, mental reaction times are now most commonly used without any explicit reference to Donders, but from time to time various investigators have made explicit psychology's methodological indebtedness to his pioneering work. These acknowledgments have come from psychologists eminent in their own right, such as James McKeen Cattell, Robert S. Woodworth, E. G. Boring, Donald E. Broadbent, Michael I. Posner, and Saul Sternberg. Citations of Donders's work continue to this day. According to the *Social Sciences Citation Index Five-Year Cumulation 1981–1985* (1987), Donders received approximately 80 citations, about 70 of which can be credited to his reaction-time methods. To put these figures into context, of 783,339 articles published in scientific journals in 1981, 81% were cited 10 times or fewer, and 47% were not cited at all between 1981 and June 1997 (Redner, 1998). So Donders produced what can easily be considered "citation classics" (Goodman, 1971).

Nonetheless, this example does urge caution in using citations as an index of impact. Because the probability of citation still tends to decay over time, a psychologist's contemporary influence must always be adjusted for his or her cohort (e.g., either birth year or year of highest degree). Thus, the most appropriate baseline for Donders should be contributors who were born in 1818 or who received their MDs in 1842. If otherwise, a Prolific psychologist of one era would convert into a Mass Producer in the next, and a Perfectionist might enter the lists of the Silents. It would then be difficult to comprehend why certain obscure psychologists attained such eminence in the history of the discipline.

EMINENCE

The use of citation indicators to assess a psychologist's impact was necessarily a recent development. The practice largely depends on the existence of professional journals with fairly explicit norms about how an author should refer to antecedent work. For example, the *Publication Manual of the American Psychological Association* (American Psychological Association [APA], 2001) spells out in considerable detail how authors of APA journal articles should assign credit to individuals who have influenced their research. Yet citation practices have not always been so explicitly formalized, especially prior to the advent of the technical journal. Before then, authors would often adopt rather casual attitudes toward their predecessors and contemporaries. Thus, it was acceptable for Descartes to use the nondescript expression "an English physician" to refer to William Harvey's revolutionary work on the circulation of blood. Indeed, in the days when people could still get executed or imprisoned for espousing iconoclastic views, overt citations might be avoided altogether. According to one history text, the French materialist thinker

> La Mettrie dared to discuss openly those ideas that were held privately by many philosophers at the time. In so doing, he offended many powerful individuals. Although it is clear that he influenced many subsequent thinkers, his works were rarely cited nor his name even mentioned. (Hergenhahn, 1992, p. 146)

These and other difficulties make it extremely challenging to use citation measures as indicators of a psychologist's greatness prior to the last century or so.

An alternative is to fall back on Galton (1869), who defined genius in terms of reputation, especially as posthumously revised by posterity. One method for implementing this definition was discussed in chapter 1—when Annin et al. (1968) asked experts to identify the "most important psychologists" in the history of the field. Alternative methods exist as well. One option is to assess how much space is devoted to each candidate in standard histories of the discipline. Thus, one study examined the average percentage of space devoted to 570 deceased contributors according to 16 texts (Zusne

& Dailey, 1982; cf. Zusne, 1987a). The texts included those by the Americans E. G. Boring and R. I. Watson, the British R. S. Peters and Robert Thomson, the German Wilhelm Hehlmann, and the Russian M. G. Yaroshevskii. Just 8 notables could claim that they averaged at least 1% of the space in these texts: Sigmund Freud, 3.23%; Wilhelm Wundt, 2.46%; William James, 1.76%; John Watson, 1.46%; Descartes, 1.35%; Gustav Fechner, 1.13%; David Hume, 1.04%; and Thomas Locke, 1.03%. Another option is to take those who have earned significant professional honors, such as those who received APA's Distinguished Scientific Contribution Award (e.g., Myers, 1970; Simonton, 1985b) or those who were elected to the APA presidency (e.g., K. R. Gibson, 1972; Suedfeld, 1985). Unlike the previous method, which relies on the judgments of posterity, this operational definition involves the direct assessments of a psychologist's contemporaries, whether by an award selection committee or the vote of members of a professional organization.

In the next section I examine more closely the implications of defining a psychologist's greatness in terms of such eminence measures. The scrutiny begins with an analysis of whether a consensus exists on the relative distinction of psychologists who have some claim to fame in the annals of the discipline. Once that question is suitably addressed, I turn to three other matters: (a) the cross-sectional distribution of eminence, (b) the correlation of eminence with lifetime output, and (c) the transhistorical stability of eminence assessments.

Galton's G: The Greatness Consensus

"Worldly renown is naught but a breath of wind, which now comes this way and now comes that, and changes name because it changes quarter," said Dante Alighieri (c. 1307/1952, p. 69). Many psychologists have echoed this cynicism with respect to the so-called greats of psychology's own past (e.g., Korn, Davis, & Davis, 1991; Ray, 1971). Furthermore, from time to time some empirical investigation will purport to show that a psychologist's fame is indeed very fickle. For instance, Roeckelein (1996b) argued that surname counts derived from introductory psychology textbooks are orthogonal to those derived from history of psychology textbooks. The intercorrelations ranged only between .19 and .51, with a median around .30. Yet these gauges of agreement are misleading for several reasons. For one thing, history and introductory texts focus on very different time periods in the development of the discipline, a factor that has been shown to contaminate indicators of eminence (Simonton, 1984g). Even more significant is that these correlations pertain to only a select group of highly eminent psychologists: A. Adler, A. Binet, W. Cannon, H. Ebbinghaus, G. Fechner, S. Freud, F. Galton, H. Helmholtz, W. James, C. Jung, W. Köhler, J. Müller, I. Pavlov, E. L. Thorndike, E. G. Titchener, J. B. Watson, and W. Wundt. That's an N of only 17, the subjects spanning only the upper end of the eminence distribution. With such a draconian truncation of the variance, these coefficients must seriously understate the degree of consensus.

In fact, a large number of studies have shown that a considerable amount of agreement exists on the differential eminence of historical figures (e.g., Farnsworth, 1969; Kynerd, 1971; Simonton, 1983c, 1986a). This consensus even transcends various civilizations, nations, and subcultures (Simonton, 1984a, 1984g). For example, the differential distinction accorded major figures in African American history differs very little across majority (White) and minority (Black) cultures (Simonton, 1998a). Similarly, the relative eminence of contributors to Japanese civilization is substantially the same in East and West (Simonton, 1996b). Furthermore, the eminence consensus transcends alternative measurement methods, whether page counts in encyclopedias or histories, line counts in biographical dictionaries, frequency of inclusion in anthologies or collections, and so forth (Simonton, 1976f, 1977b, 1984a, 1987d). Linear composites of alternative indicators, no matter how diverse, will usually boast internal-consistency reliabilities (coefficient alphas) in the upper .80s and lower .90s (e.g., Simonton, 1984g, 1990d). Indeed, confirmatory factor analyses of data sets drawn from several distinct domains of achievement have shown that all alternative indicators can be adequately explained by a single latent variable that represents individual differences in attained distinction (Simonton, 1991c). So pervasive is this underlying factor that it has been christened "Galton's G" (Simonton, 1991c). This term makes obvious reference to the similarly ubiquitous "Spearman's g," the latent variable underlying performance on various intelligence tests (Spearman, 1927). This analogy reflects the fact that the two best established operational definitions of genius entail achieved eminence and exceptional intelligence (Cox, 1926; Galton, 1869; Hollingworth, 1926; Terman, 1925).

Unfortunately, these powerful latent-variable modeling techniques have not yet been applied to multiple indicators of eminence in psychology. Even so, there is ample reason for believing that Galton's G would reappear in any sufficiently heterogeneous sample of psychologists. In the first place, the broad agreement on eminence holds for extremely diverse groups of historical figures, including 342 European monarchs (Simonton, 1984f), 39 presidents of the United States (Simonton, 1986f), 696 classical composers (Simonton, 1977b), and 772 visual artists (Simonton, 1984a). The consensus even emerges with respect to the differential eminence of two groups that include many figures in psychology's history, namely, the 2,012 philosophers (Simonton, 1976f) and 2,026 scientists (Simonton, 1991a) who populate the intellectual tradition of Western civilization. Even more significant is that inquiries into the differential eminence of psychologists reveal strong indirect evidence for the existence of a single factor underlying their distinction.

This indirect confirmation is most conspicuous in the differential distinction of 69 American psychologists active between 1879 and 1967 (Simonton, 1992b). For instance, the expert ratings of Annin et al. (1968) correlated .85 with an index of the number of textbooks that discussed the psychologist's contributions (from Zusne & Dailey, 1982). Moreover, a linear composite of these two measures plus a calculation of the amount of space devoted to each psychologist in those same textbooks (again from Zusne & Dailey, 1982) yielded an internal-consistency reliability (coefficient alpha) of .89. In addition, this 3-item composite correlated between .75 and .81 with three alternative space measures derived from Ernest R. Hilgard's (1987) more specialized text on the history of psychology in the United States. The composite measure also correlated .62 with whether the sampled psychologist had been elected APA president. This correlation between contemporary and posthumous fame is quite respectable given that it entails the relation between a continuous and a dichotomous variable, and thus it is necessarily attenuated. It is also noteworthy that the 3-item composite correlates positively with more general indicators of eminence, such as having an entry in the *World Who's Who in Science* (Debus, 1968) and *Webster's Biographical Dictionary* (1976). The two point-biserial correlations are .44 and .41, respectively, which are respectable given the highly selective nature of these two reference works. Thus, those who have outstanding reputations within the discipline also tend to have exceptional reputations in science as a whole as well as in the larger world. It is curious that the only conspicuous exception to this association was behaviorist Clark L. Hull who, despite his obvious fame as psychologist, managed not to win an entry in *Webster's*. Although Hull's influence was clearly on the wane in 1976 (Webster & Coleman, 1992), his omission must be certainly considered either an evaluative error or an editorial oversight.

It is essential to point out that the previously mentioned 69 psychologists still represented a fairly select group. The 4 who received the highest score on the 3-item composite were J. B. Watson, E. B. Titchener, C. L. Hull, and E. C. Tolman, whereas the 4 who received the lowest score were Ferree, Karwoski, Kuhlmann, and H. Seashore (but not C. Seashore, who was also among the 69). Although none of the latter is a household name in the discipline, all 4 enjoyed sufficient renown to be included in the final 538 identified as "important psychologists" by Annin et al. (1968). Certainly the sample is far more selective than most investigations into Galton's G, which number into the hundreds and even thousands of clear celebrities and near nonentities (Simonton, 1991c). Accordingly, the consensus revealed by the reliability and correlation coefficients most likely understates the true magnitude of agreement for the discipline as a whole. Readers must recall that the 538 were originally culled from an initial list of 1,040 candidates. If the same proportions hold for the American psychologists active between 1879 and 1967, the 69 could be almost doubled, augmenting the variance with the inclusion of a great many more also-rans.

Variation and Distribution

As I discussed earlier in this chapter, the cross-sectional distribution of total lifetime output is extremely skewed, with a minority of the contributors in any field deserving credit for the lion's share of the contributions. I also noted that the cross-sectional distribution of actual influence is even more elitist. In the sciences, for example, the distribution of citations to scientific publications is far more skewed than the distribution of the scientific output subject to citation. It is for this latter reason that the Ortega hypothesis was so resoundingly disconfirmed. Hence, it should come as no real surprise that eminence also displays a highly skewed distribution, the most elitist by far. This hegemony of the cream of the cream holds for both the arts and the sciences. For example, of 34,516 books written about 602 British poets, 9,118 are about Shakespeare, 1,280 about Milton, and 1,096 about Chaucer; the top 25 poets account for almost two thirds of the books, and the top 12 account for almost exactly half (Martindale, 1995b).

Psychology is no exception to the overall pattern, with a handful of psychologists striding like colossi over their less illustrious colleagues. This dominance is immediately apparent in how much space is devoted to various eminent psychologists in history of psychology textbooks. Consider the earlier study of the coverage of 570 deceased figures in 16 texts (Zusne & Dailey, 1982). The 8 top contributors who accounted for at least 1% of the space each represent only 1.4% of the total contributors, and yet they collectively receive over 13% of the coverage. Add another 10 contributors, and the proportion increases to about 22%.

A follow-up investigation demonstrated far more dramatically the extreme nature of this distribution (Zusne, 1985). Again, 16 history of psychology textbooks were used, but the sample of eminent psychologists included 697 deceased contributors plus B. F. Skinner (who was already past 80 and his place in history assured). Just 25 individuals, or 3.6%, account for half of the total number of pages in these texts. In rank order, these luminaries were S. Freud, Aristotle, W. Wundt, W. James, J. B. Watson, Plato, Descartes, G. Fechner, B. F. Skinner, Hume, Locke, E. B. Titchener, Kant, H. von Helmholtz, K. Lewin, W. McDougall, I. Pavlov, G. Berkeley, F. Galton, C. Jung, Saint Augustine, C. Darwin, J. F. Herbart, G. Leibniz, and C. L. Hull. If the average percentage of space (Y) is plotted as a function of the contributor's rank (X), it is possible to fit a hyperbola according to the equation $Y = 0.0001 + 4.251X^{-0.508}$ (Zusne, 1985). Figure 3.1 shows what this curve looks like for the first 100 eminent contributors. Needless to say, adding the remaining 598 individuals would only lengthen the righthand tail as it asymptotically approaches the 0% level. It is significant that this hyper-

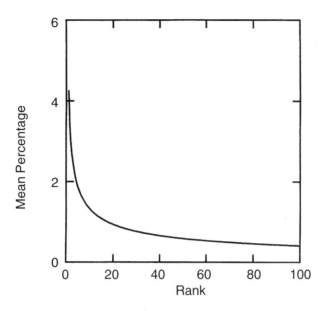

Figure 3.1. Plot of the hyperbolic function $Y = 0.0001 + 4.251X^{-0.508}$, where Y is the mean percentage of space devoted to a particular individual in 16 history of psychology textbooks and X is that individual's rank in terms of that space (Zusne, 1985). Although predicted scores for only the first 100 individuals are depicted, the curve extends to 698, approaching the 0 point asymptotically.

bolic function is not confined to history of psychology textbooks, for the same curve appears in introductory psychology texts, even when drawn from different periods (Roeckelein, 1996b; also see Coleman, 1991).

Hence, whether the measure concerns historical or contemporary fame, these eminent members among psychology's eminent constitute a most ex-alted elite.

Correlation With Lifetime Output

Yet the very extraordinary placement of psychology's greats, as so graphi-cally depicted in Figure 3.1, may lead one to wonder about the wisdom of using reputation, contemporary or posthumous, as an indicator of a psychologist's true accomplishment. "Reputation is an idle and most false imposition," warns Iago in Shakespeare's *Othello*, for it is "oft got without merit, and lost without deserving" (quoted in Evans, 1974, p. 1218). If true, this would seem to invalidate Galton's (1869) attempt to ground genius in "the opinion of contemporaries, revised by posterity." Furthermore, psychology's own history is full of cases that may provide concrete evidence for Iago's assertion.

With respect to "lost without deserving," scholars will sometimes la-ment that some relatively obscure figure is vastly underrated. This lamentation is most likely to be heard with respect to potential sexism, racism, or ethnocentrism in historical judgments (e.g., Korn et al., 1991), leading various scholars to attempt to rectify what is perceived as a social injustice (e.g., O'Connell & Russo, 1990). Yet it is curious that sometimes majority-culture men can appear the victims of posthumous neglect as well. A case in point is E. B. Twitmyer, whose independent discovery of the conditioned reflex did not earn him the same recognition in the discipline as I. Pavlov received (Coon, 1982). This differential is manifest in their opposed eponymic status: One commonly hears of Pavlovian conditioning, but never of Twitmyerian conditioning.

With respect to "oft got without merit," sometimes scholars express wonder about the elevated placement of William James in psychology's pantheon. "Everyone acknowledged his greatness, yet it is difficult to point to specific achievements in psychology as the basis of his reputation," wrote Thomson (1968, p. 125). "There is much that is paradoxical about William James and his role in American psychology," reads another history text (Schultz & Schultz, 1992, p. 173).

> On the one hand, he was certainly the leading American precursor of functional psychology. He was the pioneer of the new scientific psychology in the United States and its senior psychologist, and he is still considered by many to be the greatest American psychologist who ever lived. On the other hand, James at times denied that he was a psychologist or that there was a new psychology. He founded no formal system of psychology and had no disciples. (Schultz & Schultz, 1992, p. 173)

Such remarks suggest that James's reputation is out of keeping with his genuine achievements.

It is fortunate that an impressive accumulation of research proves quite conclusively that eminence is not capriciously bestowed (Simonton, 1994a). On the contrary, for both the arts and the sciences, differential reputation is a conspicuous function of individual differences in quantity and quality of lifetime productivity (Albert, 1975). Moreover, this linkage holds for contemporary acclaim, such as major honors and awards (Ashton & Oppenheim, 1978; S. Cole & Cole, 1973), as well as posthumous recognition, such as inclusion in biographical dictionaries, encyclopedias, and histories (Raskin, 1936; Simonton, 1977b, 1991b). These associations have been most securely demonstrated in the sciences, because a considerable amount of metascientific research has been devoted to this question (e.g., S. Cole & Cole, 1973; Feist, 1993; Simonton, 1991a).

In fact, developmental psychologist Wayne Dennis (1954a) conducted an exemplary study. He began with a random sample of 19th-century scientists with bibliographies in the *Catalog of Scientific Literature, 1800–1900*. These bibliographies were restricted to items that could be considered genuine scientific publications, namely, articles published in professional journals. The 208 sampled individuals exhibited a fairly typical range of output, from 1 to 458 publications (cf. Bringmann & Balk, 1983; Feist, 1997). Also, as should be expected, the cross-sectional distribution of output was highly skewed: Fifty percent could claim fewer than 7 publications, and 30% could boast just a single publication each. Dennis then checked to see who among these 208 attained sufficient distinction to earn a biographical entry in the *Encyclopedia Britannica*, a degree of eminence rarely achieved. Of those whose publication record placed them in the top decile, 9 of 21, or nearly half, received that honor. In contrast, only 6 of the remaining 187 attained that exclusive level of general recognition. Although Dennis (1954a) did not do so, it is easy to convert these statistics into a measure of correlation (using the phi coefficient; Simonton, 1984d). The result is .46—a fairly impressive figure given the elite nature of the eminence criterion. In addition, the advantage held by highly productive scientists persists even in the higher levels of the distribution. The top 10%, with 50–50 odds of inclusion in a prestigious encyclopedia, had produced 50 or more articles. However, of those in the top 5% in output, who published more than 140 scientific articles, the percentage so honored increased to 70%. The connection between contribution and reputation is indubitable.

Studies that specifically focus on psychologists have found comparable results. The number of citations received in the professional literature certainly correlates with peer ratings of eminence (K. E. Clark, 1957; Simonton, 1992b); election as APA president (Myers, 1970; Simonton, 1992b); having a biographical entry in *American Men of Science* (Myers, 1970), and receiving such honors as APA's Distinguished Scientific Contribution Award and the U.S. National Medal of Science (Myers, 1970). The typical correlations range in the .50s and .60s, suggesting that between one quarter and one third of the variance is shared. Even among those who were already among psychology's elite, eminence was tied to output. APA presidents who published more frequently were more prone to receive citations in 37 widely used introductory psychology textbooks (Suedfeld, 1985).

Although the positive association between productivity and eminence is firmly established, one substantive issue remains unresolved: Which is more crucial to a psychologist's ultimate eminence, quantity or quality? One plausible causal model is depicted by a simple causal chain (cf. Dennis, 1954a):

QUANTITY (publications)→QUALITY (citations)→EMINENCE (reputation)

In words, eminence is a positive function of impact, and the latter is a positive function of output. Assuming that the first two variables can be assessed with equal reliabilities, two necessary predictions follow: (a) Quality should correlate more highly with eminence than does quantity, and (b) quantity should have no independent predictive value with respect to eminence once the influence of quality is accounted for (through either partial correlation or multiple regression; see Simonton, 1997b). Are these predictions justified by the data?

Research on both scientists in general and psychologists in particular suggests that the answer is "no." In the former case, one study looked at the odds that scientists would be elected to the National Academy of Sciences (NAS; Feist, 1997). On the basis of their publication lists and citation rates, the scientists had been classified into the Silent, Perfectionist, Mass Producer, and Prolific categories discussed earlier. Only 3% of the Silents and 14% of the Perfectionists received that honor. It may seem surprising to learn that the Silents had such a good chance to attain that status, but all of the scientists in the sample had attained the rank of full professor at major U.S. research universities, and hence they already represented a fairly select group. More fascinating, therefore, are the odds for the remaining two categories of achievement: Fifty-five percent of the Prolifics and 63% of the Mass Producers had been elected to the NAS! So, quantity has an edge over quality. The same result was found for a more global measure of scientific eminence. In addition, contrary to the prediction of the simple causal-chain model, both quantity and quality were necessary for a complete prediction of differential eminence. Together the two indicators of output explained about half of the variance in eminence, with quantity explaining more than quality. It was certainly the case that quantity still predicts eminence even after quantity is statistically controlled.

Comparable results were found in a study of 69 illustrious American psychologists (Simonton, 1992b). In this instance there were two measures of output and two measures of eminence. Output was gauged by the total number of works cited in the professional journals (quantity) and by the total number of citations all of those works obtained (quality). Eminence was gauged by election to the APA presidency and by posthumous reputation, the latter determined with the 3-item composite measure discussed earlier in this chapter. Control was introduced for cohort effects (i.e., birth year). The first, contemporary eminence measure correlated .48 with total cited works and .49 with total citations—pretty much a tie. The second, posthumous measure correlated .73 with total cited works and .66 with total citations, giving quantity a slight edge over quality. However, when the predictors were placed in a multiple regression equation, somewhat different results emerged. Election to the APA presidency was a function of total citations (β = .44) but not total cited works, putting quality ahead of quantity. In contrast, for posthumous reputation total works cited (β = .34) and total citations (β = .32) came in neck and neck as predictors. These results suggest that the causal-chain model is oversimplified. The model explains election to the APA presidency fairly well but woefully misses in the case of posthumous reputation. Even so, the fact remains that eminence is prominently influenced by the quantity and quality of one's publications, either singly or in some as-yet-undefined cooperation.

The last conclusion might lead one to suppose that eminence is not whimsical. Both contemporary and posthumous reputation, after all, can be grounded in productive output and impact. A slight qualification intrudes, however. Even with both quantity and quality as predictors, a considerable amount of cross-sectional variation in eminence stays unaccounted for. Part of the remaining variance may be explained by other factors, to be discussed later, but the ugly reality persists that a significant proportion—between one quarter and one third—resists successful prediction (see, e.g., Simonton, 1992b). Moreover, the departures from prediction are most likely to reside in the upper end of the distribution, where the variation in eminence is largest. This outcome usually holds even when the eminence measures are first subjected to logarithmic transformations to shrink the upper tails. Therefore, to the extent that these statistical outliers exist, one could argue that they represent a certain amount of capriciousness in contemporaneous and posthumous assessments.

However, such a conclusion would probably be premature. The scientific study of science is still relatively young, and the psychology of science is even more recent (Feist & Gorman, 1998). A host of variables may have been inadvertently excluded from the prediction equations. In other domains of achievement, where the research has been much more extensive, the amount of unexplained variance has been reduced considerably. For instance, in the case of predicting the performance ratings of U.S. presidents, equations now can account for over 80% of the total variance, leaving much less latitude for prediction errors to occur (Simonton, 1988c). Until researchers know for sure how much of the eminence variance remains beyond their predictive grasp, it is probably best to conclude with Thomas Carlyle that "fame, we may understand, is no sure test of merit, but only a probability of such" (quoted in Sproul, 1953, p. 61). Hence, William James may really deserve his high status, and the differential between celebrated Pavlov and obscure Twitmyer may prove justified—but we don't know for sure.

Transhistorical Stability

Even if eminence is ultimately grounded in a psychologist's actual contribution, association is not static but rather dynamic. It often takes time for a psychologist's cumulative record to exert its effects on his or her colleagues. The impact often begins in a narrow circle of colleagues, expands slowly to national scope and, eventually, for the greatest psychologists, attains international prominence. For instance, after years of neglect, "the influence of Piaget's work on American psychology increased dramatically by the middle sixties because the sheer volume of his work was by then difficult to ignore" (Gilgen, 1982, p. 156). This slow growth is especially likely for the truly great innovators of psychology's history, whose work it takes time to assimilate.

Once that assimilation process is complete, the dynamic relation between contribution and reputation continues, but on a different level. The question then becomes whether the work will prove truly enduring or merely fashionable. As one history of psychology text put it, "one measure of the overall historical worth of a scientist is how well the position and conclusions stand the test of time" (Schultz & Schultz, 1987, p. 74). Will contemporary acclaim convert into posthumous fame? Or will the illustrious scientists of one generation sink into historical oblivion in the next? Even worse, will that elevated spot be replaced by some obscure colleague whose work was far ahead of his or her time and so had to await posthumous appreciation? One could alternatively argue that eminence might display considerable staying power but that the apparent transhistorical stability is specious. Once historians make an initial judgment about a psychologist's place in the discipline, subsequent historians follow suit, establishing and maintaining the received tradition.

This enforced continuity would be especially likely when the original assessments were contained in an especially well-written history. An obvious example is E. G. Boring's (1950) own *A History of Experimental Psychology*, which has greatly influenced generations of subsequent historians since its first edition appeared in 1927. As Lord Byron (1818–1821/1949) once put it,

> And glory long has made the sages smile,
> 'Tis something, nothing, words, illusion, wind—
> Depending more upon the historian's style
> Than on the name a person leaves behind.
> (p. 156)

An analogous process has been argued to occur in the case of literary criticism, with the evaluations of one generation of critics shaping the evaluations of the next (Rosengren, 1985). Any transhistorical stability then merely reflects these intergenerational borrowings of critical opinions.

My treatment of eminence opened with a discussion of Galton's G. The emphasis then was on whether a consensus transcended alternative approaches to assessing differential distinction. Yet it is clear that if Galton's (1869) conception of genius is correct, the stability must ultimately rest on the individual's powerful contributions to a domain. Each generation would have to encounter these surviving works and on that basis make their own independent assessments. If the generation concurs with the earlier judgment, then the reputation will continue, but if it does not, then the individual will have undergone a reassessment. Naturally, that reappraisal may go either way—sometimes a near-nonentity gains some approbation, and other times a celebrity will be bumped down a few steps. Even so, if a person's reputation is truly founded on a body of contributions that have genuine long-term merit, then eminence will display a corresponding amount of transhistorical stability.

Which interpretation is most correct? It just so happens that these alternative accounts are empirically distinguishable (Simonton, 1991c). The first implies that the assessments across consecutive generations will be best described by an autoregressive model. A distinguishing feature of such a model is that the farther apart are two generations, the lower their magnitude of agreement. In fact, the consensus will necessarily decay over time, asymptotically approaching the point at which the later generations will not agree at all with the earlier generations (Simonton, 1998a). The second, Galtonian interpretation, in contrast, maintains that all evaluations are a function of a single latent variable. This underlying factor reflects the intrinsic worth of a contributor's cumulative work. As a consequence, there will be no consistent tendency for the consensus to decay over time. To be sure, an individual's eminence may decline, as new findings and theories supersede his or her contributions, or as newcomers enter the competition for the attention of posterity. The old must often yield to the new. Still, on average, a person's status relative to his or her cohort will remain more or less stable over successive assessments (cf. Farnsworth, 1969; Rosengren, 1985).

So far, the little data possessed on this subject indicate that transhistorical eminence ratings are best described by the single-factor model (Simonton, 1991c). Using the advanced techniques of covariance-structure modeling, consecutive evaluations have been conclusively shown not to exhibit the correlational pattern expected of the autoregressive model (e.g., simplex or quasi-simplex matrices). Instead, in every domain of achievement examined, the observed intercorrelations can be easily explicated by a single latent variable on which all eminence measures display respectable factor loadings. Very rarely must these Galtonian models undergo modification to obtain maximal fit to the intercorrelations, and in every instance these changes involve nothing more than accommodations for method artifacts (e.g., so-called "difficulty factors" that concern whether a measure is exclusive or inclusive). There is absolutely no reason to believe that the temporal separation of two eminence measures has any substantial impact on the degree to which they agree on individual differences in reputation.

These critical tests of the two rival models admittedly did not specifically look at psychologists (Simonton, 1991c). Instead, Galton's G was fit on data involving the differential eminence of monarchs, presidents, classical composers, visual artists, scientists, and philosophers. Although psychologists were included among some of these groups, in no case were they singled out for scrutiny. Even so, I see no obvious reason to argue that the transhistorical stability of eminence operates in a totally contrary fashion in the psychological sciences. In addition, highly supportive findings were reported that specifically examined the long-term stability of the scientific reputation of contributors to our discipline (Over, 1982c). The investigation began with the eminence that 52 American psychologists had attained as of 1903, according to peer rankings solicited by James McKeen Cattell (1906).

The top 10 on this list were W. James, J. M. Cattell, H. Münsterberg, G. S. Hall, J. M. Baldwin, E. B. Titchener, J. Royce, G. T. Ladd, J. Dewey, and J. Jastrow—Cattell himself coming in second at the time! The bottom of these rankings was anchored by E. F. Buchner, A. C. Armstrong, and T. L. Bolton, psychologists not sufficiently eminent to make the list of 528 important psychologists compiled by Annin et al. (1968). The next step was to correlate these ratings with later assessments of the impact of these 52 psychologists. The main criterion chosen was the number of citations received in the journal literature from 1966 to 1970. To make the comparison more precise and just, only those citations were counted that referred to work published prior to 1903, when the peer rankings were carried out. This was necessary given that many of the rated scientists were extremely active after 1903, including J. M. Cattell himself. The correlation was .72. Hence, over half of the variance continued to be shared after more than 50 years of temporal separation. This degree of transhistorical stability is sufficient to guarantee that "there was no individual who was markedly out of favor in 1903 but markedly in favor in 1966–70, or vice versa" (Over, 1982c; also see S. F. Davis, Thomas, & Weaver, 1982).

In all likelihood, this correlation understates the true magnitude of the temporal stability. In the first place, Cattell's rankings and the citation counts represent different types of measures, with distinct psychometric properties and cross-sectional distributions that should attenuate the agreement (see Simonton, 1991c). Second, Cattell's sample included several younger psychologists whose careers had practically just begun—for example, Margaret F. Washburn was only 31, and Robert S. Woodworth was 34. Third, and last, the 52 American psychologists formed a comparatively elite group: All were "starred scientists" in Cattell's *American Men of Science* (J. M. Cattell, 1906), a status that elevated them above others who received biographical entries, which itself was a mark of distinction. The 52 included 25 APA presidents and 12 members of the NAS, and all but 2 (H. R. Marshall and A. C. Armstrong) were still receiving citations to their cumulative work in the late 1960s. It seems reasonable to assume that if many more psychologists were selected, thereby resulting in a more heterogeneous sample, this correlation might get larger. Hence, until a study is conducted that specifically tests the Galtonian and autoregressive models, the most secure conclusion is probably that eminence in psychology operates in the same manner as in other achievement domains. The transhistorical stability can be mostly credited to Galton's G.

4

LONGITUDINAL CHANGES
IN CREATIVITY

As noted in the preceding chapter, James McKeen Cattell's (1906) pioneering attempt to rank psychologists suffered from certain peculiarities that can lessen its accuracy in predicting long-term eminence. One of those peculiarities was the decision to include still-living psychologists, in contradistinction to the peer rankings conducted by Annin, Boring, and Watson (1968). This meant that some of the 52 whom Cattell's experts rated were still early in their careers when they earned such high recognition. The most remarkable of these youthful notables was not M. F. Washburn or R. S. Woodworth but rather E. L. Thorndike, who was only 29 at the time the ratings were conducted. The more cynically inclined might dismiss Thorndike's precocious inclusion on the grounds that he had earned his PhD under Cattell himself, just 5 years before. Yet with the advantage of historical hindsight, Cattell's rankings seem to display considerable foresight. After all, Thorndike's 1898 doctoral dissertation, published as a monograph supplement in the *Psychological Review*, soon became one of the classics in the field. The enduring impact of his "Animal Intelligence: An Experimental Study of the Associative Processes in Animals" is proven by the fact that the centennial of its publication was celebrated by a special commemoration in *Ameri-*

can *Psychologist*, which included both a reprint of its introductory section and several scholarly assessments (Dewsbury, 1998). The dissertation also proved prophetic with regard to the rest of Thorndike's career. He was American Psychological Association (APA) president in 1912 and was elected to the National Academy of Sciences in 1917. He died in 1949, but his cumulative publication record still received 1,093 citations in 1966–1970—appreciably more than any other of the 52 psychologists in Cattell's list of starred scientists (Over, 1982c). Even the citations of Thorndike's work when he was yet in his 20s amounted to 42, more than any other among the 52 except for William James (594), John Dewey (60), G. M. Stratton (59), J. M. Cattell (47), and G. S. Hall (43). All of these exceptions were his seniors by at least 9 years, with the biggest exception, James, only 7 years away from his death. By 1968, Thorndike was placed in the elite list of the 53 psychologists unanimously recognized as deserving to be in the top 500 of any list of the most important (Annin et al., 1968).

On the other hand, Cattell was not quite so lucky with John Dewey. Although Dewey was a major participant in the early emergence of the functionalist school of psychology, his tenure as a psychologist was virtually over in 1903, when the ratings were taken. In fact, Dewey "exerted a great influence on this school of thought, although his years of active contribution to psychology were few" (Schultz & Schultz, 1992, p. 187). The remainder of Dewey's long career—he lived for almost 50 more years and published profusely until shortly before his death—was devoted almost exclusively to education and philosophy. Indeed, although in 1966–1970 Dewey received 60 citations for the publications on which Cattell's ratings were founded, Dewey received 753 for those that came afterward, so his primary claim to fame clearly lies outside psychology per se.

The contrasting careers of Thorndike and Dewey raise a significant issue: How is a great psychologist's influence on the field distributed over the course of his or her career? At what age do great psychologists begin making major contributions to the discipline? When is their impact most likely to reach a maximum? For how long do great psychologists usually dominate their discipline? At what age do the great psychologists typically cease to be a major force in the development of psychology? These questions are important not only in themselves but also with respect to the matter of how to gauge a psychologist's greatness. A genius is often defined as someone who exerts a phenomenal influence over a given achievement domain for a considerable period of time (Albert, 1975). Thorndike himself exemplifies this linkage. According to the citations his work received in 1981–1985, Thorndike's first cited publication came at age 24, and his last at age 74, spanning 50 years, and in the first 30 years of the 20th century he rated in the top five list of active psychologists.

I begin this chapter by looking at the general relation between age and achievement in psychology. Then I turn to the question of whether this age function varies according to the psychologist's output and eminence. Do great psychologists have career trajectories that are distinguishable from those of their lesser known colleagues?

AGE AND ACHIEVEMENT

"When the age is in, the wit is out," says a character in Shakespeare's *Much Ado About Nothing*. Others have gotten more specific about when the supposed decline begins to set in. According to Oliver Wendell Holmes Jr., "if you haven't cut your name on the door of fame by the time you've reached 40, you might just as well put up your jackknife" (quoted in Lehman, 1953a, pp. 185–186). For scientific disciplines, the cutoff is sometimes placed even lower. According to Albert Einstein, "a person who has not yet made his great contribution to science before the age of thirty will never do so" (quoted in Brodetsky, 1942, p. 699). Paul Dirac, a fellow theoretical physicist, put this idea in an even more dramatic form:

Age is, of course, a fever chill
that every physicist must fear.
He's better dead than living still
when once he's past his thirtieth year.
(quoted in Jungk, 1958, p. 27)

It is significant that both Einstein and Dirac both had completed their Nobel prize-winning research when they were in their mid-20s.

Comparable opinions can certainly be found among illustrious contributors to psychology. Robert S. Woodworth was born in 1869, earned his PhD under J. M. Cattell the year after Thorndike received his, became APA president in 1914, was honored with the American Psychological Foundation Gold Medal in 1956, and died in 1962, in his 90s. During his long career he published 220 articles and 10 major books. Among the latter was his 1921 *Psychology: A Study of Mental Life*, an extremely popular introductory text that went through five editions and outsold its competitors for 25 years. In it one reads that

seldom does a very old person get outside the limits of his previous habits. Few great inventions, artistic or practical, have emanated from really old persons, and comparatively few even from the middle-aged. On the other hand, boys and girls under eighteen seldom produce anything of great value, not having as yet acquired the necessary mastery of the materials with which they have to deal. The period from twenty years up to forty seems to be the most favorable for inventiveness. (Woodworth, 1921, p. 519)

Because Woodworth was already in his 50s at the time, I suppose this means that he viewed himself as about a decade "over the hill." This would seem surprising, because his last book, *The Dynamics of Behavior*, was published when he was in his late 80s. Yet Woodworth might argue that it was only a revision of his earlier *Dynamic Psychology* and, even though he wrote the latter in his late 40s, he might not have considered it as innovative as his earlier publications.

How justified are these views? Did Woodworth capture a profound regularity of human developmental psychology, or is this a mere illustration of ageist stereotypes? Interestingly enough, the relation between age and achievement has attracted some of the earliest empirical research in the social sciences (Simonton, 1988a, 1997b). As a consequence, there has accumulated an impressive repertory of empirical and theoretical findings that shed considerable light on this significant problem. This collection deals with three topics: (a) the usual age function describing the relation between age and output, (b) the variation in this typical trajectory as a function of the type of contribution, and (c) the longitudinal association between quantity and quality of output.

Typical Career Trajectory

Adolphe Quételet was a distinguished Belgian mathematician and astronomer who is best known today for his contributions to statistics, a term that he coined. In particular, it was he, more than any other, who established the normal distribution as descriptive of the cross-sectional variation in human physical attributes. Taking his departure from the work of Laplace and Gauss on the distribution of errors about a point estimate, Quételet also developed the concept of the average individual (*l'homme moyen*), which plays an extremely critical role in the statistical analyses used in modern psychology (e.g., tests for mean differences). These contributions are found in his 1835 *A Treatise on Man and the Development of His Faculties*. It was on this classic work that Francis Galton (1869) built his case for the normal distribution of human intelligence. However, contained within the pages of the *Treatise* was a pioneering contribution not to the study of individual differences but rather to the examination of developmental changes. In particular, Quételet tabulated the lifetime output of major English and French dramatists into 11 consecutive 5-year age periods. He then showed that a consistent longitudinal pattern emerged: The output rate increased fairly rapidly to a peak productive age, after which the rate gradually declined. Almost 40 years later this fundamental age trend was replicated by George Miller Beard (1874), who is far better known for coining the diagnostic term *neurasthenia*. Yet Beard's study was oddly far less methodologically proficient than Quételet's. Indeed, the methodological sophistication of Quételet's data collection and statistical analysis was not surpassed for well over 100 years (Simonton, 1988a).

The first psychologist to build on Quételet's discovery was Harvey C. Lehman. Like his younger contemporary Wayne Dennis, Lehman must be considered among the more marginal figures in psychology's history, only even more so. Although he enjoys an entry in one biographical dictionary of eminent contributors (Zusne, 1984), Lehman is not well known today, neither does his research receive much attention in recent introductory textbooks, and even less in history texts. Similar to Wayne Dennis, Lehman started out studying child development, in his case the focus being on children's play behavior, an early contribution on that topic appearing in a 1926 issue of *Psychological Review*. He can be credited with more than 100 publications, including many articles in the *Review*, *Psychological Bulletin*, and *American Psychologist*. Yet he never obtained the same level of recognition that Dennis did. Unlike Dennis, for example, Lehman was not honored with an entry in the *World Who's Who in Science* (Debus, 1968). Lehman seems to define a lower level of eminence somewhere between a Wayne Dennis and a psychologist who never managed to make a distinctive contribution to our field.

I say "somewhere between" because Lehman's 1953 book *Age and Achievement* (Lehman, 1953a) can be considered a minor classic in adult developmental psychology (Simonton, 1988a). Still averaging about 10 citations per year, 30 years after its publication (according to the *Social Sciences Citation Index Five-Year Cumulation 1981–1985*, 1987), this work summarizes the key results of a research program that Lehman had been conducting since the 1930s. He would begin with a published list or compilation of major achievements for a particular domain—such as politics, science, the arts, sports, or entertainment—and then determine how old the individuals were at the time they made the contribution. It was then a simple matter to tabulate these facts into consecutive 5-year age periods, just as Quételet (1835/1968) had done. *Age and Achievement* essentially consists of one table and figure after another reporting the raw statistics and forms of these career trajectories for dozens of distinct areas of human accomplishment. Lehman found the same single-peaked age curve as did Quételet.

For example, in chapter 3 of the book Lehman discusses age and achievement in philosophy. He first canvassed more than 50 standard history of philosophy texts, from which he culled a list of the single greatest books by each of 52 deceased philosophers who were most frequently mentioned and discussed. Given psychology's philosophical roots, this list includes many of the masterpieces in its own past, such as John Locke's *An Essay Concerning Human Understanding*, Immanuel Kant's *Critique of Pure Reason*, René Descartes's *Meditations on First Philosophy*, Baruch Spinoza's *Ethics*, and Niccolò Machiavelli's *The Prince*. After determining the ages at which these works were composed, Lehman tabulated the number of works produced in consecutive 5-year decades from 20–24 to 25–79. A clear, single-peaked function emerged, with the maximum in the 35–39 age period. The median age for producing a philosophical masterwork was 39.6, and the mean was 41.5. The slightly higher age for the mean reflected the fact that the distribution is skewed right, with the mode appearing in the earlier portion of the philosopher's career. The remainder of this chapter is devoted to other investigations that vary the methods used, such as permitting more than one work per thinker in the tabulations, including a thinker's entire philosophical output. Lehman also broke down the results according to specialties within philosophy, namely, logic, ethics, aesthetics, metaphysics, and social philosophy. Altogether, he conducted more than 24 additional analyses, but the results were similar , with a peak in the 35–39 age period and with a median and mean somewhere between the late 30s and the early 40s.

Chapters 1 and 2 of *Age and Achievement* address science, medicine, and allied fields, also including achievement domains of interest to psychology's history. For instance, Lehman scrutinized the longitudinal distribution of 60 contributions by 55 major physiologists, obtaining results strikingly similar to that for the philosophers. The peak again fell in the 35–39 age period, with a median of 41.3 and a mean of 43.5. Also included is an agewise tabulation for 50 individuals who made 85 major contributions to psychology. The raw data in this case came from a chronological table published in *A Hundred Years of Psychology* (Flugel, 1933). This classic volume was written by John C. Flugel, a British psychologist whose approximately 80 publications were sufficient to earn him a modest place in the list of the 538 important psychologists (Annin et al., 1968; also see Zusne, 1984). Once more the peak age fell in the 35–39 period, with a median of 42.6 and a mean of 44.5. The latter two statistics are a bit older than observed for philosophy and physiology, but not substantially so. The late 30s and early 40s seem to provide a general high point to the overall career trajectory.

Although H. C. Lehman died on August 8, 1965, a follow-up investigation, serving as a fitting swan song, was published in an April 1966 issue of *American Psychologist* (Lehman, 1966). Here a greater diversity of sources was relied on. Besides using a newer edition of Flugel's (1951) work, Lehman examined tabulations derived from the contributions listed in other classic history volumes, including E. G. Boring's (1950) *A History of Experimental Psychology* and Gardiner Murphy's (1949) *Historical Introduction to Modern Psychology*. In addition, Lehman scrutinized 1,530 important contributions by 1,002 still-living psychologists as listed in the classic introductory text *Experimental Psychology* by Robert S. Woodworth and Harold Schlosberg (1954), both distinguished psychologists themselves. The results were basically indistinguishable from Lehman's 1953a findings. The peak for making a great contribution to psychology landed once more in the 35–39 age period. Furthermore, this career peak holds for both historical and contemporary contributions. Others since Lehman (1953a, 1966) have more or less replicated this finding (e.g., S. Cole, 1979; Dennis & Girden, 1954). For example, a study of more than 1,000 academic psychologists concluded that "productivity typically began at a low rate in the 20s, increased to a peak around age

40, then decreased in the later years" (Horner, Rushton, & Vernon, 1986, p. 319).

On a superficial level, this robust statistic might seem to endorse Woodworth's (1921) assertion that the innovative portion of the psychologist's career is basically over by age 40. However, there are two reasons why this developmental generalization must be viewed with considerable caution. First, one always must remember that the median and mean of the longitudinal distribution almost invariably fall in the early 40s. That signifies that more than half of a psychologist's career still remains after reaching this supposed life watermark. So, depending on whether one is a pessimist or an optimist, by this time the glass is either half empty or half full. Second, and most important, the age function is only an aggregate result averaged over numerous careers. As all psychologists know, people differ, often greatly—and psychologists are by no means an exception to that rule. In fact, there exists abundant evidence that the career trajectory is moderated by a host of other variables. These influential factors can determine the shape of the age curve, as well as the location of the peak. It is to these factors that I now must turn.

Quantity and Quality

Lehman's (1953a) *Age and Achievement* provoked considerable controversy and critical reaction. The protests centered on the apparently steep age decrement after the peak productive period has been passed. Lehman had clearly hit a nerve for many people, especially for those who found themselves on the wrong side of the great longitudinal divide. His conclusions were accordingly criticized by many within and outside the discipline (e.g., Bullough, Bullough, & Mauro, 1978; Zuckerman & Merton, 1972). Among psychologists, the most vocal critic was none other than Wayne Dennis, who was 48 years old when Lehman's book appeared (albeit Lehman himself was 64). Dennis repeatedly attacked Lehman in book reviews and articles (Dennis, 1954d, 1956a, 1958). Dennis's criticisms were not always justified, as Lehman protested more than once (e.g., Lehman, 1956, 1960, 1962). For instance, Dennis (1956a) accused Lehman of "choosing age-intervals in such a way as to maximize the effects of sampling errors" (p. 332). Yet Lehman's equally spaced, 5-year age periods (20–24, 25–29, 30–34, etc.) are quite straightforward—the same that Quételet (1835/1968) used more than 100 years before. Moreover, because Lehman subjected all of his data sets to identical longitudinal slices, Dennis's accusation becomes truly preposterous. In fact, it is not Lehman, but Lehman's critics, who can often be seen selecting arbitrary age periods that minimize the observed age decrement (see, e.g., S. Cole, 1979). Yet it was Lehman's misfortune that Dennis's critiques were frequently cited by subsequent researchers while ignoring Lehman's replies, even when published back to back in the same journal (Lehman, 1956, 1960).

This tendency was probably aggravated by the fact that Lehman died before Dennis did, enabling the latter to get the last word in their ongoing debate (Dennis, 1966).

This is not to say that all of Dennis's criticisms were unjustified. Lehman's research did suffer from a number of methodological problems (Simonton, 1988a). Among the most serious was his frequent failure to control adequately for differential life span. Because fewer individuals live to be 80 than live to be 60, the number of great contributions by 80-year-olds will necessarily be smaller than the number produced by 60-year-olds. Yet Lehman's curves typically tabulate the counts willy-nilly across individuals with vastly differing life spans, with the immediate consequence that the age decrement is exaggerated. Lehman's failure to make appropriate corrections consistently throughout all of his data analyses is all the more troublesome given that Quételet (1835/1968) introduced the same correction a century before (viz., the number of works produced each age period per number of individuals still alive that age period). Lehman apparently was unaware of Quételet's pioneering study. Obviously, science does not always progress if scientists fail to build on the advances of their predecessors. Nonetheless, subsequent investigators have introduced sophisticated methodological controls for this and other sources of artifact and still obtain an age decrement, even if a more gradual one than those that Lehman reported (S. Cole, 1979; Dennis, 1966; Simonton, 1977a, 1985b). On occasion, this elevation of the postpeak decline sometimes shifts the career optimum, so that the high point appears in the 40–44 interval rather than in the 35–39.

Another of Dennis's (1956a, 1958) criticisms is more problematic, however. It is neither clearly wrong nor obviously correct but rather requires special empirical scrutiny—especially because it raises a serious substantive issue. The problem has to do with the relation between quantity and quality of output across the course of a career. Lehman's tabulations almost invariably included only major contributions, excluding those works that failed to exert an undeniable impact on a particular domain of achievement. Dennis argued that this methodological decision underestimated the impact of scientists who were past their prime. This downward bias would take place for two reasons.

First, because the number of researchers has been growing exponentially in recent times (Price, 1963), the older an investigator gets, the more junior colleagues with whom he or she must compete. That means that later works might be less often mentioned in history and introductory texts even if they are of equal quality to the earlier works. One can address this potential artifact by introducing the appropriate controls, such as counting the number of potential competitors for attention in a given age period (e.g., Simonton, 1977a). Although this factor seems to have some effect, its impact is relatively modest, and certainly too small to account for the age decrement in any significant way (Simonton, 1988a). One reason why the repercussions are so minimal is that the frequency with which contributions are cited has more or less kept pace with the number of available contributors.

Second, it could be that the career trajectory for total output is described by a different longitudinal trend than what holds for high-impact output. Indeed, this was one point on which both Lehman and Dennis agreed. Both believed that quantity peaked later and exhibited a more gradual decline than did quality (e.g., Dennis, 1966; Lehman, 1953a). Unfortunately, this agreement was founded on data analyses that had their own methodological flaws. The developmental trends for total output were usually calculated for different samples of individuals than those for quality output only, making direct comparison impossible (Simonton, 1988a). For instance, Lehman (1953a) compared the age distribution of 85 stellar contributions by 50 historical figures (using Flugel, 1933) with the distribution of 4,687 far less significant contributions by 339 contemporary psychologists (using Murchison, 1929) and found that the peak for the latter data set fell 5 years later, in the 40–44 age period. Yet it should be obvious that Lehman confounded the quantity–quality variable with a large number of extraneous factors.

Of course, from the standpoint of psychology's history this whole debate may appear moot. After all, by definition the influential works alone leave an impact on the field. So why should one even care if the trajectory for quality might differ from that for quantity? The latter age curve would seem to lack historical consequence anyway. Yet to neglect this issue would be a grave mistake. When I discussed the quantity–quality relation with respect to cross-sectional variation, I introduced the *equal-odds rule*, which holds that quality is a constant probabilistic function of quantity: Psychologists who produce the most total work tend to produce the most influential work— as well as the most ignored work. Does the same rule have a longitudinal form? Does the ratio of high-impact publications to total publications really stay more or less constant, subject to no more than random fluctuations? Or might it not be possible that scientists can learn to increase their hit rate with accumulated professional experience? Alternatively, might the quality ratio or hit rate decline with age? This last alternative is certainly implicit in the notion, maintained by both H. C. Lehman and W. Dennis, that the age decrement is more gradual for quantity than for quality. So, which is it?

Age Distribution of Success Rates

The first scientist to investigate the quantity–quality relation was the same as the first to study the age–productivity relation: Quételet (1835/1968). Quételet considered the total work of a single great dramatist, Molière, and divided Molière's output into three categories of quality: the worst, the average, and the best. He then showed that the age trends were indistinguishable, after tabulating them into 11 consecutive 5-year age intervals. A secondary data analysis conducted more than 160 years later indicated that the three longitudinal time series correlated between .82 and .91, a high degree of agreement (Simonton, 1997a). Moreover, the ratio of top-notch work to total output exhibited a zero correlation with the dramatist's age. The hit rate neither increases nor decreases. The same age-invariant quality ratio has been found in studies of classical composers (Simonton, 1977a; Weisberg, 1994) and for scientific careers (Oromaner, 1977; Over, 1989; Simonton, 1984d). Most important of all, three studies (S. Cole, 1979; Over, 1988; Simonton, 1985b) have indicated that the same longitudinal invariance of the hit rate or quality ratio probably holds for psychology.

The first study scrutinized the articles published between 1965 and 1969 that were cited in the 1971 *Science Citation Index* (S. Cole, 1979). The articles represented the fields of chemistry, geology, mathematics, physics, psychology, and sociology. After the age of each article's author was identified, the mean numbers of publications and citations for consecutive age periods were calculated. The results for psychologists are given in Table 4.1. As is evident, both publications and citations exhibit about the same single-peaked function, with a peak in the late 30s and early 40s. The similarity of the two trends became more clear when I divided the mean citation rate by the mean publication rate to obtain the quality ratio, also shown in Table 4.1 . The average number of citations per article hovers close to unity for all age periods. The only conspicuous exception is the 60+ interval, in which the ratio declines to three fourths. This decline in the hit rate can be clearly ascribed to the unexpected publication count in this concluding interval. However, given that the sample size for this interval is understandably small, it is difficult to determine whether the decrement represents something substantially more than sampling error. Confidence in this latter inference is strengthened by the remaining two investigations.

The next study began with 227 single-authored articles published in *Psychological Review* between 1965 and 1980 (Over, 1988; also see Over, 1989). For each article the number of times it was cited in the fifth year after its publication was determined. This citation measure was then correlated with the ages of the authors, whether in terms of chronological or professional age (years since PhD). The correlation was almost exactly zero. "Although the majority of articles in *Psychological Review* were published by authors under the age of 40," the investigator (Over, 1988) concluded that

> such a bias is to be expected in terms of the age distribution of American psychologists. When allowance was made for the number of authors in different age ranges, older authors were no less likely than younger authors to have generated a high-impact article (an article cited 10 or more times in the fifth year after publication). (p. 215)

In the final investigation I (Simonton, 1985b) looked at the careers of 10 distinguished psychologists. All had received APA's Distinguished Scientific Contribution Award (and fulfilled certain other conditions): Wolfgang

TABLE 4.1

Age, Mean Publications, Mean Citations, and Quality Ratio for
Psychologists

| Age period | Mean | | Quality ratio | n |
	Publications	Citations		
> 35	5.6	5.2	0.93	151
35–39	6.4	6.6	1.03	101
40–44	6.4	6.8	1.06	92
45–49	4.9	5.1	1.04	94
50–59	3.3	3.3	1.00	79
60+	4.4	3.3	0.75	27

Note. The quality ratio is calculated here for first time. Means were taken from "Age and Scientific Performance" by S. Cole, 1979, *American Journal of Sociology, 84*, pp. 962 and 964. Copyright 1979 by University of Chicago. Reprinted with permission.

Köhler, Carl Hovland, Gordon Allport, Kenneth Spence, Edward Tolman, Carl Rogers, B. F. Skinner, J. P. Guilford, Donald T. Campbell, and Albert Bandura. Taking advantage of complete publication records published in *American Psychologist* at the time their award was announced, I divided the output into high- and low-impact works according to the citations they received in the professional literature. I then tabulated these segregated publication lists into two longitudinal time series, using 5-year intervals. After introducing necessary methodological controls I found that (a) the output of high-impact publications correlates highly with the output of low-impact publications, and (b) the ratio of high-impact publications to total output fluctuates randomly throughout the career, neither increasing nor decreasing systematically. The hit rate appeared age invariant.

These findings have some curious implications about what it takes to become a great psychologist. According to the cross-sectional version of the equal-odds rule, the most direct route to success is a high level of raw productivity. Individuals who produce more have better odds of producing a high-impact work, but they also have proportional odds of producing work that leaves no imprint on the discipline. The same principle applies to the course of an individual psychologist's career: Those periods of a career that see the most prolific output are those that are most likely to contain the psychologist's most influential work. Yet psychologists are evidently incapable of improving their success rates with practice. The odds that an octogenarian will make a major contribution are no better than the odds for a psychologist near the onset of his or her career. The consolation prize is that the likelihood is also no worse. On a contribution-for-contribution basis, age is simply irrelevant to the prediction of a psychologist's current impact.s

If psychologists evidently do not learn from experience to raise their hit rates, then they may never acquire the capacity to become good judges of their own work. At times a psychologist may feel that some current project represents a masterpiece, only to discover that his or her colleagues may not be so receptive. Another work, for which a psychologist has little regard, may have an impact far out of proportion to the originator's expectations. This discordance may remind historians of psychology what William James told his publisher, after completing the *Principles of Psychology*:

> No one could be more disgusted than I at the sight of the book. *No* subject is worth being treated of in 1000 pages! Had I ten years more, I could rewrite it in 500; but as it stands it is this or nothing—a loathsome, distended, tumefied, bloated, dropsical mass, testifying to nothing but two facts: *1st*, that there is no such thing as a *science* of psychology, and *2nd*, that W.J. is an incapable. (H. James, 1920, Vol. I, p. 294)

Although James's self-criticism may not be totally serious, other great psychologists have reported a lack of congruence between their own evaluations of their work and the work's impact on the field. Hermann von Helmholtz had this experience often enough that he even proposed a potential explanation for how personal and social assessments can diverge.

> My colleagues, as well as the public at large, evaluate a scientific or artistic work on the basis of its utility, its instructiveness, or the pleasure which it affords. An author is more inclined to base his evaluation on the labor a work has cost him, and it is but rarely that both kinds of judgment agree. Indeed, we can see from occasional statements of some of the most celebrated men, especially artists, that they assign small value to achievements which seem to us inimitable, compared with others which were difficult for them and yet which appear much less successful to readers and observers. I need only mention Goethe, who once stated to Eckermann that he did not value his poetic works as highly as the work he had done in the theory of color. (Helmholtz, 1891/1971, p. 467)

At present it is not known whether the phenomenon Helmholtz described is general. Even so, it is clear that something strange is happening. For some reason, even great psychologists cannot escape having careers that unfold with an almost random mix of successes and failures. Furthermore, their own personal opinions on their hits and misses may not agree with those of their own or later times.

Age Distribution of Career Landmarks

Given that a psychologist's career must consist of an unpredictable mix of hits and misses, an interesting and important issue necessarily arises: Certain hits will have special significance in delineating the highlights of one's career. In particular, some hits can be considered *career landmarks*. These landmarks are the first major contribution, the best contribution, and the last major contribution. The first career landmark indicates when the individual has begun to leave an imprint on the field, the last career landmark when he or she has ceased to do so, and the best contribution marks the career acme—the work for which the individual is most likely to be remembered. To be sure, for psychologists who only had one genuine success, these three landmarks will entail one and the same contribution. A one-idea great has an impact on the field that begins, peaks, and terminates with one big splash. Yet, as I pointed out in the previous chapter, the greatest of the great boast reputations that rest on much more than a single shot. For the Prolifics, whose contributions to psychology's history are the most extensive, the first, most, and last influential ideas will not be found in the same longitudinal spot in the psychologist's life. So, how are these three career landmarks distributed across the course of one's career?

Although Quételet's (1835/1968) work represents the first scientific inquiry into the age–productivity function, the earliest investigation into the three career landmarks was not published until more than 100 years later (Raskin, 1936). This study specifically looked at 120 scientists and 123 writers. Several of the scientists claim some degree of presence in the history of psychology, including J. Louis Agassiz, Charles Darwin, Michael Faraday, Karl Friedrich Gauss, Hermann von Helmholtz, Jean Baptiste Lamarck, James Clerk Maxwell, and Thomas Young (cf. Annin et al., 1968). Among the writers, in contrast, only Johann Goethe has earned some place in the annals of the discipline. In any event, the scientists typically launched their careers at age 25, produced their greatest works at age 35, stopped having an impact after 59, and died around 69. The pattern was very similar for eminent authors, with corresponding figures of 24, 34, 55, and 63. A much later investigation examined the longitudinal placement of the career landmarks in scientists, albeit in 2,026 of them (Simonton, 1991a). The scientists covered the disciplines of mathematics, astronomy, physics, chemistry, biology, medicine, technology, earth sciences, and a miscellaneous group. Across all disciplines, the first major contribution came at 31, the best at 40, and the last at 54 (with a life expectancy of 70). Nonetheless, it was the miscellaneous group that contained the largest proportion of historic figures who made contributions to psychology. Among these 102 individuals were such notable psychoanalysts as S. Freud, C. Jung, and A. Adler. The three career landmarks for this subset fell around ages 33, 42, and 55 (with a life expectancy of 69).

These figures put into proper context the results from investigations that concentrate specifically on eminent psychologists. In one investigation the sample consisted of 213 luminaries whose bibliographies appeared in R. I. Watson's (1974) *Eminent Contributors to Psychology* (Zusne, 1976a). For this group the first major publication appeared around age 30, the most significant around age 40, and the last around 65. In another investigation, the sample was also drawn from Watson's (1974) compilation but was confined to just 69 Americans (Simonton, 1992b). The study differed in another way as well: It specifically used the *Social Sciences Citation Index* to determine the first still-cited work, the most-cited work, and the last still-cited work. The first career landmark appeared around age 30, the second around age 47, and the last around age 63. The biggest discrepancy with previous findings was the age for the most-cited work, which is delayed by 5 years or so. One can determine whether this reflects a peculiarity of the sample or of the operational definition only by conducting additional studies (also see R. A. Davis, 1987). So, to best consolidate the results, the first major contribution usually occurs around age 30, the most important in the early or middle 40s, and the last major contribution in the middle 50s to early 60s. The placement of the career landmarks is asymmetrical, just like the underlying curve for total output. The second landmark most commonly arrives about 10 years after the first, whereas the third arrives between 12 and 20 years after the second.

It turns out that one cannot generate a conclusion more precise than the foregoing without introducing several complicating factors. This shall be done fairly soon. In the meantime, I discuss how the agewise position of the second career landmark links with the equal-odds rule. If quality is a positive (if probabilistic) function of quantity, then those periods in a psychologist's career in which the most works are produced should have the highest probability of containing his or her major works, and among those major works should be found the best work. Therefore, the period of maximum output during a psychologist's career should most likely contain the psychologist's single most critical contribution. In other words, the magnum opus should appear near the career peak rather than at the career's cumulation.

There exists direct evidence for this intimate connection in other creative domains (Simonton, 1991b, 1997b), but no direct tests have yet been conducted for psychology. Nonetheless, many studies have shown that psychologists attain their maximum output rate sometime in their late 30s and early 40s (e.g., Horner et al., 1986), about the same period when the second career landmark is most prone to appear. In addition, there exists anecdotal evidence that these periods may be coterminous. At least such a temporal conjunction occurred in the life of psychology's founder, Wilhelm Wundt. "The period from 1870–1879, during which Wundt published his *magnum opus* was the most productive period of Wundt's life in terms of individual publications" (Bringmann & Balk, 1983, pp. 72–73). The master work in question was the *Principles of Physiological Psychology*, which appeared in 1873–1874. Whether this tends to be typical of most great psychologists remains to be seen.

Contribution Type

So far I have been treating a publication as a publication. It matters not whether a publication is a book or a note or whether it was a contribution to physiological or social psychology. Yet a complete understanding of a psychologist's career trajectories may require adjustment for the type of contribution. Accordingly, I now scrutinize how one's career course may depend on both the genre and domain of psychological publication.

Genre

In my discussion of cross-sectional differences in output I recognized that not all publications constitute equal units of effort or impact. On the contrary, a publication may range from a research note, comment, or book review to a multivolume monograph, with the professional journal article occupying the middle range. Empirical inquiries into the publication patterns of academic researchers have consistently shown that these distinct publication genres are not distributed across the course of the career according to the same longitudinal function (Roe, 1972). For instance, according to an analysis of 30 eminent Australian academics who were 70–90 years old, "productivity increased to a peak age of 40–49 years for journal articles, 50–59 for new books and cross-disciplinary publications, and 60–69 for revised and edited books, technical publications and non-technical books" (Christensen & Jacomb, 1992, p. 681). Another investigation concentrated on an unselected group of 324 American experimental psychologists and found a similar pattern (Bayer & Dutton, 1977). "Unlike article publications, lifetime publication of books tends to increase linearly with career age for most fields, with r's ranging from approximately .30 to .50" (Bayer & Dutton, 1977, p. 275). It is interesting that there is evidence that social scientists tend to turn from refereed journal articles to book chapters as a main publication vehicle as they attain increased eminence in their fields (Rodman & Mancini, 1981). Rather than go through the sometimes-capricious hassles of the review process, eminent social scientists accept invitations to write chapters for anthologies with more assured publication.

Of these career shifts in publication genre, the most critical may be the transformation from articles to books. As observed earlier, the most influential (highly cited) work of any psychologist is more likely to be a book rather than an article. A book enables the psychologist "to put it all together in one place" in some grand synthesis or integration. It provides a superior means of showing the advances that have already been made and for highlighting the major issues that remain to be resolved. In short, the longitudinal switch may be a wise strategy for someone who aspires to become a great psychologist. It is curious, however, that this integration of progress and prospects should appear near the career peak rather than toward the career's termination. Perhaps the synthesis becomes less convincing or useful as the psychologist becomes farther removed from the real data reported in journal articles.

Domain

As I stressed in chapter 1, not all great psychologists are strictly psychologists. The history of psychology is riddled with names that should more properly be allotted to other domains of achievement. Consequently, it is essential to inquire whether there exists a one-size-fits-all career trajectory. According to a large empirical literature, expected career trajectories are not invariant across different domains (e.g., Bayer & Dutton, 1977; McDowell, 1982). The interdisciplinary variation was amply documented in Harvey C. Lehman's (1953a) *Age and Achievement*. Looking at the output of high-impact work, the career peaks for representative scientific fields are as follows: chemistry, 26–30; mathematics, physics, botany, and classical descriptions of disease, 30–34; surgical techniques, genetics, and psychology, 30–39; astronomy, geology, physiology, pathology, and medical discoveries, 35–39. For philosophical domains the peaks were located at 35–39 for logic, ethics, aesthetics, and general philosophy but at 40–44 for metaphysics. A roughly contemporary but independent investigation provided point estimates for the ages at which the best work was most likely to appear for 4,204 scientists: mathematics, 37; bacteriology and chemistry, 38; physiology and physics, 40; engineering, 43; pathology, 44, astronomy, surgery, and psychology, 45; geology, botany, and zoology, 46; and anthropology, 47 (Adams, 1946). A more recent inquiry looked at the ages at which scientists do the work for which they received the Nobel prize and obtained means of 36 for physics, 38 for chemistry, and 39 for physiology or medicine (Stephan & Levin, 1993; also see Manniche & Falk, 1957).

Wayne Dennis (1966) conducted an inquiry into the same problem but scrutinized quantity rather than quality, tabulating complete lists of contributions regardless of impact. Furthermore, he sampled only contributors who had lived to become octogenarians. These alterations were designed to overcome some of the several methodological problems he saw in Lehman's (1953a) work. Even so, his results were not dramatically different from what I just reported: Mathematicians peaked in the 30s and 40s, chemists and biologists in the 40s, geologists in the 50s, and philosophers in the 60s. S. Cole (1979) identified published articles in the sciences regardless of quality. By that standard, mathematicians peaked at 35–39, physicists and geologists at 40–44, psychologists at 40–49, and chemists and sociologists at 45–49. The same investigator determined the age at which a scientist published his or her first 5-citation article. The means were as follows: physics, 27; chemistry, 30; biochemistry, 35; experimental psychology, 34; clinical psychology, 34; and sociology, 34. S. Cole (1979) also calculated the mean age for publishing the first 10-citation article for the first three disciplines as well: physics, 28; chemistry, 34; and biochemistry, 36. Hence, domains may differ by as much as 8 years with respect to the appearance of the first career landmark. Dennis's (1966) inquiry demonstrated that substantial interdisciplinary differences also emerge at the other end of the age curve. One way of expressing the magnitude of this contrast is to compare the output in the 70s with the output at the career peak for a particular domain (see Table 2 in Dennis, 1966). For philosophy, such septuagenarians are still producing at 88% of their maximum rate. Yet in biology, chemistry, and geology the corresponding rates decline to 55%, 53%, and 53%, respectively. Dennis's (1966) study did not include psychology, but an earlier investigation found evidence that sexagenarians publish at only half the rate as seen in the 30s and 40s, the discipline's presumed career maximum (Dennis & Girden, 1954).

Although a certain degree of regularity is apparent in the above-mentioned results, the findings are not perfectly consistent. However, the age peaks given for various disciplines are not always comparable from study to study. Besides contrasts in measurement along the quantity-versus-quality dimension, the domain of achievement is often confounded with other variables that also influence the expected peak age. For example, the peak age for producing a scientific discovery or invention has increased over the years, by as much as a dozen years since the Renaissance (Zhao & Jiang, 1986). Accordingly, interdisciplinary differences could represent contrasts in the mean birth year of the individuals making up the subsamples. In addition, just because two studies both contain "physicists" does automatically mean that the groups are homogeneous, because contrasts in career trajectories can occur among subdisciplines as well. For instance, atomic and molecular physicists have peaks at 39–40, solid-state/condensed-matter physicists at 40–45, and geophysicists at 53–59 (Levin & Stephan, 1991). So, if two groups of physicists have a different mix of subdisciplines, discrepant trajectories will result. Other variables that can contaminate the results include the magnitude of eminence required, the differential life spans and contrasting nationalities of the individuals sampled, and the archival sources from which the sample was drawn.

Perhaps the most severe problem, however, concerns sampling error. Often the subgroups consist of relatively small numbers of representatives. In Dennis's (1966) study, for example, no scientific domain had as many as 50 scientists, and the chemists numbered only 24. Moreover, it is very possible that between-group variance is overwhelmed by within-group variance. Seldom are formal statistics tests performed to determine whether the group contrasts can be ascribed to chance fluctuations. However, the findings of one study provided sufficient reason for concluding that the domain differences are indeed real rather than merely apparent (Simonton, 1991a). This investigation used a large sample of hundreds of individuals who made landmark contributions to the history of science. In Table 4.2 the descriptive statistics are reported for the ages at first, best, and last major contribution for the disciplines of mathematics, astronomy, physics, chemistry, biology, medicine, technology, earth sciences, and miscellaneous (which includes most of the sampled figures who have left a name in psychology's history). It is evident from mere inspection that the longitudinal location of these three career landmarks varies substantially across these nine categories. Thus, the mean age at first significant work ranges from about 27 for mathematics to about 33 for miscellaneous. Likewise, a 7-year difference separates the discipline with the youngest last-work mean (chemistry) from the oldest (earth sciences). The interdisciplinary range in the means for the single most influential work was on the order of 5 years, from about 38 for chemistry to about

TABLE 4.2
Ages at First, Best, and Last Major Contribution for 1,884 Scientists and Inventors

	First			Best			Last			
Discipline	M	SD	Range	M	SD	Range	M	SD	Range	n
Mathematics	27.3	8.5	14–60	38.8	10.7	19–68	53.4	15.0	21–81	117
Astronomy	30.5	8.7	17–73	40.6	11.2	18–77	56.0	14.0	20–84	162
Physics	29.7	7.8	15–66	38.2	9.1	19–70	52.3	13.3	25–90	327
Chemistry	30.5	8.1	14–72	38.0	9.0	18–74	51.1	13.2	22–102	425
Biology	29.4	7.2	17–64	40.5	11.0	18–77	57.8	13.7	29–87	187
Medicine	32.3	8.2	17–62	42.1	10.4	22–81	54.5	14.0	27–92	280
Technology	31.6	9.5	11–60	39.7	10.8	20–80	53.1	14.9	21–93	229
Earth sciences	30.9	8.2	17–59	42.5	12.1	17–78	58.2	13.8	27–85	85
Other	33.4	11.0	20–67	41.6	11.1	23–69	55.2	14.4	23–86	72

Note. From "Career Landmarks in Science: Individual Differences and Interdisciplinary Contrasts" by D. K. Simonton, 1991a, Developmental Psychology, 27, p. 126. Copyright 1991 by the American Psychological Association. Adapted with permission.

43 for the earth sciences. More critical is that appropriate statistical tests demonstrate that the differences among these means are statistically reliable. They cannot be dismissed as mere products of sampling errors. In addition, the differences survived statistical controls for a host of potential artifacts, such as birth year, life span, archival source, and degree of sample selectivity.

One can consequently conclude that the career trajectory is truly contingent on the achievement domain. Eminent figures in the history of psychology who hailed from mathematics, physics, biology, medicine, or the earth sciences should have different expected career paths than those who can count as psychologists pure and simple. Yet caveat emptor: The expected career profiles should not be applied uncritically to the lives of great psychologists. A crucial complicating factor remains to be discussed.

INDIVIDUAL VARIATION IN CAREER DEVELOPMENT: A COGNITIVE MODEL

Thomas Young was just 19 when he read a paper before the Royal Society in which he experimentally established visual accommodation in terms of the changing curvature of the lens—a contribution of sufficient importance to have him elected as a Royal Society member at age 21. Darwin's greatest single contribution, *The Origin of Species*, did not appear until he was 50, and his *The Descent of Man* was more than 12 years in the future. Gustav Fechner was 75 when he published his noteworthy *Introduction to Aesthetics*, and he continued making contributions for the next 10 years. Such landmark ages do not seem to fit very well with the means shown in Table 4.2. For this reason the table also includes two measures of dispersion about each average, namely, the standard deviation and the range. These latter statistics are huge: The standard deviation varies between 7 and 15 years, and the minimum and maximum ages for each career landmark are even more impressive. In several disciplines, for example, two scientists may differ by nearly 60 years in the ages at which they made their most influential contribution. In the context of these statistics, the career trajectories anchored by the achievements of Young, Darwin, and Fechner are extraordinary but not empirically implausible.

Many empirical investigations have underlined the extreme variation that exists in career trajectories (Simonton, 1988a, 1997b). For the most part, if the goal is to predict how much a person will produce in a given time interval, it is far more critical to know *who* the individual is than *how old* he or she is (Levin & Stephan, 1989; Stephan & Levin, 1992; Over, 1982a, 1982b). Thus, in one study of more than 1,000 academic psychologists, age accounted for less than 7% of the variance in a researcher's output in consecutive career periods from ages 25 to 64 (Horner et al., 1986). This proportion may be compared with the findings reported earlier in this chapter regarding the stability of individual differences in output across consecutive decades of the career (e.g., S. Cole, 1979; Dennis, 1954b; Rodgers & Maranto, 1989). Judging from that research, between one third and two thirds of the variance in productivity in any given period may be predicted from the individual differences observed in the previous period. Hence, cross-sectional variation is probably between 5 and 10 times more powerful as a force that shapes the career trajectory. In concrete terms, Prolific psychologists in their late 50s or 60s are more productive per annum than near-Silent psychologists at their own career peaks (Simonton, 1988a, 1997b).

How can such individual differences be accommodated? Does their very existence threaten the utility of any treatment of career trajectories? To answer these questions, I turn to a cognitive model that not only integrates cross-sectional and longitudinal variation but also accounts for interdisciplinary differences. The model was developed over a 14-year period; the first version appeared in a 1984 issue of *Developmental Review* (Simonton, 1984b), and the most recent version appeared in a 1997 issue of *Psychological Review* (Simonton, 1997b), which received the 1998 George Miller Outstanding Article Award from the American Psychological Association. Several lesser refinements and amendments appeared between those dates (e.g., Simonton, 1988a, 1989a). Its original purpose was to account for longitudinal changes in creative productivity, with special emphasis on how the predicted age curve changes according to the domain of creativity. However, with only minor modifications, this cognitive model was eventually extended to explain how those career trajectories vary even for individuals working in the same field. The model is highly mathematical, relying on both differential equations and covariance algebra to derive its critical predictions. Rather than doing the math here, I present the model at only a conceptual level. I start with the longitudinal model and then extend it to the individual-differences model.

Longitudinal Model

The cognitive model begins by assuming that each individual begins his or her career with a certain amount of *initial creative potential*. In abstract terms, this hypothetical quantity gauges the total number of ideational variations a creator is capable of generating given an infinite life span. In more concrete terms, this quantity is proportional to the total number of publications a person is capable of producing, given an unrestricted amount of time. The creative potential is converted into actual products through a two-step mental process. The first step, *ideation*, involves the generation of ideational variations that provide a raw stock of "works in progress." These are the basic but rudimentary ideas that fill up notebooks and sketchbooks. The second step, *elaboration*, entails the more laborious conversion of these ideas to finished works, such as publications. The process may be summarized simply as follows:

CREATIVE POTENTIAL—Ideation→IDEAS—Elaboration→PUBLICATIONS

The coupled processes of ideation and elaboration do not take place instantaneously; rather, both consume a certain amount of time. The *ideation rate* specifies how quickly potential ideas are converted into actual ideas, whereas the *elaboration rate* indicates how fast the items in the latter repertoire become finished contributions. These two information-processing parameters will be positive decimal fractions, usually less than 0.1, and may or may not be equal. It is significant that the exact size of the ideation and elaboration rates depends on the specific nature of the concepts and techniques that define a particular domain of creative achievement. In some domains, ideational variations can be generated rather quickly, whereas in other domains the production of new ideas takes a considerable amount of time. Similar contrasts take place in how long it takes to elaborate the initial inspirations into publishable products. The ideational and elaboration rates are not necessarily correlated and, in fact, have been shown to be empirically uncorrelated across any heterogeneous collection of disciplines (Simonton, 1997b).

In any case, after a little mathematical manipulation, the foregoing two-step model yields the following equation:

$$p(t) = c(e^{-at} - e^{-bt}),$$

where $c = abm/(b - a)$. This equation specifies the publication rate p as a function of time t, where m is the initial creative potential, a is the ideation rate, b the elaboration rate, and e is the exponential constant ($= 2.718$). In the special case where the two information-processing parameters are identical ($a = b$), the equation becomes

$$p(t) = a^2 m e^{-at},$$

a slightly simpler form, but with essentially the same predicted career trajectory. Note that t is not chronological age but rather career age; that is, $t = 0$ at the moment that the individual begins generating ideational variations in a particular domain. This function permits one to formulate a number of empirically testable statements about the typical age curve, interdisciplinary contrasts in the shape of that curve, and corresponding contrasts in the longitudinal location of the three career landmarks (see Simonton, 1984b, 1997b, for details).

Specific Form of the Age Curve

Figure 4.1 shows what this curve looks like for $m = 100$, $a = .04$, and $b = .05$, which can be considered fairly typical parameters. As is immediately apparent, the model predicts an age function with the following three funda-

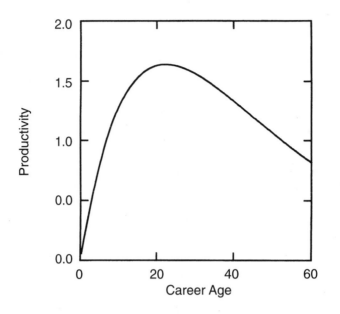

Figure 4.1. Hypothetical career trajectory according to an information-processing model of the creative process (Simonton, 1997b). Productivity *p* at career age *t* is determined by initial creative potential *m* = 100, the ideation rate *a* = .04, and the elaboration rate *b* = .05. From "Creative Productivity: A Predictive and Explanatory Model of Career Trajectories and Landmarks" by D. K. Simonton, 1997b, *Psychological Review*, *104*, p. 69. Copyright 1997 by the American Psychological Association. Adapted with permission.

mental attributes. First, the curve is single peaked rather than having two or more maxima. Second, the ascending portion of the curve is concave downward (i.e., decelerating rather than accelerating). Third, the descending portion of the curve eventually exhibits an inflexion point where the curve becomes concave upward and thereafter approaches asymptotically the zero-output point. All three of these features of the predicted age curve have been successfully verified against actual empirical data (using appropriate methodological controls; see Simonton, 1984b). The hypothesized curve was even confirmed for the psychologists of sufficient importance to have their bibliographies listed in R. I. Watson's (1974) *Eminent Contributors to Psychology* (Simonton, 1984b). For instance, the asymptotic form of the descending segment was confirmed using all 196 psychologists in Watson's book who lived to at least 70 years of age. When the predicted function is tested against data that are aggregated across many individual careers—so as to remove the random shocks that affect any one career—the correlation between expected and observed output is usually in the upper .90s (Simonton, 1984b). For example, the correlation between the observed output of American Nobel laureate scientists and the predicted output is .96 (based on the data in Zuckerman, 1977).

Information-Processing Basis for Interdisciplinary Contrasts

It is essential to realize that the high degree of correspondence between fact and theory requires that the ideation and elaboration rates be chosen to fit the typical trajectories of a given domain of achievement. Because these two information-processing parameters determine the overall shape of the age curve, such as the location of the peak and the slope of the decline, this adjustment can be accomplished by means of nonlinear estimation procedures. I actually performed this strategy using Dennis's (1966) data, obtaining estimates of the ideation and elaboration rates for 16 different domains of creative achievement (Simonton, 1989a). Thus, the 42 philosophers exhibited extremely slow rates ($a = .023$ and $b = .027$) relative to the 32 biologists ($a = .033$ and $b = .052$). Because the predicted curve is strongly determined by even the smallest changes in the two parameters, this contrast has major repercussions. In particular, the predicted age difference between the career peaks for philosophy and biology is more than 16 years. The correlations between predicted and observed levels of output are .95 for philosophers and .98 for biologists, so the agreement is very good once the adjustment is made. It presumably takes much longer to conceive and develop ideas in philosophy than it does in biology. Psychology in this respect falls closer to biology than to philosophy, as might be expected. The parameters ($a = .04$ and $b = .05$) used in Figure 4.1 are probably the most typical for the field.

Equal-Odds Rule, Output, and Career Landmarks

Once these parameters vary according to the information-processing specifics of each discipline, a great diversity of career trajectories can be supported. Peaks may be early or late, and the postpeak decrement may be gradual or steep. This tremendous interdisciplinary diversity in career trajectories permits the model to accommodate conspicuous contrasts in the longitudinal location of the three career landmarks (Simonton, 1991a, 1997b). To make this connection, it is only necessary to apply the equal-odds rule. If quality is a probabilistic function of quantity, then the single best work will be placed near the productive peak. Early-peaking disciplines will therefore differ from late-peaking disciplines in the typical location of the most influential work. Furthermore, with all other factors held constant, fields that exhibit steep ascents in the prepeak period will more likely see the first career landmark appear earlier than fields in which the ascent is much more gradual. A similar expectation holds for the last career landmark. Fields in which the postpeak decline is very gradual will most likely witness last major contributions by the most senior members of the discipline, whereas in fields where the decrement is quite substantial the last career landmark will tend to appear earlier during the contributor's life span. Even more critical is that the relative placement of the three career landmarks does not have to be consistent across different disciplines. Because the longitudinal locations of the first, best, and last major works depend on the underlying productivity curve, and given that this curve can vary appreciably according to the domain-specific information-processing rates, a large number of distinct career patterns can result. Something of this diversity is evident in Table 4.2. Although mathematicians have the earliest first contributions, their best contributions tend to come after those found among physicists and chemists, and their last contributions arrive after those of the physicists, chemists, and inventors.

The longitudinal model should help one comprehend better how career trajectories may vary for celebrities who populate the history of psychology. For instance, the slow pace of conceiving and refining great philosophical ideas sheds light on why it took so long for certain works to materialize that were to become landmarks in psychology's intellectual past. At age 24 Descartes first had his critical dream of the prospect of a unitary science, but it was not until he was 37 when he was ready to offer his ideas to the world (in the suppressed *The World*) and not until age 41 that he actually did so (in the *Discourse on the Method*)—and Descartes was actually on the precocious side for great thinkers. Locke first began to grapple with the origins of human knowledge for an informal evening discussion club when he was in his late 40s, but it was not until he was 58 when he was ready to publish his ideas in *An Essay Concerning Human Understanding*. Also in his late 40s, Kant was finally able to confide in a friend that

> I flatter myself that I have attained that conception which I have no fear that I shall ever change, though I may expand it, by means of which all kinds of metaphysical questions can be tested according to sure and easy criteria, and by means of which it can be decided with certainty how far their solution is possible. (Quoted in Hutchins, 1952, Vol. 42, p. v)

Yet it was not until more than 10 years later that Kant could start to present his new system before the world (in the first *Critique of Pure Reason*), and it took him almost another 10 years (in the remaining two *Critiques*) to put on the finishing touches.

But wait! Didn't George Berkeley publish his famed *Treatise Concerning the Principles of Human Knowledge* when he was 25? It is obvious that influential philosophical tracts are not all written by thinkers in their maturity or old age. Although it may not be possible to account for Berkeley's precocity, at least the model must be extended to accommodate a greater degree of departure from the statistical averages.

Individual-Differences Model

Although the foregoing longitudinal model was originally designed to handle longitudinal changes in output, it contains the rudiments of a more comprehensive model that can explicate individual differences as well. In particular, two distinct individual-difference variables are implicitly part of the model.

First, creative personalities must differ according to their initial amount of creative potential. Some will have a rich fund of ideas that can generate one ideational variation after another. Others are basically one-idea or "one-shot" intellects. According to the theoretical model, m should exhibit a highly skewed distribution in line with the Lotka and Price laws.

Second, creative personalities must differ according to the age at career onset, that is, the age at which $t = 0$. The most common operational definition for this variable is the age at which an individual earns his or her highest degree (e.g., Lyons, 1968). Chronological and career age admittedly often correlate very highly, often in the .80s (e.g., Bayer & Dutton, 1977). Nevertheless, by making the career trajectory a function of career age, the model can account for individual differences in the paths that cannot be explained otherwise (Simonton, 1997b).

The distinctive predictions that can be derived from the individual-difference model fall into two sets, namely, those that concern (a) the longitudinal stability of individual differences in output and (b) the longitudinal placement of the three career landmarks.

Longitudinal Stability of Individual Differences in Output

As already noted, the two information-processing parameters for ideation and elaboration account for the shape of the predicted curve. Initial creative potential (m), on the other hand, does not affect the general form of the longitudinal function. The peak remains in the same place regardless of whether creative potential is high or low. Yet the impact of creative potential on the career trajectory is quite dramatic: The higher the initial creative potential, the faster productivity accelerates in the early years of the career, the higher the output rate at the career peak, and the longer productivity is maintained in the declining years of the career. In short, creative potential determines the overall height of the curve rather than its broad shape. This consequence leads to a critical empirical test.

More than once in this chapter I have noted how publication rates exhibit appreciable stability across consecutive periods of an individual's career. Those who publish more in their 30s will also publish more in their 40s, and those who publish more in their 40s will publish more in their 50s. But why? In the sociology of science this longitudinal stability has often been considered a clear-cut illustration of the phenomenon known as *cumulative advantage* (Allison, 1980; Allison, Long, & Krauze, 1982; Allison & Stewart, 1974; also see Price, 1976). Although couched in sociological terms, this concept has a lot in common with B. F. Skinner's (1938) notion of reinforcement in operant conditioning. Those who manage to publish more early in their careers will begin to attract additional resources, such as grant support and affiliation at major research universities. This enables them to publish even more, which then brings them additional incentives and rewards. In contrast, individuals who fail to publish soon will find themselves competing unsuccessfully with their more prolific contemporaries. Unable to secure the financial resources and institutional support, they are obliged to drop out of the professional rat race. As a consequence, the rich get richer, and the poor get poorer. This has even been dubbed the *Matthew effect*, after the passage in the Gospel According to St. Matthew that says that "For unto every one that hath shall be given, and he shall have abundance: but from him that hath not shall be taken away even that which he hath" (quoted in Merton, 1968, p. 58). An interesting implication of the doctrine of cumulative advantage is that individuals who begin their careers with roughly equivalent capacities will eventually find themselves separated out into winners and losers by the luck of the draw. If not everyone can publish in the most prestigious journals, win the most remunerative grants, or receive appointments at the most select universities, then someone has to come out on the bottom. This possibility has even been styled the *Ecclesiastes hypothesis* (Turner & Chubin, 1976). This term was inspired by another passage in the Bible: "The race is not to the swift, nor the battle to the strong, neither bread to the wise, not yet riches to men of understanding, not yet favor to men of skill; but time and chance happeneth to them all" (quoted in Turner & Chubin, 1979, p. 437).

If the cumulative-advantage model is correct, then individual differences in output should correlate far higher for two consecutive age periods than for two nonconsecutive age periods. In fact, the larger the temporal separation between two age periods, the smaller should be the correlation between them. The result is a highly distinctive correlation matrix known as the *simplex* (Loehlin, 1992b): The largest correlations will be those next to the diagonal, and the off-diagonal correlations become progressively smaller the farther removed they are from the diagonal. In contrast, if the individual-differences model holds, then variation in productivity in every period of a career is a function of a single latent variable, namely, initial creative potential. The correlation matrix accordingly will not display a simplex structure, but rather the correlations will be of roughly equal magnitude throughout the correlation matrix. Confirmatory factor techniques can therefore be used to determine which alternative model best accounts for the observed interperiod correlations: the cumulative-advantage model or the information-processing model. This critical test has actually been carried out for different data sets, and the outcome uniformly supports the model advocated here (Simonton, 1997b). For example, a single-factor latent-variable model does an excellent job explaining the data that Dennis (1956b) collected on 56 scientists (yielding a comparative fit index of .994, where 1.00 indicates a perfect fit). Moreover, the factor loadings of each age period on the General

Creative Potential factor tend to be uniformly high. For instance, when the model was fit to the careers of 435 mathematicians (from S. Cole, 1979), the output in any given age period correlated between .74 and .88 with the general factor. All in all, the results flatly contradict the cumulative-advantage explanation.

I suspect that many readers may have gotten a déjà vu sensation in all this. The discussion here seems remarkably similar to my previous treatment of Galton's G (Simonton, 1991c), which concerned the causal foundation for the transhistorical stability of posthumous reputation. In that case, too, a single-factor model was pitted against an alternative, an autoregressive model in which each generation borrowed the opinions of the previous generation. Actually, autoregressive models also generate correlation matrices with a simplex structure, and hence the similarity is more than superficial. In fact, the two problems have an intimate theoretical and empirical connection. The single latent variable styled Galton's G supposedly exists because a luminary's historical reputation ultimately rests on his or her lifetime contributions. The other single factor, initial creative potential (or m), represents an individual's total capacity for generating ideational variations that can be converted into creative products. So not only must the latter factor underlie productivity in each period of a creator's career, but it must also underlie the person's ultimate achievement, especially given the strong quantity–quality association. To be sure, individuals may not live long enough to realize all of their creative potential, especially if they happened to get a late start. Even so, Galton's G must be considered a joint function of creative potential and career length. The longer the length of the career, the stronger the correspondence between m and G, between initial creative potential and ultimate posthumous eminence. This close linkage will prove to have tremendous utility in the next section.

Longitudinal Location of the Three Career Landmarks

Thus far I have focused on individual differences in creative potential and their consequences across the course of the career. Yet it is necessary to consider a second individual-difference variable, namely, variation in age at career onset. Some individuals may be "early bloomers," others "late bloomers." On both theoretical and empirical grounds the individual-differences model posits that variation on these two factors is largely uncorrelated (Simonton, 1996a); that is, a highly creative individual may bloom either early or late, and the same holds for a less creative individual. Hence, people who fall at the extremes on these two factors may be said to define a fourfold typology of career trajectories (see Figure 4.2). The *high-creative early bloomers* start young and begin producing at a fast rate, reaching their productive peak at a relatively young age, but still maintain a high level of output until late in life. The *low-creative early bloomers* have a very similar career trajectory, with the

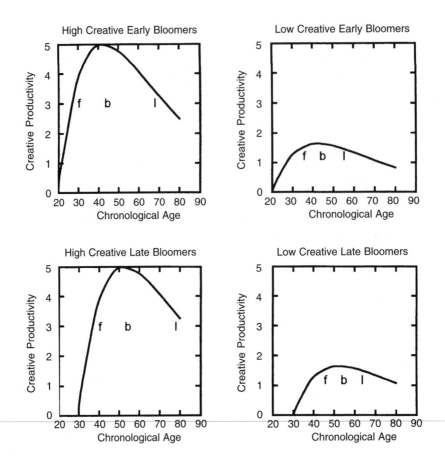

Figure 4.2. Hypothetical typology of career trajectories depending on whether the individual is high versus low in creative potential and an early versus late bloomer with respect to career onset. Corresponding to each type is a characteristic expectation regarding the most likely longitudinal placement of the three career landmarks, namely, first major contribution (f), best contribution (b), and last major contribution (l). From "Career Landmarks in Science: Individual Differences and Interdisciplinary Contrasts" by D. K. Simonton, 1991a, *Developmental Psychology, 27*, p. 121. Copyright 1991 by the American Psychological Association. Adapted with permission.

peak at the same longitudinal location but with the overall level of output consistently lower throughout the career. The *high-creative late bloomers* are older when they launch their careers, and peak correspondingly later, but maintain a high level of output throughout their career, the full realization of their potential often being cut short by death. Finally, the *low-creative late bloomers* display a similar pattern but with an appreciably lower output level throughout the career.

Furthermore, according to the equal-odds rule, the specific placement of the three career landmarks will vary across these four types of career trajectories. On the one hand, if creative potential is held constant, then all three career landmarks will be shifted earlier or later in direct proportion to whether the career onset is earlier or later. On the other hand, if age at career onset is held constant, then the higher the level of creative potential, the earlier the first major work will appear (because of the faster accumulation of output), and the later the last major work will appear (because of the higher level of output in the final years), whereas the best work will appear in the same place regardless of the level of creative potential (because the latter individual-difference variable affects only the height, not the shape, of the predicted curve). When these two orthogonal effects are combined, a rich variety of career outcomes emerges. Moreover, when these outcomes are combined with the strong positive association between creative potential and eminence, the following 10 predictions obtain (see Simonton, 1997b, for the formal derivations and additional predictions).

1. *Total lifetime productivity correlates negatively with the chronological age of the first contribution and positively with the chronological age of the last contribution.* Given the strong association between quality and quantity, this prediction holds for total high-impact contributions as well. However defined, this prediction has been repeatedly verified for both artistic and scientific forms of creative achievement (Blackburn, Behymer, & Hall, 1978; Lehman, 1946; Simonton, 1977b, 1991a, 1991b; Zhao & Jiang, 1986). It was also confirmed more specifically on a sample of 69 eminent American psychologists (Simonton, 1992b). In particular, the total number of cited publications correlated −.25 with the age at first cited work and .30 with the age at the last cited work. There is virtually no doubt that this statement is generally valid (Albert, 1975), even though there is no a priori reason why it has to be so (Simonton, 1997b). For instance, suppose that the first and last landmarks simply demarcate the onset and termination of a productive career (Raskin, 1936; Simonton, 1977b). If O is lifetime output, then it is given that $O = R(L - P)$, where R is the mean annual rate of output, L is the chronological age that output ended (longevity), and P is the chronological age that output began (precocity). Mathematically speaking, these three separate determinants of total productivity may assume a great variety of correlations without violating this identity, including associations that contradict Prediction 1. To offer a curious example, Rudolf Arnheim (1986), the eminent Gestalt psychologist, once proposed that artists with abbreviated life spans (and hence with shorter careers) may display the same general level of creative activity as do long-lived artists by

concentrating their output in a shorter period. Arnheim likened this hypothesized phenomenon to the tendency for small mammals to have faster heart rates and to breathe more rapidly than large mammals; the result is about the same number of heartbeats and breaths despite the big contrasts in life span. This assertion is equivalent to claiming that $R(L - P)$ equals some constant, in disagreement with Prediction 1. In any case, this proposition leads to Predictions 2 and 3.

2. *Individual eminence correlates negatively with the chronological age of the first contribution and positively with the chronological age of the last contribution.* This statement follows from the tight theoretical and empirical link between lifetime output and Galton's G. This prediction was first confirmed many decades ago on a sample of eminent scientists and literary figures (Raskin, 1936) and has been replicated many times since (e.g., Albert, 1975; Lehman, 1958; Simonton, 1977b, 1991b), including for a large sample of nearly 2,000 distinguished scientists (Simonton, 1991a). It has been amply confirmed for psychologists as well. For example, the posthumous reputation of American psychologists correlates $-.26$ with the age at first cited work and $.35$ with the age at the last cited work (Simonton, 1992b). This longitudinal pattern is not confined to posthumous fame. Individuals eminent enough in their own time to be elected APA president had their first hit at a younger than normal age and their last hit at an older than average age (Albert, 1975; Lyons, 1968; Simonton, 1992b).

3. *Maximum output rate correlates negatively with the chronological age of the first contribution and positively with the chronological age of the last contribution.* This claim follows immediately from the fact that creative potential is associated not only with total lifetime output but also with the height of the age curve. In fact, a career's maximum output actually provides a superior indicator of underlying creative potential, because it is not usually affected by life span (assuming that the individual dies sometime after the career peak). There exists some empirical support for this prediction (S. Cole & Cole, 1973; Simonton, 1991b), including studies conducted by both Dennis (1954b) and Lehman (1958), yet the prediction has not yet been tested for a sample of psychologists.

4. *Total lifetime productivity correlates zero with the chronological age at the maximum output rate and zero with the chronological age at the best contribution.* This is a more surprising prediction than the first, but it follows immediately from the fact that,

according to the model, only chronological age at carrier onset, not level of creative potential, determines the location of the career peak. This prediction has been amply confirmed (Christensen & Jacomb, 1962; Simonton, 1991b; Zuckerman, 1977), the first such confirmation being published by Lehman (1958) for a sample of chemists. The two predicted null relations have been demonstrated to hold in psychology as well (Horner et al., 1986; Simonton, 1992b). Hence, the great psychologists tend to attain their career optima at about the same chronological age as their less well-known colleagues.

The next two predictions follow from Prediction 4 for the same reason that Predictions 2 and 3 follow from Prediction 1 (i.e., because creative potential is assumed to have strong positive relations with lifetime output, individual eminence, and the maximum output rate at the career peak).

5. *Individual eminence correlates zero with the chronological age at the maximum output rate and zero with the chronological age at the best contribution.* This was first demonstrated for a sample of 120 scientists and 123 writers (Raskin, 1936) and later for a sample of 120 classical composers (Simonton, 1991b) and for another sample of nearly 2,000 scientists and inventors (Simonton, 1991b; also see Adams, 1946; Lehman, 1958; Zuckerman, 1977). Most important, the prediction holds for psychologists throughout the world (Simonton, 1992b; Zusne, 1976a). For example, among notable American psychologists, those who manage to earn election to the APA presidency produced their best work at the same chronological age as their less distinguished colleagues (Simonton, 1992b). Hence, even though greatness is associated with being somewhat precocious with respect to the first career landmark, the eminent and the much less so make their best contributions at the same age.

6. *Maximum output rate correlates zero with the chronological age at the maximum output rate and zero with the chronological age at the best contribution.* Empirical support for this proposition may be found in several investigations (Christensen & Jacomb, 1992; Horner et al., 1986; Lehman, 1958; Simonton, 1991b; Zuckerman, 1977), albeit only one researcher (Simonton, 1991b) addressed the issue directly and did so using a sample of 120 classical composers. Nonetheless, given the strong confirmation of Prediction 5, it is highly likely that direct tests should confirm this prediction for psychologists.

The following two predictions are derived from the fact that the output trajectories are a function of career age rather than chronological age (Simonton, 1997b).

7. *Chronological age at the maximum output rate correlates positively both with the chronological age at the first contribution and with the chronological age at the last contribution.*
8. *Chronological age of the best contribution correlates positively both with the chronological age at the first contribution and with the chronological age at the last contribution.*

At first glance, one might think that these two predictions are almost tautological, given that the career peak that contains both the maximum output rate and the best contribution must fall in the interval bounded by the first and last contributions. Given the career lengths that are typically seen, these two propositions are by no means necessary. Consider the following scenario. Suppose that the career peak is invariably placed at approximately the same chronological age, such as age 40. This placement may result from several exogenous factors, such as physiological, intellectual, or environmental influences. For instance, scores on creativity tests exhibit a distinct tendency to maximize around chronological age 40 (Simonton, 1990a). However, if the first contribution may appear any time prior to age 40, and the last contribution anytime after age 40, then both predictions would be disconfirmed, because the required positive covariances would be reduced to zero. The same null outcome would take place were the career peak randomly distributed around age 40. The only way that Predictions 7 and 8 can receive empirical confirmation is when the career peak is determined endogenously by career age rather than exogenously by chronological age. It is fortunate that both predictions have been empirically confirmed (Simonton, 1991a, 1991b, 1992b). In addition, Prediction 8 is theoretically compatible with the harmonic-mean model that Zusne (1976a) proposed and tested on a sample of 213 eminent contributors from psychology's history. In this model a psychologist's single most significant work will appear at an age that is the harmonic mean of the age at the first and the last publications (i.e., the age at best work is given by $2(P^{-1} + L^{-1})^{-1}$ where P is the chronological age at first work and L is the chronological age at last work, as in Prediction 1). The correlation between predicted and observed age at best work is .52, a fairly impressive figure. Yet if the equal-odds rule holds, then the harmonic mean of the first and last publications should closely approximate the harmonic mean of the first and last influential contributions, which in turn should provide an excellent estimate of the psychologist's career age, the sole determinant of the career peak according to the cognitive model.

I should point out, however, that the positive correlations specified in Predictions 7 and 8 should increase in magnitude once statistical control is introduced for individual differences in creative potential (using either lifetime productivity or the maximum output rate as indicators). The locations of the first and last career landmarks are determined by both initial creative potential and career age, whereas the location of the middle career landmark is determined solely by career age. Consequently, once control is introduced for creative potential, using total output or the maximum output rate, the remaining longitudinal variation in the location of the three landmarks can be assigned to career age only. In addition, if lifetime contributions are used as a gauge of underlying creative potential, then life span should be introduced as a control variable as well, to remove that source of contamination.

9. *The first-order partial correlation between the ages of first and last contributions is negative after partialing out the chronological age at the best contribution or the chronological age at the maximum output rate.*

This proposition is in many respects the most distinctive of all. Because the age at which the peak appears is a function of career age only, controlling for individual differences on this variable is tantamount to equalizing everybody with respect to career age. According to the theoretical model, this means that the sole source of variance that remains is creative potential. Stated differently, by partialing out either chronological age at best contribution or chronological age at the maximum output rate, the career trajectories become centered on the career peaks, and the only variance that remains concerns individual differences in the height of the curve, which is totally a function of creative potential. The greater the creative potential, the higher the output at the beginning of the curve, and the higher the output at the end of the curve, meaning that the first contribution comes earlier and the last contribution later. In contrast, the lower the initial creative potential, the lower the output at the beginning and at the end, putting the first contribution later and the last contribution earlier. The net result is a negative partial correlation that cannot be derived from any theory that does not simultaneously incorporate both the endogenous placement of the career peak (according to career age) and the existence of substantial individual differences in the generation of ideas (creative potential). This distinctive prediction was confirmed on a sample of nearly 2,000 scientists and inventors (Simonton, 1991a) and another sample of 120 classical composers (Simonton, 1991b). In the former case, for instance, the partial correlation between the age at first contribution and age at last contribution, controlling for the age at best contribution, is −.22.

10. *The time interval between the chronological age at career onset and the chronological age at first contribution is negatively correlated with total lifetime productivity and the maximum output rate.*

With all other factors held constant, scientists who are more prolific soon after launching their careers will be expected, according to the equal-odds rule, to obtain their first career landmark much sooner. The degree of productivity in these beginning years reflects the initial amount of creative potential, which will later manifest itself in the maximum output level attained as well as the total lifetime output achieved. Although plenty of studies indirectly support this prediction (e.g., Christensen & Jacomb, 1992), only I tested it directly, using a sample of classical composers rather than scientists (Simonton, 1991b). However, I did perform a secondary data analysis on data that had been collected on 69 eminent American psychologists (Simonton, 1992b) and found confirmatory results. The total number of cited publications correlated –.31 with the difference between the age at first publication and the age at first cited publication. One nice feature about this proposition is that it actually provides the basis for genuine prediction rather than postdiction; that is, the other predictions apply to the situation in which the careers are already complete, so that variables such as total lifetime output or at least the maximum output rate are empirically known. The last prediction reverses things, forecasting the expected maximum output rate and total lifetime productivity from the speed with which an individual first begins to leave a large and personal imprint on the field. In fact, because posthumous distinction is ultimately predicated on total output, this theoretical expectation can even be used to predict long-term impact on the discipline. Returning to the data on 69 American psychologists, posthumous reputation correlated –.26 with the time lapse between first and first-cited publications.

Taken together, Predictions 1–10 provide a baseline for evaluating whether a particular psychologist exhibits the career trajectory typical of psychology's recognized greats. Those who are most likely to make a mark on the discipline's history will begin to have an impact early, will still continue having an impact until late in their careers, and will attain an impressively high level of output throughout their careers, with an especially impressive maximum output rate. At the same time, the age at the career peak—whether gauged by the best work or the maximum output rate—is not diagnostic of a psychologist's greatness. However, the longitudinal location of the career peak is symptomatic of another crucial aspect of what it takes to make it in psychology's history: the domain of achievement. It must be stressed that these predictions uniformly posit that all of the individuals in the sample are making contributions to the same domain of creative achievement. In other words, they should all contain the qualifying phrase "holding domain constant." Hence, when examining a sample of contributors who are heterogeneous with respect to domain, then interdisciplinary contrasts in the career trajectories must be taken into account. The career peak has special utility in this regard. According to the cognitive model, the longitudinal placement of a contributor's best work appears much earlier or later than expected if the contribution comes from a discipline with either rapid or slow information-processing rates. In the latter category, for instance, are the great philosophers of psychology's past.

Even though the cognitive model provides a finely differentiated treatment of career trajectories, a precaution is in order: The predictions only approximate the complexities of reality. The approximations are evident in the correlation coefficients commonly seen in empirical tests of the model. Most correlations range in the .20s and .30s and only rarely get as high as the .40s and .50s. Indeed, it could not really be otherwise, given how few factors are explicitly incorporated into the model. Real career trajectories are influenced by a great many more factors than just domain of achievement, creative potential, and age at career onset. These additional influences deflect the course of a psychologist's career away from theoretical expectation. Some of these extraneous factors are nomothetic in nature and therefore are discussed in later chapters. However, many of the factors are idiosyncratic to a particular historical figure.

An obvious illustration is the career of John B. Watson. After earning his PhD at age 25, his career started so auspiciously that he became himself APA president at age 37. However, by age 42 his personal and professional lives were changed drastically and irreversibly by a highly publicized sex scandal: an adulterous affair with one of his students, Rosalie Rayner, who collaborated with him on the classic "Little Albert" experiment. Watson was suddenly obliged to replace the career of a university professor with a career in the advertising business. Although the theory would have predicted continued prolific output from Watson for the remainder of his very long life, the changed circumstances were to dictate otherwise. His career as a great psychologist was basically over by age 50, and much of what did appear in his late 40s must be considered more popular than professional psychology. Only if Watson's personal life had been more discreet would his career trajectory have better fit the predictions of the cognitive model. Yet it certainly is highly unlikely that one would want to include sexual discretion in even the most comprehensive theory of career trajectories.

5

THE CREATIVE PRODUCT
IN PSYCHOLOGY

The reader now knows a tremendous amount about what it takes to leave a durable impression on psychology. Individuals who are most likely to win a spot in the annals of psychology are those who begin having an impact early in their careers, produce at exceptional rates throughout their careers, and end their careers relatively late. Although their hit rates are not higher than those of their more obscure colleagues, their total influence on the field is quite substantial, in both their own and later times. In short, great psychologists have the career profiles of the typical scientific genius (Albert, 1975; Simonton, 1988d). Yet this answer is not completely satisfactory. After all, I have not really explained how it comes about that a particular psychologist's output has the influence it does. This explanation is important from the standpoint of both biography and history. From the biographical perspective, if any great psychologist generates lots of failures as well as successes—as the equal-odds rule maintains—then why are some publications in the first category and others in the second? From a historical perspective, how do contemporaries and posterity decide to praise certain privileged contributions while innumerable attempts end up in the dustbin of history?

The significance of this question is evident in the fact that histories of psychology are replete with speculations about the fundamental basis for a psychologist's long-term impact (Simonton, 1995a). It is not too surprising that most often the suggestions concentrate on the scientific value of the contributions; that is, psychologists whose ideas or works satisfy certain requirements that might enhance the discipline's advancement as a bona fide science have the greater influence (Gillispie, 1960). One such criterion is *simplicity*, a principle evoked in the following quotation: "Much of the appeal of even Guthrie's system rests upon its simplicity and its consistency over the years. It is easy to understand, especially when compared with more complex and mathematically based learning theories, such as Hull's" (Schultz & Schultz, 1992, p. 341). Another scientific criterion supposedly is *logical coherence*, as implied by this remark:

> Freud's theories, without doubt, have had greater impact on general psychology than any other single system. This was due partly to the very nature of his subject matter but, more importantly, to the creative manner in which the system was drawn together into a logical whole. (Capretta, 1967, pp. 168–169)

One other scientific asset often noted is *explanatory power*, especially with respect to a diversity of otherwise inexplicable phenomena. Thus, "one of the reasons the Gestalt movement gathered momentum so rapidly was that its major hypothesis proved to be immediately applicable to a great number and variety of perceptual phenomena with which psychologists were already familiar" (Lowry, 1982, p. 184). This explanatory breadth contrasted immensely with structuralism, which "was such a tightly knit and prefocused system that many historians regard this as the primary reason for its eventual demise" (Hillner, 1984, p. 17).

Nevertheless, textbook authors often mention the operation of criteria that are less obviously connected to the scientific worth of a psychologist's work. One such extrascientific standard is practical utility, whether real or apparent. "Freud's system has great practical application value and popular appeal because it can resolve practically every psychological phenomenon of interest and concern to the public at large," wrote one historian (Hillner, 1984, p. 201); "phrenology was also popular because, unlike mental philosophy, it appeared to offer practical information" wrote another (Hergenhahn, 1992, p. 221). Another presumably extraneous criterion is the contributor's capacity to reach an audience much more broad than fellow scientists and philosophers. As one textbook author noted, "Descartes' extraordinary influence in subsequent thought was probably due to the fact that he was one of the first major philosophers since Boethius (c. 500) to write for intelligent amateurs and gentlemen" (Capretta, 1967, p. 18, footnote 7). Besides writing in the vernacular (French), Descartes reached a wider public by adopting an attractive, nonacademic writing style. Subsequent greats in psychology's history may have followed suit (Colotla, 1980). The "overwhelming stature and influence" of William James have been ascribed to the fact that he "wrote with a brilliance and clarity rare in science, then as well as now. There [are] magnetism, spontaneity, and charm throughout his books" (Schultz & Schultz, 1987, p. 136). Indeed, being a good stylist can even help a psychologist enhance his or her standing with fellow professionals. For example, E. B. Titchener's "impact on psychology was enhanced by a writing style that was both lucid and stimulating" (Kendler, 1987, p. 53), whereas "Wundt's works are little read today [because] his writing style in German produces immediate discouragement" (Hothersall, 1990, p. 106). A similar fate awaited Kurt Koffka, whose 1935 *Principles of Gestalt Psychology* "was a difficult book to read and so did not become the definitive treatment of Gestalt psychology he had intended it to be" (Schultz & Schultz, 1992, p. 383). Being a bad read evidently is death to a psychologist's aspirations to greatness.

Complicating matters all the more is the fact that sometimes individuals occupy a large place in psychology's history despite their conspicuous failure to satisfy certain presumably essential criteria. For instance, good science is supposed to be empirically grounded, or at least capable of inspiring sound empirical research. Yet "in spite of the lack of an empirical foundation to his system, Herbart influenced subsequent psychologists" (Kendler, 1987, p. 13). Likewise, although Gordon Allport's

> theory has been more influential in psychology than the work of the early psychoanalysts, it has not inspired a great deal of research because of the difficulty in translating his concepts into specific propositions that can be tested under laboratory conditions. (Schultz & Schultz, 1992, p. 488)

Or, apart from scientific criteria, one would at least hope that it requires deep thought to become a great psychologist. However, if what one historian said is true, that requirement is not always enforced: "Though Adler worked largely on a common-sense level, and was far from an acute or profound thinker, some of his concepts have penetrated psychological thinking" (Hearnshaw, 1987, pp. 165–166).

Can this issue be addressed by some manner other than the speculation of historians? Can scientific research offer any secure insights into this difficult but important question? To find out, I deal with two related issues. First, what does it take to have a successful program of scientific research? Second, what is necessary for a particular product of a research program to have exceptional impact on the field?

GENERAL RESEARCH PROGRAMS

Although quantity (behavioral output) is strongly correlated with quality (disciplinary impact), the association is not so pronounced as to deny the existence of considerable scatter around the regression line. It is the presence of these residual errors that permits the appearance of the Perfectionists and the Mass Producers in addition to the more typical Silent and Prolific researchers. Therefore, it seems useful to ask whether certain qualities of a scientist's collective body of work increase or decrease its chances of having a major influence. But how does one assess the attributes of a program of scientific research?

One underutilized solution is to take advantage of titles. With the exception of some book reviews and commentaries, a title always graces the first page of every publication, whether it be book, book chapter, journal article, or research note. Titles are listed in everyone's curricula vitae and various bibliographic sources. More critical, according to the norms of scientific publication, is that the titles are supposed to be highly descriptive of a publication's contents (e.g., *Publication Manual of the American Psychological Association*; American Psychological Association [APA], 1994). In a sense, titles are designed to be abstracts of the abstracts found in professional journal articles. Hence, content analytical procedures can be applied to these encapsulations to discern the nature of a scientist's research program (Whittaker, 1989). I attempted this approach in an investigation of 69 eminent psychologists (Simonton, 1992b), a study already mentioned several times earlier.

Because this study (Simonton, 1992b) was designed to commemorate the 100th anniversary of the founding of the APA, it concentrated on a sample of American psychologists, including the founder and first APA president, G. S. Hall. The subjects were born between 1842 (G. T. Ladd) and 1912 (C. I. Hovland) and were publishing between 1879 and 1967. Although 10% of the subjects were born abroad, all spent most of their professional careers in the United States (e.g., E. B. Titchener). To ensure that I had adequate information on which to base a content analysis, all subjects had to claim at least 20 English-language titles spread over at least 20 years. The titles were taken from the bibliographic entries in R. I. Watson's (1974) *Eminent Contributors to Psychology*, which also provided an essential criterion for inclusion in the sample. All titles were placed in machine-readable form, and words that serve purely grammatical functions, such as prepositions, conjunctions, and articles, were deleted. These text files were then content analyzed with a program called TEXTPACK PC (Mohler & Zuell, 1990). The utility and precision of this program had been previously demonstrated in a content analysis of the 154 sonnets of William Shakespeare (Simonton, 1989b, 1990c). Like those earlier analyses, two types of measures were defined:

1. Both *primary* and *secondary* process imagery were calculated using the Regressive Imagery Dictionary of Colin Martindale (1975, 1990). This lexicon classifies words into categories for primary content (e.g., drives, sensation, defensive symbolization, and regressive cognition) and for secondary content (e.g.,

abstraction, instrumental behavior, restraint, and order). Although obviously inspired by psychoanalytic theory, the dictionary purports to capture a universal contrast between *primordial* and *conceptual* information processing (cf. S. Epstein, 1994; Suler, 1980). In any case, I used the Regressive Imagery Dictionary to compute total scores of the number of tag words in each of the two summary categories. I then divided these two scores by the total number of words in the title samples, to correct for the variable number of titles available for each of the 69 psychologists. Given the antithetical nature of primary and secondary thought, it should not surprise readers that these two transformed counts correlated −.43.

2. TEXTPACK automatically calculated, for a given unit of text, a measure known as the *type–token ratio* (TTR). The TTR consists of the ratio of types (distinct words) to tokens (total words). A high ratio means that a text is riddled with lots of different words, whereas a low ratio means that a text has many repeated words. This classic measure is normally used to assess linguistic complexity, but it acquires rather different meaning when applied to the collection of representative titles. In the latter case a high ratio indicates that a psychologist's life work addresses a considerable range of research topics, whereas a low ratio implies that the psychologist has concentrated his or her research program on a restricted number of scientific questions. I also calculated a closely related measure, namely, an index of the proportion of unique words, which can be adopted as an indicator of how often a psychologist explores distinct topics in a presumably one-shot fashion (i.e., *hapax legomena* in the content analytical literature). This measure correlated .55 with the TTR, suggesting that these two indices gauge very similar qualities of research programs. In titles, different keywords tend to be unique keywords.

To assess the differential impact of these 69 American psychologists I used the *Social Sciences Citation Index Five-Year Cumulation 1981–1985* (1987). From this source I obtained log-transformed counts of the number of total citations, the number of total cited publications, and the number of citations of the most-cited work (the middle career landmark). These three indicators correlated with two of the content analytical measures. First, the proportion of title words devoted to primary-process imagery correlated negatively with the number of citations, the number of cited publications, and the citations received by the psychologist's most cited work (*r*s = −.37, −.34, and −.41, respectively). Perhaps these negative correlations hint at why Sigmund Freud's theory has often had a rough time permeating American academic psychology, given how many of his titles are rich with primary-process tags such as *sex, anal, pleasure, eroticism, hypnotism, hysteria, dreams,* and *unconscious.* One must also recall how Clark L. Hull was obliged to forfeit his research interests in hypnosis after becoming a Yale professor. Second, the TTR also correlates negatively with the total number of citations, the total number of cited publications, and the total number of citations of the most frequently cited work ($rs = -.38, -.31,$ and $-.39,$ respectively). This content-analytical measure even correlates negatively with long-term eminence, as assessed by posthumous reputation ($r = -.30,$ after partialing out year of birth). Hence, the greatest psychologists among the 69 are those who have the same title descriptors cropping up again and again throughout their publication lists. These scientists are not dilettantes who fritter around from topic to topic.

This is a very provocative finding, for it suggests that diversity of subject matter is not highly valued as a research strategy. Rather, the results appear to be most consistent with "a commonly accepted view of the productive scientist [as] someone who continually chips away at a specific subject-matter area, becomes wedded to it, and is identified as a specialist in it by other scientists" (Garvey & Tomita, 1972, p. 379). Professional success may require a high degree of continuity in a psychologist's research program (Crane, 1965). Moreover, there is evidence that the benefits of a highly focused research program are not confined to these 69 deceased psychologists. Another investigation looked at 99 contemporary physicists, chemists, and biologists at top-rated research universities, almost one third of whom had been elected to the National Academy of Sciences (Feist, 1997). Again using TEXTPACK, the TTR was calculated using the titles contained in their complete bibliographies (taken from their curricula vitae). The TTR was negatively related to the quantity of research, the total number of citations received, membership in the National Academy of Sciences, and an indicator of global eminence (consisting of peer ratings of creativity and historical significance, professional visibility, and the prestige of the highest honor received). Although the TTR did not have an independent effect on global eminence once productivity was statistically controlled, the same consequence held for the 69 psychologists as well. This suggests that the depth of a research program affects a scientist's reputation largely through its positive influence on his or her total productivity.

Before readers jump to the conclusion that they must devote the rest of their careers to a single topic, I must warn that other evidence exists that seems to run counter to this nomothetic principle. In one investigation of 2,030 scientists from nine disciplines, those who had changed the subject-matter area of their articles actually displayed a slight increase in productivity as a consequence (Garvey & Tomita, 1972). In addition, authors of high-impact scientific contributions are more prone to display simultaneous involvement in several different research areas (Hargens, 1978; Root-Bernstein, Bernstein, & Garnier, 1993; R. J. Simon, 1974; M. S. Taylor, Locke,

Lee, & Gist, 1984). However, these findings may not necessarily conflict with the inferences drawn from the content analyses of titles. For one thing, the samples and measures are not completely comparable. More important, close attention to the discrepancies reveals that all of these results may be subsumed under a single principle—the concept of a *network of enterprises*. This idea was first proposed by Howard Gruber (1974) in the single-case analysis reported in *Darwin on Man: A Psychological Study of Scientific Creativity* (also see Gruber, 1989). The basic idea is that the great scientists neither focus on a single narrow topic nor flip randomly around from topic to topic without rhyme or reason. On the contrary, the various subjects that constitute a highly successful research program are interconnected with each other, often in subtle or inexplicit ways. Indeed, often it is not until much later that the scientist comes to realize that two research interests have more mutual relevance than originally thought. The successful resolution of one puzzle may facilitate the solution to another, seemingly unrelated problem. The great mathematician Henri Poincaré (1921) provided an illustration from his own career:

> I turned my attention to the study of some arithmetical questions apparently without much success and without a suspicion of any connection with my preceding researches. Disgusted with my failure, I went to spend a few days at the seaside, and thought of something else. One morning, walking on the bluff, the idea came to me that the arithmetic transformations of indeterminate ternary quadratic forms were identical with those of non-Euclidean geometry. (p. 388)

Two previously disconnected research interests had become suddenly united, much as Descartes unified algebra and geometry into analytic geometry.

Hence, the low TTR, the frequent subject-matter changes, and the simultaneous involvement in several research areas may all reflect the same underlining phenomenon: the operation of a network of enterprises. Such a network raises the likelihood that a scientist's research program will continue to be fruitful rather than becoming sterile. At the same time, the implicit linkages among the separate projects help ensure that discoveries will build on each other, occasionally producing significant ideational syntheses. As Walter Cannon (1945), the great physiologist, once noted,

> it seems probable that co-ordinate progress in research, process characterized by a natural development from one group of ideas to another, instead of a flitting from interest to interest in a quite inconsequential manner, is conducive to persistent effectiveness in productive scholarship. In this type of research, as studies advance and new facts are discovered, fruitful ideas accumulate and earlier ideas take on new meanings. As a result, fresh opportunities for exploration are frequently disclosed. (p. 218)

When one contemplates the careers of the truly great psychologists, the truth of Cannon's remark becomes most apparent. Sigmund Freud, Ivan Pavlov, Jean Piaget, and B. F. Skinner touched on a tremendous diversity of topics and issues throughout the course of their long careers. Yet interweaving throughout each publication was a certain set of themes, principles, or guiding metaphors. Skinner's collected publications, for instance, encompass articles and books on how to teach pigeons to exhibit "self-awareness" and "lying" behavior; the use of behavior modification to treat neurotic behavior; language acquisition and performance; the use of teaching machines in education; the design of effective cultures; the operation of poetic creativity; the nature of human free will; analyses of major figures in English literature; and even a novel, *Walden Two* (see, e.g., Skinner, 1961). Even so, permeating almost every publication is Skinner's fascination, even preoccupation, with how behavior is contingent on external reinforcement. There thus appears considerable unity in the diversity, depth combined with breadth.

In later chapters I return to the subject of what factors contribute to a highly successful research program. However, right now another issue is more urgent.

SPECIFIC SCIENTIFIC PUBLICATIONS

"The chances are that, in the course of his lifetime, the major poet will write more bad poems than the minor," observed paradoxically the English poet W. H. Auden (quoted in Bennet, 1980, p. 15). This unevenness of output even holds for a great poet like William Shakespeare (Simonton, Taylor, & Cassandro, 1998). Although some of his 154 sonnets "bear the unmistakable stamp of his genius," noted one critic (Evans, 1974, p. 1747), many others "are no better than many a contemporary could have written." To be specific, although a select few appear in almost every anthology of English poetry, a great many more are never so honored. The within-individual variation in quality of output holds for scientists, including psychologists. According to the equal-odds rule, psychologists who generate more high-impact publications should also generate more no-impact publications. For instance, an investigation into the careers of 10 illustrious psychologists—all recipients of APA's Distinguished Scientific Contribution Award—revealed that 44% of their publications received no citations whatsoever during a 5-year time interval (Simonton, 1985b). Another study of 69 eminent American psychologists divulged that the single most influential work tends to account for over one quarter of the total citations received by his or her lifetime output (Simonton, 1992b). This means that much of the differential fame attained by psychologists can be ascribed to the impact of their single best contribution. Cross-sectional variation with respect to that career landmark is immense. For the 69 psychologists, the most-cited best work received 343 times as many citations as the least-cited best work.

What can possibly account for this impressive variation in the impact of single publications? One factor has already been mentioned: namely, the fact that books tend to be more influential than journal articles (Heyduk & Fenigstein, 1984; Simonton, 1992b). However, this cannot provide a complete explanation, for even journal articles display substantial variation in citations (Redner, 1998). Another possible answer is that frequently cited articles are published in high-impact journals, that is, the journals with high citation rates per article published. These journals are usually the most prestigious refereed journals in the discipline. In psychology, such journals include *Psychological Review*, *Psychological Bulletin*, *Journal of Personality and Social Psychology*, and *Developmental Psychology* (Buffardi & Nichols, 1981; M. J. White & White, 1977). Yet such an explanation is not very satisfactory. In the first place, the variation in impact is huge even for articles published in the same journal. The variation is so large in fact, that the best articles published in second- or third-tier journals may prove more influential than the worst articles published in the top journals—in other words, the variance in article quality overlaps. Even worse, this answer begs the question. The better journals presumably have high impact because of their higher selectivity, as maintained by the editor, associate editors, editorial board, and ad hoc reviewers. Therefore, the question remains regarding the standards that must be satisfied to produce a high-impact piece of psychological science in the first place.

This question can be answered two major ways. First, one determines the criteria that psychologists claim they use to judge the merits of scientific research. Second, one can scrutinize the criteria that psychologists actually apply in such evaluations.

The Ideal: What Psychologists Say

Few scientists in modern times have not had this experience: A manuscript arrives in the mail that has been submitted for publication in a professional journal. The editor's cover letter requests that the submission's suitability for publication be evaluated according to the standards appropriate to scientific research. Often included in the package is a rating form where these criteria are explicitly stated. These criteria might include such factors as the quality of the presentation, the psychological value, social importance, theoretical significance of the results, and the competence of the methodology (Wolff, 1973). The referee—whether a member of the editorial board or an ad hoc reviewer—then applies these criteria to the best of his or her knowledge and ability. The end result is a recommendation to either accept or reject, or some editorial action between, such as the dreaded "revise and resubmit." It seems reasonable to infer, therefore, that this editorial process reveals what it takes to produce a high-impact publication.

It is fitting that research suggests that some degree of consensus exists on the most appropriate criteria (S. D. Gottfredson, 1978). Typical are the results of a survey of 66 editors of major journals in pure and applied clinical psychology, such as the *Journal of Abnormal Psychology*, *Journal of Clinical Psychology*, and the *Journal of Consulting and Clinical Psychology* (Wolff, 1970). They were asked to rank in order of importance 15 potential criteria for evaluating whether submitted manuscripts should be accepted or rejected. Top in the consolidated ratings were such standards as contribution to knowledge, research design, objectivity in reporting results, statistical analyses, writing style and readability, theoretical model, topic selection, and literature review. Toward the bottom in importance where such criteria as manuscript length, author's status and reputation, punctuation, and institutional affiliation. The coefficient of concordance was used to gauge overall interjudge consensus. It was .59, indicating a modest amount of agreement, despite the intrusion of some individual differences among the editors in their rating standards. It is significant that the rankings of the criteria were strongly correlated with those found to govern journals in counseling and guidance psychology. The rank order correlation was .91 (Wolff, 1970).

Other researchers have obtained comparable results by different means. For example, one inquiry, led by Robert J. Sternberg, first had 20 psychologists identify attributes of high-impact articles and then had 252 members of the American Psychological Society rate the resulting 45 hypothesized characteristics on 6-point scale of importance (Sternberg & Gordeeva, 1996). A principal-components analysis (followed by a varimax rotation) yielded six factors: Quality of Presentation, Theoretical Significance, Practical Significance, Substantive Interest, Methodological Interest, and Value for Future Research. Hence, it appears possible to compile a set of clear-cut do's and don'ts that detail what it takes for an article to leave an imprint on the field (see S. D. Gottfredson, 1978). Because the community of psychologists, including editors and reviewers, all agree on the criteria for success, publishing high-quality work in the discipline's most prestigious journals should be a fairly straightforward matter: Just follow these scientific norms, and any psychologist should soon be on the path to greatness.

Yet something must be amiss! Readers have seen again and again that quality of output is a function of total quantity. Whether one is looking at individual differences or longitudinal changes, the equal-odds rule reigns supreme. Yet surely psychologists must be able to internalize the rules of the game so as to increase their odds. Over the course of their careers, the hit rate should grow, and even the depressing rejections from journal editors should decrease in frequency. But this does not happen. Not only is the ratio of successes to total attempts fairly constant across the life span, but the better-established psychologists may escape painful rejections only by switching from journal articles to book chapters as a main vehicle for communicating their ideas (Rodman & Mancini, 1981). What's going on here?

The Real: What Psychologists Do

Juxtaposed against this idealized portrait of the publication process in psychological science should be the following three complications.

1. If editors and reviewers exhibit such a strong consensus on the properties of a high-impact article, then that agreement should take the form of impressive interjudge reliabilities in separate assessments of manuscripts submitted for publication. Many studies show that this is far from the case. For instance, a former associate editor of the *Journal of Personality and Social Psychology* calculated the reliability coefficients for referee evaluations of submitted manuscripts. For the evaluative criteria used for the editorial decisions, these reliabilities were: probable reader interest in problem, .07; importance of present contribution, .28; attention to relevant literature, .37; design and analysis, .19; style and organization, .25; succinctness, .31; and recommendation to accept or reject, .26 (Scott, 1974; cf. Marsh & Ball, 1989; McReynolds, 1971; Scarr & Weber, 1978). Needless to say, if a submitted manuscript reported that its measures had reliabilities this low, it (probably) would be rejected for publication on methodological grounds! So poor is this consensus that most published articles in psychology journals would suffer rejection if resubmitted for publication, as has been empirically demonstrated (Peters & Ceci, 1982). Neither is psychology the only science to have such low levels of agreement (Cicchetti, 1991). Indeed, the evaluation process that underlies all peer-reviewed journals has been generally shown to be "a little better than a dice roll" (Lindsey, 1988, p. 75). Furthermore, the same minimal concordance confronts peer review when it is applied to research proposals submitted to major funding agencies (S. Cole, 1983). Indeed, the main predictor of whether a project gets funded is the total number of grant proposals submitted, as would be expected from the operation of the equal-odds rule alone (S. Cole, Cole, & Simon, 1981).

2. The judgmental criteria by which manuscripts are actually evaluated do not always operate as implicitly claimed by the evaluators. In the first place, often the assessment of a manuscript's quality is influenced by such extraneous factors as the prestige of the institutions with which the authors are affiliated, the existence of a special relationship between the authors and the editor or reviewers, the authors' gender, the professional status of the referees, and even the length of

the submitted manuscript and the number of references it contains (Crane, 1967; Petty, Fleming, & Fabrigar, 1999; J. A. Stewart, 1983). It is irrelevant that the unfortunate effects of most of these contaminating factors can be ameliorated by the implementation of blind review process (Bowen, Perloff, & Jacoby, 1972). The fact remains that those factors can intervene elsewhere as well, such as the decision to cite someone's work once it is published (see, e.g., Ferber, 1986; Greenwald & Schuh, 1994). Second, even when a criterion is used, it is often used in the wrong way. For instance, the quality of an investigation must be judged by both the importance of its research topic and the methodological rigor by which the topic is investigated. Yet the evidence indicates that methodological flaws are more likely to be overlooked if the topic is considered a highly significant one (Wilson, DePaulo, Mook, & Klaaren, 1993). That bias can even lead to the recommendation that methodologically weak papers be accepted for publication.

3. Given the low reliability of reviewer assessments, plus the introduction of various contaminating factors, it would seem rather difficult for the peer evaluations to have much connection with a publication's actual impact on the discipline and, in fact, such ratings tend to have poor predictive validity (S. Cole, 1983; S. D. Gottfredson, 1978). At most, only about 10% of the variance is shared. For example, a study of research published in psychology journals found a correlation of .18 between rated quality and a log-transformed measure of citation counts (Shadish, 1989). Even worse, the publication attributes that predicted subjective quality evaluations were seldom the same as those that predicted objective citation measures (see e.g., Lindsey, 1978). Moreover, it was much easier to predict the quality ratings than the citation counts. On the one hand, about half of the variance in the subjective quality assessment could be predicted through a combination of predictors (although these predictors were themselves subjective and therefore shared method variance with the criterion). On the other hand, only 10% of the variance in the objective citation counts could be similarly predicted. By the way, the same low predictive power of peer evaluations applies to grant proposals as well; that is, the priority scores given research proposals fail to predict the later impact of either funded or unfunded projects (S. Cole, 1983). Despite the supposedly objective nature of science, the ultimate influence of a scientific publication is not more readily predicted than that

of a literary, artistic, or musical composition (see, e.g., Martindale et al., 1988; Simonton, 1980b, 1980c).

With the advantage of hindsight, the reasons for these discouraging results may seem obvious. First, many of the criteria require highly subjective judgments about which there must be a diversity of opinions. For instance, who can objectively judge whether a journal's readers will find a particular problem interesting? Second, some of the criteria—such as making assessments about whether a study has important implications for future research—require that the evaluator become a prophet. Third, the number of relevant criteria is very large, running into the dozens (Gottfredson, 1978; Shadish, 1989; Sternberg & Gordeeva, 1996). Although these criteria might be reduced to a subset of more inclusive judgmental factors, considerable variance is thereby left unaccounted for in the separate criteria. For example, when 45 distinct criteria are collapsed into six principal components, more than half of the variance in the items remains unexplained by the six factors (Sternberg & Gordeeva, 1996). Hence, evaluators are left with a bewildering array of standards for judging the merits of any potential contribution. This multidimensionality also implies that the attributes of a publication operate in a statistical rather than deterministic fashion to influence its ultimate success. The correlation of any one characteristic with a work's impact must necessarily be reduced as the number of participating factors increases. Finally, it is very likely that the attributes that contribute to the impact of any product operate in a complex configurational manner (Simonton, 1999b); that is, interaction effects and curvilinear functions may dominate the determination (see, e.g., Simonton, 1980c, 1990c). What might be the best method to adopt for one substantive problem may be the worst for another; what might be an ideal way to organize one discussion might be horribly ineffective for another; 20 manuscript pages might be just right for treating one topic, but too long for another and too short for a third; and so forth. To assess a manuscript's scientific worth may thus require a subtle, probabilistic manipulation of multiple dimensions interlinked in complex relationships.

None of the foregoing would be especially problematic if the human cognitive apparatus were supremely sophisticated in its information-processing capacities. Yet the human mind is not by any means an ideal processor of information (see, e.g., Bruner, Goodnow, & Austin, 1956; Faust, 1984; Fiske & Taylor, 1991; Kahneman, Slovic, & Tversky, 1982; Meehl, 1954; G. A. Miller, 1956). Instead, the human intellect is subject to many varieties of inaccuracies; constraints; and biases in perception, memory, thinking, and problem solving. Of special interest are the demonstrated human incapacities in the reliable inference of probabilistic, multidimensional, and configurational relationships among phenomena. It is interesting that many of the researchers who have made notable contributions to this convincing literature are themselves noteworthy psychologists, including Paul Meehl, Jerome

Bruner, George A. Miller, Amos Tversky, Daniel Kahneman, and Shelley Taylor, all of whom have received APA's Distinguished Scientific Contribution Award. I am not referring here to a research tradition outside the mainstream of psychological inquiry.

It also must be emphasized that these constraints, biases, and inaccuracies apply to everyone, including those who submit their manuscripts for publication. Authors are not necessarily any better at judging their own work than are journal referees, and sometimes authors may be even less adequate because of self-serving biases and other intellectual contaminants. Indeed, the historical record indicates that even the greatest scientists can get it very wrong. Gregor Mendel believed the theoretical significance of his research concerned evolution rather than inheritance. Specifically, his studies of peas were to shed light on the process of hybridization. The mathematical modeling of the inheritance process was only a secondary aspect of his classic studies. Hence, one could argue that Mendel himself was not truly a Mendelian geneticist (Brannigan, 1981; Olby, 1979). He no more appreciated the real impact of his work than did his contemporaries. It works the other way, too, of course. All too often scientists have an overly high opinion of their own work and thus find themselves cut down to size by those asked to serve as journal referees. I noted this contingency earlier when I discussed the implications of the equal-odds rule, especially in its longitudinal form.

So what should psychologists who want to attain some degree of greatness in the discipline do? Well, certainly they should make every effort to produce work that meets the highest possible scientific standards. Also, as examined earlier, it probably behooves the psychologist to engage in a network of enterprises rather than focus on an extremely narrow subject matter. Beyond that, however, a tremendous amount of uncertainty remains about which of one's publications will have a major impact on the field and which will leave little or no impression on contemporaries and posterity. To the extent that the influence of a research program is governed by the equal-odds rule, it is best to exploit the odds by being extremely productive. As Wayne Dennis (1954a) expressed it,

> the correlation between fame and fecundity may be understood in part in terms of the proposition that the greater the number of pieces of scientific work done by a given man, the more of them will prove to be important. Other things being equal, the greater the number of researches, the greater the likelihood of making an important discovery that will make the finder famous. (p. 182)

Alexander Bain put forward a similar idea nearly 100 years earlier. In his classic psychological text on *Senses and the Intellect* is found the following passage: "The greatest practical inventions being so much dependent upon chance, the only hope of success is to multiply the chances by multiplying the experiments" (Bain, 1855/1977, p. 597).

Although one might become a mere Mass Producer by adopting such a career strategy, the odds still favor one thus joining the Prolifics who may eventually figure prominently in the annals of psychology. In contrast, if one strives to become one of the Perfectionists by meticulously trying to maximize all the supposed criteria for high-impact work for every item in one's bibliography, one does so only at great risk, for one is then much more likely to end up among the Silent of psychology's history. In the final analysis, it is output that most securely and directly leads to impact.

III

PERSONAL CHARACTERISTICS THAT CONTRIBUTE TO GREATNESS AS A PSYCHOLOGIST

INTRODUCTION: PERSONAL CHARACTERISTICS THAT CONTRIBUTE TO GREATNESS AS A PSYCHOLOGIST

"Sex sells," runs one supposed motto of the advertising industry. To be sure, as noted in the previous chapter, curricula vitae that include many titles rich in primary-process imagery may receive fewer citations psychological journals, but that negative correlation may only reflect the hangups of academic culture (Simonton, 1992b). Popular culture is quite another thing, as the prominence of Sigmund Freud well illustrates. One hundred years after he published his 1900 *Interpretation of Dreams*, Freud's visage and ideas still permeate popular novels, magazines, newspapers, cartoons, and movies. No doubt a huge part of his success stems from the fact that his whole theory and therapy center on sex. Another figure from psychology's history that may have benefited from this prurient interest was Havelock Ellis. Almost Freud's exact contemporary—and, like him, a physician and a product of Victorian prudery—Ellis had a sex life even less satisfactory than Freud's, not overcoming coital impotency until he was 60 (Wallace, Wallace, Wallechinsky, & Wallace, 1981). So, quite in line with Freudian theory, Ellis became a leading authority on the psychology of sex, writing many books on the subject. The most important of these was the seven volumes of his *Studies in the Psychology of Sex* (1898–1928), a work often condemned as pornographic.

It is somewhat unfortunate, however, that these landmark works often overshadow Ellis's pioneering efforts in a totally unrelated domain: the psychology of genius. His 1902 *Study of British Genius* (Ellis, 1904/1926) contin-ued the tradition that began with Galton's 1869 *Hereditary Genius* and 1874 *English Men of Science*. Starting with a sample of 1,030 eminent figures in the *Dictionary of National Biography*, Ellis provided fairly extensive statistics re-garding the correlates of exceptional accomplishment in a diversity of do-mains. The scientific assumption permeating Ellis's investigation is that in-dividuals who attain genuine greatness in any field possess a certain well-defined set of attributes that provide the personal foundations of achieve-ment. Other investigators have followed where Ellis first feared to tread. Be-sides investigating the individual characteristics associated with eminent at-tainments in a diversity of domains (e.g., R. B. Cattell, 1963; Cox, 1926; Raskin, 1936; E. L. Thorndike, 1950), some investigators have studied which personal attributes contribute to becoming a great psychologist (e.g., Roe, 1953b; Wispé, 1963).

The upshot is a wealth of empirical findings that must enhance one's scientific understanding of psychology's history. After all, historians of the discipline frequently cite individual traits when trying to explain the impor-tance of this or that historical figure (Simonton, 1995a). A typical example is the following quotation:

> To some degree, the acceptance of Watsonian behaviorism was a func-tion of the abilities and force of Watson himself. He was charming and attractive, and he expressed his ideas with enthusiasm, optimism, self-confidence, and clarity. He was a bold and appealing figure who scorned tradition and rejected the current version of psychology. These personal qualities . . . define J. B. Watson as one of psychology's pioneers. (Schultz & Schultz, 1992, p. 327)

By the same token, the failings or limitations of a given luminary are often ascribed to some specific personality quirk. Why did William James become known as a theoretician and expositor rather than as an experimen-tal psychologist? Apparently, "James was not suited by temperament or incli-nation to be a research worker. He was a gentleman psychologist" (Hothersall, 1984, p. 254). Given this disposition, James soon felt compelled to have Hugo Münsterberg take over Harvard's laboratory for experimental psychol-ogy.

In this section I review the individual characteristics that contribute to greatness as a psychologist. I begin with chapter 6, in which I discuss cogni-tive attributes, and then in chapter 7 I deal with dispositional traits. I close the section with chapter 8, in which I discuss the worldview or belief systems of individuals who have made significant contributions to psychology.

6

COGNITION

Historic contributions to the scientific study of mind are produced by human minds—the minds of great psychologists. If psychologists are able to accumulate knowledge about psychological processes, including knowledge about how humans know, then surely psychological scientists must also possess the ability to determine the intellectual factors that contribute to the accumulation of knowledge within the discipline. To say otherwise would seem to propose a profound paradox—that psychologists can discover how all people acquire new knowledge except when those people happen to be psychologists! The latter would then have to be a separate species from the rest of humanity, an absurd proposition. So, what are the mental processes or factors that enable a psychologist to obtain valued insights?

This question can be addressed two ways. First, one can examine the repercussions of individual differences in general information-processing power—most commonly called *intelligence*. Second, one can scrutinize what specific cognitive processes and strategies contribute most to making notable contributions to psychological science.

EMINENCE AND INTELLIGENCE

Samuel Johnson (1781), the author of the first English dictionary, held that "the true Genius is a mind of large general powers, accidentally determined to some particular direction" (p. 5). This assertion sounds compatible with what is often claimed for Spearman's *g*, the general factor of human intelligence. As I noted back in chapter 3, this factor is supposed to underlie performance on an impressive variety of intellectual tasks (L. S. Gottfredson, 1997). As a consequence, general intelligence, as measured by some standardized "IQ test" loading high on *g*, will provide a consistently valid predictor of occupational attainments in a diversity of domains (e.g., Barrett & Depinet, 1991; Ree, Earles, & Teachout, 1994). Hence, it is likely that great psychologists are smart psychologists, in the sense of placement at the upper end of the distribution in general intelligence. There actually exists some evidence for this conjecture. Part of the evidence comes from psychometric studies, and part comes from historiometric investigations.

Psychometric Inquiries

Francis Galton (1869) was the first major behavioral scientist to argue that achieved eminence was strongly associated with intellectual ability. However, when he first presented this argument, in his 1869 book *Hereditary Genius*, he could make his case only indirectly, by looking at how notable achievers emerged from family pedigrees. Some time later, Galton (1883) attempted to devise direct measures of ability, but the resulting "anthropometric" instruments failed to have any predictive validity, as James McKeen Cattell, among others, was to show. It was Alfred Binet, in collaboration with Theodor Simon, who invented the true forerunner of the modern intelligence test. As originally conceived, the test was mostly dedicated to identifying schoolchildren whose intelligence fell below that of their peers. However, soon other tests began to be used to identify children whose intellectual ability was truly superior. On the basis of their test performance, children could be called "gifted" or labeled as "geniuses." Among the pioneers in this development were Leta Hollingworth (1926, 1942) and Lewis M. Terman (1917, 1925). It was this work that finally led to many dictionaries actually defining *genius* in terms of an IQ score rather than on the basis of bona fide achievement, as was the practice previously (Murray, 1989). For example, according to the *American Heritage Electronic Dictionary* (1992), a *genius* is "a person who has an exceptionally high intelligence quotient, typically above 140"—a definition that would have made no sense 100 years ago.

Of all the great psychologists, Terman is most responsible for establishing the IQ score as a criterion for genius. He initiated this lexical transformation when he converted the French Binet–Simon scale to the English-language Stanford–Binet scale. The next step was to undertake the single most ambitious longitudinal study ever conducted in the history of psychology: the series of investigations known under the collective title of *Genetic Studies of Genius*. A large sample of more than 1,500 boys and girls was selected on the basis of their performance on the Stanford–Binet, the technical threshold for inclusion being an IQ of 140 (albeit a few others with lower IQs were included as well for various reasons). The average age of the study sample was 11 years, and the average IQ was 151, with a range of 135–200. These intellectually gifted children were then followed into adulthood, with the aim of proving that they would become highly accomplished adults. The first volume, published by Terman (1925) alone, was titled *Mental and Physical Traits of a Thousand Gifted Children*. The third volume appeared 5 years later, in collaboration with two others, and was titled *The Promise of Youth: Follow-Up Studies of a Thousand Gifted Children* (Burks, Jensen, & Terman, 1930). By this time the participants had all become teenagers, and most were attending high school. Volumes 4 and 5 were also collaborative efforts, the last volume necessarily so, because Terman died before the longitudinal study could be completed. The two titles were *The Gifted Child Grows Up* (Terman & Oden, 1947) and *The Gifted Group at Mid-Life* (Terman & Oden, 1959), the latter published more than 30 years after the study had begun. Subsequent studies of these same "Termites"—for such was the name by which these participants were often called—were published by Terman's successors (e.g., Oden, 1968), including gerontological investigations of those who lived to be octogenarians (Holahan, Sears, & Cronbach, 1995).

So what happened to these children? Given the cohort, it is best to address this question by concentrating on the men, for most of the women became housewives (see Tomlinson-Keasey, 1990). Among the gifted men, 70 were eventually listed in *American Men of Science*, 9 of these for their achievements in the social sciences. Three of the men had also been elected to the National Academy of Sciences. Even more striking from the current standpoint is that 2 of the Termites eventually became distinguished psychologists, namely, Robert R. Sears and Lee Cronbach. Both Sears and Cronbach were honored with the American Psychological Association's (APA's) Distinguished Scientific Contribution Award (in 1975 and 1973, respectively), and Sears served a term as APA president in 1951. It is curious that both Sears and Cronbach eventually became investigators in the longitudinal study in which they themselves were participants (e.g., Cronbach, 1996; Sears, 1977). That unprecedented longitudinal circularity seems to operate almost as a triumphal confirmation of the study's main thesis: that a high IQ means genius.

There are several problems with this inference, however (see, e.g., Shurkin, 1992). In the first place, Terman's longitudinal study lacked a bona fide control group. He should ideally have also followed the lives of a sample of children matched on class, ethnicity, geography, and other pertinent demographic factors but who did not have genius-level IQs. Without this comparison group, the obvious intellectual ability of his gifted children was confounded with a large number of other contaminating factors. It is interesting that there was actually one child whose intelligence did not qualify him for inclusion in Terman's sample and yet who later received a Nobel prize for physics, a degree of recognition unmatched by any of the scientific Termites. That individual was William Shockley, coinventor of the transistor (Eysenck, 1995). One can only guess how many other cases like Shockley's would have emerged had Terman acquired a proper set of controls. By the same token, many of the gifted children in Terman's sample failed to grow up to become highly successful adults, and some could be considered outright failures. These negative cases did not have lower IQ scores than the positive cases. Accordingly, Terman was forced to admit that nonintellectual characteristics, such as personality, might have a very important part to play in the determination of exceptional achievement (Terman & Oden, 1959). Finally, Terman's longitudinal inquiry did not meet modern standards of scientific rigor. For instance, the scoring of the original Stanford–Binet protocols were biased upward, so that when Robert Sears had them recalculated he had to inform his fellow Termite Lee Cronbach that the latter had lived his "life with an IQ that was 10 points too high" (Hirsch, 1993, p. 1135). Making matters worse, Terman would often intervene in the lives of his Termites in various ways, such as writing letters of recommendation on their behalf. It surely must be considered more than pure coincidence that both Sears and Cronbach ended up as professors at Stanford University, where Terman had been professor and departmental chair and where he was professor emeritus.

Fortunately, it is not necessary to rely solely on Terman's classic but flawed study to address the key question of how intelligence relates to greatness. Instead, one can call on psychometric inquiries that deal with this issue using either direct or indirect assessments.

Direct Assessments

Many studies show that successful scientists tend to have IQ scores that are much higher than average—most often by about 2 standard deviations. A good example is the series of investigations conducted at the Institute for Personality Assessment and Research (IPAR) at the University of California, Berkeley, in the 1960s and 1970s. For example, Helson and Crutchfield (1970) found that creative mathematicians averaged an IQ of 135 on the Wechlser Adult Intelligence Scale (WAIS; Wechsler, 1955), whereas MacKinnon and Hall (1972) found that creative research scientists averaged WAIS IQ scores of 133. These scores are sufficiently high that they meet the standard for joining Mensa, a society for individuals who purport to have genius-grade IQs (Serebriakoff, 1985). Other researchers have reported IQ scores at least this high (e.g., J. Gibson & Light, 1967), and sometimes even higher (e.g., Roe, 1953a), with scores more in line with Terman's threshold of 140 for genius-level intelligence. Moreover, there is every reason to believe that eminent psychologists do not substantially differ from other scientists in their intellectual power (Roe, 1953a).

That's the good news. The bad news is twofold. First, the range in the IQ scores is wide: Many distinguished scientists exhibit a psychometric intelligence no higher than that of the average college graduate (e.g., an IQ of around 120). At IPAR the range for creative research scientists ranged from 121 to 142, albeit nearly three fourths had WAIS IQs $\geq$130 (MacKinnon & Hall, 1972). This variation means that many notable scientists would not qualify for membership in Mensa, and even fewer would have made it into Terman's sample of gifted children. Second, the range is so great that the IQ distributions for eminent scientists differ very little from those from their less eminent colleagues. In the IPAR studies the mean WAIS IQ scores for a comparison group of scientists was only 1 point lower (i.e., 133 vs. 132), a negligible difference (MacKinnon & Hall, 1972). Moreover, when IQ scores are correlated with some valid criterion of scientific distinction, the correlations are nearly zero. For instance, one study of 499 academic researchers in the physical, biological, and social sciences found that IQ correlated .05 with the number of published articles and .06 with the number of citations (S. Cole & Cole, 1973). Another study of research scientists actually found a slightly negative correlation ($r = -.05$) between intelligence and a citation measure of scientific achievement (Bayer & Folger, 1966). The same near-zero correlations appear if a different criterion of scientific accomplishment, such as ratings by peers and supervisors, is used (e.g., $r = -.05$; see Gough, 1976).

Although none of the above investigations singled out psychologists for special treatment, there is no prima facie reason to think that attainment in psychology operates by some principle fundamentally different than the rest of the sciences. Indeed, if an instrument devised by psychologists predicted only the differential achievement of psychologists, then one would have to seriously consider whether IQ tests have anything more than parochial value.

Indirect Assessments

Why do the direct assessments have such dismal predictive validities? There are several possible explanations. Perhaps IQ bears a curvilinear relation with achieved eminence so that someone can be *too smart* to do good psychology, a possibility that is known to hold for certain leadership domains (Simonton, 1985a, 1995c). Alternatively, intelligence may operate so that once individuals surpass a certain minimal threshold level, such as an IQ of 120, further increases do not necessarily translate into greater achievement (Barron & Harrington, 1981; Simonton, 1999d). Another possibility, however, is more critical: Perhaps the IQ tests that developed from Binet's landmark measure—in the hands of distinguished psychologists such as Charles Spearman, L. Thurstone, Lewis Terman, and David Wechsler—are no more relevant to exceptional achievement than were Francis Galton's abortive anthropometric instruments. The predictive irrelevancy of the traditional IQ test has been suggested by many psychologists, including some highly eminent ones, such as David C. McClelland (1973). If true, it is conceivable that a different type of intelligence test might do a better job of predicting scientific performance.

There exist more subtle approaches to assessing a person's intelligence than to have him or her sit down and answer the questions typical of the IQ test. One alternative is simply to ask colleagues to rate a scientist's intelligence and then determine whether this predicts achievement. In one investigation, for instance, the faculty-peer assessed intelligence of 52 full-time psychology professors correlated .40 with a composite measure of publication and citation counts (Rushton, 1990). Although this might seem to contradict what has been found with IQ tests, it is not unlikely that peer-rated intelligence is somewhat confounded with the achievement measure. Colleagues will have some idea of the more productive members of their faculty, and this may influence their evaluation of a colleague's intelligence, inflating the true correlation. A related investigation looked at the same achievement criterion for a sample of 69 Canadian psychologists, only this time with self-ratings of intelligence as the predictor (Rushton, 1990). The correlation was essentially zero ($r = .05$), suggesting, perhaps, that psychologists are not always the most dependable judges of their own capacities. Not only might some overrate themselves, but also some might underrate themselves.

Yet another indirect approach to assessing intelligence may be even more promising: the content analysis of verbal behavior. In particular, it is possible to score transcripts or written documents for individual differences in terms of *integrative complexity*, a measure of whether a person can display highly differentiated and yet fully integrative thoughts about various topics (Suedfeld, Tetlock, & Streufert, 1992). This content-analytical measure has already been applied quite successfully to political speeches, interviews, correspondence, and communiqués, most notably by psychologists Peter Suedfeld and Philip Tetlock. However, applications in the area of the psychology of science have been rather few. Of these, two examples stand out. The first inquiry found that the presidential addresses delivered by highly eminent APA presidents scored higher in integrative complexity than did those delivered by less eminent presidents (Suedfeld, 1985). Similarly, the more productive APA presidents were more integratively complex than the less productive ones. In the second inquiry interviews were scored in which a sample of physicists, chemists, and biologists talked about their research and teaching (Feist, 1994). The complexity with which a scientist spoke about his research correlated .25 with total citations and .20 with peer-rated eminence. Although it is tempting to see these results as endorsing a relation between intelligence and scientific achievement, one additional finding does not fit so easily with this generalization: The complexity reflected in the part of the interview in which a scientist spoke about his teaching correlated negatively with the total number of works that were cited in the professional literature ($r = -.21$; Feist, 1994). Hence, if the integrative complexity measure does indeed tap individual differences in intelligence, then it is doing so in a task-specific manner incompatible with the notion of Spearman's *g*. Furthermore, the possibility must be admitted that the integrative complexity a scientist brings to bear on discussions of his or her research is contaminated by the magnitude of scientific eminence attained. Scientists who receive frequent citations in the professional literature will find that many are at least partially critical (Moravcsik & Murugesan, 1975). Informed criticism received from colleagues may oblige highly visible scientists to adopt more highly differentiated and integrated views of their research program and results.

The most secure conclusion to be drawn from the direct and indirect measures is that great psychologists are certainly not less intelligent than their more obscure colleagues. The greats might even be slightly more intelligent. However, the effect size is never large for any variety of psychometric measure. Do historiometric assessments yield the same general conclusion?

Historiometric Inquiries

Earlier, when I listed the volumes making up L. M. Terman's classic *Genetic Studies of Genius*, I skipped volume 2. I did this for a very good reason: The second volume is totally unlike the rest. Besides being the only volume that does not include Terman as an author or coauthor, it is the only one that has absolutely no direct connection with the longitudinal study of 1,500 intellectually gifted children. Instead, the book is based on the doctoral dissertation of Catharine Cox (1926), one of Terman's graduate students. Cox scrutinized the intelligence of historic geniuses who were not only deceased but also were deceased before the Binet–Simon test tradition even began. Although Cox's 842-page tome is titled *The Early Mental Traits of Three Hundred Geniuses*, she actually examined 301 eminent creators and leaders of Western civilization. Despite these differences, Cox's book is not out of place in the set. It deals with the same fundamental thesis as the other volumes, only by means of an entirely different method. Rather than conducting a longitudinal study of high-IQ children to see if they developed into highly accomplished adults, Cox conducted a retrospective study of highly accomplished adults to see if they would have been identified as high-IQ children had it been possible to administer the Stanford–Binet. To pull off this seemingly impossible feat, Cox built on a study that her mentor, Terman, had published almost 10 years earlier (Terman, 1917).

Despite Terman's obvious indebtedness to the Binet–Simon tests, he remained an admirer of Francis Galton. Galton died in 1911, and a few years later Galton's pupil and collaborator, Karl Pearson, published the first volume of Galton's biography, which Terman eagerly read. As someone who had already spent a considerable amount of time assessing the intelligence of children, Terman was quite impressed with Galton's intellectual precocity. Galton learned his capital letters by the time he was 12 months old and added the lowercase alphabet 6 months later. He learned to read at age 2.5

years, was able to sign his name before he was 3, and could write without assistance at age 4. He wrote the following letter to his older sister just before his 5th birthday:

> MY DEAR ADÈLE,
>   I am 4 years old and I can read any English book. I can say all the Latin Substantives and Adjectives and active verbs besides 52 lines of Latin poetry. I can cast up any sum in addition and can multiply by 2, 3, 4, 5, 6, 7, 8, [9], 10, [11].
>   I can also say the pence table. I read French a little and I know the clock.
>   FRANCIS GALTON,
>   Febuary [sic] 15, 1827 (quoted in Cox, 1926, p. 42)

The numbers in brackets were those that Galton, in a display of second thoughts, erased from the letter; he used a knife to scratch out one number and, evidently finding this unsatisfactory, glued paper on top of the other number. Only one misspelling appears: the month that the letter was written (an error that some adults still make). When Terman carefully scrutinized all of the documentary evidence, he realized that it could be converted into an IQ score. This conversion was rendered possible because just shortly before, in 1912, William Stern had defined the intelligence quotient as a child's mental age divided by his or her chronological age, multiplied by 100 (to avoid decimal fractions). It was this same quotient that Terman adapted for his 1916 Stanford Revision of the Binet Scales. Hence, to get an IQ score out of a biography, the investigator need only determine the mental age revealed by representative childhood achievements and compare this to the corresponding chronological age. On this basis, Terman (1917) estimated that Galton's IQ was close to 200. He was doing things that children normally don't do until they were nearly twice Galton's age.

Cox (1926) improved on Terman's exploratory investigation in a manner quite worthy of a doctoral dissertation. First, she rendered the methodology far more sophisticated. For example, she used multiple and independent raters, including Terman and Florence Goodenough (a Terman student who later became famous for her eponymic Draw-a-Man test). In addition, she introduced many important statistical refinements, such as the calculation of reliability coefficients for her IQ estimates. Just as important was the large sample size she decided to study, making hers the most ambitious historiometric investigation ever undertaken, one probably unsurpassed in scope for another 50 years (Simonton, 1990b). She obtained the sample by taking advantage of a study published in 1903 by another Galton admirer, James McKeen Cattell (1903b). In it, Cattell made the first attempt at the quantitative and objective assessment of individual differences in eminence. By consulting several standard reference works in several languages, Cattell ranked the 1,000 most eminent figures in history according to the amount of space each was allotted. Starting with the top names on this list, Cox then deleted all those (a) who were born before 1450 (or who otherwise had insufficient biographical data) and (b) who attained their eminence through birth (kings, queens, and other hereditary rulers). Cox thus arrived at her final sample of 301.

The next step was the most laborious. Cox compiled for each individual the necessary biographical data, which a team of independent raters then used to provide IQ estimates. Two estimates were calculated: one for ages 0–16 and the other for ages 17–26. In addition, Cox calculated reliability coefficients that were used to provide "corrected" IQ estimates. To give an idea of the outcome, in Table 6.1 the results are shown for those among the 301 who also have figured prominently in psychology's history (according to Annin, Boring, & Watson, 1968). At the top of this list is J. S. Mill, whose IQ was about as high as what Terman estimated for Galton. The biographical data show Mill to have been a child prodigy (Cox, 1926). He began to learn Greek at 3, read Plato at 7, and studied the Greek classics until age 9. Meanwhile, he was also studying his history, so that he could discuss the relative military prowess of Marlborough and Wellington when he was 5, and he wrote a history of Rome at 6.5. He began to study Latin at 8 and was reading the Latin classics within a year. Also at 8 he began his mathematical studies with geometry and algebra, a year later advancing to conic sections, spherics, and Newton's arithmetic, so by age 11 he could begin the calculus (Newton's fluxions). Still continuing his classics studies, he wrote a synoptic table of Aristotle's *Rhetoric* at the same time, and at age 12 moved on to philosophy and logic, taking on political economy in the following year. It was now time start the modern languages, so at 14 he began reading French authors. Mill rounded out his first 16 years by commencing his legal studies.

On the other hand, this same list makes evident that many luminaries might not have made it into the Terman sample had they been tested for inclusion. Charles Darwin admitted that he was considered "much slower in learning than my younger sister" (p. 6) and that his teachers and his father viewed him "as a very ordinary boy, rather below the common standard in intellect" (F. Darwin, 1892/1958, p. 9). At school he found himself "singularly incapable of mastering any language" (F. Darwin, 1892/1958, p. 9). He also said of himself,

> I have no great quickness of apprehension or wit which is so remarkable in some clever men, for instance, [T. H.] Huxley. I am therefore a poor critic: a paper or book, when first read, generally excites my admiration, and it is only after considerable reflection that I perceive the weak points. My power to follow a long and purely abstract train of thought is very limited; and therefore I could never have succeeded with metaphysics or mathematics. My memory is extensive, yet hazy: it suffices to make me cautious by vaguely telling me that I have observed or read something opposed to the conclusion which I am drawing, or on the other hand in

TABLE 6.1
Uncorrected and Corrected IQ Scores and Reliabilities
for Ages 0–16 and 17–26

Name	Uncorrected		Reliabilities		Corrected	
	0–16	17–26	0–16	17–26	0–16	17–26
J. S. Mill	190	170	.82	.82	200	180
Johann Goethe	185	200	.82	.82	190	210
Gottfried Leibniz	185	190	.75	.75	195	205
Blaise Pascal	180	180	.75	.75	190	195
Albrecht von Haller	175	180	.82	.82	180	190
Voltaire	170	180	.75	.75	180	190
David Hume	155	160	.60	.60	175	180
George Berkeley	150	175	.60	.75	170	180
Auguste Comte	150	170	.60	.75	170	185
René Descartes	150	160	.53	.60	165	180
Denis Diderot	150	145	.60	.60	165	165
Galileo Galilei	145	165	.53	.60	160	185
Francis Bacon	145	155	.53	.53	165	180
Johannes Kepler	140	160	.53	.75	155	175
G. W. F. Hegel	140	145	.43	.43	165	165
Montaigne	140	140	.60	.43	155	165
Thomas Hobbes	140	135	.43	.43	175	180
Immanuel Kant	135	145	.60	.60	175	180
Charles Darwin	135	140	.43	.53	155	165
Isaac Newton	130	170	.43	.60	150	190
Baruch Spinoza	130	145	.20	.43	170	175
Jean-Jacques Rousseau	130	125	.53	.53	150	150
Carolus Linnaeus	125	145	.43	.60	155	165
John Locke	125	135	.43	.43	150	165
William Harvey	120	150	.20	.43	170	165
Nicolaus Copernicus	105	130	.11	.43	135	160

Note. The uncorrected and corrected estimated IQ scores and their reliabilities are taken from the entries for each of the notables reported in Cox (1926).

favour of it; and after a time I can generally recollect where to search for my authority. (F. Darwin, 1892/1958, pp. 54–55)

And yet Darwin's subgenius IQ did not prevent him from becoming one of the greatest revolutionaries in the biological and behavioral sciences.

In fact, Cox (1926) directly calculated the relation between IQ and eminence. Using the uncorrected IQ for age 17–26 and J. M. Cattell's (1903c) published rankings, she obtained a correlation of .25. Thus, about 6% of the variance is shared (also see Simonton, 1991d; Walberg, Rasher, & Hase, 1978). However, Cox recognized that this correlation might be inflated by the fact that the more eminent individuals tend to have more reliable biographical data and thereby obtain higher estimated IQ scores. So, she also calculated the partial correlation, controlling for reliability, and obtained

.16. Although this decreases the proportion of variance accounted for by more than half, the coefficient remained statistically significant. Even so, if one also partials out other variables, such as birth year, the association becomes reduced a bit more (using multiple regression, β = .14; Simonton, 1976a). So, the results are starting to appear more comparable to what was found with psychometric measures—either a null association or one that is only slightly positive. Nonetheless, it must be recognized that Cox's 301 adults form a highly select group in terms of eminence. Therefore, the eminence–intelligence correlation is seriously attenuated by range restriction. Historiometric studies of political leaders have found respectable linkages between eminence and intelligence when the former variable is allowed to vary more (i.e., by including exemplars of truly incompetent leadership). Specifically, positive relationships having about the same size as Cox's zero-order correlation have been found for both monarchs (r = .26; Simonton, 1983c) and U.S. presidents (β = .27; Simonton, 1986f). Finally, it must not be overlooked that these 301 geniuses, including the 25 who left some mark on psychology's history, define a very bright group of people. The average corrected IQ for the 0–16 age period is 153, which is 2 points higher than that for the Termites. Better yet, the average corrected IQ for the 17–26 period is 164, which is the same level as the criterion for joining the Four Sigma Society of superintelligent individuals.

All in all, the psychometric inquiries inspired by Terman's longitudinal study and the historiometric inquiries following up Cox's (1926) retrospective study have led to pretty much the same conclusion: Individuals who earn a place in the annals of the discipline's history are likely to be much more intelligent than the general population—by at least 1 standard deviation and more likely 2. Yet this is not that heavy an intellectual requirement. According to Termite Cronbach (1960), the approximate average IQ of high school graduates is 110, of college graduates 120, and of PhDs 130. Hence, when the eminent are compared to their far less illustrious colleagues, intelligence plays a minimal role, if any. One evidently needs a fairly high IQ just to become an also-ran.

MENTAL STRATEGIES AND PROCESSES

Although psychology purports to be a science, very few of the people who populate the annals of psychology have received a Nobel prize. Those who have are almost invariably honored with the Nobel for physiology or medicine. This was the case not just for Ivan Pavlov but also for S. Ramón y Cajal, Sir C. Sherrington, Antón Egas Moniz, Georg von Békésy, and Roger W. Sperry. However, there is one exception, namely, Herbert Simon, who was the recipient of the 1978 Nobel prize for economic science. It may appear odd for a psychologist to receive such an honor, but the award was given for his work on decision-making processes in economic organizations. Simon's main contribution to psychology has been his work on the cognitive processes behind decision making and problem solving. The latter research is especially important to the subject matter of this book, for Simon has devoted a considerable amount of attention to problem solving in the sciences, especially the cognitive basis of scientific discovery (H. A. Simon, 1977). He has even helped develop computer models of the discovery process that purport to simulate the manner in which real discoveries were made (Langley, Simon, Bradshaw, & Zythow, 1987; also see Shrager & Langley, 1990). Many of these discovery programs are given eponymic designations. Among these names are several that are well known in the history of psychology: OCCAM, BACON, GALILEO, and DALTON. These eponyms are not entirely incidental. For example, BACON specializes in the inductive method, yielding data-driven discoveries as advocated in Francis Bacon's 1920 *Novum Organum*. By applying Baconian induction, BACON has rediscovered Kepler's third law of planetary motion, Black's law of temperature equilibrium, Ohm's law of current and resistance, Prout's hypothesis of atomic structure, the Gay–Lussac law of gaseous reaction, the Dulong–Petit law of atomic heats, and the derivation of atomic weights by Avogadro and Cannizzaro (Bradshaw, Langley, & Simon, 1983).

The work of Simon and his colleagues is important here because it may help explain why intelligence has such a minimal association with achieved eminence in the sciences. Great scientists may not be smarter than everyone else; instead, they may have the same intellect as their less influential peers but merely know how to more effectively use their intelligence. Besides mastering the relevant knowledge and skills, so-called geniuses have acquired the necessary problem-solving expertise. In fact, Simon repeatedly argued that some of the world's greatest scientific breakthroughs were not really that special from a cognitive standpoint. For example, he claimed that "Mendeleev's Periodic Table does not involve a notion of pattern more complex than that required to handle patterned letter sequences" (H. A. Simon, 1973, p. 479). Likewise, Simon once conducted an informal experiment showing that nothing special was required to make a discovery that would win the historic discoverer a Nobel prize for physics:

> On eight occasions I have sat down at lunch with colleagues who are good applied mathematicians and said to them: "I have a problem that you can perhaps help me with. I have some very nice data that can be fitted very accurately for large values of the independent variable by an exponential function, but for small values they fit a linear function accurately. Can you suggest a smooth function that will give me a good fit through the whole range?" (H. A. Simon, 1986, p. 7)

Out of the eight lunch companions, five found an answer in only a couple of minutes or less. None was suspicious of what Simon was up to, neither did any realize the historic nature of the problem given them. Still, those five anonymous individuals had independently arrived at Planck's formula for black body radiation. In another mini-experiment a mere graduate student in chemical engineering was able to derive the Balmer formula for the hydrogen spectrum (Qin & Simon, 1990). Moreover, this student was asked to think aloud while solving the problem, and therefore protocol analysis could be applied to learn the search processes that led to the discovery. The thought processes were comparable to those that are revealed in Balmer's surviving documents, and those processes seemed to involve nothing more than straightforward logical reasoning. Anyone can do it, if he or she learns the appropriate problem-solving techniques and strategies (J. R. Hayes, 1989b).

In many respects, this work by Herbert Simon and his colleagues continues a long philosophical tradition. Ever since the time of Plato and Aristotle, thinkers have been proposing methods by which individuals can discover the truth or acquire new but valid knowledge. Philosophical fascination with these prescriptive epistemologies has accelerated since the Scientific Revolution, as one thinker after another has detailed the methods or techniques required if one wishes to do genuine science. Among these thinkers are several who have had a prominent place in psychology's own history, such as Francis Bacon, Descartes, Isaac Newton, John Locke, David Hartley, and John Stuart Mill. Where Simon departs from this epistemological tradition is his claim that the logical principles embodied in these discovery programs are descriptive rather than prescriptive. For instance, the program called KEKADA purports to model the cognitive process by which Hans Krebs arrived at the urea cycle (Kulkarni & Simon, 1988). This concordance was established by comparing the computer's output with both the notebooks and the living testimony of Krebs himself!

Herbert Simon can be certainly considered a distinguished psychologist as well as scientist. He received APA's Distinguished Scientific Contribution Award in 1969, the same year as Jean Piaget and Stanley Schachter. Consequently, Simon's claims certainly must be given their due weight. Even so, there remain considerable grounds for skepticism (Csikszentmihalyi, 1988; Simonton, 1999b; Sternberg, 1989). Not all psychologists believe that these cognitive models can capture the rich complexity of the discovery process in high-impact science. Somehow, these models make the process appear too cut and dried, orderly, and logical—all too similar to prescriptive epistemologies than bona fide descriptions of historic scientific creativity. Both the computer models and the philosophical systems have rather straitlaced ideas about what it takes to make major contributions. This prudery becomes immediately apparent when psychologists examine the notebooks of practicing scientists.

Take the commonplace claim that scientists proceed by the deliberate formulation and rejection of hypotheses (e.g., Popper, 1959). Howard Gruber (1974) had this to say after extensive examination of Darwin's notebooks:

The picture of scientific thought is often painted as being carried forward by the construction of alternative hypotheses followed by the rational choice between them. Darwin's notebooks do not support this rationalist myth. Hypotheses are discovered with difficulty in the activity of a person holding *one* point of view, and they are the expression of that point of view. It is hard enough to have one reasonable hypothesis, and two at a time may be exceedingly rare. In Darwin's case, when he is forced to give up one hypothesis, he does not necessarily substitute another— he sometimes simply remains at a loss until his point of view matures sufficiently to permit the expression of a new hypothesis. (p. 146)

Indeed, many great psychologists have made explicit that they fail to follow the rules of the abstract methodologists. B. F. Skinner (1959), for one, confessed that

the notes, data, and publications which I have examined do not show that I ever behaved in the manner of Man Thinking as described by John Stuart Mill or John Dewey or as in reconstructions of scientific behavior by other philosophers of science. I never faced a problem which was more than the eternal problem of finding order. I never attacked a problem by constructing a Hypothesis. I never deduced Theorems or submitted them to Experimental Check. So far as I can see, I had no preconceived Model of behavior—certainly not a physiological or mentalistic one, and I believe, not a conceptual one. . . . Of course, I was working on a basic Assumption—that there was order in behavior if I could only discover it— but such an assumption is not to be confused with the hypotheses of deductive theory. It is also true that I exercised a certain Selection of Facts, but not because of relevance to theory but because one fact was more orderly than another. If I engaged in Experimental Design at all, it was simply to complete or extend some evidence of order already observed. (p. 369)

Although Skinner did not receive a Nobel prize, he did earn APA's Distinguished Scientific Contribution Award in 1958 and was for a time considered the most eminent psychologist of his day. Hence, this confession must be taken as seriously as Simon's assertions.

One must delve more deeply into what great psychologists have had to say about the discovery process. These introspective reports should instruct one on how much more complicated psychological models must become before they can provide a comprehensive account of the mental processes behind great science. In addition, some of these complications will later prove useful in helping one appreciate the personality characteristics that are associated with being a great psychologist. Therefore, I next examine the roles of trial and error, free association, imagery, intuition, incubation, serendipity, and inspiration.

Trial and Error

Hermann von Helmholtz was not just an illustrious physiologist but a notable physicist and mathematician besides. If there were anyone who might be expected to follow a step-by-step reasoning process, it would be he. Yet Helmholtz (1891/1898) said that his problem-solving activities pursued a rather different path.

> I only succeeded in solving such problems after many devious ways, by the gradually increasing generalisation of favourable examples, and by a series of fortunate guesses. I had to compare myself with an Alpine climber, who, not knowing the way, ascends slowly and with toil, and is often compelled to retrace his steps because his progress is stopped; sometimes by reasoning, and sometimes by accident, he hits upon traces of a fresh path, which again leads him a little further; and finally, when he has reached the goal, he finds to his annoyance a royal road on which he might have ridden up if he had been clever enough to find the right starting-point at the outset. In my memoirs I have, of course, not given the reader an account of my wanderings, but I have described the beaten path on which he can now reach the summit without trouble. (p. 282)

Neal Miller, the eminent American psychologist, offered a very similar observation:

> Published reports of research are written with the wisdom of hindsight. They leave out the initial groping and fumbling to save journal space (and perhaps also to save face) and exclude almost all of those attempts that are abandoned as failures. Therefore, they present a misleading picture which is far too orderly and simple of the actual process of trying to extend the frontiers of science into unknown territory. (quoted in Cohen, 1977, p. 243)

These two statements were generalized by William S. Jevons. Although Jevons was an economist and logician, his work on the philosophy of science had some impact on psychology's history (Annin et al., 1968). In his book *The Principles of Science* Jevons (1877/1900) held that

> it would be an error to suppose that the great discoverer seizes at once upon the truth, or has any unerring method of divining it. In all probability the errors of the great mind exceed in number those of the less vigorous one. Fertility of imagination and abundance of guesses at truth are among the first requisites of discovery; but the erroneous guesses must be many times as numerous as those that prove well founded. The weakest analogies, the most whimsical notions, the most apparently absurd theories, may pass through the teeming brain, and no record remain of more than the hundredth part. The truest theories involve suppositions which are inconceivable, and no limit can really be placed to the freedom of hypotheses. (p. 577)

Of course, the concept of trial and error has a significant place in psychology's history. E. L. Thorndike based his classic doctoral dissertation on this idea, and it plays an important role in many behaviorist theories of learning. Especially important is its place in Skinner's theory of operant conditioning. *Operants* are trials that are reinforced only if they are not erroneous. Skinner also extended the process to encompass behaviors far more complex than kittens escaping puzzle boxes or rats pressing levers to get food pellets—including creativity (Skinner, 1959). One of his students, Robert Epstein (1990, 1991), has even developed the trail-and-error process into a generativity theory that can successfully account for the insight process observed in Wolfgang Köhler's (1925) classic studies of problem solving in chimpanzees. Just as significant is that Skinner (1938) explicitly linked this process to Darwin's theory of evolution, according to which a variation-selection process is presumed to drive the origin of species. Hence, trial and error in the creative process may be considered a form of behavioral Darwinism (Dennett, 1995). Other notable psychologists have argued the same point from nonbehavioristic perspectives. For example, Donald Campbell (1960) took this position in his blind-variation and selective-retention model of creative thought, a model later integrated with contemporary personality theory by Hans Eysenck (1995). Also, as I noted in chapter 4, this Darwinian concept of the creative process has been developed into mathematical models that explain many crucial aspects of scientific careers, such as the stochastic nature of the relation between quantity and quality of output (Simonton, 1997b, 1999b). Hence, it seems clear that any successful model of scientific discovery must incorporate some kind of trial-and-error mechanism.

Free Association

Simon and his colleagues might argue that their discovery programs already include some variation-selection process (see, e.g., Langley et al., 1987). This is true, but in an extremely constrained, non-Darwinian fashion. Just examine how BACON went about discovering Kepler's third law, which holds that the cube of a planet's distance from the sun (s^3) is proportional to the square of the planet's period of rotation squared (q^2); that is, $s^3 = kq^2$, where k is a constant. BACON is programmed to find the relation between two variables by identifying the functions for each of the variables that produce a constant ratio. In this case, the program must find a function f_1 of the distance and another function f_2 of the period such that $f_1(s)/f_2(q)$ returns about the same quotient k across all observations. It first tries the ratio of the linear functions, then the ratio of one linear and one quadratic, then the ratio of two quadratics, and so on, until the program finds that the ratio of a cubic to a quadratic returns a constant. Note that this procedure is predetermined rather than random. Furthermore, this same trial-and-error procedure would run into obstacles if BACON were given data for Fechner's law.

An authentic Darwinian trial-and-error process would be much less constrained. William James (1880) made this point clear in an essay on his own Darwinian view of the creative process:

Instead of thoughts of concrete things patiently following one another in a beaten track of habitual suggestion, we have the most abrupt cross-cuts and transitions from one idea to another, the most rarefied abstractions and discriminations, the most unheard of combination of elements, the subtlest associations of analogy; in a word, we seem suddenly introduced into a seething cauldron of ideas, where everything is fizzling and bobbling about in a state of bewildering activity, where partnerships can be joined or loosened in an instant, treadmill routine is unknown, and the unexpected seems only law. (p. 456)

A bit later, physicist Ernst Mach (1896) made a similar point from an entirely different perspective. In an article titled "On the Part Played by Accident in Invention and Discovery" he first noted the need for a scientist to have "a powerfully developed *mechanical* memory, which recalls vividly and faithfully old situations, [which] is sufficient for avoiding definite particular dangers, or for taking advantage of definite particular opportunities" (p. 167). However, he also added that

more is required for the development of *inventions*. More extensive chains of images are necessary here, the excitation by mutual contact of widely different trains of ideas, a more powerful, more manifold, and richer connection of the contents of memory, a more powerful and impressionable psychical life, heightened by use. (p. 167)

Mach then emphasized that it is

from the teeming, swelling host of fancies which a free and high-flown imagination calls forth, suddenly that particular form arises to the light which harmonises perfectly with the ruling idea, mood, or design. Then it is that which has resulted slowly as the result of a gradual selection, appears as if it were the outcome of a deliberate act of creation. (p. 174)

The process advocated by both James and Mach is clearly akin to the free-associative process discussed by Sigmund Freud. Freud himself believed that creativity required the ability to suspend judgment to so as to generate "freely rising" ideas. For instance, in the *Interpretation of Dreams* Freud (1900/ 1952) quotes at length from a letter that Friedrich Schiller, the great poet and dramatist, had written to a friend who had complained about his "lack of creative power" (p. 181). According to Schiller,

The reason for your complaint lies, it seems to me, in the constraint which your intellect imposes on your imagination. . . . Apparently it is not good—and indeed it hinders the creative work of the mind—if the intellect examines too closely the ideas already pouring in, as it were, at the gates. Regarded in isolation, an idea may be quite insignificant, and venturesome in the extreme, but it may acquire importance from an idea which follows it; perhaps, in a certain collocation with other ideas, which may seem equally absurd, it may be capable of furnishing a very serviceable link. The intellect cannot judge all these ideas unless it can retain them until it has considered them in connection with these other ideas. In the case of a creative mind, it seems to me, the intellect has withdrawn its watchers from the gates, and the ideas rush in pell-mell, and only then does it review and inspect the multitude. (quoted in Freud, 1900/1952, p. 181)

Schiller clearly describes here a variation-selection process in which first the ideas are generated willy-nilly, and only in a second stage does the tumultuous multitude undergo selection and further development.

If scientific discovery depends on such a free-association process, then it should be possible to demonstrate that highly creative scientists tend to generate unusual associations. A common way of verifying this hypothesis is to use some word-association test. It was Francis Galton who first introduced such tests into psychological science, and several other notables, such as James McKeen Cattell and Carl Jung, have proven their utility. More recently, Harrison Gough (1976) showed that the ability to produce unusual associations is positively correlated with scientific creativity. Especially interesting is the striking tendency for Nobel laureates in the sciences to provide words that are opposites, antonyms rather than synonyms (Rothenberg, 1983). Although Rothenberg's (1983) study did not include any laureate psychologists, it still suggests that to attain scientific greatness in the discipline may require the cognitive capacity to pursue unexpected, even contradictory trains of thought. Compatible results have been found using different instruments. For instance, a study of 40 eminent scientists (including 4 Nobel laureates) indicated that those who most consistently produced high-impact articles tended to be those who generated the highest number of responses to the inkblots of the Rorschach test (Root-Bernstein, Bernstein, & Garnier, 1993).

Just as James, Mach, and Freud claimed, the capacity for making great discoveries depends, in part, on the mental ability to produce a profusion of uncommon associations.

Imagery

The discovery programs constructed by Herbert Simon and his colleagues suffer from another drawback. With only one minor exception (Cheng & Simon, 1995), these computer models depend on logic statements (symbolic verbal propositions) rather than sensory imagery. Yet great scientists frequently report that their breakthrough ideas arrived by means of mental images, whether visual, auditory, or kinesthetic (Hadamard, 1945; Rothenberg, 1987). This use of imagery is amply documented in Max Wertheimer's (1945/1982) classic book *Productive Thinking*. While Wertheimer was at the University of Berlin, he became friends with fellow professor Albert Einstein, who related the thought processes by which he arrived at the theory of relativity. The original impetus came from highly visual thought experiments, such as the following;

What if one were to run after a ray of light? What if one were riding on a beam? If one were to run after a ray of light as it travels, would its velocity thereby be decreased? If one were to run fast enough, would it no longer move at all? (Wertheimer, 1945/1982, p. 169)

These questions were resolved only by what Einstein called "combinatory play" with "visual and motor" images "before there is any connection with logical construction in words or other kinds of signs which can be communicated to others" (quoted in Hadamard, 1945, p. 142). "The words or the language, as they are written or spoken, do not seem to play any role in my mechanism of thought," said Einstein (quoted in Hadamard, 1945, p. 142).

As a consequence, words and logic often come only later, as a literal afterthought. This means that discoveries that arrived by means of imagery must later be translated into words and logic. This is not always easy. According to Einstein, "conventional words or other signs have to be sought for laboriously only in a secondary stage, when the mentioned associative play is sufficiently established and can be reproduced at will" (quoted in Hadamard, 1945, p. 143). Francis Galton, who pioneered the study of visual imagery as well as word associations, reported a similar two-step process:

It is a serious drawback to me in writing, and still more in explaining myself, that I do not so easily think in words as otherwise. It often happens that after being hard at work, and having arrived at results that are perfectly clear and satisfactory to myself, when I try to express them in language I feel that I must begin by putting myself upon quite another intellectual plane. I have to translate my thoughts into a language that does not run very evenly with them. I therefore waste a vast deal of time in seeking for appropriate words and phrases, and am conscious, when required to speak on a sudden, of being often very obscure through mere verbal maladroitness, and not through want of clearness of perception. That is one of the small annoyances of my life. (quoted in Hadamard, 1945, p. 69)

Sometimes the images that rushed through Galton's head would be auditory rather than visual, but instead of sensible verbal ideas the images would sound "as the notes of a song might accompany thought" (quoted in Hadamard, 1945, p. 69). In other words, ideas would often be linked according to rhyme, alliteration, and other illogical sonic similarities, not unlike what often happens to people experiencing the tip-of-the-tongue phenomenon (R. W. Brown & McNeill, 1966).

One remarkable asset of this type of thinking is that ideas can emerge with fewer constraints than would be the case when the thoughts are confined to words. Creative scientists can generate totally anticipated juxtapositions of ideas. This is one reason why dreams are sometimes credited with the origination of major scientific breakthroughs (Koestler, 1964). As Freud (1929/1952) noted, the logical limitations imposed by secondary-process thinking are inactive during sleep, permitting diverse images to emerge in a manner that would otherwise contradict common sense. A dramatic example is how Nobel laureate Otto Loewi came up with the crucial experiment needed to demonstrate the chemical transmission of nerve impulses (i.e., neurotransmitters). When the idea appeared to him in a dream on Easter Sunday, 1920, Loewi rushed to the laboratory to carry it out. This was a fortunate decision, because the idea itself was pretty crazy. "If carefully considered in the day-time, I would undoubtedly have rejected the kind of experiment I performed. . . . It was good fortune that at the moment of the hunch I did not think but acted immediately" (Loewi, 1960, p. 18).

I hasten to point out that the ideas generated by such wild imagery do not always yield great discoveries. On the contrary, their function is more comparable to the mutations of Darwinian theory, most of which prove maladaptive (Simonton, 1999b). It is for this reason that scientific creativity is positively associated with the production of moderately uncommon associations, but not with the production of extremely bizarre associations (Gough, 1976). This also explains why drug-induced altered states of consciousness are not productive of major scientific insights. The illogical juxtapositions of ideas may fail to pass muster once normal consciousness appears and the critical faculties are reactivated. As William James (1902) reported in his *Varieties of Religious Experience,*

> nitrous oxide and ether, especially nitrous oxide, when sufficiently diluted with air, stimulate the mystical consciousness in an extraordinary degree. Depth upon depth of truth seems revealed to the inhaler. This truth fades out, however, or escapes, at the moment of coming to; and if any words remain over in which it seemed to cloth itself, they prove to be the veriest nonsense. (p. 387)

There is even some scientific doubt about the extent to which a drug-induced mind can generate ideas acceptable to artistic criteria, which are presumably less logically restrictive than those of science. For instance, although Samuel Taylor Coleridge claimed to have conceived his famous poem the "Pleasure Dome of Kublai Khan" in an opium stupor, scholarly examination of his notebooks indicates otherwise (E. Schneider, 1953). Even in the arts, the ideational variations should be free, and probably even more free than in the sciences—but not utterly random.

Incubation

So far I have written as if the whole discovery process were conscious. Trial and error, free association, and imagery all look like operations that should occupy the mind, yet great scientists often report that much of the mental work that leads to discoveries occurs at more unconscious levels (Hadamard, 1945; Poincaré, 1921). Sometimes this takes the form of so-called "imageless thought" (Roe, 1953b). "I just seem to vegetate; something is going on, I don't know what it is," reported one eminent scientist (Roe, 1953b, p. 144). Imageless thought is especially likely to take place just prior to a major insight. Often some kind unconscious information processing occurs over a much longer period of time, during what is most commonly called the *incubation period* of creativity (Wallas, 1926). A characteristic illustration may be found in *An Autobiography*, by Herbert Spencer (1904), the early evolutionist and author of the 1855 *Principles of Psychology*. A friend of his, George Eliot (Mary Ann Evans), expressed surprise that Spencer had no wrinkles on his forehead, given how much mental effort he must have engaged in when writing his great books. Spencer responded that

> it has never been my way to set before myself a problem and puzzle out an answer. The conclusions at which I have from time to time arrived, have not been arrived at as solutions of questions raised; but have been arrived at unawares—each as the ultimate outcome of a body of thoughts which slowly grew from a germ. Some direct observation, or some fact met with in reading, would dwell with me: apparently because I had a sense of its significance. It was not that there arose a distinct consciousness of its general meaning; but rather that there was a kind of instinctive interest in those facts which have general meanings. When accumulation of instances had given body to a generalization, reflexion would induce the vague conception at first framed to a more definite conception; and perhaps difficulties or anomalies passed over for a while, but eventually forcing themselves on attention, might cause a needful qualification and a truer shaping of the thought. . . . And thus, little by little, in obtrusive ways, without conscious intention or appreciable effort, there would grow up a coherent and organized theory. (pp. 463–464)

Spencer (1904) went on to say that conscious, deliberate mental process should actually prove counterproductive:

> The determined effort causes perversion of thought. When endeavouring to recollect some name or thing which had been forgotten, it frequently happens that the name or thing sought will not arise in consciousness; but when attention is relaxed, the missing name or thing often suggests itself. While thought continues to be forced down certain wrong turnings which had originally been taken, the search is in vain; but with the cessation of strain the true association of ideas has an opportunity of asserting itself. And, similarly, it may be that while an effort to arrive forthwith at some answer to a problem, acts as a distorting factor in consciousness and causes error, a quiet contemplation of the problem from time to time, allows those proclivities of thought which have probably been caused unawares by experiences, to make themselves felt, and to guide the mind to the right conclusion. (pp. 464–465)

It is significant that there exists experimental evidence that the imposition of conscious information processing can directly interfere with the solution of problems that require insight (Schooler & Melcher, 1995).

Another great psychologist who left extensive reports regarding the incubation period is Hermann von Helmholtz (1891/1971). He also described in some detail the circumstances in which incubation is most likely to come to a successful conclusion:

> As I have often found myself in the unpleasant position of having to wait for useful ideas, I have had some experience as to when and where they come to me which may perhaps be useful to others. They often steal into one's train of thought without their significance being at first understood; afterward some accidental circumstance shows how and under what conditions they originated. Sometimes they are present without our knowing whence they came. In other cases they occur suddenly, without effort, like an inspiration. As far as my experience goes, they never come to a tired brain or at the desk.
>
> I have always had to turn my problems about in my mind in all directions, so that I could see their turns and complications and think them through freely without writing them down. To reach that stage, however, was usually not possible without long preliminary work. Then, after the fatigue of the work had passed away, an hour of perfect bodily repose and quiet comfort was necessary before the fruitful ideas came. Often they came in the morning upon waking . . . But, . . . they were most apt to come when I was leisurely climbing about on wooded hills in sunny weather. The slightest quantity of alcohol seemed to frighten them away. (pp. 474–475)

I believe it crucial to any evaluation of discovery programs that they have no counterpart to the incubation process. These computer models uniformly entail an explicit and deliberate step-by-step logical analysis, persistently going through the programmed instructions until the problem is solved, if it can be under the given algorithms. The programs always work on one problem at a time, never straying from the data provided. Nothing is ever put on the back burner, to be replaced by some other problem, when some obstacle obstructs immediate solution. The whole thought process is obsessively one track, with no allowance for subliminal influences and extraneous inputs.

Yet, as I mentioned in chapter 5, great scientists tend to work simultaneously on several projects, sometimes concentrating on one, then another, going back and forth between incubation and deliberate effort (Hargens, 1978; R. S. Root-Bernstein et al., 1993; R. J. Simon, 1974; M. S. Taylor, Locke, Lee, & Gist, 1984). This parallel processing means that the progression of ideas and facts in one project will often set off a train of associations in some seemingly unrelated project, priming solutions that might not appear otherwise. For example, one detailed study of Faraday's laboratory notebooks revealed the existence of considerable cross-talk between separate projects (Tweney, 1990).

Moreover, the discovery programs do not take vacations or engage in other mundane activities that do not obviously involve the question for a solution. Helmholtz is far from the only great scientist to report how often new ideas come when someone is *not* working (Boden, 1991). Sometimes it is simply a matter of having the opportunity to become lost in thought or to daydream, as often happens when traveling. This is illustrated by the occasion when Charles Darwin arrived at his solution to the problem of the origin of species: "I can remember the very spot in the road, whilst in my carriage, when to my joy the solution occurred to me" (F. Darwin, 1892/1958, p. 43). The value of these mundane activities goes beyond just having the chance to meditate. During these irrelevant excursions or distractions the individual often receives an influx of extraneous stimuli that end up priming a major discovery. For instance, Johann Gutenberg had been trying to figure out how to mass produce Bibles for some time before he unexpectedly found the solution when, during the incubation period, he participated in the wine harvest—and found the solution he was seeking in the wine press (Koestler, 1964).

Serendipity

Judging from the preceding discussion, discovery programs will not capture the empirical complexity of the discovery process until they are designed to simulate the lives and careers actually observed in such scientists. A crucial part of that simulation must entail the allowance for the intrusion of accidental events. This necessity is made apparent in Walter Cannon's (1940) article "The Role of Chance in Discovery," in which he provides many examples of serendipitous findings in the history of science (also see Austin, 1978; Shapiro, 1986). Among these cases is Luigi Galvani's discovery of animal electricity and Claude Bernard's discovery that blood circulation is under nervous control. Cannon also provided an illustration from the accidental observation that led to his concept of homeostasis:

> About forty-three years ago, shortly after the x-rays were discovered, I was using the mysteriously penetrating light to look into animals in order to watch the little known processes of digestion. The churning and mixing of the food was clearly visible. Occasionally, however, my purposes were wholly checked because the motions came to a dead stop. That was a great annoyance; it seemed very strange, and I was at a loss to account for it. But in scientific investigation, as in daily living, obstacles may yield important values. I soon noticed that the cessation of the digestive activities was associated with signs of anxiety or other emotional disturbance. Could it be that I was seeing the harmful effects of worry on the organs which serve to make the food useful to the body? That proved to be true, for when I petted the animals reassuringly the churning waves promptly started again, and when excitement was induced the waves promptly stopped. . . . It was the beginning of many years of research on bodily functions—research which ultimately led to insight into the agen-

cies of our organism which maintain the stability of the extraordinarily unstable material of which we are composed and which give us freedom to live and carry on our various activities untrammeled by external heat or cold, by flight to high altitudes or by the internal changes produced by strenuous efforts in which we may engage. The observation of the effects of worry on digestion also resulted ultimately in a suggestive concept of the nature of emotional excitement, and, furthermore, in the demonstration of a chemical agent which acts as an intermediary between nerves and muscles when muscles are made to contract or relax. (p. 208)

Although anomalous events occur all the time, not all scientists appear capable of converting them into serendipitous discoveries. Indeed, many lucky discoveries "were seen numbers of times before they were noticed," as Ernst Mach (1896, p. 167) put it. One reason why many scientists miss out is that they do not have the requisite cognitive openness and behavioral flexibility. Not only has empirical research shown that openness and flexibility are positively correlated with scientific achievement (Feist, 1998; Feist & Gorman, 1998), but also these virtues have been repeatedly emphasized by many significant figures from psychology's past. Thus, Cannon (1940) stressed "the importance of avoiding rigid adherence to fixed ideas" (p. 208), and Skinner (1959) emphasized "a first principle not formally recognized by scientific methodologists: when you run onto something interesting, drop everything else and study it" (p. 363).

In addition, this flexibility and openness should be coupled with ample knowledge about the field. "If the psychical life is subjected to the incessant influences of a powerful and rich experience," said Mach (1896, p. 171), "then every representative element in the mind is connected with so many others that the actual and natural course of the thoughts is easily influenced and determined by insignificant circumstances, which accidentally are decisive." In fact, when these qualities are joined with an active curiosity, a great scientist may actively seek out serendipitous discoveries rather than passively waiting for them to happen. When Charles Darwin specified what he thought to be his best intellectual asset, he said "I think that I am superior to the common run of men in noticing things which easily escape attention" (quoted in S. E. Hyman, 1963, p. 373). This virtue was confirmed by his son Francis Darwin, a frequent scientific collaborator of his father. Francis took special note of his father's

> instinct for arresting exceptions: it was as though he were charged with theorizing power ready to flow into any channel on the slightest disturbance, so that no fact, however small, could avoid releasing a stream of theory, and thus the fact became magnified into importance. In this way it naturally happened that many untenable theories occurred to him; but fortunately his richness of imagination was equalled by his power of judging and condemning the thoughts that occurred to him. He was just to his theories, and did not condemn them unheard; and so it happened that

he was willing to test what would seem to most people not at all worth testing. These rather wild trials he called "fool's experiments," and enjoyed extremely. (F. Darwin, 1892/1958, p. 101)

To date, discovery programs lack the openness, flexibility, and rich knowledge base that would be required to simulate such serendipitous events.

Inspiration

It looks like it may be some time before computer models will successfully simulate the discovery process in great psychologists. However, I am by no means advocating vitalism of any kind. I personally believe that it is possible that computers might some day produce a convincing simulation—at least, such should be possible in principle. A successful discovery program would have to become far more complex, perhaps even more complicated than can be supported with current computer hardware and software. Discovery programs that make discoveries deserving of a Nobel prize may be a long way off, yet should that time come it would be interesting to know whether these programs would simulate only the cognitive side of discovery, leaving out the emotional side. Human discoverers, when they encounter a great new idea, often report reactions not unlike what Abraham Maslow (1970) called *peak experiences*. These reactions entail both cognitive and affective components. On the cognitive side there often appears a sense of unity, integration, synthesis, or harmony, combined with a focused attention so intense that the individual forfeits awareness of self. On the affective side there frequently emerges an emotional intensity that combines somewhat paradoxically a tremendous elation and excitement with a feeling of peace and relief. As might be expected, these cognitive and affective facets are often so powerful that these illuminations are described in highly rhapsodic terms. The philosopher Friedrich Nietzsche (1927) wrote that

one can hardly reject completely the idea that one is the mere incarnation, or mouthpiece, or medium of some almighty power. The notion of revelation describes the condition quite simply; by which I mean that something profoundly convulsive and disturbing suddenly becomes visible and audible with indescribable definiteness and exactness. One hears—one does not seek; one takes—one does not ask who gives: a thought flashes out like lightning, inevitably without hesitation—I have never had any choice about it. There is an ecstacy whose terrific tension is sometimes released by a flood of tears, during which one's progress varies from involuntary impetuosity to involuntary slowness. There is the feeling that one is utterly out of hand, with the most distinct consciousness of an infinitude of shuddering thrills that pass through from one head to foot;—there is a profound happiness in which the most painful and gloomy feelings are not discordant in effect, but are required as necessary colors in this overflow of light. There is an instinct for rhythmic relations which embraces an entire world of forms. . . . Everything occurs quite without volition, as if in an eruption of freedom, independence, power and divinity. The spontaneity of the images and similes is most remarkable; one loses all perception of what is imagery and simile; everything offers itself as the most immediate, exact, and simple means of expression. (pp. 896–897)

Nietzsche (1927) admitted that "this is *my* experience of inspiration" (p. 897) and that others may not have exactly the same phenomenological encounter. Yet it would be interesting to ask: When a computer program finally makes a contribution worthy of citation in the annals of science, what or who will exhibit the excitement of discovery? Will it be the program that screams out "Eureka!" and gets goose pimples all over? Or will it be the human psychologist who wrote the software whose heart skips a beat and sheds tears of joy? If the computer cannot experience the elation of great discovery, can it still be considered a great scientist?

INTERDISCIPLINARY CONTRASTS

Up to this point I have been treating the intellect of great scientists in a highly generic fashion. I have made no effort to distinguish the cognitive attributes and processes in psychology from those in other sciences. Indeed, I have not even attempted to separate scientific creativity from artistic creativity. This global treatment is compatible with Havelock Ellis's (1926) claim that "the characteristics of men of genius [are] probably to a large extent independent of the particular field their ability is shown in" (p. xv). This notion also appears consistent with the idea, already noted more than once, that generalized intelligence, or Spearman's *g*, underlies performance on a wide diversity of tasks—even those that pertain to the attainment of greatness. Nevertheless, there are several reasons for believing that this generic view of genius is highly oversimplified. For one thing, many researchers have argued that there exist more than one type of intelligence. For example, Howard Gardner (1983, 1998) discerned at least seven intelligences, including one specifically germane to psychology, namely, intrapersonal intelligence, as represented by Sigmund Freud (Gardner, 1993). Another list was suggested by L. L. Thurstone (1938), who attempted to disprove Spearman's *g* by extracting factors representing several independent "primary mental abilities" (verbal, number, spatial, perceptual, memory, reasoning, and word fluency). Even more provocative is J. P. Guilford's (1967) structure-of-intellect model, which hypothesizes 120 distinguishable abilities. What makes Guilford's model all the more striking is that he was a doctoral student of Edward Titchener, a psychologist who dedicated his career to the study of the generalized human mind completely divorced from individual differences.

There is also ample anecdotal evidence that various intellectual aptitudes may be rather differently distributed even among the greatest minds. Helmholtz (1891/1971) once confessed that

> a defect among my mental powers showed itself, however, almost early: I had a poor memory for unrelated facts. The first indication of this was, I believe, the difficulty I had in distinguishing between left and right. Later, when I began the study of languages at school, I had greater difficulty than others in learning vocabularies, irregular grammatical forms, and peculiar forms of expression. . . . This defect has, of course, grown and has been a vexation to me in my later years. (p. 468)

As observed earlier, Darwin suffered from a similar linguistic incapacity, and yet Helmholtz, unlike Darwin, was quite proficient in mathematics and physics. Hence, different great scientists can have rather contrasting cognitive profiles in a manner more akin to Thurstone's primary abilities than to Spearman's g. To some significant extent, moreover, these profile differences may reflect the distinct intellectual requirements of various scientific disciplines. A physicist and physiologist such as Helmholtz may need a different set of abilities than a biologist and geologist such as Darwin. A psychologist such as Titchener, on the other hand, had a definite capacity for languages. Besides having sufficient command of German to translate Wundt into English, Titchener knew Greek and Latin, could read French and Italian, had some familiarity with Sanskrit, and even ventured into Arabic and Chinese.

Accordingly, I next examine interdisciplinary differences in cognitive attributes of scientists. In particular, I review how scientists from different domains might vary according to intelligence, imagery, and versatility. This review should contribute to the readers' understanding of how psychology fits in with other sciences.

Intelligence

The first systematic examination of how intelligence varies across achievement domains is Cox's (1926) contribution to L. M. Terman's *Genetic Studies of Genius*. Table 6.2 shows the mean estimated IQs that Cox calculated for scientists, philosophers, nonfiction authors, and religious leaders. The last two domains are included for comparison purposes, with the nonfiction-author category encompassing essayists, historians, critics, and so on. It is evident that the philosophers tend to enjoy the highest IQs of the three groups, followed by the scientists, nonfiction authors, and religious leaders. Other domains included in Cox's sample of 301 individuals tended to have even lower averages; for example, the corresponding scores for artists were 122, 140, 135, and 160, respectively. Cox's results were replicated in a later historiometric investigation, which found the following mean IQs: phi-

TABLE 6.2
Historiometric IQs: Uncorrected and Corrected
IQ Scores for Ages 0–16 and 17–26

Achievement domain	Uncorrected		Corrected		
	0–16	17–26	0–16	17–26	n
Scientists	135	155	152	175	39
Philosophers	147	170	156	180	22
Nonfiction authors	139	160	148	170	43
Religious leaders	132	150	145	170	23

Note. The uncorrected and corrected means are taken from various statistics reported in Cox (1926).

losophers, 173; scientists, 164; nonfiction authors, 162; religious leaders, 159; and artists, 150 (Walberg et al., 1978). Neither Cox's study nor Walberg et al.'s (1978) study found a group whose IQ means exceeded those found in the two domains most intimately linked to psychology: philosophy and science.

Neither of these two studies (Cox, 1926; Walberg et al., 1978) had subsamples sufficiently large to examine the expected IQs in scientific subdisciplines. To make such fine disciplinary discriminations one needs to turn to psychometric studies of contemporary samples. A pioneering researcher in this area was Anne Roe (1953a), whose *The Making of a Scientist* can be considered the first important monograph on the psychology of scientific genius since Galton's (1874) *English Men of Science* (Mowafy & Martin, 1988). Roe studied 64 eminent American scientists: 22 physicists, subdivided into experimentalists and theoreticians; 20 biologists, including her husband, paleontologist and evolutionist George Gaylord Simpson; and 22 social scientists, namely, 8 anthropologists and 14 psychologists. Members of this last group were selected on the advice of such notable psychologists as E. G. Boring, Donald B. Lindsey, Ernest R. Hilgard, and Lewis M. Terman. Because the 64 were obviously very bright, Roe decided it might be impertinent to have them take a regular IQ test such as the WAIS. As a consequence, she made up some special tests with the help of the Educational Testing Service, the same group responsible for the Scholastic Aptitude Test. Three tests were so devised: verbal, spatial, and mathematical. The instruments were administered to all 64, with the exception that the physicists did not take the mathematical test, because Roe soon realized that it was still too easy for them.

Table 6.3 shows the resulting IQs (converted from the raw scores that Roe [1953a] provided). In terms of verbal intelligence, the illustrious psychologists were clearly in the middle of the pack: slightly lower than the anthropologists and theoretical physicists but slightly higher than the biologists, and much higher than the experimental physicists. Spatial intelligence is distributed a bit differently across the scientific disciplines, with the psychologists doing better than the anthropologists and biologists, the same as

TABLE 6.3
Psychometric IQs: Means and Ranges for
64 Eminent American Scientists

Achievement domain	Verbal		Spatial		Mathematical	
	M	Range	M	Range	M	Range
Psychologists	163	133–176	141	127–161	162	139–194
Anthropologists	165	150–175	135	123–151	142	128–154
Biologists	162	138–176	137	123–164	165	133–194
Experimental physicists	154	121–174	141	123–161		
Theoretical physicists	168	158–177	149	149–161		

Note. The standardized means and ranges were converted from the raw scores given in Roe (1952).

the experimental physicists, and not quite as well as the theoretical physicists. Finally, the eminent psychologists displayed about the same mathematical intelligence as did the biologists and substantially more than the anthropologists—by 20 points, the largest interdomain difference. No doubt the showing of the notable scientists in these three disciplines would pale in comparison to the physicists, had they taken this test. It must be noted that the within-groups variation within each scientific domain is very large, far larger than the between-groups variation. Hence, considerable overlap exists in the IQ distributions.

This last conclusion is reinforced by another investigation in which the WAIS actually was administered to scientists hailing from distinct disciplines (J. Gibson & Light, 1967). Although these scientists were not singled out for their eminence, they did hold appointments at a highly eminent university, Cambridge, and accordingly can be considered more than run of the mill. The social scientists in the sample had a mean IQ of 122, which matches that for the agricultural sciences but is otherwise lower than was found for the mathematicians, biochemists, and chemists (all 130); the physicists (128); the medical scientists (127); and the biologists (126). Nonetheless, the ranges were again large, including 112–132 for the social scientists, 112–136 for the physicists, 113–135 for the biological scientists, 116–134 for the medical scientists, and 124–136 for the mathematicians. The distributions overlap considerably.

Although Roe (1953a) did not provide much in the way of details, she did separate out the experimental psychologists from the rest of the distinguished psychologists in her sample. She found that they scored higher in spatial and mathematical intelligence, but lower in verbal intelligence, compared to their disciplinary colleagues. This contrast parallels what was found for the physicists, with the theorists being more verbal and the experimentalists more spatial. Hence, there is some tentative evidence that the IQ profile corresponds to the subdiscipline in which a psychologist is most likely to achieve distinction.

Imagery

Earlier in this chapter I noted the importance of imagery in the creative process. In fact, eminent individuals often display a rich imagination from childhood (McCurdy, 1960). At the same time, the contrasting IQ profiles across scientific domains suggest that the specific nature of this imagery might vary according to discipline. Contrasts in verbal and spatial intelligence, in particular, would seem to correspond with distinct modalities.

Roe's (1953a) study of 64 eminent scientists actually found such differences. She specifically asked them to report what mental processes they were most likely to use when coming up with their creative ideas. Scientists in all disciplines reported some amount of visual imagery, but that of eminent social scientists differed conspicuously from the other scientists in its specific nature. For the biologists and physicists, visual imagery could take the form of concrete, often three-dimensional images; geometrical and other types of diagrams; and visualized symbols, whereas for the social scientists such thoughts were confined to concrete images rather than abstract diagrams or symbols. Moreover, only 14% of the social scientists reported such concrete imagery, in contrast to 27% of the theoretical physicists, 55% of the biologists, and 78% of the experimental physicists. On the other hand, it is evident that the social scientists depended much more heavily on auditory and verbal imagery. More than half (52%) reported that they verbalized their thinking, whereas such verbal imagery was experienced by only 36% of the theoretical physicists, 30% of the biologists, and none of the experimental physicists. The physicists, however, were more likely to verbalize mathematical formulas—11% of the experimentalists and 27% of the theoreticians—something neither the biologists (0%) nor the social scientists (5%) were much inclined to do, if at all.

The more prominent verbal imagery of the social scientists was also revealed in their responses to the Thematic Apperception Test (TAT; Roe, 1953a): They tended to tell much longer stories, indicative of greater verbal fluency. Although the social scientists appear to be mostly verbalizers, there are two interesting twists. First, 19% of the social scientists reported kinesthetic imagery, an experience claimed by none of the other groups. Second, 72% reported imageless thought, relative to 67% of the experimental physicists, 55% of the theoretical physicists, and 35% of the biologists.

Because Roe (1953a) did not separate the social scientists into their subgroups, it is difficult to say to what degree these statistics reflect the cognitive attributes of the anthropologists rather than the psychologists. However, the psychologists outnumbered the anthropologists by almost 2 to 1, and so the reliance on verbalizations, kinesthetic imagery, and imageless thought probably holds for great psychologists. It would also be interesting to know how the experimental psychologists differed from their colleagues. Experimental physicists rely more on visual imagery than theoretical physicists, so the same contrast might apply to psychology as well. It would also be worth knowing whether the type of imagery influences the particular school of thought to which a psychologist is most likely to subscribe. For example, psychoanalysts appear to be intuitively disposed toward verbalizations, Gestalt psychologists toward visualizations, and Hullian behaviorists to mathematical and symbolic representations.

Versatility

Cox's (1926) 301 geniuses had another remarkable cognitive characteristic besides a high IQ: an exceptional intellectual versatility. Leonardo da Vinci was a painter, sculptor, engineer, musician, and scientist; Blaise Pascal a mathematician, physicist, inventor, philosopher, and essayist; and Johann Goethe a poet, novelist, dramatist, botanist, and government official. A secondary analysis of Cox's data indicated that most of her creators and leaders exhibited above-average attainments in 5–10 achievement domains (R. K. White, 1931). The highest level of versatility was displayed by the nonfiction writers, leaders, and philosophers, followed by the scientists, mathematicians, religious leaders, and fiction writers. Soldiers, artists, and especially musicians were by far the least versatile. Furthermore, certain types of achievement tended to cluster together. One such cluster consisted of science, mathematics, medicine, invention and, to a lesser extent, art.

Neither is versatility a thing of the past. Despite any trends toward specialization, more modern luminaries show a similar proclivity. According to one study of more than 1,000 20th-century notables,

> 10% showed competency or proficiency in three or more separate fields (or two or more different media within at least one of two fields); 28% in two separate fields; 43% in two or more related media of expression within a particular field; and 19% in only one medium or none at all. (Ludwig, 1995, p. 112)

Similarly, a survey of eminent scholars found that more than two thirds kept up with research in at least one field outside their own, where *keeping up* often meant publishing in that field as well (R. J. Simon, 1974). Philosophers boasted the widest range of active interests—statistics, physics, biology, psychology, and literature among them.

More important, the degree of versatility is positively associated with the degree of distinction achieved. This positive correlation was first demonstrated for 120 scientists and 123 writers 10 years after Cox's (1926) study (Raskin, 1936) and was later confirmed in a secondary analysis of Cox's 301 geniuses 50 years after her pioneering investigation (Simonton, 1976a). The correlation between versatility and eminence—the latter again based on James McKeen Cattell's (1903c) rankings—was .23. In addition, versatility correlated around .30 with Cox's IQ estimates, suggesting that versatility is a sign of the influx of Spearman's *g*. Comparable results are found with entirely different data sets. For instance, Manis (1951) found that the most influential social scientists are prone to express more interests in disciplines besides their own. Also, according to a historiometric study that I will describe in detail in chapter 15, the most eminent thinkers of Western civilization tended to make a name for themselves in multiple philosophical specialties (Simonton, 1976f). A lesser thinker might be satisfied by making a contribution to just epistemology, ontology, psychology, aesthetics, ethics, *or* social philosophy, but a truly great thinker will address virtually every major philosophical question that has dominated the history of ideas. Plato, Aristotle, Aquinas, Descartes, and Kant are prime examples.

The functional relation between versatility and greatness might actually be a bit more complex. According to a recent historiometric study of more than 2,250 scientists, a *U*-shaped function is superimposed over the positive linear relation, creating a *J*-curve between eminence and the number of fields in which important contributions were made (Sulloway, 1996); that is, the most famous are those who are extremely versatile, followed by those who were extremely specialized. Those who dabbled in just a couple of scientific domains attained the least renown. If you can't be a Charles Darwin, at least be a Gregor Mendel. It would be extremely interesting to learn whether this same *J*-curve holds for psychologists as well. Are the truly great psychologists those who made contributions to multiple domains, followed by extreme specialists, with those of more middling versatility suspended in a trough of relative obscurity somewhere between? If so, then the acquisition of a highly specialized expertise may more than compensate for any deficiencies in intellectual versatility.

7

DISPOSITION

Thus far I have focused on the intellectual attributes of great psychologists. This emphasis is most compatible with what Herbert Simon and many other cognitive psychologists have argued. They tend to see creativity as a special form of problem solving, a cognitive process. Indeed, many introductory psychology texts, if they discuss creativity at all, most often place it in some chapter devoted to human thinking. This orientation toward the creative process goes at least as far back as the Gestalt psychologists, such as Wolfgang Köhler and Max Wertheimer, who interpreted creative insights in terms of a perceptual restructuring process. Yet challenging this view is an entirely separate psychological tradition that conceives creativity in terms of disposition rather than cognition; that is, greatness may depend not so much on intellect as on personality (for reviews, see Barron & Harrington, 1981; Dellas & Gaier, 1970; Simonton, 1999a). Even if creative achievers think differently than the rest of us, the difference may spring from a more fundamental contrast in character. This alternative perspective also has distinguished representatives, such as Sigmund Freud, Carl Rogers, Abraham Maslow, R. B. Cattell, and Hans Eysenck.

It is fortunate that a considerable body of empirical research has accumulated on the personality characteristics of scientists, a subset of which is specifically devoted to psychologists, including those who have some claim to greatness. Better yet, comprehensive meta-analyses have already been published that have consolidated this vast literature into a set of secure empirical findings (most notably, Feist, 1998; Feist & Gorman, 1998). As a consequence, it is now possible to specify the characteristics of great psychologists with a fairly high degree of confidence. I begin by examining the diverse traits that have been associated with the attainment of eminence in psychology. I close by discussing a specific issue that has provoked much controversy, namely, whether creative geniuses have any tendency toward psychopathology.

TRAITS

A classic dictum of personality psychology is that "every man is in certain respects (a) like all other men, (b) like some other men, (c) like no other men" (Kluckhohn & Murray, 1953, p. 53). By the same token, each great psychologist is in some ways like other human beings and in other ways totally unique. Complicating matters all the more, great psychologists as a group can exhibit similarities and differences with respect to other groups of individuals. They may be compared with other historical figures or with other illustrious scientists, or they may be compared with their more obscure colleagues and even with the average human being. Each of these alternative comparison groups provides a contrasting basis for characterizing the personality profile of the typical luminary in psychology. Therefore, in attempting to portray the traits most typical of great psychologists, I take care to specify the baselines for the comparisons.

With that precaution in mind, the distinctive attributes of great psychologists may be said to fall into two broad categories: the motivational and the social.

Motivational Attributes

"Great men have great ambitions," claimed one history text (Lowry, 1982, p. 86), and the research literature concurs. Individuals who leave a mark on history almost invariably exhibit a profound desire to excel that is intimately coupled with the necessary drive and persistence to achieve the desired excellence (Ebersole & DeVogler-Ebersole, 1985; Walberg, Rasher, & Parkerson, 1980). Catharine Cox (1926) conducted the first empirical demonstration of this motivational attribute. She first abstracted from her original 301 geniuses a subset of 100 eminent creators and leaders for whom the biographical data were especially rich. The resulting subsample included several notables from psychology's history, such as Francis Bacon, René Descartes, Isaac Newton, Gottfried Leibniz, John Locke, Benjamin Franklin, Jean-Jacques Rousseau, Immanuel Kant, Johann Goethe, G. W. F. Hegel,

J. S. Mill, and Charles Darwin. Two independent judges then evaluated these luminaries on 67 character traits, as compared with other children their age. The 100 were distinguished by such attributes as "persistence," "tenacity of purpose," "perseverance in the face of obstacles," "ambition," and the "desire to excel." Moreover, Cox found evidence that this motivational attribute may prove more crucial than the intellectual capacities that were the original impetus for her whole investigation. In particular, she concluded "that high but not the highest intelligence, combined with the greatest degree of persistence, will achieve greater eminence than the highest degree of intelligence with somewhat less persistence" (p. 187, italics removed from entire quote).

Cox's (1926) pioneer study admittedly suffers from several drawbacks. The sample was small and the methodology retrospective. The character traits concerned childhood and adolescence rather than adulthood. Also, the sample included not a single individual who could be considered a psychologist in a more restricted sense. Even so, the same general conclusions have been made on the basis of studies that used contrasting samples and methods. In the specific case of science, not only are scientists more achievement oriented and driven, but also the more eminent scientists are more driven, achievement oriented, and ambitious than are their less distinguished colleagues (Feist & Gorman, 1998). Furthermore, studies that focus only on psychologists also demonstrate the significant role that exceptional motivation has in the attainment of distinction within the discipline (Wispé, 1963). For instance, Helmreich, Spence, and Pred (1988) found that the assessed achievement strivings of more than 100 contemporary psychologists were positively correlated with both the number of publications and the rate of citation within the discipline. Another survey of nearly 200 personality and social psychologists showed that publications and citations were both positively associated with orientations toward work and mastery (Helmreich, Spence, Beane, Lucker, & Matthews, 1980); that is, higher influence on the field is associated with the tendency to endorse such questionnaire items as "I like to work hard" and "I more often attempt tasks that I am not sure I can do than tasks I believe I can do" (Helmreich et al., 1980, p. 899).

The prolific output and productive longevity I discussed at great length in chapters 3 and 4 is apparently a function of the exceptional motivation notable psychologists bring to bear on their work (Blackburn, Behymer, & Hall, 1978). This drive takes the most concrete form in the exceptional amount of time they are willing to devote to research (Manis, 1951). Illustrious researchers usually spend 8–10 hr per day for 300–332 days per year (R. J. Simon, 1974). Great psychologists are no exception. As noted earlier, E. G. Boring could be placed in the upper ranks of highly productive psychologists. It should come as no surprise, then, to read the following passage in his autobiography:

I do drive perpetually for long-range goals, and my friends, my children, and my students know how I have talked about the eighty-hour week in the fifty-week year (the 4000-hour working year) and I have scorned those forty-hour academicians who take long summers off from work. I have no hobbies, except for a shop in my cellar. My vacations were never successful until I got a little study with a typewriter in it and I could answer eight letters a day and write up the waiting papers. (E. G. Boring, 1961, p. 14)

Boring's time commitment does not even represent the high point in the distribution of effort. Herbert Simon once reported to a colleague that he "spent about 100 hours per week for years doing the work for which [I] eventually won the Nobel Prize" (J. R. Hayes, 1989a, p. 137). That leaves less than 10 hr per day for Simon to have done everything else, such as eat and sleep!

How do these luminaries attain that magnitude of daily involvement in their research? Vladimir Bekhterev, the illustrious Russian psychiatrist, authored approximately 600 publications by working 18 hr per day, allotting only 5 hr of the remaining 6 to sleep. He would also accomplish a large amount of writing in bed, his wife sleeping next to him. Another bedtime worker was Edward L. Thorndike, who averaged about a publication per month during the course of his long career. According to his son, psychologist Robert L. Thorndike (1991), his father was

> in some ways the original workaholic, reading the *Encyclopaedia Britannica* in bed to locate good passages for reading comprehension tests, not because he was driven to it but because he would rather be getting or analyzing data than most anything else. (p. 151)

This qualification is important. Sometimes the motives of great psychologists have been characterized as most typical of the workaholic, coronary-prone Type A personality pattern (e.g., Matthews, Helmreich, Beane, & Lucker, 1980). Yet detailed analysis reveals that their drive and determination come from a rather different motivational core. The competitiveness, irritability, and impatience so central in conceiving the Type A personality are not what are associated with influential output; rather, the driving components are achievement, mastery, job involvement, and self-efficacy (Helmreich et al., 1988; M. S. Taylor, Locke, Lee, & Gist, 1984). As a result, eminent psychologists derive much more satisfaction from their research than do their less eminent colleagues (Chambers, 1964). This positive rather than negative commitment is a feature of distinguished scientists in general. According to Roe (1952), the individuals making up her elite 64 displayed a "driving absorption in their work" (p. 25). Each

> works hard and devotedly at his laboratory, often seven days a week. He says his work is his life, and has few recreations. . . . They have worked long hours for many years, frequently with no vacations to speak of, because they would rather be doing their work than anything else. (pp. 22, 25)

Boring, Simon, Bekhterev, Thorndike, and other great psychologists exhibited the motivational profile that best describes all illustrious scientists.

Social Attributes

Another hard-working great psychologist was R. B. Cattell, who authored more than 500 publications over a 70-year period. Among his many contributions was the development and application of the 16 Personality Factor Questionnaire (16PF; Cattell & Stice, 1955). This instrument assesses individuals on 16 bipolar personality dimensions. Some of these dimensions have self-explanatory names, such as high versus low *intelligence*, high versus low *dominance*, and *conservatism* versus *radicalism*. Other dimensions are not so obvious, at least for those who are uninitiated into Cattell's favorite terminology. These include *schizothymia* versus *cyclothymia*, *desurgency* versus *surgency*, *threctia* versus *parmia*, and *praxernia* versus *autia*. Transparent or intelligible, these dimensions can differentiate human beings according to their distinctive personality profiles. Of special relevance to this book is Cattell's use of the 16PF to determine the personality profiles of high-achieving individuals, such as creators, leaders, and athletes (R. B. Cattell & Butcher, 1968).

As part of this research program, Cattell and his colleagues have examined scientists, including highly eminent researchers. For example, R. B. Cattell and Drevdahl (1955) administered the 16PF to 140 notable scientists from the disciplines of physics, biology, and psychology (*ns* of 46, 46, and 52, respectively). Besides exhibiting a conspicuous level of general intelligence, these scientists could be distinguished from the general population according to several factors that concern social rather than motivational traits. Specifically, the eminent researchers tended to be schizothymic, desurgent, dominant, and self-sufficient. Schizothymia signifies the inclination to be "withdrawn, skeptical, internally preoccupied, precise, and critical" (R. B. Cattell, 1963, p. 121), desurgent indicates the penchant for "introspectiveness, restraint, brooding, and solemnity of manner" (R. B. Cattell, 1963, p. 121). The remaining two traits, dominance and self-sufficiency, have their everyday meanings.

R. B. Cattell (1963) complemented this psychometric study of contemporary scientists with a historiometric study of famous scientists of the past. The subjects included several major figures from psychology's own history, such as Paracelsus, F. Bacon, J. Kepler, I. Newton, G. W. Leibniz, J. Dalton, C. Darwin, S. Freud, and W. Cannon. The overall picture was virtually identical: Compared to the general population of humanity, great scientists are introverted, serious, contemplative, independent, and autonomous. It is significant that although Cattell (1963) published these results after the Cattell and Drevdahl (1955) study, the historiometric research had actually been conducted prior to the psychometric investigation. Hence, the findings regarding contemporary scientists can be said to have replicated those found for historic scientists.

R. B. Cattell's basic portrait of the great scientist has been replicated in other studies in which different samples and instruments have been used (e.g., Chambers, 1964; Van Zelst & Kerr, 1951). For example, Roe (1952) found that her 64 eminent scientists tended to avoid social activities and confined their recreation to "fishing, sailing, walking or some other individualistic activity" (p. 22). In fact, extensive meta-analyses of the empirical literature have convincingly shown that the distinctive pattern of social traits constitutes a secure empirical generalization about the scientific personality (Feist, 1998; Feist & Gorman, 1998). In general, scientists tend to be more dominant, independent, introverted, and unsociable than the typical human being, and these characteristics all tend to become accentuated in the most eminent scientists. If anything, the hard-driving autonomous personality of the great scientist often verges on arrogance and aggressiveness (Feist & Gorman, 1998). Moreover, many of these social attributes appear to be deeply rooted in the personality, for they seem to go back to childhood and adolescence. The typical notable in Roe's (1953a) sample "tended to feel lonely and 'different' and to be shy and aloof from his classmates" (p. 22). In fact, individuals who leave their mark on history often display the developmental tendency of "isolation from other children, especially outside the family" (McCurdy, 1960, p. 38).

Of course, this social profile might be expected from what readers already know about great scientists. Given that there are only 24 hr in a day, and that the creative process is to a very large extent an individualistic activity—as I documented earlier in this chapter—it would seem necessary that some price must be paid in terms of social relationships. In short, great scientists must be highly introverted rather than extroverted. Every hour spent in socializing is one less hour spent in creative contemplation. Furthermore, to pursue their own path, scientists must free themselves from the influence of others. An autonomous disposition would seem especially crucial for those who wish to promote truly revolutionary ideas. This implies that great scientists should be dominant rather than submissive, independent rather than conforming. Even when they collaborate with others, their collaborators may have to assume more subordinate positions. "I am a horse for a single harness, not cut out for tandem or teamwork," Einstein once admitted, "for well I know that in order to attain any definite goal, it is imperative that *one* person do the thinking and the commanding" (quoted in Sorokin, 1963, p. 274).

Yet there is one perplexing datum that complicates this social profile of the typical great psychologist. Research suggests that psychologists may depart from this profile in a substantial and perplexing manner. Roe (1953a) found that the social scientists in her sample were much more gregarious and extraverted than the biologists and physicists. The Rorschach indicated that the social scientists were intensely concerned with human beings, and the

Thematic Apperception Test (Roe, 1953a) indicated that they possess an unusually intense concern for interpersonal relationships. This concern contrasts strikingly with the strong tendency for eminent scientists to be "interested in things more than in persons," as Galton (1874, p. 125) concluded in his pioneer investigation (also see Barron, 1969). Furthermore, this discrepancy between social and natural scientists may appear early in individual development. Terman (1954) reported that those of his intellectually gifted children who grew up to become social scientists were very sociable as children, much more so than those who became natural scientists. Although neither Roe nor Terman presented the statistics for the psychologists in their samples of social scientists, R. B. Cattell and Drevdahl (1955) compared psychologists directly with physicists and biologists, and a similar pattern emerged. R. B. Cattell (1963) summarized the interdisciplinary contrasts in this fashion:

> The physicists are even more schizothyme than other researchers, and the psychologists, I regret to say, more dominant and less desurgent. Possibly this greater surgency accounts for the fact that on the whole psychologists have talked more and progressed less than, say, physicists! (p. 126)

R. B. Cattell's suggestion is a provocative one. Perhaps the most well-known psychologists do not have the personality profile that most typifies great scientists. Psychology then suffers as a scientific enterprise because nobody has the requisite disposition. Because Isaac Newton's mind was, in William Wordsworth's words, "for ever voyaging through strange seas of thought, alone" (quoted in Jeans, 1942, p. 711), Newton goes down in history as one of the greatest scientists of any time or place. Meanwhile, great psychologists choose chatting over creating, to the discipline's chagrin. Yet Cattell's is not the only potential explanation for this interdisciplinary contrast. Among other possibilities, the difference could merely reflect the divergent nature of psychology's subject matter. After all, psychologists are more likely to study people rather than animals or inanimate objects. In line with this truism, other social scientists seem to share psychologists' stronger attraction to things human. It may even be that those psychologists who are oriented toward people rather than things will be those who are most successful as scientists. Perhaps the best psychologists operate as human rather than natural scientists.

I return to this fascinating issue in chapter 8. Before getting there, however, it is first necessary to complete my discussion of dispositional attributes by turning to a question that has plagued the psychology of genius for millennia.

SYMPTOMS

"Those who have become eminent in philosophy, politics, poetry, and the arts have all had tendencies toward melancholia," Aristotle is reputed to have claimed (quoted in Andreasen & Canter, 1974, p. 123). Many others over the centuries have echoed this remark, from Seneca's (n.d./1932) "No great genius has ever existed without some touch of madness" (p. 285) to Shakespeare's "The lunatic, the lover, and the poet/ Are of imagination all compact" (quoted in Browning, 1986, p. 77). Toward the end of the 19th century the notion of the "mad genius" began to receive serious scientific endorsements. Thus, Cesare Lombroso (1891), the eminent Italian criminologist, asserted in *The Man of Genius* that individuals who make history had personalities associated with "degenerative psychosis," especially that of the "epileptic group." Indeed, reputable psychiatrists claimed that genius could count among the symptoms of a broad syndrome that betrays inferior genetic endowment. For instance, an article published in the *Journal of Nervous and Mental Disease* listed the four possible repercussions of a single congenital defect:

> *First*, and most prominent in the order of frequency is an early death. *Second*, he may help swell the criminal ranks. *Third*, he may become mentally deranged and ultimately find his way into a hospital for the insane. *Fourth*, and least frequently, he startles the world by an invention or discovery in science or by an original composition of great merit in art, music or literature. He is then styled a genius. (Babcock, 1895, p. 752)

With the advent of the psychoanalytic school founded by Sigmund Freud, this centuries-old thesis acquired a new form of documentation: the psychobiography. Starting with Freud's own (1910/1964) treatment of Leonardo da Vinci, one historic figure after another was submitted to psychoanalytic treatment, including such psychology notables as Socrates, Newton, Rousseau, Goethe, James, J. S. Mill, Charles Darwin, Galton, Nietzsche, Gordon Allport, and B. F. Skinner (Runyan, 1982). By a curious twist of fate, psychoanalysts themselves, such as Wilhelm Reich, Carl Jung, and Freud himself, eventually became psychobiographical subjects (Elms, 1994). Given that psychoanalytic theory was built on clinical cases, it was natural for these psychobiographers to focus on neurotic and psychotic symptoms rather than the healthy aspects of one's psychiatric makeup. Indeed, many of these analyses were more properly styled *pathographies*. Behind every great person was some even greater trauma, obsession, or defense mechanism.

Although mainstream thought seemed to side with the association of greatness with sickness, some psychologists have voiced dissent. Humanistic psychologists, especially, were prone to emphasize the healthy aspects of creativity and other forms of high achievement. Proponents of this alternative view include Rollo May (1975), Carl Rogers (1954), and Abraham Maslow (1959). For these theorists psychopathology was antithetical to the creative life. Hence, Maslow's (1970) biographical studies of eminent self-actualizing personalities included such luminaries as Baruch Spinoza, Benjamin Franklin,

Johann Goethe, Ralph Waldo Emerson, William James, and Jane Addams. These individuals were chosen precisely because they exemplified the best that could be attained by the human personality. It is odd that some of Maslow's self-actualizers were individuals whom others had identified as evincing severe psychological problems. William James certainly suffered from various emotional disorders. Often in and out of schools for diverse complaints, he once dropped out of his medical studies because he was bothered by "insomnia, digestive disorders, eye-troubles, weakness of the back, and sometimes deep depression of spirits [that] followed each other or afflicted him simultaneously" (H. James, 1926, p. 84). Frequently plagued with hypochondriasis, phobic panics, and psychosomatic disorders, he was occasionally struck by depressive episodes so severe that he would contemplate suicide—and perhaps even attempted to do so.

What is the truth of the matter? Are great creative minds "sick souls," to use a Jamesian term? More specifically, does psychopathology go hand in hand with being a great psychologist? To address this issue I first look at two kinds of scientific evidence, the first drawn from historical populations and the second from contemporary populations.

Historical Populations

It is not difficult to compile lists of historical figures who allegedly suffered from some degree of psychopathology (e.g., Prentky, 1980; Simonton, 1994a). Table 7.1 provides a listing of deceased celebrities who have also earned a secure place in psychology's history. It must be admitted that many of these diagnoses are extremely conjectural or tenuous, especially for the earlier personalities, such as Copernicus. Still, other assignments are extremely well documented. Comte, for instance, actually spent time in an asylum. Others on the list—for example, Goethe, Galton, Jung, and Mowrer—freely admitted their symptoms. Nonetheless, the first question that must be answered is not whether *some* eminent figures display some symptoms of psychopathology. After all, even extremely ordinary people can do so. Rather, the significant issue is whether the rate of psychological disorder is elevated in individuals who have some claim to greatness.

The first researcher to tackle this question systematically was Havelock Ellis, in his 1904 book A *Study of British Genius*. He noted that the incidence of some type of serious mental illness in his distinguished sample was 4.2%. Moreover, 8% displayed melancholia, and 5% showed symptoms of some type of personality disorder. These figures, according to Ellis, exceeded the incidence rates found in the general population. Ellis also noted that fully 16% of his illustrious figures suffered imprisonment, a statistic that has relevance only if one accepts the belief, prevalent at the time, that criminality, genius, and madness constituted symptoms of the same underlying pathological syndrome. In hindsight, this percentage could just as well reveal the extremely independent and anticonforming character of creative genius. Many

TABLE 7.1
Eminent Contributors With Supposed Mental Disorders

Mental disorder	Contributors
Schizophrenic disorders (and other cognitive psychoses	
Philosophers	Immanuel Kant, Friedrich Nietzsche
Scientists	Nicolaus Copernicus, René Descartes, Carolus Linnaeus, Isaac Newton, Blaise Pascal
Psychologists	Carl Jung, Wilhelm Reich
Affective disorders (depression, mania, or bipolar)	
Philosophers	Auguste Comte, Johann Goethe, William James,[a] J. S. Mill, Jean-Jacques Rousseau, Arthur Schopenhauer
Scientists	Charles Darwin, Johannes Müller[b]
Psychologists	Donald T. Campbell, Jacob Cohen, Karl Duncker,[b] Gustav Fechner, G. S. Hall, Karen Horney,[a] Hobart Orval Mowrer,[b] J. B. Watson
Personality disorders (including severe neuroses	
Philosophers	René Descartes, G. W. F. Hegel, Thomas Hobbes, David Hume, Søren Kierkegaard, Bertrand Russell, Herbert Spencer,[c] Voltaire
Scientists	Gregor Mendel, Ivan Pavlov, Havelock Ellis
Psychologists	Bruno Bettelheim,[b] Sigmund Freud,[b,c] Francis Galton

Note. Egon Brunswik and Else Frenkel-Brunswik both committed suicide, the latter 3 years after her spouse. In Else's case, at least, the suicide may have been provoked by severe depression.
[a]Attempted suicide.   [b]Suicide.   [c]Substance abuse (e.g., alcohol, opium, etc.).

of those imprisoned were paying the penalty for expressing beliefs that departed from the norms of their times.

As with most pioneer investigations, the statistics Ellis (1904) reported are subject to all sorts of methodological objections. However, from the current standpoint the most serious problem is that the figures are aggregated across a immense variety of achievement domains. It is conceivable that the high rates of psychopathology merely reflect the influence of artistic creators, such as poets and painters (Bowerman, 1947; Martindale, 1972; Post, 1996; Raskin, 1936). Hence, it is necessary to separate the psychologists from the rest, or at least separate out the scientists or even the social scientists. Two recent historiometric studies came close to attaining this segregation (also see Juda, 1949; Raskin, 1936).

The first study looked at 291 world-famous scientists, thinkers, artists, composers, and politicians (Post, 1994). Of these, 45 were scientists and 50 were thinkers. Many individuals in these two categories made unquestioned contributions to psychology as a scientific or scholarly discipline. Among the scientists were Karl Friedrich Gauss, Charles Babbage, Charles Darwin, Hermann von Helmholtz, Gregor Mendel, Francis Galton, Jean Martin Charcot, Ernst Mach, and Ivan Pavlov, and among the thinkers were Arthur Schopenhauer, Auguste Comte, J. S. Mill, William James, Friedrich Nietzsche, Sigmund Freud, Havelock Ellis, and Carl Jung [*sic!*]. For the scientists, psychopathology was severe in 17.8%, marked in 26.7%, mild in 24.4%, and absent in 31.1%. For the thinkers, the corresponding figures were 17.4%, 41.3%, 26.1%, and 15.2%. The incidence rates of psychopathology for the other achievement domains were much higher. At the same time, even the scientists experienced rates that exceeded expectation. "Scientists had the lowest prevalence of psychic abnormalities," concluded Post (1994), "but even in their case these were absent or trivial in only one-third. The amounts of psychopathology increase steadily from composers, politicians, artists, and thinkers through to writers" (p. 24). For the last group, 37.5% displayed severe psychopathology, 18.8% marked, 29.1% mild, and only 14.6% none. Hence, it would seem that great psychologists who come closest to the scientific ideal are those with the lowest proclivities toward mental illness; however, their risk would remain higher than that of the general population.

The second investigation focused on a larger and more recent sample of luminaries, chosen on the basis of whether they had biographies written about them that were reviewed in the *New York Times* (Ludwig, 1995). Having more than 1,000 subjects at his disposal, Ludwig (1995) was able to make a more refined differentiation of the domains in which eminence was attained. In particular, the subjects were subdivided into the following categories: architecture, art, business, exploration, sports, musical composing, music performance, military, public office, natural sciences, social activism, social figure, companion, social sciences, theater, nonfiction, fiction, and poetry. The social scientists numbered 73 and consisted mostly of psychoanalysts and psychiatrists (e.g., Sigmund and Anna Freud, Carl Jung, Melanie Klein, Otto Rank, Hélène Deutsch, Karen Horney, Harry Stack Sullivan, and Wilhelm Reich). However, the group also encompassed psychologists (e.g., Havelock Ellis, William James, and Cyril Burt), philosophers (e.g., Friedrich Nietzsche, John Dewey, and Jean-Paul Sartre), and sociologists and anthropologists (e.g., Herbert Spencer, Max Weber, Ruth Benedict, and Margaret Mead). Although this category is clearly heterogeneous, at least the social scientists are separated from the natural scientists. According to this inquiry, the lifetime rate of any mental disorder was 51% for the social scientists, which is comparable to rates for the social activists (49%) and business figures (49%) but noticeably higher than that for the natural scientists (28%). On the other hand, the rate was lower than seen in the arts, which got as high as 87% (for the

poets). Ludwig (1995) also did a breakdown of the most common patholo-
gies for the various domains. For the social scientists these rates fell in the
following order: depression (32%), alcoholism (10%), anxiety (8%), drug
abuse (7%), psychosis (4%), suicide (4%), and mania (1%). All in all, the
rates for the first few diagnoses exceed what would be anticipated in the
general population.

One final finding in this second historiometric investigation deserves
consideration (Ludwig, 1995). The subjects were scored on the magnitude of
psychology displayed and the level of their lifetime creative achievement.
The two variables were positively associated. Therefore, not only do eminent personalities exhibit higher than average rates of mental illness, but
also psychopathological symptoms predict ultimate success (for additional
evidence, see Juda, 1949; Raskin, 1936). Although this analysis was not conducted on the separate achievement categories, one might conjecture that
this relation would also hold for the social scientists as a subgroup. William
James and Sigmund Freud may have paid a price for their greatness.

Contemporary Populations

Psychobiographies of historic personalities are often criticized on methodological grounds (e.g., Stannard, 1980). Among those criticisms is the flimsy
nature of diagnoses made at a distance. It is one thing to interview a client
face to face but quite another to pore through the biographical record in the
hope of finding symptoms of mental illness. Needless to say, this criticism
applies just as much to the retrospective diagnoses that provide the foundation of historiometric analyses (Simonton, 1999c). Therefore, it seems that
results of stronger scientific validity should be obtained from the direct assessment of eminent contemporaries.

One potential approach is to conduct surveys that determine whether
illustrious individuals are more likely to seek or require therapy as the result
of their psychological difficulties. This line of attack has been applied to
artistic personalities, such as the creative writers who have attended the famed
Iowa Writers Workshop (Andreasen, 1987). Such studies have again found
that artistic creators exhibit higher rates of mental illness than expected,
according to the frequency that they require intervention, whether therapy
or medication (Andreasen, 1987; Jamison, 1989). Wispé and Parloff (1965)
conducted such a study for contemporary psychologists as well. The authors
surveyed all members of the American Psychological Association who had
received their PhDs between 1945 and 1951, obtaining usable responses from
966. Approximately one third of all respondents had received some form of
psychotherapy (with the clinical psychologists disproportionately represented
among those who had received treatment). This is about the same rate as
observed in a sample of eminent British artists and writers (Jamison, 1989).
To assess whether psychopathology contributed to the differential success of

the surveyed psychologists, publication counts were compiled from *Psychological Abstracts*. When the productivity of individuals who had received therapy were compared to the productivity of a comparison group that had not, but who were otherwise comparable, no significant difference was found. Hence, the results are inconclusive, except to say that members of the American Psychological Association are not disinclined to pursue therapy when they encounter psychological problems. It's nice to know that they practice what they preach!

This approach leaves much to be desired. There is often too much latitude for self-selection that can bias the sample, and it is not always easy to obtain a reasonable control group. More critical is that the assessment of psychopathology is rather crude. The symptoms must reach a level of emotional discomfort or behavioral dysfunction to cause the individuals to seek help (or, alternatively, their loved ones to get it for them). Yet it could very well be that creative genius is optimized at more moderate, subclinical symptomatology; that is, the creator may dwell at the borderline between normality and pathology. As John Dryden (1681) expressed it, "Great Wits are sure to Madness near ally'd,/ And thin Partitions do their Bounds divide" (p. 6). To test this hypothesis requires that any disposition toward psychopathology be measured along a continuous scale that covers the extremes, from the normal to the abnormal. Psychology can fortunately boast a rich inventory of psychometric instruments that purport to have just this diagnostic capacity, such as the Minnesota Multiphasic Personality Inventory (MMPI; Hathaway & McKinley, 1943). This measure has actually been applied to the eminent personalities invited to undergo intensive assessment at the Institute for Personality Assessment and Research at the University of California, Berkeley (MacKinnon, 1978). The results conform to expectation (MacKinnon, 1978). The creative writers, for example, scored in the top 10% of the general population on the scales gauging Depression, Hypomania, Schizophrenia, Paranoia, Psychopathic Deviation, Hysteria, Hypochondriasis, and Psychoaesthenia (Barron, 1969). Yet the scores were not so elevated that the writers could be considered mentally ill or emotionally unstable. Instead, they seemed to reside at Dryden's thin partition.

Another psychometric instrument that has proven useful in addressing this hypothesis is the Psychoticism scale of the Eysenck Personality Questionnaire (Eysenck, 1995). Hans Eysenck (1993, 1995) has persuasively argued that elevated but not extreme scores on Psychoticism should be positively associated with creativity. For example, Psychoticism scores are correlated with several cognitive capacities linked to the creative process, such as the ability to generate unusual associative connections between ideas (Eysenck, 1994; Woody & Claridge, 1977). More important is the fact that psychoticism is linked with creative eminence in the arts (e.g., Götz & Götz, 1979a, 1979b; Pearson, 1983). These results corroborate those obtained at the Institute for Personality Assessment and Research.

Nonetheless, these findings cannot be immediately generalized to psychologists, at least not without knowing whether psychologists fall closer to the artist rather than to the scientist end of the dispositional spectrum. Historiometric studies show that psychopathology is more common among artistic than scientific creators, and psychometric investigations have found the same result (Feist, 1998). On average, artistic creators are more emotionally unstable, sensitive, and anxious than scientific creators are. At the same time, psychologists tend to display certain characteristics that place them more toward the artistic end of the continuum. As noted earlier, psychologists seem to have undergone psychotherapy at rates comparable to artists and writers (Wispé & Parloff, 1965). In addition, compared to physical scientists, psychologists are more likely to be introverted, bohemian, unconventional, and imaginative (Chambers, 1964). So where does psychology fit in this picture?

The beginning of an answer is to be found in a two-part study of psychologists who were professors at Canadian research universities (Rushton, 1990). In the first part, 52 full-time professors of psychology at the University of Western Ontario were assessed on personality traits associated with psychoticism. A weighted composite score was then shown to correlate .26 with a creativity measure that combined each psychologist's publication and citation rate. The participants in the second part of the study were 69 psychologists who responded to a mail survey of nine leading psychology departments at English-speaking universities. Once more the Psychoticism score was based on a weighted composite of personality traits, but the creativity assessment was defined according to four measures: "(a) total number of publications, (b) mean number of publications in last 5 yr, (c) number of hours spent on research, and (d) rated enjoyment of research" (Rushton, 1990, p. 1296). Despite the changes in sample and variable definition, the findings in the second part of the study endorsed those in the first. Psychoticism correlated .43 with creative achievement. Yet it should be stressed that none of the psychologists in either inquiry could be considered psychotic. To hold down a job at a major university—and to respond to a psychologist's questionnaire—would seem to require that one be reasonably well adjusted. Hence, success as a psychologist is likely facilitated by a certain leaning toward psychopathology, without succumbing to maladaptive symptoms.

All told, a fairly consistent picture has emerged from both historiometric and psychometric inquiries. This picture should place into scientific context one's appreciation of the individuals who have made major contributions to psychology. This context is critical, because historians of psychology often betray ambivalence about people who manifest some degree of mental disorder. "In spite of, or perhaps because of, his own emotional temperament and weakness of character, he possessed great psychological insight," said one historian of Rousseau (Hearnshaw, 1987, p. 104). Wertheimer (1987, p. 86) observed how William James "suffered from poor health and to some extent from hypochondriasis throughout much of his life, but nevertheless managed an output that was both voluminous and qualitatively highly regarded both by his contemporaries and by later critics." These two statements imply that some kind of paradox exists in these personalities, that creativity and pathology don't mix. Yet the paradox vanishes if a disposition toward disorder has been shown to encourage creative achievement. A pathological proclivity alone admittedly does not suffice. The inclination must be integrated with other personal assets as well, especially those discussed previously in this chapter.

It is ironic that in his classic book *The Varieties of Religious Experience* James (1902) himself offered practically the same response to the mad-genius question:

> The nature of genius has been illuminated by the attempts to class it with psychopathological phenomena. Borderline insanity, crankiness, insane temperament, loss of mental balance, psychopathic degeneration (to use a few of the many synonyms by which it has been called), has certain peculiarities and liabilities which, when combined with a superior quality of intellect in an individual, make it more probable that he will make his mark and affect his age, than if his temperament were less neurotic. (pp. 22–23)

From what is known of James's life and career, such a bold conclusion may have been predicated as much on his personal experience as on mastery of the scientific literature of his day. I suspect that he would be pleased to learn that current psychological research has borne him out—again!

8

WORLDVIEW

What is it that drives great psychologists to devote so much time and energy to their research? It certainly is not the money: Although nobody starved to death making major contributions to the field, no one really got phenomenally rich, either. Besides, great psychologists, like other creative intellects, appear driven by intrinsic rather than extrinsic motives—but what provides the impetus behind that intrinsic motivation? Humanistic psychologists would sometimes respond by saying that the creativity comes out of the more fundamental drive for self-actualization, toward the realization of personal potential. "The mainspring of creativity appears to be the same tendency which we discover so deeply as the curative force in psychotherapy," held Carl Rogers (1954), namely *"man's tendency to actualize himself, to become his potentialities"* (p. 251). According to this conception, creativity is not a peripheral or trivial process, like tying one's shoes or doing the dishes; rather, it ensues from deeper layers of the whole personality.

In point of fact, scrutiny of the life and work of most noted creators will reveal that their work is deeply embedded in their lives. Each product coming from their minds emerges from a more encompassing worldview or ultimate concern. The symphonies of Beethoven, the sculptures of Michelangelo, and the plays of Shakespeare are stepping stones in each creator's progressive self-realization. Despite all the impersonal objectivity attached to the scientific enterprise, the same factor also operates in the careers of great scientists, including illustrious psychologists. This linkage is often hinted at when historians discuss the personal context of a psychologist's life work. A prime example is the following observation about one of psychology's pioneers: "It is a historical curiosity that Fechner's empiricism was ultimately rooted in metaphysical and mystical speculation; that in his microscopically exact experiments, there always lurked the tendency to prove the correctness of these cosmic speculations" (Capretta, 1967, p. 76). However curious historically, Fechner's case may illustrate a more universal motivational principle in the psychology of greatness.

The rest of this chapter is allotted to a more detailed discussion of this principle; that is, I examine the extent to which a psychologist's ideas emerge from a personal worldview, or *Weltanschauung*, to use the German term. I begin by discussing the impact of religious convictions and then turn to the influence of a psychologist's philosophy of science.

RELIGIOUS CONVICTIONS

In 399 BC, Socrates was condemned to drink hemlock for actions purported to undermine Athenian religious tradition and authority. It was the first notable occasion when the life of a great truth seeker was cut short because his or her truth seeking ran afoul of religious practice and dogma. Socrates' execution was sadly followed by many other examples in the history of Western civilization. In 415 AD, Hypatia, Neoplatonist philosopher and first great female mathematician, was brutally murdered by Christian zealots in the streets of Alexandria. In 1553, Michael Servetus, the great Spanish physician who discovered the lesser circulation of the blood, was burned at the stake in Geneva for espousing unconventional religious views. Even when the price was not death, religious authorities would respond with alternative means of persecution and intimidation. Galileo was forced to renounce his belief in Copernican theory and, placed under house arrest, forbidden to write further on his controversial physics. Such measures often proved efficient means of repressing the appearance of new ideas. Descartes decided not to publish his magnum opus *The World* after hearing of Galileo's fate—the work not appearing until 1664, 14 years after Descartes's death. Of course, in more recent times the antagonism between science and religion assumed a more benign form. Although certain religious authorities, such as Bishop Wilberforce, condemned Charles Darwin's evolutionary theory, they were powerless to prevent Darwin from disseminating his views.

In the history of psychology the place of religion seems to become more ambivalent. On the one hand, many great figures could be considered unambiguously religious. From Augustine to Thomas Aquinas, important Christian theologians have often provided profound reflections on psychological issues. Even after the Renaissance, priests or ministers might be notable psychological thinkers besides, such as Nicolas Malebranche, Étienne Bonnot de Condillac, James Mill, and Franz Brentano. Many other notables had once planned to enter the ministry before life's contingencies led them to pursue a different path. Examples include psychologists as diverse as Charles Darwin, Carl Stumpf, G. Stanley Hall, I. Pavlov, George Romanes, J. B. Watson, Clark L. Hull, Carl Rogers, Rollo May, and Theodore Newcomb. Also, Kant, Johann Herder, F. E. Beneke, and James Ward are among those who had first studied theology before switching to some other intellectual endeavor.

On the other hand, it seems that the connection between religion and psychology has declined over the last 100 years. For example, "the recent history of psychology includes a few clerics—like Brentano—but these were almost without exception university professors whose connection with the church was merely incidental" (MacLeod, 1975, p. 177). Moreover, psychologists often display a certain amount of suspicion toward the great psychologists whose ideas are informed or influenced by their religious beliefs, especially when those attitudes assume a mystical guise. This reaction is implicit in the following specific comment: "In spite of the strongly mystical strain in his outlook, and his flirtations with alchemy, oriental cults and occultism, Jung nevertheless made several valuable contributions to psychology" (Hearnshaw, 1987, p. 166). So, what is the connection, if any, between religion and the attainment of distinction as a psychologist? Is the association negative, positive, or neutral?

I discussed at length in chapter 4 Harvey C. Lehman's well-known research on age and achievement. Before devoting his career to that particular substantive question, however, Lehman collaborated with Paul Witty on an empirical study titled "Scientific Eminence and Church Membership" (Lehman & Witty, 1931). The sample of 1,189 eminent ("starred") scientists came from the 1927 edition of J. M. Cattell's *American Men of Science*. Information about the scientists' religious affiliations was taken from the 1926–1927 edition of *Who's Who in America*, whose editors has specifically requested that their biographies provide their religious denomination. Lehman and Witty noted at once that 75% of those sampled provided no information about church membership. From this they "inferred either that the 886 scientists, who neglected to state their church membership, belong to no church or that they did not consider the information of sufficient importance to include when they were preparing their biographical sketches" (p. 546). Of the 303 outstanding scientists for whom the data were available, the largest numbers were Congregationalist (22%), Presbyterian (20%), Episcopalian (17%), Unitarian (12%), and Methodist (10%). In contrast, "among 1,189 outstanding scientists, three only report membership in the Catholic Church" (p. 548).

However, Lehman and Witty (1931) realized that these raw percentages are misleading, because they do not take into account the distribution of church membership across the diverse denominations. When this adjustment was made using the most recent figures for the United States, the rankings altered considerably. "The Unitarians provide 81.400 times their expected quota, the Friends, 6.600, the Episcopalians, 5.701, and the Presbyterian, 2.995 times their quotas," whereas "the Roman Catholics provide the smallest number of research workers in proportion to their number" (p. 547). In fact, after adjustment, Unitarians outnumber the Catholics by 1,696 to 1. The Lutherans, Baptists, and Disciples were almost as poorly represented among eminent scientists. Lehman and Witty concluded that great scientists are not inclined to belong to established churches and, when they do, those churches are more likely to represent liberal denominations.

The low church participation rates of eminent scientists have been replicated in other investigations with different samples and methods. Of Roe's (1953a) 64 eminent scientists, only 3 displayed serious involvement in any church or synagogue. A more recent and larger sample of natural scientists found that none of the highly eminent attended religious services regularly, and even among their less eminent colleagues the figure was only 12% (Feist, 1993). Furthermore, this low attendance rate can be probably be attributed to lack of religious interests rather than the preoccupations of research (Chambers, 1964). For instance, highly creative mathematicians scored lower on measures of religious values than did their less creative colleagues (Helson & Crutchfield, 1970).

Nonetheless, it is conceivable that religious feeling lives more comfortably with some disciplines than with others. In Terman's (1954) study of 800 men who had been members of his sample of gifted children, 34% of those who pursued college majors in the social sciences reported some vocational interest in the ministry. This percentage falls in the same range as those found for those who majored in engineering (23%), the physical sciences (29%), and medicine or biology (55%), but it is half as high as found in Termites who majored in the humanities (68%). A totally different study, however, which looked at actual researchers, found that psychologists had less proclivity toward religion than did chemists (Chambers, 1964). Perhaps the safest conclusion to draw from these statistics is that great psychologists may fall somewhere in the range typical for natural scientists.

Why do most scientists, including psychologists, shy away from religion? One possible explanation is the totally contrasting attitude toward truth. For most religions, truth is contained in divinely inspired scriptures, with exegeses of those scriptures severely constrained by received traditions and institutional authorities. The truth has already been found, and that revealed truth is infallible. The Koran is Allah's revelation to Muhammad; the Old Testament contains Jehovah's revelation to the Hebrew prophets. This secure conviction differs immensely from that adopted by the scientist, who lives in a far more insecure world of hypothetical conjecture and tentative conclusions. Michael Faraday once wrote that the world little knows how many of the thoughts and theories which have passed through the mind of a scientific investigator have been crushed in silence and secrecy by his own severe criticism and adverse examinations; that in the most successful instances not a tenth of the suggestions, the hopes, the wishes, the preliminary conclusions have been realized. (quoted in Beveridge, 1957, p. 79)

Charles Darwin likewise observed that

I have steadily endeavoured to keep my mind free so as to give up any hypothesis, however much believed (and I cannot resist forming one on every subject) as soon as facts are shown to be opposed to it. Indeed, I have had no choice but to act in this manner, for with the exception of the Coral Reefs, I cannot remember a single first-formed hypothesis which had not after a time to be given up or greatly modified. (F. Darwin, 1892/1958, pp. 55–56)

Even after a scientist feels confident enough that something is worth sharing with the scientific world, the offering is given as something tentative and changeable, as new facts and theories constantly change the criteria by which any scientific idea must be judged. Each successive edition of Darwin's *Origin of Species* exhibits revisions that underline continually the fallibility of scientific knowledge. Freud's collective works reveal an intellect that could not rest content with the unmodified repetition of the same ideas, even his sacred pleasure principle, which eventually yielded ground to the death instinct. Wilhelm Wundt changed his ideas so much in his various publications as to cause William James considerable exasperation, yet James himself would sometimes collate seemingly contradictory ideas into a single publication, the *Principles of Psychology*—that inclusive and elusive compilation of surmises and guesses par excellence.

The conjectural nature of the scientific enterprise explains not only why great psychologists may be disinclined toward religion but also why when psychologists do admit religious beliefs, they tend to be of a liberal or flexible form. Unitarians subscribe to a doctrine so loose and inclusive that many more dogmatic religionists believe it cannot be considered a genuine faith. Indeed, Michael Servetus was executed for heresy because he had advocated what now would be considered Unitarian beliefs, beliefs then condemned by the Protestants and Catholics alike. Yet Unitarianism proves much more popular among scientists than those faiths in which all belief is predetermined by established dogma. Hence, great psychologists are not likely to be religious or, if they are, they are proponents of religions that remain open to novelty and controversy.

This interpretation also fits well with what the empirical research has shown about the personal characteristics of great scientists (see chapter 7). Their openness to new facts and ideas, their behavioral and cognitive flexibility, their independence, self-sufficiency, and nonconformity—these do not represent of cluster of traits that would sit comfortably with unchanging, closed, and rigid ideologies. One of the recurrent facts found in the biographies of many great psychologists is their total unwillingness to conform to the norms and expectations of their society, occupation, or church. Some daring individuals, such as L. Galvani, J. M. Cattell, and E. Tolman, lost their academic positions by advocating unpopular political views, whereas others were willing to take on powerful dictators, as when Pavlov attacked Stalin by letter or when Köhler criticized Hitler in the press. David Hartley, although trained for the Anglican ministry, could not take holy orders owing to his refusal to subscribe to all Thirty-Nine Articles, and Karen Horney found herself ousted from the New York Psychoanalytic Institute for her failure to accept its "party line." Spinoza was excommunicated from his synagogue for his "atheist" beliefs, and Johann Gottlieb Fichte was obliged to resign from the University of Jena for the same cause. The list of thinkers and researchers who have suffered arrest for expressing their unconventional views is very long and includes figures as diverse as Auguste Comte and Mustafer Sherif. Illustrations like these can go on and on. It seems that the great figures of psychology's history simply do not have the personal disposition needed to submit to the dictates of any dogmatic faith, whether it be political, professional, or religious. The conflict between science and religion is psychological rather than sociological.

My explanation for the religious orientation of great psychologists admittedly is itself only a hypothesis or theory, not proven truth and, like many other hypotheses I have held during the course of my career, it may be wrong. I cannot expect to do better than Darwin and other psychologists far greater than I!

SCIENTIFIC PHILOSOPHIES

In the foregoing argument I lumped psychologists with scientists. The implicit assumption is that each psychologist aspires to become a scientist first and foremost—or at least that's what the great ones most desire. There actually exists some empirical evidence on this score. In this study, past presidents of the American Psychological Association (APA) were asked to fill out the Strong Vocational Interest Blank (SVIB; D. P. Campbell, 1965). Of the 70 APA presidents between 1892 and 1965, 50 had completed the inventory one or more times. The sample began with Joseph Jastrow, APA president in 1900, and ended with Jerome Bruner, president in 1965. Among those assessed were such big names in the field as physiological and comparative psychologists Karl Lashley, Robert M. Yerkes, Harry Harlow, and Donald Hebb; learning psychologists Edward L. Thorndike, John B. Watson, Clark Hull, Edward Tolman, Edwin Guthrie, O. Hobart Mowrer, and Neal Miller; humanistic psychologists Gordon Allport and Carl Rogers; psychometricians

L. L. Thurstone, J. P. Guilford, and Paul Meehl; and even historians of psychology Walter B. Pillsbury, E. G. Boring, Gardner Murphy, and Ernest Hilgard. It curiously also included 2 psychologists, Robert R. Sears and Lee Cronbach, who may have taken the SVIB as part of Terman's (1954) study of the vocational interests of 800 gifted men cited in the previous section—along with Lewis M. Terman himself.

The SVIB scores for the 50 APA presidents were then contrasted with those for a large sample of psychologists at large ($N = 1,024$) who had no particular claim to distinction (D. P. Campbell, 1965). In some respects, the two groups were very similar. For example, the APA presidents "averaged 50 on the Psychologist scale, precisely the same as the total criterion group" (p. 643), and much higher the mean of 17 that a group of average male respondents received. Hence, all psychologists, eminent or not, have a strong vocational interest in psychology. Yet in other respects the two groups are rather different. On the one hand, the comparison group expressed more vocational interest in the occupations of life insurance salesman, mortician, YMCA physical director, social science teacher, and personnel manager—a rather curious mix, to say the least! These interests seem to have in common an interest in dealing with people, albeit not always in a face-to-face manner. On the other hand, the APA presidents exhibited appreciably stronger and far more coherent vocational interests in the occupations of physicist, mathematician, engineer, chemist, and physician—all pure or applied sciences.

E. G. Boring's SVIB scores are fairly typical of great psychologists in general. He had taken the SVIB in 1927, the year before he became president of APA. His five highest vocational interests were physicist, chemist, and engineer (all 54); and mathematician (53); followed closely by psychologist (48). Although it may seem odd to have Boring's own chosen profession fall in fifth place, it is not unusual. Edward K. Strong, the instrument's originator (and never an APA president), received the following scores (also in 1927): engineer, 58; chemist, 57; physicist, 48; mathematician, 48; and psychologist, 35 (D. P. Campbell, 1965). It is interesting that Boring took the SVIB two other times, in 1948 and 1965, permitting a check on the stability of his vocational interests over nearly 40 years. The profiles are basically the same, except that his interest in the occupations of mathematician, physicist, chemist, and engineer actually increased, whereas his interest in psychology remained unchanged.

Judging from these findings, great psychologists most strongly align themselves with other scientists in the exact and natural sciences. However, before one gives this conclusion unqualified acceptance, one must acknowledge that these data were collected at a time when APA was primarily a research-oriented organization, more like the American Association for the Advancement of Science than like the American Medical Association. It was after this period that APA acquired increasingly more clinical psychologists and other practitioners whose interests were aimed more at practice than research. This shift is important, because the latter psychologists may have a rather different attitude toward science than reflected in the disciplines of mathematics, physics, chemistry, and engineering. Specifically, the other psychologists may be more strongly attached to psychology as a human rather than a natural science.

This possibility was demonstrated in Gregory Kimble's (1984) investigation of "psychology's two cultures." Inspired by C. P. Snow's (1960) conception of two divergent academic cultures—the sciences versus the arts and humanities—Kimble devised a scale designed to tap the presence of conflicting values within psychology. The scale was administered to 164 APA members who belonged to only one division: either Division 3, consisting of experimental psychologists, or Division 29, consisting of psychotherapists. The scale assessed the following dimensions: (a) scientific versus human values, (b) determinism versus indeterminism, (c) objectivism versus intuitionism, (c) data versus theory, (d) laboratory investigation versus field study, (e) historical versus ahistorical, (f) heredity versus environment, (g) nomothetic versus idiographic, (h) concrete mechanisms versus abstract concepts, (i) elementism versus holism, (j) cognition versus affect, and (k) reactivity versus creativity. In line with expectation, the experimental psychologists were far more strongly governed by scientific values, with conspicuous sympathy toward determinism, objectivism, laboratory investigation, nomothetic explanation, and elementism. Moreover, subsequent investigators have found comparable results, suggesting that the division is not only real but also runs deep (e.g., Conway, 1988; Zachar & Leong, 1992).

If psychology consists of two separate cultures, then there might be two types of great psychologists, each with its own distinctive philosophy of psychological science. If so, then two questions come immediately to mind. First, is there a psychological foundation for the two types? For instance, do illustrious representatives of the two cultures differ in personality traits or developmental experiences? Second, what is the ultimate impact of the two types? Are great scientists among psychologists more influential than the great humanists, or is the reverse true?

Is There More Than One Type of Great Psychologist?

It has become almost a cliché for individuals who write history of psychology texts to suggest that a psychologist's ideas are grounded in his or her personality. The following assertion is representative: "Psychologists are human, and therefore, they have emotions, aspirations, sensitivities, and inhibitions. In later chapters, I present evidence that these personal variables have indeed influenced the development of psychological theory" (Stagner, 1988, p. 21). For instance, some psychologists might be tough minded and others tender minded, their respective philosophical orientations accordingly leaning toward either the natural or human sciences. Hence, when behaviorist B. F. Skinner and humanistic psychologist Carl Rogers once entered into a classic debate about the nature of psychology, neither could yield substantial ground. It would require a rare and drastic transformation in their personalities before any substantial change in their philosophies could be expected.

Furthermore, even when a psychologist's ideas cannot be directly ascribed to such dispositional traits, it is often argued that the credit or blame can be attributed to developmental variables, such as family background, educational experiences, or career training. "Scientists are also egocentric," wrote the above-quoted textbook author (Stagner, 1988, p. 14), and thus "their theorizing reflects their personal experiences." For example, it is frequently argued that great psychologists who have undergone medical training have their thoughts lastingly affected by the encounter. Hence, one can read of David Hartley that "as might have been expected from a medical man, his orientation was by far the most physiological of the British associationists" (Hothersall, 1990, p. 44). A similar explanation is accorded William James: "In view of his training in anatomy and physiology, it is not surprising that James emphasized physical processes in his investigations of human behavior" (S. Smith, 1983, p. 138).

Is there any evidence that psychologists' ideas have antecedents in their personality and development? The evidence is somewhat mixed.

On the one hand, some empirical studies have shown that a psychologist's scientific orientation may correlate with various personality characteristics. For example, one investigation found that scores on a measure of scientific orientation (the Organicism–Mechanism Paradigm Inventory) exhibited consistent associations with assessments of cognitive and interpersonal style, personality, and occupational interests in a large sample of behavioral scientists (J. A. Johnson, Germer, Efran, & Overton, 1988). Most telling is that behavioral scientists' views of themselves were linked with two important philosophical presuppositions: (a) whether people are passively reactive or actively purposive and (b) whether reality consists of stable, isolated elements or of changing holistic patterns. Another inquiry showed that how psychologists scored on a different measure (the Theoretical Orientation Survey) was linked with such variables as gender, age, family background, childhood experiences, education, religion, occupation, and other biographical factors (Coan, 1979). For instance, psychologists whose mothers were extremely religious are more likely to subscribe to scientifically oriented beliefs, such as behaviorism, quantification, and elementarism. This developmental boomerang effect puts into nomothetic context the extreme metaphysical behaviorism of J. B. Watson, whose mother was so devoutly religious that she named her son after the fire-and-brimstone Baptist minister John Broadus.

On the other hand, the empirical literature suffers from several drawbacks from the standpoint of a scientifically informed history of psychology.

First, the empirical results fail to cover all critical issues that make up a psychologist's worldview. For example, among the most critical distinctions in psychology's history is whether a thinker advocates materialist or idealistic beliefs. It is this issue that plays such a critical role in the mind–body problem, with some thinkers arguing for the mind (idealists such as George Berkeley) and others taking the side of the body (materialists such as Thomas Hobbes). Yet according to a pioneer study of actual philosophers conducted by Hans Eysenck (and Gilmour) in 1944, thinkers who varied along this dimension did not differ on such traits as general drive, emotionality, introversion, shyness, or depression. Second, and more important, almost all of the empirical research looked at everyday research participants (graduate students or APA members) rather than psychologists who had made a name for themselves in the discipline. Perhaps the only notable exception is Suedfeld's (1985) study of the integrative complexity of APA presidents, as assessed by content analyses of their presidential addresses. He found that integrative complexity was positively correlated with whether the psychologist had a subjectivistic rather than an objectivistic orientation. This implies that eminent figures who struggle to integrate multiple and divergent perspectives on psychological phenomena are more likely to favor treatment of human consciousness and personal experience. One cannot help but think of the contrast between the inclusiveness of a William James or Gordon Allport and the exclusiveness of an Ivan Pavlov or B. F. Skinner.

Despite these reservations, I think it is reasonable to conclude that a prima facie case has been made for the existence of distinct types of great psychologists. These types may vary along a number of dimensions, most having something to do with the distinction between scientific and humanistic views of psychology. Furthermore, to some extent yet to be fleshed out, the particular type of psychology a great psychologist represents may be embedded in his or her personal disposition and development.

Which Type of Psychologist Has the Greater Impact?

On the basis of the tentative conclusions just offered, great psychologists do not have to share identical philosophical outlooks. Even so, certain worldviews still may be more conducive to broad and enduring influence than others are. In particular, psychologists who adopt more scientific orientations may make greater contributions to psychology's progress as a science and thereby will secure more lasting fame. In contrast, psychologists who advocate more humanistic positions may be counted among those who retarded psychology's advancement toward scientific respectability.

Roeckelein (1972) actually addressed this question in a study of eponyms in psychology. His main goal was to determine how many times various psychologists' names were mentioned in eight popular textbooks for introductory psychology courses. Despite the overall eminence of the sampled psychologists, considerable variation existed in the prominence of their names in the texts. For instance, Sigmund Freud's name appeared dozens of times in every textbook, whereas Edward Titchener's name appeared in only three, and when it did appear it was mentioned only once. In a secondary part of the investigation Roeckelein (1972) examined whether this differential presence had anything to do with whether the psychologist was tender or tough minded, with 13 notables in each category. The tender-minded psychologists were Adler, Binet, Freud, Galton, Horney, Jung, Maslow, Piaget, Rogers, Sheldon, Sullivan, Terman, and Wolpe, whereas the tough-minded psychologists were Ebbinghaus, Helmholtz, Hull, James, Lashley, N. E. Miller, Pavlov, Schachter, Skinner, Thorndike, Tolman, Watson, and Wundt. Although the two groups did not significantly differ in eponymic status, subsequent analyses obtained more suggestive results; in particular, statistically significant differences were obtained when Freud was contrasted with Skinner and when Freud and Piaget were compared with Hull and Tolman. The tests showed that the tender-minded psychologists held an edge over the tough-minded psychologists according to their eponymic status in introductory psychology textbooks.

Those follow-up analyses may raise doubts about the robustness of the results—too much opportunity to pick and choose. This is not the only methodological objection. The assignment to the two orientations was based on each psychologist's subdiscipline. Personality, clinical, developmental, and testing psychologists were identified as tender minded, whereas the learning–motivation and psychophysics psychologists were classified as tough minded. In other words, the contrast was really based on whether the psychologists favored correlational or experimental methods—what Cronbach (1957) once called the "two disciplines of psychology." Making these classifications all the more crude is the fact that they were categorical rather than quantitative. Watson, Hull, and Tolman surely were not all equally tough minded, neither were Freud, Galton, and Maslow all equally tender minded. In addition, no attempt was made to control for historical time, even though the relative presence of the two types of psychologists may have shifted over the course of history. Finally, it may be preferable to use some other gauge of a psychologist's impact on the field than eponymic prominence in introductory psychology textbooks. Specifically, the magnitude of current influence might be better assessed using citation indexes, which I discussed in chapter 3. I conducted a more recent study that avoids these and many other possible objections (Simonton, 2000b).

Philosophy of Psychological Science and Long-Term Influence

The investigation (Simonton, 2000b) began with a sample of psychologists whose unquestioned eminence had been previously established through expert ratings (Coan & Zagona, 1962). The sample consisted of 54 psychologists active from the 1880s to the 1950s "who emerged among the top 50 in overall ratings or among the top 10 in the ratings for any decade" (Coan & Zagona, 1962, p. 716). The mean year of birth was around 1872, with a range from 1801 for G. Fechner to 1919 for W. Estes. Most came from the United States, and the remainder came from Germany, Britain, Austria, France, Switzerland, Canada, and Russia. The 54 represented every major subdiscipline (physiological, comparative, cognitive, personality, developmental, educational, social, clinical, etc.) as well all the major schools (structuralism, functionalism, behaviorism, Gestalt, psychoanalytic, humanistic, etc.). There was only one woman: Karen Horney.

Given this sample, it was an easy task to assess the long-term impact of these psychologists on current research using the *Social Sciences Citation Index* (1983, 1992). To obtain the most reliable measure of current influence, I used two 5-year accumulation citation indexes: one for 1976–1980 and the other 1986–1990 (Simonton, 2000b). These represent the two most recent, nonadjacent periods for which cumulative indexes were available. In each case I counted the total number of citations received (consulting various sources, such as R. I. Watson, 1974, whenever there existed any ambiguities). The correlation between these two measures is .84, indicating a conspicuous temporal stability in the long-term influence of the 54 psychologists. Because the test–retest reliability was so substantial, I was able to sum the two measures to produce a composite index of scholarly influence. The average great psychologist received 1,359 citations in the 10 years, or an average of 136 citations per year. Yet the range was substantial, from an annual rate of 6 citations for Külpe to 1,271 for Freud. Because the resulting measure was also skewed right, with an unusually extended upper tail, I submitted the citation indicator to a logarithmic transformation that made it more closely approximate the normal distribution (for scores, see Simonton, 2000b).

The next step was to see whether this log-transformed measure of total citations was contingent on the philosophy of psychological science represented by each psychologist's research program (Simonton, 2000b). This obviously requires that each of the 54 be assessed for their theoretical and methodological orientation, a seemingly prodigious task. It was fortunate that a previous investigator (Coan, 1968, 1979) had completed and published this assessment. In particular, 232 experts rated the research programs of these 54 psychologists according to 34 characteristics, such as the role of conscious processes, introspective reports, individual uniqueness, naturalistic observation, determinism, nomothetic analyses, statistical analyses, and so on. Then, with factor analysis, these 34 measures were consolidated into six nonorthogonal factors, and the corresponding factor scores were published (Coan, 1979). The six factors may be described as follows: (a) *Objectivistic Versus Subjectivistic* (emphasis on observable behavior versus emphasis on subjective experience; e.g., Watson, Pavlov, Skinner, and Hull vs. Jung, Brentano, Adler, Piaget, Fechner, and Janet); (b) *Elementaristic Versus Holis-*

tic (emphasis on molecular or atomistic analysis vs. emphasis on molar analysis; e.g., Spence, Titchener, Estes, Hull, Wundt, Pavlov, and Skinner vs. Goldstein, Koffka, G. Allport, Lewin, and Rogers); (c) *Impersonal Versus Personal* (emphasis on the nomothetic, deterministic, abstract, and tightly controlled vs. emphasis on the idiographic, emotional, and the unconscious; e.g., Hull, Skinner, Titchener, and G. E. Müller vs. Rorschach, Adler, Jung, Janet, G. Allport, and Charcot); (d) *Quantitative Versus Qualitative* (emphasis on mathematics, statistics, and precision vs. emphasis on qualitative attributes and processes; e.g., Estes, Thurstone, Spearman, Binet, and Ebbinghaus vs. Freud, Charcot, Wertheimer, Sullivan, and Köhler); (e) *Static Versus Dynamic* (emphasis on the normative and stable vs. emphasis on motivation, emotion, and the self; e.g., Wundt, Mach, Fechner, Spearman, and Külpe vs. McDougall, Mowrer, Freud, and James); (f) *Exogenist Versus Endogenist* (emphasis on environmental determinants and social influences vs. emphasis on biological determinants and heredity; e.g., Skinner, Angell, Hull, Rogers, and Watson vs. Galton, Freud, Hall, McDougall, and Cannon). The actual standardized factor scores for the 54 eminent psychologists are shown in Table 8.1.

As the original researcher, Coan (1968, 1979), pointed out, the correlations among these six factors are sufficiently high as to suggest the existence of one or more higher order factors. In fact, the first principal component accounts for nearly half of the total variance, with no loading below .49 (Simonton, 2000b). This may be considered a general factor that pits elementaristic, objectivistic, quantitative, exogenist, impersonal, and static psychologists against their holistic, subjectivistic, qualitative, personal, endogenist, and dynamic colleagues (i.e., natural vs. human science orientations). When the standardized scores on the six factors are summed to produce a composite measure, the resulting internal-consistency reliability coefficient (alpha) was .85 (see Simonton, 2000b, for actual scores).

All that was left to do was to see how the citation measure of contemporary influence correlated with the theoretical and methodological orientation represented by the general factor. I calculated this correlation after controlling for the psychologist's year of birth, so as to avoid artifacts from historical trends (Simonton, 2000b). The linear relation was negative (β = $-.23$); that is, great psychologists who adopt a human science orientation are more likely to boast long-term impact. This tendency replicates what was found earlier in the study of eponyms (Roeckelein, 1972). Nevertheless, the residuals betray substantial departures from linearity, suggesting that the relation is actually curvilinear. When a quadratic function was added to the linear function, the citation measure was a curvilinear, backward-*J* function of a psychologist's position on the natural versus human science dimension (βs = .26 for the quadratic term and $-.22$ for the linear term). Together these terms account for 11% of the total variance in long-term impact, with the curvilinear function accounting for slightly more of the curve than the linear

TABLE 8.1
Standardized Factor Scores for 54 Theorists on the
Six Factors Assessing Scientific Orientation

Theorist	Objectivistic	Elementaristic	Impersonal	Quantitative	Static	Exogenist
Gustav Fechner	−0.985	0.597	0.972	0.968	1.595	0.587
Hermann von Helmholtz	−0.269	1.090	0.582	0.445	1.093	−0.493
Francis Galton	−0.179	0.400	−0.781	0.881	0.892	−2.456
Jean-Martin Charcot	−0.448	−0.093	−1.268	−1.389	−0.918	−0.787
Wilhelm Wundt	−0.627	1.189	0.582	0.619	1.797	0.783
Franz Brentano	−1.164	−0.586	−0.391	−0.952	1.093	1.078
Ernst Mach	−0.716	0.301	0.875	−0.603	1.696	−0.002
William James	−0.448	−1.079	−0.391	−0.516	−1.119	−0.591
Granville Stanley Hall	−0.985	0.005	−1.073	0.357	−0.616	−1.769
Ivan Pavlov	2.060	1.189	0.680	0.968	0.691	−0.493
Hermann Ebbinghaus	0.179	1.386	0.485	1.318	1.394	1.372
Georg Elias Müller	−0.806	0.696	1.069	−0.341	−0.315	−0.493
Sigmund Freud	−0.090	−0.093	−0.976	−1.738	−1.320	−2.259
Alfred Binet	−0.090	0.203	−1.852	1.318	1.093	−0.394
Charles S. Sherrington	1.075	0.400	0.680	−0.603	1.093	−0.591
John Dewey	−0.627	−0.882	−0.489	−0.778	−0.918	0.194
Pierre Janet	−0.985	−0.586	−1.463	−1.738	−0.315	−0.198
James McKeen Cattell	0.179	0.400	−0.294	0.619	0.490	−0.493
Oswald Külpe	−0.358	0.696	0.290	0.183	1.294	0.587
Charles Spearman	0.090	0.696	−0.781	1.754	1.294	0.587
Edward Titchener	−0.806	1.583	1.069	−0.428	1.998	1.372
Robert S. Woodworth	−0.179	0.104	0.290	0.270	−0.516	−0.296
James Rowland Angell	−0.896	−0.488	−0.197	−1.040	−0.013	1.372
Alfred Adler	−1.075	−0.981	−1.755	−0.778	−1.622	0.391
Walter Cannon	0.448	0.104	0.388	−0.079	0.389	−1.474
William McDougall	−1.433	−1.671	−0.878	−0.778	−1.722	−1.572
Edward L. Thorndike	0.985	0.794	0.096	0.445	−0.415	0.096
Carl Jung	−1.433	−0.586	−1.657	−1.302	−1.622	−1.769
Lewis M. Terman	−0.000	0.203	−1.560	−1.667	0.490	−0.591
John B. Watson	2.239	1.090	0.777	0.532	−0.114	1.078
Kurt Goldstein	−0.896	−2.164	−0.878	−1.476	0.087	−0.689
Max Wertheimer	−0.448	−1.573	1.069	−1.214	1.495	−0.296
Hermann Rorschach	−0.896	−0.290	−1.949	0.095	−0.516	−0.198
Clark L. Hull	1.433	1.189	1.362	0.794	−0.717	1.176
Karen Horney	−0.448	−0.488	−0.976	−0.778	−0.717	0.391
Kurt Koffka	−0.716	−1.671	1.848	−1.127	0.691	−0.493
Edwin R. Guthrie	1.343	0.992	0.485	−0.079	−0.214	0.194
Edward C. Tolman	0.448	−0.784	0.777	0.794	−0.717	0.293
Wolfgang Köhler	−0.537	−1.770	1.751	−1.127	0.791	−0.787
Louis L. Thurstone	0.358	0.893	−0.489	1.929	0.289	−0.198
Kurt Lewin	−0.000	−1.474	0.680	−0.079	−0.516	0.783
Karl S. Lashley	0.985	−0.192	1.069	0.183	0.289	−0.591
Harry Stack Sullivan	−0.448	−0.488	−0.781	−1.214	−1.420	0.783
Jean Piaget	−0.985	−0.784	−0.197	−1.040	−0.315	−0.296
Gordon Allport	−0.896	−1.671	−1.365	−0.690	−0.918	−0.100
Carl Rogers	−0.627	−1.474	−0.976	−0.603	−0.817	1.176
Egon Brunswik	0.090	−0.586	0.290	0.445	0.188	0.194
B. F. Skinner	1.791	1.189	1.069	0.445	0.188	2.648

TABLE 8.1 *(continued)*

Theorist	Objectivistic	Elementaristic	Impersonal	Quantitative	Static	Exogenist
Donald O. Hebb	0.806	0.400	0.485	0.794	−0.817	−0.885
Harry Harlow	1.343	0.400	0.485	0.532	−0.616	0.096
Kenneth Spence	1.881	1.781	0.972	1.492	−0.616	1.176
Hobart Orval Mowrer	−0.179	0.301	0.388	−0.516	−1.521	0.882
Neal Miller	1.522	0.696	0.485	1.056	−1.018	0.783
William Estes	2.418	1.485	1.362	2.104	0.590	1.176

Note. All factor scores are standardized to a mean of 0 and a standard deviation of 1 (i.e., *z* scores). See text for the labels for the negative pole of each bipolar dimension. The standardized scores were computed from *T* scores reported in Coan (1979).

function (6% vs. 5%). The scatterplot and the best-fit quadratic curve are shown in Figure 8.1.

Three features of this curve deserve emphasis. First, the highest total citations tended to be received by eminent psychologists who scored lowest on the general factor. These are psychologists inclined toward the subjectivistic, qualitative, holistic, personal, dynamic, and endogenist side of psychology. Eminent figures in this group include S. Freud, C. Jung, A. Adler, W. James, G. Allport, and C. Rogers. Second, the next highest total citations tended to be received by eminent psychologists who scored highest on this same factor. These are the psychologists who leaned toward the objectivistic, quantitative, elementaristic, impersonal, static, and exogenist. B. F. Skinner, H. Harlow, L. L. Thurstone, and W. Estes are among the illustrious psychologists in this category. Third, psychologists situated at the bottom of the J-curve are those who have taken more moderate positions, with their long-term influence evidently declining as a consequence. The low point is actually off center, shifted toward individuals who score higher than average on the general factor. By applying differential calculus to the quadratic function one can show that the trough of the backward-J occurs when a psychologist scores almost exactly 0.5 standard deviation above the mean on the general factor (i.e., 0.50). In any case, the distinguished psychologists in this group are J. R. Angell, G. E. Müller, and J. M. Cattell.

Disciplinary Implications of the Backward-J Curve

What does Figure 8.1 tell us about the question at hand? Which type of philosophy of psychological science is most conducive to long-term disciplinary influence? To answer these questions one must first recognize that this question actually consists of two parts. First, why are psychologists who scored lowest on the general factor more frequently cited than those who scored highest? Second, why is the function complicated by the U-shaped curve?

One possible response to the first question is simply that the low scorers tended to produce more accessible work, not only for the researcher and prac-

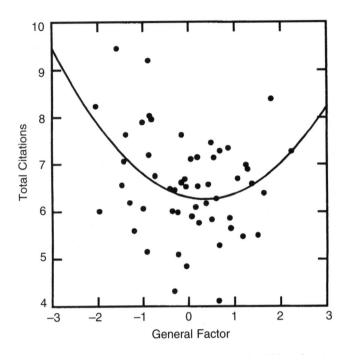

Figure 8.1. Scatterplot for total citations and scores that 54 eminent psychologists received on a general factor that gauges their human science (negative scores) versus natural science orientations (positive scores). Also shown is the best-fitting quadratic function defining the curvilinear backward-*J* curve describing the association between the two variables. From "Methodological and Theoretical Orientation and the Long-Term Disciplinary Impact of 54 Eminent Psychologists" by D. K. Simonton, 2000b, *Review of General Psychology, 4,* p. 19. Copyright 2000 by the Educational Publishing Foundation. Reprinted with permission.

titioner but also for the general scholarly community. Freud's 1900 *Interpretation of Dreams* and James's 1890 *Principles of Psychology* are certainly far more accessible works than are Hull's 1951 *Principles of Behavior* and Thurstone's 1941 *Factorial Studies of Intelligence.* Much of this accessibility may reflect a tendency for the tender-minded or human science orientation to be more broadly and enduringly attractive than the tough-minded or natural science orientation. However, it could also be that the success of the high scorers is not fully reflected in citation rates. It is in the manner of the scientific enterprise that a scientist's contributions become assimilated to such a degree that citation of his or her work would only be pedantic. As noted in chapter 3, much of the contemporary work on reaction times makes no explicit reference to F. C. Donders, because his ideas have now entered the public domain (Goodman, 1971). Of course, the same claim might be made about the eminent psychologists who occupy the low end of this general factor. The term *oedipal complex* tends to float around in the social sciences literature without specific references to any particular item in Freud's collected works. Even so, it is possible that the more personal nature of terms such as these makes this assimilation toward citation anonymity less likely than happens to an impersonal term such as *reaction time*.

What about the dip in influence seen in the psychologists who fall in the middle ranges of this broad dimension? There are at least two alternative but rather divergent responses.

On the one hand, the U-shaped portion of the curve may represent something idiosyncratic to psychology as a discipline. I already mentioned Kimble's (1984) work on psychology's "two cultures" and noted that these two cultures may reflect more fundamental contrasts in the personality traits that characterize the psychologists who typify each culture. The U-shaped curve consequently may simply reflect this fundamental bifurcation in the discipline. Eminent psychologists who can boast the most long-term success are those who can be considered exceptional exemplars of one or the other of these rival disciplinary cultures. In contrast, those who try to accommodate both sides of the division are ultimately obliged to satisfy neither and thereby undermine their influence in the long run. This interpretation implicitly assumes that the distribution of personal attributes underlying the two cultures is bimodal rather than unimodal. If most psychologists have a basic disposition focused at either one or the other extreme, with relatively few psychologists in the middle of the distribution, then the long-term reputation of the middle-of-the-roaders is clearly going to suffer as a consequence. Because so many psychological characteristics are roughly described by a normal distribution, the middle should admittedly represent the norm, and the associated pressure should push the most influential psychologists toward the golden mean between the extremes. Even so, psychologists could represent a highly biased sampling from the larger population because there actually exists more than one psychological profession—the scientist and the practitioner—each with its own distinctive requirements with respect to the orientation of its adherents.

On the other hand, this quadratic component might not be unique to psychology but rather indicate the operation of a far more universal process underlying attributions of greatness. Comparable U-functions have certainly been identified between the historical eminence of world leaders and their personal morality or idealism (Simonton, 1984f, 1987d). Saints and sinners have an advantage over those who dwell in the ambiguous compromise between good and evil. I found a parallel pattern regarding the differential eminence of more than 2,000 thinkers who make up the Western intellectual tradition (Simonton, 1976f). I describe my (1976f) inquiry in more detail in chapter 15, so may it suffice here to simply note that the most influential philosophers tend to be those who took extreme stances on the major debates that have preoccupied thinkers since the times of ancient Greece. Hence, it seems that to attain durable fame (or notoriety) demands that a person stand out from the crowd by avoiding moderate views. Long-term achievement as an eminent psychologist may operate according to the same rule.

Because the most recently born psychologists in the sample were born 80–90 years ago, one naturally might question whether the same principle operates today. Nevertheless, the residual diagnostics indicated that neither of the two most recent psychologists in the sample (N. Miller and W. Estes) departed in any significant manner from their earlier born colleagues. There was also no consistent tendency for the errors of prediction to increase as a function of birth year. As a consequence, there is no empirical reason to doubt that the findings remain applicable today (Simonton, 2000b).

Before some young, aspiring psychologist rushes off to espouse extremist positions, I must add an essential caveat: My (Simonton, 2000b) investigation examined only the long-term impact of 54 eminent psychologists. I did not address the issue of how eminent psychologists differ from their more obscure colleagues. These two questions do not necessarily have the same answer; in fact, many investigations have shown that the predictors need not be the same (see, e.g., R. B. Cattell & Butcher, 1968). For example, the factors that predict whether a politician wins an election as president of the United States are not identical to those that predict whether a president will be effective or ineffective (Simonton, 1987d, 1993; Winter, 1987). In fact, sometimes what predicts success by one criterion may predict failure by another criterion. It would consequently be most unwise for any ambitious psychologist to conclude that he or she must now adopt an extreme position on these dimensions in order to boast the same long-term impact as the 54 psychologists I investigated (Simonton, 2000b). After all, these individuals had to first make a name for themselves in the psychological science of their day (i.e., before the question of their long-term impact on contemporary psychology would have any meaning). That prerequisite signifies that they first fulfilled a far more fundamental requirement, namely, the need to make original contributions to the discipline, as amply demonstrated in chapter 3. Then and only then would anyone even care about what stand these individuals may have taken on the various theoretical and methodological matters that have provoked debate throughout psychology's history.

Nevertheless, these findings do show that once psychologists have established a solid reputation, their long-term influence may be a partial function of whether they have advocated more extremist positions (Simonton, 2000b). The irony here, of course, is that the truth may sometimes dwell at the mean rather than the extremes. An excellent case in point is the classic nature–nurture issue, a debate that dates at least to the time of Francis Galton (1874) and continues to plague the discipline today (Simonton, 1999d). Yet in the long run it may be better to claim something blatantly wrong (and thus easily attacked) than to propose a position too refined and complex for broad intellectual consumption. Insofar as the nature–nurture controversy forms an aspect of the more inclusive exogenist–endogenist dimension, one can now understand why the most distinguished contributors to the discipline tend to gravitate toward the extremes. The exogenist–endogenist dimension was specifically shown to have a curvilinear, *U*-shaped relation with the long-term influence of these same 54 psychologists (Simonton, 2000b).

This gravitation toward the antagonistic extremes contrasts dramatically with what has been learned about great discoveries in the natural sciences. In the latter, especially in physics, it is not uncommon for the breakthrough ideas to involve a synthesis of antithetical opposites. This integrative process has been called *janusian thinking*, after the Roman god who had two faces looking in opposite directions (Rothenberg, 1987). According to the son of Nobel laureate Niels Bohr, "one of the favorite maxims of my father was the distinction between the two sorts of truths, profound truths recognized by the fact that the opposite is also a profound truth, in contrast to trivialities where opposites are obviously absurd" (Bohr, 1967, p. 328). By applying this maxim, Bohr could triumphantly claim—in his complementarity principle—that the particulate and wave theories of subatomic phenomena were both correct and thereby reject the exclusive either–or position that had generated so much controversy.

One is thus led to a curious paradox: Psychology's advance as a scientific discipline may partially depend on its members' capacity to adopt more moderate, integrative positions with respect to certain key issues; yet, from the standpoint of the individual, the criteria for success may be diametrically opposed to this desideratum. To become the greatest of the great psychologists in the eyes of posterity, moderation may be an invariable vice. So, the long-term progress of the field may sometimes prove inconsistent with the long-term prominence of its participants. Great psychologists do not always make psychology a great science.

IV

LIFE SPAN DEVELOPMENT OF
GREAT PSYCHOLOGISTS

INTRODUCTION: LIFE SPAN DEVELOPMENT OF GREAT PSYCHOLOGISTS

Aristotle's father was court physician to Amyntas II, the King of Macedonia. Spinoza came from a Portuguese–Jewish family that had settled in Amsterdam. William James was the first born of 5 children. Charles Darwin's mother died when he was 8 years old. Sigmund Freud graduated from the gymnasium summa cum laude. Descartes never married. Margaret Floy Washburn earned her PhD under the supervision of Edward Titchener, himself a PhD under Wilhelm Wundt. Pavlov was in his mid-50s when he was honored with the Nobel prize for physiology.

These are some of the countless pieces of trivia that can be found in many textbooks, biographical dictionaries, and encyclopedias devoted to psychology's history. Such sporadic tidbits of information may be viewed in two contrary ways.

On the one hand, they may be considered idiographic details that help convey something of the uniqueness of a particular historical personage. These details have thus the same status as the figure's name and birth year. However curious or provocative, these idiosyncratic facts have no significance beyond the individual to whom they belong. They may give one insights into the person's quirks, or they may offer nothing more than "curious things to know."

On the other hand, these same particulars may be considered as having nomothetic implications; that is, each fact may represent a potential datum that can be subsumed under some abstract psychological process, law, or effect. Once subsumed, the fact transcends its idiographic origins. In the previously noted instances, for example, the particulars may relate to such general factors as socioeconomic class, ethnic marginality, birth order, childhood trauma, scholastic performance, marital status, mentoring, and career development. Moreover, these variables may display some useful correlation with the magnitude of a psychologist's impact on the history of the discipline. In other words, the facts become observations on variables that enable one to predict the odds that a particular individual can be considered a truly great psychologist.

It is not surprising that the second point of view is adopted in the chapters making up this part of the book. The biographical details that populate textbooks, dictionaries, and encyclopedias are seen as potential input into nomothetic equations that are relevant to the phenomenon that dominates this book. In chapter 9 I look at the family environment most strongly associated with the emergence of a great psychologist; in chapter 10 I do the same for career training and other educational experiences. Next, in chapter 11, I turn to the question of how a great psychologist's personal and professional lives most likely unfold during maturity and old age. Last, in chapter 12, I treat one of the most divisive theoretical issues in the history of psychology: the nature–nurture debate. This provides an opportunity to discuss the impact of gender on the course of psychology's history.

9

FAMILY BACKGROUND

Francis Galton's (1874) *English Men of Science* represents the first empirical study of the home environment that is most strongly associated with scientific accomplishment. Specifically, Galton sent out questionnaires to nearly 180 Fellows of the Royal Society of London (FRS)—the first such application of the survey–questionnaire method in psychology. Galton was himself an FRS and knew many great British scientists personally, such as his cousin Charles Darwin. Perhaps as a consequence he was able to attain a respectable response rate, obtaining a bit over 100 usable responses. Several of these respondents besides Galton and Darwin can claim some place in the history of psychology, namely, T. H. Huxley, William S. Jevons, Charles Lyell, James Clerk Maxwell, and Herbert Spencer (Hilts, 1975).

Because the questionnaire asked a large variety of questions about family background, it established the springboard for all subsequent research on the familial origins of eminent individuals, scientific or otherwise. Galton's successors include such researchers as Havelock Ellis (1926), James McKeen Cattell (1910), Louis M. Terman (1954), Catharine Cox (1926), Edward Thorndike (1950), and Anne Roe (1953a). Although a huge literature has thus accumulated since Galton's pioneering inquiry, relatively few studies focus on just distinguished psychologists. Even so, the research findings are probably sufficient to justify a few generalizations about the family experiences that are most strongly linked to the emergence of great psychologists. In particular, in this chapter I examine three sets of findings: (a) the general home circumstances in which a psychologist grew up, (b) the psychologist's specific birth order in the family, and (c) the occurrence of distinctive traumatic events during the psychologist's childhood or adolescence.

HOME ENVIRONMENT

Galton himself came from an old and distinguished family whose lineage included notable religious, political, and military figures. His father was a successful banker of sufficient means to leave Galton with a sizable inheritance, and his mother was a Darwin whose mother was the second wife of Erasmus Darwin. On his father's side, Galton was descended from one of the founders of the Quaker faith. Ethnically he hailed from the majority English culture, and his childhood home was in Birmingham, a major industrial and commercial city in the middle of England, approximately 110 miles from London. To put these facts into context I now examine how class, religion, ethnicity, and geography might be associated with the origins of great psychologists.

Class

The Victorian England of Galton's day was a highly stratified and class-conscious society. It was a world that placed great importance on social standing, occupational prestige, and economic advantage, with dramatic contrasts between the rich and poor, the educated and the ignorant, the wellborn and the ill-born. After all, it was during this period that Karl Marx was laboring away in London's British Museum doing his research on the class struggle. However, in the same years that Marx was writing his epochal 1867 *Das Kapital*, Galton was investigating another aspect of this socioeconomic stratification: its consequences for achieved eminence. In fact, the very first table in *English Men of Science* is devoted just to this subject (Galton, 1874, p. 22). Of the FRS he surveyed, only 2% came from farmer backgrounds, and just 8% had fathers who were noblemen and private gentlemen, whereas another 17% hailed from fathers who were in the military or government service. Almost three fourths came from just two family backgrounds: 32% from the professions (law, medicine, clergy, and teachers) and 40% from business (bankers, merchants, and manufacturers). Hence, Galton himself emerged from the largest single group, and 7% of the respondents came from bankers, counting Galton among those respondents. He fit right in.

Research since 1874 has replicated these findings many times. In Roe's (1953a) study of 64 eminent scientists, fully 53% were the sons of professional men, and not one was the son of an unskilled worker (also see Chambers, 1964; Eiduson, 1962). This is about the same percentage as holds for Nobel laureates in the sciences, with another 28% being the offspring of businessmen (Berry, 1981; also see Moulin, 1955; Zuckerman, 1977). Furthermore, the most highly represented professions among the laureate fathers are professors and physicians (Berry, 1981). It is critical to recognize that these studies usually defined socioeconomic standing in terms of the father's occupation, pretty much ignoring the mother's status. This was not due to any sexist bias on the part of the researchers. On the contrary, the one-sided definition merely reflects the place of women during the periods in which most of the scientists grew up. Almost all of these scientific luminaries came from homes in which the mother occupied the traditional role of wife, mother, and housekeeper (e.g., Eiduson, 1962), a reality that holds for even relatively recent samples (e.g., Feist, 1993). Moreover, although the mothers of eminent scientists are most likely to have been employed within the home, their own background and educational level tend to be considerably above average for their gender (e.g., Eiduson, 1962; Wispé, 1965). Hence, these mothers were obviously making significant contributions to the home environment in which the scientists experienced childhood and adolescence.

To appreciate better the role of class background in the origins of great psychologists one must examine how class origins relate to the domain of achievement and the degree of eminence achieved.

How Do Class Origins Vary Across Achievement Domains?

The specific origins of eminent figures clearly will depend on the domain in which those individuals attained eminence. Samples with a different composition than Galton's (1874) will obtain different distributions across the available classes. For instance, Havelock Ellis (1926) had a much broader sample of British geniuses and so obtained a slightly different dispersion: 3% artisans or unskilled, 6% farmers, 6% military, 9% crafts, 19% upper class, 19% business, and 35% professional (mostly clergy, law, and medicine). For the creators and leaders in Cox's (1926) sample, the breakdown was as follows: 52% nobility and professional; 29% semiprofessional, higher business, and gentry; 13% skilled workers and lower business; 4% semiskilled; and 1% unskilled. The percentages were very similar for the maternal grandfathers, except for a very slight tendency for the mother's father to come from lower socioeconomic strata. The corresponding figures are 42%, 35%, 19%, 2%, and 2%, respectively.

Several researchers have looked at how these proportions shifted according to the domain of eminence. In one early study of eminent scientists and writers (Raskin, 1936), the former were somewhat more likely to come from the homes of professionals (47% vs. 41%), whereas the latter were somewhat more likely to have fathers who were semiprofessionals (14% vs. 29%). The tendency for scientists to originate in the higher socioeconomic groups compared to other individuals in artistic domains has been found in other samples as well (e.g., Schaefer & Anastasi, 1968). However, such contrasts can even appear within various types of scientific endeavor. The anthropologists and theoretical physicists in Roe's (1953a) investigation were more prone to come from well-to-do homes. In Terman's (1954) longitudinal study, individuals who entered the physical sciences and medical–biological research tended to have somewhat better educated fathers than those who became engineers, with the social scientists being about average in class origins for the group.

This last result raises the obvious question of where the psychologists fit into this picture. If one goes by the figures whose names are most likely to grace the history of psychology, most do indeed appear to come from the homes of professionals. To offer some examples: Calkins, Fechner, Guthrie, Helvétius, Hobbes, Jung, Pavlov, Thorndike, and Wundt were all the children of ministers, priests, or clergymen; the Allports, Aristotle, E. Erikson, A. Freud, L. Galvani, C. Golgi, M. Klein, Paracelsus, C. Stumpf, and A. Vesalius were all offspring of physicians or other health professionals; G. S. Hall, H. Helmholtz, G. W. Leibniz, J. Piaget, J. Romanes, H. Spencer, E. H. Weber, M. Wertheimer, and Norbert Wiener had fathers who were professors, teachers, or other educators; and Averroës, Galen, K. Koffka, J. Locke, C. R. Rogers, and B. F. Skinner all hailed from homes where the father pursued some other learned profession, such as law, engineering, or architecture. Somewhat fewer seem to have had fathers who were in business (e.g., Bettelheim, Bruner, Ebbinghaus, Galton, Münsterberg, Schopenhauer, and Spinoza) or who served in government or military positions (e.g., Comte, Malebranche, Sartre, and Alan Turing). Fewer still emerged from the homes of skilled laborers; A. Bain, D. Diderot, A. G. Fichte, I. Kant, James Mill, and Socrates are among the examples. Even fewer could be said to have come from truly impoverished or disadvantaged backgrounds. This small group includes names like C. L. Morgan, O. Rank, and E. Titchener. By the same token, only a small number—such as A. Adler, Albertus Magnus, St. Anselm, Democritus, F. Galton, Heraclitus, W. James, J. B. Lamarck, M. Montessori, H. Murray, Plato, and E. C. Tolman—could boast status among the aristocratic or at least wealthy elite of their day.

The foregoing class distribution appears to fall in line with what might be expected from Galton's (1874) inquiry. The only important departure is that professional fathers appear somewhat more prominent than the entrepreneurial ones. In line with this switch, of the 14 eminent psychologists in Roe's (1953a) sample, 7 had fathers who were professionals (physicians, engineers, professors, and lawyers), 4 had fathers in business (2 as owners), 2 came from farming families, and only 1 had a father who was a skilled laborer. Hence, 50% came from professional families, and another 29% came from business backgrounds. Roe also noticed another curious fact about her 64 eminent scientists: Those who tended to think in words were more likely to come from homes in which the fathers pursued highly verbal occupations, such as law, the ministry, or teaching. Because psychology tends to favor verbalizations over visualizations, this linkage would suggest that great psychologists would also be more likely to have fathers with those pursuits. One of Galton's students and disciples, James McKeen Cattell, once expressed this association in a more autobiographical fashion:

> In my statistical studies I found that one who wanted to become a scientific man had the best chance if he chose a professor or a clergyman for his father. . . . My father was both a professor and a clergyman. (quoted in Sokal, 1971, p. 633)

But was Cattell more famous than his less notable colleagues as a consequence of his having chosen his father so carefully?

How Do Class Origins Vary According to Achieved Eminence?

Even if great psychologists are most likely to originate in the homes of professionals, that is not equivalent to the assertion that they are more likely to enjoy such a background than psychologists who failed to make an imprint on the discipline's history. The latter issue must be addressed separately. For example, it may simply be that people must acquire a higher education to become a scientist, and the children of professionals are most likely to obtain a college and university degree (West, 1961). In addition, the children from such backgrounds may be more likely to see the value of science as an intellectual endeavor and display an early interest in pursuing science as a career (Datta, 1967). Indeed, it is conceivable that certain kinds of professions, despite being "learned," might militate against a scientific-mindedness most supportive of doing great science. In chapter 8 I observed the potential antagonism of the scientific and religious worldviews. "It is therefore a fact," claimed Galton (1874), "that in proportion to the pains bestowed on their education generally, the sons of clergymen rarely take the lead in science. The pursuit of science is uncongenial to the priestly character" (p. 24).

The research on this question unfortunately is not totally consistent. A secondary analysis (Simonton, 1976a) of Cox's (1926) 301 geniuses found no linear or curvilinear relation between father's socioeconomic status and the genius's ranked eminence according to J. M. Cattell (1903c). This null relation even held for the subset of eminent creators in the group. A more recent study of contemporary university scientists obtained the same result, with the eminent and the noneminent exhibiting no difference in class backgrounds (Feist, 1993). In contrast, one investigation actually found that the more eminent scientists in the sample were less likely to come from the higher socioeconomic strata (Raskin, 1936). Amplifying the confusion all the more is that one study of scientists (including psychologists) discovered that the more eminent ones were more likely to have had professionals as fathers (Chambers, 1964). Even closer to home, another study found that the eminent male psychologists, relative to matched controls, had a higher likelihood of having had mothers with a high school education or better and of coming from families having three or fewer children (Wispé, 1965). This could be taken as a sign of a positive relation with social class. Yet other relevant home characteristics did not follow suit: A psychologist's eminence had nothing to do with his father's educational level or his family's financial condition.

Until additional research clarifies matters, I believe the safest conclusion is that social class helps determine who becomes a psychologist rather than how great a psychologist a person becomes. Because Galton had a banker father, he had educational opportunities that would more likely be denied a farmer's or a worker's child. However, if the latter somehow manages to overcome those obstacles and obtains the credentials necessary to secure a suitable occupation—such as physician or professor—then the socioeconomic advantage may vanish. Accordingly, many great contributors to psychology emerged from rather humble beginnings. J. P. Müller's father was a shoemaker, C. L. Hull's a poor farmer, and A. Maslow's an uneducated immigrant.

Religion

In chapter 8 I discussed the religious affiliations of great psychologists. However, an adult's religious practices may not coincide with the religious beliefs with which he or she grew up. Therefore, one still must treat the religious background most strongly associated with the attainment of success in the discipline. It should come as no surprise that Francis Galton (1874) was the first to address this question empirically. In *English Men of Science* he specifically examined the religious affiliations and origins of his distinguished survey respondents. Although the majority came from families that belonged to the Church of England, Galton was impressed with the large number of scientists with more uncommon religious backgrounds. "In confirmation of the assertion that the scientific men were usually brought up in families characterized by independence of disposition," wrote Galton (1874), "I would refer to the strange variety of small and unfashionable religious sects to which they or their parents belonged" (p. 123). Citing as examples the Sandemanians, Moravians, Bible Christians, and Unitarians among those who responded to his questionnaire, Galton could not resist noting that he found "in these returns numerous cases of Quaker pedigree" (p. 124). Besides John Dalton and Thomas Young, whom he mentioned explicitly, there was the implicit case of Galton himself (albeit his mother belonged to the Church of England). Despite the self-serving emphasis, the general conclusion remains valid: Great scientists have a higher likelihood of appearing in families that subscribe to less conventional religious faiths. In fact, this trend toward religious unconventionality has become accentuated in the 20th century: Eminent scientists are far more likely than other famous personalities to have grown up in agnostic and atheist home environments (Simonton, 1986a). Furthermore, illustrious scientists, compared to their less distinguished colleagues, are less likely to have regularly attended religious services when they were children (Feist, 1993).

Because the English of Galton's day were strongly aligned with the Protestant denominations, he did not have a whole lot to say about Roman Catholics and Jews (two groups that had suffered much persecution in generations previous to Galton's own). However, subsequent researchers have focused on broader populations of scientists, permitting generalizations about how these two faiths may contribute to the emergence of great psychologists. Two conclusions have been well established in the empirical literature.

First, notable scientists are less likely to come from Roman Catholic homes. None of Roe's (1953a) 64 scientists had such a background, for example. Among eminent mathematicians, 16% claimed such a religious heritage, an increase perhaps reflecting the fact that mathematics has seldom threatened religious dogma as much as have the natural sciences (Helson & Crutchfield, 1970). The Roman Catholic disadvantage even holds at the national level, for predominantly Protestant countries have a higher per capita output of great science than do countries in which Catholicism prevails (Berry, 1981). This is not to say that someone with a Roman Catholic background cannot become a great scientist or great psychologist. The falsity of such an assertion is disproved by such notables as Galileo, Descartes, Galvani, Volta, Golgi, and Brentano. It is simply a matter of the odds being somewhat more unfavorable.

Second, distinguished scientists are more likely to emerge from Jewish families (Berry, 1981). Of the 64 scientists in Roe's (1953a) study, 5, or about 8%, had Jewish backgrounds, a figure larger than their representation in the general population. This proportion is actually on the low side compared to what has been reported in other investigations. For instance, a survey of successful university researchers obtained the figure of 27% (Feist, 1993), and a study of eminent mathematicians obtained the figure of 38% (Helson & Crutchfield, 1970). The percentage of Protestants in these two samples was only around 45%, even though Protestants far outnumber Jews in general. Not only are Jews more numerous at the major research universities, but in addition, the more elite the university, the stronger their representation (J. R. Hayes, 1989b). Besides publishing more than Protestants and Catholics (J. R. Hayes, 1989b), Jews receive a disproportionate share of the Nobel prizes in the sciences (Zuckerman, 1977). Moreover, the advantage of having a Jewish background seems to emerge early, because Jews also represent impressive percentages of future scientists who emerge in talent searches (Datta, 1967). Of course, the contributions of Jews to psychology's history are highly conspicuous. In the 20th century alone Jewish psychologists founded (or helped found) some of the field's most influential movements, such as Gestalt psychology (Wertheimer) and humanistic psychology (Maslow). The psychoanalytic school was almost exclusively a Jewish creation, the product of such notables as Adler, Ferenczi, Rank, Fromm, Erikson, Melanie Klein,

Anna Freud, and, naturally, her father Sigmund. Other Jews among the greats of psychology's remote and recent past include Moses Maimonides, Baruch Spinoza, Henri-Louis Bergson, Stanley Milgram, and Noam Chomsky.

Ethnicity

The case of Jews is admittedly a bit ambiguous. Because they represent a people and not just a religion, Jews might just as well be considered an ethnic group. With their faith comes a distinctive language, national history, and cultural heritage that many Jews cherish even when they have given up the chief tenets of their religion. If so, then it would be most accurate to say that this particular ethnicity has an especially strong tendency to fill the ranks of the great contributors to psychology as a science.

This raises the broader question of how ethnicity is connected to the attainment of greatness as a psychologist. This, too, was an issue treated in Galton's (1874) classic survey, albeit somewhat briefly. In particular, on the basis of his FRS sample (leaving out a handful of Germans), he concluded that "out of every 10 scientific men, 5 are pure English; 1 is Anglo–Welsh; 1 is Anglo–Irish; 1 is pure Scotch; 1 includes Anglo–Scotch, Scotch–Irish, pure Irish, Welsh, Manx and Channel Islands; finally, 1 is 'unclassed'" (p. 16). However, Galton admitted that he gave "this information without being able to make much present use of it" (p. 17). Perhaps the safest generalization to draw from these data is that half of the scientists were pureblooded representatives of the majority ethnic group in the Britain of Galton's times. However, how much does this merely reflect the prejudicial manner in which British scientists were elected FRS? Is it possible that Galton's sample exhibited a certain degree of ethnocentric bias?

Because English high society was as race conscious as it was class conscious, an affirmative answer to this question cannot be dismissed. Moreover, other data lend support to this alternative account. Galton (1892/1972) himself once observed that "it is very remarkable how a large proportion of the eminent men of all countries bear foreign names" (p. 413). Empirical studies have documented the conspicuously auspicious fortune of immigrants to a new land (Bowerman, 1947). For instance, a study of 20th-century eminent personalities found that nearly one fifth were either first- or second-generation immigrants (M. G. Goertzel, Goertzel, & Goertzel, 1978). In one sample of highly eminent scientists, 25% were second-generation immigrants (Eiduson, 1962). Among distinguished mathematicians, 32% were foreign born (Visher, 1947b), and 52% were either foreign born or second-generation Americans (Helson & Crutchfield, 1970). Levin and Stephan (1999) scrutinized the origins of the most influential figures in the physical and life sciences of the United States. Judging from citation impact and membership in the National Academy of Sciences, "individuals making exceptional contributions . . . are disproportionately drawn from the foreign born" and "are also disproportionately foreign educated, both at the undergraduate and graduate level" (p. 1213).

According to the illustrious sociologist Robert Park (1928), "one of the consequences of migration is to create a situation in which the same individual . . . finds himself striving to live in two diverse cultural groups." Consequently, "the 'cake of custom' is broken and the individual is freed for new enterprises and new associations" (p. 881). Eminent psychologist Donald T. Campbell (1960) similarly maintained that

> persons who have been uprooted from traditional culture, or who have been thoroughly exposed to two or more cultures, seem to have an advantage in the range of hypotheses they are apt to consider, and through this means, in the frequency of creative innovation. (p. 391)

These explanations would also account for the pre-eminence of Jews among the Christian nations in which they reside (Veblen, 1919). Invariably strangers in a foreign land, Jews must reside forever in a bicultural world. The great philosopher Spinoza took the cultural multiplicity of the Jews to the extreme: A Portuguese second-generation immigrant in Protestant Holland, immediately descended from Jews who were forced by the Spanish Inquisition to embrace Christianity while practicing Judaism in secret, Spinoza was the polyglot product of multiple linguistic, national, and religious traditions.

Even more interesting is that these accounts suggest a way that members of the native-born population can attain some of the same advantages supposedly enjoyed by immigrants and Jews: Immerse yourself in some culture besides your own. In line with this, Havelock Ellis (1926) observed that a very high proportion of the British geniuses he studied had spent their early years living abroad for a considerable time. If one does not reside in another country early in life, at least there remains the option of studying abroad. Nobel laureates, for instance, illustrate this alternative: A very high percentage have gone to foreign universities to complete their education (Moulin, 1955; also see Poffenberger, 1930). Although Galton completed his formal education at Cambridge University, a securely English institution, perhaps his education was not really complete until he launched his significant explorations in the heart of Africa. Besides establishing his reputation as a scientist—his self-financed expedition earned him a Gold Medal from the Royal Geographical Society—Galton may have acquired a conceptual openness that he might have otherwise lacked.

Geography

Galton's fascination with geography was not confined to Africa. The very first data Galton (1874) presented in his *English Men of Science* concerned the birthplaces of his survey respondents. His goal was to discern whether eminent scientists were more likely to be born in particular parts of

England, Scotland, and Wales. Galton began by noting that "the birthplaces of scientific men and of their parents are usually in towns, away from the sea coast" (p. 19); specifically,

> out of every 5 birthplaces I find that 1 lies in London or its suburbs; 1 in an important town, such as Edinburgh, Glasgow, Dublin, Birmingham [including Galton], Liverpool, or Manchester; 1 is in a small town; and 2 either in a village or actually in the country. (p. 19)

The conclusion that great scientists are more likely to come from urban rather than rural environments has been replicated by subsequent researchers as well (e.g., Eiduson, 1962). Galton also observed that "the branch of science pursued is often in curious disaccord with the surrounding influence of the birthplace. Mechanicians are usually hardy lads born in the country, biologists are frequently pure townsfolk" (p. 19). It is surprising that Galton made no attempt to adjust his figures for population size, even though he had introduced this very correction in the analysis of the "Comparative Worth of Different Races" offered in his *Hereditary Genius* (Galton, 1869). Accordingly, it is impossible to judge from these figures whether metropolitan areas are more productive of great scientists on a per capita basis. Sometimes, when this adjustment is implemented, the primacy of the cities still emerges (Berry, 1981); at least this is true for scientists who become Nobel laureates. Yet other inquiries suggest that, notwithstanding the disadvantages apparently faced by individuals born in rural areas, birth in small towns may be more advantageous than birth in large metropolitan areas (Poffenberger, 1930). "It seems that the cities are failing to produce scientific men," noted James McKeen Cattell (1910, p. 640). Cattell himself was born in Easton, a small town in eastern Pennsylvania.

Galton's (1874) geographical interest was not confined to the question of rural-versus-urban origins. He also observed that his eminent scientists tended to originate in certain regions of the United Kingdom. In particular,

> an irregular plot may be marked on the map of England which includes much less than one-half of its area, but more than 92 per cent of the birthplaces of the English men of science or of their parents. (p. 19)

Galton had no explanation for this geographical concentration, except to note that the area roughly corresponded to the distribution of cities. Nonetheless, more than 100 years later P. H. Gray (1983) observed that the areas that were least productive of scientific eminence correspond very closely to the areas that sent the most Puritan immigrants to New England in the first part of the 17th century. In other words, these deficient regions may represent the aftermath of a massive brain drain from the mother country to the American colonies (also see Lynn, 1979).

What makes this conjecture especially intriguing is the pre-eminence of New England among the colonies in the production of great Americans.

For example, Massachusetts has been far more productive of greatness than has Virginia on a per capita basis (Woods, 1911). Furthermore, the university presidents who did the most for the establishment of scientific research in the United States were predominantly descendants of English families that had immigrated to New England in the 17th century (P. H. Gray, 1983). This list includes two eminent psychologists, namely G. S. Hall (Clark) and J. R. Angell (Yale). Even more to the point, a detailed study of the ancestry of illustrious U.S. scientists found that those with Puritan origins were by far the most conspicuous (Visher, 1947b). Of course, as the United States expanded toward the West, and with the advent of new waves of immigration, the hegemony enjoyed by Puritan New England dissipated over time (J. M. Cattell, 1933; Poffenberger, 1930). Hence, although "Massachusetts still retains its leadership in the production of scientific men," as J. M. Cattell (1910) said in the early part of the 20th century, "it has lost ground in the course of the past seven years, while the north central states have gained" (p. 639). Yet some remnants may have remained even decades later. Roe (1953a) observed that relatively few of her 64 eminent scientists came from the U.S. South.

The obvious next question is to move the analysis to another geographic level—that of the nation and civilization. Yet that topic is best left to Part V, in which I discuss the sociocultural basis for great psychologists. At that time I introduce the fascinating work of Alphonse de Candolle (1873), whose work was the direct impetus for Galton's (1874) *English Men of Science*.

ORDINAL POSITION

The preceding review focused on the home background factors that have received a respectable amount of empirical attention since Galton's (1874) survey. Naturally, not every variable that attracted Galton's fancy managed to inspire the curiosity of later researchers. Among other preoccupations, Galton examined whether the parents were in harmony with respect to the four temperaments, hair color, and body type, and from a statistical analysis concluded that "there is more purity of breed in scientific men than would have resulted from haphazard marriages" (p. 29). On the other hand, subsequent investigators have often looked at factors that attracted little or no interest on Galton's (1874) part. One of the more curious findings is the tendency for eminent personalities to be born in the cooler months of the year (Bowerman, 1947; Huntington, 1938; Kaulins, 1979), a tendency that seems to hold for illustrious scientists as well (Visher, 1947b). In line with this trend, Galton was born on February 16th and his cousin Charles Darwin on February 12th. Yet this calendrical effect is so weak that it would not have appeared in a sample of the size with which Galton had to work. Besides, the theoretical significance of this effect is not immediately clear (for further discussion, see Eysenck & Nias, 1982).

Yet Galton did pioneer the investigation of one factor that concerns the timing of one's birth in a rather different fashion: The child's order of birth in the family. Galton himself was the baby in the family, the last born of eight brothers and sisters. Perhaps as a consequence, very early in *English Men of Science* Galton (1874) took up the issue of primogeniture—doing so, in fact, immediately after his treatment of parental characteristics. Galton's analysis represents the first empirical study of the relation between birth order and exceptional achievement. Next I review his empirical findings as well as those of subsequent researchers using different samples of luminaries. Once the results are thus presented, I examine some of the explanations for birth order effects.

Empirical Findings

The research literature may be divided into three categories, depending on whether the samples consist of (a) eminent scientists from diverse disciplines, (b) great psychologists of various kinds, and (c) and more heterogeneous collections of historic personalities and geniuses. The first and the last help put in context the middle category, and all three sets of findings provide a basis for evaluating alternative theoretical interpretations.

Birth Order of Illustrious Scientists

Galton (1874) obtained usable answers from 99 of his eminent respondents. He summarized their responses as follows:

> Only sons, 22 cases; eldest sons, 26 cases; youngest sons, 15 cases. Of those who are neither eldest nor youngest, 13 come in the elder half of the family; 12 in the younger half; and 11 are exactly in the middle. (p. 33)

Given the sample size, these figures translate almost perfectly into percentages. Hence, nearly half of these scientists were eldest or only sons. Galton took this as evidence of a primogeniture effect. Two features should be noted about these figures, however. First, the numbers are expressed in terms of males only, ignoring sisters. This decision reflects the bias of Galton's times as well as the complete lack of women among the FRS. Second, Galton made no adjustment for variation in family size. This failure is unfortunate, for firstborns will outnumber laterborns in any sample that is heterogeneous with respect to family size. Nonetheless, Galton later reported that "the families are usually large to which scientific men belong" (1874, p. 36). Counting the scientist himself among their parents' offspring, their families consist of 6.3 children, or 4.8 if Galton counted only those who attained the age of 30 years. Given these statistics, there is ample room for laterborn scientists to dominate the sample. Hence, the advantage of the firstborn appears real.

Later investigators have mostly replicated Galton's results. For example, in Roe's (1953a) study 39 of the 64 eminent scientists were firstborn, and 15 of these were only children. Although Roe did not directly compare her percentages to Galton's, she did note that they were in line with what James McKeen Cattell once reported for 855 eminent American scientists (J. M. Cattell & Brimhall, 1921). Roe further observed that of the 25 who were laterborn, "5 are the oldest sons, and 2 who were second-born are effectively the oldest during their childhoods since the older children died at birth and at age 2" (p. 71), whereas another was separated by an appreciable age gap from the older brother immediately before him. In fact, for 15 of the remaining laterborns "the average number of years between the subject and his next older brother was 5" (p. 72). Hence she concluded that "most of those who are not first-born are either oldest sons, or substantially younger than their next older brothers" (p. 72). There were only 6 who do not fit this pattern. Another investigation that used a different sample of eminent scientists arrived at the same generalization (Eiduson, 1962). Out of 40, 5 were only children, and 19 were the eldest, but of the remaining laterborns, 7 saw themselves as only children because of the large age difference between them and the sibling born immediately before. It is curious that Galton himself complies with this familial pattern. He may have been the last child, but 6 years separated him from his older sister Adèle.

Like her unmentioned predecessor, Roe (1953a) did not explicitly control for family size. Even so, the primogeniture effect emerges when such control is implemented. This effect still appeared, for instance, in a study of 813 scientists at six major research organizations (West, 1960) and in another study of 197 Nobel laureate scientists (R. D. Clark & Rice, 1982). There is also evidence that the more select is the sample of scientists, the greater is the overrepresentation of firstborn and only children (e.g., Chambers, 1964; Helson & Crutchfield, 1970; West, 1960). To be sure, the literature is not always consistent with these conclusions. Feist (1993) found that although laterborns were underrepresented, the eminent scientists in the sample were somewhat more likely to be lastborns (28% vs. 10%). In addition, among Nobel laureates there is evidence that more recent prize recipients may actually be more inclined to be laterborns (R. D. Clark & Rice, 1982). These inconsistencies suggest that there may be circumstances in which the effect of ordinal position can be reversed, a point to which I attend later when I turn to the theoretical accounts of the phenomenon. First, however, I must look more closely at the subset of scientists who are the focus of this book.

Birth Order of Great Psychologists

Galton (1874) did not break down his figures on birth order according to discipline, but Roe (1953b) did. Of the 14 eminent psychologists in her sample, 6 were born first, 3 were born second, 2 were born third, and 4 were born fourth, with an average family size of 3, a median of 3, and a mode of 5. Thus, the earlier born children seem to hold an edge. Roe's (1953b) subsample here is admittedly rather small, but there is every reason to believe that her results are fairly typical. For instance, Table 9.1 provides the ordinal positions for some major figures in the history of psychology. Judging from this collection of representative names, it would seem that firstborns and only children again predominate. Many of the individuals in the table were included in a study of 79 figures who were honored by having their life stories included in the *History of Psychology in Autobiography* (Terry, 1989). Fully 52% were either firstborn or only children, a proportion that did not substantially change across various subsamples (viz., those elected president of the American Psychological Association [APA], selected for membership in the National Academy of Sciences, or honored with APA's Distinguished Scientific Contribution Award). It was also shown (Terry, 1989) that the proportion exceeds what would be expected according to the frequency distributions of the ordinal positions in their families. This correction is obviously important, especially because eminent psychologists tend to come from somewhat smaller families than do their less distinguished colleagues (Wispé, 1965).

Other investigations have obtained the same hegemony of the firstborn and only child among notable contemporary psychologists (e.g., Gupta, Gilbert, & Pierce, 1983; Helmreich, Spence, Beane, Lucker, & Matthews, 1980). Indeed, two additional findings are worth noting. First, Helmreich et al. (1980) found that the advantage was even greater for women than for men, by a contrast of 62% to 54%. Second, even after the necessary statistical controls were introduced, the asset of primogeniture is reflected in the rates at which psychologists are cited in the professional literature (Helmreich et al., 1980). Hence, firstborns and only children not only tend to outnumber the laterborns but also have more contemporary impact on the discipline of psychology.

Nevertheless, it must be emphasized that the percentages just reported represent only statistical tendencies. As is immediately obvious from inspection of Table 9.1, there are many exceptions to the rule. The nomothetic principle operating here is fundamentally probabilistic rather than deterministic; ordinal position is not destiny. Yet it is also conceivable that whenever there exist deviations from some statistical expectation, those outliers may reflect the operation of some other nomothetic regularity that functions independently of the one that generated the expectation. One such principle has already been discussed, namely, the intrusion of large age gaps that can convert a biological laterborn into a functional firstborn or only child. This possibility was noted with respect to Galton, and it may apply to other laterborns in Table 9.1. As noted there, several psychologists are separated from their older siblings by 5 years or more. Wilhelm Wundt, the "father of psychology," is a clear case. For all practical purposes he was an only child.

Another possible complicating factor may be subtler. Perhaps the impact of ordinal position depends on the domain of achievement, with some domains actually showing an advantage for children who are born later in the family lineup. To determine whether this actually happens requires that one look at studies that examine populations besides just scientists and psychologists.

Birth Order of Famous Personalities

At first glance, the primogeniture effect appears to be a universal phenomenon that is by no means confined to science and psychology. In one study of 1,000 Americans who had achieved distinction in a diversity of fields, eldest children appeared at a rate that was 172% larger than statistical expectation (Bowerman, 1947). A similar study of 227 famous Scots of the 19th century revealed that the eldest children made up almost half of the total, even though they typically came from families with 4–5 children (Bullough, Bullough, Voight, & Kluckholn, 1971). These statistics have not changed appreciably in samples consisting entirely of 20th-century notables (M. G. Goertzel et al., 1978). The asset of primogeniture even appears to hold for more narrowly defined populations. Firstborns are overrepresented among classical composers (Schubert, Wagner, & Schubert, 1977), astronauts and aquanauts (Helmreich, 1968), representatives to the U.S. Congress (Zweigenhaft, 1975), and even among First Ladies—especially women who are associated with highly powerful U.S. presidents (Simonton, 1996c).

Despite this seeming monopoly, the data also reveal that the effect of ordinal position is not always so simple. When Havelock Ellis (1926) scrutinized the birth order of his British geniuses, the youngest children had an edge over middle children, even if both categories of laterborns were less frequent than the firstborns (also see Altus, 1966). A comparable pattern was found among Terman's (1925) sample of intellectually gifted children: Although the firstborn and only children were most prominent, among those who came from large families the youngest actually outnumbered the middleborn children. Hence, the effects of ordinal placement in the family do not necessarily operate in a linear fashion. Even more critical is that some types of achievement are more likely to be occupied by laterborn and lastborn children. For instance, highly charismatic U.S. presidents are more prone to be laterborns (Simonton, 1988c). Moreover, although eminent scientists are more likely to be firstborns, eminent creative writers are more likely to be laterborns (Bliss, 1970; also see Eisenman, 1964). Even more telling is the abundant evidence the firstborn pre-eminence in the sciences has a significant qualification: The laterborns display a higher likelihood of becoming revolutionary scientists—those who overthrow the accepted scientific paradigms of their data (Sulloway, 1996). What makes this finding most provocative is that a similar finding has been found in the realm of politics: Revolutionaries who aspire to overthrow status quo governments are also

TABLE 9.1
Representative Ordinal Positions

Ordinal position	Scientist
Only child	A. Anastasi, A. Binet, D. Broadbent, L. Carmichael, E. Erikson, H. Eysenck, J. R. Hilgard, B. Inhelder, C. Jung,[a] G. W. Leibniz, J. Locke,[b] C. Mayo, B. Milner, M. Montessori, M. Rioch, J. P. Sartre, E. S. Spelke, H. Spencer, W. Stern, H. S. Sullivan,[c] S. Taylor, M. F. Washburn
First born of	
Two	Avicenna, S. Bem, R. Benedict, C. M. Bühler, B. S. Burks, C. Burt, J. M. Cattell, M. Clark, Galileo, E. Gibson, M. R. Harrower, C. L. Hull, A. Kinsey, M. Mead, W. R. Miles, C. S. Myers, B. L. Neugarten, C. Osgood, M. K. Phipps, S. L. Pressey, J. E. Purkinje, W. Reich, R. Sears, B. F. Skinner, J. T. Spence, B. R. Strickland, L. L. Thurstone, A. Treisman, H. C. Warren
Three	D. Dix, J. Dollard, J. Gibson, G. S. Hall, R. Helson, L. S. Hollingworth, J. Piaget, T. G. Thurstone, E. H. Weber, B. L. Wellman, L. Witmer, R. S. Woodworth,[d]
Four	E. S. Berscheid, J. Drever, C. H. Graham, D. O. Hebb, H. W. Helmholtz, L. J. Martin, L. Tyler, G. Watson, J. Wolpe, P. Zimbardo
Five	F. Brentano, M. Calkins, A. Gesell, E. Guthrie, W. James, C. Ladd-Franklin, I. Pavlov, P. Pinel, C. E. Seashore, R. Yerkes
Seven	J. W. Goethe, A. Maslow
Eight	S. Freud
Nine	L. M. Gilbreth
? (Unknown)	P. Abélard (oldest son), G. Berkeley (oldest son), Albertus Magnus, M. Maimonides
Middle child	
Second of 3	M. E. Bernal, R. B. Cattell, K. M. Dallenbach, E. Frenkel-Brunswik, J. P. Guilford, E. Hilgard, T. Hobbes, D. Hume, Q. McNemar, S. Milgram, H. Murray, T. Newcomb, B. Pascal
Second of 4	F. Allport, K. Lewin, E. E. Maccoby, S. Scarr, E. L. Thorndike
Second of 5	W. McDougall, J. B. Rhine, J. B. Watson
Second of 6	A. Adler, J. Garcia, J. J. Goodnow
Second of 8	W. Harvey, K. Marx, L. Vygotsky
Third of 4	J. Dewey, H. Harlow
Third of 5	N. Bayley, R. M. Elliott, E. Heidbreder, D. C. McClelland, B. Spinoza
Fourth of 4	R. A. Hinde
Fourth of 5	R. Descartes, P. S. Sears
Fourth of 6	C. Rogers
Fourth of 7	B. Rush
Fifth of 6	C. Darwin
Sixth of 10	F. J. Gall

TABLE 9.1 *(continued)*
Representative Ordinal Positions

Ordinal position	Scientist
Seventh of 8	D. Katz
Eighth of 9	D. Krech
Ninth of 12	J. F. Dashiell
Tenth of 11	J. D. Matarazzo
Twelfth of 14	L. M. Terman
Last born of	F. Denmark, F. A. Geldard (s = 9),[f] M. Henle,[g] K. Horney,[h]
Two	F. D. Horowitz, W. S. Hunter, A. E. Michotte, C. L. Morgan, C. R. Payton, H. Pièron, H. A. Simon, W. Wundt (s = 8)[f,i]
Three	J. R. Angell (s = 6),[f] C. H. Judd, H. O. Mowrer (s = 15),[f] C. W. Sherif, E. C. Tolman (s = 5)[f] M. S. Viteles
Four	G. Allport, E. G. Boring, J. Bruner (s = 14),[f] H. Deutsch, K. von Frisch, M. Klein, J. Konorski, V. S. Sexton
Five	E. Claparéde, E. A. Doll, Voltaire
Six	W. Bingham, A. Freud
Seven	T. Aquinas, F. Galton, S. A. Kierkegaard, D. Wechsler
Eight	F. L. Goodenough
Nine	W. E. Blatz
Eleven	J. B. Lamarck
? (Unknown)	N. Malebranche[j]

Note. This list comes from various sources, and not all sources agree on the ordinal position of a particular individual. The main reason for discrepancies is how to treat special circumstances, such as half-siblings and siblings who died young. I thank W. Scott Terry at the University of North Carolina at Charlotte for providing me with the raw data he used in his investigation. I also thank Rochel Gelman, Brenda Milner, Elizabeth Spelke, Shelley Taylor, and Anne Treisman for responding to my e-mail inquiries.
[a]Until age 9. [b]Older brother died in infancy. [c]Two older brothers died in infancy. [d]Third of mother.
[e]Third of father. [f]Separated from older sibling by at least 5 years (s = actual amount of separation in years). [g]With twin sister. [h]Four older stepsiblings. [i]Or only child. [j]Youngest child.

more likely to have been laterborn children (L. H. Stewart, 1977, 1991; Walberg, Rasher, & Parkerson, 1980). So both intellectual and political revolutions may constitute laterborn forms of high achievement.

Theoretical Interpretations

What theory can possibly account for the prominence usually enjoyed by the firstborn child while at the same time accommodate these apparent departures? One might best address this question by breaking it into two parts.

When Is Eldest Best?

Although Galton (1874) himself was a lastborn child, he was willing to consider the weight of the evidence obtained from his survey. Accordingly, he felt compelled to offer some explanation. Galton believed that "the elder sons have, on the whole, decided advantages of nurture over the younger sons" (p. 34). He specifically speculated that the eldest are more likely to become possessed of independent means, and therefore able to follow the pursuits that have most attraction to their tastes; they are treated more as companions by their parents, and have earlier responsibility, both of which would develop independence of character. (pp. 34–35)

This advantage would cut across socioeconomic class as well, because "the first-born child of families not well-to-do in the world would generally have more attention in his infancy, more breathing space, and better nourishment, than his younger brothers and sisters in their several turns" (p. 35).

In line with Galton's speculations, firstborns are not only more likely to attend college but also to be enrolled at highly prestigious colleges (Altus, 1966). Furthermore, performance on intelligence and academic achievement tests tends to decline as a function of ordinal position (Zajonc, 1976). Robert Zajonc (1976), the eminent U.S. psychologist, explained this trend in terms of the superior intellectual stimulation afforded those born earlier in the family. This position not only is compatible with Galton's views, but also holds that a large age gap between a youngest child and his or her older siblings would make that child more like a firstborn in the level of intellectual stimulation. In fact, Galton's older sister Adèle helped train young Francis to become a child prodigy. In other respects, too, Galton's place in the family was more like that of the firstborn son. His father left him enough money that he could become "possessed of independent means," enabling Francis to lead the life of a gentleman scientist. Moreover, owing to his father's recent conversion to the Anglican faith, the family had high hopes that Francis would become the first in the Galton family to attain a university degree at Oxford or Cambridge (Fancher, 1998). He graduated from the latter.

Galton's (1874) speculative account also suggests that birth order may affect the development of personality traits, such as "independence of character," which Galton believed was crucial to the attainment of eminence. Alfred Adler (1938), the distinguished founder of individual psychology, also thought that birth order shaped personality development, but in a somewhat different manner. As evident in Table 9.1, Adler was even less typical of great psychologists than was Galton. He was a middle child, with an older brother and sister. Adler experienced considerable sibling rivalry with his older brother but soon found himself unable to compete, especially athletically. Although his physical frailties earned him special attention from his mother, her pampering was short lived. On the birth of his younger brother, she turned her attention elsewhere, leaving Adler feeling a bit abandoned. Adler believed that this experience of abandonment was especially strong in the firstborn, who then acts as a "dethroned king." The dethroned firstborn attempts to regain parental attention and thereby becomes motivated by the need for social approval and societal prestige. The result is a child who will do everything to make his or her parents proud.

Adler's theory explains why firstborns tend to do very well in school and go on to graduate from elite institutions (Altus, 1966). According to noted social psychologist Stanley Schachter (1963), this educational repercussion alone could account for the pre-eminence of the eldest child among great scientists. After all, most domains in which eminence is attained—including psychology and other sciences—presuppose that the person attain a higher degree from a major university. In addition, if the eldest children are truly so preoccupied with obtaining recognition, then they will surely do whatever they can to attract the attention of their colleagues. This approval-seeking behavior may help account for the higher citation rates claimed by firstborns who become psychologists (Helmreich et al., 1980). Of course, well-educated firstborns who do not become scientists or psychologists may achieve distinction in some other profession instead; for example, they may become lawyers, enter politics, and become respected leaders. Whatever the specific route, the eldest children will, one way or another, come out on top, obtaining the praise and acclaim they so eagerly sought ever since they were first dethroned by a younger sibling.

Adlerian theory also addressed the other ordinal positions. Although the youngest children are often spoiled by their parents, their lowly position in the sibling pecking order means that they frequently acquire potent feelings of inferiority and thus end up with severe adjustment problems later. Only middle children experience the ordinal position most optimal for personal development. Their desire to compete with their older siblings will often make them very ambitious yet also more inclined to challenge authority and even become revolutionaries. Adler himself exemplified his own theory. Besides being the first major figure in Freud's inner circle to make a break with the master, Adler was leftist in his political outlook. A staunch feminist, he also espoused socialist positions.

When Is Youngest Best?

Adlerian theory was the first important psychological theory to perceive birth order as a significant variable in personality development; however, it was not the last. Frank Sulloway's (1996) recent book *Born to Rebel* offered an alternative developmental theory that also places major emphasis on this factor. However, Sulloway's starting point was not Adler, neither was it Freud, despite the many insights into Freudian theory that Sulloway (1979) provided in his earlier volume *Freud, Biologist of the Mind*. Instead, Sulloway's point of departure was Charles Darwin and Darwinism. Essentially, Sulloway wanted to understand why Darwin's 1859 *Origin of Species* provoked so much scientific controversy. Although many distinguished scientists praised the revolutionary work, many others, of equal distinction, condemned it in sometimes quite vicious terms. In the supportive group was T. H. Huxley, who responded to Darwin's central argument by immediately exclaiming "How extremely stupid not to have thought of that!" (quoted in Sulloway, 1996,

p. 18). In the critical group were such notables as Louis Agassiz, the great naturalist, and Pierre Flourens, the experimental physiologist who pioneered the use of ablation in the neurosciences. According to Agassiz, Darwin's theory was "a scientific mistake, untrue in its facts, unscientific in its method, and mischievous in its tendency" (quoted in Sulloway, 1996, p. 14). Flourens was even more intemperate, despite the fact that he had previously written a more balanced, empirically based critique of phrenology. Flourens needed to write a booklength monograph to attack Darwin's *Origin* with expressions like the following: "What metaphysical jargon clumsily hurled into natural history! What pretentious and empty language! What childish and out-of-date personifications!" (quoted in Sulloway, 1996, p. 14). Why was T. H. Huxley so positive and Agassiz and Flourens so negative?

Sulloway (1996) observed that the controversy that whirled around Darwinism seemed to center very little on data or deduction; instead, the differences hinged more on personality. Specifically, Sulloway surmised that the reception of Darwin's ideas reflected individual differences in openness to experience. Given this conjecture, Sulloway sought the developmental source for the cross-sectional variation on this personality factor. He believed he had found it in the scientist's ordinal position in the family—that is, on average, the later a child appears in the birth sequence, the stronger that child's disposition on this factor. Three features of Sulloway's explanation deserve special emphasis.

1. Sulloway's theory is not only grounded in the history of Darwinism but also rooted in Darwinian theory. Very much like Adler (1938), Sulloway viewed sibling competition as a critical feature in personality development. Each child in a multiple-child family must compete for the attention and resources of his or her parents. For the most part, this rivalry means that each child must find his or her special niche in the family. It is unfortunate for the laterborns that the firstborn gets the first shot at the most privileged niche, which entails the early identification with parental authority and the fulfillment of parental aspirations. Indeed, as Galton (1874) indicated, the firstborn is likely to take on family responsibilities at a relatively young age and thus obtain practice at responsible adulthood. Denied this special status, the laterborns are obliged to carve their own niches, with the result that they must remain more open to environmental possibilities and personal potentials, including more unconventional options. In a sense, each successive sibling must undergo something akin to divergent evolution, opportunistically exploiting whatever comes his or her way. This developmental thrust can explain many of the domain contrasts in the ordinal positions I noted

earlier (Simonton, 1999b). Whereas the firstborns become conventional scientists and status quo politicians, the laterborns become the revolutionary scientists, charismatic presidents, and political revolutionaries. Also, where the firstborns enter more traditional careers, such as composing classical music, the laterborns pursue the more venturesome life of the artist or creative writer. Indeed, according to a study conducted by Richard Nisbett (1968), laterborns are even more likely to engage in such high-risk activities as dangerous sports.

2. Also, not unlike Adler (1938), Sulloway's (1996) theory is far too sophisticated to rely on birth order as the sole factor in the explanatory framework. On the contrary, Sulloway's theory incorporates multiple developmental variables that combine in a complex manner to yield nonadditive and nonlinear consequences. In particular, his theory includes age gaps between adjacent siblings, gender, race, innate shyness, parent–offspring conflict, early parental loss and surrogate parenting by older siblings, and special friendships. The theory also recognizes the existence of different types of revolutions, including those that are conservative or reactionary in nature. Furthermore, all of these factors are not introduced post hoc but rather follow from Sulloway's Darwinian theory of personality development. For example, some of the factors, such as being female or extremely shy, can often prevent the firstborn child from occupying the firstborn niche, and thus the position may be taken over by the next child in the family lineup. Hence, Sulloway felt obliged to formulate his theory in terms of a multivariate prediction model. This mathematical specification sets Sulloway's theory well apart from the more qualitative and intuitive elaborations of Adlerian theory.

3. Also quite unlike Adler (1938), Sulloway (1996) actually gathered an awesome amount of data to test his theoretical model of birth order effects. All told, he analyzed "121 historical events, which encompass biographical data on 6,566 participants. These 121 events include 28 revolutions in science, 61 reform movements in American history, 31 political revolutions and the Protestant Reformation" as well as "a database on U.S. Supreme Court voting behavior, which includes biographical information on the 108 justices to date" (p. 376). Statistical analyses show the same tendency: Laterborns are much more likely to be the first to endorse revolutionary ideas (even after correcting for the fact that laterborns outnumber firstborns in the population). The firstborns, in contrast, are

more likely to support conservative movements or to join revolutionary movements once they have already been well established by laterborns. In the case of the Darwinian revolution, for example, the laterborns were almost five times more likely to support evolution by natural selection than were the laterborns. Besides T. H. Huxley, laterborn adherents of Darwinian theory included Charles Lyell, Joseph Dalton Hooker, Alfred Russel Wallace, Ernst Haeckel and, of course, Charles Darwin himself. A similar disparity is seen with respect to the Copernican heliocentric system, William Harvey's theory of blood circulation, Newton's celestial mechanics, Antoine-Laurent Lavoisier's new chemistry, James Hutton's theory of the earth, and Einstein's theory of special relativity.

Sulloway (1996) scrutinized several scientific controversies that are obviously germane to the history of psychology. Some of these were most likely to attract laterborn adherents. In addition to the Darwinian revolution, this includes the work of Francis Bacon and René Descartes on the scientific method, phrenology, and Freudian psychoanalysis up to the end of the first world war. According to Sulloway's theory, these should be considered radical revolutions. In contrast, other movements tended to appeal more to firstborn adherents, namely, mesmerism, modern spiritualism, eugenics, and Freudian psychoanalysis after 1919—what may be considered more conservative positions. Mesmerism and spiritualism tried to provide a scientific foundation for mysterious forces and experiences more compatible with older traditions, whereas eugenics attempted to justify and maintain class and racial hierarchies. The switch with respect to psychoanalysis is fairly typical of movements that are launched mostly by laterborns only to be eventually co-opted by firstborns. Movements often become entrenched and traditional, a closed system unsympathetic to new ideas. Thus Karen Horney, a laterborn, found herself excommunicated from the New York Psychoanalytic Institute for failing to conform to firstborn authority.

Sulloway's theory and data have generated considerable controversy (Simonton, 1997c). Several notable scientists view *Born to Rebel* as itself a revolutionary scientific contribution. Others are less supportive, and some are as hostile as the critics who so viciously attacked Darwin's 1859 *Origin of Species*. It would be highly instructive to see whether Sulloway's theory successfully predicts the reception his theory has received (cf. Rubin, 1970). Sulloway himself, like Darwin, was a laterborn. However, according to his theory, ordinal position is not the only factor that must be taken into consideration. Sulloway has certainly found a strong advocate in me, and I am an unequivocal firstborn (and only son, with four sisters). Yet my scores on his other predictors suggest that I may be more open to radical ideas—even those that would seem to put firstborns in a somewhat unfavorable light. Perhaps that explains why I have given his views even more attention than those of Galton and Adler. Other firstborns, with a contrasting configuration of biographical factors, may believe that my coverage is completely unwarranted. Whether this be true or not I leave to the reader to decide—whatever his or her birth order may be.

TRIALS AND TRIBULATIONS

> When Heaven is about to confer a great responsibility on any man, it will exercise his mind with suffering, subject his sinews and bones to hard work, expose his body to hunger, put him to poverty, place obstacles in the paths of his deeds, so as to stimulate his mind, harden his nature, and improve wherever he is incompetent. (quoted in Chan, 1963, p. 78)

So said the ancient Chinese philosopher Mencius (Mengzi). The basic idea expressed in this famous passage is that greatness is born out of adversity, that "what does not kill us makes us stronger." In saying this, Mencius may have had in mind the life of his great predecessor, Confucius (Kungzi). Born to an impoverished noble family, Confucius was orphaned at an early age and grew up under the most trying hardships, becoming the most erudite thinker of his day only through an arduous program of self-education.

The history of psychology is replete with major figures who likewise emerged out of exceptional adversity. Both Abraham Maslow and Henry Stack Sullivan had extremely troubled relationships with their respective mothers (the former even refusing to attend her funeral). Many were frail or sickly as children, including René Descartes, Blaise Pascal, Thomas Hobbes, Johann Friedrich Herbart, Auguste Comte, William James, Alfred Adler, Carl Rogers, and Cyril Burt. Those plagued with tuberculosis included Baruch Spinoza, Dorothea Dix, Lewis Terman, and Albert Camus. Many had to endure some physical or cognitive disability, such as polio (Clark Hull), spinal malformation (Nicholas de Malebranche), asthma (John Locke), vision problems (Socrates and Jean Paul Sartre), or such speaking difficulties as stuttering (Henry Murray), stammering (Ruth Benedict), or lisping (Anna Freud). Sometimes the person suffered from the stigma of being exceptionally unattractive, as was the case for Socrates and Bruno Bettelheim. Other times the stigma was less public, yet no less powerful, such as Harry Stack Sullivan's struggles with his homosexuality at a time when such a sexual orientation was socially unacceptable. Especially conspicuous, however, is the number of cases in which the individual lost one or both parents at an early age, as illustrated in Table 9.2. The loss may have entailed either actual death or some other dramatic and enduring absence, such as abandonment (e.g., Hobbes). However, more chronic forms of parental loss are also possible.

TABLE 9.2
Instances of Early Parental Loss

Individual	Lost parent	Age (years)
Philosophers		
R. Descartes	Mother	0
J. J. Rousseau	Mother	0
	Father	10
Montaigne	Mother	0
J. P. Sartre	Father	1
D. Hume	Father	3
B. Russell	Mother	2
	Father	3
F. Nietzsche	Father	4
G. W. Leibniz	Mother	18
	Father	6
B. Spinoza	Mother	6
Voltaire	Mother	7
T. Hobbes	Father	Childhood
M. Merleau-Ponty	Father	Childhood
G. W. F. Hegel	Mother	11
J. Bentham	Mother	12
I. Kant	Mother	13
A. Schopenhauer	Father	17
F. Bacon	Father	18
Thomas Aquinas	—	—
Aristotle	—	—
Augustine	—	—
Montesquieu	—	—
Scientists		
I. Newton	Father	0
R. Benedict	Father	2
P. Sorokin	Mother	3
	Father	11
B. Pascal	Mother	4
B. Rush	Father	5
Paracelsus	Mother	Childhood
A. Quételet	Father	7
C. Darwin	Mother	8
N. Copernicus	Mother	Childhood
	Father	10
C. S. Sherrington	Father	Childhood
J. B. Lamarck	Father	16
Psychologists		
E. Erikson	Father	Before birth
A. Anastasi	Father	1
M. Rioch	Father	1
H. Hollingworth	Mother	1
L. Hollingworth	Mother	4
G. T. Fechner	Father	5
C. Osgood	Father	6

TABLE 9.2 *(continued)*

Individual	Lost parent	Age (years)
H. Eysenck	Mother	Childhood
	Father	Childhood
J. Cohen	Father	Childhood
W. S. Hunter	Mother	12
C. Ladd-Franklin	Mother	12
J. Bruner	Father	12
R. Perloff	Father	12
H. Rorschach	Mother	12
	Father	18
J. B. Watson	Father	13
W. Wundt	Father	14
E. Hilgard	Father	14
E. Loftus	Mother	14
E. H. Weber	Mother	16
M. Klein	Father	18
H. Münsterberg	Mother	Before 20
	Father	Before 20

Note. Parental loss means loss through death or other form of separation, such as divorce or abandonment (when known). Dashes represent data that are not known.

Otto Rank's father was an incorrigible alcoholic, and Karen Horney's father, a sea captain, was absent so much that she felt that she was fatherless. Moreover, sometimes the parents, although present, were emotionally remote, as was the case for Carl Jung and Wilhelm Wundt.

And yet it must be admitted that not every eminent psychologist had to pass through such severe rites of passage. B. F. Skinner grew up in a warm, stable family environment, and R. B. Cattell claimed to have had a happy childhood. Francis Galton led a very contented life at home until he was shipped off to boarding school. These counterexamples oblige one to examine more systematically the available empirical data.

Empirical Results

Galton (1874) did not address this question in his *English Men of Science*. Perhaps it was an issue too delicate to inquire about in an impersonal questionnaire, especially in Victorian times, when private matters were usually protected by the rules of decorum. So the first to broach the topic was Havelock Ellis (1926), who noted the high frequency of "constitutional delicacy" in the early lives of his sample of British genius. Decades later, Roe (1953a) made a compatible observation about her 64 eminent scientists, a large proportion having spent their childhood suffering serious illnesses or physical handicaps—the theoretical physicists in her sample distinctively so. A totally different study of 400 eminent personalities found that about one quarter had to compensate for some disability (V. Goertzel & Goertzel, 1962). Unhappy childhoods can arise from other causes as well, such as family economic difficulties, including periods of outright poverty (Berry, 1981; V. Goertzel & Goertzel, 1962; Raskin, 1936). This developmental influence should remind psychology's historians of the financial problems often encountered in the childhood homes of such great psychologists as Sigmund Freud and Clark Hull.

Nonetheless, the bulk of the empirical research has concentrated on the high incidence of partial or complete orphanhood (i.e., the loss of one or both parents prior to attaining majority age). Several studies have suggested that orphanhood rates are especially high among eminent personalities, with rates ranging around 25%–50% (Eisenstadt, 1978; Illingworth & Illingworth, 1969; Walberg et al., 1980). Thus, an analysis of the luminaries in Cox's (1926) sample revealed that about one quarter suffered parental loss prior to attaining adulthood (Albert, 1971). Some evidence also exists that parental loss is to be found at elevated frequencies among distinguished scientists (Eiduson, 1962; Silverman, 1974). For instance, Roe (1953a) noted that "one of the first things that stands out is the frequency with which these subjects report the death of a parent during their childhood" (p. 84). The specific figure was 15%. Roe (1953a) offered statistics implying that this rate exceeded what would be expected in comparable groups. Another inquiry that looked at historical rather than contemporary scientists—including notables such as Copernicus, Descartes, Pascal, Newton, Leibniz, Quételet, and Maxwell—found that they typically lost their mothers around age 4 or their fathers around age 7 (Silverman, 1974). Among 32 famous mathematicians, moreover, one quarter lost a parent before age 10, and almost one third suffered parental loss before age 14 (Bell, 1937).

However, others have argued that when the figures are compared against the most appropriate baselines, the supposed orphanhood effect disappears (e.g., Woodward, 1974). The statistics must certainly be placed in the context of what holds for individuals born at approximately the same time and place and in about the same socioeconomic circumstances; otherwise, age at orphanhood would be confounded with the diverse factors that generally influence mortality. Although suitable comparison groups have been identified for certain domains of achievement, such as political leadership (Berrington, 1974; Simonton, 1988c), this has not been adequately attained for samples of eminent scientists, including psychologists.

Complicating the picture all the more is that the magnitude and frequency of various trials and tribulations vary according to the achievement domain. Unhappy childhoods are much more common among artistic creators than among philosophers or scientists (Post, 1994; Simonton, 1986a). This contrast holds across different specific sources, such as poverty or orphanhood (Berry, 1981; F. Brown, 1968; Eiduson, 1962; Raskin, 1936). For example, writers who receive the Nobel prize for literature are far more likely than laureates in the sciences to have "either lost at least one parent through death or desertion or experienced the father's bankruptcy or impoverishment" (Berry, 1981, p. 387). Making matters yet more complicated is the considerable variation that exists within distinct scientific activities. Among Roe's (1953a) 64 scientists, for instance, 25% of the biologists lost a parent by death before age 10, but this was the case for only 13% of the physical scientists and 9% of the social scientists. Although the last statistic seems to hint that great psychologists have happier childhoods than do great scientists in general, other empirical findings confound this simple conclusion. Chambers (1964) found that eminent psychologists, relative to other scientists, tended to come from homes in which their fathers were more emotionally remote and their parents less accepting of them. Thus, for great psychologists parental absence may assume a more subtle and chronic form. The parental neglect encountered by Wundt and Jung may not be atypical.

Theoretical Explanations

What is one to make of the foregoing findings? One possibility is simply to reject altogether any statement that the results have any relevance for a scientifically informed history of psychology. After all, few studies can be said to have established the hypothesized "unhappy-childhood effect" beyond reasonable objection, and those that have apparently done so seem to apply largely to nonscientific domains of creative achievement. None of the investigations focused specifically on individuals who attained distinction in psychology's past or present. Even so, a review of some of the offered explanations may stimulate future research on this question. These theoretical interpretations may also help direct such research toward more fruitful lines of inquiry. With that in mind, the following three accounts deserve attention.

First, various trials and tribulations in early life may make an enduring contribution to a youth's motivational development. For instance, Eisenstadt (1978) suggested that the loss of a parent in early life instills a "bereavement syndrome" that propels the individual on a lifelong journey toward compensation. One difficulty with this explanation is that it requires that the child or adolescent actually experience bereavement, something that is not always safe to assume. Certainly the death of Newton's father could leave no such impression, for Isaac had not even been born yet but rather was a posthumous child. Sometimes, too, the child does not enjoy the kind of intimate relationship that would render the parent's death truly traumatic. Charles Darwin had this to say about his own failure to face bereavement: "My mother died . . . when I was a little over eight years old, and it is odd that I can remember hardly anything about her except her deathbed, her black velvet gown, and her curiously constructed work-table" (F. Darwin, 1892/1958, pp. 5–6). Given the sentimental attitudes Victorians had toward the mother–

child relationship, it is questionable that Darwin would have admitted such emotional inertness unless it were really true. A final drawback of the bereavement explanation is that it applies only to one particular class of highly traumatic events: the loss of a loved one. Hence, other features of an unhappy childhood, such as being sickly or poor, would need some other theoretical interpretation.

The second explanation would include a wider range of untoward circumstances but still emphasize motivational development. Perhaps all those trials and tribulations, both big and small, help build a personality that has the determination and persistence that are essential for long-term success (Simonton, 1994a). As already noted, the life and career of any outstanding creator are full of obstacles and setbacks; an exceptional success may be succeeded by an equally phenomenal failure. Therefore, early and frequent encounters with various frustrations and difficulties may facilitate the growth of an individual who has the requisite robustness or hardiness. This interpretation can account for the diversity of hapless experiences. It might also accommodate the contrasts observed across creative domains. It may conceivably require more determination and persistence to become an artistic genius than a scientific genius. In fact, artists who fail to acquire the needed personal strength and willpower may be those inclined to succumb to alcoholism, a common side effect of this kind of creativity. As the Welsh poet Dylan Thomas once said, "there's only one thing that's worse than having an unhappy childhood, and that's having a too-happy childhood" (quoted in Ferris, 1977, p. 49). It is not unlikely that Thomas himself might have not drunk himself to death had he acquired a more robust personality early in childhood. He may have been a victim of having a "too-happy childhood."

The third and last explanation also handles the contrasts across creative domains but does so by emphasizing the impact that an unhappy childhood might have on cognitive development (Simonton, 1999b). This theory is predicated on a Darwinian model of the creative process first put forward by Donald T. Campbell (1960) and further elaborated by Hans Eysenck (1995). In essence, this theory assumes that: (a) creativity entails a variation–selection process; (b) different domains differ in the degree of variational freedom that they require, with scientific creativity being more constrained than artistic creativity; and (c) a creator's capacity to produce relatively unrestricted variations is a partial function of the diversity, richness, and novelty of the experiences he or she had to assimilate in childhood and adolescence. Hence, the primary importance of the various trials and tribulations is simply that they are different from what most people encounter during development. These diversifying experiences expand the range and variety of the variations that they can generate. However, because artistic creators require greater spontaneity in their variations, they should have encountered more diversifying stimulation in youth, precisely as the data suggest. Notice that this third explanation can also account for cases such as

Newton's and Darwin's. Neither had to suffer the emotional trauma of those losses for their developmental trajectories to be pushed away from the stereotypical patterns. Indeed, Darwin suddenly found himself raised by an older sister rather than by his mother, unlike most other children. Newton's case is even more dramatic and divergent: Two years after his birth, his widowed mother remarried and promptly gave him to a grandmother to raise, not wanting anything more to do with him. This caused Newton so much embitterment that he was never able to establish a normal relationship with a woman throughout his entire life. He was barely capable of having an untroubled friendship with any man as well, too often exploding in fits of paranoia.

Newton's life hints that one's childhood can indeed be excessively unhappy as well. In line with this conjecture, the eminent are not the only people who might have traumatic experiences in their early years. The rates of parental loss are also high among such unfortunate groups as juvenile delinquents, suicidal depressives, and homeless people (Eisenstadt, 1978; Roe, 1953a). Thus, perhaps if the Fates had thrown a few more life tests Newton's way, his name would not be so well known today. The operating principle appears to parallel what I observed in chapter 7 with respect to having just the right amount of mental and emotional instability. At the same time, the magnitude of trauma that a potential talent can accommodate may partly depend on his or her inherent hardiness. Unhappy experiences that might set one person on an upward path to glory might condemn another on a downward path to oblivion. English novelist Samuel Butler (1903/n.d.) suggested this contingency in his *The Way of All Flesh*:

> In quiet, uneventful lives the changes internal and external are so small that there is little or no strain in the process of fusion and accommodation; in other lives there is great strain, but there is also great fusing and accommodating power; in others great strain with little accommodating power. A life will be successful or not according as the power of accommodation is equal to or unequal to the strain of the fusing and adjusting internal and external changes. (p. 288)

Hence, the greatest psychologists may be those who experienced life challenges that were well matched to their constitutional capacity to cope constructively rather than destructively.

This latter suggestion leads to one last observation. I have noted how distinguished psychologists were more likely to have distant and unsupportive relationships with their parents, especially their fathers. Perhaps as a reaction, these same psychologists tended to have more unfavorable and rebellious attitudes toward their parents (Chambers, 1964). These results also are compatible with what Roe (1953a) reported about her social scientists on the basis of their performance on projective tests: Compared to other eminent scientists, they appeared especially hostile and overly concerned about social relationships. These results suggest that great psychologists may enter the field to work out some personal issues that originated in some less than favorable family circumstances. The life and work of Carl Rogers may best illustrate this possibility. His parents were so strict and unaccepting that he developed various psychosomatic illnesses as a youth, and Rogers later became a humanistic psychologist who placed the utmost stress on the power of giving children unconditional positive regard! Hence, unhappy childhoods can determine the content, not just the extent, of a psychologist's greatness.

10

CAREER TRAINING

Poor parent–child relationships may not be the only personal issue that shapes a great psychologist's preoccupations. Although much of a child's early years are spent in the home, as children get older their lives become ever more dominated by school. This experience, too, may be the source of either happiness or unhappiness. Francis Galton's life amply illustrates the latter possibility. He absolutely hated the boarding school to which he was shipped off at age 9. Not only was the competition there brutal, but also Galton's talents were largely out of step with its curriculum, which emphasized the classics. Neither did he do much better in his college years, despite having more opportunity to pursue his mathematical interests. Although trying his best to win honors in mathematics at Cambridge University, he found himself incapable of conquering the horrendously difficult Mathematical Tripos examinations. After the impossible quest provoked a serious nervous breakdown, Galton was compelled to lower his expectations, withdraw from the competition, and accept an ordinary degree.

Given this unfortunate experience, it seems fitting that Galton (1874) should devote the fourth and last chapter of *English Men of Science* to education. In doing so, he became the first behavioral scientist to investigate how formal education contributes to the attainment of scientific distinction. However, of course, he was by no means the last to research this topic. I review this extensive literature on a relation between education and scientific achievement next. Afterward I examine two closely related topics—self-education and professional marginality—that Galton's survey did not directly address.

FORMAL EDUCATION

Although Albert Einstein could not possibly have been among the respondents to Galton's (1874) survey, he certainly can be considered an exemplar of scientific genius. Moreover, Einstein was quite explicit when he expressed his personal attitudes toward his educational experiences. For instance, he once remarked that

> it is, in fact, nothing short of a miracle that the modern methods of instruction have not yet entirely strangled the holy curiosity of inquiry; for this delicate little plant, aside from stimulation, stands mostly in the need of freedom; without this it goes to wreck and ruin without fail. It is a very grave mistake to think that the enjoyment of seeing and searching can be promoted by means of coercion and a sense of duty. (quoted in Schlipp, 1951, p. 17)

His opinions were especially negative about the procedures most commonly used to test students' mastery of the material:

> One had to cram all this stuff into one's mind for the examinations, whether one liked it or not. This coercion had such a deterring effect on me that, after I passed the final examination, I found the consideration of any scientific problems distasteful to me for an entire year. (quoted in Hoffman, 1972, p. 31)

Given Einstein's bad attitude, it comes as no surprise that his teachers were not very impressed with him. For example, one of his university professors, Hermann Minkowski, admitted that Einstein's later scientific achievements "came as a tremendous surprise . . . for in his student days Einstein had been a lazy dog. He never bothered about mathematics at all" (quoted in Seelig, 1958, p. 28). Another exasperated professor, Heinrich Weber, told Einstein directly, after years of frustration: "You're a clever fellow! But you have one fault. You won't let anyone tell you a thing. You won't let anyone tell you a thing" (quoted in Hoffman, 1972, p. 32).

Many great figures in the history of psychology have expressed similar opinions. For instance, James McKeen Cattell (1910), in his study of 1,000 distinguished American scientists, once ventured that

> our educational methods are thus becoming more completely standardized or conventionalized. The two men who stood first on the list of 1903, Simon Newcomb and William James, had neither the regular col-

lege nor the regular university education. Whether this was favorable or harmful to their genius is unknown; but it is probable that our present educational methods do not favor individuality and its early expression. (p. 643)

Charles Darwin provided a specific anecdote illustrating the stifling effects of formal education when he complained that

during my second year at Edinburgh I attended Jameson's lectures on Geology and Zoology, but they were incredibly dull. The sole effect they produced on me was the determination never as long as I lived to read a book on Geology, or in any way to study the science. (F. Darwin, 1892/ 1958, p. 15)

These reactions are not atypical. Among the 87 scientists who responded to Galton's (1874, p. 237) question about their educational experiences, 11% complained about "want of system and bad teaching" and another 37% expressed dissatisfaction with the "narrow education" they had received. An especially common complaint was that the curriculum stressed useless subjects, such as Latin and Greek, while being largely devoid of the natural sciences and mathematics. All told, 57% had some kind of complaint. Of the remaining minority, many praised experiences that were somewhat peripheral to their formal training, such as "home teaching and encouragement." Only 10 of 87 survey responses could be placed in the category "education praised throughout, or nearly so." Moreover, individuals with more positive experiences came from institutions that provided what Einstein considered most basic to a good education. Typical praise in this vein are "freedom to follow my own inclinations, and to choose my own subjects of study, or the reverse"; "the great proportion of time left free to do as I liked, unwatched and uncontrolled"; and "unusual degree of freedom" (p. 254).

Yet these are mere opinions, not facts. Hence, to determine the impact of formal education on the emergence of great psychologists, it is necessary to look at the objective reality, not the subjective perception of that reality. I now examine the following five issues: highest degree obtained, quality of scholastic performance, degree of accelerated progress, prestige of the educational institution, and influence of distinguished mentors.

Highest Degree

It is commonly assumed that a doctoral degree is essential for eventual scientific success. Yet Einstein's own educational history proves otherwise. Having alienated too many of his college professors to have any chance to enter advanced training, he was obliged to seek employment instead, eventually procuring a full-time job at the Swiss Patent Office. In the meantime, Einstein worked independently on various projects in theoretical physics, hoping that one might be accepted as a doctoral dissertation by the University of Zurich. Even though his first attempt was rejected, the paper was afterward accepted for publication in *Annalen der Physik*, one of the premier journals in the field. His subsequent difficulties getting a higher degree later led him to tell a friend "I shall not become a Ph.D. . . . The whole comedy has become a bore to me" (quoted in Hoffman, 1972, p. 55). Yet over the next few years, this same prestigious journal accepted several additional papers of Einstein's. In 1905 came Einstein's annus mirabilis, when he completed three papers—on Brownian motion, the photoelectric effect, and the special theory of relativity—any one of which was sufficient to earn him a lasting place in the annals of physics. But it was a fourth, much less significant paper that Einstein decided to submit as a doctoral thesis. When it was again rejected, this time for being too short, Einstein persisted in his peevish cynicism. He responded by adding just one sentence, and he was hence rewarded with his PhD. All the while, he was still working away in the patent office, neither attending graduate seminars nor working in some mentor's laboratory. The lesson of this story is clear: Obtaining a PhD had nothing to do with the development of Einstein's scientific greatness. Although not nearly so dramatic, similar episodes are narrated in the history of psychology. James Rowland Angell is a favorite case, because he

> studied both abroad and under James at Harvard but never bothered to finish his PhD. His career, which included the supervision of many doctoral theses, demonstrated that one need not have those three letters after one's name to be creative, original, productive. (Wertheimer, 1987, p. 114; also see Schultz & Schultz, 1992, p. 189)

Besides supervising theses, Angell built the psychology department at the University of Chicago into the most influential of its time, served as president of the American Psychological Association (APA), and ended his career as president of Yale University, where he created its Institute of Human Relations. Not bad for a doctoral all-but-dissertation dropout. Maybe some truth is hidden in Henry David Thoreau's (1845/1942) complaint that "there are nowadays professors of philosophy, but not philosophers" (p. 39). Alternatively, cases like Einstein's and Angell's may constitute mere oddball exceptions.

To put this issue into its proper context I begin by looking at more inclusive samples of eminent personalities. Havelock Ellis (1926) reported that only 53% of his British geniuses could claim any university training whatsoever. One might think that this same statistic would not be expected in more recent samples, but that turns out not to be the case. An inquiry confined to 314 modern luminaries obtained the following breakdown: 19% graduate or professional degree, 4% some graduate or professional study, 19% college graduate, 9% some college attendance, 23% high school graduate, 11% some high school, and 15% eighth grade or less (M. G. Goertzel, Goertzel, & Goertzel, 1978). Not only do nearly half of eminent people claim no college or university education, but also those with advanced degrees are outnumbered by those who never finished high school! These figures indicate that a higher degree is not essential to the attainment of distinction.

Of course, these statistics lump together a wide array of pathways to eminence—revolutionaries, assassins, painters, poets, and so on—in which higher education may have the most minimal relevance. Research has shown, in fact, that the expected level of formal education attained varies according to the domain of achievement. Raskin (1936) directly compared eminent scientists with eminent writers and found that those in the former group were much more likely to have university training, by a differential of 73% to 65%. The latter percentage supports Vera Brittain's (1948) warning that "the idea that it is necessary to go to a university in order to become a successful writer, or even a man or woman of letters (which is by no means the same thing), is one of those phantasies that surround authorship" (p. 7). Likewise, a secondary analysis of the 314 illustrious personalities described above (M. G. Goertzel et al., 1978) revealed that the scientists and psychiatrists tended to acquire much more formal education than most other groups, especially compared to athletes, labor leaders, entrepreneurs, and mystics or psychics (Simonton, 1986a). Even so, there remains a residual of interesting exceptions, such as Erik Erikson, who managed to become a psychoanalyst without any university education whatsoever. It is interesting that Galton (1874) reported that fully one third of his eminent English scientists also lacked any university-level instruction.

Although it may be possible to attain distinction, even as a scientist, without a college or university degree, one still might wonder whether any advantage accrues to someone who has gained the privilege of adding initials such as *BA* or *PhD* to his or her name. In two secondary analyses I directly examined this issue (Simonton, 1976a, 1983b, 1984d).

In the first analysis (Simonton, 1976a) I examined the 301 geniuses in Cox's (1926) study and coded the subjects for the level of formal education they attained, using the extensive biographical data she published. I then gauged how her assessment of differential eminence (derived from J. M. Cattell's 1903b study) depended on this new measure. The 192 creators were treated separately from the 109 leaders in her sample. The result is shown in Figure 10.1. For the leaders, the linkage is strictly negative and monotonic, with the most eminent leaders having the least amount of formal education. For the creators, a rather more surprising outcome appears: The function is nonmonotonic and single peaked, yielding an inverted-*J* curve. Two features about this curve deserve emphasis. First, the optimum level of formal education appears around the last 2 years of undergraduate instruction. Second, the low point of the curve is not at zero formal training but rather at a doctoral or equivalent degree. It would seem that individuals who obtain the highest degrees are penalized for their efforts.

In the other secondary analysis (Simonton, 1984d) I used the 314 illustrious moderns already mentioned twice earlier. This time I devised a new

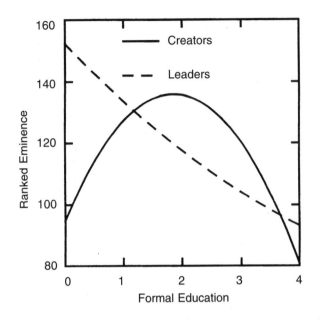

Figure 10.1. The functional association between ranked eminence and formal education for the 192 creators and 109 leaders in Cox's (1926) study of 301 geniuses (from Simonton, 1984d). The independent variable was scored as follows: 0 = no formal education, 1 = high school graduate or equivalent, 2 = bachelor's degree or equivalent, 3 = master's degree or equivalent, and 4 = doctoral degree or equivalent. A half point was awarded to individuals whose educational attainments fell between two categories (e.g., 1.5 for some college). From "Formal Education, Eminence, and Dogmatism: The Curvilinear Relationship" by D. K. Simonton, 1983b, *Journal of Creative Behavior, 17*, p. 152. Copyright 1983 by the Creative Education Foundation. Adapted with permission.

eminence measure, along the lines of J. M. Cattell's (1903b) but with several improvements. In addition, I assessed level of formal education attained in pretty much the same way as I did with the Cox (1926) data (Simonton, 1976a), but with a few refinements. Finally, I divided the sample into four groups rather than two: creators in the sciences, creators in the arts and humanities, leaders of various kinds, and miscellaneous celebrities. For the last group the function was monotonic yet positive, with greater fame associated with more formal training. In the remaining three groups, the function was curvilinear, however. Individuals who attained eminence in domains of leadership exhibited an educational peak at a modest amount of postbaccalaureate education—about the level obtained by going to law school. For subjects who achieved distinction in the arts and humanities the curve was virtually identical to what was found for the creators in Cox's sample: a curvilinear function with the peak again placed in the last couple of years of college education. Those who attained greatness in the sciences also obtained a curvilinear function, but with the optimum in a very different location, namely, the first few years of advanced training. The higher degree itself added no incremental advantage. The curve is best described as an inverted–backward J. Succeeding as a scientist in the 20th century evidently requires much more formal training than in the days of old. This conclusion is reinforced by another study of 194 technical and scientific personnel, which found that the most productive were those who had the most academic degrees, even after controlling for age (Van Zelst & Kerr, 1951).

Whether this conclusion can be extended to future psychologists is a difficult problem. The difficulty is simply that it is now rather rare for psychologists *not* to have a doctoral degree. Of 161 deceased individuals who earned obituaries in *American Psychologist* between 1979 and 1990, fully 97% had earned a PhD (Kinnier, Metha, Buki, & Rawa, 1994). This is not a recent phenomenon. Another study of 69 eminent American psychologists active between 1879 and 1967 found that 87% had the same status (Simonton, 1992b). Moreover, this percentage might be increased to 90% if one considers that 2 of the figures had actually written their doctoral dissertations but did not have them accepted. One was the already-mentioned Angell who, lacking Einstein's persistence, simply gave up trying to improve his German composition to meet his professors' high expectations. The other was Mary Calkins, to whom I shall return in chapter 12. With uneven splits such as these, there exists too little variation to give this educational factor much predictive power. Indeed, for the 69 psychologists, whether one can claim a PhD has no connection, whether positive or negative, with any standard indicator of greatness, whether eminence, citations, or productivity (Simonton, 1992b). Hence, if the goal is to predict a psychologist's greatness on the basis of his or her educational experiences, it is necessary to look elsewhere.

Scholastic Performance

Marcel Grossmann was a brilliant mathematician who earned a PhD at age 24 and at age 29 secured a mathematics professorship at Zurich Technological Institute. Yet Grossmann is not nearly so well known as his university classmate and friend, Albert Einstein. Indeed, Grossmann's fame is almost entirely confined to his having helped Einstein overcome his academic deficiencies. In the first place, it was Grossmann's meticulous lecture notes that enabled Einstein to pass the examinations he so hated. Second, when Einstein began to realize that his mathematical deficiencies were preventing him from developing his theoretical ideas, he found in Grossmann a willing and extremely capable collaborator. It is as Einstein's mathematical handyman in the development of the general theory of relativity that Grossmann is best known today. So Einstein's academic mediocrity was clearly by no means a major deficit; neither was Grossmann's scholastic proficiency a major asset.

Likewise, in the history of psychology the scholastic first may end up last and the last end up first. I have already noted Galton's academic struggles, but he is far from the only instance. Charles Darwin was another—a mediocre student throughout his years of education. Behaviorist J. B. Watson (1936) said of his own grammar school days that "I was lazy, somewhat insubordinate, and, so far as I know, never made above a passing grade" (p. 271). Alfred Adler's mathematics performance was so miserable that he was obliged to repeat the course, and Adler's father was advised by his teacher to put the boy in an apprenticeship rather than waste further education on him. Many notables had a particularly hard time in their university studies. D. O. Hebb, the distinguished physiological psychologist, graduated from college with a GPA only a hair's breadth from failing. Psychiatrist Harry Stack Sullivan was suspended from college after failing his classes. Humanistic psychologist Abraham Maslow followed up a mediocre performance in high school with even more deplorable grades in college and ended up on academic probation. When Claude Bernard, the great physiologist, took an examination to compete for an internship, he ranked 26th out of the 29 who passed. A comprehensive inventory of once-poor students who later propelled themselves into the history of psychology would be very long indeed.

All of these sad cases being what they may, there exists an ample number of major figures who could claim exceptional academic prowess. Sigmund Freud was a brilliant student, graduating summa cum laude from the gymnasium at age 17. Psychiatrist Karen Horney was an A student in both primary and secondary education, and clinical psychologist Lightner Witmer was a valedictorian. Philosopher Auguste Comte had attained one of the top spots in the examinations required to enter the École Polytechnique but at 15 he was too young to be granted admission. British luminaries John Locke, James Mill, and Edward Titchener had all won scholarships to attend college. Humanistic psychologist Carl Rogers belonged to two honor fraternities as an undergraduate. R. B. Cattell graduated from London University with honors, and both Alexander Bain and Donald T. Campbell stood at the top of their respective graduating classes. The Gestalt founder Max Wertheimer earned his PhD with highest honors. Furthermore, there are plenty of examples of "late bloomers" who may not have done well at first but performed remarkably well once some life event changed their attitude about the significance of getting a good education. Psychology's founder, Wilhelm Wundt, evinced such a dramatic conversion shortly after his father died and earned his medical degree summa cum laude. Adler became so motivated to convert a weakness into a strength that he forged himself into the best mathematics student in his class. So, is it even possible to formulate an empirically sound assertion regarding the relation between scholastic success and later greatness as a scientist?

In the main, the empirical literature suggests a somewhat ambiguous connection. On the one hand, Hudson (1958), who repeated Galton's (1874) selection procedure on a more recent sample, found that Fellows of the Royal Society had generally unimpressive undergraduate records that were certainly no better than scientists who failed to be so honored. Nonetheless, other studies have shown that indicators of undergraduate and graduate performance display modest but positive correlations with a scientist's productivity, citation rate, and eventual eminence (e.g., Chambers, 1964; Segal, Busse, & Mansfield, 1980). In particular, the more distinguished physical and biological scientists tend to boast higher GPAs, win more honors and prizes, and receive more scholarships and fellowships. Is this also true for great psychologists? One might think the answer would be negative. Besides the anecdotes given earlier, some research has shown that future psychologists do not take academics as seriously as other scientists do (Chambers, 1964). For instance, as undergraduates psychologists have lower GPAs than do chemists even though the latter had to take courses that were far more rigorous academically.

Even so, Rodgers and Maranto (1989) provided some evidence that scholastic prowess bears a positive association with the future success of psychologists. Their sample consisted of 485 APA members who were granted doctoral degrees between 1966 and 1976. For each participant the authors determined (a) the total number of citations their publications received by others and (b) the number of journal articles published in the first 6 years after the PhD was received (weighted according to quality). For each participant Rodgers and Maranto also assessed (a) how selective was the institution from which they earned their undergraduate degree, (b) whether the participant graduated with departmental honors, and (c) whether he or she graduated Phi Beta Kappa. For the most part, the two criteria of scientific impact correlated positively with the three indicators of scholastic performance. Four of the six correlations are statistically significant. Specifically, the citation measure correlated .21 with Phi Beta Kappa, whereas the productivity measure correlated .16 with selectivity, .24 with Phi Beta Kappa, and .18 with departmental honors. The consistent association with the receipt of a Phi Beta Kappa key is especially distinctive, because this honor is bestowed on U.S. undergraduates who do very well in a broad range of scholastic subjects. Eminent psychologists who have earned this distinction include G. Stanley Hall and Margaret Floy Washburn.

If these results can be generalized, mutatis mutandis, to great psychologists in other nations, then it would seem that scholastic performance should provide a weak but still positive sign of later professional success—at least, this is a reasonable assumption given what I discussed in chapter 3: Productivity and influence in the first 6 years of a psychologist's career are excellent predictors of lifetime output and impact. At the same time, with correlations in the upper teens and lower twenties, there should be ample latitude for exceptions to the rule, some of which I mentioned earlier in this section. Some scholastic stars will fail to live up to what was expected by their academic achievement, whereas some scholastic stragglers will, like Einstein, do far better than one expects on that basis alone. Because I was among the 485 participants in Rodgers and Maranto's (1989) study, and because I was among those who attended a selective college and received both Phi Beta Kappa and departmental honors, I often wonder where I fell on the regression line.

Were my own productivity and citation counts above or below prediction, or was my professional impact typical for someone with my scholastic performance? What would my situation be now, if there were a follow-up study more than 20 years later? Has my Phi Beta Kappa key any continued relevance?

Accelerated Progress

GPAs and academic honors provide one way of gauging a psychologist's scholastic performance, yet they do not exhaust the possible approaches. A largely independent alternative is to determine how rapidly an individual gets through the educational system. Judging from what I reviewed in chapter 6—especially Cox's (1926) study of 301 geniuses—individuals who claim decidedly superior information-processing skills should be able to master educational materials at an accelerated pace. This accelerated progress should show up in the precocious age at which a great psychologist advances through the key points in the educational sequence. Such educational acceleration has already been demonstrated empirically for famous scientists. In the first place, more creative scientists tend to graduate from high school at an earlier age than is the norm (C. W. Taylor & Ellison, 1967). Illustrious scientists are also more likely to complete their undergraduate education at a younger age (J. M. Cattell, 1906; Chambers, 1964; Poffenberger, 1930). Roe's (1953a) distinguished biologists, for example, received their baccalaureate degrees at a mean age of 21.8, whereas her notable physicists obtained their degrees at a mean age of 20.9. Most striking, however, are the precocious ages at which great scientists receive their doctoral degrees (Helson & Crutchfield, 1970; Roe, 1953a; Zuckerman, 1977). The average age at PhD for Roe's (1953a) biologists was 26.0, that for her physicists, 24.6. Furthermore, the more distinguished the scientist, the greater the degree of doctoral acceleration. Among U.S. scientists, those elected to membership in the National Academy of Sciences received this honor at an average age of 26.0, whereas those who received the Nobel prize did so at an average age of 24.8; both figures contrasted with the mean age of 29.5 for the typical doctorate (Zuckerman, 1977). It is curious that even Albert Einstein's academic progress could not be considered too retarded by these standards. Despite spending many years trying to get a doctoral dissertation approved, he finally succeeded at age 26, putting him in the same league as the National Academy of Science members. If his first dissertation had been accepted, then Einstein would have been 23— well within the Nobel laureate class.

Many great psychologists seem to fall into the same pattern of accelerated progress. Thus, J. M. Cattell entered college before his 16th birthday, and R. B. Cattell graduated with honors from college at age 19. J. B. Watson received his PhD at age 25 (under the PhD-less J. R. Angell), the youngest to ever do so at the University of Chicago at that time. Watson was by no means exceptional. Other notables who received their degrees at age 25 include G. Allport, S. Asch, J. R. Anderson, L. Berkowitz, C. Bühler, K. Bühler, E. DuBois-Reymond, J. Dewey, S. Fernberger, M. S. Gazzaniga, H. Harlow, S. Hecht, H. Henning, V. Henri, O. Külpe, I. Lorge, R. D. Luce, P. Meehl, A. von Meinong, H. O. Mowrer, F. Nietzsche, A. Schopenhauer, E. Titchener, and L. Witmer. Moreover, Table 10.1 gives cases of even more dramatic precocity: individuals who were doctorates at age 24 or younger. To be sure, it is always possible to cite counterexamples. Narziss Kaspar Ach, Donald T. Campbell, Wilhelm Dilthey, and George Stratton were 31; Mary Calkins and Harvey Carr were 32; John Baird, Henry Goddard, and Henry Murray were 33; Frank Angell, G. S. Hall, Clark L. Hull, and Aleksander Luria were 34; Harvey C. Lehman and Carl Murchison were 36; Alfred Binet and Eric Lennenberg were 37; Florence Goodenough was 38; Charles Spearman was 41; and Immanuel Kant was 51. Yet in many of these cases there were extenuating circumstances. Sometimes, for instance, the doctorate was received after the person first earned another advanced degree, such as an MD. In truth, numerous empirical studies show that, on average, educational acceleration is the norm for highly influential psychologists (Hirschberg & Itkin, 1978). The eminent psychologists in Roe's (1953a) sample earned their bachelor's degrees around age 21.4 and their doctorates around age 25.8 (the corresponding figures for the social scientists as a whole are 21.8 and 26.8, respectively). Illustrious contributors to psychology are more than twice as likely as their less accomplished colleagues to complete the degree requirements for the PhD in "four years or less" (Wispé, 1965). In fact, given that the average PhD in psychology is received when an individual is at least 30 years old (Gupta, Gilbert, & Pierce, 1983; Lyons, 1968; Vance & MacPhail, 1964), eminent psychologists are generally taking almost half the usual time to get through their doctoral programs (also see K. E. Clark, 1954). In addition, the earlier psychologists earned their doctoral degrees, the earlier they tend to publish their first highly cited contribution (Simonton, 1992b), the more total publications they can eventually claim (Helmreich, Spence, Beane, Lucker, & Matthews, 1980), the more citations they receive from their fellow researchers (Helmreich et al., 1980), and the higher the degree of their overall visibility in the field (K. E. Clark, 1954; Pressey, 1960). Apropos of the last point are the statistics published by Sidney Leavitt Pressey (1965), the psychologist who invented the first teaching machine. Pressey found that the first 24 APA presidents earned their doctoral degrees at a median age of 25.7.

It has been suggested that accelerated educational advancement is indicative of a scientist with exceptional intellectual ability. The greater the degree of acceleration, the more potent must be the underlying capacity.

TABLE 10.1
Precocious Doctorates in the History of Psychology

Age	Individuals
24	B. G. Anan'ev, R. Arnheim, B. M. Bass, G. Békésy, S. L. Bem, E. Brunswik, R. B. Cattell, C. N. Cofer, L. Cronbach, D. Elkind, H. B. English, W. K. Estes, H. J. Eysenck, R. M. Gagné, R. A. Gardner, P. Gassendi, K. F. Gauss, A. Gelb, J. Gibson, C. H. Graham, M. P. Haggard, R. J. Havigurst, F. Heider, H. T. Himmelweit, C. I. Hovland, W. S. Hunter, H. Kelman, D. Krech, K. L. Lashley, K. Lewin, E. A. Locke, K. Marbe, D. Marquis, D. C. McClelland, C. T. Morgan, W. B. Pillsbury, A. Pilzecker, E. H. Schein, H. Schlosberg, F. Schumann, R. R. Sears, N. W. Stock, E. L. Thorndike, F. M. Urban, M. Verworn, M. S. Viteles, H. Werner, M. Wertheimer, G. Whipple
23	G. Allport, S. Bem, F. Boas, W. J. Crozier, H. Ebbinghaus, L. Festinger, W. Hellpach, E. M. von Hornbostel, J. Jastrow, C. H. Judd, K. Koffka, F. Krüger, M. E. Lamb, T. Lipps, K. Marx, M. F. Meyer, W. Moede, G. E. Müller, Z. A. Piotrowski, W. Poppelreuter, J. Royce, J. von Neumann, R. Shank, M. F. Washburn, H. A. Witkin, T. Young, K. Zenner
22	J. L. Agassiz, A. Anastasi, V. Benussi, M. Dessoir, H. De Vries, H. A. E. Driesch, E. Fromm, E. Husserl, A. Jost, D. Katz, G. O. Klemm, W. Köhler, E. Kris, E. Mach, H. Münsterberg, W. Nagel, J. Piaget, W. Stern, D. N. Uznadze, H. Vaihinger, F. L. Wells
21	G. W. Leibniz, J. P. Müller, H. Pièron, W. T. Preyer, W. Wirth
20	P. Feuerbach, G. W. F. Hegel, C. Stumpf, M. de Unamuno
19	A. E. Michotte
18	N. Wiener

Note. The PhDs were received in several fields besides psychology.

This superior intellect then manifests itself in later achievements as well. This interpretation also accounts for the variation across fields in the expected age at receiving the various academic degrees (for evidence, see McDowell, 1982; Terman, 1954). Domains in which doctorates can be earned at the earliest ages are also the domains that tend to feature scientists with the highest IQ scores. Hence may arise the contrast between the physical sciences, on the one hand, and the social sciences and humanities on the other—with psychology and biology falling somewhere between.

Nevertheless, this is certainly not the only possible explanation. Quite a different account might be founded on the results regarding the curvilinear relation between eminence and level of formal education attained. If formal training can lead to excessive amounts of socialization and enculturation, and thus stifle the development of creative potential, as Einstein believed, then one route around this negative effect is to get through formal training as quickly as possible. Having completed the requisite academic rites of passage at the earliest opportunity, potential talents can pursue their distinctive interests at an earlier age (Pressey, 1960). James McKeen Cattell (1910) had something like this in mind when he worried about whether the increasingly more demanding requirements of the educational system were undermining the further progress of science.

> In plain English, the young man who must spend his early manhood in acquiring knowledge has passed the age at which he is most likely to have new ideas. The inherent difficulty we exaggerate by our educational methods. By our requirements for degrees, by our system of examinations, by our insistence on irrelevant information and ridicule of desirable ignorance and promising mistakes, we crowd on fat when the athlete should be relieved of every superfluous ounce. The doctor's thesis is supposed to be the first productive work; it is completed at the average age of twenty-eight years and is likely to be the working over of the old ideas of an old professor. In the meanwhile the creative instinct has atrophied. (p. 646)

Where the first explanation of acceleration–achievement gives the credit to the student, this second explanation assigns the blame to the educational system. Cattell's views are obviously more in accord with Einstein's condemnation of formal training.

Institution Prestige

Yet perhaps Einstein's problems in getting his dissertation accepted may be as much his fault as that of the institution to which he applied. The University of Zurich was no "diploma mill"; rather, it was an institution of international standing, with a reputation to maintain. This prestige extended to fields beyond physics, even encompassing psychology. More eminent psychologists have been associated with Zurich than with any other institution in Switzerland. Among the major figures with Zurich affiliations at one time or another are Carl Ludwig, Wilhelm Wundt, Eduard Hitzig, Richard Avenarius, Eugen Bleuler, Carl Jung, Karl Abraham, and Eric Lennenberg, who collectively span the period from 1849 to 1965. In any case, this biographical datum about Einstein fits a consistent empirical finding: Eminent figures are highly likely to receive their education, and especially their higher degrees, from highly prestigious institutions. This linkage was first reported by Galton (1874) in his survey of Fellows of the Royal Society scientists: "One-third of those who sent replies have been educated at Oxford or Cambridge" (p. 236). This figure becomes about 50% if those who lacked university education are excluded. Havelock Ellis (1926) found an even higher percentage in his more heterogeneous sample of British geniuses; 74% of the college graduates identified either Oxford or Cambridge as their alma mater. It is significant that it is the quality of the graduate school, not the undergraduate institution, that provides the most predictive factor (Crane, 1965). Furthermore, this is more than just a simple matter of a larger proportion of scientists hailing from certain schools. Those who earned their parchment from more prestigious institutions are more likely to become the most pro-lific and influential contributors to the field (Crane, 1965).

This same institutional advantage certainly holds for psychology as well. In Germany, the University of Berlin granted doctorates to DuBois-Reymond, Kurt Koffka, Wolfgang Köhler, Kurt Lewin, and Max Wertheimer (but de-nied one to J. R. Angell); Berlin medical degrees were bestowed on Ernst Brücke, G. T. Fritsch, Ernst Haeckel, H. Hitzig, and Karen Horney. In Aus-tria, the big academic power has always been the University of Vienna, from which Egon Brunswik, Christian von Ehrenfels, Else Frenkel-Brunswik, Edmund Husserl, Ernst Kris, Ernst Mach, and Otto Rank all earned PhDs, and Alfred Adler, Josef Breuer, Sandor Ferenczi, Sigmund Freud, Franz Jo-seph Gall, and Franz Anton Mesmer all earned MDs. Finally, Harvard has produced such doctorates as Floyd Allport, Gordon Allport, Percy Bridgman, Jerome Bruner, Mary Calkins (albeit it was never received), G. Stanley Hall, Harry Helson, Edwin Holt, Alfred Kinsey, Stanley Milgrim, B. F. Skinner, Edward Tolman, Norbert Weiner, and Robert Yerkes, while producing MDs such as Walter Cannon and William James. Of the 161 psychologists who were deemed worthy of an obituary in *American Psychologist* between 1979 and 1990, one third had obtained their doctorates from just three schools, namely, Columbia, Harvard, and Chicago (Kinnier et al., 1994).

I now move from idiographic details to nomothetic generalizations. Psychologists who obtain their advanced degrees from more prestigious insti-tutions are more likely to (a) start making contributions to the field earlier in their careers (Rodgers & Maranto, 1989; Simonton, 1992b), (b) produce more total output (Helmreich et al., 1980; Rodgers & Maranto, 1989), and (c) receive more citations of their work (Gupta et al., 1983; Helmreich et al., 1980; Rodgers & Maranto, 1989). It is essential to recognize that the impact of institution prestige on professional success is probably indirect rather than direct. According to Rodgers and Maranto's (1989) study of 485 American psychologists, mentioned earlier, the quality of the graduate program directly determines the quality of the institution where one is first hired, and the latter then has direct effects on both publications and citations (also see Bair & Boor, 1988; Helmreich et al., 1980). My study of 69 eminent American psychologists (Simonton, 1992b; cf. Rodgers & Maranto, 1989) found that the only direct influence of institution quality was to lower the age at which significant contributions began to be made, the latter result then having a more immediate impact on output and influence. Such causal chains con-sisting of direct and indirect effects are frequently found in other sciences besides psychology (S. Cole & J. R. Cole, 1973). Hence, great institutions likely make great psychologists only through a series of intermediate vari-ables.

Although psychologists who completed their education at top-flight institutions appear to hold an edge in the quest of greatness, the advantage is by no means absolute. Like other developmental correlates, the effect sizes are sufficiently modest so as to permit an abundance of exceptions. To avoid offending readers who earned their degrees at more obscure or mediocre institutions, one incontrovertible example may suffice. I already noted that Harry Stack Sullivan was an extremely poor student. Becoming a college dropout, he was obliged to obtain his medical degree from the Chicago College of Medicine and Surgery, a school that Sullivan himself called a mere diploma mill. In fact, the institution went under not long after he got his diploma. Yet that did not prevent Sullivan from becoming a distinguished American psychiatrist.

Distinguished Teachers

E. G. Boring received his PhD under Edward Titchener, who in turn had obtained his doctorate under Wilhelm Wundt, producing a three-generation sequence of mentor–pupil relations. Hence, Boring had a highly distinguished teacher who had himself studied under an even more distinguished teacher—the very founder of the discipline. In this section I scrutinize this phenomenon by addressing two questions. First, how common are such master–disciple, mentor–pupil, or teacher–student relationships? Second, what are the specific consequences of studying under a distinguished teacher?

Teacher–Student Pedigrees

Sequences such as Wundt → Titchener → Boring are far from rare in the history of psychology. For instance, in Table 10.2 some of the more famous of Wundt's doctoral students are displayed, followed by the students of those students, and the students of the latters' students. Hence, Titchener was not in any way Wundt's sole doctoral success. Moreover, Titchener had many more accomplished doctoral students besides just Boring, who himself can claim at least two notable doctoral students of his own: Harry Helson and S. S. Stevens. As a prominent historian of psychology, Boring was well aware of how rather common these relationships tend to be. In fact, he coauthored an article with his daughter, Mollie, entitled "Masters and Pupils Among the American Psychologists" (M. D. Boring & Boring, 1948), that richly documents the extent of these direct academic influences for 119 psychologists sufficiently eminent to have entries in *American Men of Science*.

So extensive are these doctoral dependencies that many contemporary psychologists are descended from Wundt, or some other notable, such as William James. For instance, Donald T. Campbell, the distinguished American social psychologist who died in 1996, was descended from both James and Wundt, according to three alternative pathways. The resulting three lines of descent are as follows:

1. W. James → E. B. Holt → E. C. Tolman → R. C. Tryon → D. T. Campbell

2. W. Wundt → H. Münsterberg → E. C. Tolman → R. C. Tryon → D. T. Campbell
3. W. Wundt → J. M. Cattell → R. S. Woodworth → H. E. Jones → D. T. Campbell

These are all direct lines of doctoral descent; that is, the arrows represent direct supervision of doctoral theses (e.g., Cattell earned his PhD under Wundt's supervision). Because Campbell himself supervised many distinguished doctoral students, this particular James–Wundt lineage continues to the present day. Among the more notable of them are Marilynn Brewer, Barry Collins, William Crano, Louise Kidder, Norman Miller, and David A. Kenny, who was my mentor in my own graduate school days. Some of these mentor–pupil relationships admittedly must pass through what some might consider "weak links." Neither Robert C. Tryon nor Harold E. Jones is quite in the same league as the others in the four lineages, which otherwise include many APA presidents, National Academy of Science members, and recipients of APA's Distinguished Scientific Contributions or Gold Medal awards. Yet both Tryon and Jones were accomplished enough as psychologists to have been included among the 119 in M. D. Boring and Boring's (1948) study, and both have had articles and obituaries written about them (e.g., Innis, 1992; Sanford, Eichhorn, & Honzik, 1944).

These lineages, as well as those given in Table 10.2, are strictly defined according to the answer to the question "under whom did you earn your PhD?" Yet one could argue that this formal definition is not the best. Indeed, M. D. Boring and Boring (1948) used a contrary definition whenever possible, namely, under whom did the psychologist feel he or she did their advanced studies, independent of the formalities. By this definition, the Borings listed Lightner Witmer not as Wundt's student but rather as J. M. Cattell's. They did this as the result of sending questionnaires to the 72 living members of their sample and asking them "Who was it who influenced you most in psychology up to the time you got your PhD?" (M. D. Boring & Boring, 1948, p. 528). According to Witmer, he went to Leipzig to study under Wundt only at Cattell's urging and because he received special funds to do so. Witmer otherwise resented Wundt and acknowledged Cattell as his true mentor.

Wundt's own career path illustrates how the mentor influences can operate along less formal paths. According to one historian,

> Helmholtz had a marked influence on the physiologists and embryonic psychologists of the day, and it is not surprising to learn that Wundt (Helmholtz's assistant for four years at Heidelberg University) incorporated much of Helmholtz's empiricism in his own system, especially the doctrine of unconscious inference. (Capretta, 1967, pp. 78–79)

If one takes this one generation farther back, Helmholtz "never undertook formal training at a university, but was close to various leading univer-

TABLE 10.2
Eminent Psychologists Among Wilhelm Wundt's Direct Doctoral Descendants

First generation	Second generation	Third generation
H. Münsterberg (1885) →		
	Boris Sidis (1897)	
	K. Dunlap (1903) →	
		C. Murchison (1923)
	L. T. Troland (1915)	
J. M. Cattell (1886) →		
	E. L. Thorndike (1898)	
		T. L. Kelley (1914)
	R. S. Woodworth (1899) →	
		D. Wechsler (1925)
		G. Razran (1933)
	S. I. Franz (1899)	
	C. Wissler (1901)	
	F. L. Wells (1906)	
	E. K. Strong, Jr. (1911)	
O. Külpe (1887) →		
	R. M. Ogden (1903)	
	M. Wertheimer (1904)	
	H. J. Watt (1904)	
F. Angell (1891)		
E. W. Scripture (1891) →		
	C. E. Seashore (1895)	
L. Witmer (1892)		
E. B. Titchener (1892) →		
	M. F. Washburn (1894)	
	W. B. Pillsbury (1896)	
	M. Bentley (1899)	
	G. M. Whipple (1900)	
	J. W. Baird (1902)	
	K. M. Dallenbach (1913)	
	E. G. Boring (1914) →	
		H. Helson (1924)
		S. S. Stevens (1933)
	P. T. Young (1918)	
	J. P. Guilford (1927)	
F. Kiesow (1894)		
C. H. Judd (1896)		
G. M. Stratton (1896)		
W. D. Scott (1900)		
W. Hellpach (1900)		
C. E. Spearman (1904)		
G. Kafka (1906)		
G. O. Klemm (1906)		
R. Pintner (1913)		

Note. Date that doctoral degree was bestowed is indicated in parentheses.

sity figures of the day, including especially the physiologist Johannes Müller at the University of Berlin" (Wertheimer, 1987, p. 55). Thus, all of the doctoral descendents of Wundt can ultimately be considered the informal intellectual descendents of Müller, the pioneer German physiologist, with Helmholtz providing the connection to Wundt.

It is worth pointing out that the pedigrees such as those shown in Table 10.2 are certainly not unique to psychology (Simonton, 1992c). On the contrary, E. G. Boring was first inspired to construct his intellectual genealogy of great psychologists after seeing one that had been published earlier with respect to the sciences in general (Pledge, 1939). An excellent illustration is those scientists who have received the Nobel prizes in physics, chemistry, and medicine or physiology (Zuckerman, 1977). Many laureates were students of previous laureates. One such sequence, for instance, is Lord Rayleigh → J. J. Thomson → Sir Ernest Rutherford → Niels Bohr → Werner Heisenberg. As always, there are exceptions. Einstein did not study under any previous laureate, and he did not receive his PhD from an illustrious mentor, although he did have some pretty distinguished teachers (Hermann Minkowski and Heinrich Weber) when he was an undergraduate. The same can be said of the history of psychology. M. D. Boring and Boring (1948) provided a pretty impressive list of great psychologists whom they counted as "self-starters," much like Einstein. This list consisted of Gordon W. Allport, J. Mark Baldwin, John Dewey, G. S. Hall, William James, H. M. Johnson, Wolfgang Köhler, George Trumball Ladd, Christine Ladd-Franklin, William McDougall, Gardner Murphey, L. L. Thurstone, and Robert M. Yerkes. This is a very impressive set of names. Even so, these are only 13 out of 119, or 11%. Also, some of these did receive their degrees *under* distinguished mentors but without feeling that they had studied *with* them. This holds for Allport (under H. S. Langfeld), Hall (under James), and Köhler (under C. Stumph). So, 92% had some relationship with a notable teacher in graduate school, whether that relationship be nominal or genuine.

M. D. Boring and Boring's (1948) study is not the only one to report the high frequency of such eminent teacher–student pairs in psychology. In the inquiry into 69 famous American psychologists active between 1879 and 1967, about three fourths earned their PhDs under an illustrious psychologist (Simonton, 1992b). In another study of 95 eminent American psychologists who obtained their degrees between 1910 and 1944, 73% said that a distinguished teacher had stimulated their intellectual development in graduate school, and 83% reported that their dissertations had been supervised by a notable psychologist (Wispé, 1965). The corresponding figures for a group of controls were 43% and 32%, respectively, even though the comparison group had been matched on year of doctorate and the university where the doctorate was obtained, so they should have enjoyed the same potential opportunities as the eminent group.

Master–Pupil Effects

But why are such teacher–student pairs so prominent? One hypothesis may go back to what I said before about the Müller → Helmholtz → Wundt chain of informal influences. Müller clearly had some highly potent ideas about developing a truly experimental physiology, so much so that he shares with von Haller the appellation of "the father of experimental physiology." Müller also had a strong inclination toward discussing physiological phenomena in psychological terms. These ideas strongly impressed his disciples, among them Helmholtz. In part through the latter's ideas, Wundt was inspired to take up the cause of a "physiological psychology," that is, an experimental psychology with deep roots in physiology. Powerful ideas that helped make Müller famous should help his followers become famous as well, as they trickled down through Helmholtz and Wundt. In short, ideas that work for the master should work for the pupil. This explanation could explain why psychologists who study under illustrious mentors are more likely to make their first important contribution at a younger age than usual (Simonton, 1992b). It would also help account for why the mentor's eminence is critical to the pupil's long-term success independent of the prestige of the graduate school where the doctoral degree was received (Crane, 1965).

Yet there are other realities that do not seem to sit well with this interpretation. First, as J. M. Cattell (1910) suggested in the quotation presented earlier in this chapter, the mentor's ideas may already be passé, so that those who convert themselves into an intellectual clone may end up trying to establish a reputation on the basis of notions that are widely considered to be out of date. This falls in line with Segal et al.'s (1980) study of biologists, which found that individuals who had served as a laboratory or research assistant in graduate school tended to receive fewer citations of their work once they launched their own professional careers. A second problem is that many of the most successful scientists tend to depart radically from their mentors' ideas. Many concrete instances can be discerned in Table 10.2. Not all of Wundt's students became Wundtian researchers. Münsterberg quickly gave up the laboratory to become an applied psychologist. From the moment J. M. Cattell arrived in Leipzig, he insisted on studying individual differences, despite Wundt's lack of sympathy for that kind of research. Witmer not only refused to acknowledge Wundt as his teacher, but he also became a pioneer in clinical psychology. Although Titchener considered himself a loyal Wundtian, many of his own doctoral students strayed far from the official line. Washburn became a comparative psychologist, whereas Guilford, like Wundt's student Spearman, became a psychometrician, with a focus on individual differences in intelligence. Other great psychologists besides this particular doctoral pedigree show a similar pattern. For example, many of Tolman's best students—including Henry Gleitman, David Krech, and Julian Hochberg—cannot be said to have clearly followed in his footsteps. There is even evidence that the most successful teachers are those who give their students the largest possible intellectual freedom. Thus, the 64 illustrious scientists in Roe's (1952) investigation asserted that they preferred most those mentors who just left them alone to do their own thing.

An alternative explanation is that the students are acquiring something far less specific, but also far more useful, namely, they are learning what one must generally do if one wants to succeed in the profession. In other words, the primary purpose of having an eminent mentor is to learn the answers to the following questions: How does one go about creating and executing a life-long research program? What are the standards that must be met to publish original research in the best journals? How does one secure a "ladder track" position at a leading university? How does one best balance research and teaching activities? What are the tricks to maintaining a scientific reputation while preserving a healthy personal life? What is the relative weight to be assigned to various professional and university responsibilities, such as reviewing manuscripts, attending conferences, or chairing time-consuming committees? At what point in the career should one think about writing a book, monograph, or textbook; who are the best publishers; and how does one secure a contract? The pearls of wisdom provided to these enigmas would have benefits independent of whether the student turns out to be the teacher's clone or an utter iconoclast. In short, the aspiring student needs "to learn the ropes," regardless of the substantive direction he or she actually takes.

This more generalized interpretation would account for the same empirical findings as the previous one, besides handling those situations when the student does not follow up the mentor's research program. This account also would accommodate other findings; most notably, studies of famous personalities of diverse kinds have shown that talent development seems nurtured by early exposure to eminent adults, even when these adults attained distinction in some domain other than that which the youth eventually pursued (Walberg, Rasher, & Parkerson, 1980). The father of William James, for example, would often invite various American luminaries to dinner, such as Ralph Waldo Emerson, exposing the young James to general models of excellence. Furthermore, this explanation would seem to fit better with the finding that not only do eminent psychologists tend to study under eminent psychologists, but they also tend to supervise more doctoral students who become eminent in their own right (Wispé, 1965). Thus, the mentor–pupil transfer of greatness can extend across multiple generations, as documented in Table 10.2. Yet the initial research program need not be continued for this transfer to take place. Indeed, it would seem very unlikely that the intellectual grandchildren and great-grandchildren would benefit much from pursuing such old-fashioned ideas. Hence, a doctoral sequence such as W. Wundt → J. M. Cattell → R. S. Woodworth → D. Wechsler can take place despite the almost complete absence of any substantive continuity in their respective research programs. This interpretation rests on the seemingly reasonable assumption that the supposed "secrets of (professional) success" do not change as rapidly over time as do the intellectual fads and fashions that shape the history of psychology. This supposition is consistent with the fact that many of the qualities that underlie the attainment are so generic as to transcend time, place, and domain of achievement (Simonton, 1994a).

Yet, for the purposes of completeness, I point to the possibility of yet another, but a bit more cynical explanation. The key asset may not entail the continuation of a proven research program or the mastery of the tricks of the trade, but rather the advantage may stem from a more basic interpersonal process—connections, connections, connections. After all, the more eminent scientists are those who sit on the editorial boards of high-impact journals, who serve on grant review panels for the most lucrative funding agencies, who attend the most conventions and conferences, and who have many close colleagues strategically placed at major research institutions. To stay in good graces with an illustrious mentor means to have freer access to this "old-boy" network of professional opportunities. It signifies that when the time comes to begin one's job quest, the mentor can provide the letter of recommendation that tips the scale in one's favor at a prestigious university. It suggests that when the beginning scientist's papers are first submitted for publication at a major journal, the editor may give the benefit of any doubt because he or she is so-in-so's best student. This interpretation might better account for why the mentor's professional activities actually do a slightly better job predicting their proteges' later scientific output and impact than does the mentor's research emphasis (Gupta et al., 1983). It would also fit better with the finding that the positive impact of eminent mentors is maximized when their students secure a position at a prestigious research institution (Crane, 1965). Furthermore, having received a degree from a prestigious institution and mentor may be more critical in securing such a high-status job than is the young scientist's actual publication record (Allison & Long, 1987). Einstein's career illustrates the potential costs to career progress should one lack such professional support. It took him a long time to work his way out of the patent office into a professorship at a prestigious university. This delay occurred despite the fact that he had already published all of the papers that were to win him the 1921 Nobel for physics. It was ironically the very Zurich professor who had first rejected and then approved Einstein's doctoral thesis who eventually secured for the future laureate his first academic appointment. This initial foothold occurred 4 years after he had earned the right to call himself Dr. Einstein.

Needless to say, it is conceivable that all three of the foregoing explanations are operative, but in varying degrees, depending on the particular mentor–pupil coupling. Moreover, it is not ruled out that some other processes are involved as well, including the genetic processes discussed in chapter 12. Right now, however, the task is to discuss two remaining features of career training: self-education and professional marginality.

SELF-EDUCATION

"I have never let my schooling interfere with my education" (quoted in Harnsberger, 1972, p. 553). Although it was Mark Twain who said this, the same sentiment—with much less humor and far more bitterness—might just as well come from the mouth of Albert Einstein. So hostile was Einstein to the interference of regular schooling that he became the equivalent of a high school dropout by withdrawing from a restrictive German gymnasium sans diploma at age 15. This risky decision was based on his belief that he would be able to pass the rigorous entrance examinations to the university by studying on his own. And why not? He had already demonstrated an impressive ability to absorb and master whatever interested him most. Indeed, by the time he was 16, Einstein had taught himself calculus. Although he was later to receive a diploma at a more liberal Swiss school, it is clear that Einstein always gave his self-education a higher priority than formal instruction.

Many key figures in the history of psychology have reported a similar proclivity. The great physicist and physiologist Hermann von Helmholtz (1891/1971) once said that

> I must confess that many times while the class was reading Cicero or Virgil, both of whom I found very tedious, I was calculating under the desk the path of light rays in a telescope. Even at that time I discovered some optical laws, not ordinarily found in textbooks, but which I afterward found useful in constructing the ophthalmoscope. (p. 469)

When a generous uncle offered to send Herbert Spencer to Cambridge to receive a college degree, the future philosopher declined, preferring to obtain his higher education through independent reading. Sometimes self-education naturally is more a matter of necessity than preference. Many great names in the history of psychology had no other choice than to educate themselves. Clark L. Hull's schooling was spotty because he often had to help out on the farm. The physicist and chemist Michael Faraday advanced his schooling by being apprenticed to a bookbinder and bookseller, taking advantage of every spare moment to read the merchandise.

Indeed, avid reading provided the primary means by which these luminaries pursued their self-education. Besides providing the basis for acquiring both general and specialized knowledge, being an avid reader will sometimes provide what has been called the *crystallizing experience*, an encounter with a field or phenomenon that sets the individual on the distinctive trajectory to eventual achievement (Walters & Gardner, 1986). Hence, several notables, such as Edward Thorndike, Clark L. Hull, and Edward Tolman, were first inspired to become psychologists by reading *The Principles of Psychology* by William James, just as Freud's *Interpretation of Dreams* played a significant role in the lives of such figures as Alfred Adler and Carl Jung. When Hermann Ebbinghaus purchased a copy of Gustav Fechner's *Elements of Psychophysics*, he soon found himself set on a new career path. In a sense, such effects should not be surprising. A main reason for publishing articles and books is to exert some influence on current and subsequent generations. Moreover, it is the avid readers who have the highest likelihood of chancing on that particular publication that will transform their lives.

In any event, there is abundant evidence that achieved eminence is associated with self-education in general and with voracious reading in particular (McCurdy, 1960). For instance, a study of more than three hundred 20th-century notables found a positive correlation between being an avid reader and degree of eminence attained (Simonton, 1984d). Likewise, Roe's (1953a) 64 illustrious scientists reported that they began to do a great deal of reading at a young age. This pattern of early avid reading is also characteristic of the intellectually gifted, such as the high-IQ children in Terman's (1925) longitudinal study (also see Schaefer & Anastasi, 1968). At the same time, investigations indicate some other common vehicles of self-education beyond mere reading. For example, one study of 335 biologists found that both publication and citation counts were positively correlated with the amount of free time spent on extra science projects or building radio sets (Segal et al., 1980). Roe (1953a) noted a strong tendency for her scientists to have developed early hobbies and interests that were closely related to their later achievements. Thus, about half of her biologists showed some early interest in natural history, much like Charles Darwin did in his youth. The social scientists, in contrast, often had early aspirations of pursing a literary career and would frequently serve as editors of yearbooks and literary magazines. These extracurricular activities are reminiscent of B. F. Skinner, who originally wanted to become a creative writer. Yet Skinner also exhibited an early fascination with constructing mechanical gadgets, an interest more in line with Roe's (1953a) eminent physicists.

These complexities should not obscure the principal conclusion: Formal education probably plays a comparatively minor role in the emergence of great psychologists. Instead, it is self-education, such as avid reading or some other extracurricular involvement, that may provide the bulk of the developmental preparation. This broadening education that goes beyond mere schooling may provide another explanation for why great scientists are so often sickly as children, as I pointed out in chapter 9. A child who has to spend much time alone, or interacting with parents rather than with peers, may be more likely to develop intellectual interests beyond the purely scholastic. Helmholtz (1891/1971) illustrated this possibility:

> During my first seven years I was a delicate boy, confined for long periods to my room and often to bed; nevertheless, I had a strong inclination toward several occupations and activities. My parents busied themselves a good deal with me, while picture books and games, especially games with wooden blocks, filled the rest of my time. In addition, reading came

fairly early, and this, of course, greatly increased the range of my occupations. (p. 468)

Another example was the great French philosopher René Descartes. While a student at a Jesuit school, he proved too sickly to follow the routine of his fellow students, and so he was allowed to stay in bed. He took advantage of this opportunity by indulging a voracious appetite for reading.

Although ill health in youth can encourage a disposition toward independent learning, the causal arrow can sometimes go in the reverse direction, albeit this may be less common. To justify withdrawing from the gymnasium, Einstein obtained from the family doctor a medical certificate affirming that he needed time for recuperation—even though there was absolutely nothing wrong with his health. Dropping out just gave Einstein the leisure to do what he wanted to do: engage in his self-education without the school's interference.

PROFESSIONAL MARGINALITY

In chapter 2 I first introduced Thomas Kuhn's (1970) internalist theory of scientific revolution, which centers on the process by which revolutionary scientists replace the old paradigm that guides normal science with a new paradigm. From a psychological perspective, one of the more interesting features of his theory is Kuhn's speculation about the characteristics of people who become a scientific revolutionaries: "Almost always the men who achieve these fundamental inventions of a new paradigm have been either very young or very new to the field whose paradigm they change" (p. 90). This is the case, Kuhn explained, because

> obviously these are the men who, being little committed by prior practice to the traditional rules of normal science, are particularly likely to see that these rules no longer define a playable game and to conceive another set that can replace them. (p. 90)

Einstein certainly serves as a prime example. At age 26, and a professional outsider, he nonetheless published two articles that revolutionized physics: one on the photoelectric effect and the other on special relativity. Newton provides another obvious instance. At about the same age, and in relative isolation from the scientific circles of his day, Newton came up with mathematical and physical ideas that were to revolutionize the exact sciences.

Historians of psychology have sometimes suggested that the same principle has operated in psychology's own past as well. Typical is this statement: "Like many innovative scientific thinkers, Skinner received little early training in his discipline" (Leahey, 1992, p. 389). B. F. Skinner was an English major in college. In a similar fashion, Carl Rogers originally pursued religious studies, L. L. Thurstone studied electrical engineering, Edward Tolman studied electrochemistry, Henry Murray studied history, and Roger Sperry studied English literature. Rogers had taken only one course in psychology as an undergraduate student—and that by correspondence—whereas Murray attended just one lecture in psychology, finding it so boring that he walked out. Even at the doctoral level there exist many conspicuous departures from the expectation that a great psychologist must receive a PhD in psychology. Exceptions include Christine Ladd-Franklin (mathematics); George Békésy and Percy Bridgman (both physics); Henry Murray (biochemistry); Karl L. Lashley (genetics); Jean Piaget, Alfred Kinsey, and Roger W. Sperry (all zoology); Herbert Simon (political science); Otto Rank (German philology); Noam Chomsky (linguistics); Leta Hollingworth (education); Erich Fromm (sociology); and Edwin Guthrie (philosophy). Furthermore, many great psychologists obtained medical rather than doctoral degrees. Pioneers such as Wilhelm Wundt, William James, Sigmund Freud, and Ivan Pavlov are among the more salient examples. Perhaps it is significant that every Nobel laureate who has some place in the annals of psychology—namely Pavlov, Békésy, Bridgman, Simon, and Sperry—had no advanced degree in psychology.

Sometimes the positive effects of such professional marginality seemed to occur simply because the newcomer could offer a fresh outlook, as Kuhn (1970) suggested. However, other times the more critical factor appears to be that the outsider could import into the discipline concepts, perspectives, or techniques that have proven useful in some other field.

> It has often happened that critical stages for advance are reached when what has been called one body of knowledge can be brought into close and effective relationship with what has been treated as a different, and a largely or wholly independent, scientific discipline,

observed the eminent psychologist F. C. Bartlett (1958, p. 98), whose own degree (an MA) was in "moral sciences." Hermann von Helmholtz (1891/1971) described such a cross-fertilization process in his own case:

> I must, however, say that I attribute my success in great measure to the fact that, possessing some geometric understanding and equipped with a knowledge of physics, I had the good fortune to be thrown into medicine, where I found in physiology a virgin territory of great fertility. Furthermore, I was led by my knowledge of vital processes to questions and points of view which are usually foreign to pure mathematicians and physicists. (pp. 472–473)

At times the outside perspective may even entail not another science but rather the humanities or even the arts:

> It has long been noted that William James, one of the founders of philosophical pragmatism as well as psychological science, had the sensibility of an artist. It has also been suggested that his artistic sensibility made a

tangible difference in the crafting of his thought, both in philosophy and in psychology. (Leahey, 1992, p. 152)

At age 18 James actually aspired to become an artist, studying painting 6 months in the art studio of William Morris Hunt, but there he discovered that his passion for drawing could not be mistaken for genuine talent.

To be sure, being a professional outsider may have its drawbacks. James's penchant for the aesthetic made Wundt conclude that his *Principles of Psychology* was more a literary than a scientific achievement, a possibility to which James himself once alluded in a letter to his brother Henry, whose 1890 novel *Tragic Muse* was published in the same year. More generally, it may take longer for professionally marginal figures to have their work appreciated by the mainstream members of the discipline. Thus, Schultz and Schultz (1992) said the following of Freud, who had to wait a very long time before his ideas began to have an impression on academic psychologists: "The fact that both the system and its originator were outsiders also complicated and delayed their acceptance" (p. 450). In a similar vein, "Kierkegaard was slow to influence the intellectual life of the west, partly because he wrote in Danish, and partly because he was in many ways an oddity, who stood outside the main movements of the time" (Hearnshaw, 1987, p. 233). Another illustration is Jean Piaget, whose "genetic epistemology" took a long time to get a firm foothold in developmental psychology, especially in the United States.

Yet the foregoing comments are nothing but anecdotes and conjectures (cf. Hudson & Jacot, 1986). There is actually very little solid evidence that the revolutionary scientists are more likely to have received training marginal to the discipline in which they eventually had their notable impact. Gieryn and Hirsh (1983) examined x-ray astronomy to determine whether the major innovators in the field were in some sense outsiders. Professional marginality was gauged by such factors as youth, recent entrance into the discipline, and affiliation with marginal institutes or with industrial laboratories rather than research universities. Although Gieryn and Hirsh concluded that marginality played no role, a reanalysis of their statistics revealed that a composite index consisting of these factors accounted for more than 20% of the variance (Simonton, 1984e). Whether similar predictive power might be found for individuals responsible for major paradigm shifts in psychology remains to be determined. The few published investigations that have any relevance to this issue fail to provide a clear picture. My study of 69 deceased eminent psychologists found that those who lacked a PhD in psychology did not have any advantage (or disadvantage) in terms of eminence, publications, or citation impact (Simonton, 1992b). Another study of 95 still-living eminent psychologists showed that they were more likely to be affiliated with major research universities (Wispé, 1965). These findings are only obliquely related to the question at hand, because eminent scientists do not have to be revolutionary scientists. Kuhnian normal scientists who make significant contributions to an established paradigm can also attain high degrees of distinction in the sciences. The most famous physicists of the 18th and 19th centuries were engaged in extending and elaborating the Newtonian paradigm, for instance.

Until empirical research directly treats this question, it may be unwise for aspiring young psychologists to seek employment at the Swiss Patent Office in the hope that it will enhance their chances of revolutionizing the field.

11

MATURITY AND AGING

Granville Stanley Hall is often considered a "champion of firsts." In 1878 he received the first doctorate in psychology to be bestowed in the United States (under William James). He then became the first American student in the first year of the first psychology laboratory anywhere in the world (with Wilhelm Wundt). Next, in 1883, Hall himself established the first working psychology laboratory in the United States (in contrast to that of James, which was used for teaching rather than research). In 1887 Hall began the publication of the *American Journal of Psychology* (AJP), the first psychological journal in the United States as well as the first English-language journal devoted entirely to psychology. The following year he became the first president of the Clark University, helping to make it one of the centers of graduate education in the field. In 1892, he helped found the American Psychological Association (APA) and became its first president. Even a few years before his death, Hall continued his participation in important firsts. In 1920, Francis Cecil Sumner, Hall's last graduate student, became the first African American to earn a doctoral degree in psychology in the United States.

Hall is also widely considered a pioneer in developmental psychology. In 1893, he founded the *Pedagogical Seminary* (later the *Journal of Genetic Psychology*), the first journal in the fields of educational and child psychology. Yet Hall made it clear during the course of his long career that he was fascinated by far more than child development. On the contrary, he strove to achieve a truly life span developmental perspective. He published his epochal two-volume book *Adolescence* in 1904, and in 1922 published another work called *Senescence*, a pioneering study in gerontology. Because Hall was then 78 years old, it is clear that his developmental studies spanned not only a whole human lifetime but also spanned his whole life.

What Hall's example shows is that this inquiry into great psychologists must not stop with the last chapter. Development does not cease once someone leaves home or graduates from a university. Accordingly, in this chapter I examine what happens to the notables of psychology's history as they mature and age. I begin with a discussion of how their careers typically develop. Once the trajectory of their professional life is thus described I look at what is most likely happening "behind the scenes," in their personal lives. I close the chapter by discussing the final stage of development that marks a psychologist's own final chapter, when the professional and personal lives must face the ever-growing prospect of death.

CAREER DEVELOPMENT

If the goal is to continue where chapter 10 left off, then part of that task has already been accomplished. In chapter 4 I reviewed what researchers have learned about how productivity—both quantity and quality—changes across the life span. From the standpoint of posterity, this creative output is the most crucial aspect of one's career. After all, I showed in chapter 3 that it is the psychologist's lifetime contributions that must ultimately carry his or her reputation in the annals of the discipline. Nevertheless, career development does not consist exclusively of simply publishing one thing after another. Most eminent contributors must earn a living as well. In the case of most research psychologists, this living consists of a position at a major university. Besides advancing up the academic ladder, such professors will also take on doctoral students, to train the next generation of psychologists. Furthermore, psychologists of all kinds, whether researchers or practitioners, may engage in various kinds of organizational activities, such as founding journals or becoming officers in professional associations. Of course, the really best researchers and practitioners will also find themselves the recipient of various awards and honors. Eventually, however, the final years will arrive. The most active part of the career comes to a close, and the long-lived psychologist may enter a period of retirement, however nominal.

G. S. Hall's career displays some of these features of career development. After receiving his PhD under James at age 34, he joined the faculty at Johns Hopkins University at age 38. He founded his first journal, *AJP*, at age 43, and his second, *Pedagogical Seminary*, when he was 47. At age 45 he became president and professor of psychology at Clark University. At both

Johns Hopkins and Clark, Hall became an active mentor to students and by age 54 had produced more than half of the psychology PhDs in the United States. Between ages 42 and 55 Hall conferred doctoral degrees on such future notables as Joseph Jastrow, William Henry Burnham, Edmund Sanford, William Lowe Bryan, Henry Donaldson, and Henry Goddard. He was 48 when he became the first president of APA. As president of Clark and one of the founders of APA, Hall demonstrated his excellent organizational skills. These appeared again at age 65, when he arranged for Sigmund Freud to deliver an address at Clark as part of the university's 20th anniversary celebrations. Freud brought along other psychoanalytic luminaries, such as Carl Jung, Sandor Ferenczi, and Ernest Jones, whereas the contingent of great American psychologists included Edward Titchener, William James, Carl Seashore, and James McKeen Cattell. Nonetheless, despite this professional triumph, Hall's career was already showing signs of decline. In his editorship of *AJP* he had antagonized many of his colleagues with his opinionated and undiplomatic critiques of their work. When Hall was 50 a rival journal, *Psychological Review*, appeared, under the leadership of James Mark Baldwin and James McKeen Cattell. This competition obliged Hall to share the *AJP* editorial responsibilities with coeditors and an editorial board. Furthermore, his research interests had begun to take a curious turn. At age 60 he founded the *American Journal of Religious Psychology and Education* which, unlike his first two journals, did not endure, lasting only 10 years. At age 73 Hall published *Jesus, the Christ, in the Light of Psychology*, a subject likely to be perceived as sacrilegious by the lay public and eccentric by fellow psychologists. Three years later he retired from Clark, and by the time he wrote *Senescence* at age 78 his own career was almost senescent. His autobiography was published 1 year later, and his death at age 80 followed shortly after. Yet, as a final career coup, Hall was elected APA president for a second time in the last year of his life—the only psychologist to be so honored besides his own teacher, William James.

There is no question that Hall secured a significant place in psychology's history. However, to what extent is this career trajectory representative of great psychologists in general? In addressing this question, of course, adjustments must be made for various altered circumstances. Psychologists who attained distinction as clinicians in private practice—such as Freud, Hall's 1909 dignitary—will certainly not exhibit the same pattern of academic achievements. Furthermore, the specific pattern of career onset, climax, and termination may vary according to the magnitude of greatness a psychologist manages to attain. It is fortunate that there already exists sufficient empirical research to permit a pretty reliable sketch of the expected career course.

Onset and Ascent

Right from the start it is apparent that Hall was atypical in one critical respect: His career as a psychologist got off to a late start. The delay was the consequence of his having originally planned to enter the ministry. To this end, at age 23 he had entered Union Theological Seminary in New York City, from which he graduated at age 26. Then, having decided to pursue an academic career instead, he worked hard to raise the necessary money, so he did not begin his graduate studies until age 32. It is more typical of both great scientists and great psychologists to make one's final career choice at a younger age than did Hall. Roe's (1952) 64 eminent scientists were most likely to make the decision to become researchers during their undergraduate education. A large-sample study of 860 scientists starred in *American Men of Science* found that about half decided to become a scientist before age 18 (Visher, 1947a). Moreover, 30% had already determined their scientific specialty before attending college, and another 50% had made that determination during college. Only 5% were more than 30 years old by the time the scientist began pursuing the area in which he or she would attain eminence. In addition, within the particular domain of psychology, the more eminent contributors tended to choose a career in psychological research at a younger age than less eminent contributors (Chambers, 1964).

Although Hall took more time than most distinguished psychologists to launch his career, he at least wasted little time once his new path was chosen. It took him only a couple of years to earn his doctoral degree. Furthermore, in other aspects Hall may follow the norm more closely. I next examine two facets of early career development: fast advancement and elite affiliation.

Fast Advancement

In chapter 10 I noted that the more distinguished scientists tend to complete their higher education at unusually young ages, and in chapter 4 I observed that those luminaries also tend to become contributors to their fields at precocious ages. Therefore, it would seem that exceptional scientists should exhibit accelerated career progress as well. As James McKeen Cattell (1910) wrote, "a man of genius is likely to do his work at an early age and to receive prompt recognition. Kelvin was appointed full professor at Glasgow at 22, Thomson at Cambridge at 26, Rutherford at McGill at 27" (p. 645). Although not quite so dramatic, Cattell's assertion has been confirmed for academic researchers. Among American Nobel laureates, for example, 36% had attained a full professorship by age 34; the corresponding figure for members of the National Academy of Sciences (NAS) is 25% and for scientists honored with entries in *American Men of Science*, 32% (Zuckerman, 1977). In contrast, only 29% of the laureates had to wait until they were 40 or older, compared to 39% of the NAS members and 42% of those featured in *American Men of Science*. These figures imply that the higher an individual's standing as a great scientist, the higher the likelihood that he or she will achieve a full professorship within 10 years or less.

Although I know of no empirical studies that have specifically addressed this issue within psychology, it is clear that many of the discipline's notables

TABLE 11.1
Precocious Full Professors in the History of Psychology

Age	Individuals
34	F. Brentano, F. C. Donders, K. S. Lashley
33	N. Chomsky, G. T. Fechner, H. Simon
32	J. F. Herbart, O. Külpe, C. L. Morgan, K. P. Moritz
31	J. G. Fichte, J. Loeb
30	E. Brücke, K. Ludwig, J. Piaget, E. L. Thorndike, J. B. Watson
29	E. Kraepelin, J. Müller
28	J. M. Cattell, H. von Helmholtz, E. Titchener, C. von Wolff
27	R. H. Lotze, I. Newton, K. Pearson, J. L. Vives
26	F. W. Bessel, E. Mach
25	F. Nietzche
23	B. Rush, E. H. Weber

also became full professors by age 34. Table 11.1 offers some prime examples. Even G. S. Hall can be said to fit this pattern if it is defined in terms of career age rather than chronological age. Although Hall was promoted to full professor at age 40, that promotion took place only 6 years after earning his PhD. Of course, as always, there exist exceptions to the general rule. Two years after Wilhelm Wundt earned his medical degree at age 24, he became assistant to Hermann von Helmholtz at Heidelberg. However, when Helmholtz left for Berlin, Wundt was bypassed in the appointment of his successor, meaning that Wundt had to seek his fortunes elsewhere. At age 42 he finally landed a professorship at the University of Zurich and the following year became professor at the University of Leipzig. Hence, despite having a more promising career onset than Hall, his promotion to professor was considerably delayed. In fact, Wundt had to use a little academic mobility as leverage in attaining that goal.

Elite Affiliation

Exceptions such as Wundt notwithstanding, great psychologists who pursue academic careers should advance quickly from assistant professor to associate professor to full professor (or their functional equivalents, depending on the particular university system). Yet this is not the only way that a disciplinary luminary can display upward mobility. There is also a striking tendency for illustrious psychologists to end up in positions at prestigious institutions as well. For example, American psychologists who are honored with election to the NAS hail predominately from Harvard, the University of California system, Stanford, Yale, Pennsylvania, Chicago, Michigan, Massachusetts Institute of Technology, and Rockefeller (Over, 1981). Most psychologists attain a job at an elite research university right from the outset of their career, on the basis of the quality of their graduate school, the distinction of their mentor, and the quality and quantity of their creative output

(Helmreich, Spence, Beane, Lucker, & Matthews, 1980; Rodgers & Maranto, 1989). However, others work their way up from lesser institutions, arduously earning their upward mobility by the impact of their research record (Gupta, Gilbert, & Pierce, 1983). Table 11.2 offers some representative examples for notable figures in various European and American universities.

The tendency illustrated in Table 11.2 also applies to G. S. Hall, albeit in a more complex manner. Hall's first academic appointment was at Johns Hopkins, a distinguished academic institution that would eventually attract many great psychologists, including James Mark Baldwin, Christine Ladd-Franklin, John B. Watson, Adolf Meyer, W. Horsley Gantt, Hans Selye, and Clifford Thomas Morgan. Yet after only 6 years, and having only 4 years to enjoy his full professorship, Hall took the risky decision to join a brand new university, Clark, that had no reputation whatsoever—good, bad, or mediocre. Yet as professor and as college president, Hall managed to recruit many distinguished faculty, even stealing a few psychologists from Johns Hopkins. Hence, in this sense, Clark University owes its elite status in psychology's history to Hall's professional influence. What Hall gained from the affiliation was the unique opportunity to exercise that influence.

Needless to say, association with prestigious institutions is not confined to psychology's notables. Great scientists, in general, tend to be affiliated with the elite research universities (Poffenberger, 1930; Zuckerman, 1977). At the same time, inquiries conducted by sociologists of science suggest that such affiliations operate in a complex fashion. Two complexities deserve mention here.

1. The prestige of the affiliation bears an inverse connection with the speed that a scientist can advance through the academic system. Top scientists who are affiliated with a less prestigious university can attain a full professorship more quickly. This differential was disclosed in a study of American Nobel laureates in the sciences (Zuckerman, 1977). For institutions below the top tier, nearly half were promoted to full professor by age 34, compared to one third for those at the most prestigious universities. Similar differentials are found for NAS members and those honored with biographies in *American Men of Science*.

2. The link between a researcher's eminence and the institution's distinction is partly causal in nature. Scientists who ascend to a more distinguished research institution tend to increase their publication rates substantially, whereas those who show downward mobility tend to decrease their output (Allison & Long, 1990). This difference reflects the fact that the elite universities emphasize research more and therefore support and encourage increased activity (Manis, 1951). Among the more

TABLE 11.2
Representative Affiliations at Distinguished Universities

Country and University	Individuals
Austria: University of Vienna (1791–1938)	Prochaska, Brücke, Meynert, Breuer, Exner, Brentano, Meinong, Ehrenfels, Mach, Benussi, K. Bühler, C. Bühler, Brunswik, Frenkel-Brunswik
Canada: University of Toronto (1890–1976)	Baldwin, Jones, Brett, Berlyne
Czech Republic: University of Prague (1818–1939)	Purkinje, Mach, Hering, Stumpf, Ehrenfels, Lindworsky
France: University of Paris (Sorbonne, 1793–1969)	Lamarck, Cabanis, Cousin, Esquirol, Flourens, Broca, Bernard, Charcot, Richet, Ribot, Beaunis, Binet, Lapicque, Janet, Lévy-Bruhl, Dumas, Bryan, Durkheim, Delacroix, Piéron, Wallon, Guillaume, Merleau-Ponty, Piaget, Berlyne
Germany: University of Berlin (1809–1948)	Fichte, Hegel, Schopenhauer, Beneke, J. Müller, Schelling, Steinthal, DuBois-Reymond, Pflüger, Dilthey, Fritsch, Bernstein, Helmholtz, Lazarus, Kries, Erdmann, Ebbinghaus, König, Bryan, Dessoir, M. Weber, Schumann, Stumpf, Hornbostel, Nagel, Pflungst, Zeihen, Ach, K. Bühler, Belb, Wertheimer, Köhler, Spranger, Lewin, von Neumann, Jaensch, Duncker, Müller-Freienfels
Great Britain: Cambridge University (1871–1957)	Maxwell, Ward, Stout, Whitehead, Rivers, McDougall, Myers, Yule, Burt, Bartlett, Fisher
Holland: University of Utrecht (1852–1922)	Donders, Zwaardmaker, Ziehen, Michotte, Révész
Hungary: University of Budapest (1908–1946)	Révész, Ferenczi, Békésy
Italy: University of Turin (1814–1922)	Rolando, Lombroso, Kiesow, Ponzo, Gemelli
Russia: Moscow State University (1888–1979)	Sechenov, Kornilov, Blonskiï, Teplov, Rubinshteïn, Luria, Leont'ev
Switzerland: University of Zurich (1849–1965)	Ludwig, Wundt, Hitzig, Avenarius, Forel, Meumann, Frey, Bleuler, Jung, Störring, Abraham, Schumann, Hess, Henri, Lennenberg
United States: Harvard University (1847–1967)	Agassiz, Brown-Séquard, Bowditch, James, Peirce, Royce, Münsterberg, Delabarre, Franz, Cannon, Holt, Urban, Yerkes, Bridgman, Langfeld, Dearborn, Elliott, Troland, F. Allport, C. L. Morgan, McDougall, Boring, Beebe-Center, Whitehead, G. W. Allport, Crozier, Rhine, Prince, Hull, Kelley, Cantril, Sachs, Wells, Lashley, Kluckhorn, Werner, Stevens, Goldstein, Sheldon, C. T. Morgan, Mowrer, F. H. Sanford, Stouffer, Békésy, Olds, Lennenberg

common means of nurturing research is to provide lighter teaching loads (Fulton & Trow, 1974).

These two findings introduce a certain dilemma for young, ambitious psychologists. If someone wishes to become a full professor fast, it is best to become a "big fish in a small pond" and accept a job offer from a institution of lesser rank. But if one is willing to face the dangers of being a "little fish in a big pond"—and especially to tolerate the prospects of delayed advancement—one's long-term impact on the field will be enhanced. It is a choice between short- and long-term gains. Yet universities that aim to raise their status among research institutions can exploit this very dilemma. Young up-and-coming faculty can be lured to less prestigious universities with assurances of lowered standards for promotion coupled with reduced teaching loads. Indeed, the latter was one of the enticements that Hall used to attract new faculty to Clark.

Climax

Once important research programs get launched in a sufficiently supportive environment, researchers find that their visibility in the discipline will steadily grow. One of the ways this growth appears is in the psychologist's participation in professional conventions and conferences. For instance, Harvey Lehman (1953b) conducted a study of the psychologists who participated in APA's 1948 Annual Convention. The modal age for participants who read papers was 34, whereas that for participants involved in symposia or who delivered invited addresses was 45. The latter group of participants had clearly attained higher status in the field. Within 10 years they presumably had gone from having to submit papers for evaluation by the program committee to receiving invitations from colleagues and program chairs.

This professional visibility eventually reaches the point at which the psychologist will be said to have reached the peak of his or her career. This career acme will have three main features: disciplinary esteem, professional service, and teaching impact.

Disciplinary Esteem

In modern times, awards and honors are bestowed on those who attain greatness as scientists. Nowadays the ultimate form of recognition are the Nobel medals bestowed each year for major contributions to physics, chemistry, physiology or medicine, and, more recently, economics. This honor typically comes about 12 years after the award-winning work appears (Manniche & Falk, 1957). Accordingly, the award is usually bestowed when the recipient is in his or her late 40s or early 50s, albeit there exists considerable variation across scientific domains (Moulin, 1955). In terms of mean ages at time of award, physicists are around 49 years old, chemists about 52, and biomedical researchers approximately 55 (Shin & Putnam, 1982). There unfortunately exists no Nobel prize for psychology. The only notables in psychology's history to receive this honor did so for either economics (Herbert Simon) or, more commonly, physiology (Ivan Pavlov, Georg von Békésy, and Roger W. Sperry). Nonetheless, it is possible to give a rough estimate of when great psychologists would earn the Nobel were one available for their discipline. Among the scientists starred in *American Men of Science*, mathematicians and physical scientists were usually so honored in their late 30s, whereas the biomedical scientists were more likely to receive that distinction in their late 40s (Visher, 1947b). The starred psychologists had a mean age of "stardom" almost exactly between these two extremes. This implies that the Nobel prize for psychology, were one to exist, would have the highest probability of being granted to psychologists who were approximately 50 years old. Nonetheless, the four figures in psychology's history who actually became laureates ranged in age from 55 to 68, with a mean and median in the early 60s. The number of relevant cases is too small to say with any confidence whether this age differential represents some statistical fluke.

Psychology happily has its own special means for recognition. One obvious example is the Distinguished Scientific Contributions Award, given out by APA since 1956, when it was bestowed on Wolfgang Köhler, Carl Rogers, and Kenneth Spence. Other recipients were B. F. Skinner, Donald O. Hebb, Nancy Bayley, Eleanor Gibson, Jean Piaget, Brenda Milner, Donald Broadbent, John Garcia, Endel Tulving, Noam Chomsky, Mary Ainsworth, and Shelley Taylor—a pretty diverse mix of notables. On the average, those so honored are about 25 years into their career, or somewhere in their early 50s (Lyons, 1968; Wispé & Ritter, 1964). Not only is this later than the norm for the Nobel prize, but it is also somewhat delayed relative to other honors. Compared to APA's highest scientific award, psychologists elected to the NAS are about 4 years younger, and those honored with the Howard Crosby Warren Medal (of the Society of Experimental Psychologists) are usually about 6 years younger (Lyons, 1968; Wispé & Ritter, 1964). On the other hand, there are other honors that great psychologists must usually wait longer to receive. Those invited to contribute to the *History of Psychology in Autobiography* (e.g., Murchison, 1936) are most often 38 years into their careers (Lyons, 1968), and those honored with the Gold Medal of the American Psychological Foundation are about 50 years into their careers (Wispé & Ritter, 1964), or at chronological ages of about 64 and 76, respectively.

It is odd that J. M. Cattell (1910), when referring to his own research on great scientists, wrote that "nearly all the men obtain recognition between the ages of 30 and 45" (p. 645). This interval is much earlier than those just given. Perhaps Cattell was thinking of lesser honors, along the lines of the various awards granted by the separate divisions of APA. There naturally also exist certain "early career awards" that are confined to individuals who have been professionally active for only a short time. Recipients of APA's Early Career Award, for instance, must have earned their PhDs only 7 or fewer years earlier. These exceptions aside, it is clear that most psychologists cannot expect to earn the highest levels of disciplinary recognition until after chronological age 45, or about 20 years into their careers.

Organizational Service

G. S. Hall was the recipient of no truly major awards for scientific achievement. To be sure, he died long before he could have received APA's Distinguished Scientific Contributions Award, yet there were other honors available in his day. For example, Hall's mentor, William James, was elected to the NAS, and so were several of Hall's younger colleagues, such as J. M. Cattell—but Hall was not. In all likelihood, Hall's research was simply not up to that level. Nevertheless, it is evident that he made some signal contribution to the development of psychology as a discipline. If otherwise, he would not have been chosen to be APA's first president. Because he was among the leaders in the initial formation of APA, this admittedly may seem less of an achievement than to be elected to a well-established and highly prestigious organization. Still, as pointed out earlier, Hall was elected to a second term more than 30 years later. More critical is that Hall's first election can be considered an explicit acknowledgment of his organizational skills. He was more a leader than a creator.

Hall's leadership is reflected in the quick success of the new organization. Hall's presidency was followed by a series of distinguished successors. A short list of his successors includes figures such as William James, J. M. Cattell, Josiah Royce, Edward L. Thorndike, Lewis M. Terman, L. L. Thurstone, Edward C. Tolman, Edwin Guthrie, and Donald T. Campbell. The list includes illustrious representatives of psychology's major schools and subdisciplines: the schools include functional (John Dewey and Harvey Carr), behaviorist (John B. Watson and Clark L. Hull), Gestalt (Wolfgang Köhler), and humanistic (Carl Rogers and Abraham Maslow); the subdisciplines include psychobiological (Karl L. Lashley, Robert Yerkes, and Harry Harlow), cognitive (Jerome Bruner and George A. Miller), psychometric (J. P. Guilford and Anne Anastasi), developmental (Robert Sears and Albert Bandura), personality and social (Gordon Allport and T. M. Newcomb), and clinical and counseling (Paul Meehl and Leona Tyler). Also listed are some of the women who have figured most prominently in American psychology, such as Mary Calkins, Margaret Washburn, Florence Denmark, and Janet Spence. Although the APA membership most often elected native-born psychologists, several foreign-born dignitaries grace the succession, including Hugo Münsterberg, Wolfgang Köhler, and D. O. Hebb. The list even includes some major contributors to the history of psychology as a specialty: J. M. Baldwin, Walter Pillsbury, E. G. Boring, Gardner Murphy, and Ernest Hilgard. Hence, the APA presidency may be counted as one of Hall's most significant historical legacies.

In terms of career development, a psychologist is most likely to be elected to the APA presidency around age 50. It is curious that Hall's successors tended to follow him in terms of the chronological age at which they were most likely to be elected president. Hall was 48, only a bit younger than the mean of 50 for those elected between 1901 and 1975 (Shin & Putnam, 1982). In terms of career age, however, Hall was much younger than the norm, namely 14 years rather than the usual 20 (Wispé & Ritter, 1964). Yet this may reflect the fact that, between Hall's day and more recent times, APA presidents have tended to be older at the time of election (Lyons, 1968; Zusne, 1976b). Thus, in the first 10 years of APA's existence the mean age for assuming the presidency was in the early 40s, an average that increased fairly steadily until the 1970s when it reached the late 50s (Zusne, 1976b). Expressing the historical shift in terms of career age, up to 1928 the average age at election was 14—making Hall absolutely typical—but this figure increased to 20 years into the career for those elected between 1929 and 1966 (Lyons, 1968).

This upward shift in the age of organizational leaders is by no means unique to APA. Harvey C. Lehman (1953a) demonstrated the existence of a consistent trend in the same direction as an organization transforms from upstart to establishment. In the United States, for instance, this historical trend toward more elevated ages occurs for senators and representatives from 1799 to 1925, for members of the president's cabinet from 1789 to 1945, the heads of federal bureaus and services from 1775 to 1945, the justices of the Supreme Court from 1789 to 1925, for ambassadors to major foreign powers from 1789 to 1900, and for army commanders and chiefs of staff from 1775 to 1945. Furthermore, because the age increment is a decade or more, this trend cannot be attributed to increases in human life expectancy (Simonton, 1994a). Rather, it seems that older institutions require or attract more mature leaders. It is ironic that Lehman (1953a) noted that these trends flatly contradict a claim that Hall (1922) made in *Senescence*: "Perhaps the world is a little too much in the hands of people who are a little too old, but this is being rapidly remedied" (p. 135). Even more ironic is the fact that Hall himself was elected to his second term as APA president shortly after making this claim—as an octogenarian!

Speaking of other organizations, it is instructive to compare the APA presidency with similar positions in other institutions of a similar nature. Judging from the data, the membership of APA appears to prefer youth over maturity when they cast their ballots. In contrast to the mean age of 50, somewhat older means are found for other professional societies. In particular, the following mean chronological ages are obtained for the following presidencies: the American Statistical Association, 52; the American Pharmaceutical Association, 54; the American Sociological Association and the Botanical Society of America, 56; the American Political Science Association, 57; the American Economic Association, the American Dental Association, and the American Chemical Society, 58; the American Medical Association, 61; the Geological Society of America, 62; and the American Society of Civil Engineers, 65 (Shin & Putnam, 1982). Not one has a lower mean age for electing their presidents. Furthermore, this preference for more youthful organizational heads is not confined to the APA presidency but rather seems to hold for other psychological associations as well. Specifically, the following median career ages have been found: APA division presidents, 14; presidents, Psychometric Society, 17; presidents of various U.S. regional psychological associations (e.g., Midwestern Psychological Association), 18; chairpersons, Society of Experimental Psychologists, 22 (Lyons, 1968; also see Wispé & Ritter, 1964). These figures contrast greatly with the mean career age of 36 that holds for those elected president of the American Association for the Advancement of Science, more than 15 years older than the typical APA president (Wispé & Ritter, 1964; also see Zusne, 1976b). Even so, not all psychological associations exhibit the same proclivity. Presidents of the International Congress of Psychology are most likely to be at career age 39, a mean much closer to that for American Association for the Advancement of Science presidents than for APA presidents (Wispé & Ritter, 1964).

Hall's assumption of the APA presidency was not the only way he displayed organizational leadership; his service as president of Clark University must be considered, too. This happened at chronological age 45 (career age 11). James Rowland Angell was somewhat older when he became president of Yale University, namely, 52. Both figures are well within the chronological ages most often found for university and college presidents in the United States (Lehman, 1953a; Shin & Putnam, 1982). For top institutions such as Berkeley, Michigan, Chicago, Stanford, and the Ivy League universities, the average chronological age is around 51, with the means ranging between 45 and 52 (Shin & Putnam, 1982). Moreover, Hall's somewhat younger age relative to Angell's can be explicated in terms of the fact that Clark was a brand new university on Hall's presidency, whereas Yale was more than 200 years old under Angell's.

So far, Hall's organizational activities appear to follow a fairly commonplace trajectory for great psychologists. According to the empirical literature, his two significant presidencies—Clark and APA—came at career and chronological ages that were well within the statistical norms. Nevertheless, two significant aspects of Hall's organizational leadership cannot be placed in a proper nomothetic context.

1. Hall was not just APA president but also played a leading role in APA's foundation. This he accomplished when he was in his late 40s. My subjective impression is that this chronological age falls pretty close to the median. At age 44 Harry Stack Sullivan helped found the Washington School of Psy-

chiatry, at age 47 Jacob Moreno established the Beacon Hill Sanitorium, at age 52 Carl Stumpf founded the Society for Child Psychology and Anna Freud founded the Child Therapy Course and Clinic, and at age 53 Robert Yerkes established the Yale Laboratories of Primate Biology. At the same time, there are instances of organizational innovations that occurred when the instigator was much younger or older than was Hall at the time of APA's birth. On the youthful end of the spectrum, at 33 Karl Abraham organized the Berlin Psychoanalytic Society, at 35 Otto Rank founded the publishing house Der Internationale Psychoanalytische Verlag, at 37 Edward Titchener founded the Society of Experimental Psychologists (as a rival to APA), and at about age 40 Plato founded his Academy in Athens. On the older end, James McKeen Cattell founded the Psychological Corporation in his late 50s, Hans Selye founded the International Institute of Stress when he was 70, and Leta Hollingworth established the Psychological Laboratories at Barnard College in her mid-70s. A study that goes beyond these specific cases is sorely needed.

2. Besides Hall's contributions to Clark and APA, he founded journals, most notably *AJP*, which he initiated at age 43. However, as in the preceding case, I know of no empirical studies that would help determine whether this accomplishment came at a typical point in the development of a distinguished career in psychology. Yet this figure also seems to conform closely to the norm, at least according to my own subjective impressions. Other journal founders or cofounders who were likewise in their 40s include Hermann Ebbinghaus (*Zeitschrift für Psychologie und Physiologie der Sinnesorgan*), Max Wertheimer (*Psychologische Forschung*), Karl Pearson (*Biometrika*), Joseph Banks Rhine (*Journal of Parapsychology*), Jacob Moreno (*International Journal of Sociometry*), and Wilhelm Wundt (*Philosophische Studien*). At the same time, some psychologists were in their 50s, 60s, and even 70s, as in the cases of B. F. Skinner's *Journal for the Experimental Analysis of Behavior*, Alexander Bain's *Mind*, Wilhelm Stekel's *Psychotherapeutische Praxis*, and E. G. Boring's *Contemporary Psychology*. Also, just as would be expected if Hall fell close to the central tendency, there are many examples of journals founded by individuals in their 30s, such as François Magendie (*Journal de Physiologie Expérmentale et Pathologie*), Moritz Lazarus (*Zeitschrift für Völkerpsychologie und Sprachwissenschaft*), and Théodule Armand Ribot (*Revue philosophique*). In fact, *Psychological Review*, which emerged as the rival publication

vehicle to Hall's *AJP*, was cofounded by James Mark Baldwin and James McKeen Cattell, who were 33 and 34, respectively. Again, more research is needed on the point in the career at which these achievements are most likely to emerge.

Before turning to the final feature of the career acme, I must pause to observe that not all great psychologists highlight their careers by getting themselves elected president or by founding new journals. Many of the greats seem perfectly content to restrict themselves to making intellectual contributions to psychological science. Ivan Pavlov, for one, confined his scientific activities almost entirely to his laboratory and thereby avoided the distractions of professional service. B. F. Skinner may have founded a journal, but it was one strictly devoted to publishing research in the Skinnerian mold; he declined the opportunity to run for APA president. Hence, a psychologist does not have to follow Hall's career emphasis to attain high status in the annals of psychology.

Teaching Influence

Between the ages of 42 and 48 Hall produced three new doctorates who were later elected to the APA presidency: Joseph Jastrow, Edmund Sanford, and William Lowe Bryan. Thus, part of Hall's impact on psychology's history was through his students, especially those who could count themselves as Hall PhDs. Naturally, not all great psychologists exerted so much influence through their teaching. The German psychologist Franz Brentano, according to one historian (Wertheimer, 1987), "did not have many students, but had a wide influence nevertheless" (p. 73). Even so, given what was covered in chapter 10, Hall may be more representative than Brentano of the norm. After all, if great psychologists are more likely to study under great psychologists, then great psychologists must teach great psychologists.

There exists evidence that excellence in research is not antithetical to excellence in teaching, as is sometimes believed. To begin, because the personality traits of good teachers are orthogonal to the personality traits of good researchers, it is possible for someone to be both a prolific researcher and an effective teacher (Rushton, Murray, & Paunonen, 1983). The two personality profiles are by no means mutually exclusive. As a consequence, it should not be surprising that the correlation between research productivity and teaching effectiveness is essentially zero (e.g., Voeks, 1962). That means that some professors will be inferior at both teaching and research, some will be inferior at one but superior at the other, and yet others will be superior at both. In line with this fourfold typology, only half of the psychologists who earn obituaries in APA's *American Psychologist* are credited with being good teachers or mentors (Kinnier, Metha, Buki, & Rawa, 1994).

Although Hall can be considered someone whose teaching skills far surpassed his research prowess, his own mentor, William James, clearly attained excellence in both. Besides writing a bestselling textbook—the famed *Principles of Psychology*—James published a work devoted to the teaching of psychology (W. James, 1900). He even took his instructional responsibilities so seriously that he introduced student evaluations to get direct feedback on his performance.

Yet a crucial contaminating factor cannot be ignored: Just as research productivity changes across the course of the career, as shown in chapter 4, so may teaching effectiveness exhibit longitudinal trends. In terms of classroom performance, there is ample reason to believe that students assign lower teaching evaluations to professors who are in the latter part of their careers (Horner, Murray, & Rushton, 1989; Kinney & Smith, 1992). With respect to the mentoring of graduate students—informal rather than formal instruction—there may appear an age for optimal effectiveness. Future Nobel laureates in the sciences tend to have been trained by mentors who were in their late 30s or early 40s (Zuckerman, 1977), a figure that corresponds closely to what happens in psychology as well (Gupta et al., 1983). Although Hall appeared to be most effective at slightly older ages, this may be ascribed to his relatively late start. His three most eminent students received their PhDs when he would have been in his late 30s and early 40s, were he to have earned his own doctorate around age 26. The students who came later in Hall's career tended to be less outstanding. Henry Goddard, for instance, who got his PhD when Hall was 55 and when he himself was 33, is now considered more infamous than famous for his work on "morons"—a term he coined. Goddard's 1912 book on *The Kallikak Family* attracted special criticism, both among contemporaries and in the eyes of posterity (Gould, 1981; J. D. Smith, 1985; cf. Goddard, 1942). Hall's last student, Francis Sumner, who got his PhD under Hall when the latter was 76, also cannot be said to rank with his best students; at least, Sumner did not become highly conspicuous as an original researcher (Guthrie, 1998).

One might think that as professors mature, they would acquire increasingly more disciplinary expertise, including enhanced knowledge and teaching skills. Yet that seems not to be the case. So what is the foundation for the apparent age decrement in teaching influence? Part of the answer may come from what I discussed at length in chapter 4: Creative productivity across the career tends to follow a single-peaked age function. It is telling that the optimal age for creative output is located at about the same point as the optimal age for teaching impact, the late 30s and early 40s. The plausible inference consequently is that the most effective mentors are those investigators who have the most active research programs. Such mentors would provide the best models for the student's emulation.

Nevertheless, this may not be the whole story. The decline in teaching effectiveness may be part of a more pervasive age trend that slowly chips away at a psychologist's greatness.

Dénouement and Epilogue

Several distinct forces may operate to undermine a psychologist's overall greatness, both as a researcher and as a teacher. The following three factors are perhaps the most noteworthy.

1. The older a scientist becomes, the less likely he or she will work hard at keeping up on the research literature. This negative trend was demonstrated empirically in a study conducted by Wayne Dennis and Girden (1954) when the former was editor of *Psychological Bulletin*. At that time the *Bulletin* was a general journal distributed to the entire APA membership. On the basis of 397 survey responses, Dennis found that those in their 20s and 30s are most likely to read widely the various articles, notes, and reviews published therein. These results were then connected to research output in two ways. First, it was shown that APA Fellows read the journal more thoroughly than other APA members. Second, the rise and fall in the reading curve tended to anticipate the rise and fall in productivity, as recorded in *Psychological Abstracts*. The latter curve was lagged about 10 years behind the first. Although Dennis and Girden did not specifically address the teaching issue, any decline in reading may have consequences for the effectiveness of any instructor and mentor. Little by little, the old professor's once arduously acquired expertise becomes ever more obsolete. Lectures are increasingly delivered from yellowed and wrinkled notes, and the laboratory increasingly uses outdated methods and techniques. The failure to keep up on the literature is especially critical in a scientific discipline such as psychology, in which knowledge becomes obsolescent at a much faster rate than in the humanities (McDowell, 1982).

2. It must be deemed ironic that a part of the decline in the research performance of scientists may be ascribed to the consequences of their very eminence. It is as if greatness self-destructs, or carries the seeds of its own destruction, in a dialectic fashion. Such a process is suggested in a study of 10 eminent social scientists (Rodman & Mancini, 1981). In the beginning of the career, the young researcher must run the professional gauntlet by submitting papers to rigorous, refereed journals, sometimes receiving acceptances but often suffering rejections as well. As social scientists attain a high degree of distinction, however, they begin to become the recipients of writing invitations. The 10 social scientists in Rodman and Mancini's (1981) sample received an average of

21 requests a year to contribute a chapter, article, book review, or other piece. As a result, more than half of the publications that they produce at this stage in their career are due to such invitations. Furthermore, only 6% of their current writing obligations involve commitments to write journal articles. They have learned that an invitation from a journal editor to write an essay is not equivalent to guaranteed publication, for the manuscript will most often still be sent out for review, with the risk of rejection or at least a request for extensive revision. This shift in publication strategy appears to be rational, even enviable, for why should luminaries expose themselves to anonymous critiques when they can publish the same thing as a book chapter? Even so, the fact that distinguished scientists become much less accountable to the peer review process means that they eventually can wallow in outmoded ideas with enviable immunity from collegial criticism. They do not even have to keep up on the research literature in their field.

3. As scientists get older, they tend to spend less time on research and correspondingly more time on administrative tasks (Zuckerman & Merton, 1972). "Well, it is a fact of life that most professors who rise in the world have to take on administrative posts," complained one of Roe's (1965, p. 316) eminent scientists when she conducted a follow-up study 12 years after her *Making of a Scientist* (Roe, 1953a). This increased assumption of major administrative responsibilities holds for psychologists as well (Horner, Murray, & Rushton, 1994). Both teaching and research will often succumb to the time-consuming and often emotionally enervating nature of these activities. A historic illustration is James Rowland Angell, whose distinguished career at the University of Chicago was not continued at Yale University when he became the latter's president. His best doctoral students—J. B. Watson, H. A. Carr, June E. Downey, and W. V. Bingham—were all Chicago PhDs (M. D. Boring & Boring, 1948), and all of his best research was published prior to his assumption of his duties at Yale (R. I. Watson, 1974). This is not to say that Angell accomplished nothing in the name of psychology. His founding of the Yale Institute of Human Relations proves otherwise. It is just that his achievements became administrative rather than scientific or instructive.

It is difficult to determine the extent to which the above three factors apply to G. S. Hall. Given his editorial duties with the journals he founded, he had to keep up on the research literature to at least some degree. Book chapters were not as important a publication vehicle in his day as they have been in more recent times (Simonton, 1992b). Perhaps Hall's administrative chores may have had more repercussions than anything else. Of the three students who later became APA presidents, two (Joseph Jastrow and Edmund Sanford) received their PhDs while Hall was a full-time professor at Johns Hopkins, and the third (William Lowe Bryan) earned his degree shortly after Hall became president at Clark. Yet, still additional factors may also be operative in Hall's case, including the developmental effect that Hall failed to discuss in his 1922 book *Senescence*.

Planck's Principle

Hall was a great admirer of the evolutionary theories of Charles Darwin, even earning the epithet "Darwin of the mind" for his insistent incorporation of Darwinism into his psychology. Of course, Hall's admiration could be considered well placed. Darwin's 1859 book *Origin of Species* has been called one of the "books that changed the world" (Downs, 1956) and was included in the collection known as the *Great Books of the Western World* (Hutchins, 1952). Darwin was even ranked 17th in a list of "the 100 most influential persons in history," a spot just behind Moses (Hart, 1987). The impact of Darwin certainly is evident in psychology's own history. "Very likely, it is no accident that the first laboratory in psychology was functioning within 20 years of the publication of the *Origin of Species*," claimed Viney and King (1998, p. 195) in their history of psychology textbook.

Nevertheless, it must be remembered that not all of Darwin's contemporaries favorably judged *Origin* to be a scientific masterpiece. Indeed, I observed in chapter 9 how the extremely mixed reception of Darwin's landmark work was what inspired Sulloway (1996) to scrutinize the psychological factors that influence whether a scientist accepts or rejects a revolutionary innovation. Although Sulloway concentrated on the scientist's ordinal position in the family, his theory incorporated several other developmental variables. Among the additional factors Sulloway (1996) examined was a developmental variable suggested by Charles Darwin himself. In *Origin* Darwin (1860/1952) anticipated the book's hostile reception with the admission that he did not "expect to convince experienced naturalists whose minds are stocked with a multitude of facts all viewed, during a long course of years, from a point of view directly opposite to mine" (p. 240). Yet Darwin did look "with confidence to the future,—to the young and rising naturalists, who will be able to view both sides of the question with impartiality." In private, Darwin would sometimes express this view even more emphatically, as is apparent in what he once told the great geologist Charles Lyell, who was 12 years his senior: "What a good thing it would be if every scientific man was to die when sixty years old, as afterwards he would be sure to oppose all new doctrines" (quoted in S. E. Hyman, 1963, pp. 375–376). When Lyell had finally converted to Darwinism after having reached age 70, he humorously informed Darwin that "he hoped that he might be allowed to live" as a consequence of his conversion (quoted in S. E. Hyman, 1963, p. 376).

Although Darwin may have been the first scientist to speculate on this developmental possibility, the hypothesis is currently known as *Planck's principle* (Hull, Tessner, & Diamond, 1978), because Planck had voiced a similar conjecture with respect to the differential response to his revolutionary quantum theory. In Planck's own words, "A new scientific truth does not triumph by convincing its opponents and making them see the light, but rather because its opponents eventually die, and a new generation grows up that is familiar with it" (1949, pp. 33–34). Indeed, so quick was the younger generation to embrace the quantum revolution that the emerging domain was for a time styled *Knabenphysiks* ("kids' physics") in German.

The eponym choice notwithstanding, the very first empirical test of the Planck principle concerned the reception of Darwin's theory of evolution by natural selection (Hull et al., 1978). In particular, Hull et al. (1978) asked whether age had any predictive value with respect to the odds that a British scientist would still reject Darwin's theory 10 years after the publication of *Origin*. Among these opponents was one major figure in the history of psychology, namely, the philosopher J. S. Mill. In contrast, those who accepted the Darwinian thesis early on included Francis Galton, T. H. Huxley, W. S. Jevons, and Charles Lyell. All told, the age of the figure at the time of *Origin*'s publication accounted for 6% of the variance in acceptance. Although a secondary analysis of these data cast some doubt on the conclusion (Levin, Stephan, & Walker, 1995), Sulloway (1996) replicated the basic finding in a far more comprehensive empirical analysis. Because Sulloway incorporated more variables into his prediction equation, he was able to gauge the relative impact of the various contributing factors. For instance, he was able to directly compare age and birth order. "Throughout the debates over evolution, 80-year-old later borns were as open to this theory as were 25-year-old firstborns. During the Darwinian revolution, being laterborn was equivalent to a 55-year dose of the openmindedness that typically resides in youth" (Sulloway, 1996, p. 36). Historians who dislike the application of quantitative techniques to historical data such as Sulloway's (1996) will probably not like to hear that Planck's principle may also apply to their very distaste; at least, age has emerged as a predictor of whether economic historians adopt cliometric methods. About 10% of the variance is explicable in terms of age (Diamond, 1980). In concrete terms, Whaples (1991) found that a 65-year-old economic historian had about one third the odds of being a cliometrician relative to a 35-year-old colleague.

What underlies the operation of Planck's principle? Barber (1961; cf. Messerli, 1988; J. A. Stewart, 1986) suggested several possibilities:

> As a scientist gets older he is more likely to be restricted to innovation by his substantive and methodological preconceptions and by his other cultural accumulations; he is more likely to have high professional standing, to have specialized interests, to be a member or official of an established organization, and to be associated with a "school." (p. 601)

This suggestion actually includes several causes, some psychological and others more sociological in nature. Especially intriguing from the present perspective is the cognitive tendency for scientists to become increasingly ensnared by the ideas that they themselves created. The creativity of their early years provides the chains of their later years, in a long-term and comprehensive form of negative transfer or functional fixedness. Sigmund Freud admitted the influence of something like this when, at age 73, he published *Civilization and Its Discontents*: "The conceptions I have summarized here I first put forward only tentatively, but in the course of time they have won such a hold over me that I can no longer think in any other way" (Freud, 1929/1952, p. 790). The same pattern of life span cognitive development may be seen in other figures besides Freud. Thus, "Golgi never abandoned his belief in the nervous system's unitary nature, despite Cajal's overwhelming evidence refuting it" (Thorne & Henley, 1997, p. 461)—and despite the irony that Golgi was obliged to share the 1906 Nobel with his scientific nemesis Ramón y Cajal. Likewise with respect to another Nobel laureate, a biographer once observed that Pavlov did not alter his theory of how the brain worked during conditioning in the light of more recent research; "it is as though, in 1900 or thereabouts, he stopped listening to what was going on elsewhere" (J. A. Gray, 1979, p. 102).

The previous two examples suggest that Planck's principle always functions in a negative manner, undermining rather than enhancing a psychologist's greatness. Yet that inference is probably misleading. There are sometimes positive benefits of becoming, with increased maturity, less than fully open to new ideas. Perhaps the most valuable asset is that a little closed-mindedness helps a scientist resist becoming intellectually overwhelmed by some highly persuasive system of thought. One illustration may be found in the following quotation:

> Unlike most of Freud's disciples, Jung had already established an impressive professional reputation of his own before he began his association with Freud. He was the best known of all the early converts to psychoanalysis. As a result, he was perhaps less malleable, less suggestible, than the younger analysts who joined Freud's psychoanalytic family. (Schultz & Schultz, 1992, p. 464)

This same advantage is implicit in a statement about Hartley's relation to Hume: "Although he was a contemporary of Hume, he was probably not strongly influenced by him since Hartley began writing and publishing in a minor way on psychological matters before the appearance of Hume's *Treatise*" (R. I. Watson & Evans, 1991, p. 207).

Although more research is needed on how Planck's principle has functioned during the course of psychology's history, I conjecture that its consequences for good or ill might partly depend on where individuals are positioned in their careers. For those who are relatively early in their careers, a little closed-mindedness would help them avoid losing their unique voice when a potent but not completely compatible perspective confronts them. However, those who are later in their careers may suffer the consequences of failing to assimilate their theories or methods to the latest advances in the discipline. They are then left behind.

In the latter part of the career, as well, Planck's principle could undermine a psychologist's effectiveness in master–disciple or teacher–student relationships. This process may be seen in the history of psychoanalysis. Josef Breuer, in his 50s when he collaborated with his younger colleague, Freud, on *Studies in Hysteria*, found himself obliged to part company with Freud as the latter began to emphasize ever more sexual etiology. By converting the latter into a dogma, Freud eventually alienated some of his best students. When Freud was 55, Alfred Adler went his separate way; when Freud was 58, Carl Jung was compelled to do the same; under slightly different circumstances, Otto Rank split with Freud when the latter was 68 years old. After that, Freud was not to mentor students who boasted nearly the same caliber.

It is tempting to apply Planck's principle to G. S. Hall's mentoring career as well, yet the application does not work very well. On the contrary, Hall seems to have maintained a very open-minded attitude toward his students' interests and aspirations until the very end of his career. This is certainly evident in his relationship with his last graduate student, Francis Sumner (Guthrie, 1998). Hall offered considerable encouragement to this talented African American, at one time even defending him when Sumner published some statements during World War I that some White Americans considered treasonous. In addition, Hall remained very flexible when Sumner had to interrupt his graduate studies to serve with the U.S. infantry in France. When Sumner was finally able to return to Clark to complete his studies, Hall was very open when Sumner decided to switch his dissertation topic from religion to psychoanalysis. Moreover, after Sumner's doctoral thesis on "The Psychoanalysis of Freud and Adler" was unanimously approved by the examining committee—which included E. G. Boring, Samuel W. Fernberger, and William H. Burnham—Hall arranged for its immediate publication in *Pedagogical Seminary*. At no time during Sumner's years under Hall's mentorship was there any suggestion that Hall was attempting to convert Sumner into an intellectual clone.

More critical is that it may not be totally fair to count Sumner as one of Hall's less accomplished protégés. After receiving his degree, Sumner faced obstacles that would not be encountered by Hall's other doctoral students.

Not only did African American universities lack the requisite resources possessed by their majority-culture counterparts, but in addition Sumner soon discovered that White funding agencies were not receptive to grant applications from Black professors. His scientific efforts thus impeded, Sumner found himself contributing to the advancement of psychological science by means other than highly prolific and influential research. Sumner served for many years as an official abstractor for psychological journals—most notably for *Psychological Bulletin*. Taking advantage of his appreciable linguistic abilities, he eventually translated thousands of articles from their German, French, and Spanish originals. More notable still was Sumner's contributions to the development of the psychology program at Howard University—whose psychology department he chaired for nearly 25 years. Under his inspiration and effort, Howard eventually graduated more Black psychologists than any other educational institution. Indeed, one of Howard's graduates, Kenneth Clark, became the first African American elected APA president. In light of these achievements, Sumner has been called the father of Black American psychologists (Guthrie, 1998). Hence, Hall's last student might easily be considered among Hall's best, at least in terms of his overall impact on the evolution of American psychology.

Late-Life Effects

Perhaps Hall (1922) never mentioned something akin to Planck's principle because it was not something he personally experienced as a consequence of aging. Although Hall's (1922) *Senescence* reports the results of questionnaire data and reviews the past literature on the subject, the work is strongly shaped by his own personal impressions, as he himself confessed. After all, Hall knew that he had approached his final years, although he could not have known that he had only 2 years left to live at the time the book was published. As a consequence, Hall's work is full of observations about aging that probably reflect his own personal experiences as much or more than those of his survey respondents. For example, according to Hall (1922),

> At sixty we realize that there is but one more threshold to cross before we find ourselves in the great hall of discard where most lay their burdens down and that what remains yet to do must be done quickly. Hence this is a decade peculiarly prone to overwork. We refuse to compromise with failing powers but drive ourselves all the more because we are on the home stretch. We anticipate leaving but must leave things right and feel we can rest up afterwards. So we are prone to overdraw our account of energy and brave the danger of collapse if our overdraft is not honored. Thus some cross the conventional deadline of seventy in a state of exhaustion that nature can never entirely make good. (p. 367)

As far as Hall's own career was concerned, the above generalization may be more be more descriptive of the last 10 years of his life. Judging from the bibliographic information provided in one reference source (R. I. Watson, 1974, p. 164), Hall's output in his 70s surpassed that in his 60s. Especially remarkable was the quantity of major books he published, including *Senescence*. Hence, Hall can be said to have ended his life and career with a final burst of creativity. Some evidence exists that Hall's late renaissance may not be unusual. Although the data published in Lehman's (1953a) *Age and Achievement* are often cited in support of the conclusion that creativity irrevocably declines with age, a secondary analysis revealed a higher than expected incidence of resurgence in the very last years (Haefele, 1962; also see R. A. Davis, 1954). For instance, the output of major philosophical works produced by thinkers between ages 80 and 84 exceeds the output in the preceding half-decades of 60–64, 65–69, 70–74, and, especially, 75–79 (in which the output becomes zero). A similar creative renaissance appeared for individuals who made great contributions to psychology, with the output of major works during the 75–79 age interval surpassing those in both the 65–69 and 70–74 intervals—the former, in fact, exceeding the preceding two half-decades put together! Thus, there is reason to believe that such a last-chance syndrome may highlight the lives of many great psychologists.

However, this late-life effect probably should not be conceived in terms of a psychologist's chronological age. Earlier in this chapter and in chapter 4 I have stressed the superior relevance of career age in describing longitudinal changes across the adult life span. Yet in the present instance career age may be no more germane than chronological age. Instead, the crucial developmental factor may be the perceived proximity of death—precisely as suggested in the preceding Hall quotation. During the final years of life any human being undergoes a number of cognitive and physiological changes that are hard not to recognize and certainly will not escape the notice of any observant psychologist. It will presumably be the onset of these developmental decrements more than a particular birthday party that will evoke the last-chance syndrome. As a consequence, the accelerated pace of creative activity that Hall discerned may take place earlier or later in the life span, depending on the status of one's intellectual and physical health. Hence, for Wilhelm Wundt, the creative intensification occurred not in the 60s, as Hall (1922) claimed, or in the late 70s, as Lehman's (1953a) data suggest, but in the middle 80s. This is evident in the rate at which Wundt wrote the 10 volumes of his *Folk Psychology* (*Völkerpsychologie*). To quote E. G. Boring (1950),

> the first volume of this work appeared in 1900 [at age 68], was later revised and finally became two volumes in a second revision. The second volume was published in 1905–1906 [age 73–74] and became two volumes on revision. Then from 1914 to 1920 [age 82–88], six more volumes appeared, making ten in all. (p. 326)

That yields an output rate of nearly a volume per year. As if finishing the last volume were not sufficient, Wundt then completed his autobiography and died, just shortly after, in the same year. Given the quickening pace in his final years, Wundt clearly was acting like someone who was obsessively driven to get all "unfinished business" off his desk before the final hour arrived.

Peter Suedfeld and his colleagues have studied how integrative complexity changes in the final 5 years of the lives of eminent personalities (C. A. Porter & Suedfeld, 1981; Suedfeld & Piedrahita, 1984). A conspicuous decline in the complexity of thought appears in those final years, according to their content analysis of private correspondence. Suedfeld (1985) later found a comparable effect when he scored 85 presidential addresses delivered before APA. Specifically, the more years the eminent psychologist had left to live after assuming the presidency, the higher was the level of integration and differentiation that he or she displayed in the speech. This finding is consistent with the implicit assumption of the last-chance syndrome that psychologists undergo certain changes that allow them to "see it coming." Of course, the fact that so many great psychologists manage to write their autobiographies in the last year or two of their lives—like Hall and Wundt did— would also imply that death's proximate arrival can often be anticipated. It usually does not make sense to write an autobiography until one can be sure that it will not have to undergo several revised editions.

The writing of autobiographies also suggests that great psychologists will often engage in a "life review" as they enter their final years (R. N. Butler, 1963). As Erik Erikson, the eminent psychoanalysist, once described the process,

> those nearing the end of the life cycle find themselves struggling to accept the inalterability of the past and the unknowability of the future, to acknowledge possible mistakes and omissions, and to balance consequent despair with the sense of overall integrity that is essential to carrying on. (E. J. Erikson, Erikson, & Kivnick, 1986, p. 56)

Mackavey, Malley, and Stewart (1991) empirically investigated this review process in a study of the autobiographies of 49 eminent psychologists. The autobiographical accounts were obtained from three volumes of *A History of Psychology in Autobiography* (e.g., E. G. Boring & Lindzey, 1967) and *Models of Achievement: Reflections of Eminent Women in Psychology* (O'Connell & Russo, 1983). These distinguished psychologists averaged around 72 years old at the time they wrote these autobiographies, and hence they were clearly approaching the final years of their lives. The investigators scrutinized their essays for autobiographically consequential experiences (ACEs). All told, researchers identified 250 ACEs, or an average of about 5 per autobiography, with a range of 1 to 9. It is significant that approximately 80% of these ACEs came from the years in which the individuals were most likely in the early stages of their career development—namely between ages 18 and 35. For instance, Gordon Allport recounted a crucial incident in which he confessed to his Harvard professor, Herbert S. Langfeld, that he had misgivings about his fitness to become a psychologist. Allport received Langfeld's reassuring response, "but you know there are many branches of psychology," as a kind of turning point (E. G. Boring & Lindzey, 1967, p. 8). He realized that the discipline was sufficiently inclusive to leave room for someone with his maverick interests. After earning his doctorate under Langfeld, Allport felt free to pursue his own brand of psychology.

So far I have shown how the final years of great psychologists may display a last-chance burst of creativity as well as an autobiographical life review. Yet it is also conceivable that their psychological worldviews might change during these concluding years. This is perhaps one of the weaknesses of the research reported in chapter 8, in which I examined the philosophies of psychological science for 54 notable figures in the discipline's history (Simonton, 2000b). Each figure had his or her beliefs characterized as if those beliefs were maintained throughout their entire life span. Yet how justified are these time-collapsed characterizations? According to one history of psychology text, "there is a literary myth that Aristotle's views were static and unchanging. We now know, however, that his thinking, like that of most creative individuals, went through various stages of development" (R. I. Watson & Evans, 1991, p. 69). Support for this latter assertion is readily found in the empirical literature on the content of creative products. A content analysis of the dramas of Aeschylus, Sophocles, Euripedes, and Aristophanes revealed that their favorite themes changed as they got older, with their early interest in practical affairs gradually giving way to a preoccupation with the divine and the mystical (Simonton, 1983a). I (Simonton, 1986e) identified a similar thematic transformation in the plays of William Shakespeare. A fascination with worldly ambition and passionate love slowly yielded ground to a more detached view of life and its conflicts. Especially intriguing is research on the transformations that can take place in the creativity that occurs in the concluding years of life. Thus, great painters may exhibit an "old age style" in their final years (Lindauer, 1999), whereas great composers may display what has been called a "swan-song phenomenon" (Simonton, 1989c). In both cases creativity often takes a shift toward greater simplicity, profundity, and spirituality.

As yet, no empirical research has specifically assessed whether analogous late-life effects might occur in the ideas expressed by great psychologists. Yet it is easy to identify possible examples in the lives of several notable figures in the field. The concluding years of Isaac Newton were given up to Biblical exegeses, especially with respect to the prophesies of Daniel and the Apocalypse of St. John. William James, in the years following the publication of *Principles* (1890/1952), replaced his psychological interests with increasingly more religious and philosophical preoccupations. This shift is evident in his 1902 book *The Varieties of Religious Experience*, his various writings on pragmatism, and his forays into psychical research. Although his ideas were more sympathetic and even accepting, great psychologists may instead decide to grapple with deeper intellectual and spiritual issues in a more critical, even rejecting manner. The 69-year-old Immanuel Kant, his three great *Critiques* already behind him, published *Religion Within the Limits of Reason Alone* in 1793, a philosophical analysis that got him into serious difficulties with the Prussian King Frederick William II. Sigmund Freud, an old man slowly dying of cancer, grappled with religion and his Jewish heritage in his 1928 *The Future of an Illusion* and 1939 *Moses and Monotheism*. Even Freud's growing theoretical fixation with the death instinct may be viewed as his own personal accommodation to death's inevitability.

G. S. Hall's life may also be taken as illustrative of these developmental trends, albeit in a more unique fashion, given that he had once aspired to enter the ministry. At age 73 Hall published his two-volume 1917 work on *Jesus the Christ, in the Light of Psychology*, and 3 years later in 1920, he published *Morale: The Supreme Standard of Life and Conduct*. Even Hall's (1922) *Senescence*, which was published when he was 78, may be considered a continuation of this shift toward concerns more profound and pervasive than those normally treated in psychology. This is apparent in the questions that Hall posed to his survey respondents. Hall first raised life-review issues such as "Are you troubled with regrets for things done or not done by or for you?" (p. 329), "What duties do you feel that you still owe either to those about you or to the world?" (p. 333), and "Would you live your life over again?" (p. 342). Hall closed the questionnaire with the queries "Do you get more or less from the clergy and the church than formerly?" (p. 353) and "Do you think or worry about dying or the hereafter more or less than formerly?" (p. 354). Hall clearly raised these issues because they were ones that he himself was contemplating as his own long life was drawing to a close. In a sense, *Senescence* was Hall's very own swan song.

MARRIAGE AND FAMILY

Now that the great psychologist's professional career has been traced from onset and acme to decline and termination, the time has arrived to look at what happens in a great psychologist's private life. How did psychology's notables manage to make their personal lives conform to their career ambitions? One response is that advanced by the English philosopher Francis Bacon (1597/1942):

> He that hath wife and children hath given hostages to fortune; for they are impediments to great enterprises, either of virtue or mischief. Certainly the best works, and of greatest merit for the public, have proceeded from the unmarried or childless men, which, both in affection and means, have married and endowed the public. (p. 29)

Bacon's statement has received some empirical endorsement. Havelock Ellis (1926) concluded from his study of British geniuses that there was "a greater tendency to celibacy among persons of ability than among the ordinary population" (p. xiv). Not counting priests, the rate was nearly 1 out of 5. Another investigation into the lives of a more elite sample of historic figures found that 55% never married (McCurdy, 1960). Of course, the history of psychology is replete with eminent contributors who avoided taking marriage vows, such as Blaise Pascal, Thomas Hobbes, Baruch Spinoza, John Locke, Gottfried Wilhelm Leibniz, Voltaire, David Hume, Immanuel Kant, Arthur Schopenhauer, Søren Kierkegaard, Herbert Spencer, Friedrich Nietzsche, and Jean Paul Sartre. Many of these confirmed bachelors would probably have agreed with Oswald Külpe's affirmation that "science is my bride" (quoted in Ogden, 1951, p. 4). Some notables admittedly managed to experience some facsimile of a family life outside the institution of marriage. Even so, these instances are often "the exceptions that prove the rule." Descartes fathered an illegitimate child through one of his Dutch servants, but the child died young. Rousseau sired five children by a servant but sent them all off to a foundling hospital.

To be sure, many of psychology's notables do get married and raise families. G. S. Hall certainly counts as an example (although he lost both his wife and one of his two children in a tragic accident). Yet a residual antagonism between family and career is suggested by the following four facts.

1. When the eminent do marry, they tend to get married at a later age than the norm, usually in their late 20s and 30s (Bowerman, 1947). The median age that influential scientists get married is 27 (Visher, 1947b), and those who earn Nobel prizes are often older still, with median ages between 29 (physiology or medicine laureates) and 31 (physics and chemistry laureates; Moulin, 1955). In line with these statistics, Freud did not get married until he was 30, and James was 35, Wundt 40, Karen Horney 44, and Rousseau 56 (when he finally married the servant who had borne him his abandoned children).

2. Even after marriage, the eminent will often have relatively few, if any, children. Francis Galton (1874) was the first to note this fact, which he reported in *English Men of Science*. He observed that the eminent scientists in his survey all had families that were smaller than those of their parents. Galton himself took this tendency to the extreme: Despite coming from a very large family, he and his wife were childless. This general trend is also apparent in the 64 eminent scientists in Roe's (1952) study: The 14 psychologists in her sample averaged only 1.6 children, with a range of 0 to 4. Naturally, there al-

ways exist exceptions to any statistical regularity, such as George Berkeley and Freud, who both had six children. On the whole, however, procreative fertility is not linked with creative productivity. In line with Freudian theory, the former seems to be sublimated in the latter.

3. Neither marriages nor general family life may come anywhere close to approaching the ideal. Whether one is a spouse or a child, it is not always easy to live with someone who works as hard as the typical eminent psychologist. As I pointed out in chapters 3 and 7, great scientists generally work many hours a week, besides displaying minimal interest in social activities. So imagine what it would be like if your spouse or parent were E. G. Boring, who insisted on working during vacations, or Edward Thorndike and Vladimir Bekhterev, who would work late at night in bed (the latter with his wife asleep beside him), or Herbert Simon, who devoted more than 100 hours per week to research, leaving less than 2 hours per day for family? Some of the consequent domestic conflicts and dissatisfaction may be revealed in an investigation into those who were sufficiently distinguished to earn obituaries in *American Psychologist* (Kinnier et al., 1994). Even though at least 72% had been married one or more times, and at least 51% had one or more children, only 35% were viewed as a valued family member. Given the eulogistic nature of obituaries, moreover, one must wonder whether the latter percentage may be somewhat exaggerated. Incidentally, there is some reason to believe that psychologists may differ from other scientists in terms of the stability of their relationships. Although one study of eminent scientists reported that 83% of those married enjoyed stable marriages (Post, 1994), and Roe (1953a) found comparable figures for her physical and biological scientists, she also noted that the social scientists in her sample had much less stable marriages than did the others. Specifically, 41% of the social scientists had divorced, in comparison to 15% of the biologists and 5% of the physical scientists.

4. Married scientists, even if they are male, may pay a price for taking on the increased responsibilities and cares of marriage and family. Kanawaza (2000) compared the creative output of 252 eminent male scientists, 70 of whom were unmarried and 182 married. All were of sufficient distinction to earn entries in a standard biographical dictionary of notable scientists (Gillispie, 1970–1980). The bachelors were just as likely to make the greatest contributions in their late 50s as in their late 20s, suggesting a minimal decline in output. In contrast,

the married scientists were far less likely to make a major discovery or invention in the later of the two life periods. This contrast also shows up in the typical ages at which scientists produce their best work. About a 6-year difference separates the peak age for the married and unmarried scientists, with the latter displaying the later peak. In concrete terms, whereas the married luminaries tended to peak around 34 years of age, the unmarried notables peaked around age 40. Empirical research needs to determine whether this differential applies to comparably eminent psychologists.

Before leaving this subject, I would like to broach a subject about which there has been virtually no empirical research: the sexual orientation of great psychologists. Homosexuality and bisexuality are practically absent among eminent scientists, unlike the relatively high percentages seen among distinguished writers and artists (M. G. Goertzel, Goertzel, & Goertzel, 1978; Ludwig, 1995; Post, 1994). The same appears to hold for psychology ; at least, the number of confirmed cases of gay men or lesbians is very small, in both absolute and relative terms. One of the few secure cases is Roger Brown, the distinguished U.S. social psychologist and psycholinguist. Brown made his sexual orientation quite public when he titled his 1996 autobiography *Against My Better Judgment: An Intimate Memoir of an Eminent Gay Psychologist.* Other instances probably exist, but they are more speculative than factually verifiable. One very probable case is Harry Stack Sullivan, who adopted a 15-year-old male who eventually became Sullivan's lifelong partner. Anna Freud's relationship with Dorothy Burlingham, with whom she lived and collaborated, is often viewed as another example, without any proof one way or the other. Needless to say, fear of social stigma, job discrimination, or legal castigation has probably encouraged many notables to keep their sexual orientation a deeply guarded secret. The consequences of failing to do so are demonstrated in the life of mathematician Alan Turing, the originator of the "Turing Test" in artificial intelligence. Besides having to undergo hormone therapy to avoid imprisonment, Turing eventually lost his security clearance for top-secret government work. These experiences may have driven Turing to commit suicide when he was just 2 weeks shy of his 42nd birthday.

LIFE'S TERMINATION

Turing's fate also is a reminder that we all are ultimately mortal, no matter how we actually end our days. Some notables in psychology's history, such as Turing, died young, even without taking their own lives. Blaise Pascal, another progenitor of artificial intelligence research, was only 39 years old. Others, in contrast, lived to ripe old ages. G. S. Hall lived to 80, but this barely octogenarian status is surpassed by Johann Wolfgang von Goethe and Sigmund Freud (both to 83); Voltaire and Jean Piaget (both 84); Gustave Theodor Fechner, Carl Jung, and B. F. Skinner (all 86); Ivan Pavlov and Anna Freud (both 87); Wilhelm Wundt (88); and R. B. Cattell (93; all life spans were calculated from birth year to birth year rather than from birthday to birthday). This extreme variation in life span leads to the final question I consider in this chapter: What is the life expectancy of great psychologists? How does the expected life span differ from what is normal in other achievement domains?

I must first establish the baselines for comparison. Most of the British geniuses studied by Havelock Ellis (1926) died in their late 60s or early 70s. Likewise, a study of eminent Americans obtained a mean of 69 (Bowerman, 1947), whereas another study, of eminent Japanese, got a mean of 66 (Simonton, 1997a), a figure virtually identical to the average life span of Catharine Cox's (1926) geniuses. Cox also showed that only 11% lived less than 50 years, whereas nearly 15% lived to be 80 or more. However, the research also shows that life expectancy is contingent on several factors.

In the first place, the predicted life span of an eminent individual varies according to the field of achievement. Ellis (1926) first pointed out that poets tend to die younger than other eminent figures, an abbreviated life that apparently holds for all of the world's major literary traditions (Simonton, 1975a; but see Simonton, 1997a). A somewhat later investigation showed that eminent scientists tend to live longer than eminent writers, by a pretty substantial margin: 69 versus 63 years (Raskin, 1936; also see Cassandro, 1998). Post (1994) found this same contrast in a much more recent study, in which he observed a life expectancy of about 72 for scientists and intellectuals but only 65 for writers and 61 for composers (see also Cassandro, 1998; Kaun, 1991). Lehman (1943) reported a similar disparity between scientists, mathematicians, and inventors, on the one hand, and oil painters, on the other, with a difference of nearly 6 years. In Cox's (1926) data, the philosophers and scientists (both around 68) were exceeded only by the statesmen (70), whereas the writers, artists, musicians, religious leaders, soldiers, and revolutionaries all died at a younger age (the last having a life expectancy of only 51 years). Yet even within specific scientific disciplines the predicted life span may vary systematically (Simonton, 1991a). Most striking is the tendency for great mathematicians to die at a younger age than most other scientists. Whereas the life expectancies in various scientific disciplines tend to range between 69 and 72 (also see Visher, 1947b), the expected life span for mathematicians is around 63. Turing and Pascal are not that unusual after all. In fact, several of the key figures in the emergence of computer science—the mathematical domain most strongly allied to psychology—suffered from shortened life spans. George Boole, of Boolean algebra fame, died at age 49, and John von Neumann, who developed both game theory and the computer model of the brain, died at age 54.

Why should life expectancies vary according to domain of achievement? One possible reason is that these interdisciplinary contrasts are merely methodological artifacts. In particular, controls must be introduced to ensure that the representatives of different domains were all born at the same time. Any heterogeneity in the average birth years across different samples will confound interdomain differences, if there are any, with any secular trends toward increased life expectancy. The temporal increase in life span for famous personalities admittedly should not be nearly as great as for the population at large (because the figures for the former necessarily exclude those who die prior to maturity), although upward trends have still been identified for eminent individuals (e.g., Simonton, 1977b). For instance, the average life span of illustrious scientists has increased from 61 years in the 16th century to 72 years in the 20th, an increment of more than 10 years (Zhao & Jiang, 1986). Even so, empirical studies have established consistent differences in life span across different domains of achievement even after introducing statistical controls for year of birth (Simonton, 1991a, 1997a).

Another possibility has to do with the empirical research on the relation between age and achievement. As I discussed at length in chapter 4, there exist substantial domain contrasts in career trajectories, including the expected location of the first, best, and last contributions. These differences cannot help but have some impact on life expectancy. For some fields, such as mathematics, it is possible to start making lasting contributions at a relatively early age, whereas in other fields, such as the earth sciences, it usually requires considerably more maturity before an individual can begin to have an influence on the field. This implies that individuals can die sooner and still leave an impression in fields that have early career onsets and perhaps early career peaks. On the whole, this appears to be the case. Poets tend to peak earlier than other prose writers and have shorter life expectancies (Simonton, 1975a). The same happens in the case of mathematics relative to other disciplines (Simonton, 1991a). A similar pattern holds in leadership domains, such as revolutionaries versus status quo politicians or the founders of major religious faiths versus the leaders of established religions. On the other hand, one reason why great philosophers tend to have longer life expectancies than creators in other fields is that the career trajectory for writing philosophy tends to be shifted toward the more mature years of life. Lending additional support to the foregoing explanation of interdomain contrasts in life expectancy is the empirical finding that, at the individual level, people who begin their careers earlier than average also tend to have shorter predicted life spans (Simonton, 1977b; Zhao & Jiang, 1986). For instance, in one large sample of eminent scientists, those who began making contributions at an unusually young age tended to live about 10 fewer years than those who launched their careers at more average years (Zhao & Jiang, 1986).

The domain of achievement is by no means the exclusive determinant of life span. The life expectancy of historical figures, like that of everybody else, certainly must be affected by severe alcoholism (Lester, 1991); chronic stress (Barry, 1969, 1983–1984; Simonton, 1997a); and violent death, including suicide (Lester, 1991; Simonton, 1997a). Besides Turing, German physiologist Johannes Müller probably died of suicide at age 57. Of course, there also exist exceptions, such as the American psychologist Hobart Orval Mowrer, who killed himself at age 75, and the American physicist Percy Bridgman, the founder of operationalism, who took his own life at age 79. Suicide need not seriously abbreviate one's life span.

Furthermore, life span is associated with other variables that are more unique to creative genius. One such factor is versatility. As I observed in chapter 6, some eminent figures are monomaniacs, focusing all their efforts on a single domain, whereas others decide to contribute to a variety of domains. A recent study of 2,102 famous personalities revealed that highly versatile scientists—especially those who make contributions outside the sciences proper—tended to have shorter life spans than the nonversatile ones (Cassandro, 1998). Another correlate of life expectancy is even more intriguing, for it gets at the very heart of greatness, namely, eminence. One might think that a longer life span would be more conducive to the attainment of distinction than would be a shorter one. This prediction follows from the fact that lifetime output is positively correlated with ultimate eminence, given that an abbreviated life would seem to mandate a truncated career. In line with this argument, there is some evidence that more eminent individuals enjoy greater longevity in both scientific and literary domains (Raskin, 1936). However, a little more thought reveals that the phenomenon may be more complex than indicated by this single consideration. As I noted before, if precocious creators have shorter life spans, then an early death will lessen their total output much less, given their early start in the first place. Moreover, there might be a "sympathy" or "tragedy" factor that could exaggerate a creator's renown if he or she dies at an unusually young age, such as happened to Pascal. In fact, if the eminence of the creators in Cox's (1926) sample is plotted against life span, a nonmonotonic U-shaped curve results (Simonton, 1976a). The least famous are individuals who died around their 60th year, whereas the most famous are those who died either younger or older than that age. Lehman (1943) observed that a similar curve has been identified for the amount of lines devoted to 1,036 deceased physicians in obituaries published in the *Journal of the American Medical Association* (cf. Mills, 1942). Hence, the sympathy or tragedy effect may be very real. Yet because no studies have concentrated on psychologists, it is impossible to say with confidence that this effect might account for a portion of the reputation of the Russian psychologist Lev Vygotsky, who died at age 38, a longevity inferior even to Pascal's.

Indeed, very few studies have focused specifically on the lives of great psychologists. A study of 69 eminent American psychologists obtained a mean life span of 71 years, with a range of 43–94 (Simonton, 1992b). However, there was a sampling bias in the data that renders this figure suspect. In particular, to qualify for inclusion in the sample, the psychologist had to be deceased, which meant that the more recently born subjects had to die younger in order to be sampled! Accordingly, the correlation between life span and birth year was –.62, a highly unlikely statistic (also see Zusne, 1976a). Kinnier et al. (1994) used a different sampling criterion and obtained a higher mean. Specifically, individuals of sufficient importance to receive obituaries in *American Psychologist* had reached a median age of 76 at time of death, and fully 58% had lived to become either septuagenarians or octogenarians. Hence, the life spans attained by G. Stanley Hall, Sigmund Freud, Jean Piaget, Ivan Pavlov, and other notables are by no means exceptional. In this respect, great psychologists fall right in the same league as great philosophers and great scientists. The emphasis on a life of the mind—in both senses of the word—is evidently good for the health.

12

NATURE VERSUS NURTURE

"Genius must be born, and never can be taught," said John Dryden (1693/1885, p. 60), the English dramatist. Dryden was expressing a very commonplace view that genius is like an extreme form of talent, an innate attribute that cannot be cultivated. Indeed, genius was often viewed as something almost divine, as something well beyond the meek powers of the mundane world to produce. In the classic *Lives of the Painters, Sculptors, and Architects*, Vasari (ca. 1550/1968) began his biography of Michelangelo by saying how "the great Ruler of Heaven looked down" and decided "to send to earth a genius universal in each art" who would be endowed with such special qualities that his works would seem "rather divine than earthly" (p. 347). This conception of the origins of genius harks all the way back to the ancient Greeks, who saw human creativity as something special, inspired by the Muses. There was a Muse for all major creative activities of classical times, including heroic or epic poetry, lyric and love poetry, sacred poetry, tragedy, comedy, music, dance, and even astronomy and history.

Even so, the picture presented in the preceding chapters seem to portray genius as being made rather than born. In particular, in chapter 9 I presented the family background most likely to encourage the development of great psychologists, and in chapter 10 I described the impact of education and other facets of career training. The implicit assumption was always that there exists a characteristic environment that shapes personal growth into the kind of individual who will leave some mark in the annals of the discipline. On occasion this environmentalist position was actually made explicit, as in my discussion of birth order and childhood trauma. However, whether implicitly or explicitly, the empirical findings seem to suggest that disciplinary achievement can be predicted by such external circumstances as socioeconomic class, religion and ethnicity, geographical origins, birth order, childhood trauma, various facets of formal education, and relationships with distinguished mentors. Maybe there was some wisdom hidden in Greek mythology, for Psyche was not one of the Muses.

So, what is the truth of the matter? Are great psychologists born or made? I address this question in two ways. First, I begin the chapter by discussing the general problem of the genetic basis of genius. Second, I close the chapter with a specific manifestation of that broad issue, namely, the relation between gender and greatness as a psychologist.

GENERAL PROBLEM: GENES AND GENIUS

In chapter 8 I treated the connection between an eminent psychologist's worldview and his or her long-term impact on the field, as gauged by the citations he or she continues to receive in the professional literature (Simonton, 2000b). I noted that psychologists were most likely to enjoy such long-term influence if they adopted extremist positions on the various critical dimensions that distinguish psychological theory and methodology. Among those dimensions was the contrast between the endogenists, who emphasize biological determinants and heredity, and the exogenists, who stress environmental determinants and social influences (Coan, 1968, 1979). An outstanding example of an extreme endogenist is Francis Galton, whereas John B. Watson and many other behaviorists count as conspicuous proponents of the extreme exogenist position. The first tells us that genius is born, whereas the second says that genius is made. I first examine these two opposed views and then turn to what modern behavioral genetics has contributed to the debate.

Genetic Determinism

The title of Galton's (1869) *Hereditary Genius* means exactly what it says: Genius is born. Indeed, the whole book is devoted to propounding this thesis. In a nutshell, Galton's argument went as follows:

1. Human beings display tremendous individual differences in what he called "natural ability." According to Galton, this term meant something a bit more complex than just intelligence. Specifically, he said that

by natural ability, I mean those qualities of intellect and disposition, which urge and qualify a man to perform acts that lead to reputation. I do not mean capacity without zeal, nor zeal without capacity, nor even a combination of both of them, without an adequate power of doing a great deal of very laborious work. (Galton, 1892/1972, p. 77)

In any large human population, natural ability would be distributed according to the normal, or bell-shaped curve. In this Galton was following the ideas of Adolphe Quételet, the Belgian pioneer in social statistics.

2. Individuals whose natural ability places them in the upper right-hand tail of the distribution would then have what it takes to be called true geniuses. Such a genius

    will, urged by an inherent stimulus, climb the path that leads to eminence, and has strength to reach the summit—one which, if hindered or thwarted, will fret and strive until the hindrance is overcome, and it is again free to follow its labour-loving instinct. (Galton, 1892/1972, p. 77)

    Galton seems to have made a big assumption here, namely, that the possession of a purely psychological attribute (high natural ability) would automatically manifest itself as a social attribute (eminence or reputation). However, he believed that the personal and social facets of genius were practically equivalent. With respect to individuals with high natural ability, "it is almost a contradiction in terms, to doubt that such men will generally become eminent" (p. 77). At the same time, "few have won high reputations without possessing these peculiar gifts," and therefore "it follows that the men who achieve eminence, and those who are naturally capable, are, to a large extent, identical" (p. 78).

3. Individual differences in natural ability are subject almost entirely to inheritance; that is, "the concrete triple event, of ability combined with zeal and with capacity for hard labour, is inherited" (Galton, 1892/1972, p. 78). So strong was Galton's belief in the genetic determination of genius that the environment had virtually no role to play.

    I believe, and shall do my best to show, that, if the "eminent" men of any period, had been changelings when babies, a very fair proportion of those who survived and retained their health up to fifty years of age, would, notwithstanding their altered circumstances, have equally risen to eminence. (p. 78)

"If a man is gifted with vast intellectual ability, eagerness to work, and power of working," Galton explained, "I cannot comprehend how such man should be repressed" (p. 79). After all, he added, "the world is always tormented with difficulties waiting to be solved—struggling with ideas and feelings, to which it can give no adequate expression. If, then, there exists a man capable of solving those difficulties, or of giving a voice to those pent-up feelings, he is sure to be welcomed with universal acclamation" (Galton, 1892/1972, p. 79). In a sense, Galton was arguing that certain individuals at the upper end of the distribution are born as great problem solvers, an exceptional ability that will necessarily be directed to some useful purpose, and thereby receive acknowledgment from contemporaries and posterity.

If the foregoing three statements are granted, then a fourth follows automatically: Eminence should run in families. In fact, the bulk of *Hereditary Genius* is devoted to listing major geniuses and their biological relatives. The geniuses themselves were taken from a recently published biographical dictionary of eminent personalities. The luminaries were grouped into several chapters, including Statesmen, Commanders, Literary Men, Men of Science, Poets, Musicians, and Painters. The chapter on scientists is most relevant here, because several of those listed have also carved out a name for themselves in psychology's history. These include Aristotle, Francis Bacon, Comte de Buffon, Charles Darwin, Benjamin Franklin, William Harvey, Gottfried Wilhelm Leibniz, and Sir Isaac Newton. All told, the number of distinguished scientists who had distinguished relatives was far greater than would be expected according to the base rate of genius in the general population.

The results for the Darwin family are perhaps most typical. Charles Darwin was the grandson of Erasmus Darwin, an early evolutionist. Moreover, Charles Darwin himself had sons sufficiently distinguished to have become knighted, an honor that Darwin himself never received (albeit Galton only mentions one by name, Sir Francis). Galton ends his list of the various notables of the lineage by adding that "I could add the names of others of the family who, in a lesser but yet decided degree, have shown a taste for subjects of natural history" (Galton, 1892/1972, p. 261). This statement could be an indication of Victorian modesty, for no doubt Galton could have included himself in this anonymous group. Galton, like Charles Darwin, was the grandson of Erasmus Darwin, although from a different grandmother.

To be sure, not every great scientist could be embedded within a notable family line. Galton specifically identified 18 who seemed to stand alone, including Roger Bacon, Tycho Brahe, Nicolaus Copernicus, Galen, Luigi Galvani, Johannes Kepler, and Thomas Young. Yet these exceptions are too rare to overthrow the general principle. Eminence in science tends to emerge from eminent pedigrees. This conclusion was strengthened by Galton's apparent demonstration that the same linkage also held for all other areas of human achievement. These results, Galton concluded, endorsed the argument that natural ability was inherited and that superior natural ability led to high distinction.

A large number of later inquiries have essentially replicated Galton's (1869) results; some have looked at inclusive groups of geniuses (e.g., Bowerman, 1947; Bramwell, 1948; Ellis, 1926; Post, 1994), others have concentrated on a particular domain of achievement (e.g., Simonton, 1983c, 1984a), including the sciences (e.g., Eiduson, 1962; Simonton, 1992c). Of these latter studies, probably the most relevant was an extensive three-part examination of family resemblances among individuals of sufficient eminence to receive entries in J. M. Cattell's *American Men of Science* (Brimhall, 1922, 1923a, 1923b). At least one quarter of those in the "starred" group—whom Cattell identified as especially distinguished—had at least one eminent relative (Brimhall, 1923b). These incidence rates were appreciably higher than in the general population. For example, the brothers of illustrious scientists are 70 times more likely to become eminent than the population baseline. Furthermore, the greater the degree of genetic proximity to the eminent scientist, the higher the odds that a relative will also be eminent (Brimhall, 1923a). It is interesting that the published genealogies include a section on 16 eminent psychologists, including James Rowland Angell, Frank Angell, James McKeen Cattell, John Dewey, G. Stanley Hall, Joseph Jastrow, Edward Lee Thorndike, and Robert Sessions Woodworth. Indeed, two of these— the two Angells—were related to each other, as cousins.

Although eminence in science thus appears to cluster into family lineages, it is not clear what exactly is being inherited. Sometimes Galton (1869) held that the pedigrees merely reflect the genetic transmission of natural ability, a rather generic combination of both intellect and disposition. Havelock Ellis (1926) drew a similar conclusion on the basis of his examination of British geniuses, holding that it was general intellectual ability that was being transferred across generations (also see Bowerman, 1947). Yet other times Galton appeared to suggest that the inheritance is more domain specific. For example, on the basis of his survey of members of the Royal Society of London, Galton (1874, p. 195) concluded that about 60% were "gifted by nature with a strong taste" for science. One problem with the notion of domain-specific inheritance, however, is that many of the distinguished family lines fail to confine themselves to a single field, or even to a closely related set of fields (Galton, 1869). According to one study of eminent scientists, for instance, eminent relatives were almost evenly divided between those who attained distinction in science and those who became famous in some other domain (Post, 1994).

If the domain is defined even more narrowly, then the degree of concordance becomes even smaller (Brimhall, 1922). Thus, although great psychologists may come disproportionately from distinguished pedigrees, it is relatively rare for those pedigrees to produce more than one great psychologist. The eponymous founder of Weber's law (Ernst Heinrich) had a younger brother of note (Wilhelm Eduard), but the latter was a famous physicist. Likewise, the eminent neobehaviorist Edward Chace Tolman had an eminent older brother, Richard Chace, who was also a physicist. Besides the Angell cousins, the only really conspicuous examples in psychology's history are the Allport brothers, Floyd and Gordon; the father–daughter pair Sigmund and Anna Freud; and the father–son pair James and John Stewart Mill. Somewhat less eminent instances include the siblings Magdalen and Philip Vernon and the father–son pairing of Edward Lee and Robert Ladd Thorndike. Hence, it is very unlikely that becoming a great psychologist is contingent on inheriting a domain-specific set of traits.

Environmental Determinism

Needless to say, all of this speculation about some genetic endowment that leads to greatness as a psychologist—whether that endowment be generic or domain specific—is premature anyway. The pedigrees may instead result from a developmental process having nothing to do with biological inheritance. Galton (1869) wrote that if a person with superlative natural ability became a changeling, and were thus raised in a totally alien environment, he or she would still become a renowned genius. The behaviorist John B. Watson (1924/1970) turned Galton's curious Gedanken experiment upside down:

> Give me a dozen healthy infants, well formed, and my own specified world to bring them up in, and I'll guarantee to take any one at random and train him to become any type of specialist I might select—a doctor, lawyer, artist, merchant chief, and yes, even a beggar-man and thief, regardless of his talents, penchants, tendencies, abilities, vocations and race of his ancestors. (p. 104)

Other behaviorists have taken a similarly strong stance in favor of environmental determinism. An especially relevant example is B. F. Skinner (1961), who has interpreted the creative process in terms of the reinforcement contingencies to which the creator was exposed. The creative individual is merely the developmental product of a supportive cumulative record. Indeed, as I noted in chapter 6, this basic Skinnerian position has been elaborated into a behavioristic theory of insight (R. Epstein, 1990, 1991). Moreover, one investigator even showed that the output of publications—in this case by writer Isaac Asimov—could be described in terms of the typical "learning curve" (Ohlsson, 1992).

Naturally, no behaviorist has actually carried out the experiment J. B. Watson (1924/1970) suggested; neither has anyone ever carefully tracked the reinforcement schedules of creative individuals throughout their life spans (cf. Simonton, 1977a). Even so, there is certainly an abundance of evidence that suggests that environmental factors must play a major role in the emergence of creative genius (Simonton, 1987a). Alphonse de Candolle (1873), the notable French botanist, offered the first empirical demonstration. It is surprising that Candolle enjoyed a genuinely distinguished pedigree, so much so that Galton (1869) listed him and his eminent father in his chapter on "Men of Science." Furthermore, at the time *Hereditary Genius* was published, Candolle's own son was well on his way to become a notable scientist in his own right. That prominent genetic background notwithstanding, Candolle believed that Galton had grossly underestimated the impact of the environment. To establish the importance, if not the primacy, of environmental forces, Candolle gathered a tremendous amount of data on the political, economic, social, cultural, and religious circumstances that were most supportive of the emergence of eminent scientists in various nations of Western civilization.

Because these conditions are best regarded as features of the sociocultural context, I save that discussion for Part V, especially for chapter 15. Nonetheless, Galton was perfectly willing to accept the weight of Candolle's evidence, at least enough to moderate his extreme genetic determinism. In fact, it was Candolle's (1873) book that inspired Galton to undertake his pioneering survey of eminent British scientists. The outcome of that survey was reported in *English Men of Science: Their Nature and Nurture* (Galton, 1874). The book's subtitle clearly reveals Galton's recognition that scientific genius is in all likelihood both born and made. The use of the words *nature* and *nurture* to indicate these two developmental forces harks back to William Shakespeare who, in *The Tempest*, has Prospero say of Caliban:

> A devil, a born devil, in whose nature
> Nurture can never stick; on whom my pains
> Humanely taken, all, all lost, quite lost.
> (quoted in Evans, 1974, p. 1631)

Nevertheless, it was Galton who used these terms explicitly to describe the nature–nurture controversy as it is currently recognized in psychology (cf. Teigen, 1984). As Galton (1874) defined the contrast,

> the phrase "nature and nurture" is a convenient jingle of words, for it separates under two distinct heads the innumerable elements of which personality is composed. Nature is all that a man brings with himself into the world; nurture is every influence from without that affects him after his birth. (p. 12)

Expertise Acquisition: Pro

Galton's own approach to addressing this question was to inquire into the familial and educational backgrounds of his notable survey respondents. He thus helped launch the vast developmental literature that I so extensively reviewed in chapters 9 and 10. However, more recently the nature–nurture debate has been rekindled from an unusual quarter: cognitive psychology. Despite all of the manifest disagreements between behaviorists and cognitive psychologists, they have tended to concur that genetic inheritance has little if any causal influence. This position emerged from the work of Herbert Simon and his colleagues on the acquisition of expertise (e.g., Ericsson, Krampe, & Tesch-Römer, 1993; H. A. Simon & Chase, 1973). According to this view, world-class experts must acquire approximately 50,000 "chunks" of domain-relevant information (H. A. Simon, 1986). As might be expected, this acquisition takes considerable effort and time in study and practice (Ericsson & Charness, 1994). Most commonly it requires approximately 10 years of intense work as an apprentice and novice before attaining expert status (J. R. Hayes, 1989b). This commitment is often referred to as the *10-year rule* (e.g., Ericsson, 1996a).

For the most part this principle was based on studies of expertise acquisition in domains such as chess, sports, and music performance (Ericsson, 1996b). Still, the same principle has been said to apply to world-class creativity as well (Ericsson, 1996a). A person may not be born a creative genius, but rather he or she is made into a genius by diligent practice and study. The British artist Sir Joshua Reynolds (1769–1790/1966) warned his students at the Royal Academy of Art:

> You must have no dependence on your own genius. If you have great talents, industry will improve them; if you have but moderate abilities, industry will supply their deficiency. Nothing is denied to well directed labour; nothing is . . . obtained without it. Not to enter into metaphysical discussions on the nature or essence of genius, I will venture to assert, that assiduity unabated by difficulty, and a disposition eagerly directed to the object of its pursuit, will produce effects similar to those which some call the result of *natural powers*. (p. 37)

In support of this idea, researchers have shown that about 10 years transpire between the time when creative individuals first begin acquiring the necessary expertise and the time when their first genuine masterpieces appear (J. R. Hayes, 1989b). For instance, one study of 120 classical composers found that their music lessons first began around 9 years old, composition around 17 years, and the first successful composition around 26 (Simonton, 1991b). Hence, by the time the typical composer had his first hit, he had been composing for 9 years and studying music for around 17.

Although no investigator has explicitly tested the 10-year rule using a sample of eminent psychologists, there has been indirect evidence respecting its descriptive accuracy. An inquiry into the career development of 69 eminent American psychologists found that the average age when they produced their first high-impact publication was around 30, whereas the average age for obtaining their highest degree was around 28 (Simonton, 1992b). When allowance is made for the amount of specialized training that likely preceded the latter figure—certainly graduate school and for most an undergraduate major in psychology besides—it would seem that something close to 10 years were usually required. Lyons (1968) scrutinized the typical career age that researchers publish articles in leading psychology journals, defining *career age* as years accumulated since receipt of the doctoral degree. The journals he examined were *Psychological Review, Psychological Bulletin*, the *Journal of Abnormal and Social Psychology*, and the *Journal of Experimental Psychology*. Although the median professional age ranged between 8 and 11 years, the bottom quartile fell between 4 and 6 years. These figures were for all articles, without respect to whether they are frequently cited. Highly cited articles would probably occur somewhat later in the career (Simonton, 1997b). In any case, it is apparent that it is uncommon for psychologists to produce a high-impact publication immediately after completing their graduate training, suggesting that their apprenticeship may continue a bit after the career officially begins.

Expertise Acquisition: Con

Like all other nomothetic principles in psychology, there certainly exist numerous exceptions to the 10-year rule. At one extreme, some great psychologists had to wait longer before their first hit. Hermann Ebbinghaus was 12 years post-PhD before he published his first great contribution, *On Memory*, and Sigmund Freud was 14 years post-MD before he collaborated with Josef Breuer on the landmark *Studies in Hysteria*. At the other extreme are those who get their careers off to a great start almost at once. Edward L. Thorndike's dissertation, as I already noted in chapter 4, was almost immediately published in *Psychological Review* and went on to become one of the classics in the psychology of learning.

Yet the existence of such individual differences would seem to cast some doubt on the expertise-acquisition model. In fact, research has shown that the amount of time usually required to acquire the necessary expertise tends to vary as a function of the degree of creative genius eventually displayed (Simonton, 1991a, 1991b). For both artistic and scientific creativity, individuals with the greatest lifetime productivity and highest levels of achieved eminence mastered the necessary information and skills in a shorter time than did their less prolific and less well-known colleagues (Simonton, 1997b, 1999d). For 69 eminent American psychologists, in particular, eminence in the field correlates $-.23$ with the amount of time that elapsed between receiving the highest degree and the first highly cited publication (Simonton, 1992b).

This is not the only empirical association that does not seem compatible with this environmental factor. Research has also shown that expertise acquisition can operate to stifle creative development rather than enhance it (Simonton, 2000a). This evidently happens because individuals can become overly specialized and thus narrow and inflexible in their thinking (Frensch & Sternberg, 1989). Indeed, this possibility was implied by some of effects discussed in earlier chapters, such as the repercussions of formal education, professional marginality, and career aging (i.e., Planck's principle). Sometimes, in fact, the detrimental effects of "overtraining" must be treated by a suitable amount of "cross-training," or the acquisition of expertise in another domain (Simonton, 2000a).

These empirical issues aside, the expertise-acquisition model must come up against another critical reality: Modern behavioral genetics suggests that genius may have indeed some foundation in biological inheritance (Simonton, 1999d).

Modern Behavior Genetics

Galton's (1869) *Hereditary Genius*, by introducing the pedigree method, became one of the pioneering works in the development of what was eventually to become known as behavior genetics. Neither was this Galton's last contribution to the emerging discipline. His work on bivariate regression was developed by his star pupil Karl Pearson into the correlational statistics that play an essential role in establishing the degree of inheritance (i.e., heritability coefficients). Furthermore, Galton pioneered the use of twins as a vehicle for helping to resolve the nature–nurture problem, a method that has a very important part to play in behavior genetics (Bouchard, Lykken, McGue, Segal, & Tellegen, 1990). Behavior genetics has naturally acquired a conception of this issue that is far more complex and sophisticated than anything Galton ever imagined. Sometimes the behavior geneticists have lent considerable support to Galton's position, but other times their results have cast doubt on many of his key ideas. I begin with the most supportive findings.

Heritability of Ability and Character

Perhaps the single most significant message to come out of recent research is how many individual-difference variables have appreciable heritability coefficients (Bouchard et al., 1990; Loehlin, 1992a; Plomin, Owen, & McGuffin, 1994). Even rather complex characteristics have genetic underpinnings, including political attitudes and musical tastes (Tesser, 1993), the amount of time devoted to watching television (Plomin, Corley, DeFries, & Fulker, 1990), job satisfaction and values (Arvey, Bouchard, Segal, & Abraham, 1989; Keller, Bouchard, Arvey, Segal, & Dawis, 1992), dispositional empathy (M. H. Davis, Luce, & Kraus, 1994), and religious interests and attitudes (Waller, Kojetin, Bouchard, Lykken, & Tellegen, 1990). To be sure, not all traits feature the same high degree of genetic inheritance. Some traits, such as intelligence, can be mostly attributed to nature, whereas other traits, such as religiosity, can be mostly attributed to nurture. Yet the inventory of characteristics with nontrivial heritability coefficients is sufficiently large and diverse that a large part of a person's personality profile will necessarily have a genetic foundation.

This inventory of genetic influences may even help historians of psychology fathom some of the personal idiosyncrasies of various notables in its history. For instance, one history of psychology textbook contained the following observation: "Despite the intellectually stimulating atmosphere in which Wundt grew up (or perhaps because of it), he remained a shy, reserved person who was fearful of new situations" (Hergenhahn, 1992, p. 237). Well, it just so happens that about half of Wundt's inclination toward a fearful and reserved shyness might be ascribed to the genes he inherited at the moment of his conception. According to behavior genetic research, about 50% of the variance in shyness, or "anxious introversion," can be ascribed to the genes, a degree of heritability noticeably higher than found for most other personality traits, which tend to feature heritabilities more around 30%–40% (Sulloway, 1996).

Shared Versus Unshared Environment

Just as crucial is the fact that behavior geneticists have clarified the nature of nurture (Plomin & Bergeman, 1991); that is, the impact of environmental factors has been partitioned into two independent influences: shared and nonshared. The former concerns aspects of the child's environment that are shared with siblings, such as their socioeconomic class. The latter concerns aspects that are distinct to each child, such as his or her respective ordinal position in the family. It is surprising that behavior geneticists have discovered that, for most personal attributes, the shared environment is far less influential than is the nonshared environment (Plomin & Rende, 1990; cf. Waller & Shaver, 1994). As a result, siblings from the same family are actually rather more different from each other than might be expected from the fact that they grew up in the same home and neighborhood.

How does this relative impotency of the shared environment square with what I have reviewed about the family background of great psychologists? Does not chapter 9 contain a long list of familial influences that concern the shared rather than nonshared environment? The solution comes from another critical finding of behavior genetics, namely, that many so-called environmental effects are actually genetic effects (Plomin & Bergeman, 1991). Nurture is often mistaken for nature (Harris, 1998). To illustrate, although great psychologists are more likely to come from the homes of parents who are professionals—ministers, physicians, lawyers, professors, and teachers—that does not necessarily mean that these homes provide a stimulating environment for the nurture of scientific talent. The children raised in these homes also inherited a superior set of genes. The same genes that enabled their parents to become professionals enabled these children to accomplish the same. That the parents provided homes well stocked with books and other reading materials, that the family often took trips to museums, art galleries, and other stimulating locales—all this is the effect rather than the cause of the high-power intellects that parent and child alike inherited. In genetic terms, the apparent association between the parental phenotype (behaviorally intelligent and inquisitive) and the offspring phenotype (also behaviorally intelligent and inquisitive) is the spurious result of the shared parent–child genotype (innate inclination toward intelligent and inquisitive behavior) rather than being a direct consequence of the parental phenotype shaping their offspring's phenotype.

This notion may even be applied to environmental factors that would seem to have their environmental status totally secure, such as immigrant status, scholastic performance, distinguished mentors, and professional marginality (Simonton, 1994a). Take the supposed developmental impact of parental loss as a case in point. It would seem that whether one or both parents died during a person's childhood or adolescence would constitute an unambiguous instance of nurture rather than nature. Yet it is very easy to recast this event as the consequence of genetic influences (Simonton, 1994a). Parents who have the attributes that Galton (1869) considered "natural ability" should tend to marry later in life and begin parenthood later still. Accordingly, those who become eminent should be born to parents who are much older than the norms, and that is demonstrably the case, as has been shown by Galton (1874), Havelock Ellis (1926) and many others (e.g., Bowerman, 1947; Raskin, 1936; Visher, 1947a). The fathers of famous people typically are in their late 30s or early 40s, the mothers in their late 20s or early 30s. For instance, the survey respondents in Galton's (1874) *English Men of Science* were born to fathers who were around 36 years old and mothers who were around 30. In general, then, it must be manifest that individuals who have older parents will be more likely to lose one or both parents while still at a minority age. This delay can also account for the tendency for the rates of parental loss to be higher among literary than scientific creators (Berry, 1981). If scientists are more likely to be firstborns and writers to be laterborns, then this contrast necessarily follows (Bliss, 1970; Galton, 1874). In line with this interpretation, the fathers of eminent scientists tend to be younger at the time the luminaries were born than the fathers of eminent literary figures (Raskin, 1936). Philosopher Jean-Jacques Rousseau best illustrates a literary rather than a scientific pattern: He was the last child of his mother, who was 40 years old at the time of his birth and who died just 5 days after he entered the world.

Psychopathological Pedigrees

The foregoing interpretation assumes that increased rates of parental loss among eminent individuals is a mere by-product of the parents' higher "natural ability," which manifests itself as a tendency to delay reproduction and thereby place their children at increased risk. However, one could also argue that the parents of eminent personalities carry genes that predispose them to die young or to exhibit some other form of parental absence. In line with this alternative genetic interpretation, research has shown that parents of the eminent who were themselves eminent (a) are more likely to have experienced early parental loss and (b) are more prone to shorter life expectancies (Eisenstadt, 1978). What might this genetic disposition be? Back in chapter 7 I discussed the literature on the "mad genius" syndrome. If creative genius is associated with a moderate infusion of madness, and if various psychopathological symptoms have high heritability coefficients, then the distinguished pedigrees that Galton (1869) identified may overlap the family lines that carry an above-average amount of genes for psychopathology. This argument has considerable empirical support (Juda, 1949; Myerson & Boyle, 1941; Richards, Kinney, Lunde, Benet, & Merzel, 1988). For instance, one comprehensive study conducted in Iceland—where genealogical and medical records are exceptionally complete—found that families that produced a disproportionate number of Icelanders suffering from mental illness also produced a disproportionate number of family members who ended up in *Who's Who in Iceland* (Karlson, 1970). In another study of 291 eminent figures of history, 56% were found to have come from family lines with conspicuous rates of psychopathology (Post, 1994). Because psychopathology is often associated with suicide, alcoholism, and other life-shortening behaviors, these pedigrees would also exhibit higher rates of early parental loss.

In agreement with this chain of reasoning, many notables of psychology's history emerged from family lines that exhibited some evidence of psychopathology. Friedrich Nietzsche's father succumbed to mental illness, and the mothers of both Ivan Pavlov and Jean Piaget suffered from nervous disorders or emotional instability. Sigmund Freud had two cousins who went insane, and Wilhelm Reich's parents both committed suicide. Not only did William James suffer from many emotional difficulties, but also his father seemed to display borderline personality disorder, and his sister Alice exhibited exceptional hypochondriasis and an incapacitating pathological dependency. Probably the most conspicuous mad-genius pedigree is that of "Darwin's bulldog," T. H. Huxley. Besides his own depressive states, his father died in an asylum; of his father's 8 children, only T. H. and his sister could be considered normal; T. H.'s daughter, Marian, became extremely melancholic, lost her sanity, and died young; one grandson, Trevenen, was also melancholic, and committed suicide; a second grandson, Julian, attempted suicide and suffered from depression; and a third, Aldous, experimented with hallucinogenic drugs and the occult. Several other temperamental disorders permeate the family history yet, all of these disturbances notwithstanding, the Huxley family is distinguished for its output of first-rate creative minds. Sir Andrew Fielding Huxley, another grandson of T. H., shared the 1963 Nobel prize for physiology or medicine. Sir Julian Huxley was a noted evolutionist who became secretary of the Zoological Society of London and the first director general of the United Nations Educational, Scientific, and Cultural Organization. Aldous Huxley, although not knighted, became a famous author, most notably of the novel *Brave New World*. In any case, the unsuccessful Huxleys inherited too much pathopathology and were debilitated as a result. The highly accomplished Huxleys were endowed with just the amount necessary to exhibit the requisite cognitive and dispositional traits—such as unrestrained imagination, introversion, and independence from social norms.

I am not arguing that early parental loss represents exclusively a genetic factor. I am stating only that, according to modern behavior genetics, things are not always what they seem. Many so-called environmental influences may actually be the consequence of underlying genetic factors. Sometimes the genetic etiology will be fairly straightforward, as in the tendency for eminent individuals to come from the homes of professionals. Other times the genes may operate by rather more roundabout routes, as in the tendency for famous people to have experienced early parental loss. Furthermore, when nurture does exert some impact on early development, that influence may involve the nonshared environment—such as birth order—far more than the shared environment.

Nurture as Nature

One final finding of modern behavior genetics puts one of Francis Galton's seemingly outlandish claims in a more favorable light. Galton (1869) believed that genetic endowment was so potent that if a highly gifted person were to become a changeling, and thus raised in a totally different environment, genius would still win out and emerge, all the obstacles notwithstanding. Although behavior geneticists would not defend so strong a position, the accumulated evidence does support a weakened form of the same proposition (e.g., Beer, Arnold, & Loehlin, 1998; Plomin, Fulker, Corley, & DeFries, 1997). In the first place, even when children are raised from infancy in a foster home, with biologically unrelated parents, their phenotype will resemble more that of their true parents than that of their foster parents (Scarr & McCartney, 1983). Furthermore, identical (monozygotic) twins reared in separate homes not only retain their genetic similarities on most individual-difference variables, but also those similarities tend to increase over time (Bouchard, 1995). In other words, the influence of genetic endowment becomes stronger as the offspring get older—precisely the opposite of what would be predicted if individual development became progressively dominated by environmental factors. As offspring mature, they evidently acquire an enhanced ability to shape the environment in a manner more consistent with their genotypic leanings (Scarr & McCartney, 1983). Toddlers are pretty much at the mercy of their parents when it comes to choosing activities and recreation, yet by the time offspring reach adolescence they take an active role in making the environment fit better with their natural inclinations. They may decide to take up this specific instrument or participate in that particular sport or read some specialized genre of books, their parents' preferences being what they may. Hence, Galton's (1869) hypothetical changelings will do whatever possible to secure the opportunities necessary to realize their full potential. Even if those changelings were raised by a John B.

Watson trying to convert them into a "beggar-man and thief," their born genius may still emerge in some form—although perhaps as a big-time drug lord rather than a great psychologist.

Emergenesis

Although it appears that Galton's views have more empirical justification than Watson's, behavior geneticists have pointed to one significant complication: Genetic inheritance may not always operate according to a simple additive process. This is apparent in the fact that, for certain personal traits, identical (monozygotic) twins are far more similar than are fraternal (dizygotic) twins, who may be on those traits no more similar than any randomly selected pair from the larger population (Lykken, 1982). This is what would be expected if inheritance were multiplicative rather than additive for these characteristics. David Lykken (1982) called this complex form of inheritance *emergenesis* and suggested that emergenic endowment underlies creative genius (Lykken, 1998). This suggestion has received some empirical endorsement (Waller, Bouchard, Lykken, Tellegen, & Blacker, 1993). One peculiar implication of emergenic inheritance is that exceptional genius should generally not run in family lines (Lykken, McGue, Tellegen, & Bouchard, 1992). Instead, great geniuses should most often emerge out of nowhere. This happens because it is very difficult to inherit the full configuration of genes that are required for the manifestation of the multiplicative composite necessary for the manifestation of true genius (Simonton, 1999d). Lykken (1998) provided some specific examples of emergenic genius, including Carl Friedrich Gauss, the great mathematician, and Michael Faraday, the great physicist and chemist, the former having uneducated parents (with an illiterate mother) and the latter coming from a humble blacksmith's family. For some reason, Galton did not even consider these two notables in his pedigree study, even though both were highly eminent. Gauss's mathematical work—the Gaussian curve—even had made a contribution to Galton's own thinking about individual differences.

It is curious that Galton (1869) himself offered a conception of genius that appears to be more multiplicative than additive. He said that natural ability required the combination of intelligence, energy, and persistence. If to this list are added certain other ingredients—such as the imagination and independence expected of individuals who hail from psychopathological pedigrees—then the odds are all the greater that genius is emergenic in nature. If so, then this process could help account for the highly skewed distribution of lifetime productivity and eminence discussed at length in chapter 3. The reason is that multiplicative inheritance implies that the emergenic trait would have a lognormal cross-sectional distribution even if the component of those traits were normally distributed. This consequence was first suggested by Cyril Burt (1943) and was more recently given considerable mathematical elaboration and empirical documentation (Simonton, 1999d).

However, if genius is emergenic, what does this imply about the distinguished pedigrees that Galton (1869) so assiduously assembled in *Hereditary Genius*? One possibility is that Galton may have overstated his case, so that the lineages are not so conspicuous as claimed. Take Isaac Newton as an example. Although Galton did not list Newton among the 18 illustrious scientists who lacked any notable kin, it becomes immediately obvious on reading Galton's description of Newton's genetic background that Newton emerged totally out of the blue, just like Gauss and Faraday. "Newton's ancestry appear[s] to have been in no way remarkable for intellectual ability," Galton (1892/1972, pp. 272–273) was forced to admit, adding that "there is nothing of note that I can find out among his descendants, except what may be inferred from the fact that the two Huttons were connected with him in some unknown way, through the maternal line." However, besides the extremely tenuous nature of the hypothesized pedigree, the Hutton lineage was so far removed from Newton that the genetic influence would be nil anyway. Other inquiries that have implemented much more strict criteria regarding what counts as a notable lineage have arrived at a much lower proportion of cases (e.g., Simonton, 1984a, 1992c). There admittedly do exist many conspicuous examples—the Darwin family to which Galton belonged conspicuous among them. Even so, these might have a totally different causal basis. Indeed, the true foundation of these lineages may be more environmental than genetic. I will pick up this possibility again in Part V. So, may it suffice to say that if Galton were still alive today, he could not consider himself to have been completely vindicated by modern behavior genetics.

SPECIFIC MANIFESTATION: GENDER AND GENIUS

Anyone who reads Galton's (1869) *Hereditary Genius* cannot avoid noting one distinctive act: Women are immensely underrepresented. The only notable case is that of the Brontë sisters, who receive their due attention in Galton's chapter on Literary Men. Given that women represent slightly more than half of human adults, far more instances would be expected. It would seem, moreover, that this dearth should cause a problem for Galton's genetic determinism. Except for a few odd "sex-linked" genes, such as those for color blindness and hemophilia, women and men inherit more or less the same genes from their parents. Galton seemed not to be sufficiently aware of this potential problem, perhaps because he had some rather curious pre-Mendelian conceptions about how inheritance worked. For instance, at one point in the book Galton stated that certain statistics "prove that the female influence is inferior to the male in conveying ability" (Galton, 1892/1972, p. 103).

Yet the problem remains: Why are women so rare in *Hereditary Genius*? Is it because a sexist bias permeated his data? Or is the differential real? If the latter, then what is the developmental cause? Are women by nature not equipped to attain greatness, or is it a matter of nurture? To address these questions I first look at the raw empirical facts and then turn to their theoretical interpretations.

The Facts

In 1903, James McKeen Cattell strove to identify the most "eminent men" of history (1903b). To avoid ethnocentric biases as much as possible, he attempted to gather an international collection of biographical dictionaries, although he was able to procure appropriate reference works only in English, French, and German. On the basis of the amount of space allotted in these sources, he produced a list of the top 1,000. Of those listed, only 32, or a bit more than 3%, were women. Moreover, many of these women were female monarchs, such as Mary Stuart of Scotland, Elizabeth I of England, Catherine the Great of Russia, Isabella of Castille, and Christina of Sweden. In fact, when Catharine Cox (1926) used Cattell's (1903b) listing to obtain her sample of eminent achievers, she deleted all the women whom she believed were born to fame and obtained a more truncated sample of eminent women. Of her final 301 geniuses, only 8 were women: Madame de Stael, Georges Sand, Madame de Sévigné, Marquise de Maintenon, Elizabeth Gaskell, George Eliot (Marian Evans), Charlotte Brontë, and Harriet Martineau. That amounts to less than 3%, or a proportional loss of about 2 women. Women are a little better represented among those included in Havelock Ellis's (1926) A *Study of British Genius*. Of the 1,030 eminent individuals, 55 are female, yielding a percentage in excess of 5%. Other heterogeneous samples of famous creators, leaders, and miscellaneous celebrities obtain percentages that fall far short of the 51% that women represent of the larger population (e.g., Eisenstadt, 1978; M. G. Goertzel, Goertzel, & Goertzel, 1978; V. Goertzel & Goertzel, 1962; J. R. Hayes, 1989b). The proportion is usually so low that small samples of notable individuals may not contain any women at all. For instance, when Edward L. Thorndike (1950) assessed the personality traits of just 91 luminaries, not one was a woman. Women did only a little better in the subsample of geniuses that Cox (1926) similarly assessed on 67 character traits: Of the 100, just 2, Stael and Sand, were women.

The proportion of women naturally varies according to the specific domain of achievement. On the one hand, women have always received more ample representation among the giants of literature. According to J. M. Cattell (1903b), about 12% of all great writers are female, a substantial increase in their usual ratio. Indeed, in the subsample of 301 geniuses that Cox (1926) drew from Cattell's 1,000, every woman but 1—Maintenon, the wife of King Louis the Great of France—was a creative writer. In a few parts of the world, female writers have attained the greatest possible heights. Japanese literature is rich in female names, among them Murasaki Shikibu, who authored the world's first novel, *The Tale of Genji*, thereby obtaining a status that compares favorably with that of William Shakespeare (Simonton, 1992a).

On the other hand, women have been rather more rare in classical music. The proportion is so small, in fact, that they appear not at all among the 120 most eminent composers (Simonton, 1991b) and are just barely represented in a sample of nearly 700 (Simonton, 1977c). Given these statistics, it comes as no surprise that not a single female composer was included among the 11 composers in Cox's (1926) historiometric inquiry. Given these statistics, it is perhaps no wonder that George Trumball Ladd, the early American psychologist, could publish in 1917 a book with the silly title *Why Women Cannot Compose Music* (Sheehy, Chapman, & Conroy, 1997).

In science women do a little better, but they still fall far short of the overall percentage. In a sample of illustrious scientists extracted from standard biographical dictionaries and encyclopedias, less than 1% were women (Simonton, 1991a). Names such as Hypatia, Caroline Herschel, Marie Curie, and Barbara McClintock are mere drops in an ocean of male scientists. Although more contemporary samples of scientists have obtained a better representation, the figures are still pretty low, especially among the truly eminent (J. R. Cole, 1987). For instance, the number of women who were members of the National Academy of Sciences (NAS) in 1991 was about 5% (Feist, 1997). Furthermore, women have received around 2% of the major scientific awards, such as the Nobel prize, the National Medal of Science, and the various awards bestowed by the NAS (J. R. Hayes, 1989b).

Yet the female representation varies even within distinct scientific disciplines. This is immediately apparent from the results that J. M. Cattell (1933) reported for a large sample of 9,785 notable American scientists. Although the overall percentage of women in this group stood at the respectable figure of 7%, the percentage remained only around 2% for physics and 4% for geology. In contrast, about 10% of the botanists and physiologists were women, and psychologists especially welcomed female participation, obtaining an impressive figure of 22%—more than twice the representation of any other scientific discipline. Nonetheless, this percentage is based on a fairly inclusive sample of 656 living psychologists. More select samples obtain lower percentages. Among 538 luminaries who obtained a place in the annals of psychology between 1600 and 1967, only 11, or about 2%, were women (R. I. Watson & Merrifield, 1973). This figure includes an anthropologist (Ruth Benedict), a psychiatrist (Freda Fromm-Reichmann), a psychoanalyst (Melanie Klein), and an educator (Maria Montessori).

More recently, of those deceased psychologists of sufficient prominence to earn obituaries in *American Psychologist* between 1979 and 1990, the percentage reaches 13% (Kinnier, Metha, Buki, & Rawa, 1994). According to a tabulation executed by one of my research assistants, women made up only 11% of those listed in a recent biographical dictionary of distinguished psychologists (Sheehy et al., 1997). Furthermore, of 69 psychologists who influenced American psychology between 1879 and 1967, the proportion declines to 4% (Simonton, 1992b). In particular, there were just 3 women in this group: Mary Calkins, June Downey, and Florence Goodenough. Of these only the first and last are still well known today. Calkins, a doctoral student of William James, was an important functionalist who studied paired-associate learning; Goodenough, a doctoral student of Lewis M. Terman, created the eponymic Draw-a-Man Test for children and was one of those who calculated IQ scores for the 301 geniuses in Cox's (1926) study.

Although psychology is highly receptive to female achievement, outstanding women psychologists are not evenly distributed across the field's subdisciplines. According to one study of 87 eminent females, 23% were clinical psychologists, 18% were developmental psychologists, 10% were personality psychologists, 8% were social psychologists, 7% were school psychologists, 5% were psychometric psychologists, and 3% were educational psychologists (Stevens & Gardner, 1985). Similar leanings toward these "soft" or "tender-minded" subdisciplines are evident in a recent compilation of 36 eminent female psychologists (O'Connell & Russo, 1990). Examples include Charlotte Bühler, Else Frenkel-Brunswik, Anna Freud, Eleanor Gibson, Leta Hollingworth, Karen Horney, Bärbel Inhelder, Eleanor Maccoby, and Maria Montessori. Out of all the eminent women covered in this reference book, less than one quarter made contributions to one of psychology's "hard" or "tough-minded" subdisciplines, such as experimental, physiological, and comparative. This list includes Mary Calkins, Christine Ladd-Franklin, and Margaret Floy Washburn. Moreover, most of these cannot be purely identified with this side of psychology, because virtually all devoted a significant portion of their careers to the other side. Mary Calkins, for instance, devoted the latter part of her career to developing a self psychology, certainly a much less scientifically rigorous topic than paired-associate learning. In any case, it is perhaps unfortunate that notable female psychologists have not been strongly attracted to the more tough-minded subdisciplines. According to an analysis of the membership of the NAS, experimental psychologists have a much greater likelihood of receiving that honor than do personality and social psychologists (Over, 1981). This alone could account for the poor representation of female psychologists in that distinguished body—a much smaller percentage than their place among great psychologists in general. The rare exceptions, such as Margaret F. Washburn and Eleanor Gibson, did a considerable amount of experimental work.

Although women may be among the highly respected researchers in certain subdisciplines of psychology, the fact persists that men dominate the annals of psychology's history. Moreover, with only one minor qualification, the hegemony of men holds no matter what the specialty may be. That one exception may be the psychology of women and gender, where women seem to predominate. Among the notables in this field are Sandra Bem, Jeanne Block, Florence Denmark, Ravenna Helson, Leta Hollingworth, Karen

Horney, Eleanor Maccoby, Clara Mayo, Virginia Sexton, Carolyn Sherif, Janet Spence, and Bonnie Strickland. Yet by its very nature this exception is itself so exceptional that it cannot seriously threaten the generalization. The overwhelming majority of great psychologists are still men. Why?

The Interpretations

As I emphatically demonstrated in chapter 3, the single most critical predictor of an individual's lasting fame is his or her total lifetime output. Thus, the most direct explanation of the low female representation in creative domains may be their low total productivity. If female psychologists are generally less productive than male psychologists, then few will enter the annals of the discipline's history, and fewer still will stand anywhere close to entering the pantheon of true greats in the field. In line with this interpretation, many notable female psychologists seem to have based their reputations on somewhat thin publication records. June Downey could claim only 76 lifetime publications and Else Frenkel-Brunswik a mere 16. Yet it is also easy to cite counterexamples. Anna Freud's bibliography contains more than 100 items, and Margaret F. Washburn's more than 200. So, is there any genuine evidence that women tend to publish less than men and thereby compromise their short- and long-term impact on the field?

There exists an abundant literature showing that female scientists tend to be less productive than men (J. R. Cole, 1987). According to one study of university faculty, the likelihood of publishing five or more articles in a 2-year period was three times greater for men than for women (Blackburn, Behymer, & Hall, 1978). Another investigation showed that men outproduced women in both articles and books by a ratio of about 2 to 1 (Clemente, 1973). Gender-based output differentials have been found in psychology as well. Rodgers and Maranto (1989) looked at the factors that predict the number of publications in the first 6 years after receiving the PhD for a sample 485 American Psychological Association (APA) members who had received their doctorates between 1966 and 1976. Whether the survey respondent was male or female was a more powerful predictor than any other factor, including quality of the first job, predoctoral publication record, and general scholastic ability. Another investigation that focused on experimental social psychologists found that gender accounted for more variance in publications than did the quality of the graduate department, the quality of the current department, and such personality traits as competitiveness (Helmreich, Spence, Beane, Lucker, & Matthews, 1980). On the whole, male psychologists appear to outpublish their female colleagues by a ratio of almost 3 to 1 (Guyter & Fidell, 1973; Helmreich et al., 1980).

The lowered quantity of output should not be equated with a lowered quality of output. In Rodgers and Maranto's (1989) study of 485 APA members, gender did not directly predict the number of citations received, but rather any contrasts in professional visibility were entirely mediated by the differences in publication rates (Rodgers & Maranto, 1989; cf. Helmreich et al., 1980). In concrete terms, men averaged 1.9 citations per article, and women averaged 1.8, a negligible difference. In another inquiry Over (1990) compared 564 high-impact articles with low-impact articles that appeared in the same journals. The articles came from leading psychology journals, such as *Psychological Review*, *Psychological Bulletin*, *Journal of Experimental Psychology*, *Journal of Personality and Social Psychology*, *Journal of Abnormal Psychology*, *Journal of Applied Psychology*, *Journal of Consulting and Clinical Psychology*, and *American Psychologist*. Although 78% of the high-impact articles had male first authors, 83% of the low-impact articles had first authors of the same gender. In other words, men publish more frequently cited articles only because they publish more ignored articles. Finally, I should mention a study of the impact of dissertation research that was published as articles in 14 top psychology journals (Over, 1982e). In the 6 years following publication, there were no gender differences in the number of citations. Although men soon pulled ahead of women in cumulative output, the number of citations received per article remained the same. In sum, gender differences in citation rates can be ascribed almost exclusively to corresponding differences in output rates. This is exactly what would be predicted according to the equal-odds rule introduced in chapter 3.

Although the productivity gap between male and female psychologists is rather substantial, it tends to be reduced when other extraneous factors are taken into consideration (Helmreich & Spence, 1982; also see Boice, Shaughnessy, & Pecker, 1985). This reduction was best demonstrated by a study that sampled 122 women and 122 men from the 1968 APA Directory (Guyter & Fidell, 1973). The men were almost three times more productive than the women, according to the publications listed in *Psychological Abstracts*. Yet most of this disparity disappeared when adjustments were made for age, area of interest (theoretical or applied), prestige of institution, and academic position (full professor, associate professor, assistant professor, lecturer–instructor, and nonacademic). The most important predictor was not gender but rather whether the psychologist's interests were theoretical or applied. Moreover, the main effect of gender essentially vanished, to be replaced by two interaction effects (gender × academic position and gender × prestige of institution). Hence, any raw gap in total output may be moderated by other factors besides gender per se.

As far as I can determine this result has not been replicated on more recent samples or elaborated with the incorporation of additional variables. Nonetheless, it suggests the possibility that women may be less likely to become great psychologists for reasons besides their productivity. In addition, even if the productivity gap is accepted, the differential output remains to be explained. Thus, in either case it becomes necessary to scrutinize the deeper causes of the phenomenon. Among the most prominent possibilities are these five: sexual dimorphism, gender socialization, gender roles, gender bias, and the gender milieu. The first of these concerns nature, whereas the last four concern nurture. This contrast is reflected in the terminology. Whereas the term *sexual* denotes the natural differences between men and women, *gender* signifies the nurtured differences.

Sexual Dimorphism

During the course of evolution, natural and sexual selection have created some very obvious morphological differences between men and women. Although the existence of contrasts in muscle mass, body fat, skeletal structure, and other secondary sexual features are uncontroversial, it is much more contentious whether men and women innately differ on anything that may account for the relative paucity of female genius. Nevertheless, for more than 100 years some psychologists have been willing to speculate that this gender disparity is born rather than made. Among the more recent examples is Hans Eysenck, the eminent personality psychologist. In his book *Genius: The Natural History of Creativity* (1995), he offered the following three biological explanations:

1. Women may be naturally less intelligent than men. Eysenck's (1995) assertion was based largely on the well-established observation that women's brains are noticeably smaller than men's. More controversial, however, is the claim that this difference cannot be totally attributed to contrasts in body size, a conspicuous correlate of brain size. Eysenck maintained that recent research (e.g., Ankney, 1992) suggests that a residual gap remains. Moreover, Eysenck (citing Lynn, 1994) argued that this gap is reflected in observable differences in performance on IQ tests. Men are reputed to enjoy an IQ at least 0.25 standard deviation higher.

2. Women display appreciably less variation in intelligence than do men. This implies that the upper tail of the intelligence distribution will extend out farther for men than for women, yielding a higher proportion of men with extremely high IQ scores. According to Eysenck's (1995) estimate, out of 10,000 randomly selected individuals, there would be 55 males with IQs of 160 or higher, but only 5 females with such IQs. In other words, men at these superlative intellectual grade would outnumber women 11 to 1. Of course, men would also be disproportionately represented among those with subnormal IQs, but that tail has no consequence of the attainment of greatness anyway. It is odd that Eysenck (1995) made no attempt to explain why the person with the highest recorded IQ according to the *Guinness Book of Records*—Marilyn Vos Sa-

vant, with a score of 228—is a woman rather than a man (McFarlan, 1989).

3. Women are constitutionally disposed toward certain personality traits that make them less likely to become creative geniuses. Eysenck (1995) put special stress on gender differences in Psychoticism, a key dimension of the Eysenck Personality Questionnaire. As noted in chapter 7, high scores on this dimension have been associated with enhanced creativity. Yet, because men tend to score twice as high as women on this factor, the former should exceed the latter in creativity as well. The consolation prize for women is that they have a lesser tendency toward the kinds of psychopathology associated with excessive scores on Psychoticism.

Although Eysenck's (1995) assertions are documented with contemporary research, the arguments themselves date back into psychology's early history (Shields, 1975). Organologist Franz Joseph Gall and phrenologist Johann Spurzheim both believed that women's brains were strikingly different from, and inferior to, men's. Pioneer neuroanatomists Paul Broca and Theodore Meynert were able to demonstrate to their satisfaction the inferior organization of female brains. The negative implications of the women's smaller brains were drawn by psychologists Alexander Bain and George Romanes. The variability hypothesis had its early beginnings in Darwin's 1871 *The Descent of Man* and was explicitly linked with intellectual ability by Havelock Ellis, notwithstanding the latter's positive attitudes toward the liberation of women. This link was endorsed and developed by Edward Thorndike (Shields, 1982), and J. M. Cattell (1903b) explicitly used this hypothesis to account for the very poor showing of women among his elite 1,000. "Women depart less from the normal than man," wrote Cattell, "a fact that usually holds for the female throughout the animal series" (p. 375). Finally, the debilitating constitution of the female personality goes back to ancient Greece and found many more modern advocates, including Spanish physician Juan Huarte and British scientist Francis Galton (Shields, 1975). Dissenters from the prevailing view admittedly would appear from time to time. Philosopher John Stuart Mill attacked the notion that women were inherently less intelligent, and the variability hypothesis was attacked by statistician Karl Pearson and psychologist Leta Hollingworth. Yet the fact remains that the idea that women are biologically inferior to men continues to be entertained by serious and illustrious psychologists at the turn of the century.

It is hard to decide why the debate has continued so long without resolution. Part of the problem is that the issue has become highly political in nature, with the stand taken seeming to reflect more general attitudes toward the place of women in society. Just as crucial may be deficiencies in the empirical evidence that make it impossible for any one side to deliver a knockout punch. Underlying Eysenck's (1995) arguments, for example, are a host of tenuous measurement assumptions. Tests are not provided a priori but rather emerge a posteriori, through various psychometric procedures that are implemented by fallible human beings (most of whom happen to be men). Last, it is not completely clear how evolution would account for the conjectured innate differences, as Karl Pearson was among the first to recognize (Shields, 1975). Indeed, it is perfectly possible to conceive evolutionary scenarios in which men and women would have to be equal on virtually all individual-difference variables (G. F. Miller, 1998; Simonton, 1999b). Perhaps only gender contrasts in physical aggressiveness can boast an empirically and theoretically secure basis, as Eleanor Maccoby and others have demonstrated (e.g., Maccoby & Jacklin, 1980; see also Hyde, 1986).

At present, the safest scientific strategy may be to adopt an agnostic attitude, at least until psychologists can devise more rigorous techniques to resolve the debate. Besides, there already exists an ample inventory of environmental factors that have a proven connection to the gender gap in creative achievement.

Gender Socialization

Parents clearly raise their children differently depending on their gender. In most literate societies across the globe, boys are socialized toward independence and achievement, whereas girls are trained to center their lives around family and relationships (Barry, Bacon, & Child, 1957). Accordingly, throughout the course of history many women of enormous talent probably never even considered the prospect of having life goals outside the home. At best, a gifted woman might hope to become the "woman behind the man," a choice made by many of the brilliant women who participated in Louis M. Terman's classical longitudinal study (Tomlinson-Keasey, 1990). Furthermore, when a family has both boys and girls, the parents traditionally invest limited resources in their sons. After all, the sons were expected to obtain occupations sufficiently well paying that they could support a wife and children. The unfortunate ramifications of this pro-son bias have been empirically demonstrated by noted female psychologist Ravenna Helson (O'Connell & Russo, 1990). In a longitudinal study of Mills College graduates, Helson (1990) found that women "who were successful in careers at age 43 were, with few exceptions, those who did not have brothers" (p. 49). Because Helson (1980) obtained similar results for eminent female mathematicians, she may have identified an important—and clearly environmental—inhibitor of talent development in women.

Something of this pro-son orientation can certainly be seen in the history of psychology. Sigmund Freud, his mother's firstborn and favorite, was given special treatment that his younger siblings could only envy. He was the only one in the family who had his own room, a room lit with an oil lamp, while the others had to use candles. Because Freud had five sisters and only one brother, who was the lastborn in the family, it was obviously his female siblings who bore most of this burden. When one of his sisters took up the piano, her older brother complained that it disrupted his studies, and so it was she, not he, who did all the compromising.

Beyond mere anecdote are the birth orders of several eminent women in the field, presented in Table 9.1. Anne Anastasi, Josephine Hilgard, Bärbel Inhelder, Clara Mayo, Brenda Milner, Maria Montessori, Margaret Rioch, Elizabeth Spelke, Shelley Taylor, and Margaret Washburn were only children. These women had no brothers at all with whom to contend. Furthermore, Sandra Bem, Ellen Berscheid, Charlotte Bühler, Barbara Stoddard Burks, Mary Calkins, Mamie Phipps Clark, Dorothea Dix, Eleanor Gibson, Lillian Gilbreth, Leta Hollingworth, Molly Harrower, Christina Ladd-Franklin, Lillien Martin, Margaret Mead, Bernice Neugarten, Janet Spence, Bonnie Strickland, Thelma Thurstone, Anne Treisman, Leona Tyler, and Beth Wellman were all firstborns—as was Ravenna Helson herself. Of these, Bem, Benedict, Burks, Gibson, Hollingworth, Spence, Treisman, and Wellman had sisters only; Gilbreth had three brothers and five sisters; Ladd-Franklin had two brothers and two sisters (one each being half-siblings); and both Berscheid and Calkins had two brothers and one sister each. Although Clark, Dix, Harrower, Helson, Martin, Neugarten, Strickland, Thurstone, and Tyler had younger brothers only, they at least enjoyed the advantage of primogeniture. Helson's two brothers (twins) were also 4 years younger than she.

The middle children in the table are Nancy Bayley, Martha Bernal, Else Frenkel-Brunswik, Hélène Deutsch, Jacqueline Goodnow, Edna Heidbreder, Eleanor Maccoby, Sandra Scarr, and Pauline Sears. Bernal, Frenkel-Brunswik, and Maccoby had only sisters. Sears had three sisters and one older brother, Scarr had an older brother and a younger sister, and Heidbreder and Bayley each had three sisters and one younger brother.

Finally, the lastborns listed are Florence Denmark, Hélène Deutsch, Anna Freud, Florence Goodenough, Mary Henle, Karen Horney, Francis Degen Horowitz, Melanie Klein, Carolyn Payton, Carolyn Sherif, and Virginia Sexton. Denmark, Horowitz, and Payton had only sisters, Sexton had only her older sister survive beyond childhood, Goodenough had five sisters and two brothers, and Deutsch and Klein had two sisters and one brother each. Henle had an older brother but also a twin sister (who became an archeologist). Horney had no sisters and one older full brother, who was 4 years her senior. Although Anna Freud had to deal with her three older brothers—Jean Martin, Ernst, and Cromwell—she also developed an extremely intimate relationship with her father that put her in a rather distinctive position.

Taken altogether, these data suggest that the "Helson effect" may constitute more than a chance observation. With only a few exceptions, most of these women came from homes in which (a) there were no brothers,

(b) there were no older brothers, or (c) sisters predominated. Therefore, it would be immensely valuable to investigate this question more systematically and in greater detail. It would be especially interesting to determine whether the developmental detriment of having brothers, especially older ones, has diminished. Societies have presumably become more egalitarian in the way they raise their children. In fact, something precisely like this has been found for women who have become presidents or prime ministers of their nations (Steinberg, 2001). Those who came to power in 1960–1989 were quite unlikely to have an older brother, but this tendency vanished for those who gained office since 1990.

The Helson effect must operate as a nonshared environmental influence. One consequence of this developmental factor would be a woman who grows up with a disposition that departs from society's feminine stereotype. Either the gender-typical socialization pressures would be less pronounced or the young talented woman would be better equipped to resist them. In support of this conjecture is the persistent finding that high-achieving women tend to be much more similar to high-achieving men than they are to women in general. Even in the case of women who became the first ladies of U.S. presidents success is not at all dependent on being "the hostess with the mostest" in the White House (Simonton, 1996c). Instead, these women's performance ratings are contingent on their establishment of independent identities and reputations as political leaders. This broad pattern holds in psychology as well. For example, one study of 212 male and 79 female psychologists found that scores on a femininity scale were negatively correlated with the citations they received in the professional literature (Helmreich et al., 1980). Another survey of 124 female psychologists concluded, on the basis of their scores on R. B. Cattell's 16 Personality Factor Questionnaire, that

> successful academic women in psychology differ from adult women in general and from women college students in many of the same personality characteristics in which they resemble successful academic men. As a group, they tend to be more intelligent, socially aloof, dominant, serious, adventuresome, sensitive, flexible, imaginative, insightful, unconventional, secure, and self-sufficient than adult women in the general population and women in college, and less anxiety prone. (Bachtold & Werner, 1970, p. 242)

It is critical that "the significant contributors among the women psychologists were more socially aloof and exacting" (p. 242) and thus departed even more from the other-directed and communal female stereotype. Furthermore, when these women did differ from comparable men, it was often in a direction away from traditional femininity. In particular, "the women psychologists score, as a group, higher than the successful academic men on intelligence, super-ego strength, and unconventionality (radicalism) and lower than the academic men on self-sentiment" (Bachtold & Werner, 1970, p. 242).

These remarks should not be interpreted as saying that great psychologists are completely equivalent. As mentioned earlier, women are more prone to make major contributions to the "soft" or "tender-minded" subdisciplines of the field. This emphasis may reflect a residual effect of gender-differentiated socialization. For instance, a survey of 510 male and 356 female psychologists revealed that the genders tend to differ on some of the methodological and theoretical dimensions that I discussed in chapter 8 (Coan, 1979). Specifically, women were much less likely than men to favor the quantitative, atomistic, objective, materialistic, deterministic, and impersonal approaches to human psychology. Hence, female psychologists may not differ from their male counterparts in having the intellect and disposition required to attain greatness, but their gender may shape the particular nature of their contributions.

Gender Roles

I have assumed that the gender differences that underlie the attainment of greatness as a psychologist can be partly ascribed to gender-based differentials in socialization practices. Men are raised one way, women in another, with corresponding consequences for the level and type of female achievement. Yet an advocate of a nature rather than nurture account might argue that the gender differences in socialization simply reflect the biological contrasts between the sexes. This argument would seem to fit what was said earlier about many so-called environmental effects actually being the spurious repercussion of deeper genetic differences. However, there are good reasons why socialization should be considered a cause rather than an effect. Not only do parents have to work so hard to make sure their children acquire what they consider to be gender-appropriate behaviors and attitudes, but also distinct cultures may have different expectations about what is gender appropriate and adjust the socialization practices accordingly (Eagly & Wood, 1999). This point was made most obvious in Margaret Mead's (1935) classic book *Sex and Temperament*. After looking at three tribes of British New Guinea, she concluded that

> many, if not all, of the personality traits which we have called masculine or feminine are as lightly linked to sex as are the clothing, the manners, and the form of head-dress that a society at a given period assigns to either sex. (p. 190)

Among the Arapesh, both males and females have what Westerners would consider feminine traits; among the Mundugumor, both men and women feature masculine personalities; and among the Tchambuli, the males were feminine whereas the females were masculine in character. To be sure, Mead may have overstated her case. Just as men hold a monopoly on physical aggressiveness, so do they monopolize war. Occasional cases, such as Joan of Arc, notwithstanding, men have constituted the principal combatants in all the world's wars throughout human history. Even so, with this lone exception, Mead's main generalization, namely, that "human nature is almost unbelievably malleable, responding accurately and contrastingly to contrasting cultural conditions" (p. 191), holds.

The socialization practices favored by any given society ultimately have one essential function: to help each child become a mature adult. This function specifically means that boys and girls must be prepared to assume the gender roles defined for men and women in their native culture. Moreover, those gender roles may exert their own independent influence on the connection between gender and genius; that is, even if a woman has the temperament necessary to achieve distinction, she may find that societal norms and expectations interfere with her realization of that potential. This obstacle is nowhere more apparent than in the repercussions of marriage and family. In chapter 11 I quoted Francis Bacon's (1597/1942) admonition that ambitious men avoid wife and children. If Bacon could recommend that gifted men shy away from domestic commitments, then how much more should this recommendation apply to women who are trained to assume far more responsibility when it comes to such family matters? As a result, many eminent women have simply avoided altogether the constraints imposed on the role of wife and mother. Prominent instances include Jane Austen, Emily Brontë, Emily Dickinson, George Eliot, Barbara McClintock, Georgia O'Keeffe, and Virginia Woolf. In more general terms, women who win an entry in Who's Who are four times more likely than similarly illustrious men to be unmarried (J. R. Hayes, 1989b). Moreover, according to the statistics calculated by Havelock Ellis (1926), those who do get married tend to do at a later age than is the norm for their social class. Charlotte Brontë did not marry until she was 38, Elizabeth Browning until age 40. In addition, the successful women who somehow fit marriage into their lives are three times more likely to be childless compared to equally successful married men (J. R. Hayes, 1989b). In fact, between 1948 and 1976 in the United States the proportion of doctorates that were granted to women correlated −.94 with the average cohort fertility, a very remarkable aggregate-level correlation (McDowell, 1982). Finally, with or without children, the marriages of high-achieving women are more prone to fail. Among the women in a sample of 20th-century luminaries, only 9% could be considered happily married (M. G. Goertzel et al., 1978). Hélène Deutsch's husband, Felix, was one of those rare men who shared childrearing responsibilities and who provided her with continual support and encouragement in her pursuit of career as a distinguished psychiatrist. In contrast, 40% of these women were divorced, and another 6% remained married but were separated from their husbands (M. G. Goertzel et al., 1978). The dissolution of a marriage did not always improve matters, for that often meant that many had to coordinate career and child care as single mothers, something Margaret Mead, among many others, had to endure.

The foregoing statistics are based on samples that were heterogeneous with respect to the domain of achievement. Several studies have focused on specific domains and have, for the most part, obtained compatible results. For instance, in a sample of 99 male and 109 female artists examined 18 years after they had completed art school, the women exhibited much more career discontinuity compared to the men, with the greatest degree of discontinuity being found among those with more children (Stohs, 1992). It is difficult to maintain a continuous career while engaged in child care. Sometimes the cost of such career interruptions can severely threaten the prospects of resuming the career once family responsibilities sufficiently diminish. In certain domains of achievement, the knowledge and techniques requisite for making creative contributions experience rapid obsolescence. In physics, a woman who interrupts her career for 4 years will see her domain-relevant expertise reduced by half, whereas to lose the same amount would require a social scientist or biologist to interrupt her career 7 years (McDowell, 1982). Better yet, an English professor can take 20 years off and still expect to sacrifice only 50% of the knowledge required to restart her career! Thus, the effort required for a woman to bring herself back up to speed after a career interruption appears to be the most severe in the physical sciences, a bit less arduous in the social and biological sciences, and negligible in the humanities.

Despite these results, research on scientific achievement has yielded somewhat more complex results (Zuckerman, Cole, & Bruer, 1991). Neither marriage nor motherhood has to be a disadvantage with respect to scientific performance, as gauged by productivity in professional journals (J. R. Cole & Zuckerman, 1987; Kyvik, 1990). In fact, both male and female scientists appear to be more productive if they are married rather than unmarried. In addition, although the responsibilities of parenthood can depress output, the costs are about the same for men as for women (Hargens, McCann, & Reskin, 1978). Furthermore, the negative consequences are long-term only if the number of children is large, a situation that also has a differential impact on men and women, the latter tending to suffer more from an exceptional increase in family responsibilities (Kyvik, 1990). Because scientists tend to have few children and to rely heavily on collaborators and students in their research, the repercussions of marriage and family are likely minimized for women.

It is unfortunate that very little research has addressed this question within the specific domain of psychology. One investigation of American psychologists found that the women were almost five times more likely to be unmarried as the men and, among the currently or previously married, the women were almost three times more likely to be childless (Helmreich et al., 1980). Yet the consequences for productivity were not reported. More research clearly needs to be carried out to determine how the gender role that women are expected to fulfill affects the likelihood of their becoming great psychologists. Besides looking at how marital and parental responsibilities influence creative output, other potentially detrimental aspects of the traditional female role should be investigated. For instance, women may feel more obliged to contribute to a variety of interpersonal relationships beyond just husband and children. One thinks immediately of the awesome task Anna Freud took on in caring for her father during the 16 years in which he fought his losing battle with cancer.

However, perhaps the most interesting empirical question is whether gender roles have converged sufficiently to lessen substantially the obstacles to female eminence in the discipline. To the extent that societal expectations have become much less strongly differentiated according to gender, women would be expected to achieve far more now than they could in the past. There certainly is suggestive anecdotal evidence of substantial gains within the 20th century alone. A concrete illustration can be found in Sandra Bem's (1998) autobiographical *An Unconventional Family*. Her marriage to eminent psychologist Daryl Bem was totally egalitarian at both personal and professional levels. At home, they coparented their three children in a truly equal fashion and did their utmost to raise them in an androgynous, non-gender-stereotypic manner. Irrevocably committed to a genuinely dual-career marriage, when Sandra was denied tenure at Stanford Daryl joined the search for a new position, giving up his own position at the same distinguished institution.

Although the marriage did not survive in the long term, Bem's experience shows how dramatically gender roles can change. Only 50 years earlier, many talented women were far more inclined to withdraw from a career in psychology once they faced the demands of being a wife and mother. This alternative outcome is well illustrated in the life of Lucy May Day, whose truncated career secured her a unique place in psychology's history (Furumoto, 1998). A very gifted student of E. M. Titchener's, in 1911 she had been first author on an article in the *Journal of Animal Behavior* (coauthored with Madison Bentley, among Titchener's more notable students, who had received his doctorate 12 years earlier). The following year Miss Day received her PhD. Her dissertation research was immediately published as an article in the *American Journal of Psychology*, and the succeeding year she was elected a member of APA. She was obviously a woman of great promise, with the potential of becoming a great psychologist, just as another of Titchener's female students, Margaret Floy Washburn, had accomplished. Yet in 1914 Miss Day married another of Titchener's graduate students, who received his own PhD in the same year they both said their marriage vows. Her career aspirations then took a very divergent course. Having taught only 1 year at Vassar College before her marriage and another year at Wells after her marriage, her first child was born in 1916, just 4 years after Lucy had become Dr.

Day. Her last publication appeared in the very next year—an article coauthored with her husband for a volume honoring Titchener.

Although Lucy lived to be nearly 110 years old, her direct contributions to psychology were over. She was soon to have 4 children to raise, and by the end of her life the family had expanded to 7 grandchildren, 4 great-grandchildren, and 2 great-great-grandchildren. Yet she could claim to have contributed indirectly to the discipline. Besides providing the supportive home environment for her hardworking spouse, she read and advised her husband on every book and article that came from his exceptionally busy pen. She thereby became the "woman behind the man," enabling him to become a highly prolific psychologist, a Harvard professor, and an APA president. She even earned enough of a reputation to have her story told in an *American Psychologist* obituary—albeit as the wife of the "great man" E. G. Boring.

It is a tempting "what if" to contemplate what would have happened if Lucy May Day and E. G. Boring had assumed the same egalitarian gender roles as did Sandra and Daryl Bem 50 years later. The history of psychology, and even the history of psychology's history, would probably have been rewritten.

Gender Bias

The counterfactual speculation that closed the preceding section may seem a little exorbitant. Why should anyone infer that Lucy May Boring might have become a great psychologist had she not become a wife and mother instead? One cue comes from something discussed in chapter 10, namely, that eminent scientists tend to earn their PhDs at relatively precocious ages. By this criterion, Miss Day had received her doctoral degree at an age fairly typical of great psychologists: 26. To put this achievement into context, her husband, E. G. Boring, and her collaborator, M. Bentley, who worked under the same mentor, were 28 and 29, respectively. The 2-year gap between Lucy and E. G. Boring was replicated by Sandra and Daryl Bem (24 vs. 26). What makes Lucy Day's doctoral performance even more impressive is that women tend to earn their doctorates at older ages than men anyway. For instance, in a sample of nearly 300 experimental social psychologists, the men were around age 28 and the women 30 when they earned their PhDs (Helmreich et al., 1980). For a more eminent sample of 69 American psychologists, the differences between the means were even greater: 28 versus 34, or a gap of 6 years (Simonton, 1992b). Thus, if anything, Day should have been older, not younger, than her husband was when she attained her highest degree.

To some extent, the environmental factors already discussed probably contribute to the woman's decelerated progression through programs that lead to the higher degree. Women are socialized to have certain priorities— and are obliged to occupy certain roles—that might compel them to assign lowered priority to the completion of degree requirements. Besides causing women to take longer to complete the requirements, this may also induce women not to finish at all, converting them into graduate school dropouts. This difference was demonstrated in an empirical study of all graduate students who entered the psychology graduate program at the University Illinois at Urbana–Champaign between 1965 and 1970 (Hirschberg & Itkin, 1978). Only 35% of the women had earned their degree by 1975, whereas the rate for the men was almost double that: 68%. Even fellow graduate students were less likely to predict that their female peers would finish the program in 4 years.

As distressing as these influences can be, it could be worse: Until recent times, women had to overcome an even more severe obstacle to greatness—outright prejudice and discrimination. Christine Ladd-Franklin obtained her bachelor's degree from Vassar, a woman's college, and later obtained a fellowship to attend Johns Hopkins for advanced study in mathematics and logic. By 1882, when she was 35, she had completed the requirements for a PhD but found that the school was not willing to award her the degree. It seems that the university did not officially recognize female candidates, and so her graduate work was discounted. She had to wait until 1926 for the injustice to be rectified.

Although Ladd-Franklin was then 78, at least she finally got what she deserved. As is well known, Mary Calkins was not nearly so lucky. Working under William James, she had fulfilled all the requirements for a PhD in 1895, at age 32. Despite the enthusiastic recommendation of her professors, Harvard would not give her the degree, because of her gender. It is astonishing how long Harvard's authorities remained adamant on this issue. By 1903 non-Dr. Calkins was rated among the top American psychologists, a reputation endorsed in 1905 when she became president of APA—the first woman to be so recognized. In 1918 she also became the first woman elected president of the American Philosophical Association, and 10 years later she became the first woman elected as an honorary member of the British Psychological Association. She obtained honorary degrees from both Columbia University and Smith College (her alma mater) in 1909 and 1910, respectively. Yet Harvard resisted repeated attempts to reverse its decision, even as late as 1927, just 3 years before she died. The sole concession was an institutional willingness to grant her a degree of Radcliff, which did not have a graduate program. Rightly, Calkins refused.

The Johns Hopkins and Harvard episodes were blatant. Both institutions made it clear that they were not in the business of bestowing doctoral degrees on women. Although such institutionalized sexism is history in most of the industrial world, more subtle forms of antifemale prejudice and discrimination are not. One guise of gender bias occurs when a woman seeks her first position at a research university. Women with identical qualifications as men are nonetheless perceived as less adequate candidates (Fidell, 1970; Glick, Zion, & Nelson, 1988). One consequence is that they tend to be appointed at inferior levels or else hired by less prestigious institutions (Helmreich et al., 1980; Simonton, 1992b). This puts women at a definite disadvantage compared to equally competent men who manage to obtain positions that are more supportive of independent research. One long-term consequence of this differential placement may be that talented women who enter the most prestigious universities will not find the female professors they need to serve as their mentors (see, e.g., Goldstein, 1979). Women, more than men, may need guidance from same-gender mentors in order to succeed in a male-dominated world.

As if this were not a sufficient handicap, the ideas of female psychologists may not receive due recognition from male psychologists. There appears to be a gender bias in citation practices, so that men are more likely to cite the work of men, whereas women are more likely to cite the work of women, a pattern that cannot be attributed to the different topics that men and women discuss (Ferber, 1986). A similar own-gender favoritism appears in the literature cited in psychology textbooks (Roeckelein, 1996c) and in praise bestowed by book reviewers (Moore, 1978). Although the bias operates both ways, it probably harms women more than men, at least so long as men dominate the scientific enterprise. A man who does not receive the appreciation he deserves from women will suffer less than a woman whose work does not receive due attention from men.

It is fortunate that the negative consequences of sexist prejudice and discrimination have been declining over the course of psychology's history. This secular trend is apparent in the changes in the representation of women among great psychologists, as displayed in Figure 12.1. This graph is based on the entries in a recent biographical dictionary of psychology (Sheehy et al., 1997). Each individual is assigned to the decade in which he or she was born; the consecutive decades span from 1800–1809 to 1950–1959. It is obvious that women were nonexistent in the days of Gustav Fechner and other German physiologists. Women did not start appearing until one third of the way through the 19th century, and even then they disappeared in mid-century. Although women recovered soon after that setback, their representation oscillated around a meager 10% until after World War II. Only in the last cohort did the percentage shoot up, and even then it maximized at 33%, still far short of the proportion of women in the general population.

Gender Milieu

Figure 12.1 provokes the question: Why does the representation of women among great psychologists fluctuate so radically over time? It is obvious that nature cannot provide the explanation, for it is difficult to imagine how the biology of being a woman could change so rapidly. Instead, the explanation must reside with nurture. The various environmental factors that enhance or inhibit female achievement must also change over the course of history. Gender socialization, roles, and bias are all embedded in a larger

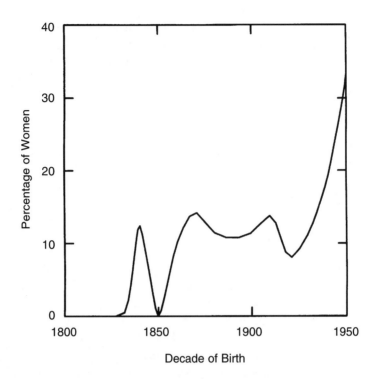

Figure 12.1. Percentage of eminent psychologists who are female as a function of birth year. The data are tabulated in consecutive decades from 1800–1809 to 1950–1959, where the sample consisted of all individuals granted entries in Sheehy, Chapman, and Conroy's (1997) *Biographical Dictionary of Psychology*. The curve was smoothed with the Spline function.

sociocultural system. This system includes economic, political, social, cultural, religious, and ideological components that provide the foundation of how women will be raised and treated at a particular time and place. I demonstrated the operation of these systemic factors in a historiometric study of the course of Japanese civilization (Simonton, 1992a). I tabulated the number of eminent women in consecutive generations since 580 AD and then compared this number witih the ups and downs in the predominance of two contextual factors that were hypothesized to affect the emergence of feminine genius. The first factor was militarism, a measure of the society's emphasis on war, conquest, military leadership, machismo, and the code of the warrior, as exemplified by the samurai. The second factor was Confucianism, an index of the predominance of a Chinese ideology that stresses the intrinsic inferiority of women vis-à-vis men. According to the generational time series analysis, both militarism and Confucianism were negatively associated with the presence of eminent Japanese women. Furthermore, this detrimental consequence even held for literary creativity, a domain in which women had made signal contributions to the civilization of Japan.

Empirical research has yet to determine whether comparable systemic factors are responsible for the fluctuations shown in Figure 12.1. Even so, it appears likely that the connection between gender and genius in psychology's history has deep roots in the more comprehensive features of the sociocultural milieu. This gender-based zeitgeist may even shape the ideas produced at a particular point in psychology's history. This assertion is nothing new, for historians of psychology often evoke such systemic effects to explain some of the strange errors that permeate the annals of the discipline. "An illustration of the effects of the zeitgeist is seen in the research of Pierre-Paul Broca," noted Hothersall (1990, p. 3). In particular, Broca was

> convinced that women are an inferior product of evolution, that their brains are significantly less developed than those of men, and that this difference in brain size increases with each generation. We now know that his conclusions not only were in error, but were based on inadequate and poorly conducted research. However, since they were in harmony with the prevailing assumptions and beliefs of the time, they went unchallenged. (Hothersall, 1990, p. 3)

Is it mere accident that Broca was born and raised in a generation in which the proportion of women among eminent psychologists was exactly zero?

Needless to say, the existence of these sociocultural influences should inspire some doubts about the scientific validity of attempts to prove that women are innately inferior to men. If the ideas that psychologists promote reflect extraneous contextual factors, can those ideas be trusted to represent truth rather than opinion? Those who still advocate the supremacy of nature over nurture admittedly might argue that an explicit connection between their theories and the larger zeitgeist has not been scientifically proven. Yet so much research demonstrates the pervasive effects of the sociocultural milieu on the history of ideas that it strains credulity to claim that gender theories are somehow insulated from these effects. The full force and relevance of these empirical findings will become apparent in Part V.

In the meantime, I think this chapter can best close with this conclusion: Although nature probably plays a big part in determining who comes a great psychologist, nurture likely claims the largest role in deciding whether that psychologist will be male or female.

V

SOCIOCULTURAL CONTEXT OF PSYCHOLOGICAL SCIENCE

INTRODUCTION:
SOCIOCULTURAL CONTEXT
OF PSYCHOLOGICAL SCIENCE

Even Francis Galton's strongest admirers cannot read *Hereditary Genius* (1869) without wincing more than once. Pure logic sometimes fails him in his arguments, and often the data fall short of supporting the inferences drawn. Galton's flimsy, even wispy conjectures about Isaac Newton's supposed pedigree is but one of numerous examples. However, the passages that cause the most embarrassment to most contemporary readers are those that gauge the relative superiority and inferiority of different human "races." In these passages Galton betrays a racism that may have been a little excessive even for the Victorian times in which he lived. These racist ideas are found in the chapter entitled "The Comparative Worth of Different Races." According to Galton's calculations, "the average ability of the Athenian race is, on the lowest possible estimate, very nearly two grades higher than our own—that is, about as much as our race is above that of the African Negro" (1892/ 1972, p. 397). Although Galton was willing to rate the ancient Athenians as superior to the British, he had no doubt that his own race was just as superior to native Africans.

To be sure, this conclusion might be said to follow inevitably from his theoretical assumptions. He assumed that exceptional natural ability would necessarily take the form of renowned genius. Therefore, if his lists of geniuses included few individuals of African ancestry, then it follows from his suppositions that the African populations had lower mean levels of natural ability. According to my own inspection of his lists, eminent figures with African roots were overlooked completely. Especially remarkable was Galton's complete omission of the two Alexandre Dumas' (father and son) from the family pedigrees of "Literary Men." Yet it should be emphasized that in compiling his pedigrees, Galton made no attempt whatsoever to gather together a truly international collection of appropriate reference works. On the contrary, he relied on a single biographical reference, the *Dictionary of the Men of the Time*, which was published in Great Britain and was dominated by entries for British luminaries.

It is not only Galton's data source that must be called into question but also the interpretation of his data. Galton was such a stalwart believer in the primacy of nature over nurture that he could not entertain the slightest doubt that the Athenian Golden Age had to have a genetic foundation. The Greeks were a master race, boasting a mean level of "natural ability" far above the norm, even for the British. His mind was completely closed to the possibility that the "Glory that was Greece" might have had an environmental cause. Faced with the historical fact of the eventual decline of Greek civilization, Galton was obliged to explicate this event in terms of dysgenic practices.

> We know, and may guess something more, of the reason why this marvellously-gifted race declined. Social morality grew exceedingly lax; marriage became unfashionable, and was avoided; many of the more ambitious and accomplished women were avowed courtesans, and consequently infertile, and the mothers of the incoming population were of a heterogeneous class. In a small sea-bordered country, where emigration and immigration are constantly going on, and where the manners are as dissolute as were those of Greece in the period of which I speak, the purity of a race would necessarily fail. It can be, therefore, no surprise to us, though it has been a severe misfortune to humanity, that the high Athenian breed decayed and disappeared; for if it had maintained its excellence, and had multiplied and spread over large countries, displacing inferior populations (which it well might have done, for it was naturally very prolific), it would assuredly have accomplished results advantageous to human civilisation, to a degree that transcends our powers of imagination. (1892/1972, p. 398)

In chapter 12 I argue that individual differences in greatness as a psychologist may have a genetic foundation, at least in part. Yet in the same chapter I also propose that gender differences in greatness are more grounded in nurture than in nature. Among those environmental influences was the sociocultural context. In the two chapters that follow, I further document the impact of these systemic factors. These factors may be divided into two kinds (Simonton, 1981). The first entails the internal milieu, that is, the circumstances specific to a particular creative enterprise, such as the state of knowledge within a given discipline at a specified point in time. The second concerns the external milieu, or factors that involve events and processes that impinge on creative activity from the outside, such as the state of the economy or the political circumstances in which the creator must function. Empirical research on these two contextual factors strongly suggests that the Golden Age of Greece, or of any other great civilization, owes far more to nurture than to nature. Some sociocultural conditions nurture the emergence of creative genius, and some snuff it out. There is no need to evoke the concept of master races and dysgenic behaviors to explain the rise and fall of the world's civilizations.

Although this research undermines Galton's genetic interpretation, the same findings are sometimes used to challenge the whole Galtonian concept of individual genius. After all, if greatness is a function of sociocultural circumstances, then how can the individual's personal qualities and capacities even be relevant? Why are chapters 3–12 even necessary to explain the phenomenon of creativity and discovery? Therefore, I close Part V with a chapter that scrutinizes the complex interplay between genius and zeitgeist. This scrutiny is especially urgent if psychologists are going to have any relevance to understanding their own history.

13

INTERNAL MILIEU

"Some are born great, some achieve greatness, and some have greatness thrust upon 'em," wrote William Shakespeare (quoted in Browning, 1986, p. 140). Of these three alternative routes to fame, the last is the most intriguing here. In some instances, the greatness of a particular luminary in the annals of psychology appears to be the consequence of being at the right place and at the right time rather than being the "right" person. For instance, "Titchener was a lesser psychologist than Wundt, but a more influential one. He lacked Wundt's originality and breadth, but he had the good fortune of residing in America where historical forces dictated the major center of psychology would be" (Kendler, 1987, p. 53). Edward B. Titchener joined the faculty at Cornell University in 1892, the same year that the American Psychological Association (APA) was founded. Just two years before, William James had published *Principles of Psychology*, and just five years previously G. Stanley Hall had established the *American Journal of Psychology*, with Titchener himself taking over the editorship in 1895. Neither was Titchener the sole foreigner attracted to the opportunities that the United States then offered. At the same time that Cornell brought in Titchener, Harvard acquired Hugo Münsterberg and the University of Chicago hired Adolf Meyer and Jacques Loeb. Of course, the decade of the 1890s also saw the emergence of several native great psychologists, including Frank and James Rowland Angell, James Mark Baldwin,

Mary Calkins, James McKeen Cattell, John Dewey, Charles H. Judd, George Herbert Mead, Edward W. Scripture, Carl E. Seashore, George M. Stratton, Edward Lee Thorndike, Margaret Floy Washburn, and Lightner Witmer. Within the first 20 years of the 20th century, American psychologists were the leading proponents of new schools of psychological thought: functionalism and behaviorism. In time, the United States began to dominate the history of psychology, exerting a hegemony that would last to the 21st century.

This confluence of greatness in a particular place and time is not unlike the Golden Age of Greece, only operating on a miniature scale and tied to a specific scientific discipline. From a purely psychological perspective, such a temporal and spatial clustering of first-rate minds would seem almost a miracle. William James (1880), for one, had this to say about the phenomenon:

> Sporadic great men come everywhere. But for a community to get vibrating through and through with intensely active life, many geniuses coming together and in rapid succession are required. This is why great epochs are so rare,—why the sudden bloom of a Greece, an early Rome, a Renaissance, is such a mystery. Blow must follow blow so fast that no cooling can occur in the intervals. Then the mass of the nation glows incandescent, and may continue to glow by pure inertia long after the originators of its internal movement have passed away. We often hear surprise expressed that in these high tides of human affairs not only the people should be filled with stronger life, but that individual geniuses should seem so exceptionally abundant. This mystery is just about as deep as the time-honored conundrum as to why great rivers flow by great towns. It is true that great public fermentations awaken and adopt many geniuses who in more torpid times would have had no chance to work. But over and above this there must be an exceptional concourse of genius about a time, to make the fermentation begin at all. The unlikeliness of the *concourse* is far greater than the unlikeliness of any particular genius; hence the rarity of these periods and the exceptional aspect which they always wear. (p. 453)

It appears as though James was operating according to the principle that if the probability of a single genius occurring is 1 out of 10,000, then the probability of a cluster of 10 geniuses occurring would be 1 out of $10,000^{10}$—very low odds indeed. Yet James may be mistaken, so that the odds of 10 geniuses appearing together may be much greater than 1 appearing in isolation. Their concourse is favored because the milieu beyond the circumscribed world of the individual's psychology is what drives the emergence of genius.

As I noted in the introduction to Part V, this milieu may consist of both internal and external factors, and in this chapter I concentrate on the former. Specifically, I discuss the following sociocultural phenomena: Kroeberian configurations, Comtian progress, Kuhnian transformations, Hegelian dialectics, and Mertonian multiples.

KROEBERIAN CONFIGURATIONS

Alfred Kroeber's 1944 book *Configurations of Culture Growth* can be considered one of the classics in the historiometric study of genius. In one respect, this book appears quite similar to Francis Galton's (1869) *Hereditary Genius*: Both contain long lists of illustrious personalities who had achieved distinction in a diversity of domains. Yet on closer examination, some striking differences appear. First, Kroeber's lists are far less ethnocentric than Galton's. Appreciative of the fact that great accomplishments have originated in all parts of the world, Kroeber devoted considerable attention to Islamic, Hindu, Chinese, Japanese, Southeast Asian, and American civilizations. Second, Kroeber's lists include many anonymous achievements, such as the relief sculpture of Ancient Egypt, the Sanskrit *Mahabharata*, and Cambodia's Angkor Wat. Third, Kroeber's chapters are titled in a less individualistic fashion than are Galton's (e.g., "Science," "Painting," "Literature," and "Music," rather than "Men of Science," "Painters," "Literary Men," and "Musicians"). Fourth, and most striking, all of Kroeber's notables are listed in chronological order, whereas all of Galton's are listed in alphabetical order.

These contrasts are not trivial. The last contrast betrays the fact that Kroeber was trying to do something very different than Galton. Kroeber was an eminent cultural anthropologist who had studied under the great Franz Boas. Boas had so emphatically rejected biological interpretations of differences between human groups that the Nazis reacted by rescinding his PhD and burning his books. Kroeber was no less opposed to such nature explanations of cultural differences and thus conceived *Configurations of Culture Growth* (1944) as a direct attack on Galton's genetic determinism. Although "Galton clearly recognized . . . the difference of genius production between fifth-century Athens and nineteenth-century England," wrote Kroeber (1944), "he misinterpreted it by giving the Athenians a hereditary rating as many degrees superior to that of the modern English as these are superior to the African negro" (p. 11). Kroeber maintained that Galton's (1869) conclusions are invalid "because there is a powerful factor of 'environment' at work which he ignored in his search for a biological cause" (Kroeber, 1944, p. 11).

Kroeber believed that the most conclusive evidence against Galton's biological determinism was the distinctive manner in which genius clustered into certain times and places. This happened far too quickly to be attributed to changes in the gene pool of the populations producing those geniuses. Therefore, these clusters must represent the impact of some environmental factor that can change rapidly. Kroeber, believed that this factor must be the sociocultural system. The coming and going of geniuses within a given civilization merely reflect underlying "configurations of culture growth"—hence the book's (1944) title. This environmentalist position also accounted for the distinctive manner in which Kroeber gathered and presented his data. In particular, whereas Galton listed his geniuses in alphabetical order to emphasize family relationships, Kroeber listed his in chronological order to emphasize the degree of clustering.

Kroeber's (1944) treatment of British science is fairly typical of the results he reported for other creative domains and other human civilizations. According to his lists, scientific genius in the British Isles falls into two clusters, the first in the 17th century and the second from the latter part of the 18th century to the end of the 19th. The first contains such notables as William Gilbert, John Napier, William Harvey, John Wallis, Robert Boyle, Edmund Halley, and, of course, the great Isaac Newton. Then, after a lull of about 50 years, British science picks up again, producing such luminaries as James Hutton, Thomas Young, John Dalton, Michael Faraday, Charles Lyell, and, naturally, the great Charles Darwin. It is curious that, according to Kroeber's figures, more British scientists were born in the 1820s than in any other decade represented by his sample. For this period Kroeber's list explicitly featured John Tyndall, Arthur Cayley, Alfred Russell Wallace, Lord Kelvin, Sir William Huggins, T. H. Huxley, Joseph Lister—and Francis Galton himself! This specific cluster demonstrates two things.

1. When Galton (1874) conducted his survey for *English Men of Science*, he had many distinguished scientists from whom to choose (see Hilts, 1975, for a list of those whom Galton surveyed). Of the contemporaries just listed, Galton actually sent out questionnaires to Tyndall, Cayley, Kelvin, Huggins, Huxley, and himself (albeit only Cayley, Huxley, and Galton returned them). In addition, Galton had access to many younger and older contemporaries. In the former group were James Clerk Maxwell and Edward Tylor (the second did not respond) and in the latter group were Richard Owen, Joseph Hooker, Charles Darwin, Charles Lyell, James Sylvester, and James Joule (the last three did not respond). All of these listed, whether respondents or not, were specifically identified by Kroeber (1944) as defining the second configuration of British scientific growth. Galton could not have picked a more propitious time to conduct the first survey of British scientists.

2. Because Galton was himself embedded in a well-defined scientific cluster, or cultural configuration, his argument about the inheritance of genius is undermined by his very own birth year. If he had been born in some forlorn period and locale, isolated from other phenomenal intellects, it would be easy to ascribe Galton's greatness to his supreme natural ability. It would be like his hypothetical changeling experiment on a larger scale. However, because Galton entered the world along

with an exceptional number of notable contemporaries, nurture appears to provide a more plausible cause than does nature. Moreover, the environmentalist explanation can handle facts that Galton's genetic determinism cannot. There certainly is no compulsion to fabricate some fanciful pedigree for Newton, when he sits atop the first great configuration of scientists in British history. Indeed, one might even argue that whatever pedigrees Galton did observe were largely a spurious consequence of the sociocultural milieu. A creative genius may be more likely to have an illustrious child than an illustrious grandchild, not because of the contrast in genetic relatedness, but because the sociocultural milieu differs most for those born farthest apart (Simonton, 1983c).

Configurations of scientific genius appear in various specialties besides. For instance, J. Schneider (1937) conducted an inquiry into the historical placement of 242 eminent English botanists and found comparable clusters for that subdiscipline. Like Kroeber, Schneider concluded that his data flatly contradicted Galton's genetic determinism:

> It is the cultural situation which produces famous men, and not breed. . . . The fact that the birth dates of all kinds of great men group themselves into galaxies is for the present ample proof of the correctness of this belief. (p. 491)

The use of the word *galaxy* is a good one, for the stars of history can be compared to the stars of the heavens. No star stands alone, but rather all stars are the products of astrophysical processes that oblige all stars to form local stellar groups, the latter forming galaxies, and the last in their turn congregating into galactic clusters.

The data are one thing, their interpretation another. Why does genius cluster so? I next examine two general types of explanations. The first assumes that creative geniuses must have predecessors on whom they build their own work. "If I have seen further, it is by standing on the shoulders of giants," said Newton (quoted in *Who Said What When*, 1991, p. 129)—a confession that might be made by all great intellects. The second explanation concentrates on the beneficial effects of having so many contemporaries who are creating ideas within the same field.

Predecessors: Lagged Effects

Alfred Kroeber (1944) himself believed that the configurations resulted from cross-generational influences. Yet when Kroeber tried to specify the reason why this positive association holds, he ended up proposing a process that appears more psychological than cultural. In particular, Kroeber quoted at length the views of Velleius Paterculus, a Roman historian who two millennia earlier had noticed the clustering of genius:

> For who can marvel sufficiently that the most distinguished minds in each branch of human achievement have happened to adopt the same form of effort, and to have fallen within the same narrow space of time. . . . A single epoch, and that only of a few years' duration, gave lustre to tragedy through the three men of divine inspiration, Aeschylus, Sophocles, and Euripedes. . . . The great philosophers, too, received their inspiration from the lips of Socrates . . . how long did they flourish after the death of Plato and Aristotle? What distinction was there in oratory before Isocrates, or after the time of his disciples and in turn of their pupils? So crowded were they into a brief epoch that there were no two worthy of mention who could not have seen each other. (p. 17)

After giving some additional examples from the history of Roman civilization, Velleius added some speculations:

> Though I frequently search for the reasons why men of similar talents occur exclusively in certain epochs and not only flock to one pursuit but also attain like success, I can never find any of whose truth I am certain, though I do find some which perhaps seem likely, and particularly the following. Genius is fostered by emulation, and it is now envy, now admiration, which enkindles imitation, and, in the nature of things, that which is cultivated with the highest zeal advances to the highest perfection. (p. 18)

Thus, according to Velleius, the florescence of creative activity is based on the sociopsychological processes of imitation, emulation, admiration, and envy. Each generation endeavors to surpass the achievements of the preceding generation, eventually reaching the heights of a Golden Age.

But why does the civilization recede from that high point? Velleius answered that

> it is difficult to continue at the point of perfection, and naturally that which cannot advance must recede. And as in the beginning we are fired with the ambition to overtake those whom we regard as leaders, so when we have despaired of being able either to surpass or even to equal them, our zeal wanes with our hope; it ceases to follow what it cannot overtake, and abandoning the old field as though pre-empted, it seeks a new one. Passing over that in which we cannot be pre-eminent, we seek for some new object of our effort. (p. 18)

Kroeber called this process *pattern exhaustion*. Each generation is engaged in conceiving products that work out the implications or potential of a given aesthetic or philosophical system. Once all the best has been extracted, and perfection reached, subsequent creators are left with the cultural dregs. Frederick C. Bartlett (1958), the distinguished British psychologist, described how this exhaustion process often takes place in scientific research:

A mass of routine thinking belonging to an immediately preceding phase [of original work] has come near to wearing itself out by exploiting a limited range of technique to establish more and more minute and specialized detail. A stage has been reached in which finding out further details adds little or nothing to what is known already in the way of opening up unexplored relations. (p. 136)

Creative minds eventually find another domain in which their talents can be better utilized, and a new configuration begins to grow (for indirect evidence, see Marchetti, 1980; Price, 1963).

Apropos of Galton's (1869) claims about the genetic superiority of the Athenian race, Velleius maintained that

a single city of Attica blossomed with more masterpieces of every kind of eloquence than all the rest of Greece together—to such a degree, in fact, that one would think that although the bodies of the Greek race were distributed among the other states, their intellects were confined within the walls of Athens alone. (quoted in Kroeber, 1944, p. 18)

Yet for Velleius, and for Kroeber, this clustering of Athenian greatness could be ascribed to the joint agency of personal emulation and cultural exhaustion.

In one respect, Velleius was in a unique position to make these observations. Active around 30 AD, he found himself situated at the tail end of the greatest period in Roman literary history: the Golden Age of Cicero, Lucretius, Vergil, Horace, and other luminaries. With the passing of Ovid in the early part of the 1st century, Latin literature seemed to have entered a period of decline. With the exception of Seneca, Velleius was without notable contemporaries. Indeed, although shortly after Velleius Roman literature experienced the "Silver Age"—containing Lucan, Martial, Tacitus, Juvenal, and other lesser lights—this resurgence was brief and far less remarkable. Within 100 years after Velleius the Classical period of Roman literature was over. Only the introduction of Christianity would resuscitate Latin as a medium of literary expression, and then in the totally different forms seen in Saint Augustine and other church fathers.

Enough of these speculations—what about scientific tests? It is fortunate that the conjectures of Velleius and Kroeber have been subjected to empirical scrutiny (Simonton, 1984d). Because investigation of this subject requires the introduction of a special methodology, and because this methodology will prove useful in this chapter and in chapters 14 and 15, it is worthwhile to devote some space to outlining its principal characteristics. After that I return to the questions raised by Velleius and Kroeber.

Generational Time-Series Analysis

Although Alfred Kroeber's (1944) raw data consisted of chronological lists of eminent figures in various domains, he realized that the cultural configurations could often be better conceived in terms of a "generation," which he took to represent one third of a century. The individuals making up his lists could then be assigned to that generation in which they attained their peak of productivity. Kroeber (1944) called this optimal career age the person's *acme* or *floruit*, for which age 40 was taken to provide "an unusually sound average estimate" (p. 27). As round numbers go, this figure certainly falls in line with the research reviewed in chapter 4. Thus, a generation consisted of geniuses who attained their career acmes within the same third of a century. In accord with Kroeber's basic thesis, genius was not randomly distributed over the generations but rather appeared to be concentrated in certain periods, whereas other periods displayed a paucity, if not total absence, of genius.

By introducing the generation concept, Kroeber was actually following an old tradition in the social sciences. Auguste Comte, John Stuart Mill, Wilhelm Dilthey, Karl Mannheim, and José Ortega y Gasset, among many others, viewed the generation as an ideal unit for conceiving transhistorical changes in the sociocultural milieu. Most of these thinkers merely viewed the generation as an aggregation of individuals, an aggregation that lacked significance at the individual level. The Spanish philosopher Ortega y Gasset (1933/1958), however, attempted to conceive the generation in a manner that would integrate aggregate and individual levels. Ortega y Gasset began with the schematic division of the person's life span into five ages of 15 years each. The first 30 years are devoted to the periods of childhood (0–15) and youth (15–30), and the last 15 years are assigned to old age (60–75). Between are the age of *initiation* (30–45) and the age of *dominance* (45–60). The former is the period of creativity and the latter of command. In Ortega y Gasset's model the characteristics of successive generations are the aggregate manifestations of underlying developmental transitions occurring in the individual's life.

Neither Ortega y Gasset nor Kroeber, or any of their predecessors, went beyond a fairly qualitative conception of the generation. As a consequence, the concept did not lend itself to the kind of precise statistical analysis that Galton (1869) could use in *Hereditary Genius*. Kroeber (1944) himself expressed begrudging admiration of Galton's quantitative analysis and certainly would have wished to have offered something comparable in his argument on behalf of sociocultural determinism. Nonetheless, with a few modifications, it is possible to integrate Kroeber's and Ortega y Gasset's ideas into a methodological strategy that lends itself to a powerful analytical technique, namely, time-series analysis. The resulting integration is called *generational time-series analysis* (Simonton, 1984c; cf. Sheldon, 1979, 1980). This technique may be described as follows:

1. The historical period under consideration is subdivided into consecutive generations. In a departure from tradition, these time units are defined by 20-year intervals, or five genera-

tions per century. Figure 13.1 shows the corresponding historical slices for the formative period of psychology's history: 1820–1839, 1840–1859, 1860–1879, 1880–1899, and 1900–1919. Then, adopting Kroeber's procedure, a given historical figure is assigned to the 20-year unit in which he or she attained age 40. Individuals who died before they turned 40 are still assigned as if they had done so, for reasons that become clearer shortly. Thus, on this basis, to the generation of 1880–1899 may be assigned William James, Josef Breuer, Camillo Golgi, G. Stanley Hall, Friedrich Wilhelm Nietzsche, Christine Ladd-Franklin, Carl Stumpf, Ivan Pavlov, Hermann Ebbinghaus, Santiago Ramón y Cajal, Sigmund Freud, Karl Pearson, Alfred Binet, Havelock Ellis, and Pierre Janet—all of whom were born between 1842 and 1859 inclusively. I now identify all the individuals who have been assigned to this period as "Generation g."

2. Assuming that the list of famous personalities is sufficiently dense, there will be a respectable number of people in most or all generations. As a result, it is possible to speak of the average characteristics of those who compose a particular generation. In particular, the average person assigned Generation g, or any other generation, will be 40 years old. Furthermore, the typical individual will be around 30 at the beginning of this period and around 50 at the end of this period. The 30–50 age interval corresponds very closely with what I discussed in chapter 4. The first career landmark tends to appear around age 30, the last around 50. Hence, the average person is assigned to the generation in which most of his or her most outstanding contributions are likely to have been made. This interval may be called the individual's *productive period*. To be sure, those whose birth years place them at the beginning of the generation will have their earlier careers truncated, just as those whose birth years put them at the end of the generation will have their later careers cut off. Yet the generational analysis works with what is average rather than with what is exceptional. In that respect, individual characteristics are submerged in the aggregate. In the specific case of Generation g in Figure 13.1, the mean age is 39, and this statistic would be even closer to 40 had even more great psychologists of the time been included.

3. If a typical member of Generation g is 40, then those members will be around 20 years old in the preceding generation, or what I designate Generation g – 1. More accurately stated, the average individual will be between ages 10 and 30 in this

DATE

1820–1839	1840–1859	1860–1879	1880–1899	1900–1919
	GENERATION $g-2$			
Developmental period (age 20 ± 10)	Productive period (age 40 ± 10)	Consolidative period (age 60 ± 10) ↓		
		GENERATION $g-1$		
	Developmental period (age 20 ± 10)	Productive period (age 40 ± 10)	Consolidative period (age 60 ± 10) ↓	
			GENERATION g	
		Developmental period (age 20 ± 10)	Productive period (age 40 ± 10)	Consolidative period (age 60 ± 10)

GENERATIONAL PLACEMENT OF SOME GREAT 19TH CENTURY PSYCHOLOGISTS

$g-2$ Fechner 1801–1887, J. Müller 1801–1858, C. Darwin 1809–1882, Bernard 1813–1878, Ludwig 1816–1895, Brown-Séquard 1817–1894, Lotze 1817–1881, Donders 1818–1889, Bain 1818–1903, DuBois-Reymond 1818–1896, Brücke 1819–1892

$g-1$ Spencer 1820–1903, Helmholtz 1821–1894, Galton 1822–1911, Liébeault 1823–1904, Broca 1824–1880, Charcot 1825–1893, Aubert 1826–1892, Pflüger 1829–1910, Sechenov 1829–1905, Wundt 1832–1920, Meynert 1833–1892, Dilthey 1833–1911, Hering 1834–1918, C. Lange 1834–1900, Lombroso 1835–1909, Hitzig 1838–1907, Mach 1838–1916, Fritsch 1838–1927, Brentano 1838–1917, Ribot 1839–1916

g Bernheim 1840–1919, Le Bon 1841–1931, James 1842–1910, Breuer 1842–1925, Golgi 1843–1926, Avenarius 1843–1896, G. S. Hall 1844–1924, Nietzsche 1844–1900, Emmert 1844–1911, Ladd-Franklin 1847–1930, Stumpf 1848–1936, Pavlov 1849–1936, Ebbinghaus 1850–1905, G. E. Müller 1850–1934, C. L. Morgan 1852–1936, Ramón y Cajal 1852–1934, Féré 1852–1907, Prince 1854–1929, Kraepelin 1856–1926, S. Freud 1856–1939, Bekhterev 1857–1927, Coué 1857–1926, Pearson 1857–1939, Binet 1857–1911, Babinski 1857–1932, Sherrington 1857–1952, Ellis 1859–1939, Loeb 1859–1924, Janet 1859–1947, Bergson 1859–1941, Dewey 1859–1952

Figure 13.1. Representative segment of a generational time series, extending five 20-year periods from 1820 to 1919. Correspondence between generational assignment and life span developmental periods are shown. Also given are illustrations of the generational placement of some notables from psychology's history.

interval. According to this scheme, this interval is labeled the *developmental period* of the individual's life. It is during this phase that the person is most susceptible to various environmental influences, especially role models and mentors, that contribute to the development of a person's creative potential (Simonton, 1997b). In terms of Kroeber's (1944) views, it would be during the developmental period that the imitation and emulation processes would presumably kick in. Who are the objects of this admiration? As is immediately apparent from inspection of Figure 13.1, the answer can be found in the individuals tallied into Generation $g - 1$. Going by the 40-year floruit assignment, this interval might include such figures as Herbert Spencer, Hermann von Helmholtz, Francis Galton, Paul Broca, Jean-Martin Charcot, Wilhelm Wundt, Cesare Lombroso, Ernst Mach, and Franz Brentano. Moreover, the members of Generation g would be ideally suited to fulfill the role required by the Velleius–Kroeber hypothesis: They will be in their own peak productive period. Hence, the count of distinguished figures in Generation $g - 1$ is tantamount to a measure of role model availability for individuals in Generation g who are at that time in their developmental period (Simonton, 1984c). During this crucial period, these individuals should be engaged in the formation of their identities, as Erik Erikson (1968) outlined in his stage theory of psychosocial development. Also during this period the person should begin to acquire the expertise required for achievement later, as I discussed in chapters 10 and 12.

4. As Figure 13.1 makes clear, it is not just Generation $g - 1$ that can provide role models for Generation g but also Generation $g - 2$. For a generational analysis of the history of psychology, this earlier generation might include Gustav Theodor Fechner, Johannes Müller, Charles Darwin, Claude Bernard, Franciscus Cornelius Donders, Alexander Bain, and Ernst Brücke. However, these individuals will generally not be at the acme of their careers. Instead, they will have entered the third period of their life according to this scheme, namely, what has been labeled, for lack of a better word, the *consolidative period*. That is, when members of Generation g are 20 ± 10 years old, members of Generation $g - 2$ will be 60 ± 10. It consequently is likely the luminaries two generations removed from those in Generation g will be less effective role models. As I noted in chapter 4, their best work is more likely behind them and, as I observed in chapter 11, scientists who are past their prime may be less effective mentors. In addition, of course, many of

the individuals in Generation $g - 2$ will already be deceased by the time those in Generation g enter their developmental period.

5. Given a sequence of consecutive generations of sufficient length, the next step is to perform a time-series analysis (Box, Jenkins, & Reinsel, 1994). Specifically, the following equation can be fit to the data (Simonton, 1990d):

$$y_g = \phi_1 y_{g-1} + \phi_2 y_{g-2} + a_g \tag{13.1}$$

This is the equation for what is called *second-order autoregression*. The data-transformed tabulations of eminent figures at Generation g provide the dependent variable y_g, which is regressed onto the corresponding tabulations at Generations $g - 1$ and $g - 2$: y_{g-1} and y_{g-2}, respectively. The autoregressive parameters ϕ_1 and ϕ_2 assess the magnitude of the same two effects. Finally, a_g represents an independent random shock, in a manner identical to the error term in a regular regression equation. If the Velleius–Kroeber interpretation is correct, then $\phi_1 > 0$; that is, the count of eminent figures in Generation g should be a positive linear function of the count at Generation $g - 1$. Under most conditions, moreover, $\phi_2 < \phi_1$, and perhaps may even approach zero. In words, predecessors in their productive period should provide role models superior to those in their consolidative period. Finally, but less obviously, when the residuals of the autoregression are closely examined they should exhibit a random temporal distribution (i.e., *white noise*, according to the jargon of the technique). This latter demonstration permits the conclusion that some other stochastic process (viz., a third-order autoregressive or even moving-average model) does not better explicate the generational time series. Instead, the clustering of genius into contiguous generations is totally explained in terms of the autoregressive process that provides the formal representation of the role modeling effects. The number of geniuses in any given generation would be a simple function of the number of geniuses in the preceding generation who are available for imitation and emulation.

That, in a nutshell, is how generational time-series analysis works. Of course, there are several complications in the actual procedure. The raw data usually must undergo several transformations, such as special operations to remove any secular trends (e.g., linear or exponential). Moreover, often the generational counts are weighted so that the more eminent figures in the field provide more points than the less eminent (e.g., C. E. Gray, 1958, 1966;

Simonton, 1975d, 1988b; Sorokin, 1937–1941). For instance, in quantifying the total genius exhibited by Generation g in Figure 13.1, it would make sense to give Pavlov more points than, say, Coué. Yet these niceties should not distract one from the main point: Generational time-series analysis provides a direct test of whether the clustering of genius can be explained in terms of the cross-generational effects described by Velleius and Kroeber (1944).

Role Model Availability

The history of psychology proper is unfortunately too short to permit the application of the technique just outlined. Even with the most liberal definition of the discipline, the units would number only 12 or so. At five generations per century, it would take a millennium before there would be sufficient degrees of freedom to apply time-series methods. Nonetheless, the technique has been applied to related domains of achievement that enjoy much longer histories. With only a few minor exceptions, these studies have supported the first-order autoregressive model (Simonton, 1975d, 1988b, 1992a). The results of my inquiry into Chinese civilization are representative (Simonton, 1988b). I began my investigation by compiling a chronological listing of all the major figures in Chinese history from 840 BC to AD 1979. In this compilation I incorporated all of the individuals listed in Kroeber's (1944) work as well as thousands more drawn from dozens of histories, chronologies, biographical dictionaries, and encyclopedias. I divided the 10,160 luminaries so selected into distinctive achievement domains and then assigned them to 141 consecutive 20-year periods.

Of special relevance were the generational time series I constructed for philosophy, mathematics, physical sciences, and the biological sciences—the four groups with the closest affinity with psychology in its own historical development (Simonton, 1988b). In every single case, the number of eminent figures at Generation g was a positive function of the number at Generation g − 1 but not of the number at Generation g − 2. The autoregressive parameters (i.e., the ϕ_1s) were as follows: philosophy, .50; mathematics, .51; physical sciences, .38; and biological sciences, .29. These results obtained for the unweighted tabulations, but pretty much the same findings appeared when the counts were weighted according to the differential distinction attained by the various philosophers, mathematicians, and physical and biological scientists. The only difference was that the autoregressive parameters were often smaller, ranging between .23 for the biological sciences and .38 for the physical sciences. For both weighted and unweighted generational time series, the first-order parameter was statistically significant and positive, whereas the second-order parameter was not statistically significant and was close to zero.

Finally, but quite important, all eight time series became random (i.e., were reduced to white noise) once the effects of the first-order autoregression were extracted (Simonton, 1988b). The clustering of genius could thus be totally explained in terms of the association between two contiguous generations. When Kroeber (1944) discussed the Chinese philosophical tradition, he pointed out the existence of several distinct clusters. Two were especially critical in the evolution of Chinese thought: the Chou period, which included such masters as Lao Tzu (Laozi), Confucius (Kongfuzi), Chuang Tzu (Zuangzi), and Mencius (Mengzi), and the Sung period, which included the great neo-Confucianist Chu Hsi (Zhu Xi). Yet when the hundreds of notable thinkers making up this tradition are assigned to their appropriate generation and a first-order autoregressive model is fitted to the resulting time series, no clustering remains in the residuals. The configurations of cultural growth are completely accounted for by the cross-generational dependency.

Given the foregoing results, it seems highly likely that a similar role modeling process has played a major role in psychology's history, however short the period in which it has had the opportunity to operate. In particular, this phenomenon can help explain the continuity that is often seen in specific disciplinary traditions. Consider, for instance, the following observation: "A succession of able pupils gave French psychiatry a supreme position during the first half of the century—and indeed down the years" (Thomson, 1968, p. 198). Role modeling effects can take many forms, but the most obvious and direct are the mentor–student or master–disciple relationships discussed in chapter 11. Hence, the greater is the availability of role models, the higher is the likelihood that these direct relationships can maintain the discipline's vitality. Several examples are apparent in Figure 13.1, such as Charcot–Janet, two exemplars of the French psychiatric tradition.

Although the autoregressive model does such a great job explicating the data, two problems remain to be addressed. The first, and least critical, is that it fails to specify the scope of the domains to which it applies. In trying to explicate a florescence in great psychologists, for instance, should one construct generational tabulations of just psychologists, or should scientists in general be included—or perhaps creative activity of all kinds? To some extent it is the creativity of the whole civilization that may stimulate the blossoming of specific cultural components (Simonton, 1996b). Also, to an even greater degree, the creativity in one scientific specialty might be responsive to the creativity in a closely related scientific specialty (Simonton, 1975c). To provide a concrete illustration, I (Simonton, 1976e) specifically looked at whether there existed any cross-generational influences that also operated across disciplines. Although I used 25-year periods and tabulated scientific discoveries rather than discoverers, the results still seem applicable to the current question. This application seems especially appropriate, because the creative activity in some scientific disciplines was actually shown to be a positive function of the amount of activity 25 years earlier in certain kindred disciplines. The best example is biological discoveries, which are responsive, after a 25-year delay, to major discoveries in medicine, chemistry, and geology. Needless to say, many concrete cases of such cross-disciplinary influences are easy to identify in psychology's own history. One prominent case is Darwin's 1859 *Origin of Species*, which was published about 25 years after Lyell's 1830–1833 *Principles of Geology*, the single most crucial work that Darwin read while he served as naturalist aboard the *Beagle*.

Second, and more critical, is the apparent fact that the autoregressive model has left something out of the Velleius–Kroeber formulation. The model captures the hypothesized impact of imitation, admiration, or emulation, but what about the notion of pattern exhaustion? Both Velleius and Kroeber argued that once a given creative domain reaches a certain climax of perfection, subsequent generations are doomed to participate in its disintegration. Florescence is followed by decadence. Yet the autoregressive model seems to account for the positive process only, not the negative. The response to this objection is simple and direct: It is completely unnecessary to include this negative process to explicate the phenomenon of clustering. The clustering of genius across history is totally explained by the autoregressive link between contiguous generations. Although one might think that this would lead to an incessant increase in the number of great intellects over time, that inference is unjustified. The secret lies in the addition of the random shock term in Equation 13.1 (i.e., a_g). This term incorporates all of the factors besides role model availability that have an impact on the number of eminent creators in Generation g. Sometimes this impact will be negative, and sometimes it will be positive, discouraging or encouraging the manifestation of creativity at a given time. Moreover, some of the factors will entail influences that operate within the discipline, whereas other factors will involve forces impinging from the outside world. Thus, a_g contains a huge inventory of potential causes, a large number of which I discuss later in this book. However, right now it is more imperative to deal with a second facet of the Kroeberian configurations.

Contemporaries: Synchronous Associations

Earlier I said that generational time series could consist of either unweighted or weighted counts of historical figures. I also stated that these alternative operational definitions of transhistorical fluctuations in creative activity yield the same basic conclusions. For both weighted and unweighted measures, the score at Generation g is a positive function of the score at $g - 1$, that is, the time series exhibit first-order autoregression. This concurrence implies that the greatest figures of history tend to appear in the same generations as do the lesser figures. I (Simonton, 1988b) found empirical support for this inference in a generational time-series analysis of 10,160 notables of Chinese civilization. For each domain of achievement I split these individuals into major and minor figures, according to the number of times they were mentioned in various sources. On average, the major figures constituted about one third of the total count. After I tabulated the major and minor figures into their separate generational time series I assessed the cross-correlations between the two series; that is, I calculated for various lags the correlations between major and minor figures.

The outcome was unambiguous: In every single domain, the synchronous correlation between the two series was the highest of all (Simonton, 1988b). The greater was the degree of lag, no matter what the direction, the smaller the size of the cross-correlation. Hence, the activity of major creators does not tend to stimulate the activity of minor creators with a delay of one or more generations, neither did the activity of minor creators stimulate the activity of major creators after some generational lag in the reverse direction. Furthermore, the synchronous correlations were all of respectable magnitude. To cite the statistics most relevant to psychological science, the correlations were .54 for the philosophers, .49 for the mathematicians, .32 for the physical scientists, and .46 for the biological scientists (or .36, .41, .31, and .26, respectively, for detrended data). Great and small tend to be contemporaries or, as one history of psychology author more dramatically expressed it, "creative geniuses are always surrounded by a host of humdrum practitioners" (Hearnshaw, 1987, p. 247).

What accounts for the generational simultaneity of major and minor figures? One possibility is simply that the appearances of both great and small are likewise contingent on the availability of role models in the previous generation; that is, if role model availability encourages the development of creative potential, then that positive effect might hold for both the stars and the dimmer lights. Another explanation might be derived from the equal-odds rule discussed in chapters 3 and 4. If quality is a function of quantity with respect to products, might not the same hold for producers? The more individuals who are active in a particular domain, the higher should be the odds that a subset of them might attain true greatness (see, e.g., Lawani, 1986). This might happen on the basis of pure chance, or it might occur according to the principle of the cross-sectional distribution of the personal traits that contribute to greatness (as discussed in chapters 6 and 7). The more individuals participate in a particular creative activity, the higher would be the probability of having someone whose intellect and character place him or her at the extreme upper tail of the curve, whether that curve be normal or lognormal. Something like this has been shown to account for the hegemony of Russians in chess (Charness & Gerchak, 1996), so the same principle might apply here, too. The more impressive the number of individuals active in a given generation, the higher are the prospects for someone to emerge at the very uppermost heights of greatness.

These explanations all view extreme greatness as a passive or incidental outcome of the sheer mass of activity in a particular generation. Yet it could be that the connection between great and small is more dynamic and direct than these interpretations imply. Once a certain "critical mass" is reached, a "chain reaction" might take place by which individuals are inspired to reach higher levels of creativity (see, e.g., Fowler, 1987). One basis for this belief is the Price law, introduced in chapter 3. The original formulation of this law was expressed in a provocative manner, namely, that "the total number of scientists goes up as the square, more or less, of the number of good ones" (Price, 1963, p. 53). The "good ones" are those who collectively account for half of all contributions to the field. Hence, if the total number of scientists within a given generation and specified field equals k, then half of all work can be attributed to $\sqrt{k}$. This implies that as k increases, the proportion of good scientists declines. If there are only 10 individuals working in an area, then about one third will account for half of all the contributions ($\sqrt{10} \approx 3.2$), whereas if the number increased to 100, the productive elite represents only 10% of the whole ($\sqrt{100} = 10$). In general, as the number of participants increases, the discipline becomes ever more elitist.

The expanded elitism predicted by the Price law suggests that the members of a given generation are doing something to simulate the creativity of the greatest thinkers of their generation. One likely explanation is that the members of a large disciplinary cohort form various kinds of professional relationships that encourage and maintain creative achievement. I illustrated this specific linkage in a study of 2,026 eminent scientists (Simonton, 1992c; also see Simonton, 1984a). For each scientist I recorded the number of professional associates of different types, such as collaborators, correspondents, friends, and even rivals. I then correlated these measures of professional relationships with three criteria of overall achievement: lifetime creative output, active career length, and posthumous reputation. The correlations were uniformly positive and statistically significant (even after controls for potential artifacts were introduced). The more eminent, enduring, and prolific scientists had more professional connections than did their less successful colleagues. This association even held for highly introverted scientists such as Isaac Newton, who accumulated more than 24 professional contacts with the leading scientists of his time. These contacts included rivalries and controversies with 5, friendships (albeit unstable) with 7, and correspondence or other collegial interactions with 21. Among the celebrities in Newton's network were Jean Bernoulli, James Bradley, Abraham DeMoivre, John Flamsted, Edmund Halley, Robert Hooke, Colin Mclauren, Olaus Rømer, John Wallis, and Christopher Wren, as well as two notables from psychology's past, Gottfried Wilhelm Leibniz and John Locke. Furthermore, these relationships were most often instrumental rather than merely incidental to Newton's scientific success. Edmund Halley, for one, had a major part to play in getting Newton to publish *Principia Mathematica*.

It is interesting that the one type of professional associate Newton lacked was a bona fide collaborator. He preferred to work completely alone on everything, whether his mathematics, celestial mechanics, or optics. However, to a very large extent Newton's failure to engage in collaborations merely reflects the state of science during the Scientific Revolution. In the day before big laboratories, the lone genius reigned supreme, and genuine collaboration was extremely rare. Copernicus, Vesalius, Galileo, Descartes, and Leibniz are other examples. Only as science became increasingly institutionalized, especially in the guise of research laboratories and academic institutions, did collaboration become a major factor in enhancing scientific creativity. This shift was already very evident in France during the first 30 years of the 19th century (Beaver & Rosen, 1979). Collaboration not only was fairly typical of the French scientific elite, but it also tended to increase a scientist's research productivity and professional visibility. In the 20th century, and particularly after World War II, this tendency toward collaboration increased in most of the sciences, with the single-authored article becoming increasingly obsolete (Beaver, 1986). In 1949, single-authored publications represented almost two thirds of the literature that year, whereas by 1979 this percentage had declined to less than one third (Zuckerman & Merton, 1972).

Similar patterns are seen in psychology as well (Over, 1982a). In 1949, the average number of authors of APA journal articles was about 1.5, but by 1979 this mean had increased to 2.2. This trend is not restricted to lesser figures in the discipline. For 69 eminent American psychologists active between 1879 and 1967, the correlation between the percentage of works that were coauthored and the year of birth was .49, a very substantial figure. James Mark Baldwin coauthored fewer than 4% of his publications, whereas Carl I. Hovland engaged in coauthorship 65% of the time, a tenfold increase in the little over 60 years that separates their birth years. Corresponding with this increased emphasis on collaboration is a tendency for collaborative research to receive slightly more recognition, including citations, compared to solo contributions (e.g., Ashton & Oppenheim, 1978; Beaver, 1986; Diamond, 1985; Smart & Bayer, 1986).

Despite these trends and tendencies, there exists as yet no empirical determination whether collaboration is a more powerful professional relationship than other varieties of contact, such as correspondence, collegial exchanges of papers, and participation in scientific symposia and conferences. Certainly these latter forms of relationship remain important, too. For example, highly productive university faculty tend to display higher rates of communication with researchers at other institutions (Blackburn, Behymer, & Hall, 1978). In addition, the more prolific was the researcher, the higher was the probability that he or she came from a large academic department (Blackburn et al., 1978). This fact should be integrated with an observation made in chapter 11, in which I noted that great scientists typically end up being affiliated with distinguished research institutions (e.g., Crane, 1965; Manis, 1951). A portion of this effect might be ascribed to the number of collegial relationships that are potentially available. This likelihood is suggested by the results of a study of 180 psychology departments in the United

States, Canada, and Great Britain (Endler, Rushton, & Roediger, 1978). The department's overall reputatial rating was highly correlated with the number of full-time faculty affiliated with the department (also see Helmreich, Spence, & Thorbecke, 1981). Faculty size was also strongly correlated with total publications and total citations earned by the department. More provocative is that faculty size was positively associated with the mean number of publications, the mean number of citations, and the median number of citations. Thus, on a per capita basis, the larger departments were more productive and more influential. This enhancement implies the existence of some synergistic process such that the output of the whole is greater than the separate parts.

This departmental impact on personal productivity helps account for a finding also noted in chapter 11, namely, that scientists who exhibited upward mobility by moving from less prestigious to more prestigious institutions tend to increase their overall productivity (Allison & Long, 1990; also see Long & McGinnis, 1981). Yet it is essential to point out that the benefits of such affiliation are not just short term. In the study of 69 eminent American psychologists, affiliation with a distinguished research institution correlated .37 with the total number of cited publications, .33 with the total number of citations, and .27 with the number of citations of the single most influential work (Simonton, 1992b). These figures are impressive because the citation measures were gauging the posthumous impact of the individuals' work—some 20 to 60 years after their deaths! Hence, the consequences of such collegial environments may be truly enduring.

All told, the clustering of genius into Kroeberian configurations may have two major sources: lagged and synchronous. The first involves the association between the amount of creative activity in Generation $g - 1$ and the amount in Generation g. This association presumably represents the influence of role model availability on creative development. The second entails the relationships among the contemporaries who are active in a given field. These professional networks operate synergistically to enhance the level of creativity displayed by each individual in the cohort.

COMTIAN PROGRESS

Alfred Kroeber (1944), like Velleius before him, believed that after a configuration reached its climax, the cultural pattern would become increasingly exhausted. The creative champions of the Golden Age would be succeeded by the runners up of the Silver Age, who in their turn would be followed by the also-rans of the period of cultural decadence and decay, receding into a Dark Age. The only upward motion in this scheme is at the very onset of the configuration, when the formative, or "pre-classical" period gradually builds up to the cultural culmination. Nonetheless, the history of any given civilization appears to be dominated by the doldrums, the long spans of time in which a civilization has lost all creative spark.

Kroeber's (1944) notion of sociocultural change seems antithetical to the modern concept of human progress—the belief that the history of civilization is a record of constant improvement. This belief has had many adherents, but among the most forceful was certainly Auguste Comte, the early 19th-century French philosopher who founded positivism. Comte argued that human progress was not a hypothesis or conjecture but rather an outright law of civilization. The history of the human mind consisted of three stages: the theological, the metaphysical, and the positive. The last stage represented the culmination of the upward progression, for knowledge would depend solely on reason and observation. In a word, human civilization culminated in science. At the same time, Comte believed that different domains of knowledge progressed through this sequence of stages at different rates. The first to reach the highest state was astronomy, followed by physics, then chemistry and, much later, physiology. Comte argued, moreover, for the emergence of a new department of positive philosophy, which he christened *sociology*.

Comte's theory of human progress thus implies an internalist history of science. Each scientific discipline advances through the theological, metaphysical, and positivist stages according to their intrinsic characteristics. Those that deal with more abstract and simple phenomena, such as astronomy, advance to the acme more quickly than those that treat more concrete and complex phenomena, such as sociology. To be sure, Comte also argued that the degree of advancement depended on the extent to which each science was contingent on other sciences. Astronomers could develop independent of what happened in other disciplines, whereas physiology depended on chemistry, and chemistry depended on physics. Nevertheless, even with this complication the progress of any given scientific domain is mainly a function of that domain's subject matter and the progress of the other domains of science on which its development depends.

This Comtian philosophy and history of science leads naturally to two sets of research questions that deserve a positivistic response.

1. What evidence is there that various scientific disciplines can be ordered into some hierarchy? Are some sciences closer to the positivistic ideal of integrated logic and fact than others? If the sciences can be ordered into a hierarchy, where does psychology fit in—between sociology and physiology, or in some more ignoble position?

2. What evidence is there that any given scientific discipline exhibits progress in a Comtian manner? Better yet, has psychology displayed an upward progression similar to the other sciences? Has psychology arrived at the stage of true positive philosophy, or must it still be considered prescientific?

These questions are obviously critical if one wishes to comprehend not only the history of psychology but also the scientific status of psychology.

Interdisciplinary Hierarchies

I first review the evidence against the existence of a hierarchy of sciences and then demonstrate that such hierarchies may indeed exist, especially if the supposedly disconfirming data are properly analyzed.

Anti-Comte

It is ironic that, although Comte viewed sociology as the top of the hierarchy—as the culmination of progress in human knowledge—that discipline is currently more often viewed as dwelling at or near the bottom of the sciences. Astronomy and physics stand at the apex, followed closely by chemistry, then physiology, with sociology far below. Even more ironic is that the first systematic attempt to determine whether the various sciences could be ordered into some scientific hierarchy was carried out by a sociologist, Stephen Cole (1983), a representative of the Mertonian school of the sociology of science. Cole (1983) began his inquiry by defining the six interrelated criteria that would be used to decide where any given discipline would be placed in the presumed hierarchy. At the top would be the sciences that (a) have well-developed or highly "codified" theories; (b) quantify ideas in mathematical language; (c) obtain high levels of consensus among practitioners with respect to theory, methods, important problems, and the like; (d) feature high rates of obsolescence as recent work quickly replaces the old; and (e) accumulate knowledge at a very rapid pace. At the bottom would be those that (a) have few generalizations and a low level of codification; (b) express key concepts in words; (c) show little consensus and hence agree little on the worth of any single person's contribution; (d) retain many references to older, so-called "classical" works that continue to be relevant to current research; and (e) accumulate knowledge at a very slow pace. These criteria, although not identical to Comte's, certainly capture the gist of his ideas that pure science is founded in rational empiricism and that the application of this positivistic approach would contribute to rapid progress in knowledge about the phenomena examined by the domain.

Before S. Cole (1983) could apply these criteria, it was first necessary to make a critical distinction regarding two types of knowledge within any given scientific discipline. The first type is the *core*, which consists of "fully evaluated and universally accepted ideas which serve as the starting points for graduate education" (S. Cole, 1983, p. 111). The second type is the *research frontier*, which includes "all research currently being conducted" (S. Cole, 1983, p. 111) at the leading edge of the discipline. This distinction was important, because Cole (1983) found that all scientific disciplines were very similar when it came to what was taking place at their respective research frontiers. In particular, there were no consistent contrasts with respect to the degree of disciplinary consensus or the rate at which new findings and concepts are incorporated into the body of disciplinary knowledge. Cole's (1983) ultimate conclusion was that "in all sciences knowledge at the research frontier is a loosely woven web characterized by substantial levels of disagreement and difficulty in determining which contributions will turn out to be significant" (p. 111). Evidently, the degree to which a discipline has implemented Comtian positivism does not ameliorate the ambiguities that attend the leading edge of research.

Other investigations appear to endorse S. Cole's (1983) generalization. For instance, Barnett, Fink, and Debus (1989) showed that citation practices in the natural sciences, social sciences, and even the arts and humanities differed very little. In all three domains the citations received by a new publication peaked within 2 years and then gradually declined, and the shape of the curve was virtually identical for the social and natural sciences. Hedges (1987) assessed whether empirical findings in the "hard sciences" were really more cumulative than findings in the "soft sciences." In line with the "physics envy" so often expressed by many psychologists, the specific comparison was between physics and psychology. Using standard statistical methods for comparing the consistency of results in multiple experiments, Hedges found no difference. In particular, the basic properties of certain elementary particles in high-energy physics were determined to be no better than various psychological parameters associated with spatial perception and visualization, verbal ability, mathematics achievement, self-concept, student-rating validities, and so forth. At least at their respective research frontiers, the hard sciences are just as soft as the soft sciences. The greatest psychologist need not be embarrassed vis-à-vis the greatest physicist.

Pro-Comte

These results notwithstanding, other researchers have offered data that imply a very different conclusion. In chapter 11 I observed that the age at which a scientist most typically receives a major award or honor varies according to the discipline. These differences might be attributed to placement in the hierarchy of the sciences. For example, the mean age at which a great scientist becomes a Nobel laureate—physics: 49, chemistry: 53, and medicine or physiology: 55—corresponds with the degree of codification that characterizes each of the three fields (Shin & Putnam, 1982). In less codified fields it presumably takes longer before a consensus is reached on the merits of a scientist's key contributions. Note, too, that this order concurs perfectly with Comte's ordering. The principal drawback to using these statistics as evidence for a scientific hierarchy is that there exists an alternative explanation, namely, interdisciplinary contrasts in the age–productivity curves (see, e.g., Simonton, 1991a).

Two other sources of evidence do not suffer from this objection. The first was a study that examined this question from the standpoint of Leon Festinger's (1954) social comparison theory (Suls & Fletcher, 1983). Briefly put, this theory states that human beings tend to compare themselves with similar others whenever they are uncertain about some belief. If the various sciences differ in the amount of consensus they display with respect to important theories, methods, and substantive issues, then the scientists will correspondingly exhibit distinctive degrees of uncertainty about the merits of their research. The higher is the magnitude of their uncertainty, the stronger will be their desire to consult with colleagues before submitting a paper for publication in the discipline's journals. This consultation is revealed in the Acknowledgment sections of the published articles. Hence, to test this hypothesis, Suls and Fletcher (1983) measured the number of colleagues who were so consulted in the journal articles of physics, chemistry, psychology, and sociology. The psychology journals were *Psychological Review, Journal of Experimental Psychology* (*Animal Behavior and Processes, Human Learning and Memory,* and *Human Perception and Performance*), *Journal of Personality and Social Psychology,* and *Journal of Abnormal Psychology*. Consistent with predictions, "social scientists were more likely to have consulted with their colleagues than were physical scientists" (p. 575).

The second evidence source involves the interdisciplinary variation in a measure called the *theories-to-laws ratio* (Roeckelein, 1997). This measure is based on the relative representation of theories and laws in the textbooks of a discipline. It is specifically defined as the count of theories cited divided by the count of laws cited. Disciplines that stand at the top of the Comtian hierarchy should have a low theories-to-laws ratio, whereas those at the bottom should have a high ratio; that is, an established science will boast many laws, whereas a struggling science will blush under the profusion of mere theories. Roeckelein (1997) applied this measure to 246 textbooks for five sciences published from 1866 to 1996. The results were fairly consistent with expectation. The average ratios across more than 100 years of textbooks were as follows: physics, 0.4:1; chemistry, 0.5:1; biology, 2.6:1; anthropology, 2.8:1; psychology, 3.8:1; and sociology, 7.3:1. Physics and chemistry clearly come out on top by this criterion, because their textbooks contain at least twice as many laws as theories. Biology and anthropology, on the other hand, land a few notches down, as theories outnumber laws by almost 3 to 1. Sociology, moreover, rests at the bottom, with a ratio of more than 7 to 1. The textbooks of psychology, finally, show a ratio of about 4 to 1, which puts it closer to biology and anthropology than to sociology. In the Comtian hierarchy, psychology is more a natural science than a social one.

Of course, Roeckelein's (1997) study differs from the rest in that it concentrated on the core rather than the research frontier of each discipline. That difference alone could explain any discrepancies with studies that failed to find evidence for a hierarchy of sciences. Nevertheless, on closer examination the results are actually not that discrepant. The problem with all of this research is that it tends to address the substantive question piecemeal, with one investigator using this criterion and another scientist using another criterion. Moreover, the specific disciplines that are examined vary from study to study, often in ways that depart significantly from Comte's original conceptions. Even worse, the various alternative rankings of the sciences are not subjected to any rigorous statistical test of the degree to which they might be in agreement. Therefore, it is conceivable that a systematic statistical comparison of multiple criteria applied to the same disciplines might demonstrate the presence of a bona fide Comtian hierarchy.

To test this conjecture, I reanalyzed previously published scores that evaluated (a) the discipline of psychology and (b) the inclusively defined disciplines of Comte's original formulation (e.g., physics as a whole rather than just the specialty of solid-state physics). The outcome was four sciences gauged by six criteria. The sciences were physics, chemistry, psychology, and sociology. The six criteria were the following:

1. One criterion was the theories-to-laws ratio measure already discussed (from Roeckelein, 1997). This was based on 23 textbooks for physics, 20 for chemistry, 136 for psychology, and 22 for sociology. The psychology texts included those by some of psychology's greats, including William James, James M. Baldwin, John Dewey, Edward Titchener, Mary Calkins, Edward Lee Thorndike, Hermann Ebbinghaus, Oswald Külpe, Robert Sessions Woodworth, William McDougall, Edward G. Boring, James M. Cattell, Gardner Murphy, Ernest R. Hilgard, and Harry Harlow (Roeckelein, 1996a).

2. The next criterion was the consultation measure based on Festinger's (1954) social comparison theory (Suls & Fletcher, 1983, Table 1). The specific measure was the number of persons acknowledged adjusted for the number of authors. Here psychology had a score of 1.21, a consultation rate higher than that for physics (0.58) and chemistry (0.53) but lower than that for sociology (2.02).

3. The remaining four criteria came from S. Cole's (1983) study. In his Table 2 Cole presented a table that gave the "proportion of scientists under 35 whose work received more than the mean number of citations for their field" (p. 118). The fields that incorporate most quickly the work of young scientists are assumed to rank higher in the hierarchy. This figure was 24% for psychology, which compares favorably with the figures for physics (25%) and chemistry (29%). The percentage for sociology, in contrast, was only 13%.

4. S. Cole's (1983) Table 3 provided data indicating a "consensus on evaluating scientists by field" (p. 120), in which 60 scientists per field were rated by colleagues in the same discipline. The consensus was gauged by the mean standard deviation of the ratings. For psychology, this was 0.74, which was smaller than that for sociology (0.76) but larger than that for physics (0.63) and chemistry (0.69). Here, the larger the standard deviation is, the greater the disagreement and hence the lower the consensus within that discipline.
5. In Table 4 of the same article (S. Cole, 1983) the consensus was assessed in a similar fashion, this time by asking scientists to mention those who "have contributed the most in past two decades" (p. 120). The specific index is the percentage of "mentions received by 5 most mentioned names" (p. 120). By this criterion, psychology did the worst, with a score of 32%, compared to 34% for chemistry, 36% for sociology, and 47% for physics.
6. The "concentration of citations to research articles" was presented in S. Cole's (1983) Table 5 (p. 122). The citations were to 10 journals in physics, 12 in chemistry, 8 in psychology, and 7 in sociology. If the citations are all concentrated in a single article, then the disciplinary consensus must be very high, whereas if it is more evenly distributed across articles, then the consensus must be minimal. The specific index (the Gini coefficient) for psychology was .16, which indicates more consensus than sociology (.09), about the same as chemistry (.15), and slightly less than physics (.18).

Because the five measures had very different scales, they were all standardized to a mean of 0 and a standard deviation of 1 to better permit direct comparisons. In addition, three of the measures—the first, the second, and the fourth—were inverted so that their scores would go in the same direction. This means that positive scores will indicate high status on the Comtian hierarchy, whereas negative scores imply low status on the same. The standardized scores are shown in Table 13.1. The general level of agreement should be immediately obvious. By all criteria, physics stands at the top and sociology at the bottom. Chemistry has a positive score on all but one criterion. Only psychology's placement is more ambiguous, with three negative scores and two positive scores.

The impression of general agreement is reinforced by the statistical tests. To begin, a principal-components analysis revealed that the first component explains 78% of the total variance in the five measures, a very remarkable figure (Simonton, 1990d). The factor loadings on the first component range from .52 to .98, indicating that all six measures are tapping the same latent

TABLE 13.1
Four Sciences Rated on Six Criteria and the Composite Rating on the Comtian Hierarchy of Sciences

Science	Criterion						Rating
	1	2	3	4	5	6	
Physics	0.79	0.73	0.33	1.29	1.45	0.90	0.92
Chemistry	0.76	0.80	0.91	0.26	−0.48	0.13	0.40
Psychology	−0.24	−0.18	0.18	−0.60	−0.78	0.39	−0.21
Sociology	−1.31	−1.34	−1.42	−0.95	−0.19	−1.42	−1.11

Note. All criterion measures were standardized to *z* scores from the statistics published in several distinct sources: 1 = theories-to-laws ratio (from Roeckelein, 1997; based on 23 textbooks for physics, 20 for chemistry, 136 for psychology, and 22 for sociology); 2 = consultation measure based on Festinger's social comparison theory (Suls & Fletcher, 1983, Table 1; viz. the number of persons acknowledged adjusted for the number of authors); 3 = the "proportion of scientists under 35 whose work received more than the mean number of citations for their field" (S. Cole, 1983, p. 118; i.e., fields that incorporate most quickly the work of young scientists are assumed to rank higher in the hierarchy); 4 = the "consensus on evaluating scientists by field" (S. Cole, 1983, p. 120), where 60 scientists per field were rated by colleagues in the same discipline (the consensus was gauged by the mean standard deviation of the ratings); 5 = the consensus gauged by asking scientists to mention those who "have contributed the most in past two decades" (S. Cole, 1983, p. 120; the specific index is the percentage of "mentions received by 5 most mentioned names"); 6 = the "concentration of citations to research articles" (S. Cole, 1983, p. 122; using the Gini coefficient).

variable. The item with the highest factor loading was the theories-to-laws ratio (Roeckelein, 1997), followed very closely by the consultation measure (Suls & Fletcher, 1983). The lowest factor loading belonged to S. Cole's (1983) Table 4, but even that loading was sizable, sharing more than 25% of its variance with the principal component. Furthermore, if the scores on the six measures are summed to produce a composite index of a discipline's status, the resulting reliability coefficient (Cronbach's alpha) is .93, a degree of internal consistency that is truly exceptional. These statistical outcomes together strongly justify the computation of an average rating across the six measures, which is also shown in Table 13.1. On this summary index, physics comes out almost 1 standard deviation above the mean, sociology more than 1 standard deviation below the mean. Chemistry is 0.4 standard deviation above the zero mean, whereas psychology is 0.2 standard deviation below. Thus, not only does a Comtian hierarchy exist, but also psychology's placement within that hierarchy appears pretty secure.

It would admittedly have been better to have ranked more disciplines and perhaps to have used more criteria to carry out those rankings. Yet the preceding secondary analysis certainly makes sense from the standpoint of Comte's positive philosophy. As a behavioral science, psychology stands somewhere between the natural sciences, represented by chemistry and physics, and the social sciences, represented by sociology. If physiology were included in the mix it would probably have come out between chemistry and psychology in the hierarchy. To the extent that even the greatest psychologists are constrained by the scientific status of their discipline, this Comtian stratification would probably guide their distinction relative to the greats of the other sciences.

Intradisciplinary Advancement

If Comte's philosophy is correct, then the positivistic status of a science is not a static phenomenon, but rather it should change over time—at least until its history culminates in pure positivism. Therefore, even if psychology falls below the natural sciences in the scale of scientific perfection, it should exhibit a transhistorical trend toward reaching the more elevated levels in the hierarchy; that is, psychology should become more scientific over the course of its history. This hypothesis might be easily tested with the theories-to-laws ratio, which has already been shown to have the highest factor loading on the 6-item principal component that gauges scientific status. Besides reporting the overall means across all the textbooks for each science, Roeckelein (1997) also provided separate means for consecutive periods. Moreover, the periods were 1866–1919, 1920–1939, 1940–1959, 1960–1979, and 1980–1996 and thus are tantamount to a generational analysis, except for the more inclusively defined first time interval. In the case of physics, chemistry, and biology the theories-to-laws ratio declines over time. When I calculated the correlations between their scores and the date of the midpoint of the five periods, I obtained the values of –.70, –.16, and –.72, respectively. Hence, despite the high status of these three sciences in the Comtian hierarchy, there remained some room for improvement, especially in the case of physics and biology. Yet the generational changes are strikingly different for the other three sciences, all of which have positive trends. In particular, the correlations between the scores and the date are .88 for sociology and .90 for anthropology and psychology! Even worse, the coefficient of .90 is statistically significant at the .05 level, the small sample size notwithstanding, so that the trend cannot be dismissed as mere chance fluctuation. Hence, despite the high theories-to-laws ratios already exhibited by psychology, its status by this criterion has been getting worse, not better.

Does this mean that the great psychologists of today are less likely to be great scientists than in the discipline's early years? Before this depressing conclusion is reached, it is first necessary to examine more indicators than just the theories-to-laws ratio. The main problem with this measure is that it concentrates on how the discipline is represented in its introductory textbooks. Yet, in line with S. Cole's (1983) distinction between the core and the research frontier, what goes on in these textbooks may differ appreciably from what is taking place in the original research of the field. If there has been any improvement in psychology's status as a scientific enterprise, it may be more evident in the articles published in the discipline's most prestigious journals. Hence, content analyses of the research literature may reveal some amount of Comtian progress. The content analytical studies that would help one address this question fall into two groups. In the first type of study the content analysis is performed with the subjective evaluations of real human beings, whereas in the second the content analysis is executed with computer programs designed to evaluate text.

Subjective (Human) Content Analyses

In 1940, Jerome Bruner and Gordon Allport scrutinized psychology's progress from this standpoint of its research literature. Although both Bruner and Allport have now left their marks on the annals of the discipline, Bruner was at that time one of Allport's graduate students, still a year away from getting his Harvard PhD. The study was titled "Fifty Years of Change in American Psychology," and in it they specifically inspected the "entire periodical output of the 'leading' psychological journals for every tenth year beginning in 1888 and ending in 1938" (p. 757). The specific journals were identified by asking 30 APA members to rate 50 different periodicals. Bruner and Allport then selected the 14 journals that came out on top of the ratings. These included *Psychological Review, American Journal of Psychology, Journal of Experimental Psychology, Journal of Comparative Psychology, Journal of Abnormal and Social Psychology, Journal of Educational Psychology, Journal of Applied Psychology*, and *Psychological Bulletin*, in which their article was itself published. Altogether, they examined the contents of 1,627 articles over the half century. As if this were not ambitious enough for a student's independent research project, the articles were all scored on 32 different categories, such as the research participants, measurement strategies, analytical approaches, theoretical concepts, and philosophical issues. Bruner scored all the materials, and Allport scored a subsample of 107 articles to determine the reliability of his student's category assignments. They agreed 92% of the time, a very reasonable degree of consensus.

Several of the categories are directly germane to the degree to which psychological research manifests the positivistic ideal. Furthermore, without exception, the trend in the representation of these categories is always in the direction that would be expected from a psychology that was growing ever more scientific. For instance, in line with the significance of quantification in the definition of genuine science, Bruner and Allport (1940) noted that "quantitatively, the most striking change in 50 years is the great increase in the use of statistical aids in psychological research" (p. 766). Even though their own data analysis was not sufficiently quantitative to specify the magnitude of this trend, it is easy to calculate the appropriate statistic from their tables. The correlation between the use of statistics and the year of publication is .93, which is statistically significant at conventional levels despite the small number of periods covered ($N = 5$, $p = .018$). In concrete terms, the percentage increased from around 2% in the late 19th century to around 44% in the 1920s and 1930s. Other trends with significant positive correlations are the use of nonverbal methods (rather than introspection) to study higher mental processes ($r = .99$, $p < .001$) and what Bruner and Allport called *methodological positivism* ($r = .88$, $p = .048$), a catch-all category that included discussion of operational definitions, formal analytical techniques in the field, and the conceptual status of the discipline's concepts. On the other hand, categories that displayed negative trends in the psychological literature were those that indicate the field's movement away from what Comte might consider prescientific notions. An example is the use of single-case studies, such as "case histories, biographies, autobiographies, diaries, etc. that attempt to obtain an *understanding* of the total personality in its *milieu*" (1940, p. 761). The correlation for this category is $-.83$ ($p = .083$).

Another irony crops up in these diverse trends. From Allport's perspective, the discipline of psychology was moving in the wrong direction. Movement toward Comtian positivism was not his preferred approach to psychological science. As apparent in Table 8.1, Allport favored the subjective, holistic, personal, and qualitative approach to psychological phenomena. This preference took the concrete form of the idiographic analysis of individual lives. In addition, Allport was among those in the forefront of the emergence of humanistic psychology in the 1960s, a movement that must be considered retrogressive from a Comtian standpoint. In contrast, once Bruner earned his doctoral degree under Allport, he moved in a direction more consistent with the general thrust of the field toward a higher placement in the hierarchy of sciences. Although Bruner's scores are not found in the Table 8.1, there is no doubt that his orientation was far more consistent with the overall direction that the field was to take in the next 60 years after he and Allport published their 1940 article.

Speaking of Table 8.1, it would seem relevant to the issue at hand to determine how scores on these six dimensions have changed from Gustav Fechner to William Estes. It turns out that the birth year of these 54 eminent psychologists correlates .39 with the objectivistic versus subjectivistic score, $-.41$ with the static versus dynamic score, and .31 with the exogenist versus endogenist score (all $ps < .05$; Simonton, 2000b). In other words, these psychologists have placed increasingly more emphasis on observable behavior, motivation and emotion, and environmental determinants. There were no significant trends on the other three dimensions. Still, these results are not strictly comparable to those of Bruner and Allport's (1940) study. Besides the difference in historical periods covered, Bruner and Allport examined all of the published literature in the leading journals, regardless of whether it was the product of a great psychologist. The 54 psychologists may not necessarily be representative of their less renowned contemporaries. I examine this critical issue in chapter 15.

Objective (Computer) Content Analyses

The effort that Bruner expended on assessing 1,627 articles on 32 categories was truly prodigious. To replicate and extend his and Allport's (1940) study by carrying the analysis all the way to the 21st century would be more monumental still. An alternative fortunately exists that is more efficient and more objective at the same time: computerized content analysis. In chapter 5 I gave an example of how computers may be programmed to content analyze written materials, and this same technique may be applied to examine historical trends in the psychological literature.

Colin Martindale (1990) implemented the first application of this method. His particular focus was stylistic changes in the prose in which psychology articles are written. He began by drawing an extensive sample of prose from the *American Journal of Psychology* from 1887—the year of its founding by G. S. Hall—to 1987, taking 10 articles at random every fifth year. Only genuine articles were chosen; obituaries, book reviews, and other miscellaneous publications were excluded. Martindale next took the first 20 lines from each article, which amounted to about 200 words per article, or nearly 50,000 words in total. He then used a computer to calculate the *composite variability index*, an objective assessment of the linguistic complexity of the writing. This measure incorporates such indicators as mean word length, variation in phrase length, number of word associates, variation in word frequency, and hapax legomena (percentage of words that occur only once in the text). Overall, scores on the composite variability index declined over 100 years covered by his data. The only exception was a slight increase in the early 20th century (when Titchener edited the journal). Martindale interpreted the downward trend as follows:

> It is reasonable to suppose that the prose has simplified as the ideas to be communicated have become more complex. The layman would find many of the earlier articles good reading—not merely because they are by writers such as William James, but mainly because the cognitive load is light and the topics are interesting. The later articles are difficult going. They are written for specialists. The topics are still interesting, but the layman can't even figure out what they are. The authors assume that you know stuff that you don't know. The style, though, is extremely simple. (1990, p. 361)

It may be a sign of scientific progress when a discipline's practitioners publish articles that hardly anyone can comprehend—but are otherwise easy to read!

I illustrated another approach to computerized content analysis in chapter 5, in my description of my study of 69 eminent American psychologists (Simonton, 1992b). Instead of sampling the main text, I used whole titles. The titles were not confined to articles appearing in a specific journal, or even to just journal articles, but all major publications, as listed given in the bibliographic entries of R. I. Watson's (1974) *Eminent Contributors to Psychology*. Using Martindale's (1975, 1990) Regressive Imagery Dictionary (RID), I scored the titles for the presence of primary- and secondary-process imagery. At that time it was recorded that primary-process content in a psychologist's titles was negatively correlated with his or her long-term impact on the field, as assessed by contemporary citations—a finding certainly complementary to psychology's scientific pretensions, insofar as primary process is antithetical to scientific thinking. However, what has not been reported yet is how primary and secondary process changed over the years represented by these 69 psychologists. This may come as a surprise, but the presence of primary process exhibited no secular trend. Even so, secondary process imagery increased prominently over time, with a correlation of .30 ($p < .05$) between the score and the psychologist's birth year. Because secondary-process thinking stresses ideas that are objective, logical, realistic, and articulate, this outcome fits nicely with the assumption that psychology has progressively moved up the Comtian scale of science.

Hence, the results of objective (computer) content analyses appear to corroborate the inferences drawn from subjective (human) content analyses. Why the theories-to-laws ratio indicated contrary conclusions may tell one more about publishing trends in psychology textbooks than about what is happening at the research frontier of the field.

KUHNIAN TRANSFORMATIONS

Fascinating though the preceding results may be, the whole question of a discipline's scientific advancement may suffer from a fatal flaw. According to Comte's internalist theory, the history of science should always move forward. Over time, each science moves closer to the positivistic ideal. Yet not all internalist theories of scientific change share this belief in inevitable progress. The most outstanding example is the theory of advocated by Thomas Kuhn (1970) in his seminal book *The Structure of Scientific Revolutions*. I briefly introduced Kuhn's theory in chapter 2, and discussed it a bit further in chapter 10, but the time has come to treat his ideas in more detail. The core concept in Kuhn's theory is the *paradigm*. This he takes to mean

> some accepted examples of actual scientific practice—examples which include law, theory, application, and instrumentation together—provide models from which spring particular coherent traditions of scientific research. These are the traditions which the historian describes under such rubrics as "Ptolemaic astronomy" (or "Copernican"), "Aristotelian dynamics" (or "Newtonian"), "corpuscular optics" (or "wave optics"), and so on. The study of paradigms, including many that are far more specialized than those named illustratively above, is what mainly prepares the student for membership in the particular scientific community with which he will later practice. . . . Men whose research is based on shared paradigms are committed to the same rules and standards for scientific practice. That commitment and the apparent consensus it produces are pre-

requisites for normal science, i.e., for the genesis and continuation of a particular research tradition. (1970, pp. 10–11)

When a discipline has a well-established paradigm it can practice "normal science," in which its members engage in "puzzle-solving research"; that is, its practitioners dedicate themselves to working out the details of the received paradigm, extending its explanatory power and testing its predictions and implications. Because all members share the same paradigm, the discipline is not divided into separate schools. This contrasts greatly with the sciences that still remain in their preparadigmatic phase. Such disciplines will usually feature two or more contending schools, owing to a lack of any consensus on the preferred theories, methods, and problems. Furthermore, the best that such sciences can accomplish is the accumulation of more or less random facts—facts that lack theoretical context or even agreed-on significance.

Thus far, Kuhn's theory appears hierarchical, with sciences falling into preparadigmatic and paradigmatic categories, the latter representing the true sciences. Yet what prevents Kuhn's scheme from being progressive, like Comte's, is the conception of anomalies. An *anomaly* is a problem that is deemed important and yet somehow cannot be readily solved within the given paradigm. On occasion, a solution arrives in sufficient time that the anomaly never poses a strong threat to the paradigm. An example is the perturbations in the orbit of Uranus that could not be explained within Newtonian gravitational astronomy. However, these departures from expectation eventually could be explained in terms of an undiscovered planet. When the unknown planet's location was predicted according to Newtonian theory, and its existence verified through telescope observations, the paradigm was vindicated. Indeed, the resolution of the anomaly became one of the paradigm's triumphs. In contrast, other anomalies are never successfully solved within the paradigm. To offer another illustration from Newtonian physics, the orbit of Mercury also had an irregularity, but one that could not be explicated in terms of an unknown planet (although such a solution was attempted). If such an anomaly cannot be dismissed as unimportant, and if it is joined by additional anomalies—such as the null results of the Michelson–Morley interferometer experiment—the discipline enters a state of *crisis*. The consensus breaks down, the paradigm's constraints are relaxed, contending theories appear, and the community of practitioners experiences a growing malaise. Hence, to a certain degree, the science retreats to its preparadigmatic period, a retrogression that has no Comtian counterpart. However, with a little luck, a new paradigm may emerge that handles all the major phenomena treated by the old paradigm and explains the anomalous findings. A case in point is Einstein's relativity theory, which subsumed Newtonian mechanics while concomitantly explaining the various anomalies that had accumulated. The discipline can then return to the status quo of puzzle-solving normal science.

Although Kuhn's theory has proven very influential, it has also provoked considerable debate, and many researchers have offered alternative theories of scientific change (e.g., Lakatos, 1978; Laudan, 1977). Furthermore, many have questioned whether the Kuhnian account is applicable to psychology's own history (Gholson & Barker, 1985; Peterson, 1981). This question can be broken into two parts. One first must ask whether psychology can be considered a paradigmatic normal science. Next one need ask whether the discipline's history has undergone scientific revolutions in a Kuhnian manner.

Paradigms

Psychologists often assume that their discipline is paradigmatic, or at least that certain subdisciplines could be considered paradigmatic at one point or another in their historical development (Peterson, 1981). For example, Hermann Ebbinghaus's classic research has been identified as providing a paradigmatic exemplar for the subfield of human memory (Young, 1985). Wilhelm Wundt had argued that the higher mental functions, such as memory, could not be studied using laboratory experiments. Instead, these processes had to be scrutinized in terms of their larger sociocultural manifestations—the motive behind his monumental 1900–1920 *Folk Psychology*. Yet by introducing the stimulus of the "nonsense syllable" and by devising such measures as a relearning "savings score," Ebbinghaus proved Wundt wrong. Although it may be an exaggeration to say that Ebbinghaus's status relative to the phenomenon of memory compares to Newton's with respect to gravitational astronomy, his paradigmatic example certainly dominated the research strategies adopted by generations of memory researchers. According to one critic, Ebbinghaus "put a stamp of this field which resulted in rigidifying, for nearly 80 years, the paradigms used to study human learning" (Young, 1985, p. 491). For instance, the nonsense syllable may have permitted investigators to bypass the contaminating influence of semantic context, yet by divorcing memory from meaning psychologists were separating the sterilized phenomenon in their laboratories from its fertile richness in real human lives.

Is it possible to go beyond mere anecdote to establish scientifically whether psychology could be considered paradigmatic in a Kuhnian sense? In one respect, I addressed this question when I examined psychology's status in the Comtian hierarchy of the sciences. Most of the criteria in Table 13.1 concern the magnitude of consensus shown by the four disciplines. Such a consensus can be adopted as an indicator of the degree to which all practitioners within the field subscribe to a unifying paradigm. By this standard, psychology would have to be considered less paradigmatic than physics or chemistry but more paradigmatic than sociology. It must be admitted, however, that this criterion is only indirect. Furthermore, even if a consensus is accepted as a rough indicator, one can argue that it makes no sense to speak of whether an entire science is paradigmatic. Some subdisciplines of psychology may be guided by strong paradigms, whereas others may remain preparadigmatic. This intradisciplinary variation is apparent in Table 5 of S. Cole's (1983) study, which was used for Criterion 6 of Table 13.1. The figures given in that column are actually averages, based on the Gini coefficients that were calculated for the leading journals of the corresponding discipline. There naturally was considerable dispersion around each mean. In the case of psychology, the coefficients ranged from .05 to .29, a spread that overlaps considerably with those of chemistry (.06–.27) and physics (.06–.35). Indeed, "the psychology journal with the highest Gini coefficient, *Journal of the Experimental Analysis of Behavior*, had a higher coefficient than any journal in chemistry, geology, or mathematics" (S. Cole, 1983, p. 121). Thus, the research appearing in the *Journal of the Experimental Analysis of Behavior* operates under such a pervasive paradigm—Skinner's radical behaviorism—that the best articles can easily be discerned from the rest, and on these articles subsequent citations can concentrate. Other subdisciplines of psychology lack the kind of paradigmatic consensus enjoyed by Skinnerian psychologists.

It is perhaps a bit strange that the psychology journal with the highest Gini coefficient was represented by the Skinnerian paradigm. At the time that this coefficient was calculated (in the late 1970s), radical behaviorism was already facing a major challenge by a newfangled psychology, a psychology that billed itself as the science of the mind, not just of behavior. Like humanistic psychology, this alternative school emerged in the 1960s but grew at a far faster pace, coming to dominate the discipline within a relatively short time. Consistent with Planck's principle, B. F. Skinner in his old age began to launch highly visible attacks on what he thought were pernicious novelties in the field. In 1987, at age 85, he wrote an *American Psychologist* article titled "Whatever Happened to Psychology as the Science of Behavior?" In it, Skinner argued that the advent of cognitive psychology—in conjunction with humanistic psychology and the helping professions—was undermining the discipline's status as a genuine science. In 1990, he closed the final year of his life with another *American Psychologist* article titled "Can Psychology Be a Science of Mind?" Yet it was already apparent by this time that Skinner was fighting a forlorn-hope rearguard action. In the 1980s and 1990s articles were appearing in the same journal arguing that psychology had undergone a "cognitive revolution." The authors of these articles were not crackpots but rather included several notables in the field, such as Karl Pribram (1986) and Nobel laureate Roger Sperry (1993). Furthermore, in 1987 Howard Gardner wrote the book *The Mind's New Science: A History of the Cognitive Revolution*—suggesting that the momentous event was already a fait accompli well before Skinner's death.

Does all this imply that the psychology had witnessed a bona fide Kuhnian paradigm shift?

Revolutions

The history of psychology often appears to contain examples of scientific change that have the superficial appearance of scientific revolutions. "In each period of psychology the research workers claimed to have new methods and new theoretical constructs," wrote Saugstad (1965, pp. 15–16), for "the Wundtian introspectionists, the phenomenologists, and the behavioristic psychologists were all . . . convinced that they conceived of psychology in a manner different from their precursors." At the same time, historians often put forward generalizations hinting that psychology's historical development may pursue patterns that depart from those put forward by Kuhn's (1970) theory. Take, for instance, the following two examples:

1. "We shall see in our review of the story of psychology that the general acceptance of a method has frequently impeded the progress of the science" (MacLeod, 1975, p. 46). According to Kuhn, the attainment of a methodological consensus is a critical part of paradigm formation. Rather than hampering progress, this consensus helps found the whole basis for the practice of normal science. It is this commitment to an accepted body of techniques that permits replication of results and the accumulation of results—and the conclusive demonstration of anomalous phenomena that inspires the extension of the paradigm or the origination of a new one.

2. "Most important to structuralism's demise . . . was its inability to assimilate one of the most important developments in human history—the doctrine of evolution" (Hergenhahn, 1992, p. 258). In Kuhnian theory, a paradigm succumbs when it fails to handle the anomalies that the paradigm itself created through its puzzle-solving devotees, whereas this quotation suggests that at least one system of psychology died because it did not make appropriate adjustments to a doctrine assuming hegemony in another scientific discipline. If the latter principle is more conspicuous than the former, then the history of psychology becomes contingent on the history of other sciences rather than constituting an autonomously evolving enterprise.

The theory that scientific change may operate differently in psychology than in the paradigmatic sciences is also suggested by an impressive and detailed philosophical analysis of authentic conceptual revolutions (Thagard, 1992). Thagard (1992) began by scrutinizing the logic of the major scientific revolutions led by Copernicus, Newton, Lavoisier, Darwin, Einstein, Wegener, and others. This analysis was frequently conducted by means of a computational model—the program ECHO—that was designed to gauge any theory's "explanatory coherence." The treatment of these secure cases thus complete, Thagard allotted a whole chapter to the question "Revolutions in Psychology?" His informed conclusion, based on the case studies and the computer model, was forthright:

> While psychology has seen much conceptual change in this century, with the replacement of the introspectionist and commonsense conceptual system by behaviorism, and the sublation of behaviorism by cognitivism, it has not had revolutions of the sort so important in the natural sciences. Behaviorism and cognitivism involved abundant conceptual change, including concept deletions and conceptual reorganization involving kind-relations. But they are best characterized as approaches rather than theories, and their ascent depended more on estimates of future explanatory coherence than on evaluation of the explanatory coherence of specific theories. (1992, p. 245)

The affirmation that no so-called cognitive revolution took place has been seconded by others. For instance, it has been argued that "the move from behaviorism to cognitivism is best represented in terms of replacement of (operationally defined) 'intervening variables' by genuine 'hypothetical constructs' possessing cognitive 'surplus meaning'" and that this replacement actually "continued a cognitive tradition that can be traced back to the 1920s" (Greenwood, 1999, p. 1). There was no "Kuhnian paradigm shift" whatsoever.

These assertions are based on conceptual analyses rather than empirical inquiries. Hence, it would be valuable to ask whether the facts support these inferences. Two distinct approaches—citation analyses and content analyses—have emerged to address empirically this question.

Citation Analysis

Kuhn (1970) himself suggested an empirical approach to testing whether revolutions indeed took place within a given scientific domain. Kuhn conjectured that when a scientific revolution takes place, and the new paradigm displaces the old, this must leave an impact on what is published in the field: "One such effect—a shift in the distribution of the technical literature cited in the footnotes to research reports—ought to be studied as a possible index to the occurrence of revolutions" (p. ix). It was 20 years before Kuhn's suggestion was specifically applied to the history of psychology. The application took the form of two successive articles that appeared in *American Psychologist*.

The first article tested the "Kuhnian displacement thesis" by gauging the citations received by the leading journals in three rival schools of psychological thought (Friman, Allen, Kerwin, & Larzelere, 1993). Psychoanalysis was represented by *Psychoanalytic Quarterly*, *Journal of American Psychoanalytic Association*, *Contemporary Psychoanalysis*, and *International Journal of Psychoanalysis*; behaviorism was represented by *Behavior Research and Therapy*,

Journal of Experimental Analysis of Behavior, Behavior Therapy, and *Journal of Applied Behavior Analysis*; and cognitivism was represented by *Cognitive Psychology, Cognition, Journal of Experimental Psychology: Learning, Memory, and Cognition*, and *Memory & Cognition*. The *Social Science Journal Citation Record* was then used to determine the impact these representative journals had on the research literature between 1979 and 1988. Despite the definition of multiple indicators (citation number, impact factor, immediacy index, etc.), the same general conclusions were obtained. Although there usually was an increase in citations to articles published in the cognitive psychology journals, and although citations to psychoanalytic journals were often lower than those to the other two, neither behaviorism nor psychoanalysis exhibited any sign of undergoing Kuhnian displacement. At least over the period studied, the citation trends for the last two schools were fairly flat. The so-called "cognitive revolution" entailed merely the increase in research on human cognition, without any corresponding decline in the scholarly activity displayed by the older schools. Scientific change in psychology consists of the accumulation of additional psychologies rather than paradigm shifts!

Friman et al.'s (1993) study essentially replicated for the whole discipline what was specifically found for B. F. Skinner (Thyer, 1991). The advent of cognitive psychology be what it may, Skinner's intellectual legacy showed no sign of languishing between 1966 and 1989, again as judged by citations in the psychological literature. Even so, such a conclusion is not immune from criticism. Perhaps the biggest problem with the test of the Kuhnian displacement thesis (Friman et al., 1993) was the methodological decision to use citations of the core journals of the three schools as an index of disciplinary displacement (Robins & Craik, 1994). A better alternative might be to look at the relative representation of the three schools in the core journals of psychology. To be concrete, how has the representation of psychoanalysis, behaviorism, and cognitive psychology changed in the articles appearing in *American Psychologist, Annual Review of Psychology, Psychological Bulletin*, and *Psychological Review*? The critics backed up their remarks by publishing a study that carried out their recommended procedure, with additional improvements (Robins, Gosling, & Craik, 1999; also see Robins, Gosling, & Craik, 1998). For good measure, they added a fourth brand of psychology: the neurosciences. Changes in the differential impact of these four psychologies were assessed three distinct ways: (a) the percentage of articles appearing in flagship publications that contain keywords relevant to the psychoanalytic, behavioral, cognitive, and neuroscientific schools; (b) the percentage of dissertations that contain the specified set of keywords for each school; and (c) the total number of annual citations by the four flagship publications of the articles that appeared in the core journals of psychoanalytic, behavioral, cognitive, and neuroscientific psychologies. The time span of the analysis varied according to the specific criterion, but the annual time series could begin as early as 1950 and end as late as 1998. Whatever the details, the results were fairly consistent across the alternative indicators. Psychoanalysis over the interval has been mostly ignored in mainstream psychology, and the neurosciences have made only the smallest impression, despite the substantial increase in neuroscientific research (and its growing citation in general scientific publications such as *Science*). More significant is that cognitive psychology began an ascent in the early 1960s, while behaviorism began a descent in the late 1960s and early 1970s.

Although this follow-up investigation (Robins, Gosling, & Craik, 1999) has drawn its share of criticisms (e.g., Martens, 2000), I think its main empirical conclusion survives unscathed: The behaviorist school has yielded ground to cognitive psychology in mainstream psychological science (Robins, Gosling, & Craik, 2000). This trend is certainly consistent with Kuhn's (1970) displacement thesis. However, do those antithetical trends prove that a paradigm shift has taken place? The citation analyses in isolation cannot really provide an answer. Accordingly, it is necessary to use an alternative methodology to see if its results corroborate what was learned from citation trends.

Content Analysis

Already in this chapter I have discussed Martindale's (1990) application of computerized content analysis to the text published in the *American Journal of Psychology*. Both in this chapter and in chapter 5 I also mentioned the utility of his RID. Use of the RID makes it possible to content analyze written material for the presence of primary- and secondary-process imagery, or what Martindale (1990) more recently named *primordial* and *conceptual content*. The usefulness of applying the RID has been illustrated in a content analysis of the publication titles of 69 eminent American psychologists (Simonton, 1992b).

Martindale (1990) himself has subjected psychological publications to this same assessment technique. In the first place, the *American Journal of Psychology* text (which he assessed with the composite variability index) was also gauged on primordial content. According to his trend analysis, "primordial content increased during the behaviorist paradigm shift and declined once the paradigm was established" (p. 363). Martindale then examined another sample of text extracted from *Psychological Review* from 1895 to 1985, using the same sampling strategy as for the *American Journal of Psychology*. Here he found that "primordial content fell throughout the behaviorist era and began to rise with the introduction of the cognitive paradigm" (p. 365). Finally, to get a better idea of what was happening to behaviorism, Martindale content analyzed the *Journal of the Experimental Analysis of Behavior*, randomly sampling 10 articles from every 2 years from 1958 to 1986. In this more specialized case, "primordial content declined during the atheoretical paradigm and began to increase with the shift to the theoretical paradigm"

(p. 366); that is, operant psychology underwent a transformation from Skinner's purely descriptive behaviorism to one that was more sympathetic to the introduction of general theoretical ideas. This change had the curious effect of rendering behaviorism more compatible with cognitive science.

Why was Martindale (1990) so interested in the transhistorical trends in the primordial (or primary-process) content in these journals? The reason is that he had already demonstrated, over a series of studies that have appeared since 1975, that fluctuations in primordial content were associated with stylistic changes in the arts, especially in such literary forms as poetry and fiction (e.g., Martindale, 1975, 1990). This association is based on the role that primary process plays in creative thought, the constraints imposed by a given artistic style, and the constant drive toward increased originality that artistic creators must face. Furthermore, Martindale wanted to show that something comparable is associated with the supposed paradigm shifts undergone by his own discipline. In fact, as is very obvious from the quotations just given, Martindale felt free to interpret his empirical results in Kuhnian terms. Accordingly, his content analyses might be said to reinforce the earlier evidence regarding Kuhn's (1970) displacement thesis. Specifically, both citation and content analyses appear to indicate the real existence of a "cognitive revolution."

Yet is this inference really justified? One might raise the objection that the trends in primordial content for the *American Journal of Psychology* and *Psychological Review* are not in complete agreement. Martindale (1990) explained the discrepancy in terms of changes in the aims of the latter journal, which transformed from a vehicle for empirical research to a place to present new theory. Yet some other reason might be responsible. Even more crucial is Martindale's demonstration that fluctuations in primordial content are associated with stylistic changes. Might it not then seem justifiable to assert that the trends observed in the *American Journal of Psychology* and *Psychological Review* reflect not paradigm shifts, in a Kuhnian sense, but rather merely mirror transformations in research styles? Like some outmoded literary genre, behaviorism became unfashionable, and cognitive psychology came in vogue. Most serious poets do not write Elizabethan sonnets anymore, and most mainstream psychologists have lost interest in describing the finest details about operant conditioning. Despite the highly paradigmatic nature of the research published in the *Journal for the Experimental Analysis of Behavior*, behaviorists did not seem to conjure up anomalies that, according to Kuhnian theory, would find resolution only with the coming of cognitive science. Cognitive psychologists did not incorporate behaviorism into a more comprehensive paradigm but simply turned to topics that have fascinated psychologists ever since the days of Wundt. In this sense, if Skinner's behaviorism was "radical," then cognitive psychology was "reactionary." The mind was revived, the mind–body problem reinstated, and introspectionism subtly reintroduced as "protocol analysis" or some similar euphemism.

Whether this alternative interpretation of Martindale's (1990) data is true cannot be decided without additional empirical studies. Perhaps both the techniques of citation and content analysis can be sufficiently improved to render more finely differentiated insights into the discipline's transformations. In the meantime, there seems no way to contradict those who say that psychology is not Kuhnian. Never having had a true paradigm, psychology's history may not contain a genuine paradigm shift. If so, then the distinction Kuhn (1970) made between normal and revolutionary science may not apply to the field. So, lists of scientific revolutionaries may include no great psychologists; neither can it be supposed that any psychologist even attained greatness as a practitioner of normal science. Psychology may not yet have reached the point to support either type. Instead, it may still be bogged down in the preparadigmatic stage, when contending schools and haphazard fact gathering abound.

The latter attribute of preparadigmatic science is reminiscent of an observation that William James (1890/1952) made in his *Principles of Psychology*:

> Within a few years what one may call a microscopic psychology has arisen in Germany, carried on by experimental methods, asking of course every moment for introspective data, but eliminating their uncertainty by operating on a large scale and taking statistical means. This method taxes patience to the utmost, and could hardly have arisen in a country whose natives could be *bored*. Such Germans as Weber, Fechner, Vierordt, and Wundt obviously cannot. . . . There is little of the grand style about these new prism, pendulum, and chronograph-philosophers. They mean business, not chivalry. . . . [T]he results have as yet borne little theoretic fruit commensurate with the great labor expended in their acquisition. But facts are facts, and if we only get enough of them they are sure to combine. New ground will from year to year be broken, and theoretic results will grow. Meanwhile the experimental method has quite changed the face of the science so far as the latter is a record of mere work done. (pp. 126–127)

The question that all psychologists must ask is whether James would have expressed the same cynicism toward the discipline's fact collectors 100 years later—after witnessing firsthand the fruits of the "cognitive revolution."

HEGELIAN DIALECTICS

The putative cognitive revolution may have another interpretation besides it being a shift in either paradigm or fashion. Instead, the advent of cognitive psychology may represent a pendulum swing, as is often said to occur in the history of ideas. At the close of chapter 8 I showed how the long-term impact of 54 great psychologists was contingent on their having advocated extremist positions on the theoretical and methodological issues that divide the discipline (Simonton, 2000b). Such advocacy must certainly have provoked considerable criticism in the psychologists' own day—criticism that may be healthy for the discipline but unwelcome by the recipient. For example, it has been said that

> Külpe's Würzburg program generated controversy, which is excellent for stimulating research. Controversy prevents the establishment of orthodoxy, which works to stifle dissent. Unfortunately for Külpe, there was a heavy personal price to pay: His unorthodox findings generated criticism, even attack, from the men he admired and liked the most. (Thorne & Henley, 1997, p. 203)

Although the particular debate in this case concerned the existence of "imageless thought" rather than one of the scientific orientations listed in Table 8.1, such negative collegial reactions are a common experience for those who depart from the scientific consensus of their time.

In many instances, moreover, this criticism may eventually elicit the appearance of new schools of thought. "Reactions to [Descartes's] notion of innate ideas were so intense," wrote Hergenhahn (1992, p. 99), "that they launched new philosophical and psychological positions (e.g., modern empiricism and modern sensationalism)." One of the long-term consequences of the imageless thought controversy was an increased dissatisfaction among psychologists who advocated introspection as a scientific method. William James (1890/1952) said that this technique was the supreme method of the discipline: "Introspective Observation is what we have to rely on first and foremost and always" (p. 121, italics removed from entire quotation). Yet when Oswald Külpe and later Alfred Binet reported imageless thought while Wilhelm Wundt and Edward Titchener protested otherwise, the controversy could not be resolved by recourse to the introspective method. The growing distrust of this technique eventually led to the reaction that became behaviorism. First John B. Watson and later B. F. Skinner emphatically proclaimed subjective states off limits for any science worthy of the name. Yet by dismissing the mind as the object of psychological science, behaviorists began to stimulate discontent of another sort. Increasingly more psychologists believed that cognitive processes were the proper province of the discipline and that these processes could be scientifically studied. Yet the cognitive revolution that ensued could not be considered a mere return to the old days. The introspective methods of Wundt, James, Külpe, and Titchener were not resurrected; instead, the methodology of the new mentalistic psychology was more tightly bound to observed behavior, such as reaction times.

In fact, this historical sequence of introspectionism → behaviorism → cognitivism has very much the appearance of the Georg Hegel's dialectic process of thesis → antithesis → synthesis. The thesis that psychologists can study the mind introduces certain contradictions that motivate the emergence of the antithesis—the notion that psychologists cannot do so and still be a science. The synthesis, cognitive psychology, brings the discipline back around to a mental science, but not without incorporating certain features introduced by the behaviorists. The pendulum has not swung back completely to its original position. Whether cognitive psychology will generate its internal conflicts that will stimulate a behavioristic revival remains to be seen.

On a superficial level, the hypothesized Hegelian movement seems quite similar to what Kuhn's (1970) theory envisioned. The practitioners of normal science, by engaging in puzzle-solving research, dig up anomalies that constitute the seeds of the paradigm's own destruction. After the scientific revolution introduces a new paradigm, that dialectic process repeats. Occasionally, a new revolution may even cause something of a pendulum swing. For instance, the particle theory of light favored by Newton eventually had to give way to the wave theory, such as was advocated by Thomas Young. This shift was provoked by the discovery of increasingly more phenomena inconsistent with the particulate paradigm (e.g., diffraction). Yet with the discovery of the photoelectric effect, Einstein was able to reinstate light as particulate in nature (i.e., photons). Again, the pendulum did not return to the exact same position, because Einstein's photons where not the same as Newton's corpuscles. Furthermore, soon a new synthesis appeared in the form of the wave–particle duality of the Copenhagen school of quantum physics. Nevertheless, despite the commonalities between the Hegelian and Kuhnian schemes, they are far from equivalent. The more critical contrast is that Kuhn's concept of paradigm is both more complex and more rigorous than what is required for the Hegelian dialectic; that is, a paradigmatic thesis contains a logically interconnected collection of theory, method, and substantive issues.

Although the Hegelian dialectic thus seems to provide a handy tool for the interpretation of historical change, it also appears to contradict what I wrote earlier about Kroeberian configurations. The clustering of genius in contiguous generations was then interpreted in terms of a social influence process involving some combination of imitation, admiration, and emulation. Yet if the notables in Generation g are using the notables in Generation $g-1$ as role models, that would seem to imply some degree of continuity in their ideas. Artists of one generation should continue forward the stylistic developments introduced by those in the preceding generation. A like continuity should hold for other domains, such as philosophy, science, and psychology. Indeed, historians often explicitly express this continuity as a given. In chapter 10 I gave the example of how Wilhelm Wundt's psychology emerged from the empiricism of Hermann von Helmholtz, under whom Wundt had served as an assistant at Heidelberg University. Why did Wundt not view Helmholtz's views as a thesis to which he would propound an antithesis? Speaking more generally, why does each generation not hold views diametrically opposed to its predecessors?

This question can be given an empirical answer that is based on a secondary analysis of extensive data published by the sociologist Pitirim A. Sorokin (1937–1941). Because these data are so crucial to the current issue, and because they are used extensively in the next two chapters, I now briefly pause to describe what the data measure and how they were collected.

Sorokin's Generational Assessments of European Intellectual History

Pitirim Sorokin was as eminent a sociologist as Alfred Kroeber was an anthropologist. Born in Russia, Sorokin had to escape to the United States after the Bolsheviks took power, and he eventually ended up at Harvard University, where he founded its sociology department. About the same time that Kroeber (1944) was working on his *Configurations of Culture Growth*, Sorokin (1937–1941) was writing his magnum opus, the four-volume *Social and Cultural Dynamics*. The main purpose of this work was to develop a theory of sociocultural change that receives due attention in chapter 14. Yet, being as much an empiricist as a theorist, Sorokin devoted a considerable amount of this work to the collection of data that he thought would demonstrate his thesis (Ford, Richard, & Talbutt, 1996).

The empirical documentation that is of most interest here is that found in Volume 2, which has the subtitle *Fluctuations in Systems of Truth, Ethics, and Law*. For this volume Sorokin and his research collaborators attempted to gauge the transhistorical changes in various philosophical beliefs from the ancient Greeks to the first 20 years of the 20th century. They began their data collection by compiling a list of more than 2,000 thinkers where were active between 580 BC and AD 1920—basically from Thales to Edmond Husserl. The next step was to rate all of these thinkers on a 1–12 scale that gauged the magnitude of their influence in Western civilization.

Table 13.2 shows the scores received by some of the thinkers in Sorokin's (1937–1941) sample who also have some prominence in the history of psychology. As Sorokin admitted, different scholars might quibble with the placement of this or that figure. Even so, four considerations should ameliorate any complaints. First, Sorokin was able to recruit raters who were professional philosophers of considerable standing in their own right, making the ratings extremely well informed. Second, his raters implemented highly objective criteria, such as the number of monographs written about each thinker. Third, the ratings concern the individuals' impact on the Western philosophical tradition, and for this reason certain great scientists or writers (e.g., Newton and Shakespeare) may appear misplaced. Fourth and foremost, Sorokin's ratings correlated very highly with alternative assessments of these same thinkers (Simonton, 1976f). In chapter 3 I introduced the concept of Galton's G, the latent variable that underlies the reputation of historical figures. Sorokin's assessment of influence boasts a factor loading of .73 on a

TABLE 13.2
Comparative Influence of Representative Western Thinkers
According to Sorokin (1937–1941)

Score	Name
12	Plato, Aristotle, Plotinus, Thomas Aquinas, Kant
10	Augustine
9	Socrates, Leibniz, Newton, Nietzsche
8	Pythagoras, Protagoras, Democritus, Epicurus, Lucretius, Origen, Erigena, Albertus Magnus, Duns Scotus, William of Occam, Copernicus, G. Bruno, Galileo, Kepler, Decartes, Hobbes, Spinoza, Locke, Berkeley, Hume, Rousseau, Fichte, Schelling, Hegel, Goethe, Gauss, Schopenhauer, Comte, J. S. Mill, Spencer, Hartmann, C. Darwin, Marx, Maxwell, Bergson
7	Heraclitus, Parmenides, Theophrastus, Galen, Anselm, F. Bacon, Pascal, Gassendi, Malebranche, Wolff, Vico, Voltaire, Herbart, Fechner, Renouvier, Bain, Wundt, Ribot, W. James, Lipps
6	Empedocles, Aristippus, Pyrrho, Epictetus, Marcus Aurelius, Boethius, R. Bacon, Petrarch, T. More, Machiavelli, Vives, Montaigne, Bayle, Buffon, Cuvier, Diderot, Lessing, Condillac, Herder, Condorcet, J. Bentham, Malthus, J. Mill, Purkinje, Helmholtz, Galton, Haeckel, Jevons, Mach, Avenarius, Pavlov
5	Anaximander, Xenophaes, Zeno of Elea, Raymond Lully, Erasmus, Mersenne, La Mettrie, Carlyle, Lotze, Quételet, Bernard, DuBois-Reymond, J. Royce, Baldwin
4	Alcuin, Abélard, Grosseteste, Pico della Mirandola, Paracelsus, Harvey, Gilbert, Hartley, Reid, B. Franklin, E. Darwin, Pestalozzi, D. Stewart, Cabanis, Coleridge, Boole, F. Brentano, Delboeuf, Lombroso, Ladd, Romanes, Binet, Pearson, Durkheim, Kierkegaard, Münsterberg
3	Ptolemy, Hypatia, Rosellinus, T. Brown, Dilthey
2	Anaximenes, Leucippus, Alcmaeon, Buridan, Leonardo da Vinci
1	Aerte

Note. The ratings come from several distinct appendexes in Sorokin (1937–1941); I took only those names considered important in the history of psychology. Sorokin did not publish the ratings for individuals in his sample who were still living at the time the study began. The group included such luminaries as Stumpf, Dewey, Janet, S. Freud, Husserl, Külpe, Stern, and Jung.

10-indicator measure of Galton's G for these 2,012 thinkers, a loading exceeded by only two other measures (Simonton, 1991c).

Sorokin's (1937–1941) purpose in calculating these scores was not to assess individual differences anyway. Instead, he merely used these scores to create weighted aggregated measures of the representation of various philosophical positions throughout the history of Western thought; that is, he assumed that, say, Aristotle was more representative of intellectual history in the late 4th century BC than was Xenocrates, and so the former counted four times as much as the latter (12 vs. 3). Likewise, René Descartes's score of 8 relative to the score of 1 received by his contemporary Henri de Roy gives the former eight times as much weight in determining the prominence of certain ideas in the early part of the 17th century. Hence, when Sorokin tabulated his large sample of eminent thinkers into consecutive 20-year periods (according to when each thinker was active), he counted each individual in proportion to his or her influence score. He thus obtained generational time series that registered the fluctuations in all the issues and beliefs that have dominated Western intellectual history since its inception.

What were these philosophical ideas in the first place? There were many; each was designed to address some particular philosophical question. There were seven issues altogether, each with two or more potential responses. The seven issues and their possible answers follow.

1. *Where does knowledge come from?* This question is the subject of epistemology, one of the fundamental issues in the Western philosophical tradition. The possible answers are (a) *empiricism* (knowledge through the sense organs; e.g., the Epicureans and the British Empiricists), (b) *rationalism* (knowledge by means of logic and reason; e.g., Plato and the neo-Platonists), (c) *mysticism* (knowledge through revelation, intuition, or divine inspiration; e.g., Ralph Waldo Emerson and Henri Bergson), (d) *skepticism* (knowledge that is unattainable; e.g., Protagoras and Pyrrho of Elis), (e) *fideism* (knowledge gained only through a "will to believe" or some "as-if" type faith; e.g., the Stoics, Blaise Pascal, and William James), and (f) *criticism* (knowledge that is transcendental, according to Immanuel Kant and the Kantians). Many analyses using these time series collapse skepticism and criticism into a single measure, given that Kantianism is so recent and that both views agree that humans cannot know things in themselves.

2. *Is the world fundamentally material or spiritual?* The main answers to this classic ontological question are the following: (a) *mechanistic materialism* (soulless or lifeless matter is the sole basis; e.g., the Greek atomists and Epicureans, Thomas Hobbes, Ivan Pavlov, and J. B. Watson), (b) *hylozoism* (matter is the sole basis, but it has some lifelike properties as derivatives; e.g., Thales, William of Occam, Julien Offroy de La Mettrie, and Denis Diderot), (c) *monistic idealism* (a unified spirit or mind is the sole basis; e.g., Parmenides, Baruch Spinoza, Georg Hegel, and Johann Goethe), and (d) *pluralistic idealism* (multiple spiritual or mental entities are the basis; e.g., Pythagoras, Plutarch, Hypatia, Gottfried Wilhelm Leibniz, and Johann Gottlieb Fichte). For most purposes, mechanistic materialism is combined with hylozoism into a single index of materialism, and monistic and pluralistic idealism are similarly combined.

3. *Is reality eternal, or is it in constant flux?* This question concentrates on another facet of the world, namely, whether change is real or only apparent. The two extreme positions on this issue are (a) *eternalism* (reality is founded in an immutable being; e.g., Parmenides, Blaise Pascal, and Arthur Schopenhauer) and (b) *temporalism* (reality is founded in ever-changing becoming or progress and evolution; e.g., Heraclitus, David Hume, and J. S. Mill). The doctrine of evolution, such as that advocated by Charles Darwin, is a clear example of temporalism applied to life.

4. *Where do abstract ideas come from?* What is the relation between the universal and particular, between abstractions (e.g., "dog") and concrete instances (e.g., "Captain, my Australian shepherd"). The three solutions to this problem are (a) *nominalism* (universals are only names given by language as labels for particulars; e.g., Protagoras, the Epicureans, Roger Bacon, Niccolò Machiavelli, and Friedrich Nietzsche), (b) *realism* (universals are actually real, of which particulars are mere facsimiles or appearances; e.g., Pythagoras, Plato, Plotinus, Augustine of Hippo, Thomas Aquinas, and Emanuel Swedenborg), and (c) *conceptualism* (universals are only mental constructs derived from particulars; e.g., Empedocles, Lucius Annaeus Seneca, Immanuel Kant, and Charles Bernard Renouvier). Note that the last solution has its counterpart in the notion of bottom-up processing in cognitive psychology, as manifested in neuronetwork models.

5. *Does the individual or society have primacy?* This a question that has considerable disciplinary importance, for it pits psychological reductionism against sociological reductionism. One manifestation of this debate is the genius-versus-zeitgeist controversy that I examine in chapter 15. Anyway, the two main answers are (a) *singularism* (only the individual person exists and acts; e.g., Epicurus, Lucretius, La Mettrie, Jean-Jacques Rousseau, and Friedrich Nietzsche) and (b) *universalism* (society takes primacy over the individual, as in statism and collectivism; e.g., Plato, Albertus Magnus, Raymond Lully, Giovanni Battista Vico, and Georg Hegel).

6. *Is everything determined, or do human beings exercise free will?* This question has two main responses: (a) *determinism* (everything is caused, whether by fate or by cause–effect sequences governed by natural laws; e.g., Democritus, Marcus Aurelius, Thomas Hobbes, Baruch Spinoza, David Hartley, and Karl Marx) and (b) *indeterminism* (at least some free will or volition exists, at least in human beings; e.g., Aristotle, August-

ine of Hippo, Alcuin, Pierre Abélard, Desiderius Erasmus, and Immanuel Kant).

7. *What are the foundations of morality?* There are three major ethical systems according to Sorokin (1937–1941): (a) the *ethics of happiness* (hedonism, eudaemonism, utilitarianism, or any other morality that uses pleasure as the criterion of good; e.g., Democritus and the Epicureans, Niccolò Machiavelli, John Locke, Herbert Spencer, and Sigmund Freud), (b) the *ethics of principles* (moral criteria based on abstract and universal principles; e.g., Pythagoras, Plato, Aristotle, Christian Wolff, Immanuel Kant, and F. W. J Schelling), and (c) the *ethics of love* (moral criteria founded on altruism and charity; e.g., Origen, Johannes Scotas Erigena, Jean-Jacques Rousseau, Johann Gottfried von Herder, and Auguste Comte). Data analyses frequently will combine the last two ethical systems, because they concur that personal happiness is not the just criterion of right and wrong.

In sum, Sorokin (1937–1941) has compiled two or more generational time series for each of seven issues, with each time series recording a weighted index of the representation of a particular answer to a given issue.

Time-Series Analyses of Sorokin's (1937–1941) Generational Measures

Not only do philosophical geniuses cluster together in contiguous generations, as Kroeber (1944) and I (Simonton, 1988b, 1997d) have shown, but also the representatives of particular philosophical positions tend to congregate in adjacent generations as well (Klingemann, Mohler, & Weber, 1982; Simonton, 1976g, 1978b). Thus, the coming and going of various intellectual movements takes so many generations to be realized that the history of ideas tends to be described by quasi-cyclic trends (Simonton, 1978b). One foundation for this transhistorical continuity is that the weighted count of thinkers advocating a particular position in Generation g is a function of the weighted count of thinkers who hold the same positions in Generation $g - 1$. This autoregressive dependency is apparent in the sizable autocorrelations for all generational time series (Simonton, 1976g). For example, nominalism, realism, and conceptualism have coefficients of .81, .75, and .45, respectively. The last is the smallest cross-generational autocorrelation of any philosophical position, whereas the largest is .89, for empiricism. Much of this transhistorical inertia, of course, is maintained by the founding of schools, such as those identified as Peripatetic (Aristotelian), Epicurean, Stoic, neo-Platonic, Thomist, and Kantian. Once a school is established, it may be generations before it withers away or is supplanted by some rival philosophical system. Thus, the empiricism, materialism, nominalism, singularism, and ethics of happiness associated with Epicureanism endured throughout antiquity, until Christianity finally overwhelmed it.

From the standpoint of a scientific history of psychology, the comparatively low autocorrelation for conceptualism must be considered provocative. Because conceptualists believe that abstract ideas are constructions of the human mind, it is essentially a psychological doctrine, in contrast to linguistic nominalism and idealistic realism. Yet the data provide a basis for comprehending the comparatively low transhistorical stability of this position (Simonton, 1978b). Conceptualism is a stance that is strongly influenced by a large number of other philosophical positions. Specifically, the representation of conceptualism in Generation g is a positive function of the representation of the following positions in Generation $g - 1$: empiricism, skepticism, criticism, materialism, temporalism, singularism, and the ethics of happiness. It is evident that when the only knowledge one has comes from the sense organs; when this knowledge cannot be trusted, especially because the underlying reality consists in a continually changing material world; and when each individual stands alone to maximize pleasure and avoid pain, it seems that the repercussion is a strengthened belief that one's ideas are nothing more than mental constructions from one's life experiences. To the extent that conceptualism is a primary concern of cognitive psychologists, then these cross-generational influences constitute an inventory of the philosophical milieu underlying that movement.

As valuable as the foregoing results may be, something appears to be missing. The original purpose behind entering this topic was to discover if there occurred any Hegelian pendulum shifts in the history of ideas. Is there any evidence that some thesis can induce the emergence of an antithesis? Can some philosophical action produce a philosophical reaction after a generational delay? Generational time-series analysis of Sorokin's (1937–1941) data have come up with one interesting example that comes close to fulfilling this requirement. Certain intellectual movements appear to have had a polarizing effect on the history of Western thought. In particular, suppose that Generation $g - 1$ has a burst of philosophical thought advocating empiricism, materialism, temporalism, nominalism, singularism, determinism, and the ethics of happiness? Then in Generation g two opposing repercussions occur simultaneously (Simonton, 1978b). First, there appears a florescence of thinkers advocating either skepticism or criticism. The human capacity to know directly the real world is thus denied. Second, there emerges a contemporary surge in thinkers advancing fideism. Rather than give up on knowing anything, fideists rely on faith alone, which cannot be undermined by arguments about the unreliability of the senses or the fallibility of reason. Fideism constitutes an almost desperate reaction to a milieu that has become excessively materialistic, transitory, arbitrary, selfish, and perhaps pessimistic.

Among the many thinkers whom Sorokin's (1937–1941) raters identified as fideists was the great psychologist William James. In line with this assignment, James grew up in a period when thinkers who espoused empiricism, materialism, temporalism, nominalism, singularism, determinism, and the ethics of happiness were becoming increasingly conspicuous in Western civilization. To give the specifics, Kroeber's (1944) 40-year floruit rule puts James in Generation 1880–1899, as in Figure 13.1. According to Sorokin's tables, during the period 1860–1879, or the preceding generation, empiricism already represented 46% of the epistemological zeitgeist. Comparable representations for the positions on the other six issues had already reached the following levels: materialism, 17%; temporalism, 41%; nominalism, 49%; singularism, 43%; determinism, 61%; and the ethics of happiness, 38%. By the first generation of the 20th century, almost all of these stances were to become the favored answers to the seven key philosophical issues (Simonton, 1976f).

Tender-minded soul that he was, James did not find this toughminded worldview totally to his liking. Scientific determinism was especially problematic for the young James, and in his late 20s he suffered a severe depression. He resolved the crisis by reading Charles Barnard Renouvier, a French philosopher who defended free will by arguing that the mind can obviously select one thought to the deliberate exclusion of other thoughts. James then affirmed that his "first act of free will shall be to believe in free will" (H. James, 1920, Vol. 1, p. 147). Hence, indeterminism was proclaimed not empirically or rationally but by means of fideism plain and simple.

This fideist orientation can be seen cropping up throughout the rest of James's career. It showed up in his philosophy of pragmatism when he argued that a belief should be judged according to whether it "works" for the person who holds that belief. In his 1907 work, *Pragmatism*, James made explicit that this loose criterion renders "theological beliefs" such as "God exists" true if someone is better off acting according to that belief. Fideism also sneaks into various places in the *Principles of Psychology* (1890/1952), as the following remark implies:

> Refuse to express a passion, and it dies. Count to ten before venting your anger, and its occasion seems ridiculous. Whistling to keep up courage is no mere figure of speech. On the other hand, sit all day in a moping posture, sigh, and reply to everything with a dismal voice, and your melancholy lingers. There is no more valuable precept in moral education than this, as all who have experience know: if we wish to conquer undesirable emotional tendencies in ourselves, we must assiduously, and in the first instance cold-bloodedly, go through the *outward movements* of those contrary dispositions which we prefer to cultivate. The reward of persistency will infallibly come, in the fading out of the sullenness or depression, and the advent of real cheerfulness and kindliness in their stead. Smooth the brow, brighten the eye, contract the dorsal rather

than the ventral aspect of the frame, and speak in a major key, pass the genial compliment, and your heart must be frigid indeed if it does not gradually thaw! (pp. 751–752)

James is expressing an "as if" philosophy here: If one pretends to have a feeling different than what one really has, one will have eventually changed one's feeling. It is what works in the end that counts. For this to work, however, one must have faith that it will work.

MERTONIAN MULTIPLES

The James quotation about how to will yourself into happiness was part of his presentation of what is now called the *James–Lange theory of emotion*. According to this theory, the subjective experience of emotion comes after the emotion has first taken bodily form as physiological and skeletal responses to the corresponding external stimuli. In concrete terms, "we feel sorry because we cry, angry because we strike, afraid because we tremble, and not that we cry, strike, or tremble, because we are sorry, angry, or fearful, as the case may be" (James, 1890/1952, p. 743). Although James shares eponymic credit with the Danish psychologist Carl Lange, the idea was not a collaborative effort. James had first proposed his version of the theory in an 1884 article in *Mind*, and Lange had independently published his own version of the theory in an 1885 pamphlet. By the time James was writing *Principles* he was aware of Lange's contribution and so discussed both versions in his chapter on emotion.

This episode is not the sole example in which two or more scientists make the same discovery independently, sometimes almost simultaneously. Perhaps the best known example from the history of psychology is also one of the most famous instances from the history of science: the theory of evolution by natural selection. In 1842, Charles Darwin first wrote a long essay describing the main features of his theory, but did not publish it at once. Knowing how controversial the theory would be, he planned to write a multivolume monograph in which the empirical support for the theory could be fully documented. Only a few of his closest colleagues were kept informed of his continual labors. Some of these colleagues, such as the geologist Charles Lyell, warned Darwin not to wait too long, or else his contribution might be pre-empted by some other scientist. In 1858, while still putting all the documentation together, Darwin received a paper from Alfred Wallace, a younger colleague. Darwin sent it to Lyell, adding the following remarks to his cover letter:

> Your words have come true with a vengeance—that I should be forestalled. You said this, when I explained to you here very briefly my views of "Natural Selection" depending on the struggle for existence. I never

saw a more striking coincidence; if Wallace had my MS. sketch written out in 1842, he could not have made a better short abstract! Even his terms now stand as heads of my chapters. Please return me the MS., which he does not say he wishes me to publish, but I shall, of course, at once write and offer to send to any journal. So all my originality, whatever it may amount to, will be smashed, though my book, if it will ever have any value, will not be deteriorated; as all the labour consists in the application of the theory. (F. Darwin, 1892/1958, p. 196)

Fortunately for Darwin, Lyell and others convinced him to contribute to a joint paper that was read along with Wallace's paper, extracts from Darwin's earlier sketch, and part of a letter to a colleague a year before in which Darwin had presented his ideas. After that presentation, made before the Linnean Society in July 1858, Darwin worked quickly to write an abstract of his unfinished treatise. The abbreviated work came out by the end of 1859, and all 1,250 copies sold the first day. So successful was the resulting *Origin of Species* that the theory is known by Darwin's name alone, rather than having to hyphenate it with Wallace's, unlike in the case of James–Lange theory.

In the above two cases everything was settled amicably, yet that is not always the outcome. Often bitter priority disputes result instead, as occurred in the vicious controversy between Isaac Newton and Gottfried Wilhelm Leibniz over who invented calculus. Priority was finally settled by a special commission of the Royal Society of London, which condemned Leibniz as a plagiarist, a charge that modern historians believe was totally unjustified. Only later was it learned that the draft of the commission's report was written by the society's president, Newton himself! Psychology's history does not contain anything quite so vicious, albeit the controversy between Pierre Janet and Sigmund Freud over the originality of the latter's psychoanalytic theory comes close. So bitter was Freud over the episode that more than 20 years later Freud refused to allow Janet to pay him a visit.

Several researchers have attempted to compile extensive lists of such phenomena. The first published list contained 148 cases (Ogburn & Thomas, 1922), but later this count was extended to 264 (Merton, 1961b) and later still to 579 (Simonton, 1979). Table 13.3 (see p. 387) provides some examples that have some relevance to the history of psychology, either because they concern significant contributions to the discipline or because they involved notable figures in the field. Although the number of reported instances is not large in psychology proper, the phenomenon cannot be considered totally exceptional either. The occurrence is certainly frequent enough to demand some explanation. I next present the traditional interpretation of these historical events, after which I present some objections to that interpretation. I conclude with a discussion of an alternative explanation that does a far better job of handling the empirical details of the multiples phenomenon.

The Traditional Interpretation: Deterministic Zeitgeist

When I discussed Kroeber's (1944) *Configurations of Culture Growth* earlier in this chapter, I noted that his intent was to disprove Galton's (1869) genetic theory of genius. As a cultural anthropologist, Kroeber strove to show that genius was merely a manifestation of the larger sociocultural system. In Sorokin's (1937–1941) terms, Kroeber was arguing for universalism, in opposition to Galton's singularism (as Galton was so identified in Sorokin's *Social and Cultural Dynamics*). However, the 1944 book was not the first time Kroeber had argued against Galton's position. The first attack came in an article entitled "The Superorganic" that Kroeber had published in a 1917 issue of *American Anthropologist*. A critical part of Kroeber's argument in this article depends on the phenomenon just described. Besides listing more than 24 cases of independent discoveries or inventions, Kroeber made much out of the near-simultaneity of so many of them. For instance, Georg Mendel's laws of inheritance were rediscovered the same year by three independent researchers: Hugo Marie De Vries, Karl Franz Correns, and Erich Tschermak. The year was 1900, and the dates were March 14, April 24, and June 2. To Kroeber, this temporal proximity seems far too great to be discounted as mere coincidence. Instead, the rediscovery must have been the product of the sociocultural system (or "superorganic") that determined that the time was ripe for that specific rediscovery to be made. Mendelian genetics "was discovered in 1900 because it could have been discovered only then, and because it infallibly must have been discovered then," claimed Kroeber (1917, p. 199). This event was not only inevitable, but it was inevitable at a narrowly demarcated moment in the history of science.

Kroeber's (1917) position was developed by subsequent anthropologists and sociologists (e.g., Lamb & Easton, 1984; L. White, 1949). Of special significance are the ideas of Robert K. Merton (1961a, 1961b), the founder of the Mertonian school of the sociology of science. For Merton, the occurrence of these independent discoveries and inventions provided an ideal research site for understanding the sociological basis of scientific creativity. Like Kroeber, he advocated a sociocultural determinism that minimized the role of the individual genius. In Merton's own words,

> discoveries and inventions become virtually inevitable (1) as prerequisite kinds of knowledge accumulate in man's cultural store; (2) as the attention of a sufficient number of investigators is focused on a problem—by emerging social needs, or by developments internal to the particular science, or by both. (1961a, p. 306)

Moreover, he deemed the phenomenon of sufficient importance to provide it with a name: *multiples*, to be distinguished from *singletons*, which were the products of a single mind (Merton, 1961b).

Merton then went on to argue that multiples are actually more typical than singletons in the history of science. To make this case, Merton (1961b) gathered a collection of 264 multiples to study their specific properties. On the basis of this study and other observations, Merton concluded that the singletons, not the multiples, constitute "the residual cases, requiring special examination," because "all scientific discoveries are in principle multiples, including those that on the surface appear to be singletons" (p. 477). Almost as conclusive proof of this claim, Merton (1961b) observed that the discovery of multiples was itself multiply discovered. In addition to Kroeber, Merton listed the French philosopher Auguste Comte, the German physiologist Emil DuBois-Reymond, and more than 12 other cases. Indeed, although Merton did not mention it, Kroeber participated in more than one multiple. At least Kroeber's (1944) use of genius clustering to attack Galton's (1869) biological determinism was independently advanced by a sociologist (J. Schneider, 1937) the same year that Kroeber (1944, p. 848) claimed to have nearly completed writing *Configurations of Culture Growth*. Although unaware of this multiple, Kroeber (1944) did view Sorokin's (1937–1941) *Social and Cultural Dynamics* as something approaching a multiple, at least in their shared analysis of the sociocultural factors behind the appearance of genius. The first volume of Sorokin's work began to emerge in 1937.

In any case, the idea that scientific contributions are rendered inevitable by the sociocultural milieu has gone beyond the confines of anthropology and sociology. It has permeated history as well. This comment of a general historian can be considered representative:

> Many scientific discoveries would have been made or sweeping theories developed by someone else had the actual discoverer or developer never lived. The first elaborate formulation of the theory of evolution appeared in 1859 in Charles Darwin's *The Origin of the Species*. Had Darwin never lived some similar book would certainly have appeared within a few years, for most of the basic conceptions in evolution had been developed in the preceding three generations. (Norling, 1970, p. 90)

What is more remarkable is that sociocultural determinism even shows up in the history of psychology as well, albeit normally under the rubric of the zeitgeist theory of history introduced in chapter 2. I say this is remarkable because histories of psychology are almost always written by psychologists. One might think that psychologists would dismiss the sociocultural explanation as just another example of anthropological and sociological universalism trying to encroach on psychological singularism. The interpretations of Kroeber, Merton, and others might be rejected as some insidious guise of disciplinary imperialism. Scientific and technological creativity would require no psychological explanation, but rather it could be totally ascribed to sociocultural processes. Therefore, it may appear almost disciplinary apostasy for a psychologist to accept the sociocultural deterministic account of the multiples phenomenon. Yet these conceptual betrayals are actually extremely common in the histories of the discipline. The following two quotations are typical of many:

1. Without Fechner's insight in 1850, a truly experimental psychology probably would have been only slightly delayed. The time was ripe for the birth of scientific psychology, and Fechner was in the right place at the right time with the right preparation. (Thorne & Henley, 1997, p. 146)

This passage appears to echo what Kroeber (1917) said of the rediscovery of Mendel's laws. The only concession to psychological singularism is the assertion that Gustav Fechner had the "right preparation," which made him the right person at the right place and time. However, certainly "preparation" is a far cry from saying Fechner's accomplishments were a mark of genius.

2. In 1847 Helmholtz published a highly significant monograph on the conservation of energy; that the concept was in the Zeitgeist is demonstrated by the fact that it was proposed independently by Mayer, a physician, who published a popular paper on it in the same year. (Wertheimer, 1987, p. 55)

What makes this quotation especially remarkable was that it came from the mouth of Michael Wertheimer, son of Gestalt psychologist Max Wertheimer. Max had devoted the last part of his life to writing the book *Productive Thinking*, which was published posthumously in 1945 and republished in 1982 under Michael's editorship. As mentioned in chapter 6, this book includes a Gestalt theory of scientific creativity that would seem incompatible with sociocultural determinism.

These two quotes reflect the pervasive influence of E. G. Boring (1963) on how the history of psychology tends to be written. Boring explicitly used the existence of multiples to support his zeitgeist interpretation of psychology's history. For instance, after discussing the James–Lange and Darwin–Wallace cases, he concluded that "you cannot get away from the fact that the times have something to do with the discovery, something more than the fact that discovery must wait upon the necessarily antecedent discoveries" (1963, p. 36). It was largely based on the multiples phenomenon that Boring believed it possible to replace a personalistic history of psychology with a naturalistic one. After all, if a discovery would have appeared regardless of the individuals involved, then it would seem superfluous, if not impertinent, to mention names or describe personal characteristics. History would become a narrative of the main discoveries that grace the annals of the discipline, plus speculations about the particulars of the zeitgeist that generated those discoveries.

Because historians of psychology could extirpate all psychology from their writings, it would seem more appropriate for the history of psychology to be written by anthropologists and sociologists than by psychologists!

Objections to Sociocultural Determinism

Although Kroeber, Merton, and Boring were all convinced that multiples undermine the individual as an agent of scientific advance, that universalist inference may go well beyond both logic and data. It is very possible that despite the prima facie plausibility of the zeitgeist explanation some other process is actually better able to explicate all the complexities of the phenomenon. In fact, there are many notables in the history of psychology who failed to draw the same conclusions from the occurrence. Two prominent examples are Charles Darwin and his cousin Francis Galton.

Darwin experienced the multiples phenomenon directly, as I noted previously. The unfortunate Wallace episode notwithstanding, Darwin's *Autobiography* contains this passage:

> It has sometimes been said that the success of the *Origin* proved "that the subject was in the air," or "that men's minds were prepared for it." I do not think that this is strictly true, for I occasionally sounded out not a few naturalists, and never happened to come across a single one who seemed to doubt about the permanence of species. Even Lyell and Hooker, though they would listen with interest to me, never seemed to agree. I tried once or twice to explain to able men what I meant by Natural selection, but signally failed. What I believe was strictly true is that innumerable well-observed facts were stored in the minds of naturalists ready to take their proper places as soon as any theory which would receive them was sufficiently explained. (F. Darwin, 1892/1958, p. 45)

This comment might admittedly appear self-serving, given that Darwin was claiming more credit than the zeitgeist interpretation would allow him. Even so, Galton (1869) observed the phenomenon in a more disinterested manner when he was writing *Hereditary Genius*. At the opening of his chapter "Men of Science," Galton (1892/1972) had this to say:

> It is notorious that the same discovery is frequently made simultaneously and quite independently, by different persons. Thus, to speak of only a few cases in late years, the discoveries of photography, of electric telegraphy, and of the planet Neptune through theoretical calculations, have all their rival claimants. It would seem, that discoveries are usually made when the time is ripe for them—that is to say, when the ideas from which they naturally flow are fermenting in the minds of many men. When apples are ripe, a trifling event suffices to decide, which of them shall first drop of its stalk; so a small accident will often determine the scientific man who shall first make and publish a new discovery. There are many persons who have contributed vast numbers of original memoirs, all of them of some, many of great, but none of extraordinary impor-

tance. These men have the capacity of making a striking discovery though they had not the luck to do so. (p. 243)

Galton (1874) returned to this topic in *English Men of Science*, in which he again recognized that "great discoveries have often been made simultaneously by workers ignorant of each other's labours. This shows that they had derived their inspiration from a common but hidden source, as no mere chance would account for simultaneous discovery" (p. 7). Galton even seemed to agree with Merton's (1961b) assertion that singletons are the exception rather than the rule, at least in terms of the underlying process.

> It would therefore appear that few discoveries are wholly due to a single man, but rather than vague and imperfect ideas, which float in conversation and literature, must grow, gather, and develop, until some more perspicacious and prompt mind than the rest clearly sees them. (Galton, 1874, p. 8)

Sometimes those ideas coalesce in a single mind and become a singleton. However, those ideas might just as well gel in two or more minds and form a multiple.

Despite the fact that Galton (1869, 1874) made these statements, he persisted in the belief that genius existed and left its mark on history. In both *Hereditary Genius* and *English Men of Science* he admitted the existence of multiples while concentrating on individual factors—genetic and developmental, respectively. Hence, psychology is not rendered irrelevant by the multiples phenomenon. On the contrary, Galton's remarks also emphasize that the discoveries occur within the human mind. Societies and cultures don't think, only people think. Moreover, some minds might be more "perspicacious and prompt" than other minds, and those at the extreme upper end of the distribution on perceptiveness and quickness may grab the idea first.

I wish to go one step further than this accommodation, however. I argue that the evidence on behalf of the zeitgeist theory is far more tenuous than most scholars—whether they be anthropologists, sociologists, historians, or psychologists—realize. Specifically, sociocultural determinism fails to deal adequately with the following four issues: generic versus specific categories, independent versus antecedent events, simultaneous discoveries versus rediscoveries, and necessary versus necessary and sufficient causes.

Universal or Particular?

Although the number of multiple discoveries looks rather impressive, the specific cases do not always bear up under scrutiny; rather, the lists of putative multiples include many clear illustrations of "a failure to distinguish between the genus and the individual" (Schmookler, 1966, p. 191). Two supposed duplicates are often not actually identical, but rather a generic category has been superficially imposed on distinct creations. In the priority dispute between Pierre Janet and Sigmund Freud, Janet argued that whatever was scientifically valid about psychoanalysis was stolen from him, whereas whatever was not so stolen was invalid. Freud made it very clear that the contrasts between their ideas were profound, all differences going in the direction of the superior scientific standing of psychoanalytic theory. For example, Freud devoted part of his 1909 lectures delivered at Clark University—a year later published as the *Origin and Development of Psycho-Analysis*—to emphasizing the differences between him and Janet. Freud's concept of the dynamic unconscious and repression cannot be subsumed under Janet's more limited and static notion of "subconscious fixed ideas."

The lack of identity of supposed multiples even holds for the Darwin–Wallace multiple, despite Darwin's spontaneous confession of the numerous similarities. In the first place, Darwin and Wallace were not stimulated by the same intellectual antecedents. Thus, although both Darwin and Wallace were influenced by Thomas Malthus, artificial selection—seen in the breeding of domestic animals—had a unique part to play in Darwin's thinking. Furthermore, it was Darwin who worked hardest at extending the explanatory power of evolutionary theory, making it encompass all of life's phenomena. Hence, it was Darwin who took the bold step of applying the theory to the evolution of human higher mental powers, something Wallace (an advocate of Spiritualism in later life) was unwilling to do. Moreover, Darwin did his utmost to provide the richest possible empirical documentation and logical argument on behalf of the theory. His 1871 *Descent of Man and Selection in Relation to Sex* and 1872 *Expression of the Emotions in Man and Animals*, in combination with the numerous editions of *Origin* and many more specialized studies, all served to establish the scientific potency of evolution by natural selection.

Without Darwin's efforts in this respect it would be doubtful that the theory would have made much headway against the prejudices of the time. For Darwin, unlike for Wallace, evolutionary theory was the "central message" of his entire career (Patinkin, 1983). Indeed, so central was Darwin's contribution that Wallace was perfectly willing to concede Darwin primary credit for the theory. As Wallace confessed in a letter written a few years after Darwin's death, "I have not the love of *work*, *experiment* and *detail* that was so pre-eminent in Darwin, and without which anything I could have written would never have convinced the world" (F. Darwin, 1892/1958, p. 201). Not long after this acknowledgment, Wallace published his 1889 book *Darwinism, an Exposition of the Theory of Natural Selection With Some of Its Applications*—and thereby conferred eponymic status on his deceased colleague.

Independent or Antecedent?

The long list of multiples suffers from another liability: that the separate contributions fail to satisfy the criterion that the products be independent. Far too often individuals cited as independent contributors were actually influenced by one or more of the other parties to the multiple. By this criterion, the Young–Helmholtz theory of color does not fall into the same category as the James–Lange theory of emotion (cf. Ogburn & Thomas, 1922). Young's work was known to Helmholtz, whose contribution was to publicize it in a slightly improved form. Helmholtz himself had no doubt about where his trichromatic theory originated.

Making this objection all the more potent is that one scientist may influence another without there being any awareness of an intellectual debt. According to E. G. Boring (1963), many "apparently independent discoveries may nevertheless depend on some degree of unconscious communication" (p. 36, italics removed from entire quotation). He specifically raised this issue with respect to the Berkeley–Titchener multiple listed in Table 13.3:

> Why did Titchener, when he formulated the context theory of meaning in 1909, feel that he was making so original a contribution when the basic relation had been noted by Bishop Berkeley in 1709? Titchener knew his British associationists and he was being just exactly two centuries late; yet he never seemed to realized this fact. (p. 36)

Titchener had probably assimilated so well Berkeley's ideas that they had become his own, without cognizance of their origins.

The fallibility of human memory that allows such events to happen is humorously illustrated in a story that Boring (1963) told of his distinguished colleague, S. Smith Stevens. The latter

> had what he thought was a brand new idea and he liked it. Starting to write it up, he searched for anticipations in the literature and failed to find any, until he discovered the very same piece of "originality" in his own files under his own authorship. (p. 11)

Stevens had formed a multiple with himself. This duplicate discovery was presumably not the Stevens's power law!

Simultaneous or Rediscovered?

Unlike independence, simultaneity is not an essential requirement for two or more products to be categorized as a multiple. Even so, a clue concerning the nature of the phenomenon may be found in the fact that supposed multiples are seldom simultaneous in any strict sense. In Merton's (1961b) study of 264 multiples, only 20% took place even within a 1-year interval. In contrast, fully 34% of the multiples required at least 10 years to elapse before the duplications ceased. In fact, occasionally hundreds of years will divide the first and last instance of a multiple—such as the discovery of the "Eustachian" tubes by Alcmaeon in the 6th century BC and by Eustachio in the 16th century AD. This frequent temporal hiatus raises two doubts, one empirical and the other theoretical.

TABLE 13.3
Some Putative Instances of Multiple Discoveries and Inventions

Discovery or invention	Discoverer/Inventor and year
Microscope	Johannides (1610?), Drebbel (1610?), Galileo (1610?)
Logarithms	Bürgi (1620), Napier and Briggs (1614)
Context theory of meaning	Berkeley (1709), Titchener (1909)
Animal electricity	Sultzer (1768), Cotuguo (1786), Galvani (1791)
Calculus	Newton (1671), Leibniz (1676)
Oxygen	Scheele (1774), Priestley (1774)
Color theory	Young (1801), Helmholtz (1856–1866)
Principle of least squares	Gauss (1809), Legendre (1806)
Evolution by natural selection	W. C. Wells (1813), P. Matthew (1831), C. Darwin (1844), Wallace (1858)
Purkinje effect	M. Koltz (1816), Purkinje (1825)
Unconscious motivation and repression	Schopenhauer (1819), S. Freud (1895)
Term *objective psychology*	Purkinje (1827), H. Spencer
Energy conservation	J. R. von Mayer (1843), Helmholtz (1847), Joule (1847), Colding (1847), Thomson (1847)
Emmert's law	Schopenhauer? (1815), Séguin (1854), Lubinoff (1858), Zehender (1856), Emmert (1881)
Ophthalmoscope	Anagnostakis (1854), Helmholtz (1851), C. Babbage (1847)
Genetic laws	Mendel (1865), De Vries (1900), Correns (1900), Tchermak (1900)
Spinal nerve root functions	C. Bell (1811), Magendie (1822)
Theory of emotions	W. James (1884), Lange (1885)
Positivist basis for introspection	Mach (1886), Avenarius (1888–1890)
Unconsciousness mind in psychopathology	Janet (1889), S. Freud (1895)
Mutation theory	Korschinsky (1899), De Vries (1900)
Classical conditioning	Pavlov (1902?), Twitmyer (1904)
Behaviorism	Piéron (1908), J. B. Watson (1913)

Note. This list concentrates on putative multiples that are of special relevance to the history of psychology and closely allied disciplines.

On the empirical side, the longer the delay separating two or more hypothesized duplicate discoveries, the more hazardous the supposition that they satisfy the essential criterion of independence. E. G. Boring (1963) raised this possibility with respect to the law of the spinal nerve roots. François Magendie's experimental work came almost 12 years after Charles Bell had published a small pamphlet presenting the law. Even if Magendie did not deliberately plagiarize Bell's work, "people do, indeed, read things, forget about them, and then later revive the idea, forgetting the source and believing it to be their very own" (Boring, 1963, p. 11). To avoid counting instances of unconscious plagiarism, perhaps historians should adopt a more conservative definition of multiples, one that requires simultaneity as well as independence. The lists might be confined, say, to only those multiples that are separated by no more than 1 year. Yet this restriction would then delete 80% of the cases, not even counting the deletions due to unacceptably generic categories and well-documented causal linkages (Merton, 1961b).

On the theoretical side, the very existence of these rediscoveries—even when truly independent—must call into question the explanatory power of sociocultural determinism. For example, if the laws of genetics become unequivocally inevitable at a specific point in history, why were they discovered first in 1865 and then rediscovered in 1900? That implies a lot of slippage in the zeitgeist's deterministic powers. Furthermore, it is begging the question to claim that Mendel was simply "ahead of his time." The times are supposed to define what products can and cannot appear. Because the zeitgeist failed to deny Mendel the discovery of the laws of genetics, it should become evident that one must segregate the creative product from whatever determines the social acceptance of that product. William James (1880) stated the difference thus:

> Social evolution is a resultant of the interaction of two wholly distinct factors: the individual, deriving his peculiar gifts from the play of psychological and infra-social forces, but bearing all the power of initiative and origination in his hands; and, second, the social environment, with its power of adopting or rejecting both him and his gifts. (p. 448)

The rejection is most likely to take place when a discovery's "implications cannot be connected by a series of simple logical steps to canonical, or generally accepted, knowledge" (Stent, 1972, p. 84). The idea is then premature, reducing the unfortunate anticipator to the status of a precursor genius.

The concept of prematurity can be applied to other multiples besides rediscoveries. In chapter 3 I mentioned the independent discovery of classical conditioning by Ivan Pavlov and Edwin Burket Twitmyer. As Table 13.3 indicates, because the two contributions appeared so close in time, and because Pavlov preceded Twitmyer, this multiple cannot be considered a rediscovery in the same pattern as Mendel's laws. Even so, Twitmyer's conditioning of the patellar reflex to a bell occurred in a different milieu than did Pavlov's conditioning of salivation to a light (Coon, 1982). Pavlov's discovery emerged directly out of his more basic research on the physiology of digestion. This Nobel prize winning research provided a secure basis for Pavlov's study of the less primitive "psychical secretions." Twitmyer, in contrast, was operating in the context of an American psychology that was still preoccupied with the content of consciousness, a subject about which the primitive knee-jerk response said nothing. Accordingly, Twitmyer's work was premature for the time and place in which he lived.

Inevitable or Eventual?

Sociocultural determinism does not adequately distinguish between necessary causes and causes that are necessary and sufficient. The occurrence of long-delayed rediscoveries implies that one must take care to distinguish between necessary and sufficient determinants of a creative product. A *necessary* cause is one that supplies a prerequisite for another event to happen. Calculus presupposes some principle of limits, but this causal claim is too weak to support the inference of determinism. To get a stronger statement, one must argue that the milieu provides necessary and sufficient causes. Such causes do not just allow an effect to take place but rather require it to happen inevitably. Yet the evidence argues against this strong form. Very often a contribution builds on a cultural substrate that has been around for decades, or even centuries. There is nothing in Copernican theory, for example, that could not have been expressed centuries earlier—neither new data nor new mathematics were required.

Individuals who believe in the inexorable advance of science might admittedly still argue that all discoveries will eventually appear once the requisite groundwork has been laid. Yet to say that something will eventually see the light of day is a far cry from claiming the inevitability of its birth at a precise point in time. Furthermore, even when one can hold that a specific discovery will happen eventually, that does not necessitate that the events will unfold in a predetermined pattern. Not just the timing, but the nature of the creative product itself may change. Stent (1972) made this point with respect to James Watson and Francis Crick's formulation of the structure of DNA:

> If Watson and Crick had not existed, the insights they provided in one single package would have come out much more gradually over a period of many months or years. Dr. B might have seen that DNA is a double-strand helix, and Dr. C might later have recognized the hydrogen bonding between the strands. Dr. D later yet might have proposed a complementary purine–pyrimidine bonding, with Dr. E in a subsequent paper proposing the specific adenine–thymine and guanine–cytosine replication mechanism of DNA based on the complementary nature of the two strands. All the while Drs. H, I, J, K and L would have been confusing the issue by publishing incorrect structures and proposals. (p. 90)

The same may be said of other multiples. The history of psychology would have been very different if Darwin had drowned on the *Beagle* voyage or if Sigmund Freud's cocaine addiction had led to a lethal overdose. The same ideas might have eventually emerged, but not in the consummate form of *Origin of Species* or *Interpretation of Dreams*. Without those seminal works and their paradigmatic sequels, how strong of a presence would evolutionary psychology or psychoanalysis currently claim in the annals of psychology?

The Modern Interpretation: Stochastic Genius

I have just shown that the empirical evidence on behalf of the zeitgeist or sociocultural determinist explanation suffers from an excessive use of generic categories to define multiples and from a tendency to overlook the essential criterion of true independence. I have also indicated how the traditional theory has problems handling the phenomenon of rediscovery and fails to distinguish between necessary causes and necessary and sufficient causes—between eventuality and inevitability. If this theory were the only one available, then it still might be necessary to retain it, at least as a working hypothesis. Yet I have shown in a series of empirical analyses and logical arguments that the multiples phenomenon can be explicated without recourse to sociocultural determinism (Simonton, 1987b, 1999b). Zeitgeist still plays a role, but a much more limited one. Just as important is that the alternative explanation is more firmly grounded in what psychologists have learned about the creative process, creative productivity, and the creative product, as I reviewed in chapters 3–6. This explanation goes as follows.

During the developmental period, the future scientist acquires a large inventory of facts, concepts, techniques, themes, and questions that provide the foundation for his or her creative potential. This inventory comes largely from the sociocultural milieu, especially as represented by formal education and available role models, but it is supplemented by various experiences that are unique to each scientist. Sigmund Freud, for instance, constructed his creative potential from: (a) general European culture, including Darwinism and Victorian sexual prudery; (b) his Jewish background, including the stories in the Pentateuch about Joseph's dream interpretations; (c) his education at the gymnasium and at the University of Vienna, such as his course from Brentano; (d) his work in Ernst Brücke's laboratory and his studies with Jean-Martin Charcot and Hippolyte Bernheim; and (e) such idiosyncratic events as the young Freud seeing his mother naked and feeling sexually aroused or urinating on his parents' bed and being ridiculed by his father. These developmental encounters, among others, produced in Freud a creative potential that is purely Freud and partly shared with many others of his generation (e.g., all MDs from the University of Vienna).

Once creative potential is established, and the productive period begins, the material that makes up this inventory is subjected to the creative process, as described at length in chapter 6. In line with Donald T. Campbell's (1960) variation–selection model of creativity, the scientist enters a process of generating various combinations of the facts, concepts, techniques, themes, and questions that constitute his or her distinctive repertoire. As shown in chapter 4, this combinatory process functions according to the equal-odds rule, with good and bad ideas being generated more or less randomly throughout the career. Moreover, as shown in chapter 3, there will exist tremendous individual differences in the amount of combinations produced, according to the amount of creative potential acquired during the developmental period. Yet this cross-sectional variation is also governed by the equal-odds rule, with individuals who produce the most good ideas also producing the most bad ideas, on average. Naturally, not all combinations that can emerge from the given creative potential will actually appear. Death is the most obvious factor that terminates the variation process, leaving much potential unactualized. Yet another pre-emptive factor—when some other scientist comes up with the same combination, or at least one that is recognizably similar—is even more critical. Once it becomes known that the wheel has been invented, the mental elements that go into conceiving the wheel will usually fuse to become the concept "wheel." This event of one scientist being anticipated by another constituted one of the major reasons why Merton (1961b) argued that many singletons are actually multiples incognito. Linus Pauling was well on his way to discovering the structure of DNA when James Watson and Francis Crick published their 1953 *Nature* article and thereby obliged him to turn his efforts elsewhere. If the announcement of their discovery had been delayed, discovery of the double helix might have become a multiple.

One immediate consequence of this model should be made explicit: It can account for rediscovery multiples, such as Mendelian genetics. Because each scientist's creative potential is a mix of shared and idiosyncratic ideas, the ideational combinations that scientists generate will likewise consist of a heterogeneous collection. The larger the proportion of idiosyncratic ideas that a creative product contains, the smaller the number of colleagues who will be able to appreciate its merits (Csikszentmihalyi, 1990). Mendel's interest in breeding peas, his willingness to quantify his observations and to calculate probabilities, and his fascination with hybridization as a mechanism for Darwinian evolution, were far too peculiar for his articles to receive wide attention in his day (Olby, 1979). More than 30 years later, several components of this Mendelian mixture became more broadly distributed across the scientific community, leading to their rediscovery by Hugo Marie De Vries, Karl Franz Correns, and Erich Tchermak. Hence, precursor geniuses such as Mendel are ahead of the time in the inventory that defines their creative potential. As I wrote before, the zeitgeist constrained not the origination but the acceptance of what was originated.

On the other side of the coin, this model helps one appreciate why multiples will seldom consist of exact duplicates. The ideational combinations produced by each scientist will probably always incorporate a few components that are idiosyncratic to that scientist. Those personal elements are evident even in the exact sciences, where one would think objectivity would filter out anything distinctive. "A mathematician will recognize Cauchy, Gauss, Jacobi, or Helmholtz, after reading a few pages, just as musicians recognize, from the first few bars, Mozart, Beethoven, or Schubert," said theoretical physicist Ludwig Boltzmann (quoted in Koestler, 1964, p. 265). Likewise, when Isaac Newton sent off an anonymous solution to a mathematical problem that had been posed as a challenge to the international community, the recipient immediately discerned "the claw of the lion." In psychology the personal side of the science is even more conspicuous. However similar may be William James's and Carl Lange's respective theories of emotion, there are certainly some differences that reflect the styles and personalities of their respective creators. In fact, part of the space James devoted to the emotions in his *Principles* (1890/1952) was assigned to detailing where he and Lange disagreed in some manner of substance or expression.

These interpretations are qualitative rather than quantitative, yet the explanatory power of this alternative model comes from its quantitative predictions (Simonton, 1987b, 1999b). The model makes specific and precise predictions with respect to three critical aspects of independent discoveries: multiple participation, multiple grades, and temporal separation.

Who Generates the Duplicates?

In chapter 3 I made quite evident that scientists exhibit considerable cross-sectional variation in lifetime creative output. Corresponding individual differences exist in the number of times a particular scientist has inadvertently duplicated the efforts of some other scientist. The stochastic-genius model can easily explicate these differences (Simonton, 1988d, 1999b). In particular, the model leads to two predictions:

1. The greater the number of scientists working within a given domain, the higher the likelihood that that those scientists will participate in one or more multiple discoveries. If there are dozens of creators all subjecting the same subset of ideas to combinatorial variation, then the odds of arriving at a duplicate variant will be very great. In contrast, a scientist who works in isolation, and thus avoids the hot topics of the day, will be less prone to duplicate the variants produced by others.

2. The greater a scientist's lifetime productivity, the higher the likelihood that he or she will participate in one or more multiple discoveries. After all, individuals who create more ideational combinations are more likely to duplicate the combinations of others. Merton (1961b, p. 484) recognized this same principle when he observed that individuals of "great scientific genius will have been repeatedly involved in multiples . . . because the genius will have made many discoveries altogether." Indeed, those of "scientific genius are precisely those . . . whose work in the end would be eventually rediscovered. These rediscoveries would be made, not by a single scientist, but by an entire corps of scientists" (1961b, p. 484). The single scientific genius is "the functional equivalent of a consider-

able array of other scientists of varying degrees of talent." Note that because eminence is strongly correlated with total output, the more eminent scientists should tend to participate in more multiples. This might be considered a corollary of this second prediction.

Empirical studies have endorsed both of these predictions (Hagstrom, 1974; Simonton, 1979). For instance, one study of 1,718 mathematicians, physicists, chemists, and biologists found that those who published the most were most likely to have had their work anticipated by other researchers (Hagstrom, 1974). Moreover, those who worked in popular research areas were also more likely to experience anticipation. These confirmatory results are strengthened all the more by the stochastic models that have been developed to explain two main aspects about the multiples themselves.

How Many Duplicates Are There?

Some multiples have more participants than others. Only two notables can claim to have devised a positivistic basis for introspection (Richard Avenarius and Ernst Mach; see E. G. Boring, 1963), whereas five might be credited with discovering Emmert's law (Emil Emmert, Edward Séguin, M. N. Lubinoff, W. Zehender, and possibly Arthur Schopenhauer; see D. T. Campbell & Tauscher, 1966). The first is a Grade 2 multiple, or *doublet*, whereas the latter is a Grade 5 multiple, or *quintuplet*. It is also apparent from the published lists of multiples that some grades may be more frequent than others. In the broadest terms, the higher the grade is, the lower the frequency. That frequency tends to decline with increased grade is clear not only in Table 13.3 but also in Table 13.4, in which the tabulations for three different collections of multiples are provided (Merton, 1961b; Ogburn & Thomas, 1922; Simonton, 1979). The highest grade ever claimed was Grade 9, or a *nonet*, but this is very rare. In contrast, Grade 2 multiples are the most common, followed by Grade 3, then Grade 4, and so on. From the combinatorial theory one can predict the specific shape of the probability distribution. In the first place, because the creative process is more or less random, a large number of variants must be generated before a useful variant survives. In other words, the probability of success is relatively small. There are many trials and many errors. Any given discipline concomitantly will consist of a fairly large number of creators independently subjecting roughly the same subset of ideas to the combinatorial process. Thus, the low probability of success for any one individual is somewhat compensated for by the large number of participants. This is essentially a form of parallel processing in which each creator is blindly generating ideational combinations but in which the discipline has "safety in numbers." Because of this redundancy, the odds will be enhanced that many of the potentially useful combinations will be found by at least one member of the field. At the same time, this same redundancy

TABLE 13.4
Observed Multiple Grades and Predicted Poisson
Values for Three Data Sets

Grade	Ogburn & Thomas (1922)		Merton (1961b)		Simonton (1979)	
	Observed	Predicted	Observed	Predicted	Observed	Predicted
0		132		159		1,361
1		158		223		1,088
2	90	95	179	156	449	435
3	36	38	51	73	104	116
4	9	11	17	26	18	23
5	7	3	6	7	7	4
6	2	1	8	2	0	0
7	2	0	1	0	0	0
8	1	0	0	0	1	0
9	1	0	2	0	0	0
μ	1.2		1.4		0.8	

Note. The predicted frequencies derived are from Equation 13.1, using the corresponding μ, and the table is adapted from "Stochastic Models of Multiple Discovery" (p. 139) by D. K. Simonton, 1986g, *Czechoslovak Journal of Physics, B 36*, p. 139. Copyright 1986 by the Czechoslovak Academy of Science. Adapted with permission.

will permit a certain number of multiples to emerge, even if the creators are truly working independently of each other. By chance alone, there will appear multiples of Grades 2, 3, 4, and so forth, up to the sole Grade 9 multiple.

Derek Price (1963), the historian of science noted for the Price law, first suggested a simple stochastic model that handles this situation. Price called it a *ripe apple model*, after Galton's (1869) remark in *Hereditary Genius*.

> If there are 1000 apples on a tree, and 1000 blindfolded men reach up at random to pick an apple, what is the chance of a man's getting one to himself, or finding himself grasping as well the hand of another picker, or even more than one? (Price, 1963, p. 66)

Given these conditions, the predicted probabilities of occurrence for multiple grades must be closely approximated by what is called the *Poisson distribution*, which is given by the formula:

$$P(i) = \mu^i e^{-\mu} / i!. \qquad (13.2)$$

Here $P(i)$ gives the probability of getting a multiple of grade i, e is the exponential constant (as seen in Equation 4.1), μ is the mean (and variance), and $i!$ is i factorial (i.e., $i! = 1 \times 2 \times 3 \times \ldots \times i$). The Poisson distribution accurately describes the occurrence of events when the number of trials is extremely large but the probability of success extremely low. This feature emerges from its derivation from the binomial distribution, with the parameter n (the number of trials) approaching infinity and p (the probability of a success) approaching zero—yielding the mean $\mu = np$. For instance, if $\mu = 1$, as Price's (1963) apple model implies, then a typical situation might be one in which there are 10 persons trying to make a discovery, each having only 1 chance out of 10 of being successful. Research has repeatedly shown that this distribution does an excellent job of predicting the observed frequencies of events when those events are so unlikely to happen that they can happen only because there are so many attempts (e.g., the number of Prussian cavalry officers killed by horse kicks in a given period of time). The same predictive success holds for multiples as well. This success is apparent in Table 13.4, in which the fit for the three data sets is presented.

The discrepancies between observed and predicted scores are so small that they can be attributed to statistical error (as demonstrated by the appropriate chi-square tests; Simonton, 1978a, 1979). Moreover, Price's original conjecture that $\mu = 1$ is not far off the mark, for the means range between 0.8 and 1.4. In addition, the same close fit between observed and predicted distributions is found when the multiples are separated by discipline (Simonton, 1978a). For example, a collection of multiples from the biological and behavioral sciences—which included almost all of the cases listed in Table 13.3—obtained an excellent fit, but with $\mu = 0.6$ (Simonton, 1978a). The lower mean signifies that the probability of making a particular discovery is much lower in this domain than in areas such as mathematics ($\mu = 1.4$), physics ($\mu = 1.2$), or chemistry ($\mu = 1.2$). The odds of producing a high-grade multiple are consequently lower. In line with this, it is evident from inspection of Table 13.3 that a much higher percentage of multiples tend to be doublets compared to what is seen in the sciences in general, as depicted in Table 13.4.

One must realize that the traditional explanation for multiples cannot accommodate these findings. After all, sociocultural determinism maintains that discoveries and inventions are inevitable, or nearly so. As a result, high-grade multiples should be not only extremely common but also much more frequent than low-grade multiples, not less so. It is equally important to recognize that the predicted distribution according to the stochastic model is not contingent on whether there exist a priori constraints on the order in which certain ideational combinations can appear. Monte Carlo simulations have shown that the same monotonically decreasing distribution emerges even if certain combinations must occur before other combinations can appear (Simonton, 1986c). Indeed, the provision for such necessary conditions serves only to lower the probability that a successful variant will emerge. Often creators will lose considerable time producing useless ideational combinations simply because one essential component is lacking from the given repertoire of ideas undergoing permutation. One wonders how many great psychologists wasted their efforts in research that was doomed to fail because they lacked the appropriate measurement techniques, statistical procedures, or other essential antecedents. One notorious example from the annals of psychology was "The Project," of Sigmund Freud in which he attempted to specify a psychodynamic model of the mind at the neuronal level. Drafted around 1895, this theoretical exercise was doomed to fail, because the neuroscience of his day fell far short of what would be necessary. It is probably safe to say that such an endeavor would be no less likely to succeed more than 100 years later, all the increased knowledge about the central nervous system notwithstanding.

Before leaving the subject of multiple grades, I should say something about the Poisson predictions that correspond with no observations. In Table 13.3, the predicted number of singletons and "nulltons" are given for each of the three data sets. Each of these categories exceeds the predicted number of doublets, or any higher grade multiple—often by a substantial margin. Hence, according to the Poisson model, multiples truly represent the exceptional cases, whereas singletons represent the statistical norm. The prediction of a substantial proportion of nulltons is certainly curious, for it implies that a significant number of potential discoveries never get made at all. These are the viable ideational combinations that never appear, owing to the low likelihood of success. Some may find this feature of the ripe-apple model unacceptable. Besides, it would seem likely that all ripe apples would eventually be picked. It is fortunate that this implication can be removed by introducing an exhaustion process into the stochastic model (Simonton, 1986c). Yet all this process does is redistribute the nulltons across the singletons and multiples in the same proportions as before. The exceptional nature of doublets, triplets, and higher grades remains in force.

What Is the Time Separation Between Duplicates?

As already noted, sociocultural determinists such as Kroeber (1917) placed a great deal of emphasis on the near simultaneity of so many multiples. To have Hugo Marie De Vries, Karl Franz Correns, and Erich Tchermak all rediscover Mendel's laws within a few months of each other must reflect a deterministic mechanism that works almost like clockwork. Yet, according to the stochastic–genius model, multiples are almost compelled to be simultaneous for the multiple to happen at all. By 1844 Darwin had written out a pretty complete version of the theory he first sketched in 1842, so perhaps by 1850 he would have been able to go public with a version not too dissimilar from the *Origin* of 1859. If he had done so, Wallace would not ever have written his own article on evolutionary theory, for he certainly would have read Darwin's treatment of the subject and be thus anticipated. Wallace would have then sent a letter to Darwin telling him how much he loved his book instead of sending Darwin a manuscript announcing the same theory. Yet the probability that Wallace might duplicate Darwin would clearly increase to the degree that the publication date for this proto-*Origin* were delayed. As the hypothetical date lengthened from 1850 to 1859, the odds of a multiple would increase from 0 to 1, assuming that Wallace still had a 100% probability of coming up with the theory independently by 1858.

In this illustration the multiple occurred because Darwin delayed publication; however, duplicates can happen even when publication is immediate. The dissemination of discoveries often takes time, especially if the information must go across barriers of language or discipline. Nonetheless, as time advances, the likelihood increases that knowledge of a discovery will become diffused throughout the scientific community and thereby lower the probability of some scientist duplicating the original contribution. Those scientists who never hear of the discovery will probably belong to disciplines so remote from the discovery's domain that they would not have the ability to participate in a multiple anyway. Hence, with a sufficient lapse of time, all potential claimants to a multiple will move to other scientific problems that remain unsolved.

It is easy to construct stochastic models that make allowances for this communication process (Brannigan & Wanner, 1983a; Simonton, 1986c, 1986d). These "contagion" models operate much like the Poisson model in that the ideational combinations are randomly generated. However, one further constraint is added: The longer the amount of time that elapses after the first appearance of a published combination, the lower becomes the likelihood of a duplicate discovery. Knowledge of the innovation is probabilistically but inevitably disseminated so as to pre-empt others from continuing further on the same project. Models based on this constraint still predict the comparative frequencies of the multiple grades, but at the same time the models accurately predict how many years will elapse before duplicates can no longer appear (Brannigan & Wanner, 1983a). Just as low-grade multiples will be more common than high-grade multiples, so will short temporal separations be more likely than long separations (Simonton, 1986c).

Because these more complex stochastic models still operate according to an underlying combinatory mechanism, this interpretation would seem to have more explanatory power than sociocultural determinism. This is especially true given how zeitgeist theory provides no a priori means of accommodating multiples with ample temporal separation. Furthermore, a stochastic model with a contagion component predicts that the temporal separation of multiples should be decreasing and that the average grade should be declining. The basis for these predictions is the simple observation that the communication process in science has become ever more efficient, with the advent of scientific journals, conferences, preprints, and, most recently, the Internet. Confirming both of these predictions is an empirical study that demonstrated "that the mean number of scientists involved in multiples has been declining, and that the time interval separating independent reports has been approaching zero" (Brannigan & Wanner, 1983b, p. 135). Although the sociocultural milieu might claim some credit for the increased simultaneity of multiples, it is difficult to see how it would explain the decline in multiple grade. Even worse, zeitgeist theory cannot accommodate the highly skewed distribution of multiple grades, neither does it make any distinctive predictions about how multiples are distributed across scientists.

Judging from everything considered in this section, E. G. Boring (1963) was hardly justified in using this phenomenon to bolster his zeitgeist theory of psychology's history. All of the characteristic attributes of multiples can be explicated without resorting to sociocultural determinism. The contributions of the zeitgeist are reduced to providing two essential items only: (a) the milieu from which scientists draw the facts, concepts, techniques, themes, and questions that constitute their creative potential and (b) the means of communication by which scientists share their most recent discoveries. Because the hypothesis of a deterministic zeitgeist is unnecessary to explain any key aspect of the phenomenon, it should be jettisoned for violating Occam's razor—the principle of parsimony in scientific explanation.

Nonetheless, to delete the deterministic zeitgeist raises a new issue. If the sociocultural milieu is no longer necessary and sufficient to produce scientific discoveries, then what is? The stochastic genius certainly cannot take over that responsibility, for the corresponding model of multiples presumes that each scientist has only a tiny probability of making any given discovery. Discoveries are eventually made because there are so many scientists subjecting the same facts, concepts, techniques, themes, and questions to the same combinatory process. This takes us back to Kroeber's (1944) cultural configurations. Golden Ages are periods in which a large number of creators, great and small, are working in a particular domain of achievement. In the specific case of science, such clusters of creators will help ensure that the discoveries that can potentially be made within that scientific milieu will in fact get made. The low odds of success of any one scientist are compensated by the high odds that at least one scientist of many will succeed. If there are enough scientists working on the same problem, and all the prerequisite elements are present in the milieu, then the appearance of a given discovery might even become inevitable in a probabilistic if not deterministic sense. The higher the number of different people who toss a coin, the higher the likelihood that someone will get heads. Yet the probability of heads never becomes unity, however close it approaches 1.0 asymptotically, and the likelihood would approach unity at an extremely slow pace were the coin so biased that a head had only 1 chance out of 100 of appearing.

14

EXTERNAL MILIEU

Alfred Kroeber (1944) conceived the clusters of genius in terms of generations. However, Kroeber also realized the necessity of delimiting these generations geographically, not just temporally. The generational time series clearly should not include all creative geniuses in the entire world who are active in a given era. The Buddha could not possibly have influenced Confucius, nor Confucius Socrates, given how isolated Indian civilization was from the Chinese and the Chinese from the Greek during that period of world history. The role modeling processes of imitation, emulation, admiration, and envy are most likely to be confined to predecessors who are seen as belonging to the same cultural system. In recognition of this fact, Kroeber tended to delimit his chronological lists of great creators in terms of apparent cultural boundaries. Most often these boundaries were demarcated by nationalities, as defined linguistically and politically. For instance, in his chapter entitled "Science," Kroeber (1944) compiled separate chronologies for ancient Egypt, Mesopotamia, Greece, and Rome; post-Renaissance Italy, Switzerland, France, the Netherlands, Great Britain, and Germany; and the civilizations of India, China, and Japan. To be sure, Kroeber would often discuss the various cross-influences among the various national traditions, in some cases collapsing data across national boundaries to produce larger aggregate counts, such as European science as a whole. Also, his treatment of

"Arab–Mohammedan" science would sometimes engage in "lumping" (e.g., by including great Persian scientists) and other times engage in "splitting" (viz., by separating "Eastern Arabic" and "Western Arabic" science into separate configurations). Nonetheless, it is clear from Kroeber's work that configurations of culture growth are meaningful only when the generations are confined to the appropriate cultural sphere in which the Velleius–Kroeber process is most likely to operate.

Other investigators have adopted the same strategy and obtained corroborating results. For instance, Harvey C. Lehman (1947b) conducted a study entitled "National Differences in Creativity" in which he traced the rise and fall of scientific and artistic creativity in dozens of nations across the world (Lehman, 1947b). In a sense, Lehman studied the cultural trajectory of national creativity in a manner that paralleled what he was already doing for the career trajectory for individual creators. In fact, Lehman (1947b) used the same raw data for this study that he used for tabulating the relation between age and achievement (e.g., Lehman, 1953a). The contributions were merely tallied into periods of a nation's history rather than into periods of a creator's life. In any case, Lehman (1947b), like Kroeber (1944), found that the ups and downs in creative activity were not synchronized across the various nations of the world, even when the analysis was confined to Europe. For example, although Italian thinkers monopolized philosophy in the 16th century, British thinkers dominated philosophy in the first half of the 17th century—yet by the second half of the 17th century the hegemony had shifted to the French, who in turn yielded to the Germans in the first half of the 18th century.

Shifting centers of national activity are also characteristic of science, as Yuasa (1974) demonstrated. Looking at Western science from 1501 to 1950, Yuasa defined the *scientific center* "as a period in which the percentage of scientific achievements of a country exceeds 25% of that in the entire world in the same period" (p. 81). According to this definition, the centers of scientific prosperity appeared in the following order: Italy, 1540–1610; Great Britain, 1660–1730; France, 1770–1830; Germany, 1810–1920; and the United States, 1920–present. This sequence parallels that seen for philosophy, suggesting that certain sociocultural factors stimulate intellectual creativity across the board. At the same time, the two sequences are not completely synchronous, implying that the ideal milieu for philosophical ferment is not identical to that for scientific activity.

What are these "factors"? No doubt some of the factors are the internal causes I discussed in chapter 13. Role model availability certainly helps explain the clustering of genius within a given country. Yet this internal factor does not account for why the center might shift from one nation to another, or why many nations could never boast that the creative center resided within their boundaries. Spain provides an excellent example, for it failed to dominate either science or philosophy even though it dominated European politics during the 1500s and early 1600s. Neither can internal factors easily explain why the center skips around so much. Why, for example, did the center of scientific activity jump from Italy to the British Isles, skipping over both intervening France and Germany? It would seem that a French scientist would be much more likely to choose an Italian as a role model than would a British scientist.

Hence, the goal of this chapter is to document the external factors that influence intellectual history. These extrinsic influences may operate in two main ways. First, some factors may affect the *level* of activity displayed by a given nation at a particular time. Second, other factors may affect the *type* of activity displayed. For instance, some characteristics of the extrinsic milieu may determine the number of thinkers active at a given time and place, whereas other characteristics may determine the epistemologies those thinkers are most likely to advocate, such as empiricism versus rationalism. The first set of factors exerts quantitative effects, the second set qualitative effects.

QUANTITATIVE EFFECTS

In chapters 9 and 12 I merely mentioned how Francis Galton's (1874) *English Men of Science* was written in response to the work of Alphonse de Candolle (1873), who had taken an environmentalist position opposed to the genetic determinism that Galton (1869) espoused in *Hereditary Genius*. Candolle's criticism was presented in the 1873 book *Histoire des Sciences et des Savants depuis Deux Siècles*. Even though relatively unknown, this work is every bit as remarkable as Galton's two books as well as those of Kroeber (1944) and Sorokin (1937–1941). Candolle's book represents the first systematic attempt to examine the circumstances that most strongly favor the emergence of eminent scientists. To carry out this investigation Candolle had to measure the comparative scientific activity of various European nations. This was no easy task, for he realized that such measures could be easily contaminated with two major artifacts. The first potential artifact was population size. It would clearly be unfair to compare the raw scientific output of Russia with that of Switzerland given the huge contrast in their populations. Accordingly, Candolle calculated scientific activity on a per capita basis. The second possible artifact is even more troublesome, namely, the intrusion of ethnocentric biases. Unlike Galton (1869), who was quite willing to assess the comparative natural ability of peoples on the basis of reference works published in Great Britain alone, Candolle realized that ethnocentrism could easily invalidate such measures. He accordingly adopted a most ingenious strategy: Scientists were considered distinguished only if their eminence was truly international, not just national, in scope.

More specifically, a nation would be credited with a scientist only if that scientist had been elected to membership in some foreign academy. Thus, no matter how famous a scientist might be in Denmark, he or she would not count in the index of Danish scientific activity unless elected to some organization, such as the French Academy of Sciences, the Berlin Academy of Sciences, or the Royal Society of London. Several notables of psychology's own history were considered internationally distinguished by this criterion. The list includes Claude Bernard, Friedrich Wilhelm Bessel, The Marquis de Condorcet, Charles Darwin, Franciscus Cornelis Donders, Benjamin Franklin, Karl Friedrich Gauss, Albrech von Haller, Hermann von Helmholtz, Christian Huygens, Gottfried Wilhelm Leibniz, Isaac Newton, Jan Erangelista Purkinje, Adolph Quételet, E. H. Weber, Christian von Wolff, and Thomas Young (but not Galton, who was only a member of his own nation's Royal Academy at the time Candolle conducted his study). Even more significant is the fact that the resulting indicators of national scientific activity appear relatively free of ethnocentrism, unlike what happened under Galton's (1869) methodology. This asset is nowhere more apparent than in Candolle's figures for his native France, which did not come out at the top. On the contrary, it was Switzerland that ended up supreme among the nations of the world, exceeding France in per capita output of great scientists by a ratio of about 5 to 1.

When these corrected cross-national measurements were compared with other attributes of the corresponding nations, Candolle (1873) was able to characterize the conditions that were most favorable to scientific creativity. The nation typically contained a substantial class of people who do not have to spend most of their time earning a living through manual labor; that is, the nation had a large proportion of people who both displayed the desire and had the leisure to devote themselves to intellectual and cultural activities. This attribute was also coupled with a long-standing cultural tradition that emphasized the value of knowing the real world rather than merely focusing on otherworldly matters. The general lay public, in particular, demonstrated a substantial curiosity about the material world rather than about the imaginary or fictitious. More specifically, public opinion tended to be favorable toward science and scientists rather than being antiscientific in tone. This favorable atmosphere tended to take concrete form as an abundant provision of institutions and equipment dedicated to scientific work, such as large libraries, observatories, laboratories, and special collections. There would also be an abundance of families that had a tradition of supporting their member's involvement in scientific or other intellectual activities.

The nation would allow sufficient freedom of intellectual inquiry so that its citizens felt free to express any opinion, at least with respect to scientific subjects, without fear of severe consequences, such as criminal prosecution. Moreover, this freedom was accompanied by the liberty to engage in any lawful profession and to travel freely within and outside the nation's borders. The nation's tolerant policies also encouraged the influx of foreign immigrants who were highly educated and who enjoyed intellectual endeavors for their own sake rather than for the income that such activities might bring them. Furthermore, the nation usually claimed an educational system that was largely if not entirely independent of political or religious control. These institutions also featured the resources and commitment to support intellectual inquiry on the part of both students and teachers. In line with these liberties, religious authority tended to play a relatively minor role. Whatever religious influence was present was benign, even supportive, rather than restrictive. In addition, the nation tended to be either a relatively small, independent country or a country that entailed the union of several independent states, rather than being subordinate to some large imperial system. The nation was typically located very close to other highly civilized nations rather than being isolated, and it was most likely to be situated where the climate was moderate rather than excessively cold or hot.

Last but not least, Candolle (1873) observed that certain languages tended to be most favorable to scientific activity, namely, English, French, and German. Because these may be considered the international languages of science, nations that had one of these as their native tongue, or that widely encouraged their citizens to acquire one of these languages as a second language, would have a definite edge. It is interesting that Candolle's complete lack of ethnocentric bias was revealed in his discussion of this factor. On the basis of his analysis of worldwide demographic trends, Candolle argued that English would eventually become the predominant language of scientific communication. He made this prophetic argument in a French book that, ironically, has never been translated into the English language. As a result, Candolle's brilliant contributions have been a bit neglected by scientists who now seldom bother to learn a language that has become much less important, just as Candolle himself predicted!

Because Candolle's (1873) work appeared about 20 years before the introduction of correlational methods, the statistical part of his inquiry admittedly falls far short of contemporary standards. Even so, many of his somewhat qualitative generalizations have been replicated in more rigorous research (Szabo, 1985). Hence, there is ample reason for concluding that cross-national contrasts in aggregate scientific creativity reflect to no small degree a broad sociocultural milieu that is favorable to science. This conclusion is reinforced by other studies that have unearthed other external factors that influence the magnitude of creativity activity exhibited at a given time and place. These diverse extrinsic effects can be grouped into three categories: transient fluctuations, inertial movements, and developmental influences.

Transient Fluctuations

Anyone who has followed the ups and downs of the stock market knows that the price of stocks and bonds can change rapidly from day to day and even from one hour to the next. These volatile shifts reflect a host of influ-

ences, such as government economic forecasts and interventions; technological news about novel products and markets; business quarterly reports,
mergers, and bankruptcies; and various current events at home and abroad.
Creative activity, too, can exhibit short-term fluctuations, albeit not nearly
so volatile as seen in the stock market. One year fewer patent applications
may be submitted than in the preceding year, and then the applications may
rebound in the year immediately after. Furthermore, these temporal insta-
bilities in creativity may be the direct consequence of underlying external
factors that display rapid changes over time.

The transient factor that has received the most attention in empirical
research is war (see extensive review in Simonton, in press). In general, this
research supports Norling's (1970) conclusion that "warfare usually tends to
produce cultural and intellectual sterility" (p. 248). This negative consequence has been most extensively demonstrated for scientific and technological creativity. One scholar to tackle this question was Derek Price, the
historian of science who proposed the Price law and the Poisson model of
multiples based on Galton's ripe-apple metaphor. In one inquiry, Price (1965)
examined the citations received by articles published between 1862 and 1961.
Two significant dips occurred in the citation rates: one during World War I
and the other during World War II. In both cases the citations declined from
the year of the war's outbreak, reaching a low point the year the war ended—
when the citation rate was about 50% below baseline. Furthermore, for both
wars a few years were required before the citation rate fully recovered. In a
second inquiry, Price (1978) scrutinized the annual fluctuations in the number of discoveries and inventions, as listed in several chronologies of science
and technology. Significant downturns in the annual count appeared during
major military conflicts, such as the Thirty Years' War, the Napoleonic Wars,
and again the two world wars. Although Price (1978) drew his conclusions
from the visual inspection of graphic representations of the transhistorical
fluctuations, the same inference obtains when these data are subjected to
rigorous multivariate time-series analyses (Simonton, 1980a). In particular,
the number of major discoveries and inventions per annum was negatively
affected by (a) balance-of-power wars among European states, such as the
War of Spanish Succession or the Seven Years' War, and (b) defensive wars
in which European civilization defended itself against incursions by non-
European civilizations, such as the various wars with the Ottoman Empire.
Even though it is sometimes claimed that "modern wars usually increase
medical knowledge" (Norling, 1970, p. 248), that claim does not survive
empirical scrutiny (Simonton, 1976e). War is negatively correlated with the
appearance of major discoveries and inventions in medicine as well.

It must be stressed that these effects are indeed temporary. The negative association between war and scientific creativity is most likely to appear
when the two phenomena are tabulated in annual units. When larger units,
such as the generations described in chapter 13, are used, the effect tends to

vanish (e.g., Simonton, 1975d, 1976b). That happens, in part, because a modest tendency exists for some compensation to appear in the postwar period (Price, 1965, 1978). Some of the ideas that failed to appear during wartime will eventually emerge later once peace has been fully restored. This certainly happened to many psychologists during the two world wars. Often recruited to serve more practical functions on behalf of the war effort, these psychologists would return to their regular work after demobilization. Ideas put on hold would then have the opportunity to be developed and presented before their colleagues.

Apropos of the last remark, Samuel W. Fernberger (1946) directly examined the connection between war and contributions to psychological science. Although Fernberger is best known for his work in psychophysics, he also conducted some pioneering statistical studies in the history of psychology (R. I. Watson, 1974; Zusne, 1984). In this particular case Fernberger tabulated the number of psychology publications appearing in various languages from 1894 to 1945. All told, 204,774 articles were thus counted. The time series exhibits depressions during the two world wars. The wartime downturns were especially prominent for German-language publications. During the height of the first world war, for example, the output of German titles decreased by two thirds. The impact of the second world war was even more devastating, with output almost vanishing altogether by the end of the war, albeit Fernberger noted that much of the additional loss could be attributed to Nazi oppression and the resulting emigration of many distinguished psychologists. The United States, of course, was one of the primary beneficiaries of this consequence, acquiring an impressive number of psychoanalysts and Gestalt psychologists. It is notable that Fernberger's (1946) data show that English-language publications were less affected by World Wars I and II. Most of the English-speaking countries involved in these two conflicts—the United States and the nations of the British Commonwealth—fought all battles beyond their shores. In fact, in line with Candolle's (1873) forecast, English titles rose throughout this period, with only minor dips during the two wars, until psychology was almost completely dominated by English-language publications.

Candolle (1873) had also concluded that scientific activity is partially contingent on economic prosperity, an inference drawn by other researchers as well (e.g., Inhaber, 1977; Rainoff, 1929; Schmookler, 1966). Yet empirical research on this topic has obtained somewhat mixed results (e.g., Naroll et al., 1971). It seems that "a certain minimum of surplus wealth must exist if any society is to support an appreciable number of people who are not economically productive" (Norling, 1970, p. 244) but, as Candolle (1873) perceived, economic prosperity will stimulate scientific output only if the sociocultural system values science. This necessary stipulation is suggested by an empirical inquiry into the circumstances that are most likely to have produced the top thinkers of Chinese civilization (Kuo, 1986). These luminaries lived during times that met the following three conditions: (a) there was a strong economic base, (b) freedom of speech was granted by the political authorities, and (c) philosophy was highly valued within the culture.

Unfortunately, I know of only one investigation concerning the correlation between the quantity of contributions to psychology and the economic milieu (Simonton, 1985b). Using a cross-sectional time-series design, I (Simonton, 1985b) examined the careers of 10 distinguished psychologists, among them Gordon Allport, Albert Bandura, J. P. Guilford, Carl I. Hovland, Carl Rogers, B. F. Skinner, Kenneth Spence, and Edward Tolman. For those whose careers overlapped with the Great Depression, a drop in the quality of their work appeared during those hard times—as gauged by the average number of citations received by their publications. Yet the decline was too small to attain conventional levels of statistical significance. A bigger sample is probably required, including a larger number of psychologists who worked before, during, and after the Great Depression.

Inertial Movements

Some external influences on scientific activity change more slowly than do the comings and goings of war and peace or economic booms and busts. Several of the factors that Candolle (1873) cited are certainly in this category. For instance, systems of government, economic production, or education tend to be relatively stable over considerable periods of time. As a consequence, the effects of these slowly changing circumstances will endure not only over a few years but for whole generations. A variety of such inertial movements are often explicitly mentioned in histories of psychology. This is one illustration: "During the Dark Ages, the material preconditions for scientific advancement no longer existed. Misgovernment, top-heavy bureaucracy, civil wars, and the encroachment of neighboring barbarian peoples led to a steady decline" (R. I. Watson & Evans, 1991, p. 122). Even if civil wars might come and go relatively quickly, it is doubtful that the other factors mentioned would change so rapidly.

Despite the great variety of potential inertial factors, I confine my discussion here to three effects that have attracted the most empirical research: population growth, national sovereignty, and cultural values.

Population Growth

When Candolle (1873) calculated the national output of great scientists on a per capita basis he was explicitly assuming that, on average, the number of scientists should increase with the total number of the nation's citizens. Because the world's population has tended to grow exponentially, it should be expected that the number of scientists should have expanded exponentially as well. This is abundantly the case, as was demonstrated by Harvey C. Lehman (1947a), again using the same data sources that he used for his studies of national output (Lehman, 1946) and the age–achievement relation (Lehman, 1953a). He tabulated the number of contributions per generation for a large number of creative domains, including several closely affiliated with psychology: genetics from 1600 to 1925, education from 1000 to 1900, and philosophy from 1250 to 1899. In almost every case the plots revealed an accelerating monotonic growth, and in every single case the curve was closely approximated by an exponential function.

Derek Price (1963) replicated Lehman's (1947a) conclusion. He noted, for instance, that the numbers of important discoveries and important physicists have doubled every 20 years; the numbers of scientific journals and scientific abstracts have doubled every 15 years; and the numbers of publications on the theory of determinants, on non-Euclidean geometry, or on x-rays have all doubled every 10 years. Price (1963) specifically observed that the literature in experimental psychology has doubled every decade as well. What is astonishing about these figures is that they exceed the growth rate of the population, which roughly doubles every half-century. Hence, if the trend continues long enough, every man, woman, and child will be a scientist— publishing research in experimental psychology! As Price himself pointed out, this accelerated growth cannot last forever and must soon be tempered by conversion into a logistic function. Yet the main point remains: To some extent the output of great scientists, including great psychologists, must depend on the general size of the population from which those luminaries must be drawn.

National Sovereignty

It is frequently observed that the contributions of the ancient Romans to psychology paled in comparison to those of the ancient Greeks. "As the Roman Empire developed with all its grandeur, it was amazing that no great philosophers or scientists had emerged," wrote Lundin (1979, p. 59). This relative dearth is all the more surprising given that the population under Imperial Rome far exceeded that of Athens during its days of glory, so the per capita output of notable figures looks even worse under the Roman Empire. Furthermore, at the time that Greek civilization reached its peak it was divided into lots of small city–states (*poli*), often engaged in internecine conflicts, such as the Peloponnesian Wars. Under the Roman Empire, in contrast, the entire Mediterranean area was unified under a single government that maintained the *Pax Romana* for considerable periods of time. Hence, the comparative infertility of Roman civilization seems to run counter to earlier conclusions about the negative repercussions of war. Why?

The answer may be found in Candolle's (1873) assertion that great scientists are most likely to appear in small, independent countries, or at least confederations of small sovereign states. Stated in an inverse fashion, subordination under large imperial systems appears antithetical to the scientific enterprise. Several social scientists have suggested that the adverse consequence of empires actually operates across the board, harming creative activity in almost every domain, with the exception of monumental architecture. After scrutinizing the various configurations of culture growth, Kroeber (1944) concluded that "it is certainly true that high achievements by suppressed nationalities are rather rare" (p. 794). Likewise, Arnold Toynbee (1946), in his magnum opus A *Study of History*, claimed that the emergence of a "universal state" was negatively correlated with the creative activity of a civilization. Nikolay Danilevsky, the great Russian historical philosopher, even styled this phenomenon the "second law of the dynamics of great cultures," namely that "in order for the civilization of a potentially creative group to be conceived and developed, the group and its subgroups must be politically independent" (quoted in Sorokin, 1947/1969, p. 543).

Empirical evidence provides some endorsement of these intuitive inductions from the historical record. The first demonstration came in the form of a study that took advantage of the lists of eminent creators that Kroeber (1944) compiled and published (Naroll et al., 1971). Specifically, the figures were drawn from Chinese, Indian, Middle Eastern, and European civilizations and then tabulated into century-long periods. The number of sovereign states was then calculated for each civilization area over the same historical intervals. The correlation between these two measures was .286, in line with Nikolay Danilevsky's second law. I found this result so provocative that I decided to attempt a replication as part of my doctoral dissertation at Harvard University (Simonton, 1974). After collecting a comprehensive inventory of approximately 5,000 eminent creators from Western civilization, I tabulated them into 127 consecutive generations, beginning in 700 BC. I also calculated the number of independent nations in each 20-year period, a measure I called *political fragmentation*. I then conducted a multivariate time-series analysis that included controls for possible contaminating variables. Political fragmentation emerged as one of the strongest predictors of the degree of creative activity. Moreover, the positive impact of this political factor was replicated across different types of creativity (e.g., scientific vs. artistic) and alternative variable definitions (e.g., weighted vs. unweighted counts).

Despite this replication, a qualification must be imposed on the applicability of this "second law." More than 10 years after I published these results (Simonton, 1975d), one of my graduate students decided to conduct his own replication, with a specific focus on the literary creativity of China. A native of Taiwan, he had access to the tremendous wealth of archival sources available only in Chinese. Thus, he managed to accumulate a collection of approximately 7,000 writers! However, the subsequent generational time-series analysis actually found a negative relation between the number of literary figures and the degree of political fragmentation (Ting, 1986). This negative result must be interpreted in light of the following two considerations:

1. Chinese history is highly distinctive in that it almost entirely represents the record of a coherent nation, culture, and a civilization. Most cultural minorities in the territorial core of China—as distinguished from those in peripheral areas, such as Tibet—all but vanished early in the emergence of Chinese civilization. As a consequence, an increase in the number of independent states is not strongly associated with nationalistic movements. On the contrary, often the emergence of new states would sometimes represent the conquest of Chinese peoples by invading non-Chinese "barbarians." This situation contrasts greatly with what tended to happen in the civilizations of India, Europe, and Islam. In these cultures imperial expansion often meant the oppression of cultures sometimes quite different from those of the conquerors. The Mogul conquest of India in the 16th and 17th centuries, for example, entailed the submission of indigenous Hindu peoples to alien Islamic invaders descended from Mongolians of Central Asia.
2. Chinese literature is also highly distinctive in its use of a writing system that transcends the spoken language. Chinese is actually a collection of mutually unintelligible languages (sometimes incorrectly called *dialects*). Although the differences among these languages are comparable to those that separate the Romance languages of Europe, the Chinese languages are all written in the same way. As a result, any tendencies toward nationalism could not take voice in a corresponding literary movement, unlike what happens in other civilization areas. When the Roman Empire began to fall apart, various vernaculars began to rival the Latin language. As nationalism increased, these vernaculars could become independent languages of new nations. With this emergence would invariably come a new national literature, beginning with epics like *The Cid* and the *Song of Roland* and eventually culminating in the masterpieces of Dante Alighieri, Francois Rabelais, Luiz Vaz de Camões, and Miguel Cervantes.

It is also conceivable that the relation between political fragmentation and creativity might have been different had my graduate student examined generational fluctuations in the appearance of major Chinese philosophers. The Golden Age of Chinese philosophy took place during the Zhou dynasty, after it had disintegrated into numerous independent states. It was then that all of the indigenous schools of thought emerged, including Taoism, Confucianism, Mohism, and Legalism. Furthermore, Chinese imperial systems displayed a distinct inclination toward imposing ideological conformity. When Shi Huangdi, founder of the Qin dynasty, finally unified China, he immediately ordered the burning of all books that were not to his liking, thereby incurring the eternal enmity of all subsequent Confucian scholars.

Cultural Values

In explaining why some nations displayed more scientific activity than others, Candolle (1873) placed great emphasis on whether the society had proscientific rather than antiscientific attitudes. Candolle actually made it pretty clear that antiscientific values often involved an excessive commitment to dogmatic religion. For instance, he stressed the importance of a fascination with this world rather than a preoccupation with the "next" world. He also emphasized the significance of the educational system being free of religious control. Candolle's assertions are not without some foundation in the history of science. The Roman Catholic Church proscribed Copernican heliocentric theory, and Galileo had to save his life before the Inquisition by abjuring any belief that the earth might indeed revolve around the sun. The Roman Catholics did not monopolize such oppression. Michael Servetus, the Spanish physician who discovered the pulmonary circulation of the blood, was burned as a heretic by John Calvin, one of the key figures of the Protestant Reformation. Later still, Darwin's theory of evolution by natural selection encountered considerable resistance on the part of devout Anglicans, such as Bishop Samuel Wilberforce, whose debate with T. H. Huxley has become one of the oft-told moments in the science-versus-religion conflict. Even in the 21st century, Christian fundamentalists continue their fight to remove evolutionary theory from the biology textbooks used in the public schools of the United States.

Rather than resorting to the citation of such anecdotes, I can demonstrate more systematically the cultural antagonism between scientific and religious values. As part of my dissertation I conducted a subsidiary study of how various creative activities were interrelated across the course of Western civilization (Simonton, 1975b). After dividing the more than 5,000 historic figures into 15 different kinds of creative achievement, I assigned each figure to 1 of 130 consecutive generations, spanning 700 BC to AD 1899. The assignment was again made according to the 40th-year floruit rule. Once general historical trends were removed, I subjected the 15 generational time series to a P-technique factor analysis. The first two factors consisted of (a) scientists, philosophers, literary figures, and composers and (b) painters, sculptors, and architects. More interesting was the third, bipolar factor, which opposed physical scientists and general philosophers against religious figures. In concrete terms, generations that featured the most religious activity were least likely to harbor great physicists and secular thinkers.

I later corroborated this inverse association using Sorokin's (1937–1941) data, mentioned in chapter 13 (Simonton, 1976c). Sorokin argued that at any given time sociocultural systems tend to be dominated by one of two great "culture mentalities"—the *sensate* and the *ideational*. Each mentality corresponds to a specific set of cultural values that determine the nature of the creativity displayed by the civilization during the corresponding era. In particular, the sensate mentality favors scientific discovery and technological invention, whereas the ideational mentality diverts creative energies toward more religious, even mystical forms of creative expression. According to Sorokin, each mentality is associated with a unique set of philosophical beliefs. Sensate culture links with empiricism, materialism, temporalism, nominalism, singularism, determinism, and the ethics of happiness, whereas Ideational culture binds with rationalism, mysticism, idealism, eternalism, realism, universalism, indeterminism, the ethics of principles, and the ethics of love. Hence, one can create composite measures of the two alternative mentalities by combining the generational time series for their corresponding philosophical positions. After making appropriate adjustments for very long-term trends, the resulting sensate and ideational measures can be correlated with the generational time series assessing scientific and religious activity, the latter coming from my dissertation data (Simonton, 1974). The results fall right in line with both Sorokin's theory and Candolle's (1873) cross-national investigation: The sensate mentality correlated .37 ($p < .01$) with scientific creativity but .04 (*ns*) with religious creativity, whereas the ideational mentality correlated .20 ($p < .05$) with religious creativity but .02 (*ns*) with scientific creativity (Simonton, 1976c).

What makes this empirical outcome especially pertinent to the current discussion is the fact that the philosophical positions that dominate a given civilization change very slowly over time. Part of this inertial movement can be ascribed to the role modeling effects I discussed in the previous chapter, which are responsible for the high autocorrelations for the generational time series (Simonton, 1976g). However, another part of this inertia may result from what Sorokin (1937–1941) theorized about the very nature of the two cultural value systems. He claimed that the sensate and ideational mentalities embody solutions to fundamental issues of human existence—most notably, how best to obtain happiness. The sensate solution is that a person should maximize personal pleasure by exerting individualistic control over the material world, whereas the ideational solution is that a person should minimize personal desires by subordinating them to a more spiritual and communal world. It takes time for individuals residing in a sensate culture to realize the inadequacies of the first solution, and so by a slow, dialectic process the sensate mentality gives way to the ideational. This is what happened when the decadent paganism of the late Roman Empire finally yielded to Christianity—as officially promulgated by the Emperor Constantine. Yet the ideational mentality contains the seeds of its own destruction, as increasingly more denizens of a civilization become dissatisfied with the constraints on sensual gratification and sensory curiosity. Thus, with the cultural pattern of Christianity finding itself exhausted at the end of the Middle Ages, the Renaissance sprang forth, with increasingly sensate attitudes, such as an appreciation for the pleasures and truths of the senses. Shortly after, that rebirth of sensate culture became the midwife of the Scientific Revolution, an epochal event that made possible the eventual emergence of psychological science.

Developmental Influences

On the basis of the theory and data presented in *Social and Cultural Dynamics*, Sorokin (1937–1941) argued that the current hegemony of sensate mentality was showing signs of decay. In time, a new ideational age would emerge, and the great age of science would be terminated. If psychology were to continue under the new milieu, it would become a rational psychology of the inner soul rather than an empirical psychology of objective behavior. Before psychologists decide to change their research programs, however, they must recognize that Sorokin's thesis suffers from several logical and empirical flaws (e.g., L. Schneider, 1964). From psychologists' standpoint the most serious is the fact that sensate and ideational mentalities do not constitute opposite ends of a bipolar dimension (Simonton, 1976c). In particular, the philosophical positions that define the sensate orientation are not negatively correlated with the positions that define the ideational orientation. Indeed, the two sets of positions are positively correlated across the course of Western civilization (at least from 540 BC to AD 1900). What this means is that thinkers who advocate sensate beliefs on the seven philosophical issues have a tendency to appear in the same generations as thinkers who advocate ideational beliefs. By the same token, some generations, such as those in the middle of the European Dark Ages, contain few thinkers at all, whether sensate or ideational. This is not to say that there do not appear periods where one or the other mentality predominates. The correlation is not that strong. Even so, the association means that at times the intellectual zeitgeist may be rich in opposing viewpoints. These are often Golden Ages of philosophical ferment, when great thinkers debate epistemology, ontology, ethics, and other key issues.

What sociocultural milieu supports such phenomenal displays of ideological diversity? One answer may be found in my earlier comments about the intellectual activity that characterized the late Zhou dynasty of ancient China. The greatest profusion of schools appeared when China was subjected to exceptional political fragmentation. A similar pattern is seen in the Western world: The greatest proliferation of new schools of thought occurred when Greek civilization was divided into numerous countries, whether the poli of Classical Greece or the Hellenistic states that emerged after the disintegration of Alexander the Great's transient empire. With respect to more recent history, it has been said that "Europe, however, with its many nations and kings, was too heterogeneous to succumb to dogmatic repression" (Leahey, 1987, p. 77). In fact, these instances embody specific cases of a general statistical association, for generational fluctuations in political fragmentation across

122 generations of Western civilization are positively associated with ideological diversity (Simonton, 1976d). The political fragmentation measure in my empirical study (Simonton, 1976d) was adopted unchanged from the data I had collected for my doctoral dissertation (Simonton, 1974), whereas the measure of ideological diversity was based on Sorokin's (1937–1941) data. Specifically, ideological diversity was taken as a count of the total number of philosophical positions represented in each generation, regardless of how many thinkers advocated each position. When this measure was cross-correlated with the previously defined measure of political fragmentation, a positive relation was observed. The higher the number of independent states there were in a given generation, the greater was the number if distinct philosophical positions represented.

It is curious that this positive association increased if the cross-correlation was lagged one generation. To be more precise, the amount of ideological diversity at Generation g correlated most strongly with the amount of political fragmentation in Generation $g - 1$ (Simonton, 1976d). According to the principles of generational time-series analysis I outlined in the previous chapter, which are schematically represented in Figure 13.1, this cross-lagged correlation implies that the number of independent states operates as a developmental-period influence. Growing up in an environment characterized by a diversity of independent states may better encourage the development of personal independence. Large imperial systems, in contrast, may nurture the development of individuals who are more disposed toward conformity to whatever ideas are most fashionable at the time. Whatever the substantive interpretation, this long-term repercussion has defined implications for the general level of creative activity displayed over the same time periods. The amount of ideological diversity in Generation g is positively associated with the number of eminent creators in the same generation. "Letting a hundred flowers blossom and a hundred schools of thought contend is the policy for promoting the progress of the arts and the sciences," said Mao Zedong (quoted in *Who Said What When*, 1991, p. 314). If Mao had practiced what he preached, China might have experienced another Golden Age but, instead of ideological diversity, a severe Marxist orthodoxy was enforced— again, behavior typical of many imperialistic systems of government.

The lagged relation between political fragmentation and ideological diversity does not by any means constitute the only instance of a developmental influence. Generational time-series analyses have revealed other sociocultural conditions that have developmental consequences. Three such factors are especially noteworthy: political anarchy, imperial instability, and foreign influence.

Political Anarchy

Sometimes political systems succumb to anarchy—to frequent coups d'etat, political assassinations, conspiracies, military revolts, and the like.

Those who make up the power elite would rather engage in internecine struggles for supremacy than govern their nation wisely. Such political instability has a devastating effect on the creative development of the youth exposed to these events (Simonton, 1975d). Expressed more precisely, the number of eminent creators in such fields as science, philosophy, literature, and music during Generation g is a negative function of the number of instances of political anarchy in Generation $g - 1$.

These negative developmental influences must also contribute to any explanation of why the Roman Empire failed to match Classical Greece in the output of figures who have earned a notable place in the annals of psychology. Augmenting the adverse consequences of the low political fragmentation was the detrimental effect of the political anarchy that often plagued the imperial system, especially in the latter part of Roman history. One general would usurp the imperial throne, only to quickly find himself overthrown by another usurper. The imperial palace in the capitol would often become a butcher shop, the emperor's own Praetorian Guard becoming a threat rather than a protector and sometimes selling the empire to the highest bidder. In one year alone, 69 AD, Rome had four emperors: Galba, Otho, Vitellius, and Vespasian—the rapid succession of rulers was determined by military revolts, usurpations, assassinations, and enforced suicides. The young generation exposed to these events produced only one notable thinker, the Stoic philosopher Epictetus, and even he had the fortune to have grown up in Asia Minor, remote from the anarchy of the capitol.

It is ironic that Epictetus also experienced the other drawback of living in an imperial state. The Emperor Domitian, Vespasian's son, decided to enforce old-fashioned Roman values. Those who practiced foreign religions, such as the Christians and Jews, were persecuted, and in 89 AD, exactly 20 years after the year of the four emperors, the philosophers were expelled from Rome, obliging Epictetus to retire to Greece. Not long after, Domitian himself was assassinated. Although the empire would enjoy a respite under the "Five Good Emperors," the death of the last of these—the Stoic philosopher Marcus Aurelius—ushered the final phase of political decay and intellectual decadence.

Imperial Instability

At various times during the course of its long history, the Roman Empire experienced other tumultuous political events besides the outbreaks of anarchy just discussed. Sometimes political violence would originate not in the power elite but in the populace; in other words, the ruled rather than the rulers would engage in revolts, revolutions, and rebellions. Especially commonplace in a culturally heterogeneous empire like the Roman Empire were various nationalistic revolts. Often, oppressed peoples would attempt to throw off the imperial yoke. Examples include revolts in Gaul in 21 AD, in Judaea from 66–77 and again from 132–135, and in Batavia from 69–71. Yet, unlike the episodes of political anarchy, these civil disturbances have a beneficial effect on subsequent creativity (Simonton, 1975d)—that is, the number of creative geniuses in Generation g tends to be a positive function of the intensity and frequency of popular revolts, revolutions, and rebellions in Generation $g - 1$.

Why should these violent civil protests against imperial rule have a positive effect on creative development while violent dissent involving the imperial rulers has a negative effect? The former events certainly challenge the political and cultural foundations of the empire in a manner that the latter events do not. The populace engaged in civil disturbances hopes to overthrow or dismantle the empire, whereas the power elite uses violent means to decide who will stand at the apex of that empire. Furthermore, those participating in such civil unrest will be less likely to subscribe to the values of the power elite, for the participants will often be drawn from the lower classes, minority groups, and oppressed nationalities. This means that civil disturbances can undermine the imperial pressure toward a homogenous culture. By reviving suppressed beliefs, customs, and mores, these events mix up the cultural broth and thereby resuscitate the cultural heterogeneity so vital to continued creative activity.

Cross-Fertilization

The interpretation just given fits very well with the third and last developmental influence. According to Sorokin (1947/1969), the creativity of individuals or groups are enhanced when they reside

> at the point of intersection of cross-currents of various appropriate or relevant systems of meanings and values. Since any new system of meanings is a blend of two or more existing systems, such a union occurs more naturally amidst several crosscurrents of different ideas, beliefs, and patterns. Such a milieu contains richer material for a new synthesis or creative combination than a cultural milieu of monotonous stereotypes. The point of junction of various cultural streams supplies a larger number of the elements necessary for a new creation. (p. 542)

Most psychologists who study creativity would probably endorse this assertion. Thus, one creativity researcher identified "creativogenic factors" such as "exposure to different and even contrasting cultural stimuli" (Arieti, 1976, p. 320, italics removed from entire quotation). This factor is also cited from time to time by historians of the field, as evident in the statement that "it was partly their familiarity, through their travelers, with a variety of seminal ideas, that made the Greek philosophers capable of the first great psychological thrust in the Western world" (Murphy & Murphy, 1969, p. 285).

Now there are several ways of obtaining this desideratum, some of which have already been mentioned. Hence, as observed in the preceding section, insofar as civil disturbances involve oppressed minorities, nationalities, or other subcultures, such events can expose all members of the society to a broader range of cultural material. Furthermore, in chapter 9 I noted the strong tendency for immigrants or the descendents of immigrants to exhibit creative genius, as discerned by Francis Galton (1869). Candolle (1873), too, saw this as an important factor underlying the scientific activity, the more creative nations being those that promoted immigration. Besides these factors, cultural cross-fertilization may be elicited when the milieu encourages individuals to study under foreign masters. As I mentioned in chapter 9, one common means of accomplishing this is studying abroad. In the early years of American psychology, a very large proportion of its most eminent representatives did their graduate work at foreign universities, especially at German institutions (Simonton, 1992b). Examples include James McKeen Cattell, Frank Angell, and Lightner Witmer. Many of those who did not earn their PhDs abroad did the next best thing, namely, study under foreigners who had immigrated to the United States. Probably the most prominent cases are all the distinguished American psychologists who earned their doctorates under Edward Titchener, an Englishman who earned his own PhD from Wilhelm Wundt in Germany. Moreover, exposure to culturally divergent perspectives does not have to be confined to formal education or training. It has been said of William James that "although he never studied psychology formally in Europe, he is considered by many to be America's greatest psychologist" (Hillner, 1984, p. 65). The implied paradox in this statement disappears once it is recognized that James had traveled extensively throughout Europe and had met informally some of the key figures of European psychology. For instance, James heard Emil DuBois–Reymond lecture in Berlin and Hermann von Helmholtz lecture in Heidelberg. He also closely followed the developments in French physiology and psychiatry and for a period could be considered a disciple of Claude Bernard.

I (Simonton, 1997a) demonstrated the group-level repercussions of cultural cross-fertilization using generational time-series analysis. In this historiometric study I examined the configurations of culture growth for 14 domains of national achievement. More specifically, I assessed the clustering of 1,803 eminent Japanese across 68 consecutive 20-year intervals from 580 to 1939 AD. I selected Japanese civilization because its history has shown unusual variation in the degree to which its culture has been open to foreign influences. At one extreme, Japan has sometimes opened the floodgates to an onrush of alien ideas, such as Chinese culture, Buddhism, and, most recently, modern Western civilization. At the other extreme, Japan has sometimes totally shut its doors to the outside world, occasionally imposing the death penalty on those who violated its policy of deliberate cultural isolation. I defined three alternative measures of Japanese openness to foreign influences: (a) the number of foreign immigrants who left a mark on Japanese history, such as Chinese Buddhist monks, Korean artists, and Christian missionaries; (b) the number of eminent Japanese who traveled abroad, that is, who left the main islands of Japan to visit civilized regions such as China, Korea, Europe, or the United States; and (c) outside influences in which native Japanese studied under foreigners, went abroad to study, or admired, developed, or imitated the style or ideas of foreigners—the most inclusive of the three measures. I then computed cross-correlations between the time series assessing fluctuations in national achievement and those gauging fluctuations in cultural openness to the non-Japanese world. Several significant cross-lagged correlations emerged. For instance, the number of eminent medical figures in Generation g was a positive function of the frequency of foreign travel in Generation $g - 2$. The two-generation lag was typical: The influx of outside ideas must be first assimilated by one generation before it can exert a developmental impact on the next generation.

Notice that this influence provides an explanation for how nascent civilizations can get a jump start on the path to a Golden Age. If the development of genius depends on the presence of suitable role models and mentors, then how does a cultural configuration even start in the first place? Who stimulated the development of the first representative of a given domain of creative activity? Most often the answer is that the culture first went through a formative period in which it was highly receptive to foreign ideas. Indeed, when Kroeber (1944) traced the course of cultural configurations he often linked their onset with some outside influence. The sciences of Egypt and Mesopotamia stimulated the emergence Greek science. The latter, in combination with Indian science, sparked the emergence of Islamic science. Of course, the same cross-fertilization process can facilitate a civilization's creative revival after it has exhausted its initial cultural patterns. One obvious illustration is the manner in which European philosophical inquiry was resuscitated by exposure to Islamic thinkers such as Averroës (Ibn Rushd) and by the rediscovery of ancient Greek thought, particularly Aristotle. The opposition of those influences to the medieval Christian tradition culminated in the great synthesis advanced by Thomas Aquinas.

Although the national benefits of cross-fertilization have been tested only on Japanese history, the results are certainly compatible with the other empirical relations that point to the value of cultural diversity in stimulating creative activity. Furthermore, the advantages of cross-fertilization are implied by two other sets of empirical findings. First, the presence of dissenting minorities has been shown to increase group-level creativity (see, e.g., Nemeth & Kwan, 1985, 1987; Nemeth & Wachtler, 1983). Hence, the intrusion of a foreign minority may undermine the normative pressures of the majority culture and thereby encourage a freer range of thought among the natives of that culture. Second, bilingualism tends to be positively associated with the capacity for creative thinking (Carringer, 1974; Lambert, Tucker, & d'Anglejan, 1973; Landry, 1972; Lopez, Esquivel, & Houtz, 1993). If a large influx of foreign ideas and people increases the overall rates of bilingualism—whether by immigrants wishing to assimilate or by natives who wish to accommodate certain features of the alternative culture—then the outcome will be a boost in cultural activity. It is interesting to recall how the psychologists who often showed the greatest creative imaginations were also those who were multilingual. The supreme example is probably Sigmund Freud, who had varying degrees of competence in Greek, Latin, Spanish, English, and French, as well as his native German.

QUALITATIVE EFFECTS

Despite all their differences in data and theory, Galton (1869, 1874), Candolle (1873), and Kroeber (1944) were largely preoccupied with the same fundamental question: What factors determine the supply of creative genius at a particular time and place? None expressed any profound interest in the nature of the creator's contribution, such as an artist's specific style or a philosopher's particular ethical stance. Yet qualitative differences in contributions certainly are very important as well. In chapter 8, for example, I showed how even great psychologists differ immensely regarding their theoretical and methodological orientations. Some, like Pavlov, may be extremely objectivistic, whereas others, like Piaget, may be extremely subjectivistic. Surely any complete scientific analysis of psychology's history must specify all external factors that might cause psychologists to take one or another position.

In fact, most histories of psychology are riddled with comments that affirm that a psychologist's ideas to a very large extent reflect the influence of factors extraneous to the discipline itself. Sometimes these supposed external influences come from other scientific disciplines, especially the much-envied "hard" or "exact" sciences. One example runs as follows:

> In the bright light of the new physics—so fully empirical and so utterly rational—and with every breath of the new cultural atmosphere so stimulating to the intellectual adventurer, one may expect to find the psychology of the eighteenth century all the more eager to proceed by rigorous self-observation and relentless logic. (Murphy & Kovach, 1972, p. 32)

This quote suggests methodological influence, but other quotes imply the cross-disciplinary impact of theoretical orientation. "The atomistic approach was surprisingly successful in several different disciplines, so it was only natural that the young psychology too would try to adopt it" (Wertheimer, 1987, p. 20). Hence, a psychologist's stance on the elementaristic-versus-holistic dimension discussed in chapter 8 may in part gauge the extent to which he or she was influenced by disciplines in which atomism has proven a valuable conceptual approach to phenomena.

On other occasions, the external input comes from outside the sciences, from the society or culture at large. Thus, the Hegelian oscillations I discussed in the previous chapter are sometimes ascribed not to an internal dialectic process but rather to changes in the larger sociocultural system. This is evident in the following remark: "Ideas and attitudes come and go in cycles that reflect the pendulum swings of societal values more than they seem to reflect new discoveries, clarifying demonstrations, or theoretical advances" (Marchman, 1993, p. 21). This statement concerns how the extrinsic zeitgeist, or "spirit of the times," may shape the history of ideas in psychological science. Other remarks, however, suggest that the decisive influence is the *ortgeist*, or "spirit of the place." Thus, American psychology is said to have taken its particular form because "since the days of the pioneers, people of the United States had emphasized individuality and practicality, and adaptation to the environment had to be a major concern" (Hergenhahn, 1992, p. 300). This distinctive American ortgeist is even said to shape the development of psychological systems imported from abroad. Hence,

> although the official Freudians adhering to the International Psychoanalytic Association . . . continued to grow in numbers, . . . rival psychotherapies increased even faster. This was particularly the case in America, where innumerable conflicts have split the psychoanalytic movement, fostered by the individualistic and anti-authoritarian streak in the American make-up. (Hearnshaw, 1987, p. 166)

In these examples, the impact of the zeitgeist or ortgeist is presumably subtle and unintended, yet sociocultural influences may intervene more forthrightly in the history of ideas. "Throughout history scientific and philosophical works have often been distorted in order to support political ideologies," wrote Hergenhahn (1992, p. 199).

I must add that not all historians agree that psychological ideas are always so intimately tied to external conditions. Concepts and orientations may occasionally emerge that seem decoupled from the milieu. For instance, "the appearance of a Russian physicalistic psychology analogous to behaviorism during the latter part of the nineteenth century is amazing when one considers that Russia was a nonwestern, nonindustrialized, totalitarian (czarist) society" (Hillner, 1984, p. 131). The wide gap between Russian and American political and economic systems notwithstanding, Russian and American psychologists have tended to be much stronger proponents of objectivistic approaches than have western European psychologists. The existence of such exceptions means that it is necessary to document which external factors do and do not influence the nature of psychological ideas at a particular time and place. As I mentioned earlier in this chapter, these effects may classed into three categories: transient fluctuations, inertial movements, and developmental influences.

Transient Fluctuations

Just as war exerts a temporary impact on the quantity of scientific output, so may it influence the qualitative nature of that output, a connection frequently mentioned by historians. For instance, it has been said that "the most dramatic catalyst for applied work, however, is usually war or the threat of war" (Gilgen, 1982, p. 7); moreover, "in a highly industrialized society, war tends to accelerate technological developments" (Gilgen, 1982, p. 59). Hence, during the first world war R. S. Woodworth designed *The Personal Data Sheet* to determine potential emotional problems of military personnel, Robert Yerkes helped develop the Army Alpha and Army Beta tests to assess the intellectual ability of new recruits, and Walter Cannon began to study the effects of severe trauma, later published in 1923 as *Traumatic Shock*. During the second world war B. F. Skinner was involved in a project to get pigeons to serve in missile guidance systems, and Henry Murray worked on the selection of undercover agents for the Office of Strategic Services. In general, the research programs of great psychologists sometimes yield to the larger urgency of the national "war effort."

Yet these transient linkages between warfare and psychological research are trivial from a theoretical perspective. In a sense, these effects are no different than the changes in artistic creations that are written under wartime conditions (Simonton, 1977c, 1983a, 1986e). That Shakespeare or any other writer talks more about war when writing during wartime does not appear to constitute a particularly profound discovery. To some extent the content of creativity will always reflect what is happening in the larger world, and scientific creativity cannot completely isolate itself from this influence. Even so, some repercussions of war are more psychologically interesting. For instance, during wartime conditions people tend to exhibit declines in the sophistication of their thinking, as assessed by the measure of integrative complexity discussed in chapter 6 (e.g., C. A. Porter & Suedfeld, 1981). Peter Suedfeld (1985) showed that this effect even holds for great psychologists. The sample consisted of 85 presidents of the American Psychological Association (APA) whose addresses were published from 1894 to 1981 in *Psychological Review, Psychological Bulletin*, or *American Psychologist*. Some of these presidential addresses were delivered during peacetime, whereas others were delivered during the Spanish–American War, one of the two world wars, the Korean War, or the Vietnam War. Suedfeld (1985) content analyzed the speeches for integrative complexity, and a consistent pattern emerged: Cognition was much more complex in the addresses given during times of peace.

Another transient external event has an even more powerful and provocative impact on psychological science: economic threat. Research on this consequence was inspired by the findings reported in *The Authoritarian Personality*, by Theodor W. Adorno, Else Frenkel-Brunswik, Daniel J. Levinson, and Nevitt R. Sanford (1950). In this classic work the investigators tried to fathom the psychodynamic roots of fascism and its various manifestations, such as antisemitism, ethnocentrism, and politico–economic conservatism. One important finding to emerge out of this inquiry was that the authoritarian personality belongs to individuals who feel threatened by powerful forces beyond their control. Subordination of their personal will to conventional authority is seen as a means of reducing the ambiguities and uncertainties elicited by those threats. Hence, authoritarianism is not only a lasting trait, a bona fide personality characteristic, but it is also a state—a temporary response to threatening external conditions. In particular, when a nation finds itself under extremely threatening conditions, the modal personality of its citizens will shift toward more authoritarian beliefs and behaviors (e.g., Jorgenson, 1975; McCann & Stewin, 1987). The external menace may be political, such as war looming on the horizon, or it may be economic, such as the onset of a major depression that threatens the livelihood of the average citizen (e.g., increased unemployment or lowered disposable income). Whatever the source, threatening circumstances can have consequences that impinge on psychology's own history, whether indirectly or directly.

Among the indirect repercussions is an increased involvement in more dogmatic religions (McCann, 1999; Sales, 1972). Certain churches demand strict adherence to a well-defined set of beliefs and practices, and members who do not conform to these expectations are ostracized or excommunicated from the congregation. Other churches have much more liberal attitudes and will tolerate an exceptional variety of behaviors and attitudes among their fold. When times are threatening—whether economically, politically, or socially—membership in the former churches tends to increase. For instance, when the unemployment rates go up, so does the religious "market share" of the most authoritarian churches. Yet, as I have discussed in earlier chapters, scientific creativity is more strongly associated with affiliation with less dogmatic faiths—or with no religious allegiance at all. Consistent with this statement, threatening circumstances are positively associated with the emergence of attitudes that can be considered antiscientific, such as increased interest in astrology, mysticism, and the occult (Padgett & Jorgenson, 1982; Sales, 1973; cf. Doty, Peterson, & Winter, 1991).

The direct effects of threatening conditions on psychology are twofold. First, because authoritarians are more superstitious and believe that human beings are subject to mysterious forces, times of threat help make parapsychology more prominent as a research topic in the psychological literature (McCann & Stewin, 1984). Here the measures of threatening circumstances included declines in per capita disposable income, increases in the unemployment rate, and the subjective assessments of historians and social critics. Because this empirical finding covered the years 1929–1975 it provides a basis for understanding the career of Joseph Banks Rhine, whose launched his research on parapsychology during the Great Depression. Specifically, he wrote his first book, *Extrasensory Perception,* in 1934, became director of the Parapsychology Laboratory in 1935, and founded the *Journal of Parapsychology* in 1937.

Second, because the symptoms of the authoritarian personality include anti-intraception, popular books and magazine articles on intraceptive topics such as psychoanalysis and psychotherapy decline during threatening times (Sales, 1973). The authoritarian bias against intraception is also apparent in changes in APA divisional membership (Doty et al., 1991). APA Divisions 12 (clinical), 17 (counseling), 29 (psychotherapy), and 32 (humanistic) have a strong intraceptive orientation, whereas Divisions 3 (experimental), 6 (physiological and comparative), 25 (experimental analysis of behavior), and 21 (applied experimental and engineering) are more nonintraceptive in nature. The relative membership growth of these two division categories corresponds to whether the times are nonthreatening or threatening. Fairly consistent with these results is the history of American behaviorism, which saw its heyday during the Great Depression and the threatening events that culminated in the entrance of the United States in World War II. In particular, neo-Behaviorists Edwin Guthrie, Clark L. Hull, B. F. Skinner, Kenneth Spence, and Edward Tolman all began to make names for themselves during the 1930s. On the other hand, more intraceptive forms of psychology, such as cognitive and humanistic psychologies, really took off in the 1960s, during a period of unprecedented peace and prosperity.

In a kind of curious twist of fate, the repercussions of a threatening milieu put into larger context the events that lead to the research on the authoritarian personality in the first place. Padgett and Jorgenson's (1982) investigation concentrated on economic threat in Germany between 1918 and 1940. They gauged the magnitude of threat using indicators of real wages, unemployment, and industrial production. These indicators traced the deteriorating conditions under the Weimar republic, conditions that got especially bad when the Great Depression struck the German economy. By 1932, unemployment had risen to an outrageous 45%, and the German people became ever more desperate—more willing to submit to a more authoritarian leadership. At the beginning of 1933, Aldolf Hitler became the chancellor of the German state, and in a short time he began to consolidate his power. With the rise of Nazi policies came the antisemitism, ethnocentrism, and politico–economic conservatism that obliged many great German and Austrian psychologists to immigrate to more tolerant nations. Among those who immigrated to the United States were Theodor W. Adorno and Else Frenkel-Brunswik, who ended up at the University of California, Berkeley. There they collaborated with Daniel J. Levinson and Nevitt R. Sanford in the research published in the 1950 work *Authoritarian Personality*, 5 years after the destruction of Hitler's regime.

Inertial Movements

Other aspects of the sociocultural milieu leave a more long-term impression on the qualitative features of creativity displayed by a civilization. Political, economic, social, and cultural systems, in particular, change only very slowly, and the creative activities they influence will tag along at a similarly glacial pace. Such an inertial movement is implicit in the following observation: "Empires tend to be pragmatic, and we find in the Romans great engineers and practical politicians rather than great thinkers" (Leahey, 1980, p. 50). Given that imperial systems often take centuries to rise and fall, a cultural favoritism toward a practical science such as engineering will not change very rapidly over the course of history. Another illustration is found in this quotation: "As people become increasingly oppressed by the miseries of life, however, they looked to philosophy and religion for greater comfort than was provided by Cynicism, Skepticism, and Epicureanism. The philosophers and theologians responded by becoming increasingly mystical" (Hergenhahn, 1992, p. 58). The slow, painful decline of the Roman Empire eventually produced chronic circumstances that encouraged a retreat from the secular and rational philosophies of life inherited from ancient Greece. The culmination of this retreat was the rise of Christianity, which replaced the Classical worldview until the Renaissance.

Earlier I described a measure of political fragmentation that spanned Western civilization from the ancient Greeks to the 20th century (Simonton, 1974, 1975d). I also mentioned more than once Sorokin's (1937–1941) indicators of fluctuations in the positions that more than 2,000 thinkers took on seven major philosophical issues. These time series are not independent of each other. On the contrary, the number of independent states in a particular generation was positively correlated with the appearance of the following eight stances: empiricism, skepticism, fideism, materialism, temporalism, nominalism, singularism, and the ethics of happiness (Simonton, 1976g). In other words, political fragmentation is associated with an increase in the number of thinkers who advocate that (a) all knowledge comes by means of the sense organs (or else that no secure knowledge can be acquired or that it can be obtained only through faith); (b) the basis of reality is matter rather than spirit, soul, or mind; (c) reality is constantly changing or evolving, rather than eternal; (d) abstract ideas are nothing but words to label collections of particulars; (e) individuals have primacy over the social system; and (f) pleasure provides the proper criterion of right and wrong. Conversely, the rise of large imperial states would be antithetical to the emergence of these same philosophical positions. This result has three valuable implications:

1. Just as Candolle (1873) concluded, division into small independent states seems again conducive to the emergence of science, albeit by a more indirect route. The epistemology of the scientific enterprise is manifestly empirical (viz., experimentation), and the ontology tends to be materialistic (e.g., atoms). Moreover, nominalism bears a close relation with the notion of operational definitions—the idea that the names given to concepts are very much matters of convention. Finally, temporalism has a strong affinity with evolutionary theories, whether biological, geological, or cosmological.

2. The obvious connection between psychology and singularism implies that political fragmentation contributed to the appearance of psychological science as well. Psychologists study individuals, not the sociological or cultural collectives favored by universalists. In a sense, the interest in the singular individuals is nurtured when a civilization is highly individualistic in its political structure.

3. The ethics of happiness is linked not only with hedonism and utilitarianism but also with all systems of psychology that posit a pleasure principle, such as Sigmund Freud's psychoanalytic theory, Clark L. Hull's drive-reduction principle, and B. F. Skinner's concept of positive reinforcers. Hence, political fragmentation may be viewed as a factor underlying the emergence of these psychological ideas.

These three implications together should help one appreciate why the first naturalistic psychologies appeared in ancient Greece and then reappeared in modern Europe. Although these statistical associations were based on Western civilization, it is possible that the same findings apply to other world cultures. The thinkers of Islamic civilization who contributed most conspicuously to the history of psychology, such as Avicenna (Ibn Sina), Averroës (Ibn Rushd), and Maimonides (Moses ben Maimon)—all lived after the disintegration of the Empire of the Caliphate but before the integration imposed by the Ottoman Empire (see Sorokin & Merton, 1935). Likewise the Buddha, who can be considered the world's first psychologist, grew up in an age prior to the advent of the great empires of Northern India. So, this external factor may have cross-cultural validity.

Developmental Influences

I must qualify the foregoing conclusion. If a cross-lagged correlation analysis is done on these generational data, then the correlation between political fragmentation and the eight philosophical positions turns out to be highest after a one-generation delay (Simonton, 1976g); that is, the number of representatives of these positions in Generation g is more strongly related to the number of sovereign nations in Generation $g - 1$ than in Generation g. The reason why both cross-lagged and synchronous correlations are significant is that political fragmentation—like a true inertial factor—is highly autocorrelated. Even after extraction of a third-order polynomial time trend, the count of independent states in Generation g correlates .77 with the count in Generation $g - 1$. This autocorrelation is sufficiently high that the synchronous correlation can be said to serve as a proxy for the cross-lagged correlation. Accordingly, it is more precise to conclude that political fragmentation operates as a developmental influence—albeit one that does not fluctuate much from generation to generation. Growing up in a milieu in which many separate nations thrive is conducive to developing ideas such as empiricism, skepticism, fideism, materialism, temporalism, nominalism, singularism, and the ethics of happiness.

This is not the sole developmental influence demonstrated in empirical research. In fact, two other factors have much less ambiguous relations with the ideas that appear in a given generation of thinkers: international war and civil disturbances.

International War

Because war and peace are much more volatile over time than are governments or dynasties, the autocorrelation for generational time series is essentially zero (Simonton, 1976g). Moreover, the amount of war in Generation $g - 1$ is negatively related to the representation of several important beliefs in Generation g, namely, empiricism, temporalism, nominalism, singularism, and the ethics of happiness. In other words, future thinkers who spent their youth in a world plagued by warfare are less likely to advocate these positions—positions that are favored by political fragmentation! It is possible that wartime conditions, including the associated propaganda and restrictions on civil liberties, discourage the development of these attitudes. The individual's perceptions, beliefs, and needs, after all, must yield to the urgency of national survival. As already noted, many great psychologists have subordinated their research programs to the general welfare under such circumstances.

Civil Disturbances

Like war, civil unrest is more randomly distributed over time; that is, generational time series that record counts of popular revolts, revolutions, and rebellions are not autocorrelated (Simonton, 1976g). Hence, unlike political fragmentation, there is less uncertainty about whether this external circumstance operates as an inertial or developmental factor. More critical is that many historians have speculated about the potential impact of civil unrest on the history of ideas. It has been said that "it cannot be mere chance that is responsible for the frequency with which periods of social turmoil and political reform are empirical in their philosophical complexion" (D. E. Robinson, 1986, p. 248) and that "the Greek cities were torn by civil revolt. As a result many intellectual citizens ceased to participate in public affairs and turned to a search for permanent and enduring qualities in their chaotic world" (Hulin, 1934, p. 11). Plato provided a specific exemplar of this second assertion. Coming from a distinguished Athenian family, but becoming disillusioned by the vicissitudes of political life, he turned to the eternal truths that transcended the mere appearances of the material world.

An even more intriguing conjecture, however, is that turbulent times might exert a polarizing influence on the course of intellectual history. Sorokin (1947/1969) called this the *law of polarization*, which he described thus:

The overwhelming majority of the population in normal times is neither distinctly bad nor conspicuously virtuous, neither very socially-minded nor extremely antisocial, neither markedly religious nor highly irreligious. In times of revolution this indifferent majority tends to split, the segments shifting to opposite poles and yielding a greater number of sinners and saints, social altruists and antisocial egoists, devout religious believers and militant atheists. The "balanced majority" tend to decrease in favor of extreme polar factions in the ethical, religious, intellectual, and other fields. This polarization is generated by revolutions in all fields of social and cultural life. (p. 487)

Sorokin never actually tested this idea, despite having collected data on both civil unrest and philosophical change for *Social and Cultural Dynamics* (1937–1941).

When the test is conducted with the generational time series I independently collected for my doctoral dissertation (Simonton, 1974, 1975d), the outcome is most provocative (Simonton, 1976g). The representation of almost every philosophical position increased one generation after a period of major civil disturbances. More specifically, the number of popular revolts, revolutions, and rebellions in Generation $g - 1$ is positively related to Generation g's representation of (a) empiricists, rationalists, and mystics; (b) materialists and idealists; (c) eternalists and temporalists; (d) nominalists and realists; (e) singularists and universalists; (f) determinists and indeterminists; and (g) advocates of the ethics of happiness and advocates of the ethics of principles or love. In short, the political conflicts that thinkers experienced when young become translated into adulthood intellectual conflicts.

These effects provide a useful context for understanding what happened in certain periods of psychology's history. For instance, one historian, in discussing the political chaos that followed the dissolution of Alexander the Great's empire, observed that "in reaction to this time of crisis, of ambiguity, and of anxiety, two opposite philosophical movements sprang up, Epicureanism and Stoicism" (Wertheimer, 1987, p. 17). These two reactions are polarized, because each school takes a rather contrary position on many philosophical questions. Epicureans tend to favor empiricism, mechanistic materialism, temporalism, nominalism, extreme singularistic individualism, indeterminism, and the ethics of happiness, whereas Stoics tend to lean toward fideism, hylozoism, eternalism, conceptualism, determinism, and the ethics of principles. The two schools are not perfect opposites, but they contain enough diametrically opposed positions to make reconciliation impossible. Just as significant is that the founders of these two schools—Epicurus and Zeno of Citium—are almost exact contemporaries, both growing up during the civil turmoil associated with the meteoric rise and fall of the Macedonian Empire. The emergence of Epicureanism and Stoicism can thus be viewed as exemplifying Sorokin's law of polarization, in its developmental form.

15

GENIUS VERSUS ZEITGEIST

How do the results of the previous two chapters fit with all the findings reported in Parts II, III, and IV? After all, in chapter 14 I provided considerable evidence that individual creativity is influenced by characteristics of the external milieu, such as the nature of the political systems, the occurrence of war or civil unrest, and the degree of economic prosperity. These extrinsic factors affect not only the quantity of creativity that appears in a given time and place but also the qualitative nature of that creativity, such as the specific philosophical positions advocated by major thinkers. To these consequences must be added the repercussions of internal factors I extensively reviewed in chapter 13. Both the level of creativity displayed and the type of creativity manifested were shown to be the function of intrinsic developments within a particular domain of creative achievement. A particularly conspicuous example is the importance of role models and mentors in creative development. Taken altogether, the results of these two chapters seem to bolster the conclusion that great psychologists are mere creatures of their times. The zeitgeist and ortgeist embody the genuine creative forces in the history of psychology. The only exception to this conclusion is the multiples phenomenon. However, even here, it was chance rather than genius that was put forward as the causal agency behind independent discovery and invention.

Against the implications of chapters 13 and 14 must be imposed virtually all of the preceding chapters. In the chapters of Part II I treated the cross-sectional variation in productivity and distinction, the longitudinal fluctuations in impact, and the attributes of influential products in psychology. Permeating this entire treatment was the explicit proposition that individuals achieve greatness in the annals of the discipline. I reinforced this proposition in Part III in my discussion of the characteristics of great psychologists—the cognitive attributes, personality dispositions, and worldviews that contribute to their long-term success. The proposition was given added weight in Part IV, in which I examined the various developmental correlates of a psychologist's attainment, including family background, career training, maturity, and aging. The last chapter of Part IV was devoted to the nature–nurture issue, a question of patent psychological relevance. Hence, to advance from chapter 12 to the two chapters of Part V seems like a quantum shift in perspectives on the etiology of psychology's history.

The goal of this chapter is therefore to attempt some reconciliation between these apparently contradictory viewpoints. This reconciliation will take two forms. First comes a theoretical discussion of various reasons why the connection between genius and zeitgeist (or ortgeist) does not lend itself to complete sociocultural reductionism. Next I describe a pair of empirical inquiries that reinforce the same inference. The history of psychology cannot be reduced to sociocultural processes any more than it can be considered a pure manifestation of individual psychology.

GENERAL THEORETICAL CONSIDERATIONS

Despite the obvious impact of the sociocultural milieu on the appearance of creative genius, a scientific psychology of psychology's history remains both tenable and important. There are at least four bases for this continued relevance: the existence of substantial individual differences, the presence of contrasting causal effects, the mediation of psychological processes in sociocultural phenomena, and the possibility that some sociocultural phenomena are actually the effects of psychological processes.

Substantial Individual Differences

As is evident in the work of Alphonse de Candolle (1873), Pitirim A. Sorokin (1937–1941), and Alfred Kroeber (1944), inquiries into the creativity of large sociocultural entities all entail the tabulation of events or people; that is, these tabulations consist of aggregate counts, such as the number of discoveries or the number of scientists per cross-sectional or time-series unit. Yet such aggregate counts overlook a very significant reality: There exist substantial and reliable contrasts in the creativity displayed by products or individuals even when they emerge at the exact same time and place (Simonton, 1991c, 1998b). Not all English plays that hit the boards at the same time as Shakespeare's *Hamlet* achieve an equivalent level of success, neither did all of Michelangelo's fellow Italian artists attain identical levels of universal acclaim. The sociocultural factors that account for an increase or decrease in the aggregate count are silent about the variation in creativity across the units making up that aggregate.

Indeed, it is somewhat ironic that the greater the magnitude of creativity exhibited at the aggregate level, the more variable is the creativity displayed within the group. This tendency emerges in two ways.

First, according to cross-cultural studies, sociocultural evolution seems to proceed from (a) relatively simple societies in which there are no geniuses per se and yet in which everybody is creative to (b) comparatively complex societies in which true creative geniuses appear and yet the masses lead relatively uncreative lives (Brenneis, 1990; Carneiro, 1970; Martindale, 1976). This increased heterogeneity in creativity is accentuated all the more by the massive increase in population size that accompanies this evolutionary transformation (J. L. Simon & Sullivan, 1989; Simonton, 1999b; Taagepera, 1979). This implies that the top-notch creators represent only a very small proportion of the entire population. According to Francis Galton's (1869) estimate, only 1 out of about 4,000 individuals could be considered deserving of the name "genius."

Second, these individual differences are not confined to the simple distinction between the producers and the consumers of creativity. As amply demonstrated in chapter 3, the cross-sectional variation in lifetime productivity is huge—far more than would be anticipated if creativity were a normally distributed trait. This is the main point of the laws of Alfred Lotka and Derek Price (Lotka, 1926; Price, 1963; H. A. Simon, 1955). Indeed, as I explained in chapter 13, the Price law says that this productive elitism must intensify as the aggregate number of active producers increases (Price, 1963). This means that as the total aggregate number of creators increases in a given nation or civilization, the more pervasive are the individual differences in total output.

These individual differences are critical, because they determine how the zeitgeist specifically manifests itself. I gave one example in chapter 13 with respect to the phenomenon of multiple discovery and invention. Because there are tremendous individual differences in total output, there also exists substantial variation in the number of multiples in which any one scientist or inventor participates. The more prolific the individual, the higher are the odds that he or she will be involved in a multiple. Because eminence correlates very highly with total output, the most famous contributors will also be involved in more multiples (Simonton, 1979, 1987b).

Another example can be inferred from chapter 7, in which I presented an inventory of the personality characteristics most commonly found among outstanding creators. Among the most critical of these is a pronounced tendency to be independent, to resist conformity pressures, to pursue one's own path without regard to societal norms. This implies that the greatest creators of a given time or place may actually be those who are least influenced by the surrounding zeitgeist or ortgeist. There is abundant evidence that this may indeed be the case. For instance, I conducted a historiometric inquiry that looked at the aesthetic impact of 15,618 melodies by 477 classical composers and found similar results (Simonton, 1980c). The most successful compositions were those that departed most from the stylistic conventions of their day. Moreover, there was a distinct tendency for composers to conform less and less to those conventions as they matured. Sticking close to the prevailing fashions may be wise in the early years of apprenticeship, but eventually composers must strike out on their own, to establish their own distinctive stylistic voice. Those who fail to free themselves from the compositional zeitgeist pay the consequence when what is fashionable becomes unfashionable (Simonton, 1998b).

Contrasting Causal Effects

Kroeber (1944) argued, on the basis of the data he had collected, that there was indeed a certain correspondence between aggregate levels of creative activity and individual differences in creative genius. In particular, the greatest creators were said to appear at the high point of the configuration, when the cultural pattern reaches a climax. Yet this conclusion was based on mere inspection of the data rather than on any sophisticated statistical analysis. When such an analysis is actually executed, a rather more complex outcome emerges (Simonton, 1996b). Specifically, I scrutinized individual differences in the eminence attained by 611 Japanese creators and leaders with respect to the configurations defined by 1,631 lesser figures active in the same domains of activity (Simonton, 1996b). The local configuration for each figure could either be a peak, a trough, an ascent, or a descent. The most eminent individuals did not display any tendency to appear during the peaks; instead, they were most likely to emerge when the civilization as a whole was on an upward trajectory (ascent) and less likely to emerge when aggregate creativity in the specific domain was on a downward trajectory (decline). Furthermore, the amount of variance explained in either case was very small, much less than 3%.

What makes the foregoing result most remarkable is that Kroeber's (1944) conjecture does seem to hold at the aggregate level, as I discussed in chapter 13; that is, the most famous creators of history tend to appear in the same generations that contain the highest numbers of also-rans in the same creative domains (Simonton, 1975d, 1988d). Moreover, the amount of variance accounted for is much higher, in the range of 10% (Simonton, 1988d). For instance, the correlation between the number of major and minor thinkers across 141 generations of Chinese philosophy is .50, which shows that 25% of the variance is shared (even after the time series is detrended).

This may seem strange to psychologists, who are mostly used to studying individual-level phenomena. Discrepancies between aggregate- and individual-level phenomena are well known to sociologists and demographers, who deal with this curiosity often (Hannan, 1971; W. S. Robinson, 1950). To illustrate, the states of the United States that have the highest economic prosperity also tend to have the highest English-language illiteracy rates. Yet at the individual level such illiteracy is negatively correlated with personal income. The aggregate and individual statistics clearly are describing two different phenomena, the first, the tendency for prosperous states to attract more immigration, the latter, the tendency for the better paying jobs in the United States to require proficiency in the English language.

To illustrate the lack of correspondence between aggregate- and individual-level effects, I return to the case of classical music. Although there is no doubt that the number of eminent composers in Generation g is a positive function of the number of eminent composers in Generation $g - 1$, that does not mean that the differential greatness of a composer active in Generation g is a simple consequence the number of great composers in Generation $g - 1$. It is evident in the fate of 696 composers active from the Renaissance to the 20th century that role model availability has much more ambivalent effects (Simonton, 1977c). On the one hand, the more role models that were available during the developmental period of a musical talent, the sooner he or she would begin to make original contributions to the repertoire. On the other hand, that same exposure has a negative effect on a composer's total output. Hence, role models leave a positive imprint on early creative precocity but a negative imprint on later productivity. Yet, complicating things all the more is that the net effect of role model availability on lifetime output is zero. This happens because total output is a positive function of precocity, yielding a positive indirect effect that cancels out the negative direct effect! Needless to say, these causal complications at the individual level have no counterpart at the aggregate level.

Intervening Psychological Processes

It must never be forgotten that the creative process is ultimately housed in the human mind. Even when several human minds are interacting to produce creative ideas—as in brainstorming sessions or collaborative research teams—it remains invariably true that single intellects are generating the ideas. By the same token, the sociocultural environment that supports the development and manifestation of creativity must somehow operate by means of the individual creator. This means that some kind of psychological process or mechanism is often involved.

I have mentioned examples of such mediating processes on several occasions in the preceding two chapters; that is, to explain the relation between the sociocultural milieu and the individual creator I cited some psychological variable as the intervening cause. Thus, in chapter 14 the benefits of cultural cross-fertilization for individual creativity were said to operate by means of the cognitive effects of bilingualism as well as the behavioral effects of exposure to minorities who do not conform to majority-culture values and beliefs. Also, in chapter 13 I discussed how Kroeber (1944) himself, following Velleius Paterculus centuries earlier, ascribed the configurations of culture growth to imitation, emulation, admiration, and envy—social learning processes that take place within individual human beings.

Psychologically Driven Sociocultural Phenomena

The preceding argument may be taken one step further. Not only may sociocultural influences operate by means of psychological processes, but also psychological processes may to some extent shape those very influences. In other words, both the zeitgeist and the ortgeist may be partly a function of the human psyche rather than the causal direction always going in the other direction. Sorokin's (1937–1941) theory of sociocultural dynamics—which I outlined in chapter 14—is a case in point. According to Sorokin, the driving force behind the transformation of culture mentalities is the relative capacity of each mentality to solve the basic problems of life faced by each person living within that culture. The most fundamental problem concerns how best to attain happiness. When the sociocultural system fails to satisfy that basic requirement of human existence, pressures will emerge to replace the old culture mentality with a new one that purports to be more satisfactory. The Roman Empire would not have become the Holy Roman Empire if the empire's citizens had not found ideational Christianity far more fulfilling than what had become a rather sensate paganism.

Of course, one might argue that to some extent the psychological variables that affect the sociocultural variables are themselves determined by other sociocultural factors. Even so, the psychological variables would still be serving a mediating function, perhaps even a role so essential that the course of history is shaped by the minds of individual creators. One case in point is Colin Martindale's (1990) work on stylistic change in the arts, which I discussed in chapter 13. Although each artistic creator works within a given aesthetic tradition, he or she can secure a reputation only by producing compositions that depart from that tradition. This pressure to be novel, even shocking, impels the artist to resort to ever more primary-process (or primordial) imagery, with corresponding consequences for the evolution of the received style. This continued drive toward ever more originality eventually destroys the style, requiring that creators come up with a new set of stylistic conventions for creativity to continue.

SPECIFIC EMPIRICAL INVESTIGATIONS

Judging from the considerations just presented, the individual creator cannot be completely subsumed under the sociocultural milieu. Besides the fact that creativity exhibits tremendous cross-sectional variation even for those who are active in the exact same zeitgeist and ortgeist, sociocultural factors often operate at the individual level in a manner strikingly different than at the aggregate level. In addition, not only may psychological processes provide intervening variables in the working out of sociocultural phenomena, but also some sociocultural phenomena might be the causal offshoot of underlying psychological mechanisms.

One weakness in this theoretical discussion should be apparent, however. Few of the research findings used to illustrate the various points had any immediate relevance to the history of psychology. What holds for great classical composers, for example, may not correspond to what applies to great psychologists. I next remedy this deficiency by providing two extended illustrations, one in which rather restricted samples of great psychologists were used and the other in which far more exhaustive samples of great thinkers were used. The first illustration concentrates on the effect of the ortgeist, the second on the impact of the zeitgeist.

The Ortgeist: Great Psychologists

In almost every chapter of this book, and especially in chapter 5, I have mentioned results taken from an intensive inquiry into the lives and careers of 69 eminent American psychologists (Simonton, 1992b). Despite the many findings already reported, one empirical outcome has yet to be discussed: the impact of the ortgeist on the differential acclaim enjoyed by these individuals. The ortgeist admittedly seems like a difficult concept to translate into objective measurements. Yet this task was not only accomplished, but also it was carried out with computerized content analysis, a technique that I have already exploited more than once in other chapters. By this means the life work of these luminaries has been gauged on the degree of focus in their research programs and the amount of primary- and secondary-process imagery. Readers should recall that these content analytical measures were all based on the titles of the principal publications of the 69 psychologists (as listed in R. I. Watson, 1974).

A measure of the American ortgeist was gauged using the same raw information (Simonton, 1992b). The first step was to perform a content analysis to determine what words had the highest frequency of occurrence in the entire set of titles. By the computer's count, the most popular words were *psychology, learning, study, mental, behavior, psychological, intelligence, studies, theory, tests,* and *experimental*. A dictionary was then constructed of all the words that occurred at least 10 times. This dictionary was used to calculate a weighted score of how much a particular psychologist's set of titles contained the keywords representative of all 2,281 titles by the 69 figures. The weight was based on the word's frequency of occurrence. Thus, the word *learning*, which appeared more than 150 times, was given a weight of 15. The resulting weighted count of keywords was then divided by the total number of words in each psychologist's collection of titles. This was then adopted as an index of each psychologist's ortgeist fit. Here *ortgeist* means the favorite topics of American psychologists active between 1879 and 1967.

It is interesting that the more recently born psychologists had lower scores than those born earlier in the period covered. This secular trend probably captures the historical shift that psychology has undergone from a relatively homogeneous field at its founding to the highly heterogeneous field that it is today. In the early days, American psychology was dominated by just a handful of research topics, whereas over time the number of topics has proliferated, especially after the second world war. This proliferation is reflected in the increase in the total number of APA divisions. APA first adopted a division structure in 1946, albeit in response to the emergence of other organizations representing psychologists with different interests (e.g., practice and policy). The number of divisions grew eventually from a mere handful until it exceeded 50 by the end of the 20th century. A similar increase in substantive pluralism is seen in APA journals. APA went from having no journals in 1892, to having 6 by 1942. By the middle of the 1980s, the number exceeded 20, and by the end of the 20th century the count surpassed 40. Needless to say, it has become increasingly difficult for any psychologist to be considered highly representative of American psychologists as a whole.

Even more interesting, however, are the correlations between the ortgeist fit and three measures of a psychologist's impact on the field. First, this content-analytical measure correlates positively with the total number of a psychologist's publications that continue to be cited in recent volumes of the *Social Sciences Citation Index*. Second, conformity to the ortgeist is positively correlated with the psychologist's posthumous reputation, as gauged by a highly reliable and valid multiple-indicator measure that I described in chapter 3. Third, ortgeist fit provides a good predictor of whether the individual was honored with election to the APA presidency. To tease out how ortgeist fit compared with other predictors of contemporary and posthumous fame, a multiple-regression analysis was conducted (Simonton, 1992b) that introduced other potential predictors, as well as control variables (especially birth year, to adjust for historical trends). A snug relationship with the ortgeist continued to make an important contribution to the prediction of both election to the APA presidency and posthumous reputation. Only continued citations to a psychologist's published work accounted for more productive power. Hence, concentrating on the most popular topics in American psychology is a good way of ensuring both contemporary acclaim and long-term distinction.

Turning to those among the 69 who scored highest and lowest on the measure can put this generalization into concrete terms. E. L. Thorndike, E.

B. Titchener, E. C. Tolman, K. W. Spence, and C. L. Hull exhibited the best fit to the American ortgeist among the 69. D. McGregor, E. Mayo, C. E. Ferree, W. v. D. Burnham, and E. K. Strong displayed the worst fit. Besides the obvious difference in name recognition, not one of those in the bottom group were ever elected to the APA presidency, whereas 3 out of the 5 in the top group—Thorndike, Tolman, and Hull—received that honor. Titchener probably would have become president, too, had not a personal dispute with James Mark Baldwin led to his resignation from APA.

These provocative results are naturally not immune from criticism. The ortgeist measure can be considered only a rough approximation. For one thing, it assessed only what topics a psychologist discussed, as revealed in the titles of his or her publications. The measure did not tap into the position taken on those topics, unlike the indicators of theoretical and methodological orientation examined in chapter 8. Just as crucial is the fact that the period covered, from 1879 to 1967, may be too long to be considered a single coherent ortgeist. In terms of generational analysis, that interval covers more than four 20-year time periods. Furthermore, no attempt was made to distinguish the American ortgeist from other disciplinary milieus, such as the British, French, German, Italian, and Russian. As a consequence, it cannot be said for sure whether the gauge of fit applies just to American psychology or to all psychology over that time period.

However, from the standpoint of the debate that is the centerpiece of this chapter, the most critical issue is whether the demonstrated impact of the ortgeist converts a great psychologist to a mere epiphenomenon of the sociocultural milieu. The answer is negative: The most consistently powerful predictor of a psychologist's impact on the field is not compatibility with the ortgeist but rather the long-term influence of his or her publications. Moreover, because the predictive power of the latter factor was estimated after controlling for the ortgeist fit, the assessment of the individual's contribution is not surviving as a proxy measure of the ortgeist fit. Also, in earlier chapters I provided a large number of cognitive, personality, and developmental variables that predict, either directly or indirectly, the impact of a psychologist's body of work. This means that great psychologists achieved the largest portion of their acclaim on the basis of their own personal characteristics, not according to the degree to which they conformed to the fashionable topics of their day. The best inference to draw from this study is that greatness as a psychologist is a matter of both genius and ortgeist, with the former holding the advantage.

The Zeitgeist: Great Psychologists, Scientists, and Philosophers

Judging from what is often said in histories of psychology, the zeitgeist should have no less impact than the ortgeist on a psychologist's ultimate

success. The following passage is illustrative of many that permeate historical narratives:

> It is now time to point out that this emphasis upon "matter in motion"
> was by no means the novel creation of Descartes, or Hobbes, or indeed of
> any other psychological thinker of the period. Every age has its vogue
> ideas, and the vogue idea of the early and middle seventeenth century
> was just this: that matter and motion constitute the warp and woof of the
> fabric of nature. (Lowry, 1982, p. 16)

Often, the only concession made to supposed geniuses is the admission
that they might manage to articulate the zeitgeist better than anyone else of
their age. "The 'great' individuals are typically those who synthesize existing
nebulous ideas into a clear, forceful viewpoint," wrote Hergenhahn (1992, p.
2). Hence, the phenomenal influence of Voltaire, the great French philosopher, has been attributed to the fact that he was "so effectively the spokes-
man of his age, so characteristically its representative, so completely its em-
bodiment" (Redman, 1968, p. 40). This notion that the zeitgeist speaks
through the genius goes back centuries. G. W. F. Hegel (1832/1952) affirmed
that "the great man of the age is the one who can put into words the will of
his age, tell the age what its will is, and accomplish it. What he does is the
heart and essence of his age, he actualizes his age" (p. 149). Johann Goethe
(1808–1832/1952) expressed this idea more poetically in *Faust*: "What you
call 'spirit of the ages' / Is after all the spirit of those sages / In which the
mirrored age itself reveals" (p. 16).

However, is this true? Are the great men and women of intellectual
history mere mirrors that reflect the times, their only claim to fame being,
perhaps, that their surfaces are more polished than the other mental reflec-
tors of the age? I addressed this question, and several other closely related
questions, in a comprehensive study of all the thinkers who dominated the
Western intellectual tradition from antiquity to the 20th century (Simonton,
1976f). I first define the study's sample and then its measures, and I conclude
by summarizing its most critical findings.

Sample

In both chapters 13 and 14 I made considerable use of Sorokin's (1937–
1941) data on the fluctuations in philosophical beliefs from the time of the
ancient Greeks to modern European culture. One generational time-series
analysis after another deciphered the diverse ways that the sociocultural milieu, both internal and external, shaped the course of intellectual history.
Yet statistical treatment of Sorokin's time series does not have to be confined to the aggregate level of analysis. The appendixes of his *Social and Cultural Dynamics* contain the original individual-level scores that were later
aggregated into the 20-year periods. Hence, it is possible to use these data for
an analysis that is confined to individuals rather than generations. The re-

sulting sample is exceptionally large, for a total of 2,012 thinkers are available for study. Furthermore, these thinkers span over two millennia of intellectual history—from Thales to Karl Pearson. In addition, the sample contains many of the key figures of psychology's history, as is evident in Table 13.2. Included are great philosophers, such as Aristotle, Thomas Aquinas, and Immanuel Kant; great scientists, such as René Descartes, Isaac Newton, and Charles Darwin; and great psychologists, such as William James and Wilhelm Wundt. If the zeitgeist → genius hypothesis has any merit, its truth should be demonstrated on this group of luminaries.

Measures

The first task was to provide an operational definition of the dependent variable, namely, each thinker's eminence. Rather than just using Sorokin's (1937–1941) assessments, I used a composite measure that consisted of 10 distinct evaluations, including those provided by Kroeber (1944) in his chapter on philosophical configurations (Simonton, 1976f). The resulting measure was highly reliable (Simonton, 1976f), as demonstrated in chapter 3, when I discussed Galton's G (Simonton, 1991c). The next step was to define the independent variables that could enter the multiple regression equation as predictors. These variables fell into four groups: external factors, internal factors, zeitgeist fit, and belief structure.

1. The external factors all came from variables discussed earlier in this chapter: political fragmentation, imperial instability, political instability (or anarchy), and war intensity (Simonton, 1975d). To apply these generational measures to the individual level of analysis, I assigned each thinker to a generation, according to the 40-year floruit rule. Each thinker's eminence could then be correlated with the scores on these variables in either the same generation (g) or the preceding generation (g – 1). The former would represent a productive-period influence, the latter a developmental-period influence. A cross-lagged analysis had been used to determine whether the relation would be synchronous or lagged.
2. The two measures of internal factors were role model availability and ideological diversity in Generation g – 1. The former was simply a count of the number of thinkers in the sample who were active in the preceding generation, whereas the latter was based on my study, discussed earlier in this chapter (Simonton, 1976d). Both were considered developmental-period factors.
3. Zeitgeist fit was assessed three distinct ways, depending on which zeitgeist the thinker was voicing. First and foremost

was a measure of representativeness, analogous to the ortgeist fit indicator on which the 69 American psychologists were assessed. A thinker's score gauged the correspondence between the positions taken on the seven core philosophical issues and the positions taken by most thinkers active in the same 20-year period (i.e., Generation g). Next was a measure of the degree of fit between the thinker's beliefs and the dominant positions of the following generation (i.e., $g + 1$) rather than the preceding generation (i.e., $g - 1$). This score was said to assess a thinker's precursiveness, that is, the extent to which he or she was ahead of the zeitgeist. The third and last measure compared the stances taken by each thinker against the most popular positions of the early 20th century. The degree of match on the seven philosophical issues assessed the thinker's modernity.

4. The last three measures concentrated on the thinker's belief structure. The first measure gauged the breadth of positions taken. Thinkers who treated all seven philosophical issues were the most broad in intellectual scope, whereas those who specialized in only one issue, such as just ethics, were the most narrow. The second was a measure of extremism, which was defined as the extent to which the thinker advocated positions that (a) were favored by less than 10% of all 2,012 thinkers in the sample and (b) occupied the endpoint of some scale of opinions on the issue (e.g., monistic idealism, extreme singularistic individualism, and the ethics of love). The third measure gauged the degree to which a thinker's package of beliefs could be considered consistent with how positions are generally put together by the thinkers of the Western philosophical tradition. Consistent belief pairs were identified if they both frequently co-occurred among all philosophers. Examples include skepticism and temporalism, mysticism and realism, empiricism and nominalism, and mechanistic materialism and the ethics of happiness. Although the consistency scores were based on an a posteriori determination, almost all belief pairs would have been judged consistent on a priori grounds as well. Perhaps the only exception is the linkage of fideism and hylozoism, which represents a pairing distinct to Stoic philosophers.

Besides the above four sets of independent variables, historical time was introduced as a statistical control. Specifically, the date of the thinker's generation was used to adjust for any timewise trends (Simonton, 1976f).

Results

In Table 15.1 the results of regressing the thinker's eminence are presented on the 13 variables just defined. The independent variables collectively account for almost 22% of the total variance in a thinker's distinction. Yet the predictors did not always have the expected effect. To begin with, of the four external factors, only political fragmentation and political instability or anarchy emerged as significant predictors. The fame of a thinker active in Generation g is a positive function of the number of independent states in the same generation. In addition, eminence was a negative function of the level of political instability in Generation $g - 1$, indicating an adverse developmental influence. These findings replicate what was found at the aggregate level (Simonton, 1975d), as already described in chapter 14. On the other hand, imperial instability did not have any effect, albeit the regression coefficient was in the right direction. This fails to replicate what holds at the aggregate level (Simonton, 1975d). Although war intensity also had no effect, this would be anticipated according to what had been found in the generational time-series analyses (Simonton, 1975d, 1976b).

In the case of the internal factors, ideological diversity had no connection with a thinker's eminence, unlike what I found using aggregate data, where this factor was linked with greater philosophical activity (Simonton, 1976d). Even more surprising is that role model availability had a statistically significant effect, but one that had the opposite sign from what was found for generational time series representing three different world civilizations (Simonton, 1975d, 1988d, 1992a). Once the effects of the other variables in the equation are partialed out one sees that the most famous thinkers are most likely to have grown up in times where there is a relative dearth of predecessors—an intellectual vacuum! Already it appears from these results that the greatest philosophers, scientists, and psychologists may prove too independent, even obstreperous, to comply with our expectations.

This judgment is strengthened by the empirical findings concerning zeitgeist fit. Only in the case of the modernity measure does the outcome comply with expectation. Holding everything else constant, the most illustrious figures of Western intellectual history tend to propound beliefs that show a high concordance with modern views. For the other two measures, in contrast, the signs of the regression coefficients are negative rather than positive. Thus, in the first place, great thinkers are less likely to be precursors of a new age, as represented by the next generation's zeitgeist. On the contrary, eminence is associated with being behind the times, of having beliefs closer to those of the generation of their youth. It is almost as if the great thinkers are engaged in synthesizing the most secure ideas of the past rather than foreseeing the tenuous novelties of the future. Even more striking is the negative effect of representativeness. It is not the truly notable thinkers but rather their obscure colleagues who are most likely to adopt majority positions. The

TABLE 15.1
Multiple Regression Analysis: Predictors of the
Eminence of a Thinker at Generation g

Independent variable	Standardized coefficient	Squared semipartial correlation
External factors		
Political fragmentation (g)	.158***	.012
Imperial instability ($g - 1$)	−.042	.000
Political instability ($g - 1$)	−.062*	.002
War intensity ($g - 1$)	−.008	.000
Internal factors		
Role model availability ($g - 1$)	−.118*	.002
Ideological diversity ($g - 1$)	.022	.000
Zeitgeist fit		
Representativeness	−.179***	.012
Precursiveness	−.053**	.003
Modernity	.210***	.017
Belief structure		
Breadth	.526***	.067
Extremism	.144***	.012
Consistency	−.276***	.028
Generation (historical period)	.130***	.004

Note. The standardized partial regression coefficients (βs) are reprinted unaltered from Table 1 in Simonton (1976f), whereas the squared semipartial correlations were calculated from the *F* ratios given in the table. The squared multiple correlation for the total regression equation is .217. From "Philosophical Eminence, Beliefs, and Zeitgeist: An Individual–Generational Analysis" by D. K. Simonton, 1976, *Journal of Personality and Social Psychology, 34*, p. 637. Copyright 1976 by the American Psychological Association. Reprinted with permission.
*$p < .05$. **$p < .01$. ***$p < .001$.

greatest minds are those who buck the ideological fashions of their time, who transcend rather than represent the zeitgeist in which they must carve out their careers.

The effects for belief structure give one even better insight into what these greats are doing to earn their acclaim. Not only are the more eminent more likely to span a broader range of philosophical issues, but also they are more likely to advocate extreme positions and to package those positions in unusual combinations. In short, their philosophical systems are broad, yet seemingly inconsistent and extremist. The latter finding is especially fascinating, because it fits with what was discovered about the worldviews 54 eminent psychologists in chapter 8. Those who had the most long-term influence on the field were those who took extreme positions on the theoretical and methodological issues that have proven most divisive in the history of psychology.

Table 15.1 provides another column of statistics that offers even more insight into the relative role of genius and zeitgeist in the course of intellectual history. The squared semipartial correlations inform one as to the proportion of variance that can be uniquely attributed to the corresponding independent variable. To illustrate, the .004 squared semipartial for generation indicates that 0.4% of the total variance in a thinker's eminence can be ascribed uniquely to the historical period in which he or she was active. Now, judging from these statistics, it should be evident that the external and internal factors account for very little of what it takes to leave a mark on Western intellectual history. Only political fragmentation exceeds 1%, and the total unique effect of all six variables remains less than 2%. Although the three measures of zeitgeist fit enhance the predictive power much more—the three together contribute a bit over 3% to the predicted variation—only one of these operates in the expected manner. Indeed, the biggest effect, that for representativeness, appears to totally contradict the hypothesis that great minds reflect their times. The results for belief structure harm even more the case for the zeitgeist. The three predictors together account for about 11% of the variance, or around half of the total predictive power. The single most potent predictor in the entire set of 13 independent variables is philosophical breadth, which accounts for almost 7% of the variance.

The differential impact of these 2,012 thinkers seems to be far more a matter of genius than of zeitgeist. Individual-level variables such as the thinker's belief system have more predictive power than do the aggregate-level variables that gauge the sociocultural milieu, whether internal or external. Even worse for zeitgeist theory, the consequences of the sociocultural milieu at the individual level are not always compatible with what happens at the aggregate level, and sometimes the effects of the milieu are utterly inverted. Moreover, the beliefs advocated by the greatest thinkers do not appear to be those that one would expect to hear from someone trying to go along with the crowd or to embody the consensus of the majority. The success of the greatest minds certainly cannot be attributed to their being mere mouthpieces of their times. Neither are they willing to adopt moderate positions or to configure their positions in a manner most friendly with the prevailing views of Western philosophy. The image that emerges is one of individuals who are firmly independent, autonomous, and resistant to the conformity pressures of their age. Here the psychological disposition associated with creative genius appears to provide the driving force behind the most influential philosophers, scientists, and psychologists. Whether the great mind is Socrates or F. Nietzsche, I. Newton or C. Darwin, G. Fechner or W. James, these are people whose personality and intellect permit them to escape the constraints and prejudices of their times.

Is it any wonder, then, that so many celebrities of psychology's history have had to pay dearly for their failure to conform to the zeitgeist and ortgeist of their day? Their extremist and unconventional positions, at least in oppressive milieu, often provoked accusations of impiety or heresy (Aristotle, R. Bacon, R. Descartes, Galileo, T. Hobbes, D. Hume, Protagoras, Socrates, etc.). Many were threatened with excommunication or were forced into exile (T. Hobbes, J. O. de LaMettrie, C. Marx, William of Ockham, Paracelsus,

Protagoras, J. Rousseau, B. Spinoza, Voltaire, etc.), or saw their books burned, proscribed, or suppressed (R. Descartes, S. Freud, T. Hobbes, D. Hume, E. Husserl, C. Marx, J. Rousseau, etc.). Many faced arrest and imprisonment (R. Bacon, A. Comte, Galileo, J. S. Mill, Voltaire, etc.), experienced the humiliation of being coerced to recant their beliefs (Galileo, C. A. Helvétius, etc.), or suffered outright execution (G. Bruno, Hypatia, M. Servetus, Socrates, etc.). These free thinkers most often endured all this for the sake of promulgating what they believed to be the truth, the responses of their contemporaries be what they may.

Yet why was the effect of the zeitgeist for these 2,012 psychologists, scientists, and philosophers so different from the effect of the ortgeist for the 69 American psychologists? Is it because the ortgeist and zeitgeist measures had different operational definitions, the former based on mere topics and the latter on actual positions? Is it because the attainment of distinction in American psychology is contingent on different factors than is the achievement of eminence in the Western intellectual tradition? These questions obviously cannot be answered without additional empirical research. Meanwhile, it should be emphasized that the two studies (Simonton, 1976f, 1992b) do share one crucial conclusion in common. For both samples the individual's actual body of work had the biggest part in the determination of his or her acclaim. This robust result reinforces all the more the most fundamental inference to be drawn from all the findings reviewed in Part V. The diverse consequences of the sociocultural milieu notwithstanding, to become a great psychologist one must indeed be the right person, and not just simply be at the right place or the right time.

VI

IMPLICATIONS FOR THE FIELD OF PSYCHOLOGY

INTRODUCTION: IMPLICATIONS
FOR THE FIELD OF PSYCHOLOGY

I have now scrutinized great psychologists from an exceptional range of scientific perspectives. To be specific, I have examined those who have exerted some influence on the discipline's history from the standpoint of cognitive psychology (chapters 5 and 6); differential and personality psychology (chapters 3 and 6–8); life span developmental psychology (chapters 4 and 9–12); and social, cultural, and political psychology (chapters 13–15). Furthermore, I made every attempt to represent the rich diversity of major contributors to the field. The exemplars of greatness are diverse with respect to subdiscipline, gender, ethnicity, nationality, civilization, and even major domain of achievement—because philosophers and scientists are treated along with psychologists per se. Finally, and most important, chapters in Parts II–V contain a huge inventory of empirical findings and theoretical analyses. Unless I have overlooked some critical publication, all of the principal facts and concepts have been granted the review and discussion they deserve.

It thus comes time to step back and look at this book's contents and aims from a broader viewpoint. What are the big implications of this whole endeavor in the first place? Why should my colleagues even care about what has been reviewed in these pages? In the chapter that immediately follows I address this issue by looking at the consequences for research and teaching.

16

RESEARCH AND TEACHING

William James did not write *Principles of Psychology* to keep his fingers busy, neither did Sigmund Freud publish *Interpretation of Dreams* with the hope that the work would be ignored. Psychologists must have much better reasons to write books, given the hours of physical and mental labor that writing involves. Because it takes more effort to put together a book than it does to compose a journal article, the endeavor is undertaken only because book writing has pronounced benefits as well as conspicuous costs. One obvious benefit is that a psychologist, if fortunate or gifted, can actually earn a little income from book royalties. Articles, in contrast, only lead to such material gains insofar as they contribute to promotions or pay increases or to the fees that clients can be charged. Even so, for most psychologists the immaterial advantages outweigh any monetary assets. According to the research reviewed in chapter 3, books tend to be more influential than journal articles (Heyduk & Fenigstein, 1984; Simonton, 1992b). Only in an entire volume does the psychologist have the latitude to "put it all together" in one place—to provide the extensive documentation and intensive argumentation necessary to make the strongest possible case for a theory or position. If Alfred Russel Wallace had written the book *Origin of Species* and Charles Darwin the article "On the Tendency of Varieties to Depart Indefinitely From the Original Type," the eponym Wallacism might be used today in lieu of Dar-

447

winism. In short, books provide the most powerful means for psychologists to exert an impact on the field.

Although I do not pretend that this volume might ever have the same influence as *Principles of Psychology*, *Interpretation of Dreams*, or *Origin of Species*, it would not have been written had I not hoped for at least a favorable cost–benefit ratio. The American Psychological Association certainly did not take this book on unless it thought that this ratio might include reasonable sales figures. However, for me the principal aspiration was to make some contribution, however modest, to psychology as a discipline, for it is my sincere belief that the scientific study of great psychologists both past and present can contribute to psychology's future greatness as an intellectual enterprise. Specifically, I believe that this book has the potential to stimulate both research and teaching.

RESEARCH

In chapter 2 I discussed the metasciences, with special emphasis on the psychology of science. A subset of this metascience quite naturally includes the psychology of one particular science, and a special case of the psychology of psychological science is the psychology of the psychologists who have contributed most to making psychology a science. Yet despite the tremendous amount of research I have reviewed in the preceding pages, much more remains to be done. Future psychological research needs both to answer many empirical questions and to develop precise and comprehensive theoretical interpretations.

Empirical Questions

The range of topics treated in Parts II–V is certainly impressive. The psychology of great psychologists already has something of the substantive scope of the typical introductory psychology text. Even so, although I treated some topics quite adequately, I could give other topics only superficial or exploratory treatment at best. Even worse, I could not examine some important topics at all, because the literature is still lacking. The only remedy for these deficiencies and gaps is a considerable amount of additional psychometric and historiometric research. I next merely suggest some of the questions that could keep researchers busy for years to come.

Output and Impact

Judging from the wealth of secure empirical findings, the main topics of Part II appear to receive the most exhaustive treatment of any in this book. A great deal is known about cross-sectional variation in creative productivity and how this variation relates to a psychologist's eminence. Furthermore, confidence in these results is reinforced by the fact that they essentially duplicate what has already been amply demonstrated in other forms of creative endeavor, in both the sciences and the arts. Perhaps the only place where a little more research might be nice concerns the equal-odds rule—the idea that the number of hits is a constant but probabilistic function of the number of attempts. Although this rule has been shown to apply to both individual differences and longitudinal changes in output and impact, the concrete and detailed workings of this principle need to be scrutinized. Why is it so difficult for a researcher to adopt a perfectionist strategy, publishing only topnotch work and keeping everything that will be merely ignored locked up in office file drawers? To what extent does the lesser work make the greater work possible? Are failures essential to success? If all psychologists were penalized for publishing unnoticed work, or if they were allowed no more than one publication per year, would the discipline gain or lose?

To illustrate one possible outcome, consider the results of the following investigation (Bayles & Orland, 1993). On the first day of class, a ceramics teacher informed his students that they would be arbitrarily divided into two groups. Those in one group would be graded solely on quality, and those in the other would be graded on quantity. The final grade for each student in the quality group would be based on a single pot, which necessarily had to represent his or her best possible work. In contrast, the final grade for each student in the quantity group would be based on the sheer weight of the total number of pots he or she produced. Hence, those in the first group spent the whole class trying to produce the most perfect pot, whereas those in the second group churned out pot after pot after pot. At the end, however, the teacher had all pots rated for quality. And guess which group produced the best pots—the students in the quantity group! Of course, they produced a lot of bad pots, but the best works by these Mass Producers were more perfect than the best works that the Perfectionists could produce. Somehow, experience with failure is essential in acquiring the expertise that leads to success. Does the same principle apply to the careers of great psychologists?

One might probe this phenomenon with a number of techniques, such as a detailed content analysis of the journal articles published by notable figures in the field. In addition, it would probably prove useful to conduct a more fine-grained study of the longitudinal distribution of a psychologist's output. For instance, John Huber (1998a, 1998b) has carried out high-resolution inquiries into the output of successful patents by hundreds of inventors. Unlike most studies reviewed in Part II, which usually aggregate output into 5- or 10-year periods of the career, Huber's analyses took advantage of information indicating the exact date (day and year) that the patent was approved. This allowed him to show that patents were randomly distributed across the career course. The number of inventions appearing in any given period was described by a Poisson distribution, with parameters compatible with those seen in my treatment of multiples (see chapter 13). This result implies that inventors manage to arrive at successful patents only because they engage in many trials, each trial having a very low probability of success. Endorsing further this interpretation was the outcome of a test for runs that showed no strong tendency for these technological hits to accumulate in one or another part of the career. Hence, the probability of success is not increasing as the inventor acquires more expertise—neither is it declining. It would be highly instructive to apply the same methodology to journal articles, taking advantage of the published information regarding the dates that the manuscript was submitted or accepted (see, e.g., Huber, 2000). Moreover, these data can be combined with additional information about the disciplinary impact of each publication, according to citation indexes.

Finally, a complete understanding of output and impact probably requires that another fundamental issue be addressed: What determines the impact of a psychologist's publications? If the criteria of an article's quality were well defined and highly objective, it would seem easy to require that psychologists share only their best work with their colleagues. Yet, as I discussed in chapter 5, it is not easy to specify what constitutes an excellent contribution. Journal referees disagree among themselves, as do the reviewers of grant applications, and neither the referees nor the reviewers can successfully predict the short- or long-term influence of a particular research study or proposal. Notwithstanding the many suggested schemes for assessing the value of specific investigations, there is no empirical evidence that these schemes correspond to how publications are judged and used by other psychologists in the real world. So, what attributes of an article actually, rather than just hypothetically, determine its scientific merit? Which of these attributes are shared with successful scientific publications in general, and which are unique to psychology?

Perhaps these questions cannot be answered fully without developing a suitable typology of contributions. For instance, Robert J. Sternberg (1998) offered a "propulsion model" that identifies several distinctive types of creativity, which he called *replication, redefinition, forward incrementation, advance forward incrementation, redirection, reconstruction/redirection,* and *reinitiation*. It is conceivable that the criteria of scientific merit are contingent on the specific type of contribution being made. An article in which the author is merely trying to redefine the way psychologists look at things may be judged by different standards than an article in which the author tries to redirect completely the course of research in a given domain. In any case, until these issues are resolved, the psychology of psychological science contains a huge paradox: On the one hand, a whole lot is known about what it takes to become a great psychologist, including the primary role played by the psychologist's lifetime contributions; on the other hand, next to nothing is known about the factors that lead a particular publication to attain the status of a contribution.

Individual Characteristics

Although a considerable amount of empirical work has examined the cognitive and dispositional attributes of great scientists, including great psychologists, there remains much to be done on this subject. Perhaps the biggest gap concerns the lack of historiometric studies directly aimed at great psychologists. All studies since Catharine Cox's (1926) ambitious assessment of intelligence and personality have followed her example by investigating inclusive samples of creators and leaders. This is true, for example, in Edward Thorndike's (1950) historiometric examination of 91 eminent personalities. Yet it is possible to concentrate these methods on achievers in a single domain of creativity or leadership. For instance, a great deal has been learned about the intellect and character of U.S. presidents by the application of historiometric methods to biographical and content analytical data (Deluga, 1998; House, Spangler, & Woycke, 1991; Simonton, 1987d, 1988c; Winter, 1987). These methods have provided the basis for successfully predicting the performance of the American chief executive in the White House. With only minor modification, this same methodology might be used to tease out the cognitive and dispositional attributes of those who have left the biggest marks on psychology's history. These assessments might also shed more light on why psychologists favor one or another scientific outlook. To what degree is a psychologist's position on the nature–nurture issue grounded in a deeper cognitive style or motivational makeup? Are psychologists with a greater proclivity toward psychopathological symptoms more likely to appreciate the power of an irrational unconscious mind?

Computer simulations that more closely capture the discovery process in psychological science might also fruitfully augment empirical studies of personal characteristics. In chapter 6 I discussed the attempts by Herbert Simon and his associates to construct discovery programs (e.g., Langley, Simon, Bradshaw, & Zythow, 1987). This fascinating work unfortunately suffers from two drawbacks from the standpoint of a scientifically informed history of psychology.

1. These programs endeavor to simulate discoveries in the physical sciences, most often in physics and chemistry. It would be valuable indeed to test models that attempt to make rediscoveries that have a notable place in the annals of the behavioral sciences. For instance, in chapter 6 I mentioned how it was possible to write a program that simulated Hans Kreb's discovery of the urea cycle and compare this simulation with Kreb's laboratory notebooks (Kulkarni & Simon, 1988). Perhaps the same can be done with respect to Charles Darwin's discovery of the theory of evolution by natural selection, a discovery that is also well documented in his exten-

sive notebooks (Gruber, 1974; see also Tweney, 1989, for a cognitive analysis of M. Faraday's laboratory notes).

2. These discovery programs operate according to rather schematic and limited models of the creative process. They all are predicated on Herbert Simon's (1973) belief that scientific discovery has a precise logic, a step-by-step procedure by which well-defined heuristics are applied to a given domain of expertise. Yet, as I pointed out in chapter 6, it is very likely that this approach does not accurately represent the richness of actual human creativity. It is telling that the computer programs that have most successfully generated true discoveries—as distinguished from rediscoveries—incorporate some kind of stochastic mechanism (Boden, 1991). The most outstanding illustrations are the programs known as *genetic algorithms* and *genetic programming* (Koza, 1992, 1994). These programs operate according to a Darwinian process that is functionally equivalent to Donald T. Campbell's (1960) blind-variation and selective-retention model of creativity. Hence, in the long run this approach may prove most promising.

So, maybe some day discovery programs will succeed in simulating some of the great moments in psychology's history. Perhaps even further off, these programs might be given cognitive styles and personality dispositions that will demonstrate how various individual-difference factors specifically shape the origination of psychological ideas.

Developmental Correlates

Although the chapters in Part IV were replete with significant findings, the results reported were often based on samples of great scientists. Hence, more research is needed that concentrates on the key contributors to psychological science. Among the topics deserving of such specialized inquiry are birth order, childhood trauma, the 10-year rule, professional marginality, and career development—such as the typical ages for founding journals or organizations. These investigations would help one better appreciate how great psychologists stack up against great scientists with respect to their life span development.

More critical still is the need for more research on the development of great psychologists from underrepresented groups. With the exception of Jews, very little is known about the origins of those who managed to emerge from minority cultures. To what extent are the developmental factors different than those that contribute to the success of psychologists from the majority culture? The answer to this question is extremely important to countries, such as the United States, that have large and growing majority populations from which future psychologists will become increasingly drawn. By the same token, considerably more needs to be discovered about what enables women to become great psychologists. In chapter 12, for instance, I provided tentative evidence on behalf of what I called the *Helson effect*—the tendency for great female psychologists to come from families where their development could not be stifled by brothers. Is this conjecture empirically valid? Does the impact of this effect lessen in more egalitarian times and places? Moreover, once a woman manages to launch her career, what is the most likely repercussion of marriage and family? Is motherhood necessarily harmful to research output? These questions have become more urgent than ever given the enormous number of women who now enter the discipline.

Many of the foregoing developmental questions can be subsumed under one all-encompassing issue: What are the relative contributions of nature and nurture to the emergence of the discipline's luminaries? To what degree is a great psychologist born or made? How do genetic and environmental forces interact to produce an individual who will make a lasting contribution to the field? There admittedly is no reason to believe that these issues will be more easily resolved for great psychologists than they have been for the general population. Even so, psychologists should at least do the best they can to fathom this big question.

Sociocultural Context

It is probably safe to say that more research needs to be carried out in this area than in any of the preceding substantive questions. The topics covered in Parts II–IV are natural ones for psychologists to investigate, whereas those treated in Part V may appear more appropriate for sociologists, anthropologists, political scientists, or historians of science. Nonetheless, work in this area can be considered a special branch of social, cultural, political, economic, and environmental psychologies. At the very least, historians of psychology who are sympathetic with quantitative and nomothetic research should take seriously the possibility of finding an empirical basis for the commonplace assertion that the discipline's history is deeply rooted in its societal, cultural, political, economic, and environmental contexts. The following remark is certainly representative of what frequently permeates historical narratives:

> We may say, as a number of historians have said, that systematic philosophy has come into existence only a few times on the face of the earth. It is in the great river mouths and coastal harbors where trade flourishes that man could "keep the jungle down" and engage in local or international trade in such a way as to develop wealth and—for a few people—leisure. (Murphy & Kovach, 1972, p. 7)

What empirical evidence, if any, supports this conjecture?

Besides discovering the external milieu that is most conducive to the emergence of great thinkers, future researchers must study how the sociocultural environment influences the qualitative aspects of the ideas those thinkers conjure up. After all, the concepts that psychologists favor and the topics they investigate may be a partial function of external conditions and circumstances. To illustrate, consider the following speculation about how the American ortgeist early on shaped the nature of psychology in the United States:

> Alexis de Tocqueville wrote in *Democracy in America* following his visit to America during 1831 and 1832: "The longer a nation is democratic, enlightened and free, the greater will be the number of these interested promoters of scientific genius, and the more will discoveries immediately applicable to productive industry confer gain, fame and even power." However, Tocqueville worried that "in a community thus organized . . . the human mind may be led insensibly to the neglect of theory." Aristocracies, on the other hand, "facilitate the natural impulse of the highest regions of thought." Tocqueville foresaw well. American psychology since its founding has neglected theory, even being openly hostile to theory at times. While Europeans such as Jean Piaget construct grand, almost metaphysical theories, B. F. Skinner argues that theories of learning are unnecessary. (Leahey, 1992, pp. 256–257)

However provocative this conjecture may be, the implicit nomothetic principle on which it is based has yet to be subjected to empirical evaluation. Are aristocratic societies more favorably disposed toward abstract thought than are democratic societies?

Chapter 13 was more than twice as long as chapter 14, and therefore one can infer that much more is known about the internal factors involved in psychology's history. True or not, there still remains a large number of questions that lack complete answers. In particular, I believe that the following four issues could benefit most from additional empirical inquiries:

1. To what extent can one objectively determine where psychology stands in a Comtian-style hierarchy of the sciences? The results reported in Table 13.1 may be fascinating, but they are also incomplete. More disciplines must be evaluated—including all those in Auguste Comte's original hierarchy—and more criteria must enter the quantitative evaluations. Moreover, this hierarchy should be examined over time to gauge its transhistorical stability. Are there periods in which the rank ordering of the sciences changes?

2. Apropos of this last question, what evidence is there that psychology is or is not paradigmatic? If paradigmatic, has the discipline undergone Kuhnian-type scientific revolutions? These questions are relevant to the preceding one, because sciences may change their status in the hierarchy depending on their

placement in the Kuhnian process (e.g., when a science enters the crisis stage). Yet, so far, speculations about the applicability of Kuhnian theory immensely outnumber investigations that directly evaluate its application.

3. To what degree is psychology's history governed by Hegelian-like pendulum swings? Can one identify the specific theoretical and methodological issues that are most susceptible to such oscillations? What dialectic forces drive these shifts? These difficult questions naturally may not be easily answered. Yet, with a little ingenuity, including the application of computerized content analyses, psychologists may come to understand better the fashion changes so conspicuous in its history.

4. How does the multiples phenomenon operate within psychology? Do the stochastic models discussed in chapter 13 apply just as well to instances specifically drawn from the annals of the discipline? When two or more psychologists come up with the same idea, what determines who gets the credit? Why, exactly, must James share credit with Lange but Darwin not share credit with Wallace? Donald Campbell once suggested that because the more eminent psychologists make a name for themselves on the basis of numerous achievements, often it is the lesser known psychologist who becomes honored with eponymic status; this happens because "the names of one-time contributors are more efficient than the names of the great who contribute many principles to science" (D. T. Campbell & Tauscher 1966, p. 62). Supposedly, this is one reason why Emil Emmert became known for "Emmert's law" rather than Arthur Schopenhauer, Edward Séguin, M. N. Lubinoff, or W. Zehender—but is that really the operative nomothetic principle?

Besides all of these issues, the central topic of chapter 15—the relation between genius and the zeitgeist (or ortgeist)—definitely demands more empirical scrutiny. What nomothetic principles are identical for both individual and aggregate levels of analysis? Which ones are dramatically different, even contradictory? What psychological processes intervene between the sociocultural system and individual behavior? To what degree do a great psychologist's personal qualities moderate the effects of the external milieu? Studies of eminent leaders have revealed how individual and situational factors can interact in intricate ways to determine leader success (e.g., Simonton, 1987d; L. H. Stewart, 1977; Winter, 1987). Are great psychologists also the complex repercussion of being the right person at the right place and at the right time? If so, what are the essential components of this winning configuration of individual and situational determinants?

Theoretical Interpretations

In line with Alexis de Tocqueville's generalization about American distrust of abstract theory, the foregoing discussion only mentioned what I, an American psychologist, considered to be the most promising questions for future empirical study. In short, I listed the areas where more facts are needed. Yet, at the risk of breaking faith with my ortgeist, I suggest the need for theoretical research as well. It may ultimately be possible to subsume the diverse empirical findings under a single, comprehensive yet precise theory, or perhaps a set of interconnected theories. The following three theoretical frameworks may have the most potential for accomplishing this integration of empirical findings, namely, the attributional, the economic, and the evolutionary.

Attributional Theories

Just as "beauty is in the eye of the beholder," so may a psychologist's greatness reside in the minds of his or her colleagues. Hence, attributional theorists would look at a psychologist's greatness in terms of the general manner in which human beings make inferences about other people's dispositions. Because these inferential processes are contaminated by all sorts of cognitive biases (e.g., the fundamental attribution error, the availability heuristic, and negativity bias), these assessments may not correspond very closely with the psychologist's true merits as represented by overt behaviors. This theoretical approach has already been applied successfully to the phenomenon of exceptional leadership, especially U.S. presidents (Simonton, 1986b, 1987d). Moreover, judgments of a person's creativity have also been explained in attributional terms (Kasof, 1995; cf. Simonton, 1995b). When historians identify someone as a "creative genius," that may prove more informative about how historians engage in myth-making attributions than about how highly creative individuals actually behave. This position is compatible with E. G. Boring's (1963) views about the arbitrary assignment of eponymic status to the various figures in psychology's history.

Economic Theories

Because creativity is a productive activity (i.e., it generates products through labor), it may be explicated in terms of investment, human capital, utility functions, and other concepts in classical economics (e.g., Diamond, 1984; Levin & Stephan, 1991; McDowell, 1982). According to this view, great psychologists invest a considerable amount of effort in acquiring expertise so that they can produce works that will obtain high-paying and prestigious positions. Some economic models do an excellent job predicting the career trajectory in creative output (Diamond, 1986). For instance, the decline in output toward the end of the career is said to occur because of changes in the cost–benefit ratio associated with productivity (e.g., works produced early in the career have a bigger impact on lifetime earnings than do works produced late in the career). Theories have recently emerged that are "psychoeconomic" in nature (Rubenson, 1990; Rubenson & Runco, 1992). As the name implies, these theories integrate economic concepts with psychological processes. An example is Sternberg and Lubart's (1991, 1995) "investment theory of creativity," in which highly successful creators operate according to the principle of "buy low, sell high."

Evolutionary Theories

In 1880 William James published an essay entitled "Great Men, Great Thoughts, and the Environment," in which he attempted to interpret greatness in terms of evolutionary theory. James specifically viewed human creativity as a variation–selection process. In 1960, Donald T. Campbell developed this notion further in his blind-variation and selective-retention model of creative thought. Because both James and Campbell concentrated on the creative process, I have endeavored to link this Darwinian theory of creativity with other aspects of the phenomenon, such as the personality, development, and sociocultural context of eminent creators. This endeavor began with my 1988 book *Scientific Genius: A Psychology of Science* (Simonton, 1988d) and continued most recently with my 1999 book *Origins of Genius: Darwinian Perspectives on Creativity* (Simonton, 1999b). Over the same time period, several other investigators have joined this theoretical enterprise (e.g., Cziko, 1998; Kantorovich, 1993; Kantorovich & Ne'eman, 1989; Martindale, 1990, 1995a). The most notable of these contributors by far is Hans Eysenck, whose 1995 book *Genius: The Natural History of Creativity* combined the "Campbell–Simonton" model of creativity with his own personality construct of psychoticism. Obviously, I believe that this expanding evolutionary system has immense explanatory potential. This belief is reinforced by the following three considerations:

First, several scholars in the philosophy of science have proposed doctrines that are explicitly evolutionary (D. L. Hull, 1988; Shrader, 1980; Stein & Lipton, 1989; Toulmin, 1981). Karl Popper (1979), for one, explicitly stated that

> the growth of our knowledge is the result of a process closely resembling what Darwin called "natural selection"; that is, *the natural selection of hypotheses*: our knowledge consists, at every moment, of those hypotheses which have shown their (comparative) fitness by surviving so far in their struggle for existence; a competitive struggle which eliminates those hypotheses which are unfit. (p. 261)

The emergence of these "evolutionary epistemologies" has also attracted the participation of psychologists (e.g., Plotkin, 1993). Perhaps the most notable among them was Donald T. Campbell (1974) himself.

Second, several historians of science have found evolutionary theory a fruitful approach to interpreting the history of scientific ideas in evolutionary terms (e.g., Bing, 1990; Parshall, 1988). In other words, Darwinian theories can provide a useful scheme for constructing historical narratives (Richards, 1981). In agreement with Popper's (1979) assertion, a selection process operates to weed out hypotheses that fail to fit the facts. In the case of psychology, however, the facts entail both objective data and subjective experience. It may even be the case that "a theory that, among other things, makes sense personally may survive longer than one that develops and is tested within the realm of science" (Hergenhahn, 1992, p. 481).

Third, increasingly more psychologists have become convinced that evolutionary theory may provide the most powerful basis for understanding human cognition and behavior (Barkow, Cosmides, & Tooby, 1992; Bradie, 1995; Crawford & Krebs, 1998). In a sense, psychology is returning to the basic tenet of the functionalist school, namely, the concept of mental processes as adaptations. The advent of connectivism in cognitive psychology also strengthens the conviction that evolutionary theory holds great promise, given the intimate conceptual linkages between connectionist models and Darwinian theories of creativity (Martindale, 1995).

If the evolutionary philosophies and histories of science become unified with a Darwinian psychology of science, the end result may be a comprehensive scientific theory of great psychologists that may not only help one explain psychology's past but also help one understand psychology's present and even predict psychology's future.

TEACHING

The empirical and theoretical questions I just raised are sufficiently rich to keep researchers busy throughout the 21st century. Besides the intrinsic interest and scientific value of these questions, their answers can make direct contributions to how psychologists educate the next generation of psychologists. These contributions take place at two levels: undergraduate instruction and graduate training.

Undergraduate Instruction

An upper division course on the history of psychology—or the history and systems of psychology—has long been a very common part of the undergraduate psychology curriculum (Riedel, 1974). According to an extensive survey of psychology programs at colleges and universities (both national and regional), such a history course was offered by 81%, and was required by 36% (Messer, Griggs, & Jackson, 1999). Often the class is conceived as a capstone course that culminates the psychology major's encounter with the discipline (Raphelson, 1982). Of course, this course can be taught in more than one manner (A. H. Smith, 1982). For instance, some instructors may prefer the great-person perspective, whereas others may favor the history-of-ideas perspective. Yet, on the basis of the research reviewed in this book, I would like to suggest another approach: the psychology-of-science perspective. This approach has implications for what kind of textbooks might be written and what kind of course assignments might be required.

Textbooks

When taught at the undergraduate level, history of psychology courses will almost always have a required textbook. Although these textbooks usually take either the great-person perspective, or the history-of-ideas perspective, it is also possible to conceive a textbook constructed around the psychology-of-science perspective. Such a textbook would take full advantage of all the nomothetic results that I have reviewed throughout this volume— the empirical findings with respect to output and impact, individual characteristics, developmental correlates, and sociocultural context. These conclusions would provide generalizations that can provide the basis for understanding a particular notable idea or famous figure (Simonton, 1995a). In different terms, the generalizations can serve as "covering laws" for comprehending the course of psychology's history (Hempel, 1965). Sometimes these covering laws might show that a particular figure simply exemplifies what one would expect on the basis of past research. For instance, in chapter 3 I mentioned how Wilhelm Wundt's phenomenal output fell right in line with what the research shows is characteristic of a major creative genius (Bringmann & Balk, 1983). Other times these covering laws might indicate how a particular luminary departs from expectation and thereby provides an exception to the rule. I gave just such an example at the close of chapter 4, when I discussed how John B. Watson's career was dramatically and suddenly terminated by the sex scandal that obliged him to resign from the academic world. Yet this very exception suggests a historical counterfact, namely, if Watson had behaved in a manner consistent with his religious upbringing, his output and influence would have been even more impressive. Watson was clearly on a fast-track career trajectory, one associated with prolific and influential productivity over the life span.

What do students gain from such specific applications of these nomothetic principles? To begin, students learn not only that psychology has discovered how people in general behave but also how psychologists behave, not excluding the great psychologists whose names fill the textbooks and lectures for all the courses they have taken in the major. Moreover, because the psychology of science encompasses the psychology of scientists, students would also acquire a superior understanding of the nature of scientific creativity, even when it reaches the level of Galileo, Isaac Newton, Louis Pasteur, or Albert Einstein. At the same time, because the generalizations that provide these covering laws are statistical rather than deterministic, students learn to appreciate that there always exist exceptions to any nomothetic statement in the behavioral sciences. This does not mean that the statement is completely overturned but only that, as the younger Alexandre Dumas humorously warned, "all generalizations are dangerous, even this one" (quoted in Esar, 1949/1989, p. 67). Specific illustrations of this precaution might be provided, such as Figure 8.1, which shows how much the data can depart from a nomothetic relation even when that association accounts for a respectable amount of variance (viz., 11%).

Instances such as these can provide ideal occasions to discuss the effect sizes typical of psychological research (Rosenthal, 1990; Rosenthal & Rubin, 1979) as well as the real-world consequences of putatively "small" effects (Abelson, 1985). To illustrate, a correlation of .40 between two dichotomous variables (with 50–50 splits) means that "only" 16% of the variance is shared. In more concrete terms, fully 30% of the cases will contradict the nomothetic association (i.e., fall in the wrong quadrant of the 2 × 2 table). Yet not only do 70% of the cases still comply with statistical expectation, but also the practical consequences can be quite substantial. If this were a drug treatment for a fatal disease, a correlation of .40 still implies that the chances of survival would be more than doubled by taking the medication (Sulloway, 1996). This enhancement is far from negligible.

Furthermore, from scrutiny of such data students can learn that departures from statistical prediction most likely indicate the effects of other factors, factors that form part of other nomothetic principles left out of the prediction (Simonton, 1990d). Thus, the reason why there exists scatter around the curvilinear function shown in Figure 8.1 is that there are many variables that systematically influence a psychologist's long-term impact besides his or her theoretical and methodological orientation. Only when all of these omitted effects are included will departures from statistical expectation presumably become negligible. In short, the psychology-of-science approach to the history of psychology can be used as a vehicle for describing the science of psychology. The history of psychology thereby becomes more closely integrated with other psychology courses, especially those in personality, developmental, and social psychology.

Not all psychologists would welcome this merger of idiographic history with nomothetic science. In fact, many historians of psychology are downright hostile to psychological science (Simonton, 1995d). Consonant with C. P. Snow's (1960) notion of the "two cultures" mentioned in chapter 8, historians commonly feel more sympathetic with the humanities than with the sciences. This sympathy fits with the history of science in general (for rare exceptions, see Donovan, Laudan, & Laudan, 1988). Nevertheless, this alignment does not mean that historians scrupulously spurn nomothetic principles when they write textbooks. On the contrary, most histories of psychology are riddled with such generalizations, however implicit their statement

(Simonton, 1995a). To make this apparent, representative quotes from these histories have been sprinkled liberally throughout this book. Neither do these generalizations come exclusively from textbook authors who cannot be considered historical scholars. Nomothetic claims are abundant in histories written by psychologists who have attained some reputation for their historical scholarship. To name names, clear examples may be found in the writings of Wolfgang Bringmann, Rand Evans, Laurel Furumoto, Thomas Leahey, Robert MacLeod, Gardner Murphy, Daniel E. Robinson, Elizabeth Scarborough, Wayne Viney, Robert I. Watson, Michael Wertheimer, and even E. G. Boring (Simonton, 1995a, 1995d). Consider the following additional instances, both coming from the pens of psychologists who were elected president of APA's Division on the History of Psychology (Division 26):

1. Many more recent views such as those of Clark Hull or Kenneth Spence were quite similar to those of Hartley, in spite of Karl Lashley's warning early in the present century that explanations of behavior in terms of reflex arcs and chains of associated neurons are doomed to failure because they are too static,

   said Michael Wertheimer, adding that "Perhaps the idea holds on so tenaciously because it is so beautifully simple" (1987, p. 42). Here the principle is that parsimony supersedes factual confirmation in the popularity of scientific ideas.

2. Daniel Robinson (1986), in discussing the ancient Greek philosophers, advised that

   we are to recognize Socrates and his pupils as the enlightened and reflective critics of an age and to realize that such philosophers, in any period, will perceive themselves as unheard by, even inaudible to "those commoner natures.". . . Seeing an entire population deluded by the trappings rather than the essence of greatness, they rejected perception as a means by which knowledge might be apprehended. Watching a world tossed in seas of change, they searched for that which never changed and called it truth. Noting the sad fate of a people moved by passion, they devoted themselves to impersonal reason. (p. 54)

   Here great thinkers are said to advocate positions that constitute Hegelian reactions to the fads and foibles of their times.

Given that even the best historians like to incorporate such explanatory statements into their narratives, it behooves them to make sure that the cited nomothetic principles have an empirical foundation. Hence, by relying on the psychology of science, historians can make their historical interpretations more scientific. To illustrate how this application might be carried out in practice, consider an essay on Christine Ladd-Franklin written by another Division 26 president, Laurel Furumoto (1992). To understand the "gender-lined societal forces that operated to exclude [Ladd-Franklin] from a career in science" as well as the "numerous enabling influences in her life . . . that served to counter them" (p. 175), Furumoto quoted extensively from the volume *Uneasy Careers and Intimate Lives: Women in Science 1789–1979* (Abir-Am & Outram, 1987). The quotations were designed to show that Ladd-Franklin fit the generic profile of the successful female scientist. According to Furumoto, these congruencies included the fact that Ladd-Franklin "had a father who displayed strong interest in his daughter's education and achievements" (Abir-Am & Outram, 1987, p. 15), that she came from "a middle-class background that became unstable through a variety of political, economic, social, or natural events" (p. 16), that she benefited from these circumstances because "a family's decreased capacity for social conformity often allowed more educational freedom for its daughters" (p. 16), and that when she entered adulthood she found that because "gender constrained [her] integration into mainstream—that is, disciplinary and empiricist—sciences" she had to "resort to transdisciplinary and theoretical strategies of claiming scientific authority" (p. 9). All in all, the fit between Ladd-Franklin's idiographic particulars and the nomothetic patterns suggests that her development had to follow much the same pathways as other talented women struggling to make a name in a male-dominated world.

In one respect, histories written along these lines would fulfill E. G. Boring's (1963) call for a purely naturalistic approach. Yet for Boring the term *naturalistic* was placed in opposition to *personalistic*. His ideal was to "extirpate" from the history of psychology "all the names of Great Men." In contrast, the history texts I foresee would be both naturalistic and personalistic. Because the psychology of science necessarily includes the psychology of the scientist, which in turn must incorporate the psychology of great scientists, the big names of history can be discussed in the context of nomothetic research. Indeed, by providing the naturalistic context of great psychologists, the personal nature of their contributions can be better appreciated. The student can then comprehend when a figure merely exemplifies an established generalization and when that same figure constitutes an exception to another generalization.

Assignments

This last statement leads to the other recommendation about how to teach an undergraduate course in the history of psychology. Instructors in such courses will frequently require a term paper. This assignment may cover any of a number of topics, some more compatible with a great-person perspective and others more consistent with a history-of-ideas perspective. For the last 10 years I have been assigning my students a term paper that operates from the psychology-of-science perspective (Simonton, 1994b). Like the great-person approach, the students commence the assignment by selecting a single major figure in the discipline's history. To facilitate their choice I provide them with lists of great psychologists drawn from various sources (e.g., O'Connell & Russo, 1990; Zusne, 1987a). The students are encouraged to find someone whom they might consider a role model—an especially valuable option for women and minorities in the major.

The students also receive a questionnaire that lists all the facts that they should attempt to obtain from biographical and autobiographical sources. As seen in Table 16.1, these items include biographical background, education and training, personal characteristics, career development, and socio-cultural context. Students are told that the information they are to gather on these topics will enable them to write a "psychobiography" that addresses the question "Was _____ a scientific genius?" This issue actually entails several subsidiary questions: Did the chosen subject's life and work look typical of a creative genius? If so, which kind of creative genius—artistic or scientific? If scientific, did he or she have the attributes of a revolutionary or normal scientist?

To help students determine how to draw the necessary inferences from their data, I do three things. First, in every single lecture I provide hints scattered here and there about the nomothetic implications of an idiographic particular. If I mention a notable's birth order, then I note whether this is characteristic of revolutionary scientists. If I give the age at which a figure received his or her doctoral degree, I compare this fact with the typical age that psychologists earn their PhDs. Second, three lectures in the latter part of the quarter are devoted to the metasciences, and two of these are specifically assigned to discussing the psychology of scientific genius. At that point I ask the students to bring their completed questionnaires to class so that we can proceed down the list of facts. I then indicate what implications may be drawn, underlining all the while that the various implications may not necessarily point in the same direction; that is, one datum might imply that the subject was a scientific creator, whereas another might hint that he or she was an artistic creator. The students must learn to balance and evaluate complex and contradictory information to arrive at a coherent assessment. Third, I assign a supplementary text that will provide the needed information about the behavioral, cognitive, motivational, developmental, and social aspects of scientific genius. I first used my 1988 book *Scientific Genius* (Simonton, 1988d), but more recently turned to my 1999 book *Origins of Genius* (Simonton, 1999b). Besides being more updated on the empirical research, the latter text provides a Darwinian framework that students use to coordinate the factual information. Moreover, because this book uses Charles Darwin as an extended illustration of the nature of scientific genius, it provides an example of how the nomothetic principles can be applied to the specific

TABLE 16.1
Sample Items from Questionnaire for Term Paper on Major Figures in the History of Psychology

Topic	Items
Family background	What was the socioeconomic class of your subject's family? His/her father's occupation? His/her mother's occupation? His/her father's educational level? His/her mother's educational level? His/her father's age at the subject's birth? His/her mother's age at the subject's birth? His/her father's interests and hobbies? His/her mother's interests and hobbies? His/her father's ethnicity? His/her mother's ethnicity? What was his/her father's religious affiliation? His/her mother's religious affiliation? Was his/her father a first-, second-, or third-generation immigrant? Was his/her mother a first-, second-, or third-generation immigrant? What language was spoken in the home? Was this the same as the culture at large? Any bilingualism? Were there any other notable achievers in the family pedigree? Is there any evidence of pathology in the family lineage, such as mental illness, suicide, drug abuse, or alcoholism? What was the subject's birth order? What was the size of the family in which he/she grew up? Where there older and younger brothers and/or sisters? Did your subject experience parental loss in childhood or adolescence? Who was (or were) the person(s) who died? How old was he/she when this happened? Any other traumatic experiences? Did he/she suffer from any physical, mental, or emotional handicaps? Was your person popular with peers or a loner? Any evidence of intellectual precocity?
Education and training	What were his/her reading habits in childhood and adolescence? What were your subject's favorite hobbies? How well did he/she do in school? How well did he/she do in college? What was the quality or prestige of the institutions in which your subject was educated? What level of formal education was attained (give highest degree)? What was the age at receiving his/her highest degree? Any honors or awards in school? Any honors or awards in college? What extracurricular activities did he/she engage in? Any important role models in youth or early adulthood? Any important mentors or teachers? Whom did he/she most admire? Any "crystallizing experiences" that decided your subject on his/her life course? Was your subject's training marginal or central to the domain in which eminence was ultimately obtained? If an outsider by training, did that marginal background leave an impression on your subject's distinctive contribution?
Personal characteristics	Was he or she highly intelligent, perhaps even possessing a genius-level intellect? Independent or nonconformist? Introverted? Risk taking? Hardworking, even workaholic? Did he or she have broad intellectual interests? Was he or she extremely versatile, contributing to more than one field? Any evidence of psychopathology, such as manic depression, neurosis, or mild psychosis? Was your subject an intuitive thinker? Any examples of leaps of imagination or inspiration? Was there a sense of purpose, or destiny underlying his or her work? Was everything

TABLE 16.1 (*continued*)
Sample Items from Questionnaire for Term Paper on
Major Figures in the History of Psychology

Topic	Items
	your subject did, no matter how diverse, connected by some central theme or preoccupation? Any examples of serendipity? What was your subject's sexual orientation? Monogamous? Married? Any children? If so, how many? Divorced? Widowed? Remarried? How did your subject die? How old?
Career development	What kind of professional positions were occupied? Did he or she attain a professorship at a distinguished university? Did your subject establish relationships with a considerable number of notable contemporaries? Did your subject have many students and disciples who attained success? Did your subject have any important collaborators? Did your subject have any important rivals? At what age did he or she first make a contribution to his or her field? At what age did your subject produce their single best work, or "masterpiece"? At what age was the last contribution made? Any instances of some "swan song"—some final work conceived shortly before death that encapsulated in a distinctive manner the entire course of a career? What was the total number of works produced? Did the rate of productivity rise to some peak and then decline in a fashion you would anticipate, or were there some surprises? As your subject got older, did he or she become the defender of the status quo, rejecting innovative ideas?
Sociocultural context	Did your subject work in times of economic prosperity? Did your subject work in times of peace or war? Did you subject work in times of political freedom? Did your subject work in times of cultural diversity? Did your subject work in times when his/her field was experiencing a "Golden Age"? Did your subject fit in with the mood of the times or was your subject ahead of the zeitgeist? Were the ideas rejected by contemporaries so that he or she experienced an uphill fight to fame, or did acceptance come easily? Can you identify any examples of "multiples"; that is, did anyone else come up with the same ideas as your subject at roughly the same time? Did a priority dispute result?
Influence on field	How influential were the works produced in your subject's own time and ours? Did your subject have failures as well as successes? To what extent was your subject's impact due to taking extremist positions on certain theoretical or methodological issues? Did your subject receive any contemporary recognition, such as special honors or awards? Any posthumous honors or memorials? What was the ultimate impact of your subject to making psychology a genuine science? Did your subject make any contribution that remains important today?

Note. From "Scientific Eminence, the History of Psychology, and Term Paper Topics: A Metascience Approach" by D. K. Simonton, 1994b, *Teaching of Psychology, 21*, pp. 170–171. Copyright 1990 by Lawrence Erlbaum Associates, Inc. Reprinted with permission.

case. As a result, Charles Darwin is the only subject whom the students cannot select for their term papers.

The final papers are graded on how well each student formulates and defends a thesis based on the general theory and the specific facts. To make this determination, the students are required to attach their completed questionnaire to their term paper when they turn it in. I also make very clear that they can take any stand they want as long as it is adequately argued and documented. Thus, one student might hold that Sigmund Freud was a genius but not a scientist, whereas another might maintain that he was a scientist but not a genius—and still both might earn top grades. I have even assigned "As" to papers that took positions that I personally found unacceptable (e.g., that Francis Galton was not a scientific genius), so long as the fact and logic formed a coherent thesis.

This assignment has several assets. First, the students must learn a tremendous amount of information about a single major figure in psychology's history. At the same time, all of these numerous facts must be logically integrated with an abstract theoretical scheme. That means that the student cannot just regurgitate undigested facts; rather, the paper requires critical thinking. Moreover, the assignment teaches students the elusive connection between a single person's behavior and empirical generalizations based on statistical analyses. Even robust statistical results with impressive effect sizes can allow the existence of numerous outliers. Thus, students learn firsthand the distinction between what happens on average and what happens in the singular case. "You can never foretell what any man will do," said Sherlock Holmes, "but you can say with precision what an average number will be up to. Individuals may vary, but percentages remain constant" (quoted in Doyle, 1890/1986, p. 175). The assignment also has a favorable impact on how students react to the lectures. Every lecture contains clues about what kinds of things to look for in their chosen subject and what those things might mean. Indeed, with biographical details tied to theoretical implications, facts acquire a meaningfulness that might otherwise be considered mere historical trivia. Finally, the students both enjoy and value the term paper. In fact, the popularity of the course increased after I adopted this particular assignment, and it has now become one of the most highly rated classes in the department (i.e., on a 5-point scale, the mean rating of course and instructor are 4.8 and 4.9, respectively). As further testimony of its instructional utility, the article in which I first described this approach (Simonton, 1994b) was subsequently reprinted in the second edition of the *Handbook of Demonstrations and Activities in the Teaching of Psychology* (Ware & Johnson, 2000, Vol. 1, pp. 302–305).

Perhaps as psychologists discover increasingly more about what it takes to become a great psychologist, this psychology-of-science assignment will become more widely disseminated in history of psychology courses. I believe that it is an excellent way to instruct undergraduates in both history and science.

Graduate Training

Undergraduate majors are often required to take a course in the history of psychology, but it is rare for such a course to be an integral part of a psychology graduate program, except in those few programs that offer higher degrees in the field. Yet I would argue that the history of psychology, when combined with the psychology of science, could make a very critical contribution to graduate training. Besides suggesting fascinating and significant research questions for doctoral dissertations, a scientific history of psychology could contribute to both professional and personal advancement. I must confess at once that these contributions are highly speculative and perhaps constitute pure fantasy. Still, the possibilities deserve exploration.

Professional: Psychology as Science

A PhD in psychology is, like all doctorates, a research degree. The degree is awarded to students who have learned how to make an original scientific contribution to the field, as represented by their doctoral dissertation. For many psychology PhDs this will be their last contribution to psychological science—particularly the new doctorates heading toward practice. For other students, however, the graduate training will provide the foundation for entire careers dedicated to scientific inquiry. It is for this reason that so much of graduate education is devoted to mastering the latest theories, the most current ("hot") research topics, and the most leading-edge techniques of measurement and analysis. The graduate student must learn the do's and don'ts of scientific research. So, how do individuals active in graduate education really know what works and what does not? What are the optimal theoretical and methodological approaches for the advancement of science? What is it that the graduate students must acquire en route to becoming outstanding scientists in their own right?

One response is to have graduate students become familiar with the philosophy of science (e.g., Danto & Morgenbesser, 1960). Philosophers of science have been writing prescriptions about how to do great science ever since the days of Francis Bacon and René Descartes. Yet how do the philosophers know what to prescribe? After all, the philosophers usually formulate their prescriptions on a priori grounds—based on logic rather than on data. Descartes, for instance, supposedly deduced the rules of his "method" from first principles. This approach ironically appears to contradict the whole spirit of the scientific enterprise. The Scientific Revolution was in no small part a reaction to the a priori reasoning of the scholastic philosophers. Instead of relying on what had to be true "logically"—such as the existence of God or the immortality of the soul—early scientists proposed direct appeals to nature. These appeals took the form of systematic observation or experiment. Perhaps the same empiricist approach can provide the foundation for a philosophy of science based on fact rather than theory.

This position was taken by Paul Meehl, the distinguished clinical psychologist (Meehl, 1992; also see Faust & Meehl, 1992). Meehl has long been critical of the methodologies that often dominate the discipline (e.g., Meehl, 1978, 1990a, 1990b). In his classic article entitled "Theoretical Risks and Tabular Asterisks: Sir Karl, Sir Ronald, and the Slow Progress of Soft Psychology," Meehl (1978) lamented that

> it is simply a sad fact that in soft psychology theories rise and decline, come and go, more as a function of baffled boredom than anything else; and the enterprise shows a disturbing absence of that cumulative character that is so impressive in disciplines like astronomy, molecular biology, and genetics. (p. 807)

To make sure that psychology eventually shows the same cumulation of knowledge that is so conspicuous in the "hard" sciences it is necessary to adopt the most rigorous methodologies. It is at this point that a scientific history of psychology may come into play. Meehl (1992) persuasively argued for the need to develop a "cliometric metatheory," that is, an "empirical, history-based philosophy of science" (p. 339). In essence, this would entail the application of historiometric methods to episodes drawn from the history of science. By applying appropriate actuarial methods the outcome would be a determination of what theoretical and methodological approaches have the highest likelihood of advancing science. Meehl's cliometric metatheory would establish what works best empirically rather than attempt to do so analytically. This could resolve numerous enigmas about how to do great science. To what extent does a scientist's confirmation bias help or hinder scientific progress? Does having a strong theoretical basis for empirical research increase or decrease the odds of making important discoveries? When is quantification appropriate, and when is it premature or misleading? On what occasions is a holistic perspective superior to an atomistic one? The historical record, if properly analyzed, may contain some or all of the answers.

Of course, the development of Meehl's (1992) cliometric metatheory would not be easy. Indeed, the successful creation of such a discipline might itself be considered a substantial scientific achievement. Moreover, there is no guarantee that psychologists would reform how they train their graduate students along the lines suggested by any results. Yet, according to the oft-quoted remark of philosopher George Santayana, "those who cannot remember the past are condemned to repeat it" (quoted in *Who Said What When*, 1991, p. 211). Hence, psychologists should realize that by adopting a scientific approach to psychology's history they might make the future history of psychology more scientific.

Personal: Psychologists as Scientists

The historical record contains more lessons than just what theories and methods have proven most useful. History also records the lives and careers of people who have made notable contributions to science. The historiometric study of these data, when joined with psychometric studies of eminent contemporaries, can thus provide a complete psychology of distinguished scientists, great psychologists among them. Besides the intrinsic interest of this metascientific knowledge, the resulting research literature would probably have practical implications for graduate education. One application might be the identification of the most promising scientific talents for admission into graduate programs. The more one knows about the developmental and dispositional correlates of scientific success as a research psychologist, the less hit-or-miss the selection process needs to be. For instance, if there are certain personality traits that are most strongly associated with scientific eminence, these traits might be useful supplements to the indicators of promise in current use (see, e.g., Gough, 1992). To be sure, psychologists of truly historic stature are so relatively rare that the odds of any graduate program admitting a notable-to-be must be rather small. Even so, it would be wise to use any reasonable means to increase the likelihood of that happening. At the very least, many of us involved in graduate education would love to see one of our former students become one of the discipline's genuine stars.

Even if the foregoing suggestion turns out to be hopelessly impractical, there is another, more personal application of this metascientific literature. Much of the discussion in chapter 13 was allotted to the developmental impact of role models and mentors. Although graduate advisors would certainly provide mentors, and various active researchers might serve the function of role models, these do not exhaust the potential sources of career guidance. It also may be helpful to possess a generic picture of what it takes to become a successful contributor to psychological science; that is, a nomothetic profile of the great psychologist might provide a young, aspiring talent with a more secure basis for social comparison than any single psychologist, however great. This profile would offer a comparative baseline not only during graduate training but also throughout the subsequent career course. The profile would provide responses to questions such as the following.

Under whom should I study, the well-established senior scientist or the promising younger scientist? Would it really help if my mentor were the same race or gender as I? How much should I be publishing as a graduate student? At what age should I expect to finish my degree, and at which institutions should I end up? When should I get married and raise a family? How conscientious must I be about my teaching? Should I take on those administrative duties or found a new journal? Is it more critical for me to focus on a single question at any one time, or is it more advantageous for me to work on several projects at once? Do those rejection letters and unnoticed publications mean that I am a failure, or do they mean I'm ahead of my time? Should I collaborate on this project, or work as a solo author as much as possible? When should I start writing books at the expense of journal articles? How critical is it that I attend this convention or that conference? What are the chances of my work being anticipated by another researcher? When in my career should I get an inkling of whether I am going to leave my own imprint on the discipline? How do my accomplishments compare with notable psychologists both past and present? What honors should I reasonably expect given my publication record and citation visibility? Which qualities and experiences should I look for in the graduate students whom I decide to mentor? What kinds of tips and pearls of wisdom can I give those of my students who aspire to become great psychologists?

Needless to say, the contemplation of these questions can become normative, not just comparative. A young psychologist can strive to live up to implied expectations. As a consequence, the generic picture of the great psychologist might promote the appearance of new great psychologists. If so, the scientific study of psychology's history may increase the chances that the discipline will have a prominent place in the history of science well into the future.

REFERENCES

Abelson, R. P. (1985). A variance explanation paradox: When a little is a lot. *Psychological Bulletin, 97*, 129–133.

Abir-Am, P. G., & Outram, D. (Eds.). (1987). *Uneasy careers and intimate lives: Women in science, 1789–1979.* New Brunswick, NJ: Rutgers University Press.

Abt, H. A. (1983). At what ages do outstanding American astronomers publish their most cited papers. *Publications of the Astronomical Society of the Pacific, 95*, 113–116.

Adams, C. W. (1946). The age at which scientists do their best work. *Isis, 36*, 166–169.

Adler, A. (1938). *Social interest: A challenge to mankind* (J. Linton & R. Vaughan, Trans.). London: Faber & Faber.

Adorno, T. W., Frenkel-Brunswik, E., Levinson, D. J., & Sanford, R. N. (Eds.). (1950). *The authoritarian personality.* New York: Harper.

Albert, R. S. (1971). Cognitive development and parental loss among the gifted, the exceptionally gifted and the creative. *Psychological Reports, 29*, 19–26.

Albert, R. S. (1975). Toward a behavioral definition of genius. *American Psychologist, 30*, 140–151.

Allison, P. D. (1977). The reliability of variables measured as the number of events in an interval of time. In K. F. Schuessler (Ed.), *Sociological methodology 1978* (pp. 238–253). San Francisco: Jossey-Bass.

Allison, P. D. (1980). Estimation and testing for a Markov model of reinforcement. *Sociological Methods and Research, 8*, 434–453.

Allison, P. D., & Long, J. S. (1987). Interuniversity mobility of academic scientists. *American Sociological Review, 52*, 643–652.

Allison, P. D., & Long, J. S. (1990). Departmental effects on scientific productivity. *American Sociological Review, 55*, 469–478.

Allison, P. D., Long, J. S., & Krauze, T. K. (1982). Cumulative advantage and inequality in science. *American Sociological Review, 47*, 615–625.

Allison, P. D., & Stewart, J. A. (1974). Productivity differences among scientists: Evidence for accumulative advantage. *American Sociological Review, 39*, 596–606.

Allport, G. W. (1937). *Personality: A psychological interpretation.* New York: Holt.

Allport, G. W. (1962). The general and the unique in psychological science. *Journal of Personality, 30*, 405–422.

Altus, W. D. (1966, January 7). Birth order and its sequelae. *Science, 151*, 44–48.

American heritage electronic dictionary (3rd ed.). (1992). Boston: Houghton Mifflin.

American Psychological Association. (2001). *Publication manual of the American Psychological Association* (5th ed.). Washington, DC: Author.

Andreasen, N. C. (1987). Creativity and mental illness: Prevalence rates in writers and their first-degree relatives. *American Journal of Psychiatry, 144,* 1288–1292.

Andreasen, N. C., & Canter, A. (1974). The creative writer: Psychiatric symptoms and family history. *Comprehensive Psychiatry, 15,* 123–131.

Ankney, C. D. (1992). Sex differences in relative brain size: The mismeasure of women, too? *Intelligence, 16,* 329–336.

Annin, E. L., Boring, E. G., & Watson, R. I. (1968). Important psychologists, 1600–1967. *Journal of the History of the Behavioral Sciences, 4,* 303–315.

Arieti, S. (1976). *Creativity: The magic synthesis.* New York: Basic Books.

Arnheim, R. (1986). *New essays on the psychology of art.* Berkeley: University of California Press.

Arvey, R. D., Bouchard, T. J., Segal, N. L., & Abraham, L. M. (1989). Job satisfaction: Environmental and genetic components. *Journal of Applied Psychology, 74,* 187–192.

Ashton, S. V., & Oppenheim, C. (1978). A method of predicting Nobel prizewinners in chemistry. *Social Studies of Science, 8,* 341–348.

Austin, J. H. (1978). *Chase, chance, and creativity: The lucky art of novelty.* New York: Columbia University Press.

Aydelotte, W. O. (1971). *Quantification in history.* Reading, MA: Addison-Wesley.

Babcock, W. L. (1895). On the morbid heredity and predisposition to insanity of the man of genius. *Journal of Nervous and Mental Disease, 20,* 749–769.

Bachtold, L. M., & Werner, E. E. (1970). Personality profiles of gifted women: Psychologists. *American Psychologist, 25,* 234–243.

Bacon, F. (1942). *Essays* and *The New Atlantis.* Roslyn, NY: Black. (Original works published 1597 and 1620)

Bacon, F. (1952). Novum organum. In R. M. Hutchins (Ed.), *Great books of the Western world* (Vol. 30, pp. 105–195). Chicago: Encyclopedia Britannica. (Original work published 1620)

Bain, A. (1977). *The senses and the intellect* (D. N. Robinson, Ed.). Washington, DC: University Publications of America. (Original work published 1855)

Bair, J. H., & Boor, M. (1988). Psychology of the scientist: LIX. The academic elite in psychology: Linkages among top-ranked graduate programs. *Psychological Reports, 63,* 539–542.

Barber, B. (1961, September 1). Resistance by scientists to scientific discovery. *Science, 134,* 596–602.

Barkow, J. H., Cosmides, L., & Tooby, J. (Eds.). (1992). *The adapted mind: Evolutionary psychology and the generation of culture.* New York: Oxford University Press.

Barnett, G. A., Fink, E. L., & Debus, M. B. (1989). A mathematical model of academic citation age. *Communication Research, 16,* 510–531.

Barrett, G. V., & Depinet, R. L. (1991). A reconsideration of testing for competence rather than for intelligence. *American Psychologist, 46,* 1012–1024.

Barron, F. X. (1963). The needs for order and for disorder as motives in creative activity. In C. W. Taylor & F. X. Barron (Eds.), *Scientific creativity: Its recognition and development* (pp. 153–160). New York: Wiley.

Barron, F. X. (1969). *Creative person and creative process.* New York: Holt, Rinehart & Winston.

Barron, F. X., & Harrington, D. M. (1981). Creativity, intelligence, and personality. *Annual Review of Psychology, 32,* 439–476.

Barry, H., III (1969). Longevity of outstanding chess players. *Journal of Genetic Psychology, 115,* 143–148.

Barry, H., III (1983–1984). Predictors of longevity of United States presidents. *Omega: Journal of Death and Dying, 14,* 315–321.

Barry, H., Bacon, M. K., & Child, I. L. (1957). A cross-cultural survey of some sex differences in socialization. *Journal of Abnormal and Social Psychology, 55,* 327–332.

Bartlett, F. (1958). *Thinking: An experimental and social study.* New York: Basic Books.

Barzun, J. (1974). *Clio and the doctors: Psycho-history, quanto-history, and history.* Chicago: University of Chicago Press.

Bayer, A. E., & Dutton, J. E. (1977). Career age and research—Professional activities of academic scientists: Tests of alternative non-linear models and some implications for higher education faculty policies. *Journal of Higher Education, 48,* 259–282.

Bayer, A. E., & Folger, J. (1966). Some correlates of a citation measure of productivity in science. *Sociology of Education, 39,* 381–390.

Bayles, D., & Orland, T. (1993). *Art & fear: Observations on the perils (and rewards) of artmaking.* Santa Barbara, CA: Capra.

Beard, G. M. (1874). *Legal responsibility in old age.* New York: Russell.

Beaver, D. de B. (1986). Collaboration and teamwork in physics. *Czechoslovak Journal of Physics, B36,* 14–18.

Beaver, D. de B., & Rosen, R. (1979). Studies in scientific collaboration: Part II. Scientific co-authorship, research productivity and visibility in the French scientific elite, 1799–1830. *Scientometrics, 1,* 133–149.

Beer, J. M., Arnold, R. D., & Loehlin, J. C. (1998). Genetic and environmental influences on MMPI factor scales: Joint model fitting to twin and adoption data. *Journal of Personality and Social Psychology, 74,* 818–827.

Bell, E. T. (1937). *Men of mathematics.* New York: Simon & Schuster.

Bem, S. L. (1998). *An unconventional family.* New Haven, CT: Yale University Press.

Bennet, W. (1980, January–February). Providing for posterity. *Harvard Magazine,* pp. 13–16.

Berrington, H. (1974). Review article: *The Fiery Chariot:* Prime ministers and the search for love. *British Journal of Political Science, 4,* 345–369.

Berry, C. (1981). The Nobel scientists and the origins of scientific achievement. *British Journal of Sociology, 32,* 381–391.

Beveridge, W. I. B. (1957). *The art of scientific investigation* (3rd ed.). New York: Vintage.

Bing, R. J. (1990). Evolution in cardiology: Triumph and defeat. *Perspectives in Biology and Medicine, 34,* 1–16.

Blackburn, R. T., Behymer, C. E., & Hall, D. E. (1978). Correlates of faculty publications. *Sociology of Education, 51,* 132–141.

Bliss, W. D. (1970). Birth order of creative writers. *Journal of Individual Psychology, 26,* 200–202.

Boden, M. A. (1991). *The creative mind: Myths & mechanisms.* New York: Basic Books.

Bohr, H. (1967). My father. In S. Rozental (Ed.), *Niels Bohr: His life and work as seen by his friends and colleagues* (pp. 325–335). Amsterdam: North-Holland.

Boice, R., Shaughnessy, P., & Pecker, G. (1985). Women and publishing in psychology. *American Psychologist, 40,* 577–578.

Bonzi, S. (1992). Trends in research productivity among senior faculty. *Information Processing and Management, 28,* 111–120.

Boring, E. G. (1950). *A history of experimental psychology* (2nd ed.). New York: Appleton-Century-Crofts.

Boring, E. G. (1961). *Psychologist at large: An autobiography and selected essays.* New York: Basic Books.

Boring, E. G. (1963). *History, psychology, and science* (R. I. Watson & D. T. Campbell, Eds.). New York: Wiley.

Boring, E. G., & Lindzey, G. (1967). *A history of psychology in autobiography* (Vol. 5). New York: Appleton-Century-Crofts.

Boring, M. D., & Boring, E. G. (1948). Masters and pupils among the American psychologists. *American Journal of Psychology, 61,* 527–534.

Boswell, J. (1952). The life of Samuel Johnson. In R. M. Hutchins (Ed.), *Great books of the western world* (Vol. 44). Chicago: Encyclopaedia Britannica. (Original work published 1791)

Bouchard, T. J., Jr. (1995). Longitudinal studies of personality and intelligence: A behavior genetic and evolutionary psychology perspective. In D. H. Saklofske & M. Zeidner (Eds.), *International handbook of personality and intelligence* (pp. 81–106). New York: Plenum.

Bouchard, T. J., Jr., Lykken, D. T., McGue, M., Segal, N. L., & Tellegen, A. (1990, October 12). Sources of human psychological differences: The Minnesota study of twins reared apart. *Science, 250,* 223–228.

Bowen, D. D., Perloff, R., & Jacoby, J. (1972). Improving manuscript evaluation procedures. *American Psychologist, 27,* 221–225.

Bowerman, W. G. (1947). *Studies in genius.* New York: Philosophical Library.

Box, G. E. P., Jenkins, G. M., & Reinsel, G. C. (1994). *Time series analysis: Forecasting and control* (3rd ed.). Englewood Cliffs, NJ: Prentice Hall.

Bradie, M. (1995). Epistemology from an evolutionary point of view. In E. Sober (Ed.), *Conceptual issues in evolutionary biology* (2nd ed., pp. 454–475). Cambridge, MA: MIT Press.

Bradshaw, G. F., Langley, P. W., & Simon, H. A. (1983, December 2). Studying scientific discovery by computer simulation. *Science, 222,* 971–975.

Bramwell, B. S. (1948). Galton's "Hereditary Genius" and the three following generations since 1869. *Eugenics Review, 39,* 146–153.

Brannigan, A. (1981). *The social basis of scientific discoveries.* Cambridge, England: Cambridge University Press.

Brannigan, A., & Wanner, R. A. (1983a). Historical distributions of multiple discoveries and theories of scientific change. *Social Studies of Science, 13,* 417–435.

Brannigan, A., & Wanner, R. A. (1983b). Multiple discoveries in science: A test of the communication theory. *Canadian Journal of Sociology, 8,* 135–151.

Brems, C., Johnson, M. E., & Gallucci, P. (1996). Publication productivity of clinical and counseling psychologists. *Journal of Clinical Psychology, 52,* 723–725.

Brenneis, D. (1990). Musical imaginations: Comparative perspectives on musical creativity. In M. A. Runco & R. S. Albert (Eds.), *Theories of creativity* (pp. 170–189). Newbury Park, CA: Sage.

Bridgwater, C. A., Walsh, J. A., & Walkenbach, J. (1982). Pretenure and posttenure productivity trends of academic psychologists. *American Psychologist, 37,* 236–238.

Brimhall, D. R. (1922). Family resemblances among American men of science. *American Naturalist, 56,* 504–547.

Brimhall, D. R. (1923a). Family resemblances among American men of science: III. The influence of the nearness of kinship. *American Naturalist, 57,* 137–152.

Brimhall, D. R. (1923b). Family resemblances among American men of science: II. Degree of resemblance in comparison with the generality: Proportion of workers in each science and distribution of replies. *American Naturalist, 57,* 74–88.

Bringmann, W. G., & Balk, M. M. (1983). Wilhelm Wundt's publication record: A re-examination. *Storia e Critica della Pssichologia, 4,* 61–86.

Brittain, V. (1948). *On being an author.* New York: Macmillan.

Brodetsky, S. (1942). Newton: Scientist and man. *Nature, 150,* 698–699.

Brown, F. (1968). Bereavement and lack of a parent in childhood. In E. Miller (Ed.), *Foundations of child psychiatry* (pp. 435–455). Oxford, England: Pergamon.

Brown, R. (1996). *Against my better judgment: An intimate memoir of an eminent gay psychologist.* New York: Haworth.

Brown, R. W., & McNeill, D. (1966). The "tip of the tongue" phenomenon. *Journal of Verbal Learning and Verbal Behavior, 5,* 325–337.

Browning, D. C. (1986). *The complete dictionary of Shakespeare quotations.* New York: New Orchard Editions.

Bruner, J. S., & Allport, G. W. (1940). Fifty years of change in American psychology. *Psychological Bulletin, 37,* 757–776.

Bruner, J. S., Goodnow, J. J., & Austin, G. A. (1956). *A study of thinking.* New York: Wiley.

Buffardi, L. C., & Nichols, J. A. (1981). Citation impact, acceptance rate, and APA journals. *American Psychologist, 36,* 1453–1456.

Bullough, V. L., Bullough, B., & Mauro, M. (1978). Age and achievement: A dissenting view. *The Gerontologist, 18,* 584–587.

Bullough, V. L., Bullough, B., Voight, M., & Kluckholn, L. (1971). Birth order and achievement in eighteenth century Scotland. *Journal of Individual Psychology, 27,* 80.

Burks, B. S., Jensen, D. W., & Terman, L. M. (1930). *The promise of youth: Follow-up studies of a thousand gifted children.* Stanford, CA: Stanford University Press.

Burt, C. (1943). Ability and income. *British Journal of Educational Psychology, 12,* 83–98.

Burt, C. (1963). Is intelligence distributed normally? *British Journal of Statistical Psychology, 16,* 175–190.

Busse, T. V., & Mansfield, R. S. (1984). Selected personality traits and achievement in male scientists. *Journal of Psychology, 116,* 117–131.

Butler, R. N. (1963). The life review: An interpretation of reminiscences in the aged. *Psychiatry, 26,* 65–76.

Butler, S. (n.d.). *The way of all flesh.* Roslyn, NY: Black. (Original work published 1903)

Butterfield, H. (1951). *The Whig interpretation of history.* London: Bell.

Byron, Lord. (1949). *Don Juan.* London: Lehmann. (Original work published 1818–1821)

Campbell, D. P. (1965). The vocational interests of American Psychological Association presidents. *American Psychologist, 20,* 636–644.

Campbell, D. T. (1960). Blind variation and selective retention in creative thought as in other knowledge processes. *Psychological Review, 67,* 380–400.

Campbell, D. T. (1974). Evolutionary epistemology. In P. A. Schlipp (Ed.), *The philosophy of Karl Popper* (pp. 413–463). La Salle, IL: Open Court.

Campbell, D. T., & Tauscher, H. (1966). Schopenhauer (?), Séguin, Lubinoff, and Zehender as anticipators of Emmert's Law: With comments on the uses of eponymy. *Journal of the History of the Behavioral Sciences, 2,* 58–63.

Candolle, A. de (1873). *Histoire des sciences et des savants depuis deux siècles* [History of the sciences and scientists in the last two centuries]. Geneva, Switzerland: Georg.

Cannon, W. B. (1940). The role of chance in discovery. *Scientific Monthly, 50,* 204–209.

Cannon, W. B. (1945). *The way of an investigator: A scientist's experiences in medical research.* New York: Norton.

Capretta, P. J. (1967). *A history of psychology in outline.* New York: Dell.

Carlyle, T. (1841). *On heroes, hero-worship, and the heroic.* London: Fraser.

Carneiro, R. L. (1970). Scale analysis, evolutionary sequences, and the rating of cultures. In R. Naroll & R. Cohn (Eds.), *A handbook of method in cultural anthropology* (pp. 834–871). New York: Natural History Press.

Carringer, D. C. (1974). Creative thinking abilities in Mexican youth. *Journal of Cross-Cultural Psychology, 5,* 492–504.

Cassandro, V. J. (1998). Explaining premature mortality across fields of creative endeavor. *Journal of Personality, 66,* 805–833.

Cattell, J. M. (1903a, April 10). Homo scientificus Americanus. *Science, 17,* 561–570.

Cattell, J. M. (1903b). A statistical study of eminent men. *Popular Science Monthly, 62,* 359–377.

Cattell, J. M. (1903c). Statistics of American psychologists. *American Journal of Psychology, 14,* 574–592.

Cattell, J. M. (1906). *American men of science: A biographical directory.* New York: Science Press.

Cattell, J. M. (1910, November 4). A further statistical study of American men of science. *Science, 32,* 633–648.

Cattell, J. M. (1933, March 10). The distribution of American men of science in 1932. *Science, 77,* 264–270.

Cattell, J. M., & Brimhall, D. R. (Eds.). (1921). *American men of science: A biographical directory* (3rd ed.). Garrison, NY: Science Press.

Cattell, R. B. (1963). The personality and motivation of the researcher from measurements of contemporaries and from biography. In C. W. Taylor & F. Barron (Eds.), *Scientific creativity: Its recognition and development* (pp. 119–131). New York: Wiley.

Cattell, R. B., & Butcher, H. J. (1968). *The prediction of achievement and creativity.* Indianapolis, IN: Bobbs-Merrill.

Cattell, R. B., & Drevdahl, J. E. (1955). A comparison of the personality profile (16 P. F.) of eminent researchers with that of eminent teachers and administrators, and of the general population. *British Journal of Psychology, 46,* 248–261.

Cattell, R. B., & Stice, G. F. (1955). *The sixteen personality factor questionnaire and handbook.* Champaign, IL: Institute for Personality and Ability Testing.

Chambers, J. A. (1964). Relating personality and biographical factors to scientific creativity. *Psychological Monographs: General and Applied, 78*(7, Whole No. 584).

Chan, W. (Ed.). (1963). *A source book in Chinese philosophy* (W. Chan, Trans.). Princeton, NJ: Princeton University Press.

Charness, N., & Gerchak, Y. (1996). Participation rates and maximal performance: A log-linear explanation for group differences, such as Russian and male dominance in chess. *Psychological Science, 7,* 46–51.

Cheng, P. C.-H., & Simon, H. A. (1995). Scientific discovery and creative reasoning with diagrams. In S. M. Smith, T. B. Ward, & R. A. Finke (Eds.), *The creative cognition approach* (pp. 205–228). Cambridge, MA: MIT Press.

Christensen, H., & Jacomb, P. A. (1992). The lifetime productivity of eminent Australian academics. *International Journal of Geriatric Psychiatry, 7,* 681–686.

Chubin, D. E., Porter, A. L., & Broeckmann, M. E. (1981). Career patterns of scientists: Comment on Long et al., *ASR,* October 1979. *American Sociological Review, 46,* 488–496.

Cicchetti, D. V. (1991). The reliability of peer review for manuscript and grant submissions: A cross-disciplinary investigation. *Behavioral and Brain Sciences, 14,* 119–186.

Clark, K. E. (1954). The APA study of psychologists. *American Psychologist, 9,* 117–120.

Clark, K. E. (1957). *America's psychologists: A survey of a growing profession.* Washington, DC: American Psychological Association.

Clark, R. D., & Rice, G. A. (1982). Family constellations and eminence: The birth orders of Nobel Prize winners. *Journal of Psychology, 110,* 281–287.

Clemente, F. (1973). Early career determinants of research productivity. *American Journal of Sociology, 79,* 409–419.

Coan, R. W. (1968). Dimensions of psychological theory. *American Psychologist, 23,* 715–722.

Coan, R. W. (1973). Toward a psychological interpretation of psychology. *Journal of the History of the Behavioral Sciences, 9,* 313–327.

Coan, R. W. (1979). *Psychologists: Personal and theoretical pathways.* New York: Irvington.

Coan, R. W., & Zagona, S. V. (1962). Contemporary ratings of psychological theorists. *Psychological Record, 12,* 315–322.

Cohen, D. (1977). *Psychologists on psychology.* London: Routledge & Kegan Paul.

Cole, J. R. (1987). Women in science. In D. N. Jackson & J. P. Rushton (Eds.), *Scientific excellence: Origins and assessment* (pp. 359–375). Beverly Hills, CA: Sage.

Cole, J., & Cole, S. (1971). Measuring the quality of sociological research: Problems in the use of the *Science Citation Index. American Sociologist, 6,* 23–29.

Cole, J. R., & Cole, S. (1972, October 27). The Ortega hypothesis. *Science, 178,* 368–375.

Cole, J. R., & Zuckerman, H. (1987, February). Marriage, motherhood and research performance in science. *Scientific American, 256,* 119–125.

Cole, S. (1970). Professional standing and the reception of scientific discoveries. *American Journal of Sociology, 76,* 286–306.

Cole, S. (1979). Age and scientific performance. *American Journal of Sociology, 84,* 958–977.

Cole, S. (1983). The hierarchy of the sciences? *American Journal of Sociology, 89,* 111–139.

Cole, S., & Cole, J. R. (1973). *Social stratification in science.* Chicago: University of Chicago Press.

Cole, S., Cole, J. R., & Simon, G. A. (1981, November 20). Chance and consensus in peer review. *Science, 214,* 881–886.

Coleman, S. R. (1991). Contributions to the history of psychology: LXXX. The hyperbolic structure of eminence updated, 1975–1986. *Psychological Reports, 68,* 1067–1070.

Colotla, V. A. (1980). Psychology of the scientist: XLII. Scientific eminence and reading ease. *Psychological Reports, 46,* 211–216.

Conway, J. B. (1988). Differences among clinical psychologists: Scientists, practitioners, and scientist–practitioners. *Professional Psychology: Research and Practice, 19,* 642–655.

Coon, D. J. (1982). Eponymy, obscurity, Twitmyer, and Pavlov. *Journal of the History of the Behavioral Sciences, 18,* 255–262.

Cox, C. (1926). *The early mental traits of three hundred geniuses.* Stanford, CA: Stanford University Press.

Craig, H., & Bevington, D. (Eds.). (1973). *The complete works of Shakespeare* (rev. ed.). Glenview, IL: Scott, Foresman.

Crandall, R. (1978). The relationship between quantity and quality of publications. *Personality and Social Psychology Bulletin, 4,* 379–380.

Crane, D. (1965). Scientists at major and minor universities: A study of productivity and recognition. *American Sociological Review, 30,* 699–714.

Crane, D. (1967). The gatekeepers of science: Some factors affecting the selection of articles for scientific journals. *American Sociologist, 2,* 195–201.

Crawford, C. B., & Krebs, D. (Eds.). (1998). *Handbook of evolutionary psychology: Ideas, issues, and applications.* Mahwah, NJ: Erlbaum.

Cronbach, L. J. (1957). The two disciplines of scientific psychology. *American Psychologist, 12,* 671–684.

Cronbach, L. J. (1960). *Essentials of psychological testing* (2nd ed.). New York: Harper & Row.

Cronbach, L. J. (1996). Acceleration among the Terman males: Correlates in midlife and after. In C. P. Benbow & D. J. Lubinski (Eds.), *Intellectual talent: Psychometric and social issues* (pp. 179–191). Baltimore: Johns Hopkins University Press.

Crowther, J. G. (1968). *Science in modern society.* New York: Schocken Books.

Csikszentmihalyi, M. (1988). Motivation and creativity: Toward a synthesis of structural and energistic approaches to cognition. *New Ideas in Psychology, 6,* 159–176.

Csikszentmihalyi, M. (1990). The domain of creativity. In M. A. Runco & R. S. Albert (Eds.), *Theories of creativity* (pp. 190–212). Newbury Park, CA: Sage.

Cziko, G. A. (1998). From blind to creative: In defense of Donald Campbell's selectionist theory of human creativity. *Journal of Creative Behavior, 32,* 192–208.

Dante, Alighieri (1952). Divine comedy (C. E. Norton, Trans.). In R. M. Hutchins (Ed.), *Great books of the western world* (Vol. 21). Chicago: Encyclopaedia Britannica. (Original work published c. 1307)

Danto, A., & Morgenbesser, S. (Eds.). (1960). *Philosophy of science.* Cleveland, OH: Meridian Books.

Darwin, C. (1859). *On the origin of the species by means of natural selection, or, The preservation of favoured races in the struggle for life.* London: Murray.

Darwin, C. (1952). The descent of man and selection in relation to sex. In R. M. Hutchins (Ed.), *Great books of the western world* (Vol. 49, pp. 253–600). Chicago: Encyclopedia Britannica. (Original work published 1871)

Darwin, C. (1952). The origin of species by means of natural selection. In R. M. Hutchins (Ed.), *Great books of the western world* (Vol. 49, pp. 1–251). Chicago: Encyclopaedia Britannica. (Original second edition published 1860)

Darwin, F. (Ed.). (1958). *The autobiography of Charles Darwin and selected letters.* New York: Dover. (Original work published 1892)

Datta, L. (1967). Family religious background and early scientific creativity. *American Sociological Review, 32,* 626–635.

Davis, M. H., Luce, C., & Kraus, S. J. (1994). The heritability of characteristics associated with dispositional empathy. *Journal of Personality, 62,* 369–391.

Davis, R. A. (1954). Note on age and productive scholarship of a university faculty. *Journal of Applied Psychology, 38,* 318–319.

Davis, R. A. (1987). Creativity in neurological publications. *Neurosurgery, 20,* 652–663.

Davis, S. F., Thomas, R. L., & Weaver, M. S. (1982). Psychology's contemporary and all-time notables: Student, faculty, and chairperson viewpoints. *Bulletin of the Psychonomic Society, 20,* 3–6.

Debus, A. G. (Ed.). (1968). *World who's who in science.* Chicago: Marquis.

Dellas, M., & Gaier, E. L. (1970). Identification of creativity: The individual. *Psychological Bulletin, 73,* 55–73.

Deluga, R. J. (1998). American presidential proactivity, charismatic leadership, and rated performance. *Leadership Quarterly, 9,* 265–291.

Dennett, D. C. (1995). *Darwin's dangerous idea: Evolution and the meanings of life.* New York: Simon & Schuster.

Dennis, W. (1954a, September). Bibliographies of eminent scientists. *Scientific Monthly, 79,* 180–183.

Dennis, W. (1954b). Predicting scientific productivity in later maturity from records of earlier decades. *Journal of Gerontology, 9,* 465–467.

Dennis, W. (1954c). Productivity among American psychologists. *American Psychologist, 9,* 191–194.

Dennis, W. (1954d). Review of *Age and Achievement. Psychological Bulletin, 51,* 306–308.

Dennis, W. (1955, April). Variations in productivity among creative workers. *Scientific Monthly, 80,* 277–278.

Dennis, W. (1956a). *Age and Achievement:* A critique. *Journal of Gerontology, 9,* 465–467.

Dennis, W. (1956b, July 5). Age and productivity among scientists. *Science, 123,* 724–725.

Dennis, W. (1958). The age decrement in outstanding contributions: Fact or artifact? *American Psychologist, 9,* 457–460.

Dennis, W. (1966). Creative productivity between the ages of 20 and 80 years. *Journal of Gerontology, 21,* 1–8.

Dennis, W., & Girden, E. (1954). Current scientific activities of psychologists as a function of age. *Journal of Gerontology, 9,* 175–178.

Dewsbury, D. A. (1998). Celebrating E. L. Thorndike a century after *Animal Intelligence. American Psychologist, 53,* 1121–1124.

Diamond, A. M., Jr. (1980). Age and the acceptance of cliometrics. *Journal of Economic History, 40,* 838–841.

Diamond, A. M., Jr. (1984). An economic model of the life-cycle research productivity of scientists. *Scientometrics, 6,* 189–196.

Diamond, A. M., Jr. (1985). The money value of citations to single-authored and multiple-authored articles. *Scientometrics, 6,* 315–320.

Diamond, A. M., Jr. (1986). The life-cycle research productivity of mathematicians and scientists. *Journal of Gerontology, 41,* 520–525.

Donovan, A., Laudan, L., & Laudan, R. (Eds.). (1988). *Scrutinizing science: Empirical studies of scientific change.* Dordrecht, The Netherlands: Kluwer.

Doty, R. M., Peterson, B. E., & Winter, D. G. (1991). Threat and authoritarianism in the United States, 1978–1987. *Journal of Personality and Social Psychology, 61,* 629–640.

Downs, R. B. (1956). *Books that changed the world.* New York: Mentor.

Doyle, A. C. (1986). The sign of four. In *Sherlock Holmes: The complete novels and stories* (Vol. 1, pp. 107–205). New York: Bantam. (Original work published 1890)

Dryden, J. (1681). *Absalom and Achitophel: A poem.* London: Davis.

Dryden, J. (1885). Epistle to Congreve. In W. Scott & G. Saintsbury (Eds.), *The works of John Dryden* (Vol. 11, pp. 57–60). Edinburgh, Scotland: Paterson. (Original work published 1693)

Eagly, A. H., & Wood, W. (1999). The origins of sex differences in human behavior: Evolved dispositions versus social roles. *American Psychologist, 54,* 408–423.

Ebbinghaus, H. (1908). *Psychology: An elementary text-book* (M. Meyer, Ed. & Trans.). Boston: Heath.

Ebersole, P., & DeVogler-Ebersole, K. (1985). Meaning in life of the eminent and the average. *Journal of Social Behavior and Personality, 1,* 83–94.

Eiduson, B. T. (1962). *Scientists: Their psychological world.* New York: Basic Books.

Einstein, A., & Infeld, L. (1938). *The evolution of physics: The growth of ideas from early concepts to relativity and quanta.* New York: Simon & Schuster.

Eisenman, R. (1964). Birth order and artistic creativity. *Journal of Individual Psychology, 20,* 183–185.

Eisenstadt, J. M. (1978). Parental loss and genius. *American Psychologist, 33,* 211–223.

Ellis, H. (1904). *A study of British genius.* London: Hurst & Blackett.

Ellis, H. (1926). *A study of British genius* (rev. ed.). Boston: Houghton Mifflin. (Original work published 1904)

Elms, A. C. (1994). *Uncovering lives: The uneasy alliance of biography and psychology.* New York: Oxford University Press.

Endler, N. S., Rushton, J. P., & Roediger, H. L., III. (1978). Productivity and scholarly impact (citations) of British, Canadian, and U.S. departments of psychology (1975). *American Psychologist, 33,* 1064–1082.

Epstein, R. (1990). Generativity theory and creativity. In M. Runco & R. Albert (Eds.), *Theories of creativity* (pp. 116–140). Newbury Park, CA: Sage.

Epstein, R. (1991). Skinner, creativity, and the problem of spontaneous behavior. *Psychological Science, 2,* 362–370.

Epstein, S. (1994). Integration of the cognitive and the psychodynamic unconscious. *American Psychologist, 49,* 709–724.

Ericsson, K. A. (1996a). The acquisition of expert performance: An introduction to some of the issues. In K. A. Ericsson (Ed.), *The road to expert performance: Empirical evidence from the arts and sciences, sports, and games* (pp. 1–50). Mahwah, NJ: Erlbaum.

Ericsson, K. A. (Ed.). (1996b). *The road to expert performance: Empirical evidence from the arts and sciences, sports, and games.* Mahwah, NJ: Erlbaum.

Ericsson, K. A., & Charness, N. (1994). Expert performance: Its structure and acquisition. *American Psychologist, 49,* 725–747.

Ericsson, K. A., Krampe, R. T., & Tesch-Römer, C. (1993). The role of deliberate practice in the acquisition of expert performance. *Psychological Review, 100,* 363–406.

Erikson, E. H. (1958). *Young man Luther: A study in psychoanalysis and history.* New York: Norton.

Erikson, E. H. (1968). *Identity, youth, and crisis.* New York: Norton.

Erikson, E. J., Erikson, J., & Kivnick, H. Q. (1986). *Vital involvement in old age.* New York: Norton.

Esar, E. (Ed.). (1989). *The dictionary of humorous quotations.* New York: Dorset. (Original work published 1949)

Evans, G. B. (Ed.). (1974). *The Riverside Shakespeare.* Boston: Houghton Mifflin.

Eysenck, H. J. (1993). Creativity and personality: Suggestions for a theory. *Psychological Inquiry, 4,* 147–178.

Eysenck, H. J. (1994). Creativity and personality: Word association, origence, and psychoticism. *Creativity Research Journal, 7,* 209–216.

Eysenck, H. J. (1995). *Genius: The natural history of creativity.* Cambridge, England: Cambridge University Press.

Eysenck, H. J., & Gilmour, J. S. L. (1944). The psychology of philosophers: A factorial study. *Character & Personality, 12,* 290–298.

Eysenck, H. J., & Nias, D. K. B. (1982). *Astrology: Science or superstition?* London: Smith.

Fancher, R. E. (1979). *Pioneers of psychology.* New York: Norton.

Fancher, R. E. (1998). Biography and psychodynamic theory: Some lessons from the life of Francis Galton. *History of Psychology, 1,* 99–115.

Farnsworth, P. R. (1969). *The social psychology of music* (2nd ed.). Ames, IA: Iowa State University Press.

Faust, D. (1984). *Limits of scientific reasoning.* Minneapolis: University of Minnesota Press.

Faust, D., & Meehl, P. E. (1992). Using scientific methods to resolve questions in the history and philosophy of science: Some illustrations. *Behavior Therapy, 23,* 195–211.

Feist, G. J. (1993). A structural model of scientific eminence. *Psychological Science, 4,* 366–371.

Feist, G. J. (1994). Personality and working style predictors of integrative complexity: A study of scientists' thinking about research and teaching. *Journal of Personality and Social Psychology, 67,* 474–484.

Feist, G. J. (1997). Quantity, quality, and depth of research as influences on scientific eminence: Is quantity most important? *Creativity Research Journal, 10,* 325–335.

Feist, G. J. (1998). A meta-analysis of personality in scientific and artistic creativity. *Personality and Social Psychology Review, 2,* 290–309.

Feist, G. J., & Gorman, M. E. (1998). The psychology of science: Review and integration of a nascent discipline. *Review of General Psychology, 2,* 3–47.

Ferber, M. A. (1986). Citations: Are they an objective measure of scholarly merit? *Signs, 11,* 381–389.

Fernberger, S. W. (1938). The scientific interests and scientific publications of the members of the American Psychological Association, Inc. *Psychological Bulletin, 35,* 261–281.

Fernberger, S. W. (1946, August 23). Scientific publication as affected by war and politics. *Science, 104,* 175–177.

Ferris, P. (1977). *Dylan Thomas.* London: Hodder & Stoughton.

Festinger, L. (1954). A theory of social comparison processes. *Human Relations, 7,* 117–140.

Fidell, L. S. (1970). Empirical verification of sex discrimination in hiring practices in psychology. *American Psychologist, 25,* 1094–1098.

Fisch, R. (1977). Psychology of science. In I. Spiegel-Rösing & D. Price (Eds.), *Science, technology, and society* (pp. 277–318). London: Sage.

Fisher, D. H. (1970). *Historians' fallacies: Toward a logic of historical thought.* New York: Harper & Row.

Fisher, R. A. (1930). *The genetical theory of natural selection.* Oxford, England: Oxford University Press.

Fiske, S. T., & Taylor, S. E. (1991). *Social cognition* (2nd ed.). New York: McGraw-Hill.

Flugel, J. C. (1933). *A hundred years of psychology, 1833–1933.* New York: Macmillan.

Flugel, J. C. (1951). *A hundred years of psychology, 1833–1933: With additional part on developments 1933–1947* (2nd ed.). London: G. Duckworth.

Folly, G., Hajtman, B., Nagy, J. I., & Ruff, I. (1981). Some methodological problems in ranking scientists by citation analysis. *Scientometrics*, *3*, 135–147.

Ford, J. B., Richard, M. P., & Talbutt, P. C. (Eds.). (1996). *Sorokin and Civilization: A centennial assessment*. New Brunswick, NJ: Transaction.

Fowler, R. G. (1987). Toward a quantitative theory of intellectual discovery (especially in physics). *Journal of Scientific Exploration*, *1*, 11–20.

Frensch, P. A., & Sternberg, R. J. (1989). Expertise and intelligent thinking: When is it worse to know better? In R. J. Sternberg (Ed.), *Advances in the psychology of human intelligence* (Vol. 5, pp. 157–188). Hillsdale, NJ: Erlbaum.

Freud, S. (1952). *Civilization and its discontents* (J. Riviere, Trans.). In R. M. Hutchins (Ed.), *Great books of the western world* (Vol. 54, pp. 767–802). Chicago: Encyclopaedia Britannica. (Original work published 1929)

Freud, S. (1953). A difficulty in the path of psycho-anlaysis (J. Riviere, Trans.). In J. Strachey (Ed.), *The standard edition of the complete psychological works of Sigmund Freud* (Vol. 17, pp. 137–144). London: Hogarth Press. (Original work published 1917)

Freud, S. (1964). *Leonardo da Vinci and a memory of his childhood* (A. Tyson, Trans.). New York: Norton. (Original work published 1910)

Friman, P. C., Allen, K. D., Kerwin, M. L. E., & Larzelere, R. (1993). Changes in modern psychology: A citation analysis of the Kuhnian displacement thesis. *American Psychologist*, *48*, 658–664.

Fulton, O., & Trow, M. (1974). Research activity in American higher education. *Sociology of Education*, *47*, 29–73.

Furnham, A., & Bonnett, C. (1992). British research productivity in psychology 1980–1989: Does the Lotka–Price law apply to university departments as it does to individuals? *Personality and Individual Differences*, *13*, 1333–1341.

Furumoto, L. (1989). The new history of psychology. In I. S. Cohen (Ed.), *The G. Stanley Hall lecture series* (Vol. 9, pp. 9–34). Washington, DC: American Psychological Association.

Furumoto, L. (1992). Joining separate spheres—Christine Ladd-Franklin, Woman–Scientist (1847–1930). *American Psychologist*, *47*, 175–182.

Furumoto, L. (1998). Lucy May Boring (1886–1996). *American Psychologist*, *53*, 59.

Galton, F. (1869). *Hereditary genius: An inquiry into its laws and consequences*. London: Macmillan.

Galton, F. (1874). *English men of science: Their nature and nurture*. London: Macmillan.

Galton, F. (1883). *Inquiries into human faculty and its development*. London: Macmillan.

Galton, F. (1972). *Hereditary genius: An inquiry into its laws and consequences* (2nd ed.). Gloucester, MA: Smith. (Original work published 1892)

Gardner, H. (1983). *Frames of mind: A theory of multiple intelligences*. New York: Basic Books.

Gardner, H. (1987). *The mind's new science: A history of the cognitive revolution*. New York: Basic Books.

Gardner, H. (1993). *Creating minds: An anatomy of creativity seen through the lives of Freud, Einstein, Picasso, Stravinsky, Eliot, Graham, and Gandhi.* New York: Basic Books.

Gardner, H. (1998). Are there additional intelligences? The case for naturalist, spiritual, and existential intelligences. In J. Kane (Ed.), *Education, information, and transformation* (pp. 111–131). Upper Saddle River, NJ: Merrill.

Garvey, W. D., & Tomita, K. (1972). Continuity of productivity by scientists in the years 1968–1971. *Science Studies, 2*, 379–383.

Gaston, J. (Ed.). (1978). *The sociology of science.* San Francisco: Jossey-Bass.

Gholson, B., & Barker, P. (1985). Kuhn, Lakatos, and Laudan: Applications to the history of physics and psychology. *American Psychologist, 40*, 755–769.

Gholson, B., Shadish, W. R., Jr., Neimeyer, R. A., & Houts, A. C. (Eds.). (1989). *The psychology of science: Contributions to metascience.* Cambridge, England: Cambridge University Press.

Gibson, J., & Light, P. (1967). Intelligence among university scientists. *Nature, 213*, 441–443.

Gibson, K. R. (1972). Eminence of the APA presidents. *American Psychologist, 27*, 582–583.

Gieryn, T. F., & Hirsh, R. F. (1983). Marginality and innovation in science. *Social Studies of Science, 13*, 87–106.

Gilgen, A. R. (1982). *American psychology since World War II: A profile of the discipline.* Westport, CT: Greenwood.

Gillispie, C. C. (1960). *The edge of objectivity: An essay on the history of scientific ideas.* Princeton, NJ: Princeton University Press.

Gillispie, C. C. (Ed.). (1970–1980). *Dictionary of scientific biography* (16 vols.). New York: Scribner's.

Glick, P., Zion, C., & Nelson, C. (1988). What mediates sex discrimination in hiring decisions? *Journal of Personality and Social Psychology, 50*, 178–186.

Goddard, H. H. (1912). *The Kallikak family: A study in the heredity of feeblemindedness.* New York: Macmillan.

Goddard, H. H. (1942, June 5). In defense of the Kallikak study. *Science, 95*, 574–576.

Goertzel, M. G., Goertzel, V., & Goertzel, T. G. (1978). *300 eminent personalities: A psychosocial analysis of the famous.* San Francisco: Jossey-Bass.

Goertzel, V., & Goertzel, M. G. (1962). *Cradles of eminence.* Boston: Little, Brown.

Goethe, J. (1952). Faust (G. M. Priest, Trans.). In R. M. Hutchins (Ed.), *Great books of the western world* (Vol. 47). Chicago: Encyclopaedia Britannica. (Original work published 1808–1832)

Goldstein, E. (1979). Effect of same-sex and cross-sex role models on the subsequent academic productivity of scholars. *American Psychologist, 34*, 407–410.

Goodman, E. S. (1971). Citation analysis as a tool in historical study: A case study based on F. C. Donders and mental reaction times. *Journal of the History of the Behavioral Sciences, 7*, 187–191.

Gottfredson, L. S. (1997). Why g matters: The complexity of everyday life. *Intelligence, 24*, 79–132.

Gottfredson, S. D. (1978). Evaluating psychological research reports: Dimensions, reliability, and correlates of quality judgments. *American Psychologist, 33*, 920–934.

Götz, K. O., & Götz, K. (1979a). Personality characteristics of professional artists. *Perceptual & Motor Skills, 49*, 327–334.

Götz, K. O., & Götz, K. (1979b). Personality characteristics of successful artists. *Perceptual & Motor Skills, 49*, 919–924.

Gough, H. G. (1976). Studying creativity by means of word association tests. *Journal of Applied Psychology, 61*, 348–353.

Gough, H. G. (1992). Assessment of creative potential in psychology and the development of a Creative Temperament Scale for the CPI. In J. C. Rosen & P. McReynolds (Eds.), *Advances in psychological assessment* (Vol. 8, pp. 225–257). New York: Plenum.

Gould, S. J. (1981). *The mismeasure of man.* New York: Norton.

Gray, C. E. (1958). An analysis of Graeco–Roman development: The epicyclical evolution of Graeco–Roman civilization. *American Anthropologist, 60*, 13–31.

Gray, C. E. (1966). A measurement of creativity in western civilization. *American Anthropologist, 68*, 1384–1417.

Gray, J. A. (1979). *Ivan Pavlov.* New York: Viking.

Gray, P. H. (1983). *Hereditary Genius* revisited: Were Galton's missing scientists the aftermath of the Puritan brain drain to America? *Bulletin of the Psychonomic Society, 21*, 120–122.

Green, G. S. (1981). A test of the Ortega hypothesis in criminology. *Criminology, 19*, 45–52.

Greenwald, A. G., & Schuh, E. S. (1994). An ethnic bias in scientific citations. *European Journal of Social Psychology, 24*, 623–639.

Greenwood, J. D. (1999). Understanding the "cognitive revolution" in psychology. *Journal of the History of the Behavioral Sciences, 35*, 1–22.

Grover, S. C. (1981). *Toward a psychology of the scientist.* Washington, DC: University Press of America.

Gruber, H. E. (1974). *Darwin on man: A psychological study of scientific creativity.* New York: Dutton.

Gruber, H. E. (1989). The evolving systems approach to creative work. In D. B. Wallace & H. E. Gruber (Eds.), *Creative people at work: Twelve cognitive case studies* (pp. 3–24). New York: Oxford University Press.

Guilford, J. P. (1967). *The nature of human intelligence.* New York: McGraw-Hill.

Gupta, N., Gilbert, L. A., & Pierce, C. A. (1983). *Protégés, mentors, and academic success: A feedback report to participants.* Austin: University of Texas at Austin.

Guthrie, R. V. (1998). *Even the rat was white: A historical view of psychology* (2nd ed.). Boston: Allyn & Bacon.

Guyter, L., & Fidell, L. (1973). Publications of men and women psychologists. *American Psychologist, 28*, 157–160.

Hadamard, J. (1945). *The psychology of invention in the mathematical field*. Princeton, NJ: Princeton University Press.

Haefele, J. W. (1962). *Creativity and innovation*. New York: Reinhold.

Hagstrom, W. O. (1974). Competition in science. *American Sociological Review, 39*, 1–18.

Hall, G. S. (1922). *Senescence: The last half of life*. New York: Appleton.

Hannan, M. T. (1971). Problems of aggregation. In H. M. Blalock (Ed.), *Causal models in the social sciences* (pp. 473–508). Chicago: Aldine-Atherton.

Hargens, L. L. (1978). Relations between work habits, research technologies, and eminence in science. *Sociology of Work and Occupations, 5*, 97–112.

Hargens, L. L., McCann, J. C., & Reskin, B. F. (1978). Productivity and reproductivity: Fertility and professional achievement among research scientists. *Social Forces, 57*, 154–163.

Harnsberger, C. T. (Ed.). (1972). *Everyone's Mark Twain*. New York: Barnes.

Harris, J. R. (1998). *The nurture assumption: Why children turn out the way they do*. New York: Free Press.

Hart, M. H. (1987). *The 100: A ranking of the most influential persons in history*. Secaucus, NJ: Citadel Press.

Hathaway, S. R., & McKinley, J. C. (1943). *Manual for the Minnesota Multiphasic Personality Inventory*. Minneapolis: University of Minnesota Press.

Hayes, J. R. (1989a). Cognitive processes in creativity. In J. A. Glover, R. R. Ronning, & C. R. Reynolds (Eds.), *Handbook of creativity* (pp. 135–145). New York: Plenum.

Hayes, J. R. (1989b). *The complete problem solver* (2nd ed.). Hillsdale, NJ: Erlbaum.

Hayes, S. C. (1983). When more is less: Quantity versus quality of publications in the evaluation of academic vitae. *American Psychologist, 38*, 1398–1400.

Hearnshaw, L. S. (1987). *The shaping of modern psychology*. London: Routledge & Kegan Paul.

Hedges, L. V. (1987). How hard is hard science, how soft is soft science? *American Psychologist, 42*, 443–455.

Hegel, G. W. F. (1952). *The philosophy of history* (C. F. Atkinson, Trans.). New York: Dover. (Original work published 1832)

Helmholtz, H. von (1898). An autobiographical sketch. In *Popular lectures on scientific subjects, second series* (E. Atkinson, Trans., pp. 266–291). New York: Longmans, Green. (Original work published 1891)

Helmholtz, H. von (1971). An autobiographical sketch. In R. Kahl (Ed.), *Selected writings of Hermann von Helmholtz* (pp. 466–478). Middletown, CT: Wesleyan University Press. (Original work published 1891)

Helmreich, R. L. (1968). Birth-order effects. *Naval Research Reviews, 2*, 1–6.

Helmreich, R. L., & Spence, J. T. (1982). Gender differences in productivity and impact. *American Psychologist, 37,* 1142.

Helmreich, R. L., Spence, J. T., Beane, W. E., Lucker, G. W., & Matthews, K. A. (1980). Making it in academic psychology: Demographic and personality correlates of attainment. *Journal of Personality and Social Psychology, 39,* 896–908.

Helmreich, R. L., Spence, J. T., & Pred, R. S. (1988). Making it without losing it: Type A, achievement motivation, and scientific attainment revisited. *Personality and Social Psychology Bulletin, 14,* 495–504.

Helmreich, R. L., Spence, J. T., & Thorbecke, W. L. (1981). On the stability of productivity and recognition. *Personality and Social Psychology Bulletin, 7,* 516–522.

Helson, R. (1980). The creative woman mathematician. In L. H. Fox, L. Brody, & D. Tobin (Eds.), *Women and the mathematical mystique* (pp. 23–54). Baltimore: Johns Hopkins University Press.

Helson, R. (1990). Creativity in women: Outer and inner views over time. In M. A. Runco & R. S. Albert (Eds.), *Theories of creativity* (pp. 46–58). Newbury Park, CA: Sage.

Helson, R., & Crutchfield, R. S. (1970). Mathematicians: The creative researcher and the average Ph.D. *Journal of Consulting and Clinical Psychology, 34,* 250–257.

Hempel, C. G. (1965). *Aspects of scientific explanation, and other essays in the philosophy of science.* New York: Free Press.

Henley, T. B., & Thorne, B. M. (1992). Eminent psychologists or psychological eminence? *American Psychologist, 47,* 1147–1148.

Hergenhahn, B. R. (1992). *An introduction to the history of psychology* (2nd ed.). Belmont, CA: Wadsworth.

Heyduk, R. G., & Fenigstein, A. (1984). Influential works and authors in psychology: A survey of eminent psychologists. *American Psychologist, 39,* 556–559.

Hilgard, E. R. (1987). *Psychology in America: A historical survey.* San Diego, CA: Harcourt Brace Jovanovich.

Hillner, K. P. (1984). *History and systems of modern psychology: A conceptual approach.* New York: Gardner.

Hilts, V. L. (1975). *A guide to Francis Galton's* English Men of Science. Philadelphia: American Philosophical Society.

Hirsch, J. (1993). Terman's questionable evidence. *Contemporary Psychology, 38,* 1135.

Hirschberg, N., & Itkin, S. (1978). Graduate student success in psychology. *American Psychologist, 33,* 1083–1093.

Hoffman, B. (1972). *Albert Einstein: Creator and rebel.* New York: Plume.

Holahan, C. K., Sears, R. R., & Cronbach, L. J. (1995). *The gifted group in later maturity.* Stanford, CA: Stanford University Press.

Hollingworth, L. S. (1926). *Gifted children: Their nature and nurture.* New York: Macmillan.

Hollingworth, L. S. (1942). *Children beyond 180 IQ: Origin and development.* Yonkers-on-Hudson, NY: World Book.

Horner, K. L., Murray, H. G., & Rushton, J. P. (1989). Relation between aging and rated teaching effectiveness of academic psychologists. *Psychology and Aging, 4,* 226–229.

Horner, K. L., Murray, H. G., & Rushton, J. P. (1994). Aging and administration in academic psychologists. *Social Behavior and Personality, 22,* 343–346.

Horner, K. L., Rushton, J. P., & Vernon, P. A. (1986). Relation between aging and research productivity of academic psychologists. *Psychology and Aging, 1,* 319–324.

Hothersall, D. (1984). *History of psychology.* New York: Random House.

Hothersall, D. (1990). *History of psychology* (2nd ed.). New York: Random House.

House, R. J., Spangler, W. D., & Woycke, J. (1991). Personality and charisma in the U.S. presidency: A psychological theory of leader effectiveness. *Administrative Science Quarterly, 36,* 364–396.

Howard, A., Pion, G. M., Gottfredson, G. D., Flattau, P. E., Oskamp, S., Pfafflin, S. M., Bray, D. W., & Burstein, A. G. (1986). The changing face of American psychology: A report from the Committee on Employment and Human Resources. *American Psychologist, 41,* 1311–1327.

Huber, J. C. (1998a). Invention and inventivity as a special kind of creativity, with implications for general creativity. *Journal of Creative Behavior, 32,* 58–72.

Huber, J. C. (1998b). Invention and inventivity is a random, Poisson process: A potential guide to analysis of general creativity. *Creativity Research Journal, 11,* 231–241.

Huber, J. C. (1999). Inventive productivity and the statistics of exceedances. *Scientometrics, 45,* 33–53.

Huber, J. C. (2000). A statistical analysis of special cases of creativity. *Journal of Creative Behavior, 34,* 203–225.

Hudson, L. (1958). Undergraduate academic record of Fellows of the Royal Society. *Nature, 182,* 1326.

Hudson, L., & Jacot, B. (1986). The outsider in science. In C. Bagley & G. K. Verma (Eds.), *Personality, cognition and values* (pp. 3–23). London: Macmillan.

Hulin, W. S. (1934). *A short history of psychology.* New York: Holt.

Hull, D. L. (1988). *Science as a process: An evolutionary account of the social and conceptual development of science.* Chicago: University of Chicago Press.

Hull, D. L., Tessner, P. D., & Diamond, A. M. (1978, November 17). Planck's principle: Do younger scientists accept new scientific ideas with greater alacrity than older scientists? *Science, 202,* 717–723.

Huntington, E. (1938). *Season of birth: Its relation to human abilities.* New York: Wiley.

Hutchins, R. M. (Ed.). (1952). *Great books of the western world.* Chicago: Encyclopaedia Britannica.

Hyde, J. S. (1986). Gender differences in aggression. In J. S. Hyde & M. C. Linn (Eds.), *The psychology of gender: Advances through meta-analysis* (pp. 51–66). Baltimore: Johns Hopkins University Press.

Hyman, B., & Shephard, A. H. (1980). Zeitgeist: The development of an operational definition. *Journal of Mind and Behavior, 1*, 227–246.

Hyman, S. E. (Ed.). (1963). *Darwin for today: The essence of his works.* New York: Viking.

Illingworth, R. S., & Illingworth, C. M. (1969). *Lessons from childhood.* Edinburgh, Scotland: Livingston.

Inhaber, H. (1977). Scientists and economic growth. *Social Studies of Science, 7*, 514–526.

Innis, N. K. (1992). Tolman and Tryon: Early research on the inheritance of the ability to learn. *American Psychologist, 47*, 190–197.

James, H. (Ed.). (1920). *The letters of William James.* Boston: The Atlantic Monthly Press.

James, H. (Ed.). (1926). *The letters of William James.* Boston: Little, Brown.

James, W. (1880, October). Great men, great thoughts, and the environment. *Atlantic Monthly, 46*, 441–459.

James, W. (1900). *Talks to teachers on psychology and to students on some of life's ideals.* New York: Holt.

James, W. (1902). *The varieties of religious experience: A study in human nature.* London: Longmans, Green.

James, W. (1952). Principles of psychology. In R. M. Hutchins (Ed.), *Great books of the western world* (Vol. 53). Chicago: Encyclopaedia Britannica. (Original work published 1890)

Jamison, K. R. (1989). Mood disorders and patterns of creativity in British writers and artists. *Psychiatry, 52*, 125–134.

Jeans, J. (1942). Newton and the science of to-day. *Nature, 150*, 710–715.

Jevons, W. S. (1900). *The principles of science: A treatise on logic and scientific method* (2nd ed.). London: Macmillan. (Original work published 1877)

Johnson, J. A., Germer, C. K., Efran, J. S., & Overton, W. F. (1988). Personality as the basis for theoretical predilections. *Journal of Personality and Social Psychology, 55*, 824–835.

Johnson, S. (1781). *The lives of the most eminent English poets* (Vol. 1). London: Bathurst.

Jorgenson, D. O. (1975). Economic threat and authoritarianism in television programs: 1950–1974. *Psychological Reports, 37*, 1153–1154.

Juda, A. (1949). The relationship between highest mental capacity and psychic abnormalities. *American Journal of Psychiatry, 106*, 296–307.

Jungk, R. (1958). *Brighter than a thousand suns* (J. Cleugh, Trans.). New York: Harcourt Brace.

Kahneman, D., Slovic, P., & Tversky, A. (Eds.). (1982). *Judgment under uncertainty: Heuristics and biases.* Cambridge, England: Cambridge University Press.

Kanazawa, S. (2000). Scientific discoveries as cultural displays: A further test of Miller's courtship model. *Evolution and Human Behavior, 21*, 317–321.

Kant, I. (1952). Critique of pure reason (2nd ed., T. K. Abbott). In R. M. Hutchins (Ed.), *Great books of the western world* (Vol. 42, pp. 1–250). Chicago: Encyclopedia Britannica. (Original work published 1787)

Kantorovich, A. (1993). *Scientific discovery: Logic and tinkering*. Albany: State University of New York Press.

Kantorovich, A., & Ne'eman, Y. (1989). Serendipity as a source of evolutionary progress in science. *Studies in History and Philosophy of Science, 20*, 505–529.

Karlson, J. I. (1970). Genetic association of giftedness and creativity with schizophrenia. *Hereditas, 66*, 177–182.

Kasof, J. (1995). Explaining creativity: The attributional perspective. *Creativity Research Journal, 8*, 311–366.

Kaulins, A. (1979). Cycles in the birth of eminent humans. *Cycles, 30*, 9–15.

Kaun, D. E. (1991). Writers die young: The impact of work and leisure on longevity. *Journal of Economic Psychology, 12*, 381–399.

Keller, L. M., Bouchard, T. J., Arvey, R. D., Segal, N. L., & Dawis, R. V. (1992). Work values: Genetic and environmental influences. *Journal of Applied Psychology, 77*, 79–88.

Kendler, H. H. (1987). *Historical foundations of modern psychology*. Chicago: Dorsey.

Kimble, G. A. (1984). Psychology's two cultures. *American Psychologist, 39*, 833–839.

Kinney, D. P., & Smith, S. P. (1992). Age and teaching performance. *Journal of Higher Education, 63*, 282–302.

Kinnier, R. T., Metha, A. T., Buki, L. P., & Rawa, P. M. (1994). Manifest value of eminent psychologists: A content analysis of their obituaries. *Current Psychology: Developmental, Learning, Personality, Social, 13*, 88–94.

Klingemann, H.-D., Mohler, P. P., & Weber, R. P. (1982). Cultural indicators based on content analysis: A secondary analysis of Sorokin's data on fluctuations of systems of truth. *Quality and Quantity, 16*, 1–18.

Kluckhohn, C., & Murray, H. A. (1953). Personality formation: The determinants. In C. Kluckhohn & H. A. Murray (Eds.), *Personality in nature, society, and culture* (2nd rev. ed., pp. 53–67). New York: Knopf.

Knapp, R. H. (1962). A factor analysis of Thorndike's ratings of eminent men. *Journal of Social Psychology, 56*, 67–71.

Koestler, A. (1964). *The act of creation*. New York: Macmillan.

Köhler, W. (1925). *The mentality of apes* (E. Winter, Trans.). New York: Harcourt, Brace.

Korn, J. H., Davis, R., & Davis, S. F. (1991). Historians' and chairpersons' judgments of eminence among psychologists. *American Psychologist, 46*, 789–792.

Koza, J. R. (1992). *Genetic programming: On the programming of computers by means of natural selection*. Cambridge, MA: MIT Press.

Koza, J. R. (1994). *Genetic programming II: Automatic discovery of reusable programs*. Cambridge: MIT Press.

Krasner, L., & Houts, A. C. (1984). A study of the "value" systems of behavioral scientists. *American Psychologist, 39*, 840–850.

Kroeber, A. L. (1917). The superorganic. *American Anthropologist, 19*, 163–214.

Kroeber, A. L. (1944). *Configurations of culture growth.* Berkeley: University of California Press.

Kuhn, T. S. (1970). *The structure of scientific revolutions* (2nd ed.). Chicago: University of Chicago Press.

Kulkarni, D., & Simon, H. A. (1988). The process of scientific discovery: The strategy of experimentation. *Cognitive Science, 12*, 139–175.

Kuo, Y. (1986). The growth and decline of Chinese philosophical genius. *Chinese Journal of Psychology, 28*, 81–91.

Kynerd, T. (1971). An analysis of presidential greatness and "President rating." *Southern Quarterly, 9*, 309–329.

Kyvik, S. (1990). Motherhood and scientific productivity. *Social Studies of Science, 20*, 149–160.

Lakatos, I. (1978). *The methodology of scientific research programs.* Cambridge, England: Cambridge University Press.

Lamb, D., & Easton, S. M. (1984). *Multiple discovery.* Avebury, England: Avebury.

Lambert, W. E., Tucker, G. R., & d'Anglejan, A. (1973). Cognitive and attitudinal consequences of bilingual schooling: The St. Lambert project through grade five. *Journal of Educational Psychology, 65*, 141–159.

Landry, R. G. (1972). The enhancement of figural creativity through second language learning at the elementary school level. *Foreign Language Annals, 4*, 111–115.

Langley, P., Simon, H. A., Bradshaw, G. L., & Zythow, J. M. (1987). *Scientific discovery.* Cambridge, MA: MIT Press.

Laudan, L. (1977). *Progress and its problems.* Berkeley: University of California Press.

Lawani, S. M. (1986). Some bibliometric correlates of quality in scientific research. *Scientometrics, 9*, 13–15.

Leahey, T. H. (1980). *A history of psychology: Main currents in psychological thought.* Englewood Cliffs, NJ: Prentice Hall.

Leahey, T. H. (1987). *A history of psychology: Main currents in psychological thought* (2nd ed.). Englewood Cliffs, NJ: Prentice Hall.

Leahey, T. H. (1992). *A history of psychology: Main currents in psychological thought* (3rd ed.). Englewood Cliffs, NJ: Prentice Hall.

Leahey, T. H. (1997). *A history of psychology: Main currents in psychological thought* (4th ed.). Englewood Cliffs, NJ: Prentice Hall.

Lehman, H. C. (1943, September 24). The longevity of the eminent. *Science, 98*, 270–273.

Lehman, H. C. (1946). Age of starting to contribute versus total creative output. *Journal of Applied Psychology, 30*, 460–480.

Lehman, H. C. (1947a). The exponential increase of man's cultural output. *Social Forces, 25,* 281–290.

Lehman, H. C. (1947b). National differences in creativity. *American Journal of Sociology, 52,* 475–488.

Lehman, H. C. (1953a). *Age and achievement.* Princeton, NJ: Princeton University Press.

Lehman, H. C. (1953b). The ages of scheduled participants at the 1948 APA annual meeting. *American Psychologist, 8,* 125–126.

Lehman, H. C. (1956). Reply to Dennis' critique of *Age and Achievement. Journal of Gerontology, 11,* 128–134.

Lehman, H. C. (1958, May 23). The chemist's most creative years. *Science, 127,* 1213–1222.

Lehman, H. C. (1960). The age decrement in outstanding scientific creativity. *American Psychologist, 15,* 128–134.

Lehman, H. C. (1962). More about age and achievement. *The Gerontologist, 2,* 141–148.

Lehman, H. C. (1966). The psychologist's most creative years. *American Psychologist, 21,* 363–369.

Lehman, H. C., & Witty, P. A. (1931). Scientific eminence and church membership. *Scientific Monthly, 33,* 544–549.

Lester, D. (1991). Premature mortality associated with alcoholism and suicide in American writers. *Perceptual & Motor Skills, 73,* 162.

Levin, S. G., & Stephan, P. E. (1989). Age and research productivity of academic scientists. *Research in Higher Education, 30,* 531–549.

Levin, S. G., & Stephan, P. E. (1991). Research productivity over the life cycle: Evidence for academic scientists. *American Economic Review, 81,* 114–132.

Levin, S. G., & Stephan, P. E. (1999, August 20). Are the foreign born a source of strength for U.S. science? *Science, 285,* 1213–1214.

Levin, S. G., Stephan, P. E., & Walker, M. B. (1995). Planck's principle revisited—A note. *Social Studies of Science, 25,* 35–55.

Lindauer, M. S. (1999). Old age style. In M. A. Runco & S. Pritzker (Eds.), *Encyclopedia of creativity* (Vol. 2, pp. 311–318). San Diego, CA: Academic Press.

Lindsey, D. (1976). Distinction, achievement, and editorial board membership. *American Psychologist, 31,* 799–804.

Lindsey, D. (1978). *The scientific publication system in social science.* San Francisco: Jossey-Bass.

Lindsey, D. (1980). Production and citation measurements in the sociology of science: The problem of multiple authorship. *Social Studies of Science, 18,* 145–162.

Lindsey, D. (1988). Assessing precision in the manuscript review process: A little better than a dice roll. *Scientometrics, 14,* 75–82.

Lindsey, D. (1989). Using citation counts as a measure of quality in science: Measuring what's measurable rather than what's valid. *Scientometrics, 15,* 189–203.

Loehlin, J. C. (1992a). *Genes and environment in personality development*. Newbury Park, CA: Sage.

Loehlin, J. C. (1992b). *Latent variable models: An introduction to factor, path, and structural analysis* (2nd ed.). Hillsdale, NJ: Erlbaum.

Loewi, O. (1960). An autobiographical sketch. *Perspectives in Biology and Medicine, 4,* 3–25.

Lombroso, C. (1891). *The man of genius*. London: Scott.

Long, J. S., & McGinnis, R. (1981). Organizational context and scientific productivity. *American Sociological Review, 46,* 422–442.

Lopez, E. C., Esquivel, G. B., & Houtz, J. C. (1993). The creative skills of culturally and linguistically diverse gifted students. *Creativity Research Journal, 6,* 401–412.

Lotka, A. J. (1926). The frequency distribution of scientific productivity. *Journal of the Washington Academy of Sciences, 16,* 317–323.

Lowry, R. (1982). *The evolution of psychological theory: A critical history of concepts and presuppositions* (2nd ed.). New York: Aldine.

Ludwig, A. M. (1995). *The price of greatness: Resolving the creativity and madness controversy*. New York: Guilford Press.

Lundin, R. W. (1979). *Theories and systems of psychology* (2nd ed.). Lexington, MA: Heath.

Lykken, D. T. (1982). Research with twins: The concept of emergenesis. *Psychophysiology, 19,* 361–373.

Lykken, D. T. (1998). The genetics of genius. In A. Steptoe (Ed.), *Genius and the mind: Studies of creativity and temperament in the historical record* (pp. 15–37). New York: Oxford University Press.

Lykken, D. T., McGue, M., Tellegen, A., & Bouchard, T. J., Jr. (1992). Emergenesis: Genetic traits that may not run in families. *American Psychologist, 47,* 1565–1577.

Lynn, R. (1979). The social ecology of intelligence in the British Isles. *British Journal of Social and Clinical Psychology, 18,* 1–12.

Lynn, R. (1994). Sex differences in intelligence and brain size: A paradox resolved. *Personality & Individual Differences, 17,* 257–271.

Lyons, J. (1968). Chronological age, professional age, and eminence in psychology. *American Psychologist, 23,* 371–374.

Maccoby, E. E., & Jacklin, C. N. (1980). Sex differences in aggression: A rejoinder and reprise. *Child Development, 51,* 964–980.

Mach, E. (1896, January). On the part played by accident in invention and discovery. *Monist, 6,* 161–175.

Mackavey, W. R., Malley, J. E., & Stewart, A. J. (1991). Remembering autobiographically consequential experiences: Content analysis of psychologists' accounts of their lives. *Psychology and Aging, 6,* 50–59.

MacKinnon, D. W. (1978). *In search of human effectiveness*. Buffalo, NY: Creative Education Foundation.

MacKinnon, D. W., & Hall, W. B. (1972). Intelligence and creativity. In *Proceedings of the XVIIth International Congress of Applied Psychology* (Vol. 2, pp. 1883–1888). Brussels, Belgium: EDITEST.

MacLeod, R. B. (1975). *The persistent problems of psychology*. Pittsburgh, PA: Duquesne University Press.

MacRae, D., Jr. (1969). Growth and decay curves in scientific citations. *American Sociological Review, 34*, 631–635.

Mahoney, M. J. (1976). *Scientist as subject*. Cambridge, MA: Ballinger.

Manis, J. G. (1951). Some academic influences upon publication productivity. *Social Forces, 29*, 267–272.

Manniche, E., & Falk, G. (1957). Age and the Nobel prize. *Behavioral Science, 2*, 301–307.

Mansfield, R. S., & Busse, T. V. (1981). *The psychology of creativity and discovery: Scientists and their work*. Chicago: Nelson-Hall.

Marchetti, C. (1980). Society as a learning system: Discovery, invention, and innovation cycles. *Technological Forecasting and Social Change, 18*, 267–282.

Marchman, J. N. (1993). Clinical psychology in its historical context. *Contemporary Psychology, 38*, 20–21.

Marsh, H. W., & Ball, S. (1989). The peer review process used to evaluate manuscripts submitted to academic journals: Interjudgmental reliability. *Journal of Experimental Education, 57*, 151–169.

Martens, M. P. (2000). Difficulties in analyzing trends in psychology. *American Psychologist, 55*, 272–273.

Martindale, C. (1972). Father absence, psychopathology, and poetic eminence. *Psychological Reports, 31*, 843–847.

Martindale, C. (1975). *Romantic progression: The psychology of literary history*. Washington, DC: Hemisphere.

Martindale, C. (1976). Primitive mentality and the relationship between art and society. *Scientific Aesthetics, 1*, 5–18.

Martindale, C. (1990). *The clockwork muse: The predictability of artistic styles*. New York: Basic Books.

Martindale, C. (1995a). Creativity and connectionism. In S. M. Smith, T. B. Ward, & R. A. Finke (Eds.), *The creative cognition approach* (pp. 249–268). Cambridge, MA: MIT Press.

Martindale, C. (1995b). Fame more fickle than fortune: On the distribution of literary eminence. *Poetics, 23*, 219–234.

Martindale, C., Brewer, W. F., Helson, R., Rosenberg, S., Simonton, D. K., Keeley, A., Leigh, J., & Ohtsuka, K. (1988). Structure, theme, style, and reader response in Hungarian and American short stories. In C. Martindale (Ed.), *Psychological approaches to the study of literary narratives* (pp. 267–289). Hamburg, Germany: Buske.

Marx, K. (1952). Capital (3rd ed., F. Engels, Trans. & Ed.). In R. M. Hutchins (Ed.), *Great books of the western world* (Vol. 50, pp. 1–411). Chicago: Encyclopaedia Britannica. (Original work published 1873)

Maslow, A. H. (1959). Creativity in self-actualizing people. In H. H. Anderson (Ed.), *Creativity and its cultivation* (pp. 83–95). New York: Harper & Row.

Maslow, A. (1966). *The psychology of science*. New York: Harper & Row.

Maslow, A. H. (1970). *Motivation and personality* (2nd ed.). New York: Harper & Row.

Matthews, K. A., Helmreich, R. L., Beane, W. E., & Lucker, G. W. (1980). Pattern A, achievement striving, and scientific merit: Does Pattern A help or hinder? *Journal of Personality and Social Psychology, 39,* 962–967.

May, R. (1975). *The courage to create*. New York: Norton.

McCann, S. J. H. (1999). Threatening times and fluctuations in American church memberships. *Personality and Social Psychology Bulletin. 25,* 325–336.

McCann, S. J. H., & Stewin, L. L. (1984). Environmental threat and parapsychological contributions to the psychological literature. *Journal of Social Psychology, 122,* 227–235.

McCann, S. J. H., & Stewin, L. L. (1987). Threat, authoritarianism, and the power of U.S. presidents. *Journal of Psychology, 121,* 149–157.

McClelland, D. C. (1962). On the psychodynamics of creative physical scientists. In H. E. Gruber, G. Terrell, & M. Wertheimer (Eds.), *Contemporary approaches to creative thinking* (pp. 141–174). New York: Atherton.

McClelland, D. C. (1973). Testing for competence rather than for "intelligence." *American Psychologist, 28,* 1–14.

McCurdy, H. G. (1960). The childhood pattern of genius. *Horizon, 2,* 33–38.

McDowell, J. M. (1982). Obsolescence of knowledge and career publication profiles: Some evidence of differences among fields in costs of interrupted careers. *American Economic Review, 72,* 752–768.

McFarlan, D. (Ed.). (1989). *Guinness book of world records*. New York: Bantam.

McReynolds, P. (1971). Reliability of ratings of research papers. *American Psychologist, 26,* 400–401.

Mead, M. (1935). *Sex and temperament*. New York: Morrow.

Meehl, P. (1954). *Clinical versus statistical prediction: A theoretical analysis and a review of the evidence*. Minneapolis: University of Minnesota Press.

Meehl, P. E. (1978). Theoretical risks and tabular asterisks: Sir Karl, Sir Ronald, and the slow progress of soft psychology. *Journal of Consulting and Clinical Psychology, 46,* 806–834.

Meehl, P. E. (1990a). Appraising and amending theories: The strategy of Lakotosian defense and two principles that warrant it. *Psychological Inquiry, 1,* 108–141.

Meehl, P. E. (1990b). Why summaries of research on psychological theories are often uninterpretable. *Psychological Reports, 66,* 195–244.

Meehl, P. E. (1992). Cliometric metatheory: The actuarial approach to empirical, history-based philosophy of science. *Psychological Reports, 71,* 339–467.

Merton, R. K. (1968, January 5). The Matthew effect in science. *Science, 159,* 56–63.

Merton, R. K. (1961a). The role of genius in scientific advance. *New Scientist, 12,* 306–308.

Merton, R. K. (1961b). Singletons and multiples in scientific discovery: A chapter in the sociology of science. *Proceedings of the American Philosophical Society, 105,* 470–486.

Messer, W. S., Griggs, R. A., & Jackson, S. L. (1999). A national survey of undergraduate psychology degree options and major requirements. *Teaching of Psychology, 26,* 164–171.

Messerli, P. (1988). Age differences in the reception of new scientific theories: The case of plate tectonics theory. *Social Studies of Science, 18,* 91–112.

Miller, G. A. (1956). The magical number seven, plus or minus two: Some limits on our capacity for processing information. *Psychological Review, 63,* 81–97.

Miller, G. F. (1998). How mate choice shaped human nature: A review of sexual selection and human evolution. In C. B. Crawford & D. Krebs (Eds.), *Handbook of evolutionary psychology: Ideas, issues, and applications* (pp. 87–129). Mahwah, NJ: Erlbaum.

Mills, C. A. (1942, October 23). What price glory? *Science, 96,* 380–387.

Mohler, P. P., & Zuell, C. (1990). *TEXTPACK PC.* Mannheim, Germany: ZUMA.

Moore, M. (1978). Discrimination or favoritism? Sex bias in book reviews. *American Psychologist, 33,* 936–938.

Moravcsik, M. J., & Murugesan, P. (1975). Some results on the function and quality of citations. *Social Studies of Science, 5,* 86–92.

Moulin, L. (1955). The Nobel Prizes for the sciences from 1901–1950: An essay in sociological analysis. *British Journal of Sociology, 6,* 246–263.

Mowafy, L., & Martin, J. (1988). Anne Roe: The making of a scientist. *Journal of the History of the Behavioral Sciences, 14,* 13–17.

Mulkay, M. (1980). Sociology of science in the West. *Current Sociology, 28,* 1–184.

Murchison, C. (Ed.). (1929). *The psychological register* (Vol. 1). Worcester, MA: Clark University Press.

Murchison, C. (Ed.). (1932). *The psychological register* (Vol. 3). Worcester, MA: Clark University Press.

Murchison, C. (Ed.). (1936). *A history of psychology in autobiography* (Vol. 3). Worcester, MA: Clark University Press.

Murphy, G. (1949). *Historical introduction to modern psychology* (rev. ed.). New York: Harcourt Brace.

Murphy, G., & Kovach, J. K. (1972). *Historical introduction to modern psychology* (3rd ed.). New York: Harcourt Brace Jovanovich.

Murphy, G., & Murphy, L. B. (Eds.). (1969). *Western psychology: From the Greeks to William James.* New York: Basic Books.

Murray, H. A. (1943). *Thematic apperception test manual.* Cambridge, MA: Harvard University Press.

Murray, P. (Ed.). (1989). *Genius: The history of an idea.* Oxford, England: Blackwell.

Myers, C. R. (1970). Journal citations and scientific eminence in contemporary psychology. *American Psychologist, 25,* 1041–1048.

Myerson, A., & Boyle, R. D. (1941). The incidence of manic-depression psychosis in certain socially important families: Preliminary report. *American Journal of Psychiatry, 98,* 11–21.

Naroll, R., Benjamin, E. C., Fohl, F. K., Fried, M. J., Hildreth, R. E., & Schaefer, J. M. (1971). Creativity: A cross-historical pilot survey. *Journal of Cross-Cultural Psychology, 2,* 181–188.

Nemeth, C. J., & Kwan, J. (1985). Originality of word associations as a function of majority vs. minority influence. *Social Psychology Quarterly, 48,* 277–282.

Nemeth, C. J., & Kwan, J. (1987). Minority influence, divergent thinking and detection of correct solutions. *Journal of Applied Social Psychology, 17,* 788–799.

Nemeth, C. J., & Wachtler, J. (1983). Creative problem solving as a result of majority vs. minority influence. *European Journal of Social Psychology, 13,* 45–55.

Nickerson, R. S. (1998). Confirmation bias: A ubiquitous phenomenon in many guises. *Review of General Psychology, 2,* 175–220.

Nietzsche, F. W. (1927). *The philosophy of Nietzsche* (C. Fadiman, Trans.). New York: Modern Library.

Nisbett, R. E. (1968). Birth order and participation in dangerous sports. *Journal of Personality and Social Psychology, 8,* 351–353.

Norling, B. (1970). *Timeless problems in history.* Notre Dame, IN: Notre Dame Press.

O'Connell, A. N., & Russo, N. F. (Eds.). (1983). *Models of achievement: Reflections of eminent women in psychology* (Vol. 1). New York: Columbia University Press.

O'Connell, A. N., & Russo, N. F. (Eds.). (1990). *Women in psychology: A bio-bibliographic sourcebook.* New York: Greenwood Press.

Oden, M. H. (1968). The fulfillment of promise: 40-year follow-up of the Terman gifted group. *Genetic Psychology Monographs, 77,* 3–93.

Ogburn, W. K., & Thomas, D. (1922). Are inventions inevitable? A note on social evolution. *Political Science Quarterly, 37,* 83–93.

Ogden, R. M. (1951). Oswald Külpe and the Würzberg school. *American Journal of Psychology, 64,* 4–19.

Ohlsson, S. (1992). The learning curve for writing books: Evidence from Professor Asimov. *Psychological Science, 3,* 380–382.

Olby, R. (1979). Mendel no Mendelian? *History of Science, 17,* 53–72.

Oromaner, M. (1977). Professional age and the reception of sociological publications: A test of the Zuckerman–Merton hypothesis. *Social Studies of Science, 7,* 381–388.

Oromaner, M. (1985). The Ortega hypothesis and influential articles in American sociology. *Scientometrics, 7,* 3–10.

Ortega y Gasset, J. (1957). *The revolt of the masses* (M. Adams, Trans.). New York: Norton. (Original work published 1932)

Ortega y Gasset, J. (1958). *Man and crisis* (M. Adams, Trans.). New York: Norton. (Original work published 1933)

Over, R. (1981). Affiliations of psychologists elected to the National Academy of Sciences. *American Psychologist, 36,* 744–752.

Over, R. (1982a). Collaborative research and publication in psychology. *American Psychologist, 37,* 996–1001.

Over, R. (1982b). Does research productivity decline with age? *Higher Education, 11,* 511–520.

Over, R. (1982c). The durability of scientific reputation. *Journal of the History of the Behavioral Sciences, 18,* 53–61.

Over, R. (1982d). Is age a good predictor of research productivity? *Australian Psychologist, 17,* 129–139.

Over, R. (1982e). Research productivity and impact of male and female psychologists. *American Psychologist, 37,* 24–31.

Over, R. (1988). Does scholarly impact decline with age? *Scientometrics, 13,* 215–223.

Over, R. (1989). Age and scholarly impact. *Psychology and Aging, 4,* 222–225.

Over, R. (1990). The scholarly impact of articles published by men and women in psychology journals. *Scientometrics, 18,* 71–80.

Padgett, V., & Jorgenson, D. O. (1982). Superstition and economic threat: Germany 1918–1940. *Personality and Social Psychology Bulletin, 8,* 736–741.

Pardek, J. T., Chung, W. S., & Murphy, J. W. (1996). An examination of the scholarly productivity of social work journal editorial board members and guest reviewers. *Research on Social Work Practice, 5,* 223–234.

Park, R. E. (1928). Human migration and the marginal man. *American Journal of Sociology, 33,* 881–893.

Parshall, K. H. (1988). The art of algebra from al-Khwarizmi to Viète: A study in the natural selection of ideas. *History of Science, 26,* 129–164.

Patinkin, D. (1983). Multiple discoveries and the central message. *American Journal of Sociology, 89,* 306–323.

Pearson, P. (1983). Personality characteristics of cartoonists. *Personality and Individual Differences, 4,* 227–228.

Peritz, B. C. (1983). Are methodological papers more cited than theoretical or empirical ones? The case of sociology. *Scientometrics, 5,* 211–218.

Peters, D. P., & Ceci, S. J. (1982). Peer-review practices of psychological journals: The fate of published articles, submitted again. *Behavioral & Brain Sciences, 5,* 187–255.

Peterson, G. L. (1981). Historical self-understanding in the social sciences: The use of Thomas Kuhn in psychology. *Journal of the Theory of Social Behaviour, 11,* 1–30.

Petty, R. E., Fleming, M. A., & Fabrigar, L. R. (1999). The review process at *PSPB:* Correlates of interreviewer agreement and manuscript acceptance. *Personality and Social Psychology Bulletin, 25,* 188–203.

Piaget, J. (1970). *Genetic epistemology* (E. Duckworth, Trans.). New York: Columbia University Press.

Planck, M. (1949). *Scientific autobiography and other papers* (F. Gaynor, Trans.). New York: Philosophical Library.

Platz, A. (1965). Psychology of the scientist: XI. Lotka's law and research visibility. *Psychological Reports, 16,* 566–568.

Platz, A., & Blakelock, E. (1960). Productivity of American psychologists: Quantity versus quality. *American Psychologist, 15,* 310–312.

Pledge, H. T. (1939). *Science since 1500: A short history of mathematics, physics, chemistry, biology.* London: Clowes.

Plomin, R., & Bergeman, C. S. (1991). The nature of nurture: Genetic influence on environmental measures. *Behavioral and Brain Sciences, 14,* 373–386.

Plomin, R., Corley, R., DeFries, J. C., & Fulker, D. W. (1990). Individual differences in television viewing in early childhood: Nature as well as nurture. *Psychological Science, 1,* 371–377.

Plomin, R., Fulker, D. W., Corley, D. W., & DeFries, J. C. (1997). Nature, nurture, and cognitive development from 1 to 16 years: A parent–offspring adoption study. *Psychological Science, 8,* 442–447.

Plomin, R., Owen, M. J., & McGuffin, P. (1994, June 17). The genetic basis of complex human behaviors. *Science, 264,* 1733–1739.

Plomin, R., & Rende, R. (1990). Human behavioral genetics. *Annual Review of Psychology, 42,* 161–190.

Plotkin, H. C. (1993). *Darwin machines and the nature of knowledge.* Cambridge, MA: Harvard University Press.

Poffenberger, A. T. (1930). The development of men of science. *Journal of Social Psychology, 1,* 31–47.

Poincaré, H. (1921). *The foundations of science: Science and hypothesis, the value of science, science and method* (G. B. Halstead, Trans.). New York: Science Press.

Popper, K. (1959). *The logic of discovery.* New York: Basic Books.

Popper, K. (1979). *Objective knowledge: An evolutionary approach* (rev. ed.). Oxford, England: Clarendon.

Porter, A. L. (1977). Citation analysis: Queries and caveats. *Social Studies of Science, 7,* 257–267.

Porter, C. A., & Suedfeld, P. (1981). Integrative complexity in the correspondence of literary figures: Effects of personal and societal stress. *Journal of Personality and Social Psychology, 40,* 321–330.

Post, F. (1994). Creativity and psychopathology: A study of 291 world-famous men. *British Journal of Psychiatry, 165,* 22–34.

Post, F. (1996). Verbal creativity, depression and alcoholism: An investigation of one hundred American and British writers. *British Journal of Psychiatry, 168,* 545–555.

Prentky, R. A. (1980). *Creativity and psychopathology: A neurocognitive perspective.* New York: Praeger.

Pressey, S. L. (1960). Toward earlier creativity in psychology. *American Psychologist, 15,* 124–127.

Pressey, S. L. (1965). Two basic neglected psychoeducational problems. *American Psychologist, 20,* 391–395.

Pribram, K. H. (1986). The cognitive revolution and mind/brain issues. *American Psychologist, 41,* 507–520.

Price, D. (1963). *Little science, big science.* New York: Columbia University Press.

Price, D. (1965, July 9). Networks of scientific papers. *Science, 149,* 510–515.

Price, D. (1976). A general theory of bibliometric and other cumulative advantage processes. *Journal of the American Society for Information Science, 27,* 292–306.

Price, D. (1978). Ups and downs in the pulse of science and technology. In J. Gaston (Ed.), *The sociology of science* (pp. 162–171). San Francisco: Jossey-Bass.

Qin, Y., & Simon, H. A. (1990). Laboratory replication of scientific discovery processes. *Cognitive Science, 14,* 281–312.

Quételet, A. (1968). *A treatise on man and the development of his faculties* (reprint of 1842 Edinburgh translation of 1835 French original). New York: Franklin.

Rainoff, T. J. (1929). Wave-like fluctuations of creative productivity in the development of West-European physics in the eighteenth and nineteenth centuries. *Isis, 12,* 287–319.

Randall, J. H. (1940). *The making of the modern mind: A survey of the intellectual background of the present age* (rev. ed.). Boston: Houghton Mifflin.

Raphelson, A. C. (1982). The history course as the capstone of the psychology curriculum. *Journal of the History of the Behavioral Sciences, 18,* 279–285.

Raskin, E. A. (1936). Comparison of scientific and literary ability: A biographical study of eminent scientists and men of letters of the nineteenth century. *Journal of Abnormal and Social Psychology, 31,* 20–35.

Ray, A. J., Jr. (1971). Scientific eminence versus scientific notoriety. *American Psychologist, 26,* 666–667.

Redman, R. R. (Ed.). (1968). *The portable Voltaire.* New York: Viking.

Redner, S. (1998). How popular is your paper? An empirical study of the citation distribution. *European Physical Journal B, 4,* 131–134.

Ree, M. J., Earles, J. A., & Teachout, M. S. (1994). Predicting job performance: Not much more than *g. Journal of Applied Psychology, 79,* 518–524.

Reynolds, J. (1966). *Discourses on art.* New York: Collier. (Original work published 1769–1790)

Richards, R. J. (1981). Natural selection and other models in the historiography of science. In M. B. Brewer & B. E. Collins (Eds.), *Scientific inquiry and the social sciences* (pp. 37–78). San Francisco: Jossey-Bass.

Richards, R., Kinney, D. K., Lunde, I., Benet, M., & Merzel, A. P. C. (1988). Creativity in manic-depressives, cyclothymes, their normal relatives, and control subjects. *Journal of Abnormal Psychology, 97,* 281–288.

Riedel, R. G. (1974). The current status of the history and systems of psychology courses in American colleges and universities. *Journal of the History of the Behavioral Sciences, 10,* 410–412.

Robins, R. W., & Craik, K. H. (1994). A more appropriate test of the Kuhnian displacement thesis. *American Psychologist, 49*, 815–816.

Robins, R. W., Gosling, S. D., & Craik, K. H. (1998, July–August). Psychological science at the crossroads. *American Scientist, 86*, 310–313.

Robins, R. W., Gosling, S. D., & Craik, K. H. (1999). An empirical analysis of trends in psychology. *American Psychologist, 54*, 117–128.

Robins, R. W., Gosling, S. D., & Craik, K. H. (2000). Trends in psychology: An empirical issue. *American Psychologist, 55*, 276–277.

Robinson, D. E. (1986). *An intellectual history of psychology*. Madison: University of Wisconsin Press.

Robinson, W. S. (1950). Ecological correlations and the behavior of individuals. *American Sociological Review, 15*, 351–357.

Rodgers, R. C., & Maranto, C. L. (1989). Causal models of publishing productivity in psychology. *Journal of Applied Psychology, 74*, 636–649.

Rodman, H., & Mancini, J. A. (1981). The publishing patterns of eminent social scientists. *Sociology and Social Research, 65*, 381–389.

Roe, A. (1952, November). A psychologist examines 64 eminent scientists. *Scientific American, 187*(5), 21–25.

Roe, A. (1953a). *The making of a scientist*. New York: Dodd, Mead.

Roe, A. (1953b). A psychological study of eminent psychologists and anthropologists, and a comparison with biological and physical scientists. *Psychological Monographs, 67*(2, Whole No. 352).

Roe, A. (1965, October 15). Changes in scientific activities with age. *Science, 150*, 113–118.

Roe, A. (1972, May 26). Patterns of productivity of scientists. *Science, 176*, 940–941.

Roeckelein, J. E. (1972). Eponymy in psychology. *American Psychologist, 27*, 657–659.

Roeckelein, J. E. (1996a). Citation of laws and theories in textbooks across 112 years of psychology. *Psychological Reports, 79*, 979–998.

Roeckelein, J. E. (1996b). Contributions to the history of psychology: CIV. Eminence in psychology as measured by name counts and eponyms. *Psychological Reports, 78*, 242–253.

Roeckelein, J. E. (1996c). Gender differences in naming and eponymy in psychology. *Psychological Reports, 79*, 435–442.

Roeckelein, J. E. (1997). Psychology among the sciences: Comparisons of numbers of theories and laws cited in textbooks. *Psychological Reports, 80*, 131–141.

Rogers, C. R. (1954). Toward a theory of creativity. *ETC: A Review of General Semantics, 11*, 249–260.

Root-Bernstein, R. S., Bernstein, M., & Garnier, H. (1993). Identification of scientists making long-term, high-impact contributions, with notes on their methods of working. *Creativity Research Journal, 6*, 329–343.

Rosengren, K. E. (1985). Time and literary fame. *Poetics, 14,* 157–172.

Rosenthal, R. (1990). How are we doing in soft psychology? *American Psychologist, 45,* 775–777.

Rosenthal, R., & Rubin, D. B. (1979). A note on percent variance explained as a measure of the importance of effects. *Journal of Applied Social Psychology, 9,* 395–396.

Ross, D. (1969). The "Zeitgeist" and American psychology. *Journal of the History of the Behavioral Sciences, 5,* 256–262.

Rothenberg, A. (1983). Psychopathology and creative cognition: A comparison of hospitalized patients, Nobel laureates, and controls. *Archives of General Psychiatry, 40,* 937–942.

Rothenberg, A. (1987). Einstein, Bohr, and creative thinking in science. *History of Science, 25,* 147–166.

Rubenson, D. L. (1990). The accidental economist. *Creativity Research Journal, 3,* 125–129.

Rubenson, D. L., & Runco, M. A. (1992). The psychoeconomic approach to creativity. *New Ideas in Psychology, 10,* 131–147.

Rubin, Z. (1970). The birth order of birth-order researchers. *Developmental Psychology, 3,* 269–270.

Ruja, H. (1956). Productive psychologists. *American Psychologist, 11,* 148–149.

Runyan, W. M. (1982). *Life histories and psychobiography.* New York: Oxford University Press.

Rushton, J. P. (1984). Evaluating research eminence in psychology: The construct validity of citation counts. *Bulletin of the British Psychological Society, 37,* 33–36.

Rushton, J. P. (1990). Creativity, intelligence, and psychoticism. *Personality and Individual Differences, 11,* 1291–1298.

Rushton, J. P., Murray, H. G., & Paunonen, S. V. (1983). Personality, research creativity, and teaching effectiveness in university professors. *Scientometrics, 5,* 93–116.

Rushton, J. P., & Roediger, H. L. (1978). An evaluation of 80 psychology journals based on the *Science Citation Index. American Psychologist, 33,* 520–523.

Sales, S. M. (1972). Economic threat as a determinant of conversion rates in authoritarian and non-authoritarian churches. *Journal of Personality and Social Psychology, 23,* 420–428.

Sales, S. M. (1973). Threat as a factor in authoritarianism: An analysis of archival data. *Journal of Personality and Social Psychology, 28,* 44–57.

Sanford, R. N., Eichhorn, D. H., & Honzik, M. P. (1944). Harold E. Jones. *Journal of Consulting Psychology, 8,* 198.

Saugstad, P. (1965). *An inquiry into the foundations of psychology.* New York: Bedminster.

Scarr, S., & McCartney, K. (1983). How people make their own environments: A theory of genotype $\rightarrow$ environmental effects. *Child Development, 54,* 424–435.

Scarr, S., & Weber, B. L. R. (1978). The reliability of reviews for the *American Psychologist*. *American Psychologist, 33,* 935.

Schachter, S. (1963). Birth order, eminence, and higher education. *American Sociological Review, 28,* 757–768.

Schaefer, C. E., & Anastasi, A. (1968). A biographical inventory for identifying creativity in adolescent boys. *Journal of Applied Psychology, 58,* 42–48.

Schlipp, P. A. (Ed.). (1951). *Albert Einstein: Philosopher–scientist*. New York: Harper.

Schmookler, J. (1966). *Invention and economic growth*. Cambridge, MA: Harvard University Press.

Schneider, E. (1953). *Coleridge, opium, and Kubla Khan*. Chicago: University of Chicago Press.

Schneider, J. (1937). The cultural situation as a condition for the achievement of fame. *American Sociological Review, 2,* 480–491.

Schneider, L. (1964). Toward assessment of Sorokin's view of change. In G. K. Zollschan & W. Hirsch (Eds.), *Explorations in social change* (pp. 371–400). Boston: Houghton Mifflin.

Schooler, J. W., & Melcher, J. (1995). The ineffability of insight. In S. M. Smith, T. B. Ward, & R. A. Finke (Eds.), *The creative cognition approach* (pp. 97–133). Cambridge, MA: MIT Press.

Schubert, D. S. P., Wagner, M. E., & Schubert, H. J. P. (1977). Family constellation and creativity: Firstborn predominance among classical music composers. *Journal of Psychology, 95,* 147–149.

Schultz, D. P., & Schultz, S. E. (1987). *A history of modern psychology* (4th ed.). San Diego, CA: Harcourt Brace Jovanovich.

Schultz, D. P., & Schultz, S. E. (1992). *A history of modern psychology* (5th ed.). San Diego, CA: Harcourt Brace Jovanovich.

Scott, W. A. (1974). Interreferee agreement on some characteristics of manuscripts submitted to the *Journal of Personality and Social Psychology*. *American Psychologist, 29,* 698–702.

Sears, R. R. (1977). Sources of life satisfactions of the Terman gifted men. *American Psychologist, 32,* 119–128.

Seelig, C. (1958). *Albert Einstein: A documentary biography* (M. Savill, Trans.). London: Staples.

Segal, S. M., Busse, T. V., & Mansfield, R. S. (1980). The relationship of scientific creativity in the biological sciences to predoctoral accomplishments and experiences. *American Educational Research Journal, 17,* 491–502.

Seneca. (1932). On tranquillity of mind. In *Moral essays* (J. W. Basore, Trans., Vol. 2, pp. 203–285). Cambridge, MA: Harvard University Press.

Serebriakoff, V. (1985). *Mensa: The society for the highly intelligent*. London: Constable.

Shadish, W. R., Jr. (1989). The perception and evaluation of quality in science. In B. Gholson, W. R. Shadish, Jr., R. A. Neimeyer, & A. C. Houts (Eds.), *The psychology of science: Contributions to metascience* (pp. 383–426). Cambridge, England: Cambridge University Press.

Shadish, W. R., Jr., & Fuller, S. (Eds.). (1994). *The social psychology of science*. New York: Guilford Press.

Shapiro, G. (1986). *A skeleton in the darkroom: Stories of serendipity in science*. San Francisco: Harper & Row.

Sheehy, N., Chapman, A. J., & Conroy, W. (Eds.). (1997). *Biographical dictionary of psychology*. London: Routledge.

Sheldon, J. C. (1979). Hierarchical cybernets: A model for the dynamics of high level learning and cultural change. *Cybernetica, 22*, 179–202.

Sheldon, J. C. (1980). A cybernetic theory of physical science professions: The causes of periodic normal and revolutionary science between 1000 and 1870 AD. *Scientometrics, 2*, 147–167.

Shields, S. A. (1975). Functionalism, Darwinism, and the psychology of women: A study in social myth. *American Psychologist, 30*, 739–754.

Shields, S. A. (1982). The variability hypothesis: The history of a biological model of sex differences in intelligence. *Signs, 7*, 769–797.

Shin, K. E., & Putnam, R. H. (1982). Age and academic–professional honors. *Journal of Gerontology, 37*, 200–229.

Shockley, W. (1957). On the statistics of individual variations of productivity in research laboratories. *Proceedings of the Institute of Radio Engineers, 45*, 279–290.

Shrader, D. (1980). The evolutionary development of science. *Review of Metaphysics, 34*, 273–296.

Shrager, J., & Langley, P. (Eds.). (1990). *Computational models of scientific discovery and theory formation*. San Mateo, CA: Kaufmann.

Shurkin, J. N. (1992). *Terman's kids: The groundbreaking study of how the gifted grow up*. Boston: Little, Brown.

Silverman, S. M. (1974). Parental loss and scientists. *Science Studies, 4*, 259–264.

Simon, H. A. (1954). Productivity among American psychologists: An explanation. *American Psychologist, 9*, 804–805.

Simon, H. A. (1955). On a class of skew distribution functions. *Biometrika, 42*, 425–440.

Simon, H. A. (1973). Does scientific discovery have a logic? *Philosophy of Science, 40*, 471–480.

Simon, H. A. (1977). *Models of discovery: And other topics in the methods of science*. Boston, Reidel.

Simon, H. A. (1986). What we know about the creative process. In R. L. Kuhn (Ed.), *Frontiers in creative and innovative management* (pp. 3–20). Cambridge, MA: Ballinger.

Simon, H. A., & Chase, W. G. (1973). Skill in chess. *American Scientist, 61*, 394–403.

Simon, J. L., & Sullivan, R. J. (1989). Population size, knowledge stock, and other determinants of agricultural publication and patenting: England, 1541–1850. *Explorations in Economic History, 26*, 21–44.

Simon, R. J. (1974). The work habits of eminent scientists. *Sociology of Work and Occupations, 1*, 327–335.

Simonton, D. K. (1974). *The social psychology of creativity: An archival data analysis.* Unpublished doctoral dissertation, Harvard University.

Simonton, D. K. (1975a). Age and literary creativity: A cross-cultural and transhistorical survey. *Journal of Cross-Cultural Psychology, 6*, 259–277.

Simonton, D. K. (1975b). Interdisciplinary creativity over historical time: A correlational analysis of generational fluctuations. *Social Behavior and Personality, 3*, 181–188.

Simonton, D. K. (1975c). Invention and discovery among the sciences: A p-technique factor analysis. *Journal of Vocational Behavior, 7*, 275–281.

Simonton, D. K. (1975d). Sociocultural context of individual creativity: A transhistorical time-series analysis. *Journal of Personality and Social Psychology, 32*, 1119–1133.

Simonton, D. K. (1976a). Biographical determinants of achieved eminence: A multivariate approach to the Cox data. *Journal of Personality and Social Psychology, 33*, 218–226.

Simonton, D. K. (1976b). The causal relation between war and scientific discovery: An exploratory cross-national analysis. *Journal of Cross-Cultural Psychology, 7*, 133–144.

Simonton, D. K. (1976c). Do Sorokin's data support his theory?: A study of generational fluctuations in philosophical beliefs. *Journal for the Scientific Study of Religion, 15*, 187–198.

Simonton, D. K. (1976d). Ideological diversity and creativity: A re-evaluation of a hypothesis. *Social Behavior and Personality, 4*, 203–207.

Simonton, D. K. (1976e). Interdisciplinary and military determinants of scientific productivity: A cross-lagged correlation analysis. *Journal of Vocational Behavior, 9*, 53–62.

Simonton, D. K. (1976f). Philosophical eminence, beliefs, and Zeitgeist: An individual–generational analysis. *Journal of Personality and Social Psychology, 34*, 630–640.

Simonton, D. K. (1976g). The sociopolitical context of philosophical beliefs: A transhistorical causal analysis. *Social Forces, 54*, 513–523.

Simonton, D. K. (1977a). Creative productivity, age, and stress: A biographical time-series analysis of 10 classical composers. *Journal of Personality and Social Psychology, 35*, 791–804.

Simonton, D. K. (1977b). Eminence, creativity, and geographic marginality: A recursive structural equation model. *Journal of Personality and Social Psychology, 35*, 805–816.

Simonton, D. K. (1977c). Women's fashions and war: A quantitative comment. *Social Behavior and Personality, 5*, 285–288.

Simonton, D. K. (1978a). Independent discovery in science and technology: A closer look at the Poisson distribution. *Social Studies of Science, 8*, 521–532.

Simonton, D. K. (1978b). Intergenerational stimulation, reaction, and polarization: A causal analysis of intellectual history. *Social Behavior and Personality, 6,* 247–251.

Simonton, D. K. (1979). Multiple discovery and invention: Zeitgeist, genius, or chance? *Journal of Personality and Social Psychology, 37,* 1603–1616.

Simonton, D. K. (1980a). Techno-scientific activity and war: A yearly time-series analysis, 1500–1903 A.D. *Scientometrics, 2,* 251–255.

Simonton, D. K. (1980b). Thematic fame and melodic originality in classical music: A multivariate computer-content analysis. *Journal of Personality, 48,* 206–219.

Simonton, D. K. (1980c). Thematic fame, melodic originality, and musical zeitgeist: A biographical and transhistorical content analysis. *Journal of Personality and Social Psychology, 38,* 972–983.

Simonton, D. K. (1981). Creativity in Western civilization: Extrinsic and intrinsic causes. *American Anthropologist, 83,* 628–630.

Simonton, D. K. (1983a). Dramatic greatness and content: A quantitative study of eighty-one Athenian and Shakespearean plays. *Empirical Studies of the Arts, 1,* 109–123.

Simonton, D. K. (1983b). Formal education, eminence, and dogmatism: The curvilinear relationship. *Journal of Creative Behavior, 17,* 149–162.

Simonton, D. K. (1983c). Intergenerational transfer of individual differences in hereditary monarchs: Genes, role-modeling, cohort, or sociocultural effects? *Journal of Personality and Social Psychology, 44,* 354–364.

Simonton, D. K. (1984a). Artistic creativity and interpersonal relationships across and within generations. *Journal of Personality and Social Psychology, 46,* 1273–1286.

Simonton, D. K. (1984b). Creative productivity and age: A mathematical model based on a two-step cognitive process. *Developmental Review, 4,* 77–111.

Simonton, D. K. (1984c). Generational time-series analysis: A paradigm for studying sociocultural influences. In K. Gergen & M. Gergen (Eds.), *Historical social psychology* (pp. 141–155). Hillsdale, NJ: Erlbaum.

Simonton, D. K. (1984d). *Genius, creativity, and leadership: Historiometric inquiries.* Cambridge, MA: Harvard University Press.

Simonton, D. K. (1984e). Is the marginality effect all that marginal? *Social Studies of Science, 14,* 621–622.

Simonton, D. K. (1984f). Leaders as eponyms: Individual and situational determinants of monarchal eminence. *Journal of Personality, 52,* 1–21.

Simonton, D. K. (1984g). Scientific eminence historical and contemporary: A measurement assessment. *Scientometrics, 6,* 169–182.

Simonton, D. K. (1985a). Intelligence and personal influence in groups: Four nonlinear models. *Psychological Review, 92,* 532–547.

Simonton, D. K. (1985b). Quality, quantity, and age: The careers of 10 distinguished psychologists. *International Journal of Aging and Human Development, 21,* 241–254.

Simonton, D. K. (1986a). Biographical typicality, eminence, and achievement style. *Journal of Creative Behavior, 20*, 14–22.

Simonton, D. K. (1986b). Dispositional attributions of (presidential) leadership: An experimental simulation of historiometric results. *Journal of Experimental Social Psychology, 22*, 389–418.

Simonton, D. K. (1986c). Multiple discovery: Some Monte Carlo simulations and Gedanken experiments. *Scientometrics, 9*, 269–280.

Simonton, D. K. (1986d). Multiples, Poisson distributions, and chance: An analysis of the Brannigan–Wanner model. *Scientometrics, 9*, 127–137.

Simonton, D. K. (1986e). Popularity, content, and context in 37 Shakespeare plays. *Poetics, 15*, 493–510.

Simonton, D. K. (1986f). Presidential personality: Biographical use of the Gough Adjective Check List. *Journal of Personality and Social Psychology, 51*, 149–160.

Simonton, D. K. (1986g). Stochastic models of multiple discovery. *Czechoslovak Journal of Physics, B36*, 138–141.

Simonton, D. K. (1987a). Developmental antecedents of achieved eminence. *Annals of Child Development, 5*, 131–169.

Simonton, D. K. (1987b). Multiples, chance, genius, creativity, and Zeitgeist. In D. N. Jackson & J. P. Rushton (Eds.), *Scientific excellence: Origins and assessment* (pp. 98–128). Beverly Hills, CA: Sage.

Simonton, D. K. (1987c). Presidential inflexibility and veto behavior: Two individual–situational interactions. *Journal of Personality, 55*, 1–18.

Simonton, D. K. (1987d). *Why presidents succeed: A political psychology of leadership.* New Haven, CT: Yale University Press.

Simonton, D. K. (1988a). Age and outstanding achievement: What do we know after a century of research? *Psychological Bulletin, 104*, 251–267.

Simonton, D. K. (1988b). Galtonian genius, Kroeberian configurations, and emulation: A generational time-series analysis of Chinese civilization. *Journal of Personality and Social Psychology, 55*, 230–238.

Simonton, D. K. (1988c). Presidential style: Personality, biography, and performance. *Journal of Personality and Social Psychology, 55*, 928–936.

Simonton, D. K. (1988d). *Scientific genius: A psychology of science.* Cambridge, England: Cambridge University Press.

Simonton, D. K. (1989a). Age and creative productivity: Nonlinear estimation of an information-processing model. *International Journal of Aging and Human Development, 29*, 23–37.

Simonton, D. K. (1989b). Shakespeare's sonnets: A case of and for single-case historiometry. *Journal of Personality, 57*, 695–721.

Simonton, D. K. (1989c). The swan-song phenomenon: Last-works effects for 172 classical composers. *Psychology and Aging, 4*, 42–47.

Simonton, D. K. (1990a). Creativity and wisdom in aging. In J. E. Birren & K. W. Schaie (Eds.), *Handbook of the psychology of aging* (3rd ed., pp. 320–329). New York: Academic Press.

Simonton, D. K. (1990b). History, chemistry, psychology, and genius: An intellectual autobiography of historiometry. In M. Runco & R. Albert (Eds.), *Theories of creativity* (pp. 92–115). Newbury Park, CA: Sage.

Simonton, D. K. (1990c). Lexical choices and aesthetic success: A computer content analysis of 154 Shakespeare sonnets. *Computers and the Humanities, 24,* 251–264.

Simonton, D. K. (1990d). *Psychology, science, and history: An introduction to historiometry.* New Haven, CT: Yale University Press.

Simonton, D. K. (1991a). Career landmarks in science: Individual differences and interdisciplinary contrasts. *Developmental Psychology, 27,* 119–130.

Simonton, D. K. (1991b). Emergence and realization of genius: The lives and works of 120 classical composers. *Journal of Personality and Social Psychology, 61,* 829–840.

Simonton, D. K. (1991c). Latent-variable models of posthumous reputation: A quest for Galton's G. *Journal of Personality and Social Psychology, 60,* 607–619.

Simonton, D. K. (1991d). Personality correlates of exceptional personal influence: A note on Thorndike's (1950) creators and leaders. *Creativity Research Journal, 4,* 67–78.

Simonton, D. K. (1992a). Gender and genius in Japan: Feminine eminence in masculine culture. *Sex Roles, 27,* 101–119.

Simonton, D. K. (1992b). Leaders of American psychology, 1879–1967: Career development, creative output, and professional achievement. *Journal of Personality and Social Psychology, 62,* 5–17.

Simonton, D. K. (1992c). The social context of career success and course for 2,026 scientists and inventors. *Personality and Social Psychology Bulletin, 18,* 452–463.

Simonton, D. K. (1993). Putting the best leaders in the White House: Personality, policy, and performance. *Political Psychology, 14,* 537–548.

Simonton, D. K. (1994a). *Greatness: Who makes history and why.* New York: Guilford Press.

Simonton, D. K. (1994b). Scientific eminence, the history of psychology, and term paper topics: A metascience approach. *Teaching of Psychology, 21,* 169–171.

Simonton, D. K. (1995a). Behavioral laws in histories of psychology: Psychological science, metascience, and the psychology of science. *Psychological Inquiries, 6,* 89–114.

Simonton, D. K. (1995b). Exceptional personal influence: An integrative paradigm. *Creativity Research Journal, 8,* 371–376.

Simonton, D. K. (1995c). Personality and intellectual predictors of leadership. In D. H. Saklofske & M. Zeidner (Eds.), *International handbook of personality and intelligence* (pp. 739–757). New York: Plenum.

Simonton, D. K. (1995d). Spread-eagle over the disciplinary chasm. *Psychological Inquiry, 6,* 135–141.

Simonton, D. K. (1996a). Creative expertise: A life-span developmental perspective. In K. A. Ericsson (Ed.), *The road to expert performance: Empirical evidence from the arts and sciences, sports, and games* (pp. 227–253). Mahwah, NJ: Erlbaum.

Simonton, D. K. (1996b). Individual genius and cultural configurations: The case of Japanese civilization. *Journal of Cross-Cultural Psychology, 27,* 354–375.

Simonton, D. K. (1996c). Presidents' wives and First Ladies: On achieving eminence within a traditional gender role. *Sex Roles, 35,* 309–336.

Simonton, D. K. (1997a). Achievement domain and life expectancies in Japanese civilization. *International Journal of Aging and Human Development, 44,* 103–114.

Simonton, D. K. (1997b). Creative productivity: A predictive and explanatory model of career trajectories and landmarks. *Psychological Review, 104,* 66–89.

Simonton, D. K. (1997c). Evolution, personality, and history [Review of *Born to rebel: Birth order, family dynamics, and creative lives* by F. Sulloway]. *American Journal of Psychology, 110,* 457–461.

Simonton, D. K. (1997d). Foreign influence and national achievement: The impact of open milieus on Japanese civilization. *Journal of Personality and Social Psychology, 72,* 86–94.

Simonton, D. K. (1998a). Achieved eminence in minority and majority cultures: Convergence versus divergence in the assessments of 294 African Americans. *Journal of Personality and Social Psychology, 74,* 804–817.

Simonton, D. K. (1998b). Fickle fashion versus immortal fame: Transhistorical assessments of creative products in the opera house. *Journal of Personality and Social Psychology, 75,* 198–210.

Simonton, D. K. (1999a). Creativity and genius. In L. A. Pervin & O. John (Eds.), *Handbook of personality theory and research* (2nd ed., pp. 629–652). New York: Guilford Press.

Simonton, D. K. (1999b). *Origins of genius: Darwinian perspectives on creativity.* New York: Oxford University Press.

Simonton, D. K. (1999c). Significant samples: The psychological study of eminent individuals. *Psychological Methods, 4,* 425–451.

Simonton, D. K. (1999d). Talent and its development: An emergenic and epigenetic model. *Psychological Review, 106,* 435–457.

Simonton, D. K. (2000a). Creative development as acquired expertise: Theoretical issues and an empirical test. *Developmental Review, 20,* 283–318.

Simonton, D. K. (2000b). Methodological and theoretical orientation and the long-term disciplinary impact of 54 eminent psychologists. *Review of General Psychology, 4,* 1–13.

Simonton, D. K. (in press). Creative cultures, nations, and civilizations: Strategies and results. In P. B. Paulus & B. A. Nijstad (Eds.), *Group creativity.* New York: Oxford University Press.

Simonton, D. K., Taylor, K., & Cassandro, V. (1998). The creative genius of William Shakespeare: Historiometric analyses of his plays and sonnets. In A. Steptoe (Ed.), *Genius and the mind: Studies of creativity and temperament in the historical record* (pp. 167–192). New York: Oxford University Press.

Skinner, B. F. (1938). *The behavior of organisms: An experimental analysis.* New York: Appleton-Century.

Skinner, B. F. (1959). A case study in scientific method. In S. Koch (Ed.), *Psychology: A study of a science* (Vol. 2, pp. 359–379). New York: McGraw-Hill.

Skinner, B. F. (1961). *Cumulative record* (rev. ed.). NY: Appleton-Century-Crofts.

Skinner, B. F. (1987). Whatever happened to psychology as the science of behavior? *American Psychologist, 43*, 824–825.

Skinner, B. F. (1990). Can psychology be a science of mind? *American Psychologist, 45*, 1206–1210.

Smart, J. C., & Bayer, A. E. (1986). Author collaboration and impact: A note on citation rates of single and multiple authored articles. *Scientometrics, 10*, 297–305.

Smith, A. H. (1982). Different approaches for teaching the history of psychology course. *Teaching of Psychology, 9*, 180–182.

Smith, J. D. (1985). *Minds made feeble: The myth and legacy of the Kallikaks*. Rockville, MD: Aspen Systems.

Smith, S. (1983). *Ideas of the great psychologists*. Cambridge, MA: Barnes & Noble.

Snow, C. P. (1960). *The two cultures and the scientific revolution*. New York: Cambridge University Press.

Social science citation index. (1975). Philadelphia: Institute for Scientific Information.

Social science citation index five-year cumulation 1976–1980. (1983). Philadelphia: Institute for Scientific Information.

Social science citation index five-year cumulation 1981–1985. (1987). Philadelphia: Institute for Scientific Information.

Social science citation index five-year cumulation 1986–1990. (1992). Philadelphia: Institute for Scientific Information.

Sokal, M. M. (1971). The unpublished autobiography of James McKeen Cattell. *American Psychologist, 26*, 626–635.

Sorokin, P. A. (1937–1941). *Social and cultural dynamics* (Vols. 1–4). New York: American Book.

Sorokin, P. A. (1963). *A long journey: The autobiography of Pitirim A. Sorokin*. New Haven, CT: College and University Press.

Sorokin, P. A. (1969). *Society, culture, and personality*. New York: Cooper Square. (Original work published 1947)

Sorokin, P. A., & Merton, R. K. (1935). The course of Arabian intellectual development, 700–1300 A.D. *Isis, 22*, 516–524.

Spearman, C. (1927). *The abilities of man: Their nature and measurement*. New York: Macmillan.

Spencer, H. (1904). *An autobiography* (Vol. 1). New York: Appleton.

Sperry, R. W. (1993). The impact and promise of the cognitive revolution. *American Psychologist, 48*, 878–885.

Sproul, K. (Ed.). (1953). *The shorter Bartlett's familiar quotations*. Garden City, NY: Permabooks.

Stagner, R. (1988). *A history of psychological theories*. New York: Macmillan.

Stannard, D. E. (1980). *Shrinking history: On Freud and the failure of psychohistory*. New York: Oxford University Press.

Stein, E., & Lipton, P. (1989). Where guesses come from: Evolutionary epistemology and the anomaly of guided vision. *Biology & Philosophy, 4*, 33–56.

Steinberg, B. S. (2001). The making of female presidents and prime ministers: The impact of birth order, sex of siblings, and father–daughter dynamics. *Political Psychology, 22*, 89–110.

Stent, G. S. (1972). Prematurity and uniqueness in scientific discovery. *Scientific American, 227*, 84–93.

Stephan, P. E., & Levin, S. G. (1991). Inequality and scientific performance: Adjustment for attribution and journal impact. *Social Studies of Science, 21*, 351–368.

Stephan, P. E., & Levin, S. G. (1992). *Striking the mother lode in science: The importance of age, place, and time*. New York: Oxford University Press.

Stephan, P. E., & Levin, S. G. (1993). Age and the Nobel prize revisited. *Scientometrics, 28*, 387–399.

Sternberg, R. J. (1989). Computational models of scientific discovery: Do they compute? [Review of *Scientific discovery: Computational explorations of the creative process*]. *Contemporary Psychology, 34*, 895–897.

Sternberg, R. J. (1998). A propulsion model of types of creative contributions. *Review of General Psychology, 3*, 83–100.

Sternberg, R. J., & Gordeeva, T. (1996). The anatomy of impact: What makes an article influential? *Psychological Science, 7*, 69–75.

Sternberg, R. J., & Lubart, T. I. (1991). An investment theory of creativity and its development. *Human Development, 34*, 1–31.

Sternberg, R. J., & Lubart, T. I. (1995). *Defying the crowd: Cultivating creativity in a culture of conformity*. New York: Free Press.

Stevens, G., & Gardner, S. (1985). Psychology of the scientist: LIV. Permission to excell: A preliminary report of influences on eminent women psychologists. *Psychological Reports, 57*, 1023–1026.

Stevens, S. S. (1939). Psychology and the science of science. *Psychological Bulletin, 36*, 221–263.

Stewart, J. A. (1983). Achievement and ascriptive processes in the recognition of scientific articles. *Social Forces, 62*, 166–189.

Stewart, J. A. (1986). Drifting continents and colliding interests: A quantitative application of the interests perspective. *Social Studies of Science, 16*, 261–279.

Stewart, L. H. (1977). Birth order and political leadership. In M. G. Hermann (Ed.), *The psychological examination of political leaders* (pp. 205–236). New York: Free Press.

Stewart, L. H. (1991). The world cycle of leadership. *Journal of Analytical Psychology, 36*, 449–459.

Stocking, G. W. (1965). On the limits of "presentism" and "historicism" in the historiography of the behavioral sciences. *Journal of the History of the Behavioral Sciences, 1*, 211–218.

Stohs, J. H. (1992). Career patterns and family status of women and men artists. *Career Development Quarterly, 40*, 223–233.

Suedfeld, P. (1985). APA presidential addresses: The relation of integrative complexity to historical, professional, and personal factors. *Journal of Personality and Social Psychology, 47*, 848–852.

Suedfeld, P., & Piedrahita, L. E. (1984). Intimations of mortality: Integrative simplification as a predictor of death. *Journal of Personality and Social Psychology, 47*, 848–852.

Suedfeld, P., Tetlock, P. E., & Streufert, S. (1992). Conceptual/integrative complexity. In C. P. Smith (Ed.), *Motivation and personality: Handbook of thematic content analysis* (pp. 393–400). Cambridge, England: Cambridge University Press.

Suler, J. R. (1980). Primary process thinking and creativity. *Psychological Bulletin, 88*, 144–165.

Sulloway, F. J. (1979). *Freud, biologist of the mind: Beyond the psychoanalytic legend.* New York: Basic Books.

Sulloway, F. J. (1996). *Born to rebel: Birth order, family dynamics, and creative lives.* New York: Pantheon.

Suls, J., & Fletcher, B. (1983). Social comparison in the social and physical sciences: An archival study. *Journal of Personality and Social Psychology, 44*, 575–580.

Szabo, A. T. (1985). Alphonse de Candolle's early scientometrics (1883, 1885) with references to recent trends in the field (1978–1983). *Scientometrics, 8*, 13–33.

Taagepera, R. (1979). People, skills, and resources: An interaction model for world population growth. *Technological Forecasting and Social Change, 13*, 13–30.

Taylor, C. W., & Ellison, R. L. (1967, March 3). Biographical predictors of scientific performance. *Science, 155*, 1075–1080.

Taylor, M. S., Locke, E. A., Lee, C., & Gist, M. E. (1984). Type A behavior and faculty research productivity: What are the mechanisms? *Organizational Behavior and Human Performance, 34*, 402–418.

Teigen, K. H. (1984). A note on the origin of the term "nature and nuture": Not Shakespeare and Galton, but Mulcaster. *Journal of the History of the Behavioral Sciences, 20*, 363–364.

Terman, L. M. (1917). The intelligence quotient of Francis Galton in childhood. *American Journal of Psychology, 28*, 209–215.

Terman, L. M. (1925). *Mental and physical traits of a thousand gifted children.* Stanford, CA: Stanford University Press.

Terman, L. M. (1954). Scientists and nonscientists in a group of 800 gifted men. *Psychological Monographs: General and Applied, 68*(7, Whole No. 378), 1–44.

Terman, L. M., & Oden, M. H. (1947). *The gifted child grows up.* Stanford, CA: Stanford University Press.

Terman, L. M., & Oden, M. H. (1959). *The gifted group at mid-life*. Stanford, CA: Stanford University Press.

Terry, W. S. (1989). Birth order and prominence in the history of psychology. *Psychological Record, 39*, 333–337.

Tesser, A. (1993). The importance of heritability in psychological research: The case of attitudes. *Psychological Review, 100*, 129–142.

Thagard, P. (1992). *Conceptual revolutions*. Princeton, NJ: Princeton University Press.

Thomson, R. (1968). *The Pelican history of psychology*. Harmondsworth, England: Penguin Books.

Thoreau, H. D. (1942). *Walden* (G. H. Haight, Ed.). New York: Black. (Original work published 1845)

Thorndike, E. L. (1921). Measurement in education. *Teachers College Record, 22*, 371–379.

Thorndike, E. L. (1936). The relation between intellect and morality in rulers. *American Journal of Sociology, 42*, 321–334.

Thorndike, E. L. (1950). Traits of personality and their intercorrelations as shown in biographies. *Journal of Educational Psychology, 41*, 193–216.

Thorndike, R. L. (1991). Edward L. Thorndike: A professional and personal appreciation. In G. A. Kimble, M. Wertheimer, & C. L. White (Eds.), *Portraits of pioneers in psychology* (pp. 138–151). Hillsdale, NJ: Erlbaum.

Thorne, B. M., & Henley, T. B. (1997). *Connections in the history and systems of psychology*. Boston: Houghton Mifflin.

Thurstone, L. L. (1938). *Primary mental abilities*. Chicago: University of Chicago Press.

Thyer, B. A. (1991). The enduring intellectual legacy of B. F. Skinner: A citation count from 1966–1989. *Behavior Analyst, 14*, 73–75.

Ting, S.-S. (1986). *The social psychology of Chinese literary creativity: An archival data analysis*. Unpublished doctoral dissertation, University of California, Davis.

Tomlinson-Keasey, C. (1990). The working lives of Terman's gifted women. In H. Y. Grossman & N. L. Chester (Eds.), *The experience and meaning of work in women's lives* (pp. 213–239). Hillsdale, NJ: Erlbaum.

Toulmin, S. (1981). Evolution, adaptation, and human understanding. In M. B. Brewer & B. E. Collins (Eds.), *Scientific inquiry and the social sciences* (pp. 18–36). San Francisco: Jossey-Bass.

Toynbee, A. J. (1946). *A study of history* (2 vols., abridged by D. C. Somervell). New York: Oxford University Press.

Trimble, T. (1986). Death comes at the end—Effects of cessation of personal influence upon rates of citation of astronomical papers. *Czechoslovak Journal of Physics, B36*, 175–179.

Turner, S. P., & Chubin, D. E. (1976). Another appraisal of Ortega, the Coles, and science policy: The Ecclesiastes hypothesis. *Social Science Information, 15*, 657–662.

Turner, S. P., & Chubin, D. E. (1979). Chance and eminence in science: Ecclesiastes II. *Social Science Information, 18*, 437–449.

Tweney, R. D. (1989). A framework for the cognitive psychology of science. In B. Gholson, W. R. Shadish, Jr., R. A. Neimeyer, & A. C. Houts (Eds.), *The psychology of science: Contributions to metascience* (pp. 342–366). Cambridge, England: Cambridge University Press.

Tweney, R. D. (1990). Five questions for computationalists. In J. Shrager & P. Langley (Eds.), *Computational models of scientific discovery and theory information* (pp. 471–484). San Mateo, CA: Kaufmann.

Tweney, R. D. (1999). Toward a cognitive psychology of science: Recent research and its implications. *Current Directions in Psychological Science, 7,* 150–154.

Tweney, R. D., Doherty, M. E., & Mynatt, C. R. (Eds.). (1981). *On scientific thinking.* New York: Columbia University Press.

Vance, F. L., & MacPhail, S. L. (1964). APA membership trends and fields of specialization of psychologists earning doctoral degrees between 1959 and 1962. *American Psychologist, 9,* 654–658.

Van Zelst, R. H., & Kerr, W. A. (1951). Some correlates of technical and scientific productivity. *Journal of Abnormal and Social Psychology, 46,* 470–475.

Vasari, G. (1968). *Lives of the painters, sculptors, and architects* (A. B. Hinds, Trans.; W. Gaunt, Rev.; E. Fuller, Ed.). New York: Dell. (Original work published ca. 1550)

Veblen, T. (1919). The intellectual preeminence of Jews in modern Europe. *Political Science Quarterly, 34,* 33–42.

Viney, W., & King, D. B. (1998). *A history of psychology: Ideas and content* (2nd ed.). Boston: Allyn & Bacon.

Visher, S. S. (1947a). *Scientists starred, 1903–1943, in "American men of science": A study of collegiate and doctoral training, birthplace, distribution, backgrounds, and developmental influences.* Baltimore: Johns Hopkins University Press.

Visher, S. S. (1947b, Autumn). Starred scientists: A study of their ages. *American Scientist, 35,* 543, 570, 572, 574, 576, 578, 580.

Voeks, V. W. (1962). Publications and teaching effectiveness: A search for some relationship. *Journal of Higher Education, 33,* 212–218.

Wainer, H. (1976). Estimating coefficients in linear models: It don't make no nevermind. *Psychological Bulletin, 83,* 213–217.

Walberg, H. J., Rasher, S. P., & Hase, K. (1978). IQ correlates with high eminence. *Gifted Child Quarterly, 22,* 196–200.

Walberg, H. J., Rasher, S. P., & Parkerson, J. (1980). Childhood and eminence. *Journal of Creative Behavior, 13,* 225–231.

Walberg, H. J., Strykowski, B. F., Rovai, E., & Hung, S. S. (1984). Exceptional performance. *Review of Educational Research, 54,* 87–112.

Wallace, I., Wallace, A., Wallechinsky, D., & Wallace, S. (1981). *The intimate sex lives of famous people.* New York: Delacorte.

Wallas, G. (1926). *The art of thought.* New York: Harcourt, Brace.

Waller, N. G., Bouchard, T. J., Jr., Lykken, D. T., Tellegen, A., & Blacker, D. M. (1993). Creativity, heritability, familiality: Which word does not belong? *Psychological Inquiry, 4*, 235–237.

Waller, N. G., Kojetin, B. A., Bouchard, T. J., Jr., Lykken, D. T., & Tellegen, A. (1990). Genetic and environmental influences on religious interests, attitudes, and values: A study of twins reared apart and together. *Psychological Science, 1*, 138–142.

Waller, N. G., & Shaver, P. R. (1994). The importance of nongenetic influences on romantic love styles: A twin-family study. *Psychological Science, 5*, 268–274.

Walters, J., & Gardner, H. (1986). The crystallizing experience: Discovering an intellectual gift. In R. J. Sternberg & J. E. Davidson (Eds.), *Conceptions of giftedness* (pp. 306–331). New York: Cambridge University Press.

Ware, M. E., & Johnson, D. E. (Eds.). (2000). *Handbook of demonstrations and activities in the teaching of psychology* (2nd ed., Vol. 1). Mahwah, NJ: Erlbaum.

Watson, J. B. (1936). John Broadus Watson. In C. Murchison (Ed.), *A history of psychology in autobiography* (Vol. 3, pp. 271–281). Worcester, MA: Clark University Press.

Watson, J. B. (1970). *Behaviorism.* New York: Norton Library. (Original work published 1924)

Watson, R. I., Sr. (1963). *The great psychologists: From Aristotle to Freud.* Philadelphia: Lippincott.

Watson, R. I., Sr. (1974). *Eminent contributors to psychology* (Vol. 1). New York: Springer.

Watson, R. I., Sr., & Evans, R. B. (1991). *The great psychologists: A history of psychological thought* (5th ed.). New York: HarperCollins.

Watson, R. I., Sr., & Merrifield, M. (1973). Characteristics of individuals eminent in psychology in temporal perspective: I. *Journal of the History of the Behavioral Sciences, 9*, 339–359.

Webster, S., & Coleman, S. R. (1992). Contributions to the history of psychology: LXXXVI. Hull and his critics: The reception of Clark L. Hull's behavior theory, 1943–1960. *Psychological Reports, 70*, 1063–1071.

Webster's biographical dictionary. (1976). Springfield, MA: Merriam.

Wechsler, D. (1955). *Manual for the Wechsler adult intelligence scale.* New York: Psychological Corporation.

Weisberg, R. W. (1994). Genius and madness? A quasi-experimental test of the hypothesis that manic-depression increases creativity. *Psychological Science, 5*, 361–367.

Welsh, G. S. (1975). Adjective Check List descriptions of Freud and Jung. *Journal of Personality Assessment, 39*, 160–168.

Wertheimer, M. (1982). *Productive thinking* (M. Wertheimer, Ed.). Chicago: University of Chicago Press. (Original work published 1945)

Wertheimer, M. (1987). *A brief history of psychology* (3rd ed.). New York: Holt, Rinehart & Winston.

West, S. S. (1960). Sibling configurations of scientists. *American Journal of Sociology,* 66, 268–274.

West, S. S. (1961). Class origin of scientists. *Sociometry, 24,* 251–269.

Whaples, R. (1991). A quantitative history of the *Journal of Economic History* and the cliometric revolution. *Journal of Economic History, 51,* 289–301.

White, K. G., & White, M. J. (1978). On the relation between productivity and impact. *Australian Psychologist, 13,* 369–374.

White, L. (1949). *The science of culture.* New York: Farrar, Straus.

White, M. J., & White, K. G. (1977). Citation analysis of psychology journals. *American Psychologist, 32,* 301–305.

White, R. K. (1931). The versatility of genius. *Journal of Social Psychology, 2,* 460–489.

Whitehead, A. N. (1929). *Process and reality: An essay in cosmology.* New York: Macmillan.

Whittaker, J. (1989). Creativity and conformity in science: Titles, keywords, and co-word analysis. *Social Studies of Science, 19,* 473–496.

Who said what when: A chronological dictionary of quotations. (1991). New York: Hippocrene Books.

Wilson, T. D., DePaulo, B. M., Mook, D. G., & Klaaren, K. J. (1993). Scientists' evaluations of research: The biasing effects of the importance of the topic. *Psychological Science, 4,* 322–325.

Winer, B. J. (1962). *Statistical principles in experimental design.* New York: McGraw-Hill.

Winter, D. G. (1987). Leader appeal, leader performance, and the motive profiles of leaders and followers: A study of American presidents and elections. *Journal of Personality and Social Psychology, 52,* 196–202.

Wispé, L. G. (1963, September 27). Traits of eminent American psychologists. *Science, 141,* 1256–1261.

Wispé, L. G. (1965). Some social and psychological correlates of eminence in psychology. *Journal of the History of the Behavioral Sciences, 7,* 88–98.

Wispé, L. G., & Parloff, M. B. (1965). Impact of psychotherapy on the productivity of psychologists. *Journal of Abnormal Psychology, 70,* 188–193.

Wispé, L. G., & Ritter, J. H. (1964). Where America's recognized psychologists received their doctorates. *American Psychologist, 19,* 634–644.

Wolff, W. M. (1970). A study of criteria for journal manuscripts. *American Psychologist, 25,* 636–639.

Wolff, W. M. (1973). Publication problems in psychology and an explicit evaluation schema for manuscripts. *American Psychologist, 28,* 257–261.

Woods, F. A. (1909, November 19). A new name for a new science. *Science, 30,* 703–704.

Woods, F. A. (1911, April 14). Historiometry as an exact science. *Science, 33,* 568–574.

Woodward, W. R. (1974). Scientific genius and loss of a parent. *Science Studies, 4,* 265–277.

Woodworth, R. S. (1921). *Psychology: A study of mental life.* New York: Holt.

Woodworth, R. S., & Schlosberg, H. (1954). *Experimental psychology* (rev. ed.). New York: Holt.

Woody, E., & Claridge, G. (1977). Psychoticism and thinking. *British Journal of Social and Clinical Psychology, 16,* 241–248.

Young, R. K. (1985). Ebbinghaus: Some consequences. *Journal of Experimental Psychology: Learning, Memory, and Cognition, 11,* 491–495.

Yuasa, M. (1974). The shifting center of scientific activity in the West: From the sixteenth to the twentieth century. In. N. Shigeru, D. L. Swain, & Y. Eri (Eds.), *Science and society in modern Japan* (pp. 81–103). Tokyo: University of Tokyo Press.

Zachar, P., & Leong, F. T. L. (1992). A problem of personality: Scientist and practitioner differences in psychology. *Journal of Personality, 60,* 665–677.

Zajonc, R. B. (1976, April 16). Family configuration and intelligence. *Science, 192,* 227–235.

Zhao, H., & Jiang, G. (1986). Life-span and precocity of scientists. *Scientometrics, 9,* 27–36.

Zuckerman, H. (1977). *Scientific elite.* New York: Free Press.

Zuckerman, H., Cole, J. R., & Bruer, J. T. (Eds.). (1991). *The outer circle: Women in the scientific community.* New York: Norton.

Zuckerman, H., & Merton, R. K. (1972). Age, aging, and age structure in science. In M. W. Riley, M. Johnson, & A. Foner (Eds.), *Aging and society: Vol 3. A sociology of age stratification* (pp. 292–356). New York: Russell Sage Foundation.

Zusne, L. (1976a). Age and achievement in psychology: The harmonic mean as a model. *American Psychologist, 31,* 805–807.

Zusne, L. (1976b). A footnote to Lehman's *Age and achievement. Perceptual & Motor Skills, 43,* 409–410.

Zusne, L. (1984). *Biographical dictionary of psychology.* Westport, CT: Greenwood Press.

Zusne, L. (1985). Contributions to the history of psychology: XXXVIII. The hyperbolic structure of eminence. *Psychological Reports, 57,* 1213–1214.

Zusne, L. (1987a). Contributions to the history of psychology: XLIV. Coverage of contributors in histories of psychology. *Psychological Reports, 61,* 343–350.

Zusne, L. (1987b). *Eponyms in psychology: A dictionary and biographical sourcebook.* New York: Greenwood Press.

Zusne, L., & Blakely, A. S. (1985). Contributions to the history of psychology: XXXVI. The comparative prolificacy of Wundt and Piaget. *Perceptual & Motor Skills, 61,* 50.

Zusne, L., & Dailey, D. P. (1982). History of psychology texts as measuring instruments of eminence in psychology. *Revista de Historia de la Psicología, 3,* 7–42.

Zweigenhaft, R. L. (1975). Birth order, approval-seeking, and membership in Congress. *Journal of Individual Psychology, 31,* 205–210.

AUTHOR INDEX

SUBJECT INDEX

negative effect on creative development, 413–414
Andreasen, N. C., *161–162*
Angell, J. R.
    denouement of career of, 269
    on doctoral degree, *228*
Annin, E. L., 8, *54*, *57*
Arieti, S., *415*
Aristotle, 8, 277
Attributional theories
    future research on, 456
Authoritarianism
    impact on psychological science, 420–422
Authoritarian personality
    anti-intraception, 421–422
    manifestations of, 420–422
Authoritarian Personality, The, 420
Autobiographically consequential experiences (ACEs)
    in life-review, 276–277
Autobiography
    as life-review, 276–277
Awards and honors
    age and, 261
    in career development, 260–261
    Nobel prize, 260–261
    women and, 304

Bachtold, L. M., *312, 313*

Bacon, F.
    on marriage and family, *278*
BACON discovery program
    induction in, 134, 138
    limitations of, 138
Bain, A., *116*
Barron, F. X., *45*
Bartlett, F. C., *334, 335*
    on cross-fertilization and outside perspective, *249–250*
Behavior genetics, 296–302
    emergenesis in, 301–302
    environment in, shared and unshared, 297–298
    Galton's contributions to, 296
    heritability of ability and character, 296–297
    nuture as nature in, 300–301
    psychopathological pedigrees in, 298–300
Behaviorism

environmental determinism in, 292–293
    sociopolitical context of, 422
Bem, S.
    marriage of
        gender roles in, 316
Bennet, W., *110*
Beveridge, W. I. B., *175*
Bevington, D., *33*
Bilingualism
    creativity and, 417–418
Binet-Simon scale, 124, 129
Biographical details
    examples of, 193
    nomothetic implications of, 104
Birth order, 206–217
    Adler on, 212–213
    of eminent women, 210–211, 311
    empirical findings, 207–211
    of famous persons, 210–211
    first born, 207, 208, 209, 210–212, 311
    in Galton, *207*
    later born as first or only child, 209
    middle, 311
    of psychologists, 208–210
    of scientists, 207–208
    theoretical interpretations
        for eldest child, 211–213
        for youngest child, 213–217
Bohr, N., *189*
Boring, E. G., *18*, 270, 276, 277, 386, *387–388*, *1058*
    on history of psychology, 382, 383
    on late-life productivity of Wundt, *275*
    motivational attributes of, *158*
    on rediscovery in multiple discovery, *388*
    Strong Vocational Interest Blank scores for, 177
    Zeitgeist *vs.* genius in, 16, 18
Boswell, J., *24*
Brannigan, A., *397*
Browning, D. C., *162*
Brunner, J. S., *356, 357*
Butler, S., *223*
Butterfield, H., *20*
Byron, Lord, *64*

Campbell, D. T., *204, 455*
Candolle, A. de
    conditions for scientific creativity
        language, 403

national characteristics, 402–403
environmental determinism in, 292–293
as response to genetic determinism, 401
on population growth and output, 406–407
quantitative effects on creativity
nation states *vs.* imperial states, 407–408
Cannon, W. B., *109*
on flexibility, *146*
on homeostasis, *145–146*
Capretta, P. J., *104, 172, 241*
Career development
awards and honors in, 260–261
children and, 279–280
climax of, 260–267
disciplinary esteem and, 260–262
organizational service and, 262–266
teaching influence and, 266–267
contribution type and, 80–85
domain, 81–85
genre, 81
denouement and epilogue of, 268–278
Planck's principle and, 270–274
elite affiliation and, 257–260
fast advancement of, 256–257
formal education in, 226–245
at graduate training level, 468–469
of Hall, 254–256
individual variation in
cognitive model of, 85–101 (*See also* Cognitive model)
interdisciplinary variation in peaks
Dennis study of, 82–83
Lehman study of, 81–82
Simonton study of, 83–85
late-late effects on, 274–278
late start and, 255–256
marriage and family and, 278, 279
women and, 314–315
organizational service in
Hall, G. S. and, 262–265
professional marginality and, 248–251
cross-fertilization of ideas and, 249
negative effects of, 251
outside perspective and, 249–250
positive effects of, 248–250
research on
birth order in, 452
Helson effect, 453
for minorities, 452–453
self-education in, 246–248
sexual orientation and, 281
Career landmarks
age and
first, best, last major contribution, 78–80, 83–84
Raskin study of, 79
consolidative, 339–340
developmental, 339
domain and
first, best, last major contribution, 83–84
individual variation in, 89–90
longitudinal location of, 93–100
productive, 337
Career training. *See* Education
Career trajectory
achievement domain in, 81–85
age and, 70–73, 98
longitudinal location of
predictions from, 95–101
typology in, 93–94
Carlyle, T., *16*
Catell, R. B.
portrait of great scientist, 159–160
Cattell, J. M., *36, 205*
on career advancement, *256*
on education, *226–227*
eminence ranking of psychologists, 65–66, 67
on formal education, *236, 237*
individual differences
quantitative and objective evaluation of, 130
16 Personality Factor Questionnaire, *159*
ranking of psychologists, 67–68
on recognition, *261*
social attributes
interdisciplinary contrasts of, 161
on women *vs.* men, *309*
Cattell, R. B., *161*
Chan, W., *217*
Christensen, H., *81*
Christian theologians
on psychological issues, 172–173
Chubin, D. E., *92*
Citation
elitist distribution of, 46
gender and, 307
and uncited publications, 46

of women, 319
Citation analysis
   and cognitive revolution, 364–366
   of neuroscience
      for impact, 365–366
   of scientific revolution, 364–366
   as test of Kuhnian displacement thesis
      application in history of psychology,
         364–366
Citation counts
   citation decay over time and, 53–54
   correlation with age, 86
   of eminence
      pre-twentieth century, 54
   of long-term influence
      anomalies in, 51–53
   in quality assessment, 44–45
      criticisms of, 44
      intercorrelations of, 44–45
Citation rate
   correlation with persistence, 157
   longitudinal stability of, 47–48
   temporal stability of, 48
   war and, 404
Civil disturbances
   influence on intellectual history, 425,
      426
Class origins
   eminence and
      in psychology, 199–200
      in science, 199
   variation in
      achieved eminence and, 199–200
      across achievement domains, 197–
         199
Cliometrics
   as quantitative method in history, 23
Clustering
   in Chinese philosophical tradition,
      341, 342
   of contemporaries, 343–347
   from cross-generational influences,
      333
   of eminence in science
      inheritance and, 291
   generational time-series analysis of,
      335–342
   of genius, 400
      in Velleius, 334
   James on, *330*
   Kroeber on, 331–333
   lagged through predecessors, 333–343

pattern exhaustion and, 333, *335*
of psychologists
   1890s, 329–330
   twentieth century, 330
of representatives of philosophical positions in adjacent generations,
   375–376
role model availability and, 341–343
Schneider on, *333*
scientific centers and, national, 400
synchronous of contemporary figures
   collaborators and, 345–346
   collegial association and, 346–347
   professional associations and, 345–
      346
Cognitive model
   of career trajectory variation
      purpose of, 86
   individual-differences model in, 90–91
      age at career onset and, 91
      doctrine of cumulative advantage
        and, 92
   longitudinal model in
      age curve in, specific form, 87–89
      elaboration in, 86–87
      equal-odds rule, output, career land-
        marks, 89–90
      ideation in, 86
      information-processing basis for in-
        terdisciplinary contrasts, 89
      initial creative potential in, 86
Cognitive psychology, 27
Cognitive revolution
   citation analysis and, 364–366
   content analysis of, 366–367
Cohen, D., *137*
Cole, S., 113, *352, 353*
   Comtian hierarchy study, *352, 353*
Computer analysis
   applications of
      Martindale and, 358
      Simonton and, 358–359
   of conceptual revolutions, 363
   of intradisciplinary advancement, 357–
      358
Computer simulation programs
   of discovery process in psychological
      sciences, 451–452
Comte, and sociology, 348
Comtian progress
   hierarchies of sciences in, 348
   humanistic perspective on, 357

interdisciplinary hierarchies, 349–355
(*See also* Hierarchies of sciences)
intradisciplinary advancement
    objective (computer) content
        analysis, 357–358
    subjective (human) content analy-
        ses and, 356–357
    intradisciplinary advancement and,
        355–359
        methodological positivism and, 357
        use of statistical aids in research, 356
    research questions on, 348–349
    theory of, 348
Content analysis
    of cognitive revolution, 366–367
    of intradisciplinary advancement, 357–
        358
    of paradigm shift, 366–367
    of titles in research programs, 106–
        108
    of verbal behavior, 128
Copernicus, N., contribution to psychology,
    10–11
Cox, C.
    derivation of IQ from biographical
        data, 131
    study of geniuses, 129–131
Craig, H., *33*
Creative activity
    nation states *vs.* imperial states, 407–408
    political fragmentation and, 408–410
    in Chinese literature, 408–410
Creative process
    information-processing model of
        steps in, 86–88
    variation-selection model of, 390–391
        rediscovery multiples and, 391
Creative product. *See also* Research programs
    research programs
        assessment of, 106–110
    scientific publications, 110–117 (*See
        also* Scientific programs)
    scientific value of
        criteria for, 104–105
Creativity
    age and transformation of, 277
    aggregate, 428
        individual differences in, 428–430
    creative potential in, 390
    developmental period in, 390
    discrepancies between aggregate and
        individual levels, 431

    expertise acquisition effect on, 295–
        296
    interdisciplinary contrasts in, 148–
        154
    late-life effect on, 275–276
    national differences in, 400
    and personality, 155–156
    productive period in, 390
    from self-actualization, 171
    stimulation of
        cross-fertilization in, 413, 415–418
        imperial instability in, 414–415
Cross-fertilization
    creativity and, 413, 415–418
    foreign study and, 416
    in Japanese history
        generational time-series analysis of,
        416–417
Crowther, J. G., *35*
Cultural values
    scientific *vs.* religious
        creative activity and, 410
Cumulative-advantage model, of individual
    differences, 92–93

Darwin, C., 26, *131–132*, *175*, *227*, *378–
    379*, *383*, *385*
    on bereavement, *221*
    educational experience of, *227*
    on flexibility and openness, *146–147*
    on his intelligence, *132–133*
    impact of, *270*
    on new ideas, *270–271*
Darwin, F., 26, *131–132*, *146–147*, *175*,
    227, *378–379*, *383*, *385*
Darwin family
    natural ability and eminence in,
        290
Dennis, W., *39*, *40*, *73*, *116*
Developmental psychology, 27
    Hall and, 253–254
    Lehman and, 71–72
Discovery
    altered states of consciousness in, 142
    drug-induced, 142
    emotion in, 147–148
    parallel processing and, 144
Discovery process
    computer simulation of, 134, 451–452
        deficiencies of, 138, 140
    trial and error in
        Jevons on, *137*

and developmental psychology, 253–254

journal founder
American Journal of Psychology, 255, 265
Pedagogical Seminary, 253

late life
interest in religion 278
Senescence in, 274, 278

late-life
productivity of, 275
Senescence, 254

life-review issues in, 278

marriage and family of, 279

organizational service of, 262–265
in American Psychological Association foundation, 262, 264–265
American Psychological Association presidency, 255, 258, 262
Clark University presidency, 255, 258, 264

teaching influence of, 266, 267

Hearnshaw, L. S., *105, 172, 250, 344, 419*
religion and psychology, *173*

Hegel, G. W. F., *436*

Hegelian dialectics
application to psychological schools, 369–370
comparison with Kuhn's transformations, 370
in generational succession, 370
in imageless thought controversy
behaviorism as reaction to, 369
Kroeber's clustering of genius and, 370
as reaction to extreme positions, 368
Sorokin's generational assessments and, 371–375 (*See also* Sorokin, P.A.)

Helmholtz, H. von
on intellectual aptitudes, *149*
problem-solving process of, *137*
on self-education, *247–248*
self-education and, *246*

Helsen effect
eminence in women without brothers, *310*, 311

Henley, T. B., *272, 382*

Hergenhahn, B. R., *54, 297, 363, 419, 423, 458*
on evolution *vs.* structuralism, *363*

Heritability
of ability and character, 296–297
of genius, 290–291

Heyduk, R. G., *51*

Hierarchy of sciences
anti-Comte, 349–350
Comtian
four sciences in, 352
rating criteria for, 352–354, 361
interdisciplinary contrasts in
in age-productivity curves, 350
social comparison theory and, 351
theories-to-law ratio and, 351–352, 354
pro-Comte, 350–354

Hillner, K. P., *419*

Historicism
in history, *21*

Historiometric studies
definition of, 29

History
in combination with science, 22
deterministic physical science *vs.* stochastic psychological science, 25–26
genius *vs.* Zeitgeist in
as causal agents, 16–19
idiographic *vs.* nomothetic analyses in, 21–22
presentist *vs.* historicist narratives in, 20–21
quality *vs.* quantity in science, 22–24
quantification in, 23–24
scientific analyses of, 26–29
transhistorical perspective on, 21

History of psychology
eponyms in, 16, 17
internal *vs.* external influences in, 19–20
scientific psychology of
contrasting causal effects and, 430–431
individual differences and, 428–430
mediation of psychological processes in, 431–432
psychologically driven sociocultural phenomena in, 432–433
Zeitgeist interpretation of, *382, 383*

Hoffman, B., *226, 227, 228*

Home environment
brothers in, *310*, 311
class and, 196–200
Galton study of, 195
mothers in, 197

Hothersall, D., *105, 122, 179, 321*

Jungk, R., 69

Kant, I., *90*
Kendler, H. H., *105, 329*
King, D. B., *270*
Kivinick, H. Q.
    psychologists' life-review, *276*
Knowledge
    and Comtian progress, 349–350
    core, 349
    progression of, 348
    research frontier, 349
Koestler, A., *391*
Kovach, J. K., *418, 453*
Kroeber, A. L.
    on British scientific genius, 332–333
    on clustering of genius, 331–335
        generational and cultural boundaries of, 399–400
        pattern exhaustion and, 334, *335*
        Velleius Paterculus and, 334
    genius
        correspondence of individual differences in with aggregate levels of creativity, 430
    sociocultural determinism of, 380
Kuhn, T. S., *359–360, 364*
    on cross-fertilization of ideas, *249*
    theory of scientific revolutions, 359–368
Kuhnian transformations
    paradigm in, 359–360
    anomaly and, 360
Külpe, O.
    marriage and science, *279*

Language
    and creativity
        bilingualism and, 417–418
        scientific activity and, 403
Leahey, T. H., *248, 249–250, 412, 423, 454*
Lehman, H. C.
    Age and Achievement
        adult developmental psychology, 71–72
        criticisms of, 73–75
        longitudinal distributions in, 72
        replication by others, 72–73
    "Scientific Eminence and Church Membership," *173* 174
Levin, S. G., *203*
Life review

by great psychologists, *276*
Life span
    comparison of psychologists and scientists, 284
    domain of achievement and, 282–283
    precocity and, 284
    suicide and, 284
    versatility and, 284
Lindsey, L., *277*
Loewi, O., *142*
Lombroso, C., *42, 162*
Longevity
    examples of eminent psychologists, 281–282
Loss of parent, 217
    effect of, 298–299
    instances of, 218–219
    variation by achievement domain, 221
Lotka law, 41–42
Lowry, R., *436*
Ludwig, A. M., *153*
Lundin, R. W., *407*

Mach, E., *139*
    on flexibility and openness, *146*
MacLeod, R. B., *173, 363*
Mancini, J. A., *81*
Marchman, J. N., *419*
Marriage and family, 278–285
    vs. career, 279–281
    women and scientific achievement and, 314–315
    women in psychology and, 315–316
Martindale, C., *366–367*
    content analysis of paradigm shift, 366–367
Marx, K., *20*
Mass producers, 43–44, 48, 117
Master-pupil effects
    connection building, 245
    nuturance of talent, 244–245
    transfer of greatness, 244–245
Matthew effect, 92
Matthews, K. A., *37*
Maturity
    career development and, 254–258
    and keeping abreast of research literature, 268
    marriage and family and, 287–291
McCurdy, H. G., *160*
Mead, M.
    Sex and Temperament

gender roles in, *313, 314*

Meehl, P. E.
    cliometric metatheory of, *468*
    hard *vs.* soft psychology, *468*

Mental strategy(s) and process(es)
    and eminence, 133–148
    free association, 138–140
    imagery, 140–142
    incubation, 142–145
    inspiration, 147–148
    serendipity, 145–147
    trial and error, 136–138

Mentors
    age and, 267
    teachers as, 241–242

Merton, R. K., *380, 392–393*

Mertonian multiples. *See* Duplicate Discoveries; Multiple discoveries

Minkowski, H., *226*

Minnesota Multiphasic Personality Inventory (MMPI)
    for tendency toward psychopathology, 167

Motivation
    of great psychologists, 157–159
    in psychology of greatness, 172

Multiple discoveries
    deterministic Zeitgeist interpretation of, 380–383
    historical examples of
        Darwin-Wallace, evolution, 378–379, *379*
        James-Lange, theory of emotion, 378
        Newton-Leibniz, calculus, 379
    Kroeber and
        clustering of genius *vs.* Galton's determinism, 380, 381
        cultural configurations and, 398
    Merton on, *380*
    sociocultural determinism and
        Darwin and, *383, 385*
        Galton on, *383–384*
        independent or antecedent, 385–386
        inevitable or eventual, 389
        simultaneous or rediscovered, 386–388
        time elapsed and rediscovery, 387–388
        universal or particular, 384–385
    stochastic genius interpretation of, 390–398

Zeitgeist contribution to, 398

Murphy, G., *415, 418, 453*

Murphy, L. B., *415*

National Academy of Science (NAS)
    age at membership in, 256
    election to, 262

Nations
    clustering of creativity and, 400

Nature and nuture
    defined by Galton, *293*
    environment as nuture, 297
    in Galton, *293*
    in Shakespeare, *293*

Newton, I.
    multiple discovery of calculus, 379
    as psychologist, 10

Nietzsche, F. W., *147–148*

Nobel laureates
    teacher and mentor pedigrees and, 242

Nobel prize
    in career life-span, 260–261

Norling, B., *381, 404, 405*

Nuture *vs.* nature
    greatness and, 326–327

Ogden, R. M., *279*

Ortega y Gasset, J.
    generation concept in, 336
    hypothesis of advancement of many *vs.* few, *35, 42, 46, 58*

Ortgeist
    American Psychological Association divisions and, 434
    fit with psychologist's impact, 434–435
    measure of American, 433–434, *435*
    and nature of psychology in U.S., *454*

Output. *See* Productivity

Over, R., *76*

Parapsychology
    response to threatening conditions, 421

Park, R., *204*
    on immigration, *204*

Pathographies
    of historic figures, 162

Peak experiences, 147

Pedigree method
    Galton and, 296

Perfectionists, 43–44, 48, 117

Persistence

in Cox study of genius, 156–157
drawbacks in, 157
Personality
and eminence in women, *312, 313*
gender and genius and, 309, 310
and psychologist type, 178–180
Personality development
Darwinian theory of, 214–216
Personality psychology, 27
Personality traits
and psychologist's philosophies, 179
Philosophy
contributions to psychology, 6–9
Philosophy of psychological science
study of long-term influence of
assessment of scientific orientation
in, 182–185
correlation of current influence
with theoretical and methodological orientation, 183–184
correlation of six factors, 183
disciplinary implications of backward J-curve, 185–189
factors in, 182–185
measure of current influence and,
182–183
Piaget, J.
output of, 36, 37
Planck, M., *271*
Planck's principle
in career denouement, 270–274
definition of, *271*
in master-disciple, teacher-student
relationships, 273
mentorship and, 273
negative operation of, 272
operation of, *271, 272*
test of, Darwin's theory evolution in, 271
Poincaré, H., *109*
Political fragmentation
implications of, 423–424
Popper, K., *457*
Population growth
output of great scientists and, 406
Presentism
in history, 20–21
Price, D., *394*
ripe apple model of duplicates, *394*
Price law, 41
definition of, 345
individual differences and aggregate
numbers, 429

Productivity, 36–54. *See also* Quality
contribution type and, 49–51
citation measure of books, 50–51
comparison across disciplines, 49–
50
peer identification of impact, 51
elite affiliation and, 258, 260
gender and, 306, 307–308
individual differences in, 86
longitudinal stability of, 91
late-life effect on, 275–276
lifetime
correlation with age of contributions, 95
correlation with chronological age
at maximum output and best
contribution, 96–97
longitudinal stability of, 47–49
long-term influence
citation measures of, 51–53
marriage and family and, 280–281
gender and, 315
maximum output rate and
correlation with chronological age,
97
correlation with chronological age
at best contribution, 96–97
measurement of, 36–37
multiple authorship and, 38
publication counts in, 37–38
as ratio scale, 36–37, 42
weighting of publications, 38
motivation and, 157
output rate
correlation with chronological age
of first and last contributions, 96
output trajectories
as function of career age *vs.* chronological age, 98
perfectionists and mass producers and,
43–44, 48
quality as function of quantity, 45
quantity and quality in, 42–47
quantity-quality relation
cross-sectional distribution and, 46
equal-odds rule and, 45
scatter around bivariate regression
line and, 46–47
silents and prolifics and, 43–44, 48
variation and distribution in, 39–42
elitist distribution in, 40–42
genius *vs.* mediocrity in, 42

Jewish, 201–202
Protestant, 203
Roman Catholic, 201
"Scientific Eminence and Church Membership," *173, 174*
truth in *vs.* scientific truth, 174–175
Research
    empirical questions for, 448–455
        developmental correlates, 452–454
        history of psychology and Hegelian pendulum swings, 455
        individual differences, 451–452
        operation of multiples within psychology, 455
        output and impact, 448–450
        position of psychology in hierarchy of sciences, 454
        psychology as paradigmatic, 454–455
        relation of genius and Zeitgeist, 455
        sociocultural context, 453–455
    on individual characteristics
        computer simulations in, 451–452
        lack of historiometric studies of, 451
    theoretical interpretations in
        attributional, 456
        economic, 456–457
        evolutionary, 457–458
Researchers, aging, and decline in performance, 268–269
Research programs
    content analysis of titles in
        correlation with counts of citations, cited publications, citations of most-cited work, 107–108
        primary and secondary process imagery and, 106–107
        TEXTPACK PC program in, 106–107
        type-token ratio in, 107
    network of enterprises in, 109
Revolution
    citation analysis of, 364–366
    computer analysis of, 363–364
    conceptual
        philosophical analysis of, 363, *364*
    content analysis of
        behaviorist and cognitive paradigms in, 366–367
    Kuhn's internalist theory of, *248*
    paradigm in
        examples of, 361

formation and demise of, 363
    in psychology
        cognitive, 363, 364
        Skinnerian behaviorism, 363
Revolutionaries
    in science, 215
    in science and government, 210, 212
Reynolds, J., on acquisition of expertise, *294*
Robinson, D. E., *425, 461*
Rodman, H., *81*
Roe, A., *158, 160, 208*
Rogers, C. R., *171*
Role model
    in clustering, 341–343
Rushton, J. P., *72–73*

Saugstad, P., *363*
Schlipp, P. A., *226*
Schmookler, J., *384*
Schneider, J., *333*
Schultz, D. P., *18, 60, 104, 105, 228, 250, 272*
Schultz, S. E., *18, 60, 104, 105, 228, 250, 272*
Science
    advancement of
        through the many or genius of few, 35–36
    definition of, *27*
    history of
        evolutionary theory in, 458
    philosophy of
        evolutionary epistemologies in, 457
    women representation in, 304
Scientific achievement
    flexibility and openness and, 146–147
Scientific publications
    criteria for evaluation of submissions, 111–112
    evaluation of
        contaminating factors in, 113–114
        ideal, 111–112
        inaccuracies, constraints, biases in, 115–116
        real, 113–117
        reliability of review and, 113
        subjective quality *vs.* objective citation evaluation, 114–115
    variation in impact of, 110–111
        factors in, 112
Scientific revolutions
    Kuhn's theory of, 359–368

paradigm in (*See* Paradigm)
Scientists
    cognitive attributes of, 148–143
        imagery, 152–153
        intelligence, 149–151
        versatility, 153–154
    contributions to psychology, 9–11
    eminence of
        international recognition require-
            ment for, 401–402
        first born, 210
        later born, revolutionary, 210
    openness and flexibility of
        in conflict with religious dogma,
            175
    social attributes of, 159–160
Self-actualization
    Maslow and, 162–163
    Rogers and, 162, *171*
Self-education. *See also* Formal education;
    Graduate training
    Einstein and, 245
    extra-curricular activities in, 247
    Helmholtz and, *246*
    reading in, 246–248
Seneca, *162*
Sensate mentality
    and creative output, 410, 411
Serendipity
    Cannon on homeostasis, *145–146*
Sexual dimorphism
    in Darwin, *The Descent of Man*, 309
    Eysenck's explanation of, 308–309
    as issue, 309–310
    origins of theory, 309–310
Sexual orientation
    career and, 281
    of great psychologists, 281
Shin, K. E., *350*
Simon, H. A., *134*
    motivational attributes of, *158*
    Nobel prize
        for cognitive processes in problem
            solving and decision making,
            133–135
Simonton, D. K., *24*
Skinner, B. F., *136*
    environmental determinism in, 292
    on flexibility, *146*
Smith, S., *179*
Social attributes
    of great psychologists, 159–161

historiometric study of past scientists,
    159–160
    interdisciplinary contrasts in, 161
    psychometric study in contemporary
        scientists, 159
    of scientists
        individualism, 160
Socialization
    pro-son orientation in, 310–311
Social psychology, 27
Social Sciences Citation Index, 434
Sociocultural determinism
    in history, *381*
    in history of psychology, 381–382
    of Kroeber, 380
    of Merton, *380*
Sociocultural milieu
    qualitative effects of
        cross-disciplinary, 418
        developmental influences, 424–426
        economic threat, 420–422
        inertial movements, 422–424
        religion, 421
        transient fluctuations, 419–422
        war, 419–420
        Zeitgeist or ortgeist, 419
    quantitative effects of, 401–418
        cultural values, 410–412
        developmental influences, 412–418
        economic milieu, 405–406
        imperial instability, 414–415
        inertial movements, 406–412
        national sovereignty, 407–410
        political anarchy, 413–414
        population growth, 406–407
        transient fluctuations, 403–406
        war, 404–405
    research on, 453–455
Sociocultural phenomena
    Comte's theory of human progress,
        347–359 (*See also* Comtian
        progress)
    Hegelian dialectics, 368–378
    Kroeber's *Configurations of Culture
        Growth*, 331–347 (*See also* Cluster-
        ing)
    Kuhn's structure of scientific revolu-
        tions, 359–368
    Merton's multiples, 378–398
    psychologically driven, 432–433
    psychological processes in, 431–432
Socioeconomic stratification

merger of idiographic history with
nomothetic science in, 460–461
term paper in
defense of thesis in, 466
psychology-of-science perspective
in, 463
questionnaire for, 463, 464–465
range of topics in, 462
supplementary text for methodology, 464–465
textbooks for
naturalistic *vs.* personalistic approach to, 460
nomothetic results in, 459
psychology-of-science perspective
in, 459–460

Vasari, G.
on Michelangelo, 287
Velleius
influence of predecessors on creative
activity, 334, 335
Versatility
correlation with eminence
and Spearman's g, 153–154
functional relation with greatness, 154
in geniuses, 153
Viney, W., 270

Wanner, R. A., 397
War
as catalyst for applied psychology, 420
citation rates and, 404
and contribution to psychological science, 405
negative effects of, 404–405
psychological research during, 425
Watson, J. B., 232
environmental determinism and, 292
Watson, R. I. Sr., 106, 406
on Aristotle's creativity, 277
on Hartley's relation to Hume, 272–
273
Wechsler Adult Intelligence Scale (WAIS)
of scientists
across domains, 151
Werner, E. E., 312, 313
Wertheimer, M., 168–169, 266, 382, 418,
426, 461
Wechsler Adult Intelligence Scale (WAIS),
126–127

Whitehead, A. N., 8
Who Said What When, 333, 413, 468
Witty, P. A., 173
Women. *See also* Gender and Genius
citation of, 306
doctoral degree
age and, 317–318
discrimination and, 318–319
domain representation of, 303–304
eminence in
personality factors and, 312–313
without brothers, 310, 311–312
eminent in psychology, 304
percentage as function of birth year,
319, 320
and genius
facts, 302–306
interpretation, 306–321
influence on American psychology,
304–305
institutional sexism and, 318
productivity of, 306, 307
in science, 304
socialization and eminence, 310–313
in studies of eminence, 303
in subdomains of psychology, 313
Woodworth, R. S., 69
age and achievement in, 69–70
Worldview
religious convictions, 172–176
scientific philosophies, 176–189
Wundt, W.
career development of, 257
doctoral descendants of, 239, 241
late-life productivity of, 260, 275
master-pupils effect of, 243
output of, 36, 37

Yuasa, M., 400

Zeitgeist
gender-based
and women, 321
study of impact on psychologist's success, 435–442
study of impact on success of psychologist, philosopher, scientist
belief structure, 438, 440
external factors in, 437
historical time as statistical control
in, 438

individual- *vs.* aggregate-level variables and, 441
internal factors in, 437, 439
measures of variables in, 437–438
population sample in, 436–437
predictors of eminence at generation g, 439, 440

results, 439–440
vs. effect on ortgeist of American psychologist, 442
Zeitgeist fit, 437–438, 439–440
transmission through genius, 436

ABOUT THE AUTHOR

Dean Keith Simonton, PhD, is currently a professor of psychology at the University of California, Davis. He obtained his PhD in social psychology from Harvard University in 1975. His research program is mostly devoted to the application of historiometric methods to the study of genius, creativity, leadership, talent, and aesthetics. He has studied eminent scientists and inventors, philosophers, poets and dramatists, painters and sculptors, classical composers, presidents, monarchs, generals, and other notables drawn from the cultures of Europe, Asia, Africa, and the Americas. In these studies he examines such factors as intelligence, precocity, personality, values, motivation, family environment, education, political circumstances, and the broad sociocultural milieu. This research program has been very fruitful, producing approximately 250 publications, including well over 100 articles in the technical journals of psychology, education, sociology, anthropology, political science, the natural sciences, and the humanities.

In addition, Dr. Simonton is the author of eight books, including *Genius, Creativity, and Leadership* (1984); *Scientific Genius* (1988); *Psychology, Science, and History* (1990); *Greatness* (1994); and *Origins of Genius* (1999). He has served as editor of the *Journal of Creative Behavior*; was guest editor of the *Leadership Quarterly* for a special issue on "Political Leadership"; and has served on the editorial boards of the *Creativity Research Journal, Empirical Studies of the Arts,* the *Leadership Quarterly, Political Psychology,* the *Review of General Psychology,* the *Journal of Personality,* and the *Bulletin of Psychology and the Arts.* He is Fellow of the American Association for the Advancement of Science, the American Psychological Association (Divisions 1, 2, 7, 8, 9, 10, and 20), the American Psychological Society, the American Association of Applied and Preventative Psychology, and the International Association of Empirical Aesthetics. His research has earned him the William James Book Award, the George A. Miller Outstanding Article Award, the Rudolf

Arnheim Award for Outstanding Contributions to Psychology and the Arts, the Sir Francis Galton Award for Outstanding Contributions to the Study of Creativity, the Award for Excellence of the Mensa Education and Research Foundation, and the UC Davis Prize for Teaching and Scholarly Achievement.